PENSIONS ACT 2004

www.lnepusanregulabr.gov.
uh

PENSIONS ACT 2004

A Guide to the New Law

Jane Marshall, Catherine McKenna and Elizabeth Graham

Hammonds

The Law Society

© Hammonds 2005

ISBN 1 85328 923 X

Published in 2005 by the Law Society
113 Chancery Lane, London WC2A 1PL

Typeset by J&L Composition, Filey, North Yorkshire
Printed by TJ International Ltd, Padstow, Cornwall

CONTENTS

ACKNOWLEDGEMENTS

All of the pension lawyers at Hammonds have contributed to this book, and their hard work and commitment is gratefully acknowledged. The following members of the team either worked in groups to research the provisions of the Act under the various topic headings covered by this book or contributed to the book in other ways: Jane Marshall, Andrew Powell, Jay Doraisamy, Catherine McKenna, Terry Saeedi, Andrew Ashley Taylor, Steve Southern, Pauline Anning, Francois Barker, Ian Forrest, Philip Sutton, Jayne Willetts, Graham Wrightson, Oliver Reece, Georgina Rankin, Rhys Thomas, Fraser Sparks, Jessica Cheek, Wendy Eyre, Chris Jackson, Emma King, Michael Salters, Gino Rocco, Clare Grice, Mark Ridler, Clifford Sims, Kate Ive, Nita Champaneri, Charmian Johnson, John Sabel, Ian Jackson, Laura Millington, Jayne Reilly, Claire Rogers, Carol Jones, Fiona James, Matthew Giles, Gemma Hanley, Graeme Tricker, Emma Shopland, Elizabeth Graham, Frances Phillips-Taft, Caroline Foster, Ian O'Toole, Tom Collinge, Jane Briggs and Navneet Bassan.

Particular thanks also go to Jane Marshall, Catherine McKenna and Elizabeth Graham who contributed to and edited the material produced by the team in order to create this book.

This book refers extensively to the Explanatory Notes to the Pensions Bill as brought from the House of Commons on 21 May 2004, the text of which is Crown Copyright. The book does not refer to any of the numerous sets of draft regulations which will accompany the Act and which will no doubt have been published since the date of writing. We have aimed to state the law as at 31 December 2004.

Hammonds
January 2005

LIST OF ABBREVIATIONS

1992 Act	Social Security Contributions and Benefits Act 1992
1993 Act	Pension Schemes Act 1993
1995 Act	Pensions Act 1995
1999 Act	Welfare Reform and Pensions Act 1999
Act	Pensions Act 2004
2004 Regulations	Information and Consultation of Employees Regulations 2004, SI 2004/3426
Board	The Board of the Pension Protection Fund
DWP	Department for Work and Pensions
ERISA	Employment Retirement Security Act 1974 (USA)
Explanatory Notes	Explanatory Notes to the Pensions Bill as brought from the House of Commons on 21 May 2004
FAS	Financial Assistance Scheme
FSD	Financial support direction
FSMA 2000	Financial Services and Markets Act 2000
GMP	Guaranteed minimum pension
IDR procedure	Internal dispute resolution procedure
IORP Directive	Directive 2003/41/EC on the Activities and Supervision of Institutions for Occupational Retirement Provision
LPI	Limited price indexation
MFR	Minimum funding requirement
MNT	Member nominated trustee
Myners Review	The Myners Review of institutional investment in the UK published on 6 March 2001
OPRA	Occupational Pensions Regulatory Authority
Panel	Determinations Panel
PPF	Pension Protection Fund
Regulator	Pensions Regulator
RPI	Retail Prices Index
s.75 debt	A debt due from an employer pursuant to s.75 Pensions Act 1995
SIP	Statement of Investment Principles
Tribunal	Pensions Regulator Tribunal
TUPE	Transfer of Undertakings (Protection of Employment) Regulations 1981, SI 1981/1794

TABLE OF CASES

TABLE OF STATUTES

TABLE OF STATUTORY INSTRUMENTS

TABLE OF EUROPEAN LEGISLATION

1 THE BACKGROUND TO THE ACT

1.1 INTRODUCTION

1.1.1 Nearly a decade ago, the Pensions Act 1995 (the 1995 Act) was enacted to improve pension fund security. Legislation was the end of a chain of events which started with the disappearance of £600m from pension schemes operated by the Mirror Group. The House of Commons Select Committee on Social Security, which had at that time already been considering occupational pension schemes, decided to look more closely at pension fund security and recommended a government inquiry to review the law. The Pension Law Review Committee, chaired by Professor Roy Goode, was commissioned by the Secretary of State for Social Security in June 1992 to investigate and to report on the state of UK pensions law. The result was the 1995 Act.

1.1.2 At the time the legislation came into effect, there were, broadly, two schools of thought. One was that the Goode Committee proposals embodied in the 1995 Act merely strengthened and built on existing legal frameworks. After all, the six key recommendations of the Goode Committee had provided that:

- trust law should continue to provide the basic framework of pensions law, albeit reinforced and strengthened by a pensions regulator, OPRA;
- pension rights already earned should be protected and some trustees should be nominated by members;
- there should be more and better information;
- there should be minimum solvency levels and greater responsibilities placed on scheme advisers;
- employers should continue to have the right to determine benefits including reducing or stopping future benefits entirely; and
- pensions law and administration should be simplified and flexibility increased.

1.1.3 With the possible exception of the minimum solvency standard, none of this appeared contentious. Most pension lawyers agreed that past service rights were protected by trust law in any event, and many pension schemes already included member representation. The Goode Committee had acknowledged the key role of the scheme sponsor, and its freedom to change future benefits or discontinue a scheme entirely. There was even recognition that investment policy in a balance of cost scheme directly affected the employer – hence the appearance for the first time of an express statutory duty to consult the employer on these matters.

1.1.4   The other school of thought believed the 1995 Act represented a sea change in the way in which pension schemes in the UK were to be run. While familiar principles of trust law would continue, the imposition of penalties was likely to mean that the administration of pension schemes would become defensive. Those administering and advising pension schemes, however well intentioned, were likely to be drawn into a 'box ticking' culture rather than focusing on the quality of the decision-making. Even though the Goode Committee's solvency standard was watered down and became the 1995 Act's minimum funding requirement (MFR), there were concerns that pension schemes would in future be run on a radically different basis.

1.1.5   In the event, the latter view has proved correct. With hindsight the 1995 Act indeed represented a major change in the relationship between scheme sponsors, trustees and members.

1.2   PRESSURE FOR REFORM

1.2.1   All might have continued in an evolutionary rather than revolutionary pattern, had it not been for very significant changes which were occurring in investment markets. Until the partial recovery in the equity markets in early 2003, UK pension schemes had suffered from three consecutive years of losses in the UK equity market. In addition to negative investment performance and increasing longevity, sponsoring employers also found themselves under the spotlight with the introduction of the new accounting standard FRS17, which obliges them to report more clearly on the actual state of funding of their schemes and the cost of benefits.

1.2.2   The result has been an acceleration of the existing trend towards closure and termination of defined benefit schemes (in many cases with significant deficits) and the reduction of benefit accrual in continuing schemes. The abolition of dividend tax credit in the Labour government's first budget in 1997 (coincidentally the same year when many provisions of the 1995 Act came into force) destroyed a long-held consensus on the tax treatment of pension schemes.

1.2.3   While arguments raged about the actual impact of the tax change, it was undoubtedly the catalyst for an examination by many companies of the continued rationale for providing increasingly expensive defined benefit schemes. Notwithstanding these pressures, government maintained that its policy objective was the encouragement of more private pension provision, and introduced a completely new product, the stakeholder pension. Change also continued in other aspects of pensions management, and the Treasury asked Paul Myners to examine the role of trustees in pension scheme investment.

The Myners Review eventually concluded that more training for trustees and greater professionalism was needed.

1.2.4   Steps were also under way to try to deal with some of the unintended consequences of the 1995 Act. The MFR, for example, was found to be rather inflexible. It had also led some employers to conclude that a statutory minimum was also an acceptable maximum. There was some criticism of the new regulator, the Occupational Pensions Regulatory Authority (OPRA), not because of its integrity, professionalism and commitment, which were clear, but rather due to the inflexible legislative framework within which it had to work.

1.2.5   Concern was also growing about the complexity of the requirements, since compliance with the 1995 Act had led to significantly increased costs for both schemes and sponsors. The Department for Work and Pensions (DWP) appointed Alan Pickering in September 2001 to look at ways in which social security legislation could be simplified. Both the Pickering Report (*A Simpler Way to Better Pensions*) and the Sandler Report (*Medium and Long Term Retail Savings in the UK*) were published in July 2002. Pickering concluded that employer-sponsored pension provision should be encouraged. The increasing burden of new requirements, desirable in themselves, but which had not been considered or costed when schemes were set up, had unfortunately produced the opposite effect.

1.2.6   The tax system and its different regimes was acknowledged to be a factor in this complexity. The government decided to deal with this along with its more general proposals for reform, by publishing in December 2002 a Green Paper *Simplicity, Security and Choice: Working and Saving in Retirement* at the same time as Inland Revenue proposals *Simplifying the taxation of pensions: increasing choice and flexibility for all*. A tight timetable of consultation followed, and in June 2003 the DWP published an 'action plan' following such consultation. Later that year it also began consultation on implementing the EU Pensions Directive which had passed through the Council of Ministers some months earlier.

1.2.7   The Pensions Bill was introduced into Parliament in February 2004 and, after an eventful passage through both Houses, received Royal Assent on 18 November 2004.

2 THE PENSIONS REGULATOR

2.1 INTRODUCTION

2.1.1 Section 1 of the Pensions Act 2004 (the Act) establishes the Pensions Regulator (referred to in this book as the Regulator), which will replace OPRA from 6 April 2005.

2.1.2 In the December 2002 Green Paper, *Simplicity, Security and Choice: Working and Saving for Retirement*, the Government observed that OPRA had laid good foundations for the regulation of pensions, but recognised that OPRA had been restricted by the current legislation which obliged OPRA to take action in respect of minor breaches of law, without the flexibility that would often be desirable.

2.1.3 The provisions of the Act relating to the Regulator, detailed below, are intended to remove these restrictions and make the Regulator more proactive and responsive, and better able to target its resources on those cases where the members' benefits are at greatest risk. The Regulator's powers are wide ranging, and will be heavily supplemented by regulations.

2.2 CONSTITUTION OF THE REGULATOR

2.2.1 Under s.2 of the Act, the Regulator will consist of the following members:

(a) a Chairman appointed by the Secretary of State;
(b) a Chief Executive; and
(c) at least five other members appointed by the Secretary of State after consulting with the Chairman and who should represent certain groups (employer and employee representatives and persons knowledgeable about pension schemes and their management and administration).

2.2.2 At least two of the five other members must be appointed from the staff of the Regulator and the majority must be non-executive members (i.e. not the Chief Executive or members appointed from the staff of the Regulator). The Chairman must not be appointed from the staff of the Regulator or be the Chairman of the Board of the Pension Protection Fund (PPF). In addition, no member of the staff of the PPF is eligible for appointment as a member of the

Regulator. David Norgrove has been appointed as the first Chairman of the Regulator, and Tony Hobson has been appointed as its first Chief Executive.

2.3   THE REGULATOR'S FUNCTIONS

2.3.1   The Regulator's functions under the Act are potentially very wide. In exercising its functions, it will also operate in accordance with wide objectives, as follows (s.5):

(a) to protect the benefits of members of work-based pension schemes;
(b) to reduce the risk of situations arising which may lead to compensation from the PPF; and
(c) to promote and improve the understanding of the good administration of the schemes it regulates.

2.3.2   The Regulator will have the functions that are transferred to it from OPRA and any other functions conferred by the Act or any other legislation. This will include the functions of OPRA under the Pensions Schemes Act 1993 (the 1993 Act), the 1995 Act and the Welfare Reform and Pensions Act 1999 (the 1999 Act).

2.4   THE NON-EXECUTIVE COMMITTEE

2.4.1   The Regulator must establish and maintain a non-executive committee (s.8) which will consist of the Chairman and the other non-executive members of the Regulator. The role of the non-executive committee is:

(a) to keep under review the strategic direction of the Regulator;
(b) to scrutinise the performance of the Chief Executive;
(c) to monitor the extent to which the Regulator is meeting its objectives and targets;
(d) to monitor the Regulator's reporting to the Secretary of State under section 11 of the Act; and
(e) to keep under review the Regulator's internal financial controls to ensure it secures the proper control of its finances.

2.5   THE DETERMINATIONS PANEL

2.5.1   The Regulator must establish and maintain a Determinations Panel (the Panel) (ss.9 and 10). The Panel is a committee consisting of a Chairman and at least six other persons. The appointments committee of the Regulator is to nominate a person suitable for appointment as Chairman of the Panel.

2.5.2   The Chairman of the Panel must decide the number of persons to be appointed as members of the Panel and nominate a person suitable for each of those appointments. To ensure transparency of the Panel and separation of functions, the following persons are ineligible for appointment as members of the Panel:

(a) any member of the Regulator;
(b) any member of staff of the Regulator;
(c) any member of the Board of the PPF; and
(d) any member of the staff of the Board of the PPF.

The function and purpose of the Panel

2.5.3   The function of the panel is to exercise 'reserved regulatory functions' on behalf of the Regulator. Reserved regulatory functions are detailed in Sched.2 to the Act. By way of example, they include powers to:

(a) prohibit a person from being a trustee under s.3(1) of the 1995 Act;
(b) require a person to pay a penalty under s.10 of the 1995 Act;
(c) make an order under section 11 of the 1995 Act to direct and authorise an occupational pension scheme to be wound up; and
(d) make an order under s.69 of the 1995 Act authorising the modification of an occupational pension scheme.

2.5.4   In addition, reserved regulatory functions include new functions of the Regulator under the Act, including the power to make a freezing order under s.23, the power to issue a contribution notice under s.38 and the power to issue a financial support direction under s.43.

2.5.5   The purpose of the Panel is to separate the decision makers from the investigatory staff of the Regulator. Currently, there is a lack of detail in the Act as to who will serve on the Panel, how the Panel will operate in practice and whether any kind of 'Chinese wall' mechanism will be established to ensure proper separation of functions. Further detail is awaited in regulations.

2.6   THE REGULATOR'S PROCEDURES IN RELATION TO ITS REGULATORY FUNCTIONS

2.6.1   The Regulator will determine the procedures that it proposes to follow in the exercise of its regulatory functions (ss.93–101). The Panel will determine its own procedures. Procedures of the Regulator and the Panel must provide for 'standard procedure' and 'special procedure'. Throughout the rest of **para.2.6**, references to the Regulator include the Panel.

Standard procedure (s.96)

2.6.2   The standard procedure applies where notice is given to individuals directly affected by potential regulatory action – referred to as a 'warning notice'. The procedure must ensure that individuals affected are given a chance to make representations to the Regulator. In addition, the Regulator has to take into consideration the evidence provided and notify the individuals concerned of its decision and whether or not it will take the proposed action. This is known as a determination notice. If the proposed action is taken, the determination notice must contain:

(a) notification of the right of referral to the Pensions Regulator Tribunal (the Tribunal);
(b) the form and content of further warnings and determination notices;
(c) details of when further warning and determination notices will be given; and
(d) any time limits which apply throughout the process.

2.6.3   The determination may be referred to the Tribunal, either by anyone to whom the determination notice is given or by anyone who is directly affected by the determination.

Special procedure (s.97)

2.6.4   The special procedure applies where the Regulator determines that it is necessary to exercise its regulatory functions immediately. This will be the case where the Regulator considers it likely that, if a warning notice were given, there would be an immediate risk to the interests of members or to the assets of an occupational or personal pension scheme. Accordingly, the Regulator will not issue a warning notice and there will be no opportunity for persons affected by the regulatory function to make representations. Section 97(5) sets out the regulatory functions to which the special procedure applies.

2.6.5   The determination notice following the special procedure must be given to all individuals who appear to be directly affected by it. The notice must contain details of the Regulator's requirement to review the determination under s.99 of the Act (compulsory review) and the right of referral to the Tribunal. Individuals who receive a determination notice have the right to make representations, before the Regulator undertakes the compulsory review of the determination under s.99. The Regulator will consider these representations before the compulsory review and the final notice is given.

2.6.6   The compulsory review may confirm, change or revoke a determination of the Regulator or substitute a different determination. When the Regulator has completed the review of the determination, a final notice must be sent to all the individuals who are affected by the determination notice.

2.6.7   The regulatory function in question may not be exercised in the period during which individuals have the right to have the determination referred to the Tribunal or if it is referred whilst the Tribunal process is ongoing. There are certain exclusions to this provision highlighted in s.96(5) of the Act.

2.6.8   The Regulator, in exercising its functions, has a duty to have regard to the interests of the members and the interests of the persons the Regulator considers to be directly affected by the exercise.

2.7   THE PENSIONS REGULATOR TRIBUNAL

2.7.1   The Act also establishes a Tribunal which will hear appeals on determinations (s.102).

Composition of the Tribunal

2.7.2   The Lord Chancellor will appoint a panel of persons for the purposes of serving as Chairmen of the Tribunal. The Lord Chancellor must appoint one of the members of the panel of Chairmen to preside over the exercise of the Tribunal's functions and who will be known as the President of the Tribunal. The Lord Chancellor must also appoint a panel of persons who appear to him to be qualified by experience to deal with matters of a kind that may be referred to the Tribunal (known as the 'lay panel').

2.7.3   On a reference to the Tribunal, members of the Tribunal are to be selected from the panel of Chairmen and the lay panel, with at least one member being selected from the panel of Chairmen.

Tribunal procedure

2.7.4   The procedure of the Tribunal will be set by rules made by the Lord Chancellor although the President may give directions as to the practice and procedure to be followed by the Tribunal in relation to references to it.

2.7.5   A reference to the Tribunal following a determination under the standard procedure (see **para.2.6.2**) must be made within 28 days beginning with the day on which the determination notice in question is given. In the case of a reference following determination under the special procedure (see **para.2.6.4**) it must be made within 28 days beginning with the day on which the final notice in question is given. The Tribunal also has the discretion to hear a reference after the end of the periods specified above.

2.7.6   On a reference, the Tribunal may consider any evidence relating to the subject matter of the reference, whether or not it was available to the Regulator at the material time. The Tribunal has power to summons a person to attend, to give evidence, or to produce any documents in his or her custody. In addition, the Tribunal may take evidence on oath.

2.7.7   A person who, without reasonable excuse, refuses or fails to attend the Tribunal following a summons, or to give evidence, is guilty of an offence which is liable to a summary conviction or a fine. If a person alters, suppresses, conceals or destroys a document which is liable to be produced for the purposes of proceedings of the Tribunal, or refuses to produce the document, then that person will be guilty of an offence and liable on summary conviction to a fine or on conviction on indictment to imprisonment for a term not exceeding two years.

2.7.8   Any decision of the Tribunal may be taken by a majority and the decision must state whether it was a unanimous decision or taken by a majority. The decision must be recorded in a document which contains a statement of the reasons for the decision and be signed and dated by the member of the panel of Chairmen dealing with the reference.

2.7.9   If the Tribunal considers that a party to any proceedings on a reference has acted frivolously or unreasonably it may order that party to pay to another party to the proceedings the whole or part of any costs or expenses incurred by that other party in connection with the proceedings. In addition, if the Tribunal considers that a determination of the Regulator that is the subject of the reference is unreasonable, it may order the Regulator to pay to another party to the proceedings the whole or part of any costs or expenses incurred by the other party in connection with the proceedings.

2.7.10   On determination of the reference, the Tribunal must remit the matter to the Regulator with such directions as the Tribunal considers appropriate to give effect to its determination. These directions may include directions to the Regulator to confirm its determination, vary or revoke its determination or substitute a different determination.

2.7.11   A party to a reference may appeal only on a point of law with the leave of the Tribunal.

The legal assistance scheme

2.7.12   The Lord Chancellor may establish a scheme governing the provision of legal assistance in connection with proceedings before the Tribunal. It may be a condition of such legal assistance that the recipient of the aid makes a contribution.

2.8   INFORMATION POWERS

Provision of information, education and assistance

2.8.1   Section 12 of the Act deals with the Regulator itself providing information to others. The Regulator may provide such information, education and assistance as it considers appropriate to those involved in:

(a) the administration of 'work-based pension schemes' (i.e. occupational pension schemes, stakeholder pension schemes or personal pension schemes where 'direct payment' arrangements exist); or

(b) advising the trustees or managers in relation to such schemes' operation.

Register of schemes

2.8.2 Sections 59–65 of the Act deal with the maintenance by the Regulator of a register of pension schemes. Section 59 requires the Regulator to compile and maintain a register of occupational and personal pension schemes.

2.8.3 The Register must contain 'registrable information' (s.60), being:

(a) the scheme's name and address;
(b) the trustees' and participating employers' names and addresses;
(c) whether the scheme is closed to new members;
(d) whether benefit accrual and the payment of contributions is frozen;
(e) whether the scheme has any active members;
(f) the categories of benefits; and
(g) the number of members.

2.8.4 The trustees or managers must provide the Regulator with the necessary 'registrable information' within three months after the establishment of the scheme (s.62).

Collecting information relevant to the PPF Board

2.8.5 Section 68 provides that the Regulator may collect any information which appears to it to be relevant to the exercise of the functions of the PPF Board.

2.8.6 Section 69 provides that (except where the Regulator otherwise directs) the 'appropriate person' (essentially, the trustees or managers) must give written notice to the Regulator of any 'notifiable event' as soon as reasonably practicable after becoming aware of such event. 'Notifiable events' are to be prescribed by regulations and will concern the scheme itself or the employer in relation to the scheme. Notifiable events will presumably include, for example, information about a scheme's or employer's underfunding which could indicate to the PPF that it might need to become involved with the scheme.

Gathering, using and disclosing information

2.8.7 Sections 72–89 of the Act deal with the provision of information to the Regulator.

2.8.8 The key provisions are contained in s.72 which provides that the Regulator may (by notice in writing) require the following persons to provide any information/documentation relevant to the exercise of the Regulator's functions:

(a) the trustees/managers of an occupational or personal pension scheme;
(b) an employer in relation to an occupational pension scheme or a personal pension scheme where 'direct payment' arrangements exist;
(c) a professional adviser in relation to an occupational pension scheme; and
(d) any other person appearing to the Regulator to be a person who holds (or is likely to hold) information relevant to the exercise of the Regulator's functions.

2.8.9   Sections 73–76 contain provisions enabling the Regulator (at any reasonable time) to enter and inspect premises for the purpose of investigating whether various specified statutory requirements are being complied with in relation to an occupational or stakeholder pension scheme (and when on the premises, to require the production of and/or seize documents). These statutory requirements include, for example:

(a) the member-nominated trustee requirements (as amended in s.241 of the Act);
(b) any of the requirements of Part 1 of the 1995 Act apart from the indexation and equal treatment requirements;
(c) the transfer value provisions of the 1993 Act; and
(d) the employer duty to facilitate access to a stakeholder pension scheme.

2.8.10   Perhaps surprisingly, such statutory requirements also include, for example:

(a) the new trustee requirement for 'knowledge and understanding' under ss.247 and 248 of the Act; and
(b) the new 'employer consultation' requirements under ss.259–261 of the Act.

2.8.11   It is an offence under s.77 to refuse a request for information/obstruct an inspection of premises under ss.72–76. Such an offence is punishable by a fine or (in the case of a person who, without reasonable excuse, alters, suppresses, conceals or destroys a document which he is, or is liable to be, required to produce) to imprisonment. Section 80 makes it an offence (punishable by fine or imprisonment) knowingly or recklessly to provide the Regulator with false or misleading information. Section 78 enables a Justice of the Peace to issue a warrant authorising the Regulator to enter and inspect premises or, for example, to require persons to provide explanations in relation to documents obtained in the course of such an inspection.

2.8.12   Information held by the Regulator in the exercise of any of its functions (or contained in the register of pension schemes) may be used by the Regulator for the purposes of, or for any purposes connected with or incidental to, the exercise of its functions (s.81).

2.8.13   The Regulator may not disclose 'restricted information' except with the consent of the person to whom it relates (and, if different, the person from whom the Regulator obtained it) (s.82). This requirement is also extended to anyone who receives such information (whether directly or indirectly) from the Regulator. 'Restricted information' is defined as any information obtained by the Regulator in the exercise of its functions which relates to any person's business or other affairs. Unsurprisingly, however, this non-disclosure requirement is made subject to a long list of exceptions. In particular:

(a) information which has (at the time of disclosure) already been made available to the public from other sources (s.82(4)(a));

(b) summary information where particular information relating to individual people cannot be identified (s.82(4)(b));

(c) information which is disclosed for the purpose of enabling or assisting the Regulator (s.84) or the PPF Board (s.85) to exercise its functions;

(d) information which is disclosed to persons specified in Sched.3 to the Act (e.g. the Financial Services Authority or the Pensions Ombudsman) if the Regulator considers that the disclosure would enable or assist such person to exercise the functions also specified in that Schedule (s.86); and

(e) information which is disclosed, for example, to the Secretary of State or the Inland Revenue (s.87).

2.8.14 It is worth noting that s.83 makes it more difficult to take advantage of an exception to the non-disclosure requirement in the case of information received from 'corresponding overseas authorities'.

2.8.15 A breach of the disclosure of information requirements is punishable by a fine and/or imprisonment.

2.9 THE REGULATOR'S POWERS

2.9.1 As already noted, all of OPRA's functions will be transferred to the new Regulator under the Act. However, as well as having all of OPRA's powers, the Pensions Regulator will be given a range of additional powers.

Improvement notices

2.9.2 If the Regulator believes that a person is contravening or has contravened (and is likely to continue contravening) pensions legislation, then it has the power to issue an improvement notice (s.13). 'Pensions legislation' means the 1993 Act, Part 1 of the 1995 Act (other than the equal treatment provisions set out in ss.62–66A), Part 1 or s.33 of the 1999 Act or the Act itself.

2.9.3 An improvement notice will be issued directly to a person who satisfies the above conditions and the Regulator can direct that person to take, or refrain from taking, specific steps in order to remedy or prevent a recurrence of the contravention. An improvement notice must contain a statement as to why the Regulator believes that the pensions legislation is being contravened, and state the evidence on which that opinion is based. In addition, where the Regulator requires any specific steps to be taken, the improvement notice must specify the period (which cannot be less than 21 days) within which each step must be complied with.

2.9.4 Improvement notices may also refer to any Code of Practice issued by the Regulator under s.90 and can also give the party to whom the notice is addressed a choice as to how he wishes to remedy or prevent the recurrence of any contravention.

2.9.5   An improvement notice may also be conditional on a third party comply-ing with any of the directions which the Regulator might specify. Those directions will be contained in a notice under s.14 (third party notices) (see **para.2.9.7**).

2.9.6   Improvement notices can also direct the person to whom they are issued to inform the Regulator of how he has complied or is complying with the terms of the notice. The Regulator can specify the time period for doing this. If trustees fail to comply with an improvement notice issued to them, the Regulator can impose civil penalties under s.10 of the 1995 Act where there is no 'reasonable excuse' for non-compliance. It should be noted that 'reasonable excuse' has not been defined in the legislation; it is assumed that this will be left to the courts to decide.

Third party notices

2.9.7   Where the Regulator believes that a person is contravening or has contravened the pensions legislation and that contravention may be due to the failure of a third party who has not, themselves, contravened the pensions legis-lation, then the Regulator can issue a third party notice (s.14). The third party notice can be used to direct a third party to take or refrain from taking the steps specified in the notice in order to remedy or prevent any recurrence of the failure on the part of the third party.

2.9.8   As with improvement notices, the third party notice is required to state which part of the pensions legislation the Regulator believes that the third party is contravening and the evidence on which that assertion is based. Again, a time limit for complying with each step can be imposed (but cannot be less than 21 days beginning with the date of the notice). The third party may be given a choice of ways for remedying or preventing a recurrence of any failure. Interestingly, s.14(3) only appears to give a choice to third parties as to the ways of remedying or preventing the recurrence of any 'failure to do something'. It remains to be seen whether this will be extended to the actions of third parties which contravene the pensions legislation. The notice may also require the third party to notify the Regulator once he has complied with or is complying with any third party notice.

2.9.9   Perhaps the major difference between third party notices and improve-ment notices (other than the parties to whom they are directed) is set out in s.14(7). This section makes it clear that, where a third party is required to com-ply with the third party notice, any other duty which is imposed on them will not be regarded as contravened simply because they are complying with the third party notice.

2.9.10   The requirements to comply with a third party notice are also subject to legal professional privilege (s.311).

2.9.11   Non-compliance with a third party notice can lead to a penalty under s.10 of the 1995 Act.

2.9.12   Third party notices are a fairly significant extension of the powers currently open to OPRA under the 1995 Act. At present, OPRA is only able to act against trustees or employers. The Regulator will be able to take action against those who have a duty to do something in relation to the scheme (and the section is drafted so widely that it will almost certainly apply to all professional advisers and to almost any other third party).

Injunctions and (in Scotland) interdicts

2.9.13   The Regulator may apply to court for the grant of an injunction restraining any particular person from doing any act which constitutes a misuse or misappropriation of any pension scheme (occupational or personal) assets (s.15). Similarly, if a person has done any such act and there is a 'reasonable likelihood' of it continuing or being repeated, an injunction may also be granted. The power granted to the Regulator under s.15 is useful but is likely only to have a limited scope given that, where any action taken in relation to a scheme is neither a misuse nor a misappropriation of assets, the Regulator will find its hands tied. If members' benefits are prejudiced in a way which cannot be said to amount to misuse or misappropriation then, in those circumstances, s.15 will not assist the Regulator.

Restitution

2.9.14   The Regulator may apply to a court for an order that any person who has been involved in the misuse or misappropriation of any scheme assets should restore the parties to the position they would have been in had the misuse or misappropriation not occurred (s.16). For the purposes of s.16, a person is 'involved' if the court takes the view that he has been knowingly concerned in the misuse or misappropriation of assets.

Recovery of unpaid contributions

2.9.15   Section 17 allows the Regulator to stand in the shoes of the trustees or managers of a scheme and to recover from any employer any contribution payable towards that scheme which has not been paid on or before its due date. An employer contribution in relation to an occupational pension scheme includes any contribution payable in accordance with the schedule of contributions (s.227) or payment schedule (s.87 of the 1995 Act).

2.9.16   This power would extend to allow the Regulator, on behalf of the trustees or managers, to recover, for example, any debt due to the scheme under s.75 of the 1995 Act. Assuming that the Regulator will be better placed to recover debts, this power could be exercised by the Regulator in a way which would ease financial pressure on the PPF. The Regulator may well choose to pursue debts as a first line of action before allowing schemes to move into the PPF.

Powers in relation to winding up, contribution notices and financial support directions

2.9.17   These particular powers are dealt with in **Chapter 10**.

2.10   TRUSTEES OF OCCUPATIONAL PENSION SCHEMES

Prohibition orders

2.10.1   Section 33 of the Act replaces s.3 of the 1995 Act and considerably widens the ambit of the original s.3. Under s.3 of the 1995 Act, OPRA was only able to prohibit a person from being a trustee if that person had been 'in serious or persistent' breach of certain duties under the pensions legislation.

2.10.2   The new s.3 allows the Regulator to prohibit a person from being a trustee of a particular scheme, a particular description of trust schemes or of trust schemes in general if it is satisfied that the person is 'not a fit and proper person to be a trustee'. The Regulator must prepare and publish a statement of the policies it intends to adopt in relation to its exercise of its powers under s.3.

2.10.3   In the event that the Regulator decides that a prohibition order is appropriate, the person affected is removed as a trustee although he may apply to the Regulator to revoke its order. The Regulator can do so either generally or in relation to a particular scheme or description of schemes.

Suspension orders

2.10.4   The Regulator's power to make suspension orders under s.4 of the 1995 Act has been extended by s.34 of the Act. In addition to the powers already granted under s.3 of the 1995 Act, the Regulator may now suspend a trustee where consideration is being given to the institution of proceedings against him for an offence involving dishonesty or deception. This is wider than the original wording which went only so far as to allow suspension to occur where such proceedings had been instituted.

Appointment of trustees

2.10.5   Where a person has been removed as a trustee under s.3 of the 1995 Act or has been disqualified as a trustee, the Regulator may appoint a trustee in his place. For the most part, the requirements of s.7 of the 1995 Act continue to apply in this respect (i.e. to secure that the trustees as a whole have the necessary skill and knowledge for the proper administration of the scheme and are sufficient in number and to secure the proper use or application of scheme assets).

2.10.6   Section 35 of the Act inserts a new s.7(5A) into the 1995 Act and allows the trustees, employer or any member of the scheme to apply to the Regulator for the appointment of a trustee.

2.10.7   Section 8 of the 1995 Act (consequences of appointment of trustees under s.7) is also amended by s.35 of the Act. Where the Regulator makes an order appointing a trustee under s.7, it can require any of the trustee's fees and expenses to be paid by the employer, out of scheme resources, or both. The order can also provide that any amount paid out of scheme resources can be treated as a debt due from the employer (which was basically the position under ss.8(1) and 8(2) of the 1995 Act).

Independent trustees

2.10.8   Sections 22 to 26 of the 1995 Act currently require an independent trustee to be appointed where an insolvency practitioner (or the official receiver) has been appointed in relation to a scheme employer and there is currently no independent trustee in place.

2.10.9   Those provisions are extended by s.36 of the Act to allow the Regulator to appoint an independent trustee where a scheme is being assessed to see if it qualifies for entry into the PPF or is continuing as a closed scheme under s.153. Where an insolvency practitioner (or the official receiver) begins or ceases to act in relation to the scheme he must notify the Regulator, the Board and the scheme trustees. The details of that notification are still to be prescribed.

2.10.10   Another point to note is that, under the 1995 Act, whilst s.22 applies to a scheme an independent trustee must be appointed by the insolvency practitioner. Sections 23 and 24 of the 1995 Act are amended to allow the Regulator to appoint the independent trustee from a register which the Regulator is required to maintain in relation to independent trustees. There will be prescribed conditions for registration and compilation of the register.

2.10.11   Section 25 of the 1995 Act remains relatively unchanged and continues to allow the independent trustee to exercise powers vested in the trustees or the employer. The two relatively minor changes are: first, if an independent trustee ceases to be independent, the trustee is required to notify the Regulator and, second, the Regulator can make an order as to who should pay the independent trustee's fees and the method of payment.

Disqualification

2.10.12   Sub-section 30(1) of the 1995 Act has been substituted such that, where a trustee is disqualified in relation to a scheme, it has the effect of automatically removing him as a trustee (rather than his simply ceasing to be a trustee). See s.37 of the Act. This brings the disqualification provisions into line with the prohibition conditions.

2.11   REPORTING BREACHES OF THE LAW

Duty to report

2.11.1   Section 70(1) of the Act details those people who will have a reporting requirement imposed upon them, namely:

(a) a trustee or manager of an occupational or personal pension scheme;
(b) a person who is otherwise involved in the administration of such a scheme;
(c) the employer in relation to an occupational pension scheme;
(d) a professional adviser in relation to such a scheme; and
(e) a person who is otherwise involved in advising the trustees or managers of an occupational or personal pension scheme.

2.11.2   Where any of the persons listed above has reasonable cause to believe that a duty relevant to the administration of the scheme which is 'imposed by or by virtue of an enactment or rule of law' has not been, or is not being, complied with and the failure is likely to be of 'material significance' to the Regulator in the exercise of any of its functions, then that person must give a written report to the Regulator as soon as reasonably practicable.

2.11.3   'Professional adviser' has the same meaning as s.47(1) of the 1995 Act. It will therefore include the scheme actuary, the scheme auditor, actuarial advisers, legal advisers, fund managers and any custodian appointed in relation to the scheme. Section 70 is therefore considerably wider than the current whistleblowing requirements of s.48 of the 1995 Act which imposes a duty to notify only on auditors and actuaries (the other professional advisers could, but were not required to, whistle blow).

2.11.4   However, it is not clear under s.70 exactly which duty or duties are relevant. The wording of s.70(2)(a) refers to a duty which is 'relevant to the administration of the scheme in question'. Clearly, any duty imposed under the pensions legislation would fall under the ambit of this wording. However, legislation such as the data protection legislation and employment legislation generally will probably also be caught. To compound the problem, the duty referred to is one which has been 'imposed by or by virtue of an enactment or rule of law'. Insofar as any duty has been imposed by an enactment, it should be reasonably easy to pin down the duty in question. That is not so easy in respect of a duty which has been imposed by a rule of law. Are implied duties included? It is probably fair to assume that any fiduciary duties imposed on trustees would fall within this wording. Suffice it to say, the position is vague and could extend much further than originally thought.

2.11.5   Section 70(2)(b) also requires the failure to comply with a duty to be 'of material significance' to the Regulator. The wording is intended to avoid the situation in which OPRA often found itself i.e. it was spending a disproportionate amount of time dealing with minor breaches while fairly significant breaches were going unchecked. The Regulator is expected to adopt a much more proportionate approach to its duties. In due course, the Regulator will be issuing a Code of Practice giving guidance as to how it considers these sections should operate. The Regulator will certainly have to give some thought to what it considers to be materially significant in terms of what should be reported to it; otherwise it could be inundated with reports of minor breaches which could hamper it in exercising its functions.

2.11.6   Section 10 of the 1995 Act will apply to any person who, without reasonable excuse, fails to comply with s.70 of the Act.

2.11.7   One final point to note is that there are exclusions in s.70 relating to the disclosure of information contained in privileged communications between a legal adviser and his client, provided it is in connection with the giving of legal advice to the client.

Reports by skilled persons

2.11.8   Section 71 provides that the Regulator may issue a notice (a 'report notice') requiring trustees, employers or any other person involved in the administration of a scheme to provide the Regulator with a report prepared by a skilled person nominated or approved by the Regulator and who must have the skills necessary to make a report on the matters concerned. Report notices will be issued by the Regulator to obtain information about specified matters which are relevant to the exercise of its functions. Even though a report notice may be issued to, say, the trustees, any person who is providing services to the trustees in relation to a matter on which a report is required is also required under the Act to give the person appointed to make the report such assistance as he may reasonably require.

2.11.9   The person to whom the report notice is issued must meet the costs of providing the report. However, the report notice can require any person specified (other than the Regulator) to reimburse those costs.

2.11.10   If the trustees fail to comply with any report notice issued to them, penalties can be imposed under s.10 of the 1995 Act. In addition, s.10 will apply to any person who, without reasonable excuse, fails to comply with any report notice issued to him.

Publishing reports

2.11.11   Section 89 of the Act gives the Regulator power to publish a report on the consideration given by it to the exercise of its functions in relation to any particular case, together with the results of that consideration. The report can take whatever form the Regulator considers appropriate.

2.11.12   For the purposes of the law of defamation, the publication of any matter by the Regulator is privileged unless the publication is shown to be made with malice.

2.12   CONCLUSION

2.12.1   As already noted, a large amount of the detail as to the operation of the Regulator, how it will carry out its functions and the administration of its procedures is still to be fleshed out in regulations. What is clear is that the Regulator's powers will allow it to be more pro-active in protecting the interests of pension scheme members and to take a targeted and proportionate approach in doing so. Early indications are that the Regulator intends to make full use of its powers.

2.12.2   The Regulator's information powers are more extensive than the powers which OPRA previously had and, if used wisely, could allow the Regulator to make significant inroads in ensuring that pension arrangements are properly administered. However, the greatest change in the way the Regulator will operate as compared to OPRA is likely to come from the raft of new powers which it has been granted. Improvement notices and third party notices may be useful weapons in the Regulator's armoury, allowing it to take direct action against those who have a duty to do something in relation to a scheme (including professional advisers). The Regulator's powers in relation to winding up, and issuing contribution notices and financial support directions (see **Chapter 10**) have already received a great deal of attention and will, no doubt, receive more as and when the Regulator makes use of them.

2.12.3   Finally, s.70 of the Act (duty to report) may cause difficulties for, amongst others, professional advisers in the short (and, perhaps, long) term. The section is considerably wider than the current whistle-blowing requirements of the 1995 Act and it may have consequences which were not originally intended. In this respect, the Regulator's Code of Practice will be of significant interest.

3 THE PENSION PROTECTION FUND

3.1 INTRODUCTION

3.1.1 One of the key reforms proposed by the Government in its 2003 paper *Action on Occupational Pensions* was the establishment of a compensation scheme to be known as the Pension Protection Fund (PPF). The aim was to protect private sector defined benefit scheme members whose employers become insolvent with unfunded liabilities in the pension scheme. The Government promised to legislate accordingly.

3.1.2 The resulting provisions are contained in Part 2 of and Scheds. 5–9 to the Act. They cover the establishment of the PPF Board (the Board) and its powers, detailed provisions regarding the protection to be afforded by the PPF and new fraud compensation provisions. Part 2 also contains provisions regarding the review of Board decisions, including the creation of a new PPF Ombudsman. See **Chapter 4** for a discussion of these provisions.

3.1.3 It is understood that the PPF provisions of the Act and related regulations will be implemented in April 2005.

3.2 ELIGIBILITY

3.2.1 The Act prescribes certain eligibility criteria that a scheme must satisfy before the Board is required to assume responsibility for it as follows:

(a) the scheme must have been an eligible scheme throughout the prescribed period (s.126);
(b) the Board has become involved with the scheme because either:
   (i) a qualifying insolvency event has occurred in relation to the scheme and the insolvency practitioner has issued a scheme failure notice which has become binding; or
   (ii) the Board has received an application from the trustees or a notice from the Regulator and the Board has issued a scheme failure notice which has become binding;

(c) the scheme's assets are less than the value of its protected liabilities;

(d) no withdrawal notice has been issued since the occurrence of the qualifying insolvency event and the occurrence of a withdrawal event before the issue of a scheme failure notice is not a possibility; and

(e) the scheme is not a new scheme.

Eligible schemes

3.2.2   Eligible schemes are defined in s.126. To be eligible, an occupational pension scheme must not be a money purchase or a prescribed scheme. Prescribed types of scheme will also be excluded. The Explanatory Notes indicate that prescribed schemes or schemes of a prescribed type will be, in the main, those schemes currently exempted from the application of the MFR.

3.2.3   In addition, the scheme must not have commenced winding up before a day to be appointed by the Secretary of State by order ('appointed day'), which is expected to be 6 April 2005.

3.2.4   Section 126 is subject to regulations which may provide that an otherwise eligible scheme will not be admitted to the PPF. According to debate in the House of Lords the intention is to exclude schemes whose trustees have compromised a debt arising under s.75 of the 1995 Act but whose assets are still insufficient to meet the scheme's protected liabilities, unless (according to OPRA Update 10) the compromise is part of a scheme of arrangement or it takes place during a scheme's assessment period when the Board is acting as creditor of the employer in place of the scheme's trustees.

Qualifying insolvency event

3.2.5   An insolvency event is 'qualifying' if it occurs on or after the appointed day and either it is the first insolvency event to occur in relation to the employer on or after the appointed day or it does not occur within the scheme's assessment period. See ss.120–122 and 127.

3.2.6   This requirement may reduce the scope for trustees to be able to compromise a debt on the employer arising under s.75 of the 1995 Act. If the trustees believe that members may receive a greater share of their benefits by being admitted to the PPF than if the trustees compromise the debt and the scheme subsequently commences winding up, the trustees may be obliged (under their duties as trustees) to demand a debt from the employer that will be sufficient to push the employer into insolvency.

Delaying the occurrence of a qualifying insolvency event

3.2.7   If, prior to the commencement of the PPF, an employer finds itself in financial difficulties both the employer and the trustees of an underfunded scheme sponsored by the employer may be tempted to prolong the life of the employer until after the appointed day, when an insolvency event would then be engineered, in the hope that the scheme would qualify for entry into the PPF.

3.2.8   Note that the incentive for taking such action may be reduced when further details of the Financial Assistance Scheme (see **Chapter 13**) are available, depending on the eligibility requirements and compensation available from that scheme. Also note that this could create a real dilemma for trustees in setting employer contribution rates, whether in consequence of statutory or scheme based powers.

3.2.9   However, trustees and employers should be aware that they are at risk of incurring personal liability by intentionally delaying the otherwise inevitable insolvency of the employer. In particular, trustees may be at risk of claims from members for breach of trust, and directors of the employer may face court action for wrongful trading.

Breach of trust

3.2.10   Trustees risk committing an actionable breach of trust if, as a result of an intentional delay, members eventually receive a lower level of benefits from the scheme or compensation from the PPF than they would have received if the trustees had compromised the debt when they first had the opportunity to do so.

3.2.11   In addition, trustees may also have an obligation under their trust deed and rules to trigger the winding up of the scheme in circumstances where there is no reasonable prospect of the employer being able to meet the scheme's on-going costs. They will commit a breach of trust if they do not act in accordance with the terms of the trust deed.

3.2.12   Arguably such breaches of trust may be wilful default, which may prevent the trustees relying on any exoneration or indemnity provisions contained in the trust deed and the rules of the scheme in the case of claims by members. This is also likely to prevent a successful claim under any trustee indemnity insurance policy, as insurers tend to exclude claims in relation to wilful breach.

Wrongful trading

3.2.13   The employer risks committing the offence of wrongful trading under s.214 of the Insolvency Act 1986. This occurs where:

(a) a company enters into insolvent liquidation; and
(b) at some point prior to entering into liquidation the directors knew or ought reasonably to have concluded that the company could not avoid going into insolvent liquidation; and
(c) from that point the directors did not take every step with a view to minimising the loss to creditors.

3.2.14   If the offence of wrongful trading is committed, the directors of the employer will be personally liable and they may be required to contribute personally to the assets of the employer.

3.2.15   However, if the liquidation of an employer is delayed because the employer and the trustees are in negotiations regarding the compromise of a debt, for example, the directors may be able to justify their decision to continue trading during this time as, until such time as a compromise is agreed or negotiations break down, it may not be inevitable that the company will enter into insolvent liquidation. However, directors in such circumstances should be made fully aware of the potential risks.

3.2.16   Also note that the potential for a contribution demand under scheme powers may create a similar debate i.e. if the potential for a material contribution demand by scheme trustees is known to the directors.

Notice of insolvency event

3.2.17   When an insolvency event occurs in relation to the employer of an occupational pension scheme, the insolvency practitioner appointed in relation to the employer must give notice of that event to the Board, the Regulator and the trustees. The notice must be issued within a prescribed notice period and contain prescribed content to be set out in regulations (ss.120–121).

Scheme rescue

3.2.18   Under s.122, if an insolvency practitioner is able to confirm that a scheme rescue has already occurred he must issue a withdrawal notice to the Board. If an insolvency practitioner is able to confirm that a scheme rescue is not possible he must issue a scheme failure notice to the Board. There will be prescribed matters contained in regulations to determine whether or not a scheme rescue is possible. The relevant 's.122 notice' must be issued within a prescribed notice period and contain prescribed content.

3.2.19   If, in prescribed circumstances such as the end of insolvency proceedings, the insolvency practitioner is unable to confirm either that a scheme rescue has already occurred or that one is not possible he must issue a notice to that effect to the Board, the Regulator and the trustees. The s.122 notice must be issued within a prescribed notice period and contain prescribed content.

3.2.20   If the insolvency practitioner fails to issue a s.122 notice in circumstances when he ought to have done or the Board does not approve the s.122 notice, the Board must issue a notice instead.

3.2.21   When a s.122 notice is issued, the Board must determine whether or not to approve it (s.123). The notice must be approved if the insolvency practitioner was required to issue the notice and the notice complied with prescribed requirements. Where the Board makes a determination it must issue a determination notice to the Regulator, the trustees, the insolvency practitioner who issued the notice, any insolvency practitioner appointed in relation to the employer, or the employer if there is no insolvency practitioner in relation to it.

3.2.22   Section 122 notices are not binding as to the status of the scheme until the Board has issued a determination notice (or a s.122 notice itself) and the review period under Chapter 6 of the Act (Reviews, Appeals of Maladministration) has expired or any review has been finally disposed of.

3.2.23   Once the s.122 notice has become binding the Board must deliver a copy of the s.122 notice and a notice that it has become binding, to the Regulator, the trustees, the insolvency practitioner, any insolvency practitioner appointed in relation to the employer, or the employer if there is no insolvency practitioner in relation to it.

Application from the trustees

3.2.24   If trustees become aware that the employer is unlikely to continue as a going concern and prescribed requirements are met, the trustees must apply to the Board for it to assume responsibility for the scheme (ss.128–129). The application must be issued within a prescribed period and contain prescribed content.

3.2.25   According to the Explanatory Notes this provision is aimed at schemes whose employer cannot be subject to insolvency events, for example public sector schemes without a crown guarantee and schemes with overseas employers which are subject to foreign insolvency proceedings. However, the obligation is not currently limited to the trustees of such schemes.

3.2.26   Section 128 appears to place an onerous obligation on trustees, who may not have access to sufficient information about the employer's financial situation to be able to draw such a conclusion. In addition, it is unlikely that lay trustees would have the necessary experience or expertise to be able to process financial information in such a way, even if they did have access to it.

3.2.27   This requirement may cause additional difficulties for those trustees who are officers of the employer and who are likely to be much more aware of the future trading prospects of the employer. The Act does refer to 'trustees' rather than an individual trustee, but it is unclear what obligations will be placed on a trustee who has individually become aware that the employer is unlikely to continue as a going concern. One would generally expect such a person to find himself facing a serious conflict of interests.

3.2.28   Any provision which discourages managers and directors from becoming trustees of their company's occupational pension scheme cannot be good news for the future of such schemes. On the other hand, it may be argued that this dilemma already exists i.e. that duties owed by a company officer to the company and his duties as a trustee are not resolvable.

Notice from the Regulator

3.2.29   If the Regulator becomes aware that the employer is unlikely to continue as a going concern and prescribed requirements are met, the Regulator must give notice to this effect to the Board (s.129).

Scheme rescue

3.2.30   If the Board receives an application from the trustees or a notice from the Regulator it must seek to confirm whether or not a scheme rescue is possible and issue either a scheme failure notice (if no scheme rescue is possible) or a withdrawal notice (if a scheme rescue has already occurred) to the Regulator, the trustees and the employer (s.130). There will be prescribed matters to determine whether or not a scheme rescue is possible or has already occurred.

3.2.31   The Board's notice is not binding until the review period under Chapter 6 has expired or any review has been finally disposed of. The Board must notify the Regulator, the trustees and the employer when the notice becomes binding.

Protected liabilities

3.2.32   To be eligible for the PPF the value of a scheme's assets must be less than the value of its protected liabilities, which are, according to s.131:

(a) the cost of securing benefits which correspond to the compensation that would be payable if the Board assumed liability for the scheme;
(b) other liabilities of the scheme which are not liabilities to members; and
(c) the estimated cost of winding up.

The method of valuation may be prescribed by regulation.

Actuarial valuation

3.2.33   To determine whether a scheme's assets are sufficient to meet its protected liabilities the Board must as soon as reasonably practicable obtain an actuarial valuation as at the relevant time (ss.143–145).

3.2.34   A scheme's assets may include debts due to the scheme under the moral hazard and restoration order provisions of the Act and any debt due under s.75 of the 1995 Act. Regulations are to provide for how such 'assets' will be valued.

3.2.35   Once the Board is satisfied that the actuarial valuation has been prepared in accordance with prescribed requirements it must approve the actuarial valuation and provide copies of it to the Regulator, the trustees and the insolvency practitioner or employer as appropriate.

3.2.36   The actuarial valuation is not binding until it is approved and the period for review of the approval has passed or, if a review is required, all matters in relation to the review have been disposed of. A binding valuation is conclusive as to whether a scheme's assets are sufficient to meet its protected liabilities.

Board ceases to be involved

3.2.37   If a withdrawal event occurs during an assessment period the Board must cease to be involved with the scheme (ss.149–150).

New schemes

3.2.38   The Board cannot assume responsibility if it is satisfied that the scheme is a new scheme i.e. it has been set up to become eligible for the PPF (ss.146–147).

3.3   THE ASSESSMENT PERIOD

3.3.1   Under s.132, if a qualifying insolvency event has occurred in relation to the employer the assessment period commences at the start of the qualifying insolvency event.

3.3.2   If the Board has received an application from the trustees or a notice from the Regulator under s.129, the assessment period begins when the application is made or the notice received (unless the application is made or notice given during an existing assessment period).

3.3.3   During an assessment period certain actions are prescribed or prohibited.

Frozen scheme

3.3.4   No new members may be admitted and no benefits may accrue (except benefit increases or money purchase benefits derived from investment gains).

Payment of benefits

3.3.5   Benefits payable are reduced to the level that would be payable by the PPF if the Board had assumed responsibility for the scheme, although regulations may provide otherwise. Similarly regulations may provide for death benefits to be paid unreduced.

3.3.6   Where, on the commencement of the assessment period, a member becomes a deferred member who is entitled to a cash equivalent transfer or a return of contributions under the new Chapter 5, Part IV of the 1993 Act (inserted by s.264 of the Act), no right or power conferred by that Chapter may be exercised and no duty imposed by that Chapter may be discharged. In addition, no benefits are payable to or in respect of such a member during the assessment period. These provisions are limited to people who become deferred members on the commencement of the assessment period and appear to exclude existing deferred members or those who become deferred during the duration of the assessment period.

3.3.7   If the scheme was being wound up prior to the commencement of the assessment period the benefits payable during the assessment period must disregard the effects of the winding up i.e. benefits must be paid at a level comparable to the level of compensation which members would receive if the scheme were admitted into the PPF (s.138(6)).

3.3.8   Except in relation to money purchase benefits, commencement of pensions and payment of lump sum benefits may, in prescribed circumstances, be postponed if a member remains in service after his normal retirement age under the scheme. This seems inconsistent with members' increased freedom to remain in employment whilst drawing their pension which has been introduced as part of the government's tax simplification exercise.

3.3.9   If the scheme has insufficient assets to pay reduced benefits as they fall due the trustees may apply to the Board for a loan (s.139).

3.3.10   The trustees are not prevented from discharging their liability under Part 4 of the 1999 Act in respect of pension sharing (s.135(8)).

Review of ill health pensions

3.3.11   The Board may review reviewable ill health pensions pursuant to ss.140–142 if:

(a) the member would be entitled to compensation if the Board assumed responsibility for the scheme;
(b) the member had not attained his normal pension age prior to the commencement of the assessment period; and
(c) the pension is attributable to service under the scheme or another scheme.

3.3.12   An ill health pension is a reviewable ill health pension if it was awarded to the member in the three years preceding the assessment date, or before the end of a prescribed period beginning with the assessment date in response to an application made before that date.

3.3.13   Following the review, if the Board assumes responsibility for the scheme, it may determine that reviewable ill health pensions will be terminated in a prescribed manner. One of the conditions for terminating a reviewable ill health pension is that the award was made in ignorance of, or based on a mistake as to, a material fact relevant to the decision and that had the trustees known, or not been mistaken as to that fact, they could not reasonably have decided to make an award. This condition makes it vital that the trustees keep full records of the facts that are available to them when they make any decision to award an ill health pension and also a record of the reasons that they rely upon in coming to their decision.

3.3.14 Such a decision may be open to review and reconsideration under ss.206–208 (see **Chapter 4**).

3.3.15 Any review of ill health pensions undertaken by the Board, and any subsequent reviews or reconsiderations of the Board's decisions will delay the valuation, as the review may affect the scheme's liabilities.

Contributions

3.3.16 No further contributions may be paid during the assessment period (although they may be payable in respect of the assessment period following cessation of the assessment period if the Board does not assume liability for the scheme).

Investment

3.3.17 The Board may issue directions to relevant persons in relation to the investment, expenditure, legal proceedings and other prescribed matters. 'Relevant persons' for these purposes includes not only the trustees of the scheme but also the employer and such other persons as may be prescribed.

Debt due from employer

3.3.18 Any rights and powers of the trustees in relation to any debt due to them from the employer are exercisable only by the Board (s.137).

Prohibited actions

3.3.19 Winding up cannot commence during an assessment period, except by order of the Regulator (s.135). This effectively takes away all the power that the trustees or the employer might have under the scheme rules to wind up a scheme.

3.3.20 No transfers may be made except in prescribed circumstances, and no other steps may be taken to discharge any liability. Furthermore, the Regulator may not make a freezing order in respect of the scheme.

Consequences of breach

3.3.21 Action taken in contravention of ss.133–135 is void (unless validated by the Board) and s.10 of the 1995 Act applies to trustees who fail to take all reasonable steps to secure compliance.

End of assessment period

3.3.22 The assessment period ends on the first of when:

(a) the trustees receive a transfer notice (see **para.3.4** below);

(b) the Board ceases to be involved with the scheme (see **para.3.5** below); or

(c) it is determined that no scheme rescue is possible but there are sufficient assets to meet the protected liabilities (see **para.3.5** below).

3.4   ADMISSION TO THE PPF

Transfer notice

3.4.1   When the Board is required to assume responsibility for a scheme it must issue a transfer notice to the trustees under s.160. A transfer notice cannot be issued within the first 12 months of the assessment period. Furthermore, no transfer notice may be issued if an application has been made under the fraud compensation regime, until the application has been finally disposed of (s.172).

Effect of admission to PPF

3.4.2   The property, rights and liabilities of the scheme are transferred to the Board with effect from the time that the trustees receive the transfer notice (s.161 and Sched.6).

3.4.3   Liabilities are defined as excluding 'any liability to, or in respect of, any member of the scheme, other than liabilities in respect of money purchase benefits and such other liabilities as may be prescribed' (s.161(3)). So liabilities of the scheme will transfer to the PPF under s.161(2)(a) but liabilities for and in respect of individual members will not except in relation to money purchase benefits or other prescribed liabilities.

3.4.4   The transfer is automatic and does not require the completion of any legal formality or the consent of any person which would otherwise have been required. Section 161 provides that the trustees are discharged from their pension obligations from the time of the transfer and that the Board is responsible for securing that compensation is paid in accordance with the pension compensation provisions.

3.4.5   However, Sched.6 provides that trustees are not discharged in respect of any existing or future cause of action against them if, disregarding the transfer, the trustees would have been personally liable and in respect of which they would not have been indemnified from the assets of the scheme. This presumably means that if, but for the transfer, the trustees would have benefited from an exoneration clause in the scheme's trust deed and rules, the trustees will not become liable as a result of the transfer. However, if the scheme's exoneration and indemnity provisions are insufficient to protect them, the trustees will be left in the vulnerable position of being without scheme assets or (in most cases) a solvent employer, from which the premiums on a trustee insurance policy may be paid.

3.4.6 The scheme is treated as having been wound up immediately after the time of the transfer. However, Sched.6 provides that the trustees must continue to hold the property or rights for the benefit of the Board until such time as they can be legally vested in the Board. It is the Board's responsibility to ensure that foreign assets are vested.

3.4.7 Schedule 6 provides that where any rights or liabilities under a contract of employment between the trustees and an individual would be transferred to the Board as part of the automatic transfer, that contract shall instead be treated as terminated on the day preceding the day on which the trustees receive the transfer notice.

3.4.8 The Act makes no specific provision as to the allocation of liability for any breach of an employee's statutory or contractual rights. It seems logical to assume that the liability must transfer from the trustees (who would now be without scheme funds to meet any claims) to the Board, either by virtue of the general transferring provisions in the Act or because such a situation would fall under the Transfer of Undertakings (Protection of Employment) Regulations 1981, SI 1981/1794.

Levels of compensation

3.4.9 Sections 162–171 and Sched.7 contain the PPF pension compensation provisions.

3.4.10 Generally, if a person has reached his normal pension age as at the assessment date, he will receive 100 per cent of the benefits that would usually have been provided to him by the scheme, with no cap on this amount. All other members (regardless of whether they have actually retired) will receive 90 per cent of their benefits, subject to a maximum which is known as the 'compensation cap'.

3.4.11 There was pressure from the House of Lords to reduce the level of compensation paid to people over their normal pension age to bring it into line with the compensation paid to other scheme members. The argument for providing such members with 100 per cent of their benefits is that it would be unfair to take benefits away from members who have no chance to build up further benefits by contributing to another pension arrangement. On the other hand, people who are currently in receipt of benefits having taken early retirement will have their benefits reduced in circumstances where it may be no fairer to do so than it would be to reduce the benefits of those over their scheme's normal pension age (see below).

3.4.12 Pensions accrued on or after 6 April 1997 will be increased in line with the retail prices index, capped at 2.5 per cent. There are no increases in respect of pre-6 April 1997 pensions.

3.4.13 Widow's and widower's pensions will be 50 per cent of the member's pension. There is no provision to increase this figure or increase the member's pension in circumstances where a member has taken a reduced pension to provide an increased survivor's pension. Regulations may provide for survivor's pensions not to be paid in certain circumstances.

3.4.14   Regulations may prescribe the payment of benefits to partners of pre-scribed descriptions. House of Lords debates suggest that the intention here is to provide survivor's benefits in the case of civil partnerships and unmarried part-ners if this is provided for by the scheme rules. However, if the scheme rules only provide for widow's/widower's pensions, the PPF will only provide survivor's pensions in the case of marriage or civil partnerships and not for unmarried partners.

3.4.15   Section 171 contains an equal treatment provision which will apply to any function conferred on the Board which may treat a woman less favourably than a man (or vice versa).

3.4.16   Regulations will prescribe how money purchase benefits will be dealt with where a member is entitled to money purchase benefits under a scheme admitted to the PPF. Presumably, this will include money purchase AVC benefits, as they are not dealt with elsewhere in the Act for these purposes.

3.4.17   Where a person becomes a deferred member on the commencement of the assessment period and becomes entitled to a cash equivalent transfer or a refund of contributions, Chapter 5 of Part 4 of the 1993 Act is excluded in re-lation to such a member and the member is treated as not having an accrued right (although para.32 of Sched.7 provides otherwise). Such a person is entitled only to compensation in the form of a lump sum, being 90 per cent of the value of either the transfer value or the return of contributions. Compensation is payable immediately after the issue of the transfer notice.

3.4.18   There is provision for Sched.7 (the compensation provisions) to be amended by regulation in relation to prescribed schemes or schemes of a pre-scribed prescription. House of Lords debate indicated that this is intended to cover cash balance schemes and other future arrangements which cannot currently be anticipated, but at the moment this provision contains no such restriction.

Definition of normal pension age

3.4.19   Normal pension age is defined in para.34 of Sched.7 as being the age specified in the admissible rules as the earliest age at which the pension or lump sum becomes payable without actuarial adjustment.

3.4.20   This will not necessarily be the normal pension age defined in the scheme rules. For example, if a member may take early retirement as of right based on his pensionable salary and service as at the date of retirement, without actuarial adjustment, this date will be the members' normal pension age for the purposes of the PPF.

Reducing the level of compensation

3.4.21   As mentioned above, the amount of compensation payable may be subject to the compensation cap and details of the cap are set out in para.26 of Sched.7. The amount of cap is not specified in the Act and will be set out in an order made by the Secretary of State. However, it has been speculated that the compensation cap will be £25,000 (to be increased in line with earnings) if a member's normal pension age is 65. The figure will be adjusted if a person's normal pension age is higher or lower than 65.

3.4.22   The compensation cap applies not only on the amount that will be paid by the PPF by way of compensation in respect of a benefit under the scheme, but it will also apply to any other benefits that a member will receive from the same or a connected scheme (connected scheme is not defined). If the aggregate of the benefits from the scheme or schemes exceeds the compensation cap, the benefits payable from the PPF will be reduced accordingly.

3.4.23   There is also a power for the Secretary of State to vary the levels of compensation payable from the PPF. Although a reduction cannot be imposed retrospectively, if the Board anticipates that it will have to assume responsibility for a large and severely underfunded scheme it could potentially apply to the Secretary of State to amend the levels of compensation prior to admitting the scheme. This has created understandable controversy, as the intention of creating the PPF is to provide a specific level of benefits, in the form of compensation, for members of final salary pension schemes. If the level of the compensation were to fluctuate, the PPF will surely fail to achieve this fundamental aim.

Invalidating scheme amendments

3.4.24   Paragraphs 31 and 35 of Sched.7 contain provisions enabling pensions in payment to be reduced on certain conditions. In some cases members over their normal pension age may not be entitled to the whole of the benefits prescribed by the scheme rules.

3.4.25   The first condition is that the scheme rules must have been subject to amendments (except those required by legislation or of a prescribed description) made within the three years preceding the assessment date (even if the amendments took effect by reference to an earlier date) or that there are scheme rules which only came into effect on the winding up of the scheme, the insolvency of the employer, or any prescribed event in relation to the future of the employer as a going concern.

3.4.26   Secondly, there must have been a recent discretionary increase (above that required by legislation or provided for by the scheme rules disregarding the recent amendment) in the rate of any pension in payment or postponed pension which took effect within the three years preceding the assessment date.

3.4.27   Thirdly, the amendment and the increase combined must have increased the protected liabilities of the scheme.

3.4.28   If the effect of disregarding the amendment would be that the pensioner member would cease to be entitled to a certain part of his pension, regulations may provide that the Board does not have to pay compensation for that part of his pension.

3.5   IF ADMISSION TO THE PPF IS REFUSED

3.5.1   The Board may refuse to accept responsibility for a scheme at the termination of the assessment period either because a withdrawal event has occurred or because the Board has determined that, although no scheme rescue is possible, there are sufficient assets to meet the protected liabilities.

Withdrawal events

3.5.2   The Board ceases to be involved with a scheme on the occurrence of the first withdrawal event following the commencement of the assessment period (s.149). The Board must issue a withdrawal notice if any of the following withdrawal events occur:

(a)   notice by an insolvency practitioner that a scheme rescue has occurred;
(b)   determination by the Board that a scheme rescue has occurred;
(c)   the expiry of 6 months from the date on which an insolvency practitioner gave notice that he was unable to confirm whether a scheme rescue was possible or had occurred and provided that no further insolvency event occurs within that 6 month period. Where the Board receives notice from the insolvency practitioner that he cannot determine whether or not a scheme rescue is possible the Board must review whether any insolvency event has occurred in relation to the employer since the date of the notice, or is likely to occur within 6 months of the date of the notice. If it determines that no insolvency event has occurred or is likely to occur in that period, the Board must issue a withdrawal notice to that effect. This means that the Board must have to carry out some review of the employer's financial position and prospects in order to be able to determine the likelihood of an insolvency event occurring in relation to it within 6 months;
(d)   determination by the Board that a scheme has not been eligible throughout the prescribed period or that the scheme is a new scheme;
(e)   determination by the Board that no insolvency event has occurred or is likely to occur within six months of the date on which a s.122(4) notice became binding.

3.5.3   A withdrawal notice is not binding until the review period in respect of Chapter 6 of the Act has expired or any review has been finally disposed of. Once the withdrawal notice becomes binding the Board must issue a notice to this effect (s.148(7)).

Effect of withdrawal: payment of benefits

3.5.4   Where reduced benefits have been paid to or in respect of a member during the assessment period, the balance of the benefits due under the scheme are payable when the Board ceases to be involved with the scheme.

3.5.5   Where a scheme was being wound up prior to the commencement of the assessment period s.138(6) requires the trustees to ignore the effects of the winding up when determining the level of benefits payable during the assessment period and to pay benefits at a level comparable to the level of compensation that would have been paid if the scheme had been admitted to the PPF. This may have resulted in overpayments to members retiring during the assessment period, compared to the benefits that they would otherwise have received on wind up. When the Board ceases to be involved with the scheme, the trustees may take such steps as they consider appropriate, including adjusting future payments from the scheme, to recover any excess.

Effect of withdrawal: retrospective accrual

3.5.6   Regulations may prescribe that benefits may accrue in respect of service during the assessment period which, apart from the provisions of the Act, would have counted under the scheme as pensionable service.

3.5.7   Such regulations may also prescribe that accrual may be dependent upon the payment of retrospective contributions (by both employer and employee). The Explanatory Notes provide that any retrospective contributions may have to be paid within a prescribed timeframe. Depending on the timeframe, this may not give trustees the freedom to allow members to pay retrospective contributions at an appropriate rate, bearing in mind the length of time for which contributions were put on hold. The employer and/or the trustees could consider providing some facility for active members to make equivalent monthly contributions to a separate account during the assessment period, repayable if the scheme is accepted into the PPF, to avoid the need for a lump sum contribution on the cessation of the assessment period.

3.5.8   If the employer is capable of continuing to pay the contributions that it would otherwise have been obliged to pay to the scheme under the schedule of contributions, these sums could similarly be provided for during the assessment period to avoid the need for the employer to make a lump sum contribution to the scheme at the cessation of the assessment period. Depending on the amount required and the solvency of the employer, this requirement in itself may lead to the occurrence of a relevant insolvency event and so start the whole process over again.

3.5.9   Regulations may provide for the modification of s.31 of the 1999 Act (reduction of benefit where a person's shareable rights under a pension arrangement are subject to be a pension debit) in its application to cases where benefits accrue in respect of service during the assessment period.

Effect of withdrawal: repayment of loans

3.5.10   Any loans that were made from the Board to the trustees to allow them to pay benefits as they fell due during the assessment period now fall due for repayment, together with interest (s.139(3)). However, it is hard to see how a scheme that, during the assessment period, did not have sufficient funds to pay capped benefits as they fell due, will suddenly be able to repay a loan plus interest, at the same time as paying back-dated full benefits to members in respect of the assessment period. This will undoubtedly put an enormous strain on such schemes at a time when the Board has refused to accept liability for its members.

Scheme rescue not possible but sufficient assets to meet the protected liabilities: application for reconsideration

3.5.11   If the Board has ceased to be involved with an eligible scheme because there is a scheme failure notice which has become binding but the valuation shows that the scheme has sufficient assets to meet the protected liabilities, the trustees may apply to the Board for it to assume responsibility for the scheme (s.151). The application must be made within the authorised period.

3.5.12   In applying for reconsideration the trustees must provide a protected benefits quotation setting out the cost of providing, in respect of each member, either the scheme benefits or the PPF level of benefits (whichever, in the case of that member, would cost less to provide) and audited scheme accounts for a prescribed period.

3.5.13   Once the application has been made the Board may obtain a further valuation of the scheme as at the reconsideration date, thus prolonging the application further. Considering that to produce a full actuarial valuation from raw data can take anywhere between three to eight months, a scheme may not receive a final decision as to its admittance into the PPF for some considerable time after the commencement of the assessment period.

3.5.14   If the value of the scheme assets is less than the total of the amount quoted in the protected benefits quotation, the amount of the scheme's liabilities other than those to or in respect of members and the estimated costs of winding up the scheme, the Board must generally assume responsibility for the scheme and must issue a determination notice accordingly.

Continuing as a closed scheme

3.5.15   As part of their above application, the trustees must submit a full buy-out quotation. If they are unable to do so, having taken all reasonable steps, they must apply to the Board for authority to continue as a closed scheme (ss.153, 155–159). The Explanatory Notes envisage that this will usually apply to schemes that are unable to obtain a buy-out quotation due to the large level of the scheme's liabilities.

3.5.16   Regulations will require the trustees of a closed scheme to obtain valuations at such times and in a manner to be prescribed.

3.5.17   If, whilst the scheme is continuing as a closed scheme, the trustees become aware that the assets of the scheme are less than the value of the protected liabilities the trustees must apply to the Board for it to assume responsibility for the scheme (s.157(1)). If the trustees fail to take all reasonable steps to secure compliance with this requirement s.10 of the 1995 Act will apply.

3.5.18   If the Regulator becomes aware that the assets of the scheme are less than the value of the protected liabilities the Regulator must notify the Board (s.157(3)).

3.5.19   The making of an application or the giving of a notice triggers another assessment period in relation to the scheme.

3.5.20   Where the Board receives an application from the trustees or a notice from the Regulator and if the value of the scheme's assets is less than the value of the protected liabilities, the Board must assume responsibility for the scheme. To determine this the Board must obtain an actuarial valuation.

Compulsory wind up

3.5.21   If no application is made to the Board to reconsider its withdrawal or, if an application has been made, it has been withdrawn or turned down by the Board (and finally determined), the trustees must wind up the scheme or continue with a wind up which had commenced prior to the start of the assessment period (s.154).

3.5.22   This overrides any provisions in the rules of the scheme, or any enactments or rules of law that would normally prevent a scheme from winding up. Where a public service pension scheme is wound up, modifications may be made to any enactment in which the scheme is contained or under which it is made.

3.5.23   The Board has the power to give directions to the trustees relating to the manner of winding up the scheme, and the Regulator may issue orders to direct any person specified in the order to take such steps as it consider necessary. Section 10 of the 1995 Act will apply to any person who fails to comply with such directions.

3.5.24   A winding up which commences on the cessation of the assessment period is deemed to have commenced immediately before the commencement of the assessment period. This will mean that the priority order will be determined as at that date. See **para.10.5** for more on the statutory priority order under s.73 of the 1995 Act.

3.6   CONSTITUTION OF THE BOARD

3.6.1   The Board will be a body corporate made up of a chairman, a chief executive and at least five 'ordinary members' (at least two of whom must be appointed from the Board's staff) (s.108). The constitution of the Board must be such that the majority of its members are 'non-executives'. The executive members of the Board will be the chief executive and the ordinary members who are Board employees.

The chairman

3.6.2   The Board's chairman will be appointed by the Secretary for State (on terms and conditions determined by the Secretary of State) and must be a person who is not on the Board's staff. The chairman must not be the chairman of the Regulator. Lawrence Churchill has been appointed as the first chairman of the PPF.

The chief executive

3.6.3   The first chief executive will be appointed by the Secretary of State but subsequent chief executives will be appointed by the Board with the approval of the Secretary of State (Sched.5, para.12). The Secretary of State determines the terms and conditions of the appointment, although the chief executive's remuneration will be decided by the non-executive committee with the approval of the Secretary of State. Myra Kinghorn has been appointed as the first chief executive of the PPF.

The ordinary members

3.6.4   The first five ordinary members will be appointed by the Secretary of State and subsequent appointments will be made by the Board in accordance with any procedure they may decide (Sched.5, para.2). If, at any time, the number of ordinary members falls below five, the Secretary of State will intervene to bring the number back up to five.

3.6.5   The terms and conditions of appointment for executive members will be determined by the chief executive. The terms and conditions for non-executive members will be determined by the chairman with the approval of the Secretary of State, save for remuneration which will be set by the Secretary of State alone.

3.6.6   In addition, the Board will employ staff, the number of which will have to be approved by the Secretary of State. The chief executive will determine the staff's terms and conditions of employment.

3.7   PROCEEDINGS OF THE BOARD

Committees

3.7.1   The Board may establish committees for any purpose and those committees may establish sub-committees (Sched.5, para.3). The Board may delegate any of its functions to these committees, save for its 'non-executive functions' (see below).

Accounts

3.7.2   The Board must keep proper accounts and prepare a statement of accounts for each financial year, which must contain actuarial valuations of the PPF, undertaken by an actuary appointed by the Board (Sched.5, para.22).

Validity

3.7.3   The validity of the Board's proceedings is not affected by vacancies on the Board, its committees or sub-committees or by a defect in the appointment of Board members. The Board and its members (including members of committees and sub-committees) have no liability in damages for anything done or omitted to be done in the exercise or purported exercise of its functions, as conferred on it by legislation. This exclusion of liability is, however, limited so that it will not apply where an act or omission was in bad faith or where to prevent an award of damages would be unlawful under the Human Rights Act 1998.

3.8   NON-EXECUTIVE FUNCTIONS OF THE BOARD

3.8.1   The Board is required to establish a committee to discharge the non-executive functions on its behalf and only non-executive members of the Board may sit on that committee (s.112). The non-executive functions are:

(a) to keep under review the question of whether the Board's internal financial controls secure the proper conduct of its financial affairs;
(b) to determine, with the approval of the Secretary of State, the remuneration of the chief executive and other executive members of the Board; and
(c) to determine the remuneration of certain members of staff.

3.8.2   The committee must prepare a report on its discharge of these functions for inclusion in the Board's annual report to the Secretary of State.

3.9   INVESTMENT

3.9.1   Section 113 of the Act states that the Board may invest PPF assets, but does not oblige the Board to do so. Assuming the Board decides to make use of this power, it must appoint at least two fund managers who must have appropriate knowledge and experience for managing the PPF.

3.9.2   It remains to be seen whether any changes will be made to the financial services legislation so as to require the Board to delegate all routine and day-to-day investment decisions to a fund manager in order for it not to be regarded as under-taking the regulated activity of managing assets belonging to another by way of business, in the same way that pension scheme trustees are required to do.

3.9.3   As part of its investment strategy, the Board may borrow money from banks and grant security over its assets. However, a borrowing limit may be pre-scribed in regulations. Furthermore, the Board must prepare, maintain and, from time to time, revise a statement of investment principles in accordance with regulations yet to be published.

3.10   ANNUAL REPORT

3.10.1   The Board must prepare a report for each financial year covering the activities of the Board during the year for which the report is prepared (s.119). The report must be laid before Parliament by the Secretary of State and must include sections on the following issues:

(a) the strategic direction of the Board and the manner in which this has been reviewed;
(b) the steps taken to scrutinise the performance of the chief executive in securing the Board's functions are exercised efficiently and effectively; and
(c) the Board's objectives and targets and the steps taken to monitor whether they are being met.

3.11   INFORMATION GATHERING

3.11.1   Regulations will set out the persons who will be required to provide the Board with information at prescribed times (s.190). In particular, this information will enable the Board to determine the level of compensation payable to scheme members from the PPF. The Board may issue notices requiring information from trustees, professional advisers, employers, insolvency practitioners and any other people likely to hold information which is relevant to the discharge of the Board's functions.

3.11.2   Members of the Board's staff may enter 'scheme premises' and ask ques-tions of people they find there (s.192). Scheme premises are those premises which are, or are reasonably believed to be, used by a relevant employer, scheme admin-istrator or insolvency practitioner, or are premises where relevant documents are kept. Any documents taken can be retained for up to 12 months and for a further 12 months if the Board directs. Any person who obstructs this process or fails to assist may be fined and, any person who intentionally conceals or destroys docu-ments may also be imprisoned for up to two years. The Board may obtain a warrant to use reasonable force to enter and search premises where there are reasonable grounds for believing documents would not otherwise be provided (s.194).

3.11.3   Although there is a presumption that this information shall not be disclosed, the Board may disclose 'restricted information' in a wide range of situations, including where it would assist either the Board or the Regulator in its functions (ss.197–203). In addition, regulations may require the Board to issue information to prescribed people or require trustees to issue information to members of their scheme.

3.12   LEVIES

3.12.1   The PPF is to be partly funded by levies which will be imposed by the Board on the trustees, managers or other prescribed persons of eligible schemes.

3.12.2   There are various levies payable under the Act. The first is the 'initial levy', which will apply for approximately a year following the introduction of the PPF. The second is the 'pension protection levies', which can be either risk-based or scheme-based.

3.12.3   The initial levy and the pension protection levies are payable to the Board by the trustees or managers of a scheme or by any other person prescribed by regulation. The Board or the Regulator (if the Board so determines) may recover any outstanding levies. The Board is also responsible for deciding which schemes the levies will apply to, the amount of the levies and notifying the persons who are liable to pay the levies how much and when they must pay. The Board may require the Regulator to carry out these functions on its behalf.

3.12.4   In addition to the two categories of levy referred to above, the Act also introduces an administration levy and a fraud compensation levy. The administration levy will be applied to schemes to cover the set up and ongoing costs of the PPF and the PPF Ombudsman. The fraud compensation levy will replace the current Pensions Compensation Board levy and will be paid by both defined benefit and defined contribution schemes.

The initial levy

3.12.5   The initial levy is introduced by ss.174 and 181 of the Act. Section 174 provides that regulations must make provision for the imposing of a levy in respect of eligible schemes for the 'initial period'. The 'initial period' is to begin on a date to be appointed by regulation and will end either on the following 31 March or, if regulations so provide, 12 months after the appointed date.

3.12.6   Much of the detail regarding the initial levy will be contained in regulations, such as the factors by reference to which the initial levy is assessed, the rate at which the initial levy will be set and the time or times at which it is payable.

According to the Explanatory Notes, the initial levy will be based on scheme-factors only (i.e. no risk-based factors will be taken into account), and the intention is to collect approximately half of the amount that the Board will need to collect in future years to meet its liabilities.

Pension protection levies

3.12.7 The pension protection levies (ss.175–181 of the Act) will apply once the initial period has passed. Following this initial period there will be a 'transitional period', within which certain rules that govern the payment of pension protection levies may be modified by regulation, in accordance with s.180. The length of the transitional period is to be prescribed by regulation. However, if the transitional period begins on a date other than 1 April, regulations may be made which would modify ss.175–180 (i.e. the key provisions relating to the pension protection levies) in relation to the period beginning at the same time as the transitional period and ending with the following 31 March and the following financial year.

3.12.8 The pension protection levies comprise a risk-based pension protection levy ('risk-based levy') and a scheme-based pension protection levy ('scheme-based levy'). Broadly, the risk-based levy will be based on the likelihood of a scheme making a claim from the PPF, whereas the scheme-based levy is applied to schemes in accordance with objective scheme factors such as the size of the scheme.

3.12.9 Different risk factors, scheme factors and rates may be set for different types of pension scheme which could include a pension protection levy rate of nil (see s.175(6) and (7)).

3.12.10 For each financial year following the initial period, the Board must impose both a risk-based levy and a scheme-based levy in relation to eligible schemes. The Board will also determine the factors by reference to which the pension protection levies will be assessed, the rates to be applied and when the levies will become payable. Where it is the first year that the Board is to impose pension protection levies, or where there is to be a change in the levy rates or factors from the previous year, or where no such consultation has been required for the previous two financial years, then the Board must consult such persons as it considers appropriate and in a prescribed manner before making these determinations.

3.12.11 Sections 177 and 178 of the Act govern the amount that will be raised by the pension protection levies. Each year the Board will estimate the amount that will be raised by the pension protection levies that it proposes to impose. The risk-based levy must be in a form which the Board estimates will amount to at least 80 per cent of the total amount estimated to be raised by both levies.

3.12.12 The total estimated amount to be raised from the pension protection levies cannot exceed what is termed the 'levy ceiling' for that financial year. The levy ceiling will be set by order of the Secretary of State for each year. Treasury approval is required for the order imposing the levy ceiling in the first financial year in which the pension protection levies are imposed. In subsequent years, the levy ceiling will either be the same amount as the previous year or will be that amount increased in line with the percentage increase in earnings (calculated in accordance with s.178(4)–(7)), although the Secretary of State may impose a higher levy ceiling by order, on the recommendation of the Board, after consultation with and the approval of the Treasury. During the transitional period (with the approval of the Treasury) and the first financial year following that transitional period, regulations may provide for the reference to the levy ceiling to be read as a reference to a lower amount for the purposes of restricting the amount estimated by the Board to be raised by the pension protection levies.

3.12.13   A limit of 25 per cent has been placed on any increase to the total estimated amount to be raised from the pension protection levies, when compared with the equivalent estimate from the previous financial year. However, this restriction will not apply until the second financial year after the transitional period. The Secretary of State may by order specify a percentage other than 25 per cent after consulting such persons as he considers appropriate and obtaining Treasury approval.

3.12.14   As previously mentioned, many of these provisions may be amended by regulation (in accordance with s.180) during the transitional period. In addition, the Secretary of State has certain powers to alter the restrictions applied to the amount of the pension protection levies.

Scheme-based levy

3.12.15   The scheme-based levy will be calculated for each scheme by reference to the amount of a scheme's liabilities to or in respect of members (other than liabilities relating to money purchase benefits) and, if the Board considers it appropriate, by reference to one or more other 'scheme factors'.

3.12.16   The Act provides a list of additional scheme factors which the Board may select at the beginning of each financial year, when determining the factors by reference to which the levy is to be assessed. These additional scheme factors are listed at s.175(4) of the Act and are as follows:

(a) the number of persons who are members, or fall within any description of member, of a scheme;
(b) the total annual amount of pensionable earnings of active members of a scheme; and
(c) such other factors as may be prescribed.

Risk-based levy

3.12.17   The risk-based levy will be assessed by reference to the difference between the value of a scheme's assets (excluding assets which represent the value of any rights to money purchase benefits under the scheme rules) and the amount of its protected liabilities, and unless the scheme is a prescribed scheme or of a prescribed description, the likelihood of an insolvency event occurring in relation to the employer. If the Board considers it appropriate, the risk-based levy will also be set by reference to one or more other 'risk factors' (see below).

3.12.18   The Act provides for regulations which will prescribe how the assets and protected liabilities of schemes will be calculated and will require the trustees or managers of a scheme to provide the Board (or the Regulator on its behalf) with information regarding the scheme's assets and protected liabilities, including actuarial valuations (see s.179).

3.12.19   Other 'risk factors' that the Board may select and by reference to which the risk-based levy will be calculated are set out in s.175(3) of the Act as follows:

(a) the risks associated with the nature of a scheme's investments when compared with the nature of its liabilities; and
(b) such other matters as may be prescribed.

Administration levy

3.12.20   The purpose of the administration levy is to meet the Secretary of State's expenses in setting up the Board and to meet the Board's expenses which have initially been met by the Secretary of State. This levy is payable directly to the Secretary of State by or on behalf of the trustees or managers of those pension schemes which are eligible for inclusion within the PPF or any other prescribed person. The amount of this levy is yet to be prescribed but will be set by the Secretary of State after having consulted with the Board.

3.13   FRAUD COMPENSATION

3.13.1   Sections 182–189 of the Act set out the provisions relating to the payment of fraud compensation by the Board to the trustees or managers of a scheme. Unlike much of the rest of the PPF provisions, these sections are applicable to both defined benefit and defined contribution pension schemes. The pension scheme does not therefore have to be eligible for compensation from the PPF in order to be eligible for fraud compensation.

3.13.2   These provisions will replace the current Pensions Compensation Board. The Pensions Compensation Board will be dissolved and its assets will become part of the Fraud Compensation Fund.

The Fraud Compensation Fund

3.13.3   Section 188 provides that the Fraud Compensation Fund will be funded by the following:

(a) the transfer of property and rights from the Pension Compensation Board;

(b) the fraud compensation levy;

(c) money borrowed by the Board;

(d) interim payments that have been recovered from the trustees or managers of a scheme (see below); and

(e) any income or capital gain arising from the assets of the Fraud Compensation Fund.

The fraud compensation levy

3.13.4   Section 189 allows for regulations to be made which will provide for the imposition of a levy to meet the expenditure payable out of the Fraud Compensation Fund. Schemes that are not eligible to receive fraud compensation will not have to pay the fraud compensation levy.

3.13.5   The levy will be payable to the Board by the trustees, managers or other prescribed persons in relation to a scheme. The timing and amount of the payments will be prescribed by regulation and determined by the Board. The Board (or the Regulator at the Board's request) will determine which schemes will pay this levy, the amount of the levy and notify persons liable to pay it of the amount and the times at which it will be payable. The recovery of unpaid levies will be carried out by the Board or, if the Board so determines, by the Regulator on its behalf.

Eligibility

3.13.6   Section 182 sets out the conditions necessary for a payment of fraud compensation to be made in respect of a scheme:

(a) *Type of scheme* – the scheme must not be a prescribed scheme or a scheme of a prescribed description.

(b) *Reduction of assets as a result of a prescribed offence* – the value of the scheme's assets must have been reduced since 6 April 1997 (or such other date as appointed by the Secretary of State by order) and the Board must consider that there are reasonable grounds for believing that this was a result of a 'prescribed offence'.

(c) *Employer insolvent or likely to become insolvent* – a 'qualifying insolvency event' (defined at section 182(8)) must have occurred in relation to the employer, or the employer is unlikely to continue as a going concern, in the circumstances set out in s.182(2), (3) or (4).

(d) *Application* – an application must be made for fraud compensation by a person and in a form to be prescribed by regulation and within the time scale described below.

Prescribed offences

3.13.7   As the name suggests, offences which are prescribed offences will be set out in regulations. However, in response to a query during a meeting of the Lords Grand Committee, Baroness Hollis of Heigham gave what she described as the 'scantiest of backgrounds' to what is likely to constitute a prescribed offence. She said that:

> 'A prescribed offence will be an offence that involves dishonesty. It is not about mistakes or something being one day late but about dishonesty. That test is well established in common law.'

Time limits on applying for fraud compensation

3.13.8   Unless the Board decides that a longer period of time should apply, the application for fraud compensation must be made within 12 months of the later of:

(a) the 'relevant event'; or
(b) the time when the auditor, actuary, trustees or managers of the scheme knew or ought reasonably to have known that the reduction of the scheme's assets had taken place (s.182(6)).

3.13.9   The 'relevant event' is defined in s.182(10) as one of the events listed below, depending on whether s.182(2), (3) or (4) applies.

(a) If s.182(2) applies and the scheme is an eligible scheme, the relevant event is the qualifying insolvency event.
(b) If s.182(2) applies and the scheme is not an eligible scheme, the relevant event is the issuing of a notice by the insolvency practitioner, confirming that a scheme rescue is not possible under s.122(2)(a).
(c) If s.182(3) applies then the relevant event is either the application by the trustees to the Board for it to assume responsibility for the scheme on the basis that the employer is unlikely to continue as a going concern (s.129(1)) or notification from the Board to the trustees that the Regulator has become aware that the employer is unlikely to continue as a going concern (s.129(5)(a)).
(d) If s.182(4) applies then the relevant event is the trustees or managers of the scheme becoming aware that the employer is unlikely to continue as a going concern and that prescribed requirements are met in relation to the employer.

Payment of compensation

3.13.10   No fraud compensation payments may be made until the 'settlement date' (s.184(2)). This is the date after which the Board determines that the trustees or managers of the scheme will be unlikely to obtain any recovery of value (s.184) for the scheme without disproportionate cost or within a reasonable period of time. The Board must consult the trustees or managers of the scheme before setting this date.

3.13.11   The Board may make fraud compensation payments to the trustees or managers of the scheme on such terms (including the repayment of all or part of the compensation) as the Board considers appropriate.

3.13.12   The fraud compensation paid by the Board cannot exceed the amount of the reduction in the scheme's assets which the Board has reasonable grounds for believing is attributable to the prescribed offence, taking into account any recoveries of value obtained before the settlement date (see s.185). The Board must determine the amount of the compensation in line with the appropriate regulations and must take account of any interim payments already made to the trustees or managers of the scheme. According to commentary on these provisions, it is intended that there will be 100 per cent compensation for all schemes which qualify for it.

3.13.13   The Board may make interim payments (within prescribed limits) to the trustees or managers of a scheme when the trustees or managers have made an application for fraud compensation and the Board is of the opinion that their application will or may be successful and that without the interim payment the trustees or managers of the scheme would not otherwise be able to meet liabilities of a prescribed description (s.186). The Board may impose conditions on the payment of interim payments such as terms relating to the repayment of all or part of the sum. In addition, in order to make interim payments the Board must not have already determined the settlement date. The Board may, except in prescribed circumstances, recover all or part of an interim payment from the trustees or managers of the scheme if it later determines that the amount of the interim payment was excessive or the scheme does not qualify for fraud compensation.

Relationship of the Fraud Compensation Fund with the PPF

3.13.14   No application for fraud compensation may be made once the Board has issued a transfer notice in relation to the scheme, i.e. the notice issued when the Board assumes responsibility to pay compensation to members of the scheme from the PPF (s.182(7)).

3.13.15   Similarly, no transfer notice relating to the Board assuming responsibility for the scheme can be made where there is an outstanding application for fraud compensation (s.172). If fraud compensation becomes payable during the assessment period (during which the Board will determine whether to admit the scheme to the PPF) then, in the circumstances outlined in s.172(4), it is to be regarded as an asset of the scheme for the purposes of deciding whether the scheme is sufficiently underfunded to qualify for entry into the PPF. However, this provision does not apply where fraud compensation is payable in relation to a reduction in the value of money purchase assets of the scheme.

3.13.16   Section 187 provides for the transfer of assets from the Fraud Compensation Fund to the PPF. The amount of the transfer cannot exceed the amount of the reduction believed to be attributable to the prescribed offence (taking into account any recoveries in value obtained by the Board). The Board may make such a transfer where it believes that the assets of a scheme for which it has assumed responsibility were reduced before the transfer notice was issued and after 6 April 1997 (or such other date as appointed by the Secretary of State) and there are reasonable grounds for believing that the reduction was attributable to a prescribed offence. In addition, no application must have been made under s.182 for fraud compensation, unless such an application was withdrawn.

3.13.17   Similar rules apply as regards the transfer of assets from the Fraud Compensation Fund to the PPF as apply to the payment of fraud compensation to the trustees or managers of a scheme. For example, the Board is obliged to obtain recoveries of value (see above) to the extent that it may do so without incurring disproportionate costs and delay. No transfer of assets may be made from the Fraud Compensation Fund to the PPF until the date after which the Board determines further recoveries of value are unlikely to be obtained without disproportionate costs and delay.

4 COMPLAINTS, APPEAL PROCEDURES AND EVIDENCE

4.1 GENERAL

This Chapter pulls together the various provisions of the Act which impact on the forum, management and resolution of disputes.

4.2 INTERNAL DISPUTE RESOLUTION (IDR)

Introduction

4.2.1 Currently, most occupational pension schemes are required under s.50 of the 1995 Act to provide a procedure by which disputes can be resolved. The Occupational Pension Schemes (Internal Dispute Resolution Procedures) Regulations 1996, SI 1996/1270, provide detailed requirements on the form and content of the IDR procedure.

4.2.2 The current procedure is available to scheme members, widows/widowers of members, surviving dependants of deceased members or prospective members who have disputes about matters concerning the scheme. The existing procedure deals with complaints in two stages, each requiring a response within two months (although there is no penalty for non-compliance with this deadline). Certain prescriptive information must be provided. Under Stage One, a nominated individual is appointed by the trustees of the scheme to consider the dispute. If the member is not satisfied with the first stage decision, the member has six months from the date that the decision is communicated within which to lodge an appeal. If a member appeals the Stage One decision, under Stage Two the trustees must consider the complaint and make a decision.

4.2.3 The general rule is that the IDR procedure should be used before the Pensions Ombudsman will investigate a complaint.

4.2.4 Various consultation papers prior to the preparation of the Act expressed views that the IDR procedure required under the 1995 Act was too restrictive. The Government has endorsed these views and acknowledged that the existing requirements should be simplified.

Changes in the Act

4.2.5   Section 273 of the Act covers internal pension scheme disputes. It provides for s.50 of the 1995 Act to be repealed and replaced with a new s.50, s.50A and s.50B. It is currently envisaged that the new style of IDR procedure required under the Act must be in place for all complaints made on or after 6 April 2005. However, it may be that the introduction of the changes to the IDR procedure will not be effective until September 2005. Any cases being dealt with under IDR procedure at the time of the change will continue to be dealt with under the existing criteria. The principal changes implemented by the Act are as follows.

(a)   The IDR procedure is no longer required to be in two stages. The trustees or managers of the scheme must make the IDR decision. The requirement for a nominated 'adjudicator' who dealt with the first stage decision process in the old system is removed.

(b)   The categories of complainant have been extended to include a non-dependent beneficiary of a deceased member who is entitled to death benefits.

(c)   The new procedure must include a provision that allows a complaint to be made or continued by a complainant's personal representative following the complainant's death, or by a nominated representative if the complainant is a minor or otherwise wishes to be represented.

(d)   There are no detailed time limits set out in the Act. Trustees can set their own time limits provided that these are reasonable. A Code of Practice will provide guidance on what periods are deemed to be reasonable.

(e)   The new procedure must provide details about the way in which complainants should make an application for a dispute to be considered, what the application should include and the way in which decisions will be reached and communicated.

(f)   The new procedure requires trustees to inform members of their right to obtain OPAS assistance and to take their complaint to the Pensions Ombudsman at the time the IDR procedure is concluded.

Implications for trustees and others

4.2.6   Trustees or managers must implement the new style of IDR procedure for all complaints made on or after the new rules come into force. The penalty for failing to do so will be a fine of up to £1,000 for individuals and up to £10,000 for corporate trustees. However, these figures are under review and may be changed to bring them in line with other 1995 Act civil penalties, ie £5,000 and £50,000 respectively.

4.2.7   The new style procedure gives schemes the opportunity to provide a more streamlined approach to the resolution of disputes. It should accelerate dispute resolution and reduce expense. The increased flexibility in the content of the IDR procedure will allow the trustees to adopt bespoke procedures that are more suitable to their scheme and members.

4.2.8   In principle, it will still be possible for non-trustees to be involved in IDR decisions provided that this is possible within the trustees' powers of delegation under their trust deed, and that the trustees properly delegate authority. However, since the Act requires the trustees or managers to take decisions, these decisions should be approved by the trustee board, perhaps after consideration of a recommendation from the non-trustee.

Action required

4.2.9   Trustees and managers should review and redraft their existing IDR procedures. It may be sufficient simply to drop stage one of the existing procedure. Any changes should be communicated to members, as the IDR procedure amounts to basic scheme information under the Occupational Pension Schemes (Disclosure of Information) Regulations 1996, SI 1996/1655. Any material changes to such information should be communicated, in advance if practicable, or otherwise no later than three months after the change has taken effect.

4.3   PENSIONS OMBUDSMAN

Introduction

4.3.1   The Office of the Pensions Ombudsman was established under the 1993 Act. His powers and responsibilities are currently set out in: s.146 of the 1993 Act, the Personal and Occupational Pension Schemes (Pensions Ombudsman) Regulations 1996, SI 1996/2475; and ss.157–160 of the 1995 Act.

4.3.2   Provision was included within the Child Support, Pensions and Social Security Act 2000 to extend the Pensions Ombudsman's powers and jurisdiction to allow him to make determinations that would affect not only the complainant but also other members of the scheme, in other words class actions. These provisions were not brought into force. Sections 274–276 of the Act contain a few minor provisions that relate to the Pensions Ombudsman.

Deputy Pensions Ombudsman

4.3.3   Section 274 of the Act introduces a new provision that will amend s.145 and introduce a new s.145A to the 1993 Act. The provision allows the appointment of Deputy Ombudsmen who will be appointed on such terms as decided by the Secretary of State. A Deputy Ombudsman will be able to perform the functions of the Pensions Ombudsman when:

(a) the Office of the Pensions Ombudsman is vacant;
(b) at any time when the Pensions Ombudsman is unable to discharge his functions; or
(c) at any other time with the consent of the Secretary of State.

4.3.4   The purpose behind introducing the role of Deputy Ombudsmen is to provide assistance to the Pensions Ombudsman with his heavy workload.

Jurisdiction

4.3.5   Section 275 of the Act introduces a new section to the 1993 Act. New s.146(4A) provides a definition of persons 'concerned with the administration of an occupational pension scheme'. The definition extends this category to any person or body who is responsible for carrying out an act of administration concerned with the scheme.

4.3.6   The effect of this amendment is to extend the jurisdiction of the Pensions Ombudsman to cover disputes with those who are responsible for carrying out single acts of administration for a pension scheme. This provision is likely to be a direct response to the case of R (*Britannic Asset Management*) v. *Pensions Ombudsman* [2002] 90 PBLI, in which the Court of Appeal held that an insurer of an occupational pension scheme did not act as an administrator with reference to that scheme and therefore came outside the jurisdiction of the Pensions Ombudsman.

4.3.7   This section will apply to any matter which arises on or after the day upon which the new rules come into force.

Investigations

4.3.8   Section 276 of the Act repeals s.54 of the Child Support, Pensions and Social Security Act 2000, which envisaged extending the Pensions Ombudsman's jurisdiction to deal with class actions. This provision has therefore been repealed before ever coming into force.

Implications for trustees, employers and others

4.3.9   There was much expectation within the pensions industry that the Act would substantially extend the Pensions Ombudsman's powers and jurisdiction. The minor provisions provided are disappointing and will have little impact on the current position.

4.3.10   The introduction of Deputy Pensions Ombudsmen may reduce the time it takes for complaints to the Pensions Ombudsman to be determined. The extension of the Pensions Ombudsman's jurisdiction to include those involved in single acts of administration will allow members to bring actions directly against culpable administrators rather than the trustees. However, the Act does not extend the jurisdiction of the Pensions Ombudsman to allow him to consider class actions, as had been expected. Class actions will therefore remain the preserve of the courts.

4.4   REVIEWS AND RECONSIDERATION BY THE BOARD OF THE PPF IN REVIEWABLE MATTERS

Introduction

4.4.1   The Board of the PPF exercises various statutory functions under the Act that affect, for example, schemes' entry into the PPF and the amount of members' benefits available under the PPF. The Board will undertake a two-stage review and reconsideration process at the request of an affected party (who will be prescribed by regulations) where the Board acts or fails to act in respect of a reviewable matter.

4.4.2   Once that process is exhausted, the matter can be taken to the PPF Ombudsman.

Reviewable matters

4.4.3   The Board is permitted by s.207 to review 'reviewable matters'. There is a list of 30 reviewable matters set out in Sched.9 to the Act. Broadly, reviewable matters are those that relate to the exercise by the Board of its statutory functions under the Act. Key examples of reviewable matters include issues which affect the scheme, such as those listed below.

- The issue or failure to issue a notice under s.130 stating that scheme rescue (prior to the admission to the PPF) is not possible.
- The approval or failure to approve a valuation in respect of an eligible scheme under s.144(2).
- The amount of the initial levy or any pension protection levy determined by the Board under s.181(3)(b).

Reviewable matters will also include issues that affect the member, such as the determination of compensation under the pension compensation provisions.

Review and reconsideration of reviewable matters

4.4.4   Regulations will prescribe who may apply to the Board to have each type of reviewable matter reviewed (s.207(2)). It is likely that these persons will include trustees and members. Similarly, where a review decision has been made, an interested person may apply to have that decision reconsidered by a committee of the Board (s.207(1)(b)).

Powers of the Board in respect of a review and reconsideration

4.4.5   The Board's powers on reviewing or reconsidering a decision set out in s.207(4) will include the power to do the following:

(a) Vary or revoke the determination, direction or other decision already made by the Board in respect of the reviewable matter.

(b) Substitute a different determination, direction or decision.
(c) Generally to deal with the matters arising on the review decision or reconsideration decision as if they had arisen on the original determination, direction or decision.
(d) Pay such compensation as the Board considers appropriate to such persons as it may determine.

4.4.6   Regulations will also be introduced to govern the procedure and time limits for applications and ensure that members of the Board involved in the reconsideration decision were not concerned with the original earlier decisions (s.207(5)).

4.5   REVIEW OF COMPLAINTS OF MALADMINISTRATION

Introduction

4.5.1   The Act enables the Board of the PPF to review and reconsider complaints brought against it in respect of its own maladministration in respect of certain specific actions. Thereafter, any continuing complaints may be referred to the PPF Ombudsman (see below). As with maladministration under the jurisdiction of the Pensions Ombudsman, 'maladministration' is not defined in the Act. In the context of the Board of the PPF, maladministration would be expected to cover the Board's conduct of the matters within its jurisdiction, such as the timeliness of its actions.

Review and reconsideration of complaints of maladministration

4.5.2   The only persons who may bring a complaint of maladministration are (s.208(2)):

(a) a person who is or might become entitled to compensation under the pension compensation provisions; or
(b) a person who has, or may make an application for fraud compensation under s.182.

4.5.3   These are also reviewable matters under s.206 (see **para.4.4.3**). The basis for approaching the Board in these instances will depend on the nature of the breach.

4.5.4   Regulations will also govern the procedure and time limits for applications and ensure that members of the Board involved in the review decision were not concerned with the original decision (s.208(4)). When a complaint of maladministration is reviewed, it will also be reconsidered before it may be referred to the PPF Ombudsman.

Powers of Board

4.5.5   The Act does not specify the extent of the Board's powers when making a decision. However, these include the power to award compensation.

4.6   THE PPF OMBUDSMAN

Introduction

4.6.1   Where a reviewable matter or a complaint of maladministration has been reviewed and reconsidered, the matter may then be referred to the PPF Ombudsman (ss.213(1) and 214(1)). The PPF Ombudsman is appointed by the Secretary of State and is independent from the Board of the PPF. In addition, the Secretary of State may appoint one or more persons to act as a deputy to the PPF Ombudsman (s.210). Regulations will set out whether any deputy may only perform the functions of the PPF Ombudsman when he is unable to act (or there is a vacancy), or whether he may assist the PPF Ombudsman with his day-to-day caseload.

Procedure

4.6.2   Regulations will govern who may refer reviewable matters or claims of maladministration to the PPF Ombudsman, but this is clearly likely to be the person who brought the initial complaint. There is also scope for prescribed persons to bring a complaint when the complainant has died.

4.6.3   The regulations will give the PPF Ombudsman the ability to conduct oral hearings or dispose of the matter by way of written representations. The PPF Ombudsman will also be able to consider expert evidence and require the production of documents (ss.213(2)–(4) and 214(2)). He will also be able to refer questions of law to the High Court in England and Wales and to the Court of Sessions in Scotland (s.215).

Determination of the PPF Ombudsman

4.6.4   Any order of the PPF Ombudsman is enforceable as if it were an order of the Court. Where a reviewable matter is appealed to the PPF Ombudsman he will remit the matter to the Board with directions to give effect to his determination (s.213(1)(b)). In respect of complaints of maladministration, the PPF Ombudsman may direct the Board to take or refrain from taking certain steps (s.214(2)(d)).

4.6.5   In respect of both types of complaint, the PPF Ombudsman may direct the Board to pay compensation (ss.213(5) and 214(2)(d)).

4.6.6   The PPF Ombudsman may publish reports of any investigation he has carried out. Interestingly, these will be absolutely privileged under the laws of defamation (s.216).

Appeal from determination of PPF Ombudsman

4.6.7   Appeals may be made to the High Court in England and Wales and to the Court of Session in Scotland on a point of law from a determination of the PPF Ombudsman (s.217).

Obstructing the PPF Ombudsman

4.6.8   If any person obstructs the PPF Ombudsman in the performance of his functions or is guilty of an act or omission which would constitute contempt of court if the matter were a proceeding in the court, the PPF Ombudsman may certify an offence to the County Court (s.218). The County Court may consider the matter and deal with the person as if the offence had been committed in the County Court. Under s.14 of the Contempt of Court Act 1981, the County Court may jail a person for up to two years for contempt of court and fine the person up to £2,500.

4.7   ADMISSIBILITY OF STATEMENTS

Introduction

4.7.1   The Act imposes a number of obligations to provide information to bodies such as the Pensions Regulator, the Board of the PPF and the PPF Ombudsman, as well as powers which permit the inspection of premises and seizing of documents under certain circumstances. These are known as 'information requirements' and are set out in s.310(4).

4.7.2   Section 310 sets out the provisions dealing with the admissibility of the evidence which has been gathered by those involved with an investigation.

General provisions in relation to admissibility

4.7.3   Where a person makes a statement in accordance with one of the information requirements, that statement will be admissible in any proceedings except:

(a)   certain criminal or civil proceedings as outlined below, and

(b)   where the statement does not comply with any requirement governing the admissibility of evidence in the circumstances in question. This appears to be a reference to the general rules of admissibility of evidence, such as the rule that the evidence must be relevant.

Proceedings where statements are only admissible in certain circumstances

4.7.4   Where a person makes a statement in accordance with one of the information requirements in the following proceedings:

(a) criminal proceedings in which that person is charged with a 'relevant offence' (relevant offences are all criminal offences except certain offences under the Act, listed at s.310(4) and specific perjury offences); or
(b) proceedings as a result of which that person may be required to pay a financial penalty under or by virtue of:

(i) s.168 of the 1993 Act (which provides that regulations under the 1993 Act may provide for contravention of them to be an offence); or
(ii) s.10 of the 1995 Act;

no evidence may be adduced relating to the statement and no question may be asked in relation to it by or on behalf of the prosecution or the Regulator unless evidence relating to it has been adduced, or a question has been asked on behalf the person charged with the offence.

Implications for trustees

4.7.5   Trustees will be provided with limited protection by these provisions. Statements made under the information requirements will not be used in evidence against them in certain criminal and civil proceedings unless they raise that evidence themselves. However, trustees will not receive this protection in relation to the offences under the Act relating to neglect or refusal to provide information, or providing false or misleading information to the Regulator or the Board (s.310(4)).

4.8   LEGAL PRIVILEGE

Documents that do not have to be disclosed under the Act

4.8.1   Section 311 of the Act contains provisions specifying which documents do not have to be disclosed by virtue of any provision of the Act, due to legal privilege. They are as follows:

(a) communications between a professional legal adviser and his client or any person representing his client which were made:

(i) in connection with the giving of legal advice to the client; or
(ii) in connection with, or in contemplation of, legal proceedings and for the purpose of those proceedings; or

(b) a communication between a professional legal adviser, his client or any person representing his client and any other person which is made in connection with legal proceedings and for the purpose of those proceedings.

4.8.2   Items that are enclosed with, or referred to, in those communications are also privileged. Communications held with the intention of furthering a criminal purpose will not be privileged.

4.8.3   These provisions potentially give greater protection in respect of legal advice privilege than that available at common law. This is because they extend to communications between a legal adviser and a third party who is not the client. It is likely to be simpler for trustees to rely on this statutory provision to protect privileged communications from disclosure rather than relying on the more unwieldy common law arguments.

5 FUNDING AND ACTUARIAL ISSUES

5.1 INTRODUCTION

5.1.1 The Minimum Funding Requirement (MFR), which was introduced by the 1995 Act, came into effect in April 1997 and applied to most defined benefit occupational pension schemes. It was intended to provide a common measure of a scheme's funding position, if not its solvency, and set down the basis on which schemes could be tested. In the event that an MFR valuation showed any shortfall in funding, the shortfall was to be corrected over a prescribed period.

5.1.2 However, the MFR has proved to be unsuccessful as a test of individual schemes' financial positions and, following industry pressure, it was generally accepted that a more scheme-specific replacement should be sought. In addition, it also became necessary to introduce into UK law the requirements of Directive 2003/41/EC on the Activities and Supervision of Institutions for Occupational Retirement Provision (the IORP Directive) on scheme funding. Sections 221–233 of the Act contain the new legislation intended to address these and related matters.

5.1.3 As the IORP Directive must be passed into domestic UK law by September 2005, it is anticipated that the Act's provisions on funding, which largely derive from that Directive, will be introduced with effect from September 2005.

5.2 STATUTORY FUNDING OBJECTIVE

5.2.1 The Act provides for a new statutory funding objective (s.222) which will apply to all occupational schemes except for money purchase arrangements and other prescribed schemes. Generally, schemes which were subject to the MFR will be covered by the statutory funding objective.

5.2.2 Each scheme will be required to have sufficient and appropriate assets to cover its 'technical provisions'. This term is lifted directly from the IORP Directive and is defined in the Act as being the amount required, on an actuarial calculation, to make provision for the scheme's liabilities. Regulations will dictate which assets may be included and how their value should be calculated. Liabilities relative to a scheme's technical provisions will also be calculated in a prescribed manner. It is anticipated that this will involve trustees or managers, on receipt of actuarial advice, choosing from a range of potential calculation bases that could be applied to their scheme.

5.2.3   In addition, the Regulator is required under s.90(2)(d) to issue a Code of Practice giving advice to trustees on the discharge of their duties under the scheme funding provisions contained in Part 3 of the Act, which will include guidance on the selection of a suitable basis for calculating the scheme's technical provisions.

5.2.4   Given that none of the regulations referred to above nor the Code of Practice on funding have been issued at the time of writing, much of the detail of the new scheme specific funding standard is still unknown. It therefore remains to be seen how tough the new standard will be, both in its own right and as compared with the MFR.

5.2.5   The legislation will override any scheme rules that might seek to limit the amount of liabilities relative to assets that can be valued under the statutory funding objective.

5.2.6   The intention behind the introduction of the statutory funding objective is to enable greater flexibility in scheme funding. One criticism of the MFR was that it was inflexible because it applied a generic test which was too restrictive in relation to individual schemes. However, whilst the new test introduces a less restrictive approach, it clearly also operates within given parameters.

5.2.7   Trustees or managers acting on actuarial advice will need to agree the relevant methods and assumptions with the sponsoring employer. In the event that agreement cannot be reached the issue must be referred to the Regulator who can direct how the calculation of the scheme's technical provisions is to be undertaken. Under the MFR regime, trustees could impose a contribution rate at least targeted to meet MFR levels of funding, if they were unable to agree this with the employer.

5.3   STATEMENT OF FUNDING PRINCIPLES

5.3.1   The Act requires trustees to prepare, keep under review and when necessary revise a statement of funding principles (s.223). Essentially, this will require production of a written statement of the trustees' policy on how to achieve the statutory funding objective. The trustees must obtain actuarial advice before preparing or revising the statement of funding principles (s.230(1)(b), and they must obtain the agreement of the employer to any matter to be included in the statement (s.229(1)(b)). The statement of funding principles should not be confused with the statement of investment principles (SIP), which continues to be required.

5.3.2   The details to be covered by the statement of funding principles will include:

(a) how the trustees propose to ensure that the statutory funding objective is met;

(b) how the employer's agreement on funding will be arranged;

(c) the implications of the scheme's funding policy on the scheme's investment policy;

(d) the methods and assumptions to be used in calculating the scheme's technical provisions; and

(e) how any failure to meet the statutory funding objective should be remedied.

5.3.3   It is proposed that the statement of funding principles be reviewed every three years. However, regulations will also require a review and, if necessary, a revised statement to be prepared in prescribed situations.

5.3.4   Trustees may be subject to penalties by the Regulator for failing to take reasonable steps to comply with these provisions.

5.4   ACTUARIAL VALUATIONS AND REPORTS

5.4.1   The occasions when actuarial advice is required will increase as a result of the Act. The current requirement to obtain a scheme valuation every three years will continue. However, unless actuarial reports on developments in relation to a scheme's technical provisions are provided annually, the Act requires an actuarial valuation to be obtained every year. This reflects the requirements of the IORP Directive.

5.4.2   The preparation of both valuations and reports will require the advice of the scheme actuary. The effective date of a valuation will be the date on which the assets are valued and the technical provisions calculated, and the effective date for a report will be governed by the information to which it relates. The precise content of such actuarial valuations and reports will be prescribed by regulations.

5.4.3   Regulations will require that the scheme actuary provides valuations or reports within a prescribed period. Trustees will be required to provide the sponsoring employer with copies of such valuations or reports within seven days of their receipt.

5.4.4   The Regulator may impose penalties under s.10 of the 1995 Act where a trustee or manager has failed to take reasonable steps to comply with these requirements.

5.4.5   Nothing in the legislation will prevent trustees seeking additional actuarial advice if so required. However, the ongoing need for annual reports now necessitates a level of actuarial monitoring that was not previously formalised, even if best practice may have suggested that it was appropriate in given circumstances.

5.5   CERTIFICATION OF TECHNICAL PROVISIONS

5.5.1   As part of the valuation process, the scheme actuary will be required to certify the calculation of the scheme's technical provisions, which must have been valued according to prescribed methods and assumptions (s.225). This again reflects the requirements of the IORP Directive.

5.5.2   If the actuary is unable to give such a certificate, he must report that fact to the Regulator and s.10 of the 1995 Act will apply to an actuary who fails to do so without reasonable excuse.

5.6   RECOVERY PLAN

5.6.1   The Act requires trustees to prepare a recovery plan if a scheme valuation reveals that the statutory funding objective was not met on the effective date (s.226), although this does not seem to apply if an actuarial report discloses a failure to meet the objective. The recovery plan must be prepared within a given timescale and must set out the necessary steps to meet the statutory funding objective and the time within which this objective should be achieved.

5.6.2   Actuarial advice should be obtained in relation to the preparation or revision of a recovery plan. Regulations will prescribe the factors trustees should take into account when assessing these matters.

5.6.3   Except in certain circumstances, the plan must be provided to the Regulator and, if required, must be subject to review or revision following subsequent actuarial valuations. Regulations are expected to require the plan to be accompanied by other specified information when it is provided to the Regulator. Civil penalties may be imposed in relation to any failure to meet these requirements.

5.6.4   A recovery plan will need to be consistent with the scheme's statement of funding principles and should be agreed with the scheme employer (s.229(1)(c)). If agreement cannot be reached, the matter must be reported to the Regulator who can direct the way in which the statutory funding objective is to be attained. This will therefore alert the Regulator to schemes which are in potential financial difficulty.

5.7   SCHEDULE OF CONTRIBUTIONS

5.7.1   Trustees are already required to prepare schedules of contributions subject to actuarial advice under the MFR regime. Section 227 of the Act maintains the requirement for a schedule of contributions, showing the rates of contribution payable by the employer and the scheme's active members, along with the due dates for payment.

5.7.2   It is understood (from the Explanatory Notes) that regulations will set out provisions which mirror existing requirements, in that the schedule should be agreed with the employer within eight weeks of the actuarial valuation and then certified by the scheme actuary within another four weeks. Similarly, it is proposed that the schedule should cover a five-year period where the valuation shows that the statutory funding objective was met on the effective date. However, where a recovery plan is in operation, the schedule will be required to cover a period no shorter than the plan.

5.7.3   Regulations will be introduced which will, for example, require employers to sign the schedule and require that deficit correction contributions under any recovery plan are shown separately in the schedule.

5.7.4   The schedule will only come into force when the scheme actuary has certified that either the valuation confirms that the statutory funding objective has been met and the schedule will maintain this status, or that the funding objective has not been met but the contributions payable under the recovery plan are sufficient to restore the position.

5.7.5   A copy of the schedule of contributions must be sent within a reasonable time to the Regulator if a valuation shows that the funding objective was not met. Equally, if a scheme actuary cannot certify a schedule of contributions within a reasonable period the actuary must notify the Regulator of that fact. An actuary failing to make such a report may face a penalty, and civil penalties may be imposed by the Regulator on trustees failing to meet the above requirements.

Implications for trustees

5.7.6   Under the MFR regime, trustees could impose a schedule of contributions – at least to the level required by the MFR – on an employer who failed to agree the schedule of contributions. Under the new statutory funding objective provisions, the agreement of the employer is required to any matter included in the schedule of contributions, and the employer will be required to sign the schedule. If the employer's agreement is not obtained within the relevant period, the trustees have power to modify the future accrual of benefits under the scheme, subject to certain conditions and to obtaining actuarial advice, but with the employer's agreement (s.229). This power would override any scheme rule prohibiting amendment to future benefit accrual.

5.7.7   The absence of any agreement from the employer on matters included in the schedule of contributions must be reported to the Regulator within a reasonable time. The Regulator then has various powers, including the power to modify the scheme as regards future accrual, or to impose a schedule of contributions on the employer and the trustees.

5.7.8   Reaching agreement on the schedule of contributions is likely to be a strategic issue for trustees, who will be anxious to seek an appropriate level of contributions from the employer. Negotiations in this area will have to be conducted within the parameters set by the Act and by the Code of Practice on funding to be issued by the Regulator. To a lesser extent, negotiations will also be influenced by the way the Regulator deals in practice with situations where schedules of contributions cannot be agreed by the trustees and the employer.

5.8   DISCLOSURE TO MEMBERS

5.8.1   The Act amends s.41 of the 1995 Act (provision of documents for members) to provide that the statement of funding principles, any actuarial valuation or report prepared under s.224, any actuarial certificate of technical provisions and the schedule of contributions must be made available to scheme members and others: see s.319 of and Sched.12 to the Act. The effective date of this change is not yet known, but it will probably be the same date as applies to the funding provisions generally, namely September 2005.

5.9   FAILURE TO MAKE PAYMENT

5.9.1   Under the 1995 Act, if an employer failed to pay contributions or if contributions were late, trustees were required to make a report to OPRA. The new legislation will also require breaches to be reported to the Regulator but only in instances when the trustees have reasonable cause to believe that the failure is likely to be of material significance to the Regulator. It is anticipated that a Code of Practice will provide more precise guidance on how trustees should make such a decision. Furthermore, regulations may specify instances of when a report to the Regulator is *not* required. Actuaries and auditors will also be required to report in certain circumstances.

5.9.2   Civil penalties will apply in relation to any breach of these provisions. Employers failing to make payments will be subject to civil penalties, whilst unpaid contributions will constitute a debt against the employer.

5.10   POWERS OF THE REGULATOR

5.10.1   As discussed in **Chapter 2**, the Regulator will have more extensive powers than its predecessor, OPRA, which is likely to result in the Regulator taking on a more proactive role. In relation to scheme funding, this is likely to become apparent if trustees have failed to prepare or review documents relating to the funding requirements, or the actuary cannot certify relevant matters, or the employer has failed to make contributions under the schedule of contributions, or where the trustees and the employer cannot reach agreement.

5.10.2   Depending upon the relevant circumstances, the Regulator will have power to: modify the scheme for the purposes of future accrual; direct how the calculation of technical provisions is to be undertaken; set the duration of the recovery period; and/or impose a schedule of contributions.

5.11   CONCLUSION

5.11.1   The new funding requirements are significant for both trustees and sponsoring employers, and much of the detail is yet to be made available in the form of draft regulations. Whilst the Regulator appears to have wide powers to intervene in relation to scheme funding issues where agreement cannot be reached between employer and trustees, it seems clear that these powers are only intended to be used as a last resort, and that trustees and employers will be expected to try hard to reach agreement.

5.11.2   It should be remembered that the overall legislative framework governing scheme funding will incorporate primary legislation, secondary legislation, one or more Codes of Practice issued by the Regulator, not to mention any additional guidance from the Regulator and the actuarial profession's own professional guidance. Therefore, an analysis of the Act in isolation will not present the whole picture on scheme funding. In particular, the Code of Practice to be issued by the Regulator on funding and any related guidance will form a key part of the legal framework in relation to scheme funding in the future.

6 INVESTMENTS

6.1 INTRODUCTION

6.1.1 This Chapter looks at how ss.244–246 of the Act change ss.35 and 36 of the 1995 Act, which deal with the statement of investment principles (SIP) and choosing investments. These sections also introduce new provisions on borrowing by trustees. The main purpose of these amendments is to bring UK law in line with the IORP Directive, with which the UK must comply by September 2005. The DWP therefore expects that these provisions will come into effect from September 2005.

6.1.2 The Act also deals with other aspects relating to investments which are covered elsewhere in this book. Trustees' obligations to have knowledge and understanding of the principles of the investment of scheme assets are dealt with in **Chapter 11** (Trustees' Standard of Care). Investment in relation to the PPF is covered in **Chapter 3** (The Pension Protection Fund), and financial planning for retirement is dealt with in **Chapter 9** (Employment-Related Issues).

6.2 STATEMENT OF INVESTMENT PRINCIPLES

6.2.1 Section 244 of the Act replaces the current s.35 of the 1995 Act with a new section. In terms of structure, many of the substantive provisions relating to the new section will be set out in regulations made under s.35 of the 1995 Act. As none of the regulations have yet been published, the Explanatory Notes and the requirements of the IORP Directive provide the best indication of what might be in the final regulations.

Preparation, review and revision of an SIP

6.2.2 Trustees will be obliged under the new s.35 of the 1995 Act to ensure that an SIP governing decisions about investments for the purposes of the scheme is prepared and maintained (s.35(1)(a) of the 1995 Act). This express investment duty applies to the trustees as a body, to any investment committee established under s.34(5)(a) of the 1995 Act comprising two or more of their number to which they may have delegated their investment powers, and to any fund manager to whom the trustees have delegated the exercise of their discretionary investment powers.

6.2.3   The trustees must ensure that the SIP is reviewed at such intervals and on such occasions as may be prescribed and, if necessary, revised. In order to comply with the IORP Directive, the SIP must be reviewed at least every three years and after any significant change in the investment policy of the fund.

The form of a SIP

6.2.4   The SIP requirements have historically been interpreted differently by different schemes and their investment advisers. Some SIPs are quite short, while others are much more extensive documents. The new s.35 states that regulations will set out the prescribed form of the SIP (s.35(4) of the 1995 Act).

6.2.5   The Myners Review conceded that the SIP represented a valuable step towards formalising a scheme's policies on a number of important issues, and that it may also inhibit the worst sorts of mismanagement. However, under the current law, Myners concluded that the SIP 'will not by itself promote proper discussion of the fund's investment strategy'. Accordingly, it recommended a material strengthening of the SIP in such a way that the annual report should 'develop into a forum for decision-makers to explain and justify their approach, and for stakeholders to exercise oversight of the decisions made on their behalf'. This quasi-corporate approach to the governance of pension schemes (for 'stakeholders', one could draw an analogy with 'shareholders' although he was presumably referring to members and the employer) is a constant theme in the Myners Review.

Requirements for a SIP

6.2.6   The matters which the SIP must cover will be set out in regulations (s.35(4) of the 1995 Act). These will provide that the SIP must cover:

(a) the kind of investments to be held;
(b) the balance between the different types of investments to be held;
(c) risk;
(d) the expected returns on investments;
(e) the extent (if at all) to which social, environmental or ethical considerations are taken into account in the selection, retention and realisation of investments;
(f) their policy (if any) in relation to the exercise of the rights (including voting rights) attaching to investments; and
(g) the requirement to state the extent (if at all) to which the trustees take social, environmental or ethical considerations into account.

6.2.7   Another aspect of investment strategy and philosophy which also raises questions of fiduciary duties is the area of ethical investments. The SIP has been required, since July 2000, to refer to the trustees' policy on social, environmental or ethical considerations. The obligation is relatively modest, but has been perceived in some quarters as potentially the 'thin end of the wedge'. The concern, often voiced privately, is that trustees will come under pressure to embrace positive ethical strategies, and will find themselves being lobbied for or against different investment classes or specific investments.

6.2.8   It has been suggested in some quarters that trustees should consult their members on such matters, apparently following the reasoning of the dicta in *Cowan* v. *Scargill* [1984] 2 All ER 750, that if beneficiaries had strong views '. . . it might not be for the "benefit" of such beneficiaries to know that they are obtaining rather larger financial returns under the trust by reason of investments in those activities than they would have received if the trustees had invested the trust funds in other investments'. While the Myners Review suggested that, for a defined contribution scheme, members' attitude towards risk should be assessed by trustees in the selection of investment vehicles, there are major practical and legal difficulties which would be involved in generally consulting on ethical investments and few trustee boards have decided that it is an appropriate way forward. In both *Cowan* and the other leading case in this area, *Martin* v. *City of Edinburgh District Council* 1988 SLT 329, the courts decided that members' best interests were synonymous with their best financial interests.

6.2.9   That said, there is risk of embarrassment for sponsoring employers as a result of the investment policies of their pension trustees (for example, if a political party's pension fund was invested in a company engaged in animal experiments). It is desirable to use the opportunity for consultation with the employer to check that, where possible, there is an understanding of the ethical and social stance being adopted.

Consulting the employer

6.2.10   Regulations will provide that, as currently, before preparing or revising their SIP, trustees will be required to consult the employer. What is the extent of the employer's right of consultation? Many employers take the view that, in a final salary scheme, the right to be consulted about the investment strategy of the fund flows from the balance of cost obligation imposed on the employer. Indeed, prior to the 1995 Act this view was sometimes reflected in scheme documents which required the employer's consent to strategic investment decisions. The right of consultation for the employer as regards the content of the trustees' SIP under s.35 of the 1995 Act was therefore intended to meet a legitimate concern of the employer.

6.2.11   However, there are grey areas. For example, if the trustees were investing the entire assets of a large scheme in building society deposits or in an underperforming mode of investment, the employer could legitimately urge the trustees to rectify the position so as to comply with their duty to maximise the return to the fund having regard to their duty of prudence and diversification. The fact that the company could benefit from improved performance by paying a lower employer contribution rate is quite consistent with the company's duty of good faith. If, on the other hand, a cash-strapped employer encouraged the trustees of a mature fund to pursue a high-risk investment strategy so as to minimise employer contributions, where this was unsuited to its liabilities in relation to the entire scheme assets, it would clearly be imprudent for the trustees to agree to such a request without additional security of some sort.

6.2.12   This is not to say that the financial position of the employer is irrelevant – merely that the trustees' prime duty is to have regard to member security. It is also the case that judgements are rarely clear cut, since a strategy which rigidly matched the asset mix to the scheme's liabilities could, in some circumstances, produce the need for greater employer contributions which would undermine the employer's business.

6.2.13   It is not yet apparent whether the current consultation requirements in respect of multi-employer schemes will continue. At present, reg. 11 of the Occupational Pension Schemes (Investment) Regulations 1996, SI 1996/3127, provides that the employers may nominate one person as their representative for consultation purposes. If they do not do so, all employers have to be consulted unless they notify the trustees that this is unnecessary. It is also open to the trustees to specify a reasonable period (at least 28 days) within which they must receive representations from the employer. They need not consider representations received after the end of that period (reg. 11(2)).

Taking advice

6.2.14   The regulations will provide that, before preparing or revising a SIP, trustees will have to obtain and consider the written advice of someone who they reasonably believe to be qualified by their ability in and practical experience of financial matters and who has the appropriate knowledge and experience of the management of investments of such a scheme.

Exemption from s.35

6.2.15   The IORP Directive allows member states to opt out, in certain circumstances, of its provisions for small schemes (defined as having fewer than 100 members). The UK Government has stated in its response to consultation on the implementation of the IORP Directive (published in June 2004) that it does not intend to seek exemptions in many circumstances. However, it may do so in relation to the requirements of Art.12 (Statement of Investment Policy Principles) of the IORP Directive and it is also considering the position of pension schemes which are wholly insured or invested in pooled funds. Whether defined contribution schemes will be exempted from the requirement, regardless of how they invest, remains to be seen.

Features of the current s.35 which are not replicated in the new section

6.2.16   The existing s.35 of the 1995 Act provides that the SIP must cover the trustees' policy for securing compliance with the MFR. As the MFR will be abolished in favour of the statutory funding objective, in future trustees will have to prepare a separate statement of funding principles to set out their policy for ensuring that the statutory funding objective is met and will not have to include this information in the SIP.

6.2.17   The current s.35 of the 1995 Act provides that the SIP must contain a statement on:

(a) the trustees' policy for securing compliance with their duty of diversification and of ensuring the suitability of investments pursuant to s.36 of the 1995 Act; and
(b) the realisation of investments.

6.2.18   There is no mention of these in the Explanatory Notes, so it is not apparent whether they will be contained in the new regulations. However, it is not clear why these would not be carried forward to the new section. There would appear to be nothing in the IORP Directive that would prevent these from being requirements of a revised SIP.

Risk

6.2.19   Currently, trustees of UK pension schemes are only required to set out in general terms their policy in relation to 'risk' (which is not defined) in the SIP, whereas the IORP Directive requires information to be given as to investment risk measurement methods used, the risk management processes which are implemented by trustees, and the strategic asset allocation with respect to the nature and duration of pension liabilities. This requirement is not apparent on the face of the Act or the Explanatory Notes, but we would expect it to become part of the relevant regulations.

Shareholder activism

6.2.20   Traditionally, occupational pension fund trustees have left the question of the voting of pension fund shares to their investment managers. Indeed, under paragraph G9 of the Investment Management Association's IMA1 Terms and Conditions, an investment manager may decide to procure the exercise of any voting rights attaching to the investments of the fund either:

(a) at its discretion, subject always to any specific instructions of the trustees; or
(b) only with the agreement, or on the specific instructions, of the trustees as the customer.

6.2.21   With effect from 3 July 2000 the trustees' SIP has had to state any policy they have on exercising voting rights. However, historically the record of UK pension funds and other institutional investors in voting has been very poor when compared to their US counterparts.

6.2.22   The question of whether the trustees have a legal duty to exercise the voting rights which are attached to shares held within the portfolio of the fund has long been discussed. Certainly it has been recognised there is a fiduciary element, since voting rights have a value. Voting of shares was seen as merely a part of a wider issue by Myners, that of shareholder activism.

6.2.23   The Myners Review drew on US Department of Labor Interpretive Bulletin 26 and ss.402–404 of the US Employment Retirement Security Act 1974, which it felt correctly articulated the element of duty of care which fund managers owed to their clients, and in particular the principle that 'the fiduciary obligations of prudence and loyalty to plan participants and beneficiaries require the responsible fiduciary to vote proxies on issues that may affect the value of the plan's investment'. In other words, investment managers should routinely consider the possibility of intervening in investee companies as one of the means of adding value for their clients.

6.2.24   It would help to ensure that this change was made if pension schemes themselves recognised the value of active intervention and asked their managers for evidence that they had been pursuing such a course. Myners recommended that the terms of the Bulletin which deal with shareholder activism should be incorporated into English law, making it a duty to intervene in the affairs of companies where it is in shareholders' and beneficiaries' interests. The Government initially proposed that this new legal duty of activism would be imposed on both trustees and fund managers, but subsequently compromised the position by agreeing to endorse the Institutional Shareholders' Committee (ISC) Principles published in October 2002 which maintains the voluntary nature of compliance with the activism requirements. In December 2004, it proposed that trustees incorporate a reference to the ISC Principles into their investment management agreements where relevant. The ISC Principles only apply to UK equities.

6.2.25   In a Department of Trade and Industry (DTI) consultative document on company law reform, *Company Law: Flexibility and Accessibility*, published in May 2004, the Government announced that in a new Companies Bill it will 'embed' in law the concept of an enlightened shareholder value, which will 'ensure that regard has to be paid by directors to the long term as well as the short term, and wider factors where relevant, such as employees, effects on the environment, suppliers and customers'. It remains to be seen whether trustees will take up this concept in assessing the merits of a particular investment or whether this will be an issue for their fund managers alone.

6.3   CHOOSING INVESTMENTS

6.3.1   Section 36 of the 1995 Act regulates trustees' exercise of their powers in respect of the selection and retention of investments and also that of any fund manager to whom a discretion has been delegated. Section 36 is modified by s.245 of the Act in order to ensure compliance with Art.18(1) of the IORP Directive which requires investments to be carried out in accordance with the 'prudent person principle' set out in that Article.

Exercise of the power of investment

6.3.2   Trustees, and any fund manager to whom any discretion has been delegated, must exercise their powers of investment in accordance with regulations which may specify criteria to be applied when choosing investments and require the diversification of investments. The regulations will include requirements that:

(a) an investment should not adversely affect the overall quality of the investment fund;
(b) investments should be made predominantly on regulated markets; and
(c) any investments in derivatives should contribute towards a strategy of risk reduction or efficient portfolio management.

Requirements for investments to be diversified

6.3.3   The current s.36(2) provides that the trustees or fund manager must have regard to the need for diversification insofar as appropriate to the circumstances of the scheme. It appears that the new requirements on diversification might be wider, in that s.36(1A) provides simply that regulations may require diversification of investments.

6.3.4   However, it is likely that there will be a caveat in the regulations as there are circumstances where diversification is not justified, such as in relation to a mature scheme or a scheme that is in winding up.

Derivatives

6.3.5   The new restriction on investment in derivatives, namely, that they should only be used to contribute towards a strategy of risk reduction, or efficient portfolio management, is a requirement of Art.18(1) of the IORP Directive.

6.3.6   Derivatives are widely used by pension schemes (and other institutional investors) for the creation of 'synthetic' securities. For example, many pension schemes wish to buy index-linked gilts because of the nature of their pension obligations, which tend to increase in line with inflation. The market in index-linked gilts is currently too small to meet demand. The private sector tends not to issue index-linked gilts and the UK Government has not done so in any quantity for some time. This results in a shortage of supply, leading to upwards price pressure. Further, index-linked gilts tend now not to have long periods to maturity. Institutional investors will therefore often buy a corporate bond and enter into a swap transaction with an investment bank, exchanging the fixed interest income flow under the bond for an index-linked income flow provided by the investment bank (i.e. swaps).

6.3.7   In our view, investment in derivatives for these purposes would represent efficient portfolio management. However, we are aware that some commentators take the view that the position is not clear-cut. Our view is supported by the Inland Revenue's Tax Bulletin No.66 (August 2003), which states that where an approved pension scheme uses interest rate, currency or equity swaps, the Revenue will normally regard such swaps as investments if the purpose of entering into the swap falls into one of the following categories:

(a) to hedge risk inherent in the scheme's existing investment portfolio;
(b) as part of an investment strategy to enhance the returns from the existing investment portfolio; or
(c) to create a synthetic exposure to investments of a particular type or in a particular market, in line with the fund's normal policies of investing directly in such instruments.

6.3.8   Using swaps to create a synthetic exposure to investments of a particular type is therefore expressly referred to in the third category of permitted purposes.

Taking advice

6.3.9   As a matter of common law, trustees are expected to take advice, where appropriate, before exercising their investment powers (*Cowan v. Scargill* [1984] 2 All ER 750).

6.3.10   Section 36 of the 1995 Act currently provides that, before investing in any manner (except in a manner mentioned in Part I of Sched.1 to the Trustee Investments Act 1961), trustees must obtain 'proper advice' on the question of whether the investment is satisfactory, having regard to the requirements of the regulations made under s.36 of the 1995 Act so far as they relate to the suitability of investments and also the principles contained in the SIP.

6.3.11   If the advice relates to investments which are regulated under the Financial Services and Markets Act 2000 (FSMA 2000), 'proper advice' for this purpose is advice given by a person authorised or exempt under that Act. As regards investments which are not regulated under FSMA 2000 (e.g. cash and direct property holdings), there is still a requirement to take 'proper advice'; however, in this case it must be given by a person who is reasonably believed by the trustees to be qualified by his ability in and practical experience of financial matters and who they believe to have the appropriate knowledge and experience of the management of the investments of occupational pension schemes. In both cases, the advice must be given or confirmed in writing (s.36(6) and (7) of the 1995 Act).

6.3.12   The requirement to take such advice applies equally where the trustees are considering whether to retain or sell a particular investment or class of investments. The trustees may determine at what intervals 'proper advice' ought to be taken, but they are under an express duty to obtain and consider such advice at such intervals as they determine (s.36(4) of the 1995 Act).

Disapplication of s.36 of the 1995 Act

6.3.13   The new s.36(9) contains a power to permit regulations to exclude the application of s.36 to prescribed schemes. The Explanatory Notes state that an exemption would be considered, for example, for small schemes where all active members are trustees.

6.4   BORROWING BY TRUSTEES

6.4.1   Section 36A is inserted into the 1995 Act by s.246 of the Act to ensure compliance with Art.18(2) of the IORP Directive. It provides that regulations may prohibit trustees, or the fund manager to whom any discretion has been delegated, from borrowing money or acting as a guarantor, except in prescribed cases.

6.4.2   The regulations will:

(a) specify that trustees may only borrow where this is on a temporary basis and for liquidity purposes; and
(b) prohibit trustees from guaranteeing loans.

6.4.3   The Explanatory Notes provide that an exemption from the requirements would again be considered, for example, for small schemes where all of the active members are trustees.

6.5   KNOWLEDGE AND UNDERSTANDING OF INVESTMENT PRINCIPLES

6.5.1   Section 90 of the Act provides, amongst other things, that the Regulator must issue a Code of Practice in relation to the obligations imposed by ss.247 and 248 in respect of the requirements for knowledge and understanding, which provide that individual and corporate trustees have knowledge and understanding of the principles relating to the investment of the assets of pension schemes.

6.5.2   Originally, OPRA published two 'scope' documents for consultation, one for self-administered schemes and one for those schemes which were exclusively invested in insurance policies. The reaction to this artificial distinction, which is not supported by any statutory provision, was universally negative and OPRA has indicated that only one code will be issued. However, the distinction may well be preserved in respect of the principles of investment governing the two different types of scheme. These are given below.

Defined benefit and defined contribution self-administered schemes (including AVCs): investment

6.5.3   (a) How capital markets behave and how, broadly, they react to economic cycles.

(b) The major asset classes and their characteristics:

(i)   equities;
(ii)   bonds;
(iii)   cash; and
(iv)   property.

(c) The nature of risk and the risk/reward profile of each asset class.
(d) The implications of overseas investment for some specialised asset classes.
(e) Specialised asset classes, instruments and techniques (as appropriate).
(f) Valuation mechanisms for each asset class.

Defined contribution self-administered schemes (including AVCs): investment choices

6.5.4   (a) Factors which will influence investment choices include:

(i)   the choice of contribution level available including the effect of employer contribution;
(ii)   the age of the members and their proximity to retirement;
(iii)   the financial awareness of members, including the risk/reward balance;
(iv)   the availability of advice;
(v)   the selection of an appropriate number and range of funds;
(vi)   the implications of choice for members;
(vii)   the appropriateness of default or lifestyle options; and
(viii) how techniques for communication with members will impact upon their ability to make financial decisions.

(b) The capability of the administration system to manage the arrangements.

Defined benefit and defined contribution wholly insured schemes (including AVCs): investment

6.5.5   (a) How capital markets behave and how, broadly, they react to economic cycles.

(b) The major asset classes and their characteristics:

(i)   equities;
(ii)   bonds;

   (iii) cash; and
   (iv) property.

(c) The nature of risk and the risk/reward profile of each asset class.
(d) The nature of pension funds offered by providers:

   (i)   pooled funding;
   (ii)   with profits/unit linked;
   (iii) managed;
   (iv)   equity;
   (v)   fixed interest;
   (vi)   cash; and
   (vii) property.

Defined contribution wholly insured schemes (including AVCs): investment choices

6.5.6   (a) Factors which will influence investment choices, including:

   (i)   the choice of contribution level available including the effect of employer contribution;
   (ii)   the age of the members and their proximity to retirement;
   (iii) the financial awareness of members, including the risk/reward balance;
   (iv)   the availability of advice;
   (v)   the selection of an appropriate number and range of funds;
   (vi)   the implications of choice for members;
   (vii) the appropriateness of default or lifestyle options;
   (viii) how techniques for communication with members will impact upon their ability to make financial decisions.

   (b) The capability of the administration system to manage the arrangements.

6.6   IMPLICATIONS FOR TRUSTEES AND FUND MANAGERS

6.6.1   The changes proposed under the Act to the investment provisions contained in the 1995 Act are not especially onerous. Perhaps of more significance will be an amendment to the financial services regime to restore the position which applied under the Financial Services Act 1986, so that trustees will have to delegate only all day-to-day investment management decisions, rather than all 'routine or day-to-day' decisions, as required under FSMA 2000.

SIP

6.6.2   Trustees have been required to produce an SIP since the 1995 Act came into force in 1997. The new provisions do not radically alter that obligation. The main changes that trustees will have to bear in mind are the obligation to review the SIP every three years and the scope for additional content requirements for the SIP (following on from Myners' recommendations). Regulations will also prescribe the form of the SIP.

Choosing investments

6.6.3   Whilst the basic principle underlying the existing s.36 is preserved in the new section, trustees and fund managers will have to consider new criteria in relation to the selection and retention of investments, and also seek advice based on those new criteria. Trustees whose schemes hold derivatives will also have to seek advice on whether they do so in a way which is consistent with a strategy of risk reduction or efficient portfolio management.

Borrowing

6.6.4   Trustees will have to ensure that any borrowing is on a temporary basis and for liquidity purposes only.

6.7   EMPLOYER-RELATED INVESTMENTS

6.7.1   Article 18(1)(f) of the IORP Directive provides that trustees may invest no more than 5 per cent of the assets of the scheme in the sponsoring employer and, where the sponsoring employer belongs to a group, investment in that group of companies may not be more than 10 per cent of the portfolio.

6.7.2   The IORP Directive also provides that, for multi-employer schemes, investment in the employers must be made prudently, taking into account the need for proper diversification.

6.7.3   This requirement is a departure from the current requirements of the Occupational Pension Schemes (Investment) Regulations 1996, SI 1996/3127, which prescribe that not more than 5 per cent of the assets of a scheme may be invested in employer-related investments. It is therefore likely that these regulations will be amended in order to comply with the IORP Directive.

7 AMENDING PENSION SCHEMES

7.1 INTRODUCTION

7.1.1 Pension schemes often have a long life and can go through many changes in the light of economic, social and statutory changes. Although this book is principally concerned with the Act, no review of scheme amendments is complete without consideration of other related issues which impact on scheme amendments. Therefore, this Chapter includes a brief overview of a scheme's power of amendment. It then covers s.67 of the 1995 Act, as amended by the Act. It then deals with the powers of the Regulator, and other statutory, Regulator and court powers of modification. It finishes with a brief review of employer consultation and other regulatory controls.

7.1.2 In this Chapter, the word 'amendment' is construed widely to include any change, revocation or addition to the trust deed or rules of a trust-based occupational pension scheme (approved or unapproved). References to sections are to sections of the 1995 Act as amended by the Act. References to regulations are to the Occupational Pension Schemes (Modification of Schemes) Regulations 1996, SI 1996/2517 unless otherwise stated.

7.2 SCHEME'S POWER OF AMENDMENT

Express power required

7.2.1 Unless a power of amendment is expressly provided in the trust documentation there is no power for employers or trustees to amend the provisions of a scheme (subject to statutory powers outlined at **para.7.5**). If there is no explicit power of amendment, a power could be implied in limited circumstances depending on the construction of the trust deed and rules of the scheme but this must be done with extreme care.

Exercising the amendment power

7.2.2   If the power prescribes a method of exercise, this must be followed. For example, if the power is required to be exercised by deed, a deed is needed; a simple resolution would be inadequate.

7.2.3   Where a resolution of the trustees or of the board of an employer is required care must be taken to ensure that this is validly obtained. In *Municipal Mutual Insurance Ltd* v. *Harrop* [1998] PLR 149, the exercise of a power of amendment was nearly invalidated because it was supposed to be made by resolution of the board of the principal employer and instead was agreed to as an informal arrangement by some of the directors of the board. The amendment was only validated retrospectively by a subsequent board resolution ratifying the previous informal consent.

7.2.4   Amendment powers often require the consent of another party, such as the principal employer or, more infrequently, a representative group or proportion of the membership. Actuarial certificates as to the effect of making a particular amendment are sometimes required by the terms of the power of amendment. These requirements should be strictly complied with.

7.2.5   The old s.67(6) and reg.5 provide a useful let out where the consent of members is required by the power of amendment and members do not respond. Consent can be treated as given if the trustees have sent notices of the proposed amendment to a member's last known address (with at least two months between the notices) and no response is received within a month of the date when the last notice is sent. This method of deeming consent is relevant only where consent of members is required by the scheme's power of amendment, not in relation to the consent requirements of s.67(2).

7.2.6   Any amendment to accrued rights or subsisting rights under s.67 will be subject to the express provisions of the trust deed and rules.

Express limitations on express powers of amendment

7.2.7   It is important to consider carefully the wording of a power of amendment in order to determine its precise scope.

7.2.8   Some schemes contain powers which permit amendment of only the deed or only the rules. Others may impose different requirements and limitations for amendments of the deed or the rules. Often the power will be expressed in a way which limits the power to make amendments. Many, particularly older, schemes include express restrictions prohibiting amendment of particular clauses or rules. In such cases it is important to determine whether the wording of the prohibition is so precise that it is impossible to change even a word of the protected clauses or rules, or whether in fact the proper construction of the restriction is that the meaning of the clause or rule in question cannot be altered.

7.2.9   The most common type of express restriction is one which prohibits amendments which would have a particular result. Two common examples are considered below.

(a) *No amendment of the main object or purpose of the scheme.* Where a restriction prevents alteration of the main purpose of the scheme, great care needs to be taken when considering what is that main purpose. Often, the main purpose is expressly stated in a substantive provision or a recital of the trust deed, but sometimes it needs to be gathered from the totality of the provisions of the trust deed and rules, by extraneous circumstances, or just over the passage of time.

(b) *No amendment to reduce pensions in payment or accrued benefits.* A restriction on amendments which reduce the value of benefits is extremely common. Usually the restriction refers to the amendment of benefits or rights accrued at the date of amendment, but the particular wording chosen can have significant implications and care must be taken when considering the precise interpretation of the limitation in question.

Implied limitations on power of amendment

7.2.10   Even if there is no express prohibition on amendment of the main object or purpose of the scheme, such a prohibition will be implied. The purpose of the scheme is a question of construction. It does not depend just on any particular statement of the purpose, but also on the totality of the scheme in the light of the circumstances at the time of a proposed amendment.

Reduction of past service benefits

7.2.11   If there is no express protection of past service benefits, it is possible that, as a matter of trust law, a power of amendment cannot be used to reduce the rights of beneficiaries in respect of past service without their consent. Certainly, in *Municipal Mutual Insurance Ltd* v. *Harrop* [1998] PLR 149, it was felt that a retrospective amendment could not be made which would have the effect of divesting vested rights. It was also held that it was not even possible to do so to correct a previous amendment erroneously made. It is worth noting that there were some very particular facts in this case.

Change of circumstances

7.2.12   Whilst there may be a power of amendment, circumstances may prevent its use. It is possible that the power has simply ceased to be available for use, and an example of this is where a scheme has gone into winding up. Care should always be taken to consider whether the power is still exercisable.

Amending the power of amendment

7.2.13   There is no total bar on exercising the power of amendment to amend the power itself. However this is subject to an implied restriction (in the absence of an express power to amend the power). It seems unlikely that an amendment to remove express or implied restrictions on a power of amendment would be permissible; if it were, the consequence would be that restrictions on the amendment powers would be pointless.

7.2.14   It is also arguable that the power of amendment cannot be widened or extended. This is logical, bearing in mind the need for the power to be expressly stated in the first place. Similarly, in the absence of an express power to do so, it is possible that the power of amendment can be used to introduce further restrictions or to reduce a power of amendment already existing. There are no cases in which these issues have been properly debated.

Retrospective amendments

7.2.15   Retrospective amendments may be made where the power of amendment expressly provides for such amendments. For the reasons given above, it is unlikely that a retrospective power can be introduced into a power of amendment which did not previously permit it.

7.2.16   It is likely that there is no generally implied power to make retrospective amendments. However, it might be possible to imply such a power into a scheme, depending on the specific construction of that scheme's governing documentation, for example, the power to administer the scheme in the manner announced to members pending the execution of a deed. Careful consideration will be needed to determine whether the power is truly being exercised retrospectively or whether it is effectively being exercised by interim means by the issue of the announcements, especially when considering whether there is any change to subsisting rights (see **para.7.3.7**) for the purposes of any restriction under the scheme or s.67 of the 1995 Act and, if so, when the amendment is effective.

Effect of winding up

7.2.17   It will often be the case that the power of amendment will be lost on a scheme going into winding up. This depends on the construction of the provisions of the scheme, in particular, the winding-up rule. However, there is no reason why an express power of amendment or the winding-up rule could not include a provision that the power of amendment should continue to be available once the scheme has gone into winding up, and this type of provision is normally included in new schemes. If winding up is contemplated, then the scheme provisions should be checked beforehand to see whether any amendment should be made. It may also be possible to amend the provisions to enable changes to be made during the winding up.

7.3   STATUTORY PROTECTION: s.67

7.3.1   One of the principles of the 1995 Act was to protect against adverse changes to members' accrued rights. The old s.67 prevented a scheme being modified in a manner which 'would or might affect any entitlement, accrued right or pension credit right of any member of the scheme acquired before the power is exercised' unless the actuarial certification and/or the member consent requirements were satisfied. Section 262 of the Act substitutes an entirely new s.67 of the 1995 Act. It is expected that the new s.67 will come into effect on 6 April 2006. It will apply to occupational pension schemes other than public service pension schemes.

7.3.2   In contrast to the Government's stated intentions to promote simplicity, the new s.67 now extends to 10 sections (9 pages) and is highly prescriptive.

Who will be protected?

7.3.3   Section 67 of the 1995 Act will protect the subsisting rights of all members of pension schemes, i.e. active, deferred and pensioner members, as well as other categories of members such as pension credit members and those in receipt of surviving spouse's or dependant's pensions (new s.67A(5) and (10) of the 1995 Act).

7.3.4   Section 67A(5) does not expressly refer to contingent beneficiaries (e.g. a spouse or child who would be entitled to a benefit if the member died) as a separate protected category. However, the benefits of contingent beneficiaries would be protected during the member's lifetime to the extent that they form part of the member's subsisting rights (therefore falling within s.67A(5) and (6)).

7.3.5   Therefore, if a modification would or might affect contingent benefits, the member and not the contingent beneficiaries would have to be notified and allowed to make representations. If the consent requirements are applied (see **para.7.3.32** below), it is the member and not the contingent beneficiaries who would have to consent. If the actuarial equivalence requirements are used (see **para.7.3.46** below), the actuary is likely to have to consider the actuarial value of the member's total benefits, rather than the contingent benefits separately.

7.3.6   This is important for trustees from a practical point of view, as they are very unlikely to know who all of the contingent beneficiaries are, and the class of contingent beneficiaries may be very wide.

'Subsisting rights'

7.3.7   Section 67 protects the 'subsisting rights' of a member. These are defined in s.67A(6) as:

(a) any right which at that time has accrued to or in respect of a member to future benefits under the scheme rules;

(b) any other entitlement to benefits which a member has at that time under the scheme rules; or

(c) in relation to the survivor of a member, any entitlement to benefits, or right to future benefits, which he has at that time under the scheme rules.

7.3.8   Section 67 must be considered in respect of each individual member's or survivor's subsisting rights. It is not possible to consider the total subsisting rights of all affected members when determining whether there has been an adverse effect on subsisting rights.

7.3.9   The meaning of each component of the term 'subsisting rights' is discussed below.

Rights which have accrued to or in respect of a member to future benefits under the scheme rules

7.3.10   It has always been necessary to consider carefully on a case by case basis whether the right in question is a right that has accrued to the member. It is beyond the scope of this book to include a comprehensive review on whether each specific benefit under a scheme is an accrued right. The subsisting rights of an active member are to be determined as if he had opted to terminate his service immediately before the modification took effect (s.67A(7) of the 1995 Act).

7.3.11   Subsisting rights cannot include incapacity early retirement benefits or death in service benefits, on the basis that these benefits would not be payable after leaving pensionable service. However, benefits on death in deferment (or early payment of deferred pension) form part of both active and deferred members' accrued rights.

Entitlements of members or survivors to benefits under the scheme rules

7.3.12   'Entitlement' means the entitlement to the present payment of a pension or other benefit (s.67A(6)(a)(ii) of the 1995 Act). This clarifies a previous uncertainty under the old s.67.

What are the 'scheme rules'?

7.3.13   The scheme rules are the rules of the scheme, as overridden by the various statutory provisions referred to in s.67A(8) and (9), including in relation to equal treatment, preservation, pension credits, and pension increases. In essence, the scheme rules are also deemed to contain any provision that they do not contain but must do if the scheme is to conform to the various overriding requirements referred to.

Rights excluded from subsisting rights

7.3.14   Section 67 does not apply in relation to the exercise of a power for a purpose connected with debits under the 1999 Act (i.e. a pension sharing order), or in any manner to be set out in regulations (s.67(3) of the 1995 Act).

Should the security of a member's subsisting rights be taken into account?

7.3.15   In our view the security of benefits need not be considered when determining whether the amendment adversely affects subsisting rights. Section 67 is concerned with the value of subsisting rights; other provisions of the 1995 Act (particularly those relating to the statutory funding objective) safeguard security.

7.3.16   When s.67 was originally enacted there was much debate as to whether the effect of a modification on the security of benefits should be taken into account. The authors have always taken the view that it should not.

Does s.67 apply to a change in the order of priorities in the winding-up provisions?

7.3.17   Section 67 of the 1995 Act does not apply to an amendment of the order of priorities on winding up. This is because such an amendment alters only the potential security of a member's benefits not the value. Such a change may still be prevented by the scheme's trust documentation or where it is not in members' interests.

'Regulated modifications'

7.3.18   Section 67 of the 1995 Act applies to two types of modification, 'protected modifications' and 'detrimental modifications', which are together known as 'regulated modifications'. If an amendment is a protected modification, the trustees will have to follow the consent requirements. If the amendment is a detrimental modification, they may apply either the consent requirements or the actuarial equivalence requirements (see **para.7.3.32** and **para.7.3.46** respectively).

What is a 'modification'?

7.3.19   In our opinion, a modification to a scheme is effected whenever there is a change to the governing documentation of the scheme. In this context the governing documentation is not limited to just the trust deed and rules; it extends to any document which contains the benefit promise. For example, if the rules refer to a benefit being of an amount notified by the trustees to the member (as might be the case on the receipt of a transfer in), a subsequent re-notification to change the amount of the benefit could amount to a modification of the scheme and therefore would be subject to s.67 of the 1995 Act.

7.3.20   This does not mean that all promises in booklets or announcements become part of the scheme. The status of such documents will depend on the construction of the totality of the scheme documentation. Unless the type of situation described above applies, the booklet or announcement will probably be explanatory or illustrative only and will not form part of the governing documentation.

7.3.21   A problem occasionally encountered is where a booklet promises more benefits than are provided by the deed and rules. Unless the deed and rules contain a power permitting the alteration of benefits in this way, the 'incorrect' statement could amount to misrepresentation or give rise to an estoppel. However the issuing of the booklet would not be a modification to the scheme and nor would its correction.

7.3.22   The position in respect of modifications has been complicated by the recent High Court decision on *Aon Trust Corporation Limited* v. *KPMG & Ors* [2004] EWHC 1844. It was held in this case that the exercise by the trustees of a power under the scheme to adjust or amend benefits (which the court said included pensions in payment) if an actuarial valuation showed a deficiency, amounts to a 'modification' for the purposes of s.67 of the 1995 Act as it was an 'omission' from the scheme. This was even though the benefit change could be made without an amendment to the scheme documentation (the definition of modification comes from s.181 of the 1993 Act and includes any 'additions, omissions and amendments' from a scheme). The authors do not share the court's view, and as the decision is being appealed it is to be hoped that the Court of Appeal will clarify the situation.

7.3.23   Using the court's logic, any exercise of a power under the rules to, for example, withdraw an ill-health early retirement pension on the basis that the member had recovered would be a 'modification' of the scheme for the purposes of s.67 of the 1995 Act. This would mean that every exercise of a power in a scheme to withdraw an ill-health pension (e.g. because the member has recovered) or a change to early retirement factors would fall within the scope of s.67. Similarly, we do not consider that the exercise of a power to modify a scheme includes the exercise of any power which would result in a change to benefits.

'Protected modifications'

7.3.24   'Protected modifications' are defined in s.67A(3) of the 1995 Act as certain significant amendments which can only be made by using the consent requirements. These types of amendments are modifications which:

(a) would or might result in any subsisting right of a member or a survivor which is not a right or entitlement to money purchase benefits becoming, or being replaced with, a right or entitlement to money purchase benefits under the scheme (e.g. accrued final salary rights being altered to money purchase);

(b) would or might result in a reduction in the prevailing rate of any pension in payment; or

(c) is of a prescribed description (note that there are not currently any prescribed types of amendment).

7.3.25   If trustees wish to make a protected modification, they may only do so if they satisfy the consent requirements (see **para.7.3.32**) (s.67(2)(a)(i) of the 1995 Act).

'Detrimental modifications'

7.3.26   A 'detrimental modification' is defined in s.67A(4) of the 1995 Act as any modification (other than a protected modification) that would or might adversely affect the subsisting rights of a member or a survivor. Detrimental modifications may be made using either the consent requirements or the actuarial equivalence requirements (s.67(2)(a)(ii) of the 1995 Act). If it is not possible to satisfy one set of requirements, the trustees may use the other.

Is an augmentation a regulated modification?

7.3.27   This question was unclear under the old s.67. Under the new provisions an augmentation is not a regulated modification. This is because detrimental modifications require an adverse effect on members' subsisting rights, which, clearly, would not include an augmentation. In addition, augmentations do not fall within the defined categories of protected modifications.

Are changes of commutation or early retirement factors regulated modifications?

7.3.28   Before considering whether changes to commutation factors or to early retirement factors are regulated modifications, it is first necessary to consider whether the changes amount to a modification of the scheme. There would be no modification if the factors were changed in line with a specific power or direction under the governing documentation given to the trustees or employer to revise the factors from time to time, or where they fall to be determined by the actuary from time to time (although see the comments in respect of *Aon Trust Corporation Limited* v. *KPMG & Ors* in **para.7.3.22**). Conversely, if the factors are set out in the trust deed and rules or some other formal document with no mechanism for their alteration (other than the scheme's power of amendment), then a change would amount to a modification of the scheme.

7.3.29   It is likely to be rare that such a change would amount to a modification, but if it does then it is necessary to consider whether it would, or might, affect a member's subsisting rights and comprise a regulated modification.

7.3.30   The authors do not share the view sometimes expressed that, where the early retirement or commutation is subject to the consent of the trustees or the employer there is no right to the early retirement or commutation, and so the factors cannot form part of the accrued rights or entitlement.

Does s.67 of the 1995 Act apply to modification by trustee resolution under s.68 or s.69, by the Regulator under s.69 or by the court?

7.3.31   Neither the current nor the new s.67 apply to modifications by trustee resolution under s.68 or s.69, or by the Regulator under s.69 or by the court. This is because s.67 applies only to a power to modify conferred by an occupational pension scheme (s.67(1)) and the powers to amend given by s.68 and s.69 or held by the court are not 'conferred' by the scheme.

Consent requirements (s.67B)

7.3.32   Trustees wishing to make a protected modification to a scheme must comply with the consent requirements. If they wish to make a detrimental modification, they may either use the consent requirements set out below or the actuarial equivalence requirements (see **para.7.3.46**). The consent requirements are made up of the informed consent requirement and the timing requirement. In addition, the trustees must comply with the trustee approval requirement and the reporting requirement.

'The informed consent requirements'

7.3.33   Where a member must give informed consent before a modification is effected, s.67(B)(4) of the 1995 Act sets out the requirements for the trustees. Prior to the effective date of the change, the trustees must have given the member written information adequate to explain the nature of the modification and its effect on him. The trustees must also have notified the member in writing that he may make representations to the trustees about the modification, afforded him a reasonable opportunity to make representations, and notified him in writing that the consent requirements apply to him. The affected members must then give their written consent to the modification.

7.3.34   Trustees will probably wish to give members as much information as possible in order to ensure that it is 'adequate to explain the nature of the modi-fication and its effect on him' (s.67B(4)(a)(i) of the 1995 Act). If a member is not given enough information there is a risk that he may complain at some point in the future that he was not properly informed about the nature of the change, and that the modification should be voided. It is possible that the Code of Practice to be issued on s.67 will provide some guidance on the necessary level of detail.

7.3.35   Members must be given a reasonable time in which to make representa-tions. This time will be set out in the Code of Practice on s.67 to be issued by the Regulator. However, as the amendment cannot be made without member consent this does not seem to be relevant. There is no specific requirement in the informed consent requirements for the trustees to consider representations made by members. However, s.67 separately requires trustees to consent to regulated modifications before they are made. When giving their consent, trustees will be subject to their general trust law duties to take all relevant considerations into account. Therefore, if members raise considerations that are relevant, trustees should take these into account.

7.3.36   Once a member has been given the notifications above, he must provide his written consent to the amendment. It appears that, unlike the situation under the old s.67, members will have to actively provide their consent. Currently, if trustees have sent two notifications to members and no response is received within a certain period of the second notice, a member is deemed to have given consent. The DWP has confirmed that new regulations on the new s.67 will not contain similar deemed consent provisions.

7.3.37   If a member dies after having given his consent, the trustees will not have to obtain the consent of the member's survivors, who will be deemed to have given their consent (s.67(5) and (6) of the 1995 Act).

The timing requirement

7.3.38   In order to satisfy the timing requirement, the modification must take effect in respect of each affected member within 'a reasonable period' after the member has given his consent (s.67B(6) of the 1995 Act). This period will be set out in the Code of Practice on s.67 to be issued by the Regulator.

Trustee approval requirement

7.3.39   Once the trustees have fulfilled the informed consent requirements, if the scheme's governing documents give the power of amendment to the trustees, they must then determine to exercise that power. If the power is vested in the employer, the trustees must also consent to the making of the amendment (ss.67E and 67(2)(b) of the 1995 Act).

7.3.40   Trustees must do this within 'a reasonable period' from the first consent given by an affected member (s.67E(3) of the 1995 Act). This period will be set out in the Code of Practice on s.67 to be issued by the Regulator.

7.3.41   Where the trustees have determined to exercise the power or consented to its exercise in respect of a member who then dies, this determination also applies to the member's survivors and no separate determination is necessary in respect of them (s.67(5) and (6) of the 1995 Act).

The reporting requirement

7.3.42   After determining to exercise the power of amendment, or consenting to its exercise, the trustees must notify each affected member that they have made the determination or given their consent (ss.67F(1) and 67(2)(c) of the 1995 Act).

7.3.43   The trustees must give this notification within a reasonable period from their determination or consent to the exercise of the power of amendment, and before the modification takes effect (s.67F(2) of the 1995 Act). This period will be set out in the Code of Practice on s.67 to be issued by the Regulator. It is arguable that the requirement to give notification before the amendment takes effect might prohibit retrospective amendments because if a retrospective amendment is to take effect, from, say, five years ago, the trustee would not be able to give this notification before the amendment takes effect. However, the DWP has confirmed that the intention is that the notice should be given before the deed or other amending document is executed, rather than before the effective date of the amendment.

What if the trustees cannot fulfil the consent requirements?

7.3.44   If none of the members consent to the amendment, the consent requirements will obviously not have been satisfied. If some members consent to the amendment and some do not, then the trustees can choose to amend the scheme only in respect of those members who have consented. This is because s.67 applies separately to each affected member. However, the trustees should consider whether they can agree to the amendment under these circumstances from a trust law perspective and seek appropriate advice.

7.3.45   If the amendment is a protected modification, s.67 will not permit the amendment to be made in respect of members who do not give their consent. If the amendment is a detrimental modification, the trustees may (if consent is not obtained) decide to use the actuarial equivalence procedure requirements. If the trustees wish to use that alternative procedure then, when they give members the notifications referred to in **para.7.3.33**, they should state that the actuarial equivalence requirements will apply if members do not give their consent. This will avoid the need to give members information about the modification again when the trustees seek to make the amendment using the actuarial equivalence requirements.

The actuarial equivalence requirements (s.67C)

7.3.46   Where trustees wish to make a detrimental modification (which would or might affect subsisting rights), they may use either the consent requirements or the actuarial equivalence requirements which are set out below. In addition to the actuarial equivalence requirement, the trustees must also comply with the trustee approval requirement and the reporting requirement. The actuarial equivalence requirements and the other requirements, in the order in which they must be satisfied, are:

(a) actuarial value requirement (s.67C(5));
(b) information requirement (s.67C(4));
(c) trustee approval requirement (s.67E);
(d) reporting requirement (s.67F); and
(e) actuarial equivalence statement requirement (s.67C(6)).

Actuarial value requirements

7.3.47 In order to satisfy the actuarial value requirements, before the modification is made, trustees must make such arrangements or take such steps as are adequate to secure that actuarial value will be maintained (s.67C(5) of the 1995 Act). In respect of each affected member, actuarial value is maintained if the actuarial value of the member's subsisting rights immediately after the amendment takes effect will be equal to or greater than the actuarial value immediately before that time (s.67C(8) of the 1995 Act).

7.3.48 The two fundamental questions are therefore how the actuarial value of subsisting rights is calculated and how the trustees should take steps or make arrangements to ensure that the actuarial value is maintained.

7.3.49 Section 67D(4) and (5) provides that regulations may prescribe requirements for the purpose of calculating actuarial value, which may include requirements for calculations to be made in accordance with guidance prepared by a prescribed body and, if so required, approved by the Secretary of State. It therefore appears that an actuarial guidance note will be prepared to set out how actuarial value will be calculated.

7.3.50 It is likely that trustees will want to satisfy themselves that actuarial value will be maintained by obtaining written confirmation of this from the scheme actuary. It can therefore be seen that the willingness of actuaries to provide such confirmation, and to issue actuarial equivalence statements, will be fundamental to the success of the new s.67.

'Information requirement'

7.3.51 The information requirement is satisfied in respect of each affected member if, before the modification has been made, the trustees have taken all reasonable steps to give the member written information adequate to explain the nature of the modification and its effect on him; notify the member in writing that he may make representations to the trustees about the modification; afford the member a reasonable opportunity to make representations; and notify the member in writing that the actuarial equivalence requirements apply to him (s.67C(4) of the 1995 Act).

7.3.52 The factors the trustees will wish to consider regarding the information to provide, the position on the death of a member, and their response to any representations to be made by members, are similar to those outlined in relation to informed consent (see **paras. 7.3.33–7.3.37**). The Code of Practice on s.67 may provide some guidance on the necessary level of detail. It is more likely that members will make representations in respect of the actuarial equivalence requirements as the restructuring of benefits is likely to advantage some members and disadvantage others. If it appears from representations that the modification will disadvantage a large proportion of the membership, this is a relevant factor for the trustees to take into account.

7.3.53 Where the original proposed modification has changed after the information requirements have been satisfied, and before the trustees have made a determination to exercise the power or given their consent as set out in **para.7.3.39**, the information requirement is taken to have been satisfied in relation to the revised modification. This will only be the case where the revised modification does not differ from the original modification in any material respect (s.67D(2) of the 1995 Act). It is possible that the Code of Practice to be issued by the Regulator will set out what is 'material' for these purposes.

Trustee approval requirement

7.3.54 Once the trustees have fulfilled the actuarial value requirements and the information requirement:

(a) if the scheme's governing documents give the power of amendment to the trustees, they must determine to exercise that power; or
(b) if the power is vested in the employer, the trustees must consent to the making of the amendment.

7.3.55 Where the trustees have determined to exercise the power or consent to its exercise in respect of a member who then dies, this determination also applies to the member's survivors and no separate determination is necessary in respect of them (s.67(5) and (6) of the 1995 Act).

The reporting requirement

7.3.56 After determining to exercise the power of amendment, or consenting to its exercise, the trustees must take all reasonable steps to notify each affected member that they have made the determination or given their consent.

7.3.57 The trustees must do this within a reasonable period from their determination or consent to the exercise of the power of amendment, and before the modification takes effect (s.67F(2) of the 1995 Act). This period will be set out in the Code of Practice on s.67 to be issued by the Regulator. It is arguable that the requirement to give notification before the amendment takes effect might prohibit retrospective amendments as, if a retrospective amendment is to take effect, say, from five years ago, the trustees will not be able to give their consent before the amendment takes effect but the DWP has confirmed that the intention is that notice should be given before the deed is executed.

Actuarial equivalence statements

7.3.58   Trustees must, once the detrimental modification takes effect, obtain a statement from the scheme actuary (or person with prescribed qualifications) which certifies that the actuarial value of each affected member's subsisting rights is equal to or greater than the value immediately before the amendment took effect (s.67C(6) of the 1995 Act). The actuarial equivalence statement must be given within a reasonable period from the amendment taking effect. This period will be set out in the Code of Practice on s.67 to be issued by the Regulator. A single actuarial equivalence statement may be given in respect of all affected members, certain affected members or groups of affected members.

7.3.59   In practice, trustees will want to obtain a draft actuarial equivalence statement before the amendment is made, and may want to append the draft to the deed of amendment.

What if the actuarial equivalence requirements cannot be used?

7.3.60   If it transpires that the proposed detrimental modification will not maintain the actuarial value, the trustees may choose to make the amendment using the consent requirements.

7.3.61   It is unlikely that the trustees would choose to give the notices to members in accordance with **para.7.3.51** above unless they were sure that the actuarial value requirements would be satisfied. However, if for whatever reason, the trustees felt that it might be necessary to make the amendment using the consent requirements at a later date, they should specify in the notices to members that, if the actuarial equivalence requirements do not apply, the consent requirements will apply. This will prevent trustees from having to give information about the modification again for the purposes of the consent requirements. The trustees will nevertheless have to write to members in order to ask for their consent.

Implications for trustees and employers

7.3.62   The new s.67 has the effect of permitting certain amendments to be made to the accrued rights and entitlements of members where the overall actuarial value of each member's benefits is maintained. It is generally considered that this is not permitted by the current s.67. However, the highly prescriptive nature of the procedural requirements could potentially have the effect of limiting the circumstances in which this is actually used. Employers should consider making any amendments which would be a protected modification (such as a switch to money purchase or to pensions in payment) before the new s.67 is effective.

7.3.63   The new s.67 will not affect scheme amendments relating to future service which is not covered by s.67. Whilst the new s.67 will provide the power to modify subsisting rights where the actuarial value of each member's benefits is at least maintained, it remains to be seen how many schemes will seek to do this in practice. This will be partly dependent on how willing actuaries will be to provide actuarial equivalence statements.

7.4   POWERS OF THE REGULATOR

7.4.1   The Regulator's wide ranging powers under the Act extend to matters relating to the new s.67 of the 1995 Act. Sections 67G and 67H enable the Regulator to declare void/prohibit modifications which fail to meet the requirements of s.67(2). Also, s.67I provides for the imposition of civil penalties under s.10 of the 1995 Act when purported modifications are made in breach of the requirements of s.67(2).

7.4.2   Perhaps the most notable point about the Regulator's powers is that he is able to take pre-emptive action i.e. to issue a prohibitive notice in advance of a purported modification being effected.

Regulator's power to declare modifications void

7.4.3   Section 67G of the 1995 Act provides that the Regulator may make an order declaring that a modification that has been made is void (to the extent the Regulator specifies and in respect of such persons as the Regulator specifies) where:

(a) the modification fails to meet the requirements of s.67(2) (i.e. because member consent is not obtained, the actuarial equivalence test is not satisfied, trustee approval is not obtained or the member reporting requirement is not required); or
(b) such modification contravenes an order made under s.67H (see below).

7.4.4   Such an order must specify the affected member or members or a description of affected members to which the order applies. The order may be made before or after the time the purported modification would have taken effect, but for it being void. In addition, the Regulator may declare void the grant of any rights under the scheme in connection with the modification in question. He may also require the trustees to take (within the time specified) such steps as may be specified for the purpose of giving effect to the order. He may also declare that anything done by the trustees after the time the purported modification would have taken effect were it not void, and which would under the scheme's trust deed and rules otherwise be valid, is not, for such purposes as may be specified, to be taken as having contravened the scheme's trust deed and rules.

Regulator's powers to issue directions to trustees

7.4.5   Section 67H of the 1995 Act enables the Regulator, where he has reasonable grounds to believe that a modification that fails to meet the requirements of s.67(2) either has been made or will be made, to make an order:

(a) directing the trustees (or other person who has power to make the modification) not to make the modification; and/or

(b) requiring the trustees to take such steps as may be specified (and within such time as may be specified) to secure that any of the requirements of s.67(2) are satisfied.

Imposition of civil penalties

7.4.6   Where a purported modification is made in breach of the requirements of s.67(2), civil penalties under s.10 of the 1995 Act may be imposed on any trustee where the modification was made either by the trustees of the scheme or (in certain circumstances, any other person) and such trustees failed to take all reasonable steps to secure that the modification met the requirements of s.67(2).

7.4.7   Civil penalties under s.10 of the 1995 Act may also be imposed on any trustee who fails to take all reasonable steps to secure compliance with an order made by the Regulator. Section 67I also enables civil penalties to be imposed on any other persons in limited circumstances.

7.5   STATUTORY, REGULATOR AND COURT POWERS TO MODIFY PENSION SCHEMES

7.5.1   Trustees have certain statutory powers to modify schemes. Modification can also be made by the Regulator or by the court. There must be compliance with Inland Revenue, contracting out and regulatory requirements. These provisions go beyond the scope of this book, but are outlined here as they are relevant to proper consideration of any proposed amendment.

Section 68 of the 1995 Act

7.5.2   Section 68 of the 1995 Act introduced powers enabling trustees in specific circumstances to modify schemes where no power exists to do so. The principal areas of overlap with the Act are:

(a) *Member nominated trustee arrangements.* Currently, under ss.16(1) and 17(1) of the 1995 Act the provisions of the scheme are overridden to enable it to comply with the member nominated trustee requirements (s.68(2)(b) of the 1995 Act). These provisions will be superseded in 2006 by the provisions of ss.241 and 242 of the Act.

(b) *Compliance with terms and conditions imposed by the Board of the PPF (s.68(2)(c) of the 1995 Act).* The power under s.68(2)(c) allows the trustees to modify the scheme to enable the scheme to comply with any terms and conditions that the Board of the PPF decides to impose in relation to any payments made by it under s.185 of the Act or interim payments made by it under s.186 of the Act (fraud compensation).

Powers of the Regulator to modify or authorise modification

7.5.3   Section 69 of the 1995 Act gives OPRA power to modify or authorise the modification of a pension scheme. These powers will under the Act vest in the Regulator. The ability of the Regulator to modify is limited to two specific purposes (the power of OPRA to modify a pension scheme to reduce/eliminate an excessive surplus under s.69(3)(a) is removed). In order to make a modification order, the Regulator must be satisfied either that the desired result cannot be achieved either without the order, or that the procedure for doing so would be unduly complex or protracted or would involve obtaining of consents which would be difficult to obtain (s.70 of the 1995 Act).

7.5.4   The Regulator's order may modify the scheme retrospectively or authorise others to modify the scheme retrospectively, and can be made or complied with even if the scheme's rules or other legal requirements would otherwise prevent it (s.71 of the 1995 Act).

7.5.5   The two specific purposes are as follows:

(a) *Section 69(3)(b) – to distribute excess assets on winding-up to an employer.* This power can be exercised to enable excess assets on winding up to be distributed to the employer but only on application from the trustees. Regulation 11 of the Occupational Pension Schemes (Payment to Employers) Regulations 1996, SI 1996/2156, specifies a number of additional requirements which must be met including compliance with s.76(3) and (4) of the 1995 Act, covering the notice and information to be provided to members. Perhaps the most significant requirement is that the trustees must be satisfied that the payment to the employer will be in the interests of the members (reg.11(b)). The circumstances in which trustees will reach this conclusion will be rare.

(b) *Section 69(3)(c) – to allow members' employment to be treated as contracted out.* The Regulator may exercise its power under s.69 to enable the scheme to be treated in such a way as to allow members' employments to be treated as contracted out on the application of the trustees, managers, employer or anyone else with power to alter the scheme's rules.

Powers of the court to modify

7.5.6   The court has an inherent jurisdiction to vary the trust. This power is usually only exercised where some matter concerning the scheme has already come before the court e.g. in settlement of litigation and where the terms are approved by the court on behalf of all interested parties. However, it might also be used in emergency situations where trustees are facing a difficulty which was unforeseen when the trust was set up, and the proposed course of action is seen as being in the best interests of the beneficiaries. The main guidance on the court's inherent jurisdiction is in *Chapman* v. *Chapman* [1954] AC 429.

7.5.7   The trustees may apply to the court under s.1(1) of the Variation of Trusts Act 1958 for the court to amend the trust if it thinks fit. Section 1(1) enables the court to approve amendments on behalf of beneficiaries. This power is not normally used in relation to pension schemes, since it requires the consents of all beneficiaries under the trusts who are living and *sui juris*.

7.5.8   The court can amend a trust, on application by the trustees or beneficiaries under s.57 of the Trustee Act 1925, to permit the trustees to take some action in relation to trust property which they do not have power to do under the scheme's provisions. The court will need to be convinced that the proposed transaction is expedient.

7.5.9   The court has jurisdiction to grant the equitable remedy of rectification. It can modify the terms of a written instrument so as to give effect to the real intention of the parties to it. This remedy is generally only available if there has been a clear and unambiguous mistake which is mutual or common to all parties to the instrument. The aim of the court will be to put the parties in the position they would have been in if the mistake had not been made i.e. to reflect what was in the minds of the parties at the time of execution of the document.

7.5.10   Applying to the court for rectification is a very rare course of action. It is expensive and the court, it seems, has traditionally been very reluctant to grant the requested remedy. However, since 'correcting' amendments are perhaps now harder to make using the scheme's power of amendment in view of s.67 and in the light of the purposive approach taken by the court in *AMP* v. *Barker* [2001] PLR 77, rectification is likely to be sought more frequently.

7.6   CONSULTATION BY EMPLOYERS

7.6.1   Prior to the Act, the Government stated in its December 2002 Green Paper that it was good practice for employers to consult their employees and/or employee representatives before making changes to pension arrangements. The Government also said that it did not seem unreasonable for employees to be given the opportunity to put their views forward before employers made such important decisions. Unfortunately, not all employers follow such good practice and this has led to the inclusion of provisions in the Act requiring employers to consult their employees or their representatives before making changes to the pension scheme.

7.6.2   See **Chapter 9** which deals with the proposed consultation requirements.

7.7   REGULATORY CONTROLS

Revenue approval

7.7.1   Inland Revenue approval of a scheme automatically ceases on amendment of the scheme unless the amendment is a type of amendment not requiring Inland Revenue approval (s.591B(2) of the Income and Corporation Taxes Act 1988).

7.7.2   In Pensions Update 29 the Inland Revenue announced that amendments which only introduce 1995 Act requirements need not be submitted for approval. Equally, arrangements to implement ss.16(1) or 17(2) dealing with member nominated trustees (but not member nominated directors) or modifications under s.68(2)(d) (see para.4.1(e) of the Practice Note) do not trigger the loss of continuing approval.

7.7.3   Note that the requirement for Inland Revenue approval is relevant even where the amendment is made under the trustees' statutory powers to modify their scheme (except under s.68(2)(d) of the 1995 Act) or by the court.

7.7.4   All amendments should be submitted to the Inland Revenue unless it is absolutely clear that they fall within the rare exemptions mentioned. If there is any doubt as to whether the Inland Revenue would approve the amendment, the Inland Revenue's opinion on the principle of the amendment should be sought in advance, or the amendment introduced but on a basis which is conditional on receipt of Inland Revenue approval.

Contracted-out schemes

7.7.5   Specific restrictions on amendments to contracted-out schemes or schemes which used to be contracted out and continue to provide benefits in respect of the contracted-out period are imposed by s.37 of the 1993 Act. Generally amendments which relate to contracted-out rights may not be made if the amendment would prevent the scheme continuing to satisfy the contracting-out requirements or adversely affect accrued contracted-out rights.

Disclosure

7.7.6   Information about amendments must usually be disclosed to members. Under reg.4 of the Occupational Pension Schemes (Disclosure of Information) Regulations 1996, SI 1996/1655, trustees must give members basic information about the scheme as specified in Sched.1 to those regulations. If an amendment will result in a 'material alteration' to some of that information the trustees must notify members of the change either before the change takes effect or at the latest within the following three months.

7.7.7   In addition, it is a condition of Inland Revenue approval of a scheme that any employee who is or has a right to be a member must be given 'written particulars of the scheme which concern him' (s.590(2)(b) of the Income and Corporation Taxes Act 1988). It is thought that this imposes a continuing duty on the 'administrator' to notify the same categories of people of any changes to those essential features.

8 ADMINISTRATIVE AND MISCELLANEOUS CHANGES

8.1 INDEXATION

Current position

8.1.1   The 1995 Act currently provides that pensions under approved occupational pension schemes, other than public sector schemes, which accrue on or after 6 April 1997 must generally be increased by the lesser of 5 per cent per annum and the annual increase in the Retail Prices Index (RPI), which is known as limited price indexation or LPI (see s.51 of the 1995 Act).

8.1.2   AVCs are excluded from the above requirements, as is a pension in payment to a member who is below the age of 55, unless the member has retired on the grounds of ill-health.

8.1.3   In relation to certain personal pension schemes, the 1995 Act currently requires the protected rights element of a personal pension (derived from contributions made after 6 April 1997) to be increased in line with LPI. There is no statutory requirement to index non-protected rights in respect of a personal pension.

Changes in the Act

8.1.4   Section 278 of the Act amends s.51 of the 1995 Act (annual increase in rate of certain occupational pensions) and s.279 amends s.162 of the 1995 Act (annual increase in rate of certain personal pensions).

8.1.5   In relation to defined benefit occupational schemes, the Act splits pensionable service into two parts. Pensionable service accrued up to the commencement day (the day when s.278 comes into effect, which is expected to be 6 April 2005) must be increased by at least the lesser of the annual increase in the RPI or 5 per cent. This period of pensionable service is referred to as 'Category X pension'. Pensionable service accrued on and from the commencement day must be increased by at least the lesser of the annual increase in the RPI or 2.5 per cent. This period of pensionable service is referred to as 'Category Y pension'.

8.1.6   Where part of a pension referred to above is attributable to pensionable service before the commencement day and part is attributable to pensionable service after the commencement day, each part is to be treated as if it were a separate pension (s.51(4C) of the 1995 Act).

8.1.7   The Act removes the requirement to provide statutory increases in respect of money purchase benefits under occupational schemes which come into payment on or after the commencement day (expected to be 6 April 2005). Where a pension derived from money purchase benefits is in payment before 6 April 2005, it must be increased by the lesser of the annual increase in the RPI and 5 per cent.

8.1.8   In relation to personal pensions, s.279 of the Act requires an annual increase to be applied to the protected rights element of any personal pension in payment before 6 April 2005. The whole or part of any such pension must be attributable to contributions in respect of employment carried out on or after 6 April 1997. The rate of such increase must be at least the lesser of the annual increase in the RPI and 5 per cent.

Pension sharing

8.1.9   Section 40 of the 1999 Act (power of the Secretary of State to increase pensions provided to give effect to certain rights) enables the Secretary of State to protect an occupational pension in payment that is derived from a pension share against inflation. Section 40 allows similar inflation protection in relation to a personal pension in payment which is derived from safeguarded rights.

8.1.10   Section 280 of the Act amends s.40 of the 1999 Act. In particular, s.280 provides for a pension derived from a pensions sharing order made before the commencement day (expected to be 6 April 2005) to be increased by at least the lesser of the annual increase in the RPI or 5 per cent. However, a pension derived from a pension sharing order where entitlement arises on or after the commencement day is to be increased by at least the lesser of the annual increase in the RPI or 2.5 per cent.

8.2   DEFERRING STATE PENSIONS

Current position

8.2.1   State pension is currently payable from age 60 (women) and 65 (men) provided that the person concerned makes a claim. With effect from 2010, state pensions will be payable to women born after 5 April 1955 from age 65, when state pension ages are equalised. Women born between 5 April 1950 and 5 April 1955 will attain state pension age in accordance with a sliding scale of ages set out in Sched.4 to the 1995 Act.

8.2.2   No pension will be paid in respect of any period between state pension age and the date when the person claims the pension, but the pensioner will instead be eligible to receive an increase to the weekly pension. Alternatively, a person may become eligible for a pension increase where he cancels his entitlement to state pension.

8.2.3   The amount of the increase (or 'increment') is, broadly, one-seventh of 1 per cent of the person's weekly pension for each week the pension is deferred. Increments of less than 1 per cent are not awarded. Increments may relate to both category A and category B pensions, shared additional pension and Guaranteed Minimum Pension (GMP). (Category A pension is payable to a person by virtue of their own National Insurance contributions, and Category B pension is payable to a person by virtue of someone else's National Insurance contributions.) Increments may currently be earned for up to five years.

8.2.4   With effect from April 2010, the weekly rate of the increment was set to rise to one-fifth of 1 per cent (amounting to an annual rate of 10.4 per cent) and the five-year limit on deferring state pension was to be removed. These changes were contained in the 1995 Act.

Changes in the Act

8.2.5   Section 297 of, and Sched.11 to, the Act relate to the deferral of state pensions. They amend the Social Security Contributions and Benefits Act 1992 (the 1992 Act).

8.2.6   The new provisions make various changes. They bring forward the increase in the incremental rate contained in the 1995 Act from April 2010 to April 2005. Similarly, they remove the five-year limit on deferring state pension with effect from April 2005. Finally, they enable people to defer state pension in return for a taxable lump sum, in certain circumstances, instead of receiving the weekly increments outlined above.

Section 297: deferral of retirement pensions and shared additional pensions

8.2.7   Section 297(1) of the Act replaces s.55 of the 1992 Act and Sched.11 amends Sched.5 to that Act. The new s.55 and Sched.5 provide that an increment or lump sum may be payable where a person's entitlement to their Category A or Category B pension is deemed to be deferred. Such entitlements will be deemed to be deferred where:

(a) the person concerned has not claimed the pension but, that apart, would be entitled to the pension; or
(b) the entitlement to a Category B pension is derived from the spouse's contributions, if the spouse has not claimed a pension; or
(c) the person has cancelled his entitlement under s.54 of the 1992 Act.

8.2.8   Increments or a lump sum may also be payable where entitlement to a shared additional pension is deferred.

8.2.9   Each person may defer his own Category A pension. In the case of a married person, this applies irrespective of what the person's spouse elects in respect of his own Category A pension. Where a person dies whilst deferring state pension, the surviving spouse will be able to elect to inherit either a lump sum or increments based on the spouse's deferred entitlement. The inheritable proportion will depend upon the pension component to which the increments relate.

Schedule 11: deferral of entitlement to retirement pension

8.2.10   A person who defers his Category A or B pension for at least 12 months must choose to receive either increments or a lump sum (Sched.11, para.4). The lump sum option will not be available where benefits are deferred for less than 12 months. Regulations will set out how the choice must be made and any time limits. If the person does not choose within the time allowed, he will be deemed to have chosen the lump sum.

8.2.11   Regulations may permit a person to reverse an election or a deemed election. However, it is expected that the circumstances will be limited, and that once an election is made, it should normally be regarded as binding.

8.2.12   Where a person's deferred pension includes increments inherited from a deceased spouse relating to a deferred GMP, only increments will be payable for that element. The lump sum option will not be available. This limitation is necessary because pension schemes will not be required to change their rules to permit the payment of a lump sum instead of increments in respect of deferred GMPs.

8.2.13   As at present, no increment of less than 1 per cent will be payable (para.1(2) of Sched.5). The effect of this paragraph combined with the new incremental rate of one-fifth of 1 per cent per week is that the minimum period of deferral on which increments can be earned is five weeks.

8.2.14   Where a person has elected to receive a lump sum or is treated as having made such an election (having deferred entitlement for more than 12 months), new para.3B of Sched.5 provides for calculation of the lump sum in accordance with a complex formula.

8.2.15   Broadly, a rate of return which is 2 per cent higher than the Bank of England base rate will be applied to the weekly amount that the person would have received had payment not been deferred. A higher rate may be prescribed by affirmative regulations (para.19). A change in the Bank of England base rate will automatically lead to a corresponding change in the rate of return on the lump sum so as to retain the 2 per cent difference. There is, however, a regulation-making power to enable the old rate to continue if it is not practical to introduce the new rate quickly enough. This would allow the old rate to remain lawful until the new rate could take effect.

8.2.16   The new provisions insert a definition of 'Bank of England base rate' into the 1992 Act for this purpose (Sched.11, para.18).

8.2.17   Increments payable to a deceased spouse arising from the spouse having deferred his GMP cannot be inherited as a lump sum. They will be paid to the surviving spouse as an increase to pension.

8.2.18   Regulations may be made so that the lump sum may be adjusted to take account of circumstances which would have led to the claimant's pension being reduced. Examples given in the Explanatory Notes are where another benefit which overlaps with the retirement pension had been in payment, or where the person had been in prison.

8.2.19   A surviving spouse of a person who has deferred his pension for a minimum of 12 months may choose to inherit either increments or a lump sum in respect of that deferment. The choice can only be made when the widow or widower is claiming his or her own pension. If the deferrer dies while the surviving spouse is still under state pension age, the amount of increase or lump sum which would have been awarded had the surviving spouse been entitled to his pension at the time when the deferring pensioner died will be increased in line with prices for the period between the date of death of the deceased and the date on which the survivor claims his pension.

8.2.20   The surviving spouse is deemed to have chosen the lump sum if the surviving spouse does not make an election within a time limit to be prescribed. The surviving spouse may be allowed to change the election in prescribed circumstances.

8.2.21   Where the deceased person would have been entitled to increments on deferred GMPs, surviving spouses can only inherit an increase to their weekly pension in respect of that element irrespective of whatever choice the surviving spouse made in relation to the rest of the deceased's deferred entitlement.

Schedule 11: deferral of entitlement to shared additional pension

8.2.22   Since December 2000, it has been possible to share the additional component of the state pension as part of a divorce settlement. The weekly pension payable as a result of a cash equivalent transfer of all or part of an ex-spouse's additional state pension is called the 'shared additional pension'.

8.2.23   Paragraph 15 of Sched.11 to the Act introduces a new Sched.5A to the 1992 Act. The new provisions give persons who have deferred their entitlement to shared additional pension for at least 12 months a choice between a lump sum or pension increase, along similar lines to those applying on deferment of retirement pension.

8.2.24   The provisions in Sched.5A are broadly equivalent to the corresponding paragraphs of the amended Sched.5, setting out when and how a person becomes entitled to a lump sum or increments and how the lump sum or increments are to be calculated.

8.2.25   However, there is a key difference between the provisions applying to a lump sum payable in respect of deferred pension entitlement under Sched.5 to the 1992 Act and a lump sum payable in respect of shared additional pension. As is currently the case in relation to shared additional pension increments, if the person entitled to the shared additional pension dies after remarrying and leaves a widow (or widower), the surviving widow/widower will not be entitled to inherit the lump sum.

8.2.26   The new provisions extend the definition of 'deferred' and 'period of deferment' in the 1992 Act to cover deferment of shared additional pension (Sched.11, para.18).

Transitional provision

8.2.27   Schedule 11, para.27 enables the Secretary of State to make regulations setting out such transitional provision as he thinks fit.

8.2.28   In particular, regulations may modify the provisions outlined above where the deferment of a retirement pension or shared additional pension starts before 6 April 2005 and continues after that date. According to the Explanatory Notes, regulations made under this power will provide that any period of deferment which precedes 6 April 2005 will be subject to the pre-6 April 2005 rules. For any such period, only increments at the then current rate may be paid. However, for the period beginning on 6 April 2005, the new provisions will apply. If the deferment period starting on 6 April 2005 lasts for at least 12 months, the deferrer will have the choice of a lump sum or increments at the new rate. Equivalent provisions will be made in respect of surviving spouses entitled to inherited increments or a lump sum.

8.3   ENTITLEMENT TO MORE THAN ONE CATEGORY B PENSION

8.3.1   At present, where a person is entitled to more than one retirement pension, s.43 of the 1992 Act enables that person to choose which of those pensions he wishes to receive and notify the Secretary of State accordingly, but only where the retirement pensions are of a different category (e.g. Category A and Category B). In the absence of such a notification, the person will receive whichever retirement pension is the most favourable to him from time to time.

8.3.2   However, no such choice is available where a person is entitled to more than one retirement pension in the same category (e.g. where a widow who is entitled to receive a Category B pension remarries and becomes entitled to receive another Category B pension). Note that a Category B pension is payable to someone by virtue of somebody else's National Insurance Contributions.

8.3.3   Section 296 of the Act amends s.43(3) of the 1992 Act by allowing such a person to choose which of the two Category B pensions they wish to receive.

Where no choice is made, the person will be entitled to whichever pension is most favourable to that person.

8.3.4   This change came into force on 18 November 2004 (the date on which the Act was passed) in accordance with s.322 of the Act.

8.4   VESTING

Current position

8.4.1   Part IV of the 1993 Act currently gives employees who leave an occupational pension scheme within two years of commencement of service a statutory entitlement to a refund of their contributions only. Such employees do not acquire the right to preserved pension benefits in the scheme, nor are they permitted to transfer their benefits to an alternative pension arrangement.

8.4.2   However, it has for some time been acknowledged that this situation is out of step with the employment pattern for many UK workers, who may change jobs several times during their working lives. This results in employees losing the ability to build up valuable pension benefits where their pensionable service in a particular job amounts to less than two years. The Act makes various changes to redress the balance in favour of such shorter-serving employees.

Changes in the Act

8.4.3   Section 264 of the Act relates to early leavers, and introduces a fifth chapter into Part IV of the 1993 Act which contains new ss.101AA to 101AI (early leavers: cash transfer sums and contribution refunds).

8.4.4   The Act allows an early leaver whose rights have not yet vested in a scheme to opt for a cash transfer out of the scheme after a minimum of three months' service (referred to in s.264 as the 'three month condition'). This therefore enables an early leaver to benefit from the employer contributions made in respect of him and tax relief after only three months of service. The member may still opt to take a refund of his own contributions instead if he wishes.

8.4.5   However, the Act does not give such a member a right to a preserved pension in the scheme. It remains the case that a scheme is only required to provide vested pension rights on completion of two years' pensionable service.

8.4.6   The new provisions will apply to any member of an occupational pension scheme whose pensionable service ends at least one year before normal pension age. Furthermore, the requirement for three months' service will include current and previous pensionable service under the scheme, together with any period of linked qualifying service (i.e. pensionable service in a previous scheme which gave rise to a transfer credit in the scheme).

8.4.7   It is expected that these provisions will come into force on 6 April 2006.

Duties of trustees

8.4.8   Pursuant to new s.101AC of the 1993 Act, on cessation of a member's pensionable service, the trustees of the scheme must, within a reasonable period, give the member a written statement. The statement must set out the amount of the cash transfer sum or contribution refund to which the member is entitled, together with details of the permitted ways in which he may use the cash transfer sum, and such other information as may be prescribed. In addition, the statement must specify the latest date by which the member should notify the trustees of his decision ('the reply date').

8.4.9   The member must notify the trustees in writing of his choice of cash transfer sum or contribution refund. If he opts for the cash transfer sum, he must specify in which of the permitted ways, outlined in the statement, he wishes to use the transfer sum. The member must reply by the reply date, otherwise the trustees may discharge their liability to the member by paying a refund of employee contributions only, provided that they notified the member of that fact in the written statement (new s.101AH of the 1993 Act).

8.4.10   If the member fails to respond by the reply date, he may apply to the trustees for permission to respond by such later date as the trustees may determine (new s.101AI(2) of the 1993 Act).

8.4.11   Where the member opts for the cash transfer sum, the amount of the transfer sum will be the cash equivalent of the benefits which would have accrued to, or in respect of, him under the applicable rules had the two-year vesting rule not applied (new s.101AB(3) of the 1993 Act).

8.4.12   A cash transfer sum may be used to acquire rights under another occupational scheme or a personal pension scheme, providing the relevant scheme is willing and able to accept the transfer and providing the scheme meets prescribed requirements. It may also be used to purchase one or more appropriate annuities from an insurer chosen by the member or for subscribing to such other pension arrangements as may be prescribed.

8.4.13   If the member decides to take a contribution refund, the refund will represent the member's employee contributions to the scheme and, where rights were transferred into the scheme, any employee contributions to the former scheme which relate to the transfer payment. 'Employee contributions' is defined in new s.101AB(5) of the 1993 Act as contributions made to the scheme by or on behalf of the member on his own account, but the definition excludes any transfer payment and any pension credit or amount paid to the scheme which is attributable (directly or indirectly) to a pension credit.

8.4.14   Trustees may be able to deduct administrative costs from cash transfer sums, if regulations so permit. It may also be possible for cash transfer sums and contribution refunds to be increased or reduced in prescribed circumstances. This would, for example, enable a cash transfer sum or contribution refund to be reduced (to nil, if necessary) where a scheme has a funding deficit.

8.4.15   When the trustees receive the written reply from the member within the time limit, they must take whatever steps are needed to comply with the member's request within a reasonable period. The trustees will then be discharged from any obligation in respect of any rights (other than pension credit rights) the member may have in the scheme (see new s.101AG of the 1993 Act). Similar provisions apply where the trustees pay a contribution refund to a member because he failed to respond.

8.4.16   A member will lose any right acquired under these provisions to a cash transfer sum or contribution refund in the event that the scheme is wound up (new s.101AI(1) of the 1993 Act).

Implications for trustees and employers

8.4.17   Under the new provisions, trustees will have to offer all members who have more than three months' pensionable service the choice of either a cash transfer value or a refund of contributions. This will inevitably lead to an element of increased costs for schemes where the cash transfer option is exercised. Employers may wish to seek actuarial advice on the extent of any such increase in costs to the scheme.

8.4.18   Given that the Act does not go so far as to grant a preserved pension entitlement to members with less than two years' pensionable service, the costs of administering early leaver benefits should not increase significantly. However, there will be an additional administrative burden in terms of informing members of their options on leaving the scheme and calculating and paying out a transfer value where relevant. It remains to be seen whether trustees will be permitted to deduct such administrative costs from the member's cash transfer sum.

8.4.19   Should trustees or managers fail to take all reasonable steps to comply with their duties under s.264 of the Act, s.10 of the 1995 Act (civil penalties) will apply.

8.5   SURPLUS REPAYMENTS

Current position

8.5.1   Schemes are currently required to take appropriate steps to reduce surpluses that are deemed to be excessive by the Inland Revenue (known as 'statutory' surpluses). One of the ways in which a scheme may reduce such a surplus is by making a payment to the scheme employer, the amount of such payment currently being taxable at 35 per cent. Section 37 of the 1995 Act sets out the conditions which must be satisfied before any such payment can be made.

8.5.2   However, as part of a general change in legislative direction relating to the funding of occupational pension schemes, ss.250 and 251 of the Act provide new rules governing payments to an employer from surplus in an ongoing occupational pension scheme.

8.5.3   It is anticipated that these new provisions will come into force on 6 April 2006.

Payment of surplus to an employer

8.5.4   Section 250 adds a new s.37 to the 1995 Act. The new s.37 will broadly reflect the tax simplification measures contained in the Finance Act 2004 and, in particular, will remove the requirement for schemes to dispose of excessive surplus.

8.5.5   Whereas under the current regime, surpluses are measured on a basis prescribed by the Inland Revenue, surpluses under the revised s.37 will be measured by reference to the ability of the scheme to meet all of its accrued liabilities by way of purchasing immediate and deferred annuities for all of its pensioner and non-pensioner liabilities. Given the current economic climate, the legislators have, in effect, made it more difficult for there to be a surplus repayment in an ongoing scheme.

8.5.6   The new s.37 will continue (as at present) to require that payments can only be made from an ongoing scheme if the scheme rules permit the payment of surplus to an employer, and that any power under the rules for the payment of surplus to the employer must be exercised by the trustees.

8.5.7   New s.37(3) provides that payments to an employer cannot be made unless:

(a) the trustees have obtained a written valuation of the scheme's assets and liabilities and there is in force a certificate from a 'prescribed person' of the assets and liabilities of the scheme, calculated and verified in accordance with prescribed requirements and stating the maximum amount of the payment that may be made;
(b) the payment does not exceed the maximum amount given on the certificate;
(c) the trustees are satisfied that it is in the interests of the members for the payment to be made;
(d) where appropriate, the employer has requested, or consented to, the payment;
(e) the Regulator has not issued a freezing order against the scheme; and
(f) the scheme members have been notified in accordance with prescribed requirements.

8.5.8   Regulations may provide for, amongst other things, how the scheme's assets and liabilities are to be valued; which assets and liabilities should be taken into account for valuation purposes; and the circumstances surrounding the prescribed manner in which the valuation is to be carried out by the prescribed person. In addition, it is expected that regulations will require the trustees to inform both the Inland Revenue and the Regulator when a payment is to be made.

8.5.9 The Regulator may impose sanctions under s.10 of the 1995 Act where trustees purport to exercise a power to pay surplus to the employer without complying with the requirements of s.37, or where they fail to comply with requirements set out in regulations, if the trustees fail to take all reasonable steps to secure compliance.

8.5.10 According to the Explanatory Notes, the intention is for regulations to require defined benefit schemes to have assets which are more than sufficient to allow the liabilities of the scheme to be secured by way of immediate and deferred annuities. The amount of any payment to the employer must be less than the excess of the value of the assets over the value of the liabilities on this basis on the date at which the prescribed person provides his certificate. As previously noted, this is likely to be more restrictive than the current Inland Revenue requirements, thereby reducing the number of schemes to which a surplus repayment may become relevant in the future.

8.5.11 The current s.37 requires that all scheme members are provided with LPI increases to pensions once they come into payment, before any surplus repayment can be made. However, the new s.37 will not reproduce that requirement. Instead, the valuation of the scheme's assets and liabilities by the prescribed person will reflect the increases provided by the scheme either under its own rules or by virtue of the relevant legislation.

Transitional power to amend scheme

8.5.12 Section 251 of the Act introduces a transitional power for trustees to amend scheme rules to take account of the new provisions described above.

8.5.13 Before s.37 of the 1995 Act was introduced, some schemes had rules which allowed payments to the employer other than in order to comply with Inland Revenue requirements. Section 37 constrained such powers, leaving them unusable except in the circumstances envisaged by s.37. However, s.251 of the Act proposes that trustees may choose to revive their original powers, limit them, or leave them unrevived.

8.5.14 For those schemes which, apart from the statutory surplus compliance requirements, were not permitted to make payments of surplus to the employer, trustees will now be allowed to choose whether and, if so, how they wish to have power to make such payments to the employer.

8.5.15 In either case, trustees must be satisfied that such a rule change is in the interests of the scheme members. In addition, trustees may only make one such decision and must make it within five years of the commencement of s.251. Written notice must be given to the employer and the scheme members if the trustees intend to change the scheme rules with regard to payments to an employer. Naturally, any new rules introduced under s.251 will become subject to the overriding provisions of the new s.37 of the 1995 Act.

Implications for trustees/employers

8.5.16   Trustees may wish to consider whether, and if so, how, they intend to exercise the transitional power given to them by s.251 to amend the scheme rules, bearing in mind that the power ceases to be exercisable five years after commencement of s.251.

8.5.17   The new s.37 of the 1995 Act continues the trend in recent years towards reducing the scope for an employer to recover assets from a scheme whilst the scheme is ongoing. The raising of the threshold at which a scheme is categorised as being in surplus for the purposes of a surplus repayment further reflects the legislators' desire to focus on the winding-up liabilities of the scheme, even though the scheme in question may not be in any imminent danger of being wound up.

8.6   REVALUATION

Current position

8.6.1   Revaluation is a measure introduced to protect the preserved benefits of members of occupational pension schemes from the impact of inflation in respect of the period from leaving pensionable service up to normal retirement date.

8.6.2   The current provisions are found in Chapters II and III of Part IV of the 1993 Act. In essence, two separate systems of revaluation apply.

8.6.3   GMPs (accrued prior to 6 April 1997) are subject to revaluation under Chapter III of Part IV. GMPs are currently revalued either by means of revaluation of the earnings factor used to calculate the GMP (by reference to orders made under s.148 of the Social Security Administration Act 1992), or by means of fixed-rate revaluation (a fixed percentage depending on the date of termination of contracted out employment). A third method, limited rate revaluation is available, but only in respect of members for whom limited revaluation premiums were being paid prior to 6 April 1997. This provides for increases at the rate of the lesser of 5 per cent and the s.148 rate.

8.6.4   Non-GMP benefits are subject to revaluation under Chapter II of Part IV, and Sched.3 to the 1993 Act. The revaluation requirements apply where benefits are payable to or in respect of an occupational pension scheme member, and:

(a) the member's pensionable service terminates on or after 1 January 1986;
(b) the member has accrued rights to benefits under the scheme;
(c) there is at least a year between date of leaving to normal pension age; and
(d) in the case of benefit payable to any other person in respect of the member (e.g. spouse or dependant), the member dies after normal pension age.

8.6.5   Revaluation applies to the total period of pensionable service where the member left service on or after 1 January 1991, but it only applies to benefits accrued from 1 January 1985 where the member left pensionable service before 1 January 1991.

8.6.6   There are four different revaluation methods to be applied, as appropriate, to the underlying benefit structure of the scheme: the average salary method; the flat rate method; the money purchase method; and the final salary method.

8.6.7   Under the final salary method, the non-GMP preserved benefit is increased in line with the 'revaluation percentage' specified in the last calendar year before the date on which the member attains normal pension age as being the appropriate percentage for the period between termination of pensionable service and normal pension age. The revaluation percentage is to be specified by the Secretary of State in each calendar year, being the lesser of the increase in the general level of prices in the UK during the reference period (the 12-month period from 1 October in the preceding calendar year) or 5 per cent.

8.6.8   For the purposes of preservation, short service benefit must be payable from the scheme's 'normal pension age' or, where that age is earlier than age 60, from age 60. 'Normal pension age' is defined in s.180 of the 1993 Act as being the earliest age at which the member is entitled to receive benefits (other than GMP) on his retirement from such employment. The former Occupational Pensions Board's guidance (in memorandum 78) is generally still followed in interpreting this definition: i.e. that it is the earliest date on which the member has an un-qualified right to retire on an unreduced pension (other than on special grounds such as ill-health or redundancy).

8.6.9   The revaluation requirements override scheme rules in the event of any inconsistency.

Changes in the Act

8.6.10   Section 281 of the Act amends s.84 of the 1993 Act and allows schemes to revalue all benefits (excluding GMPs) by reference to the retail prices index (RPI). RPI is defined as the general index of retail prices (for all items) published by the Office for National Statistics. Where the index is not published for a month, any substitute index or figures published by that Office should be used.

8.6.11   This change came into force on 18 November 2004 (the day the Act was passed) as provided by s.322 of the Act.

Implications for trustees/employers

8.6.12   The amendment to s.84 of the 1993 Act enables schemes to revalue the pension or other benefit by reference to the RPI. This change effectively restores the situation to that which existed before a similar provision was repealed by the 1995 Act.

8.6.13 Trustees and employers should bear in mind that, whilst the option may confer administrative benefits in removing a layer of complexity, this should be weighed against any increase in the cost of funding increases on a full RPI basis.

8.6.14 Scheme rules will require amendment in order to take advantage of this option.

8.7   MEMBER-NOMINATED TRUSTEE PROVISIONS

8.7.1 The existing requirements in relation to member-nominated trustees (MNTs) and directors contained in ss.16–21 of the 1995 Act will be repealed in their entirety by the Act (as will ss.43–46 of the Child Support, Pensions and Social Security Act 2000, which were never actually brought into force). In their place will be new MNT provisions contained in ss.241–243 of the Act.

Applicability

8.7.2 The new MNT provisions will apply to all occupational pension schemes set up under trust, except:

(a) those schemes where every member of the scheme is a trustee of the scheme and no other person is such a trustee;
(b) those schemes where every trustee of the scheme is a company; or
(c) those schemes where regulations are in force excluding them from compliance with the MNT regime.

The new MNT requirements

8.7.3 An employer will no longer be able to put in place alternative trustee arrangements. All occupational pension schemes established under trust will be required to have member-nominated trustees who have been selected and appointed in accordance with the new provisions.

8.7.4 The DWP has issued a press release stating, inter alia, that discussions with industry, employers and schemes will take place about how best the changes can be implemented, especially for those small and medium sized schemes that may not have member-nominated trustee representation at present.

8.7.5 Under the Act, the Trustees are required to ensure that arrangements are in place which provide for at least one third of the total number of trustees to be member nominated. The DWP has stated that the one-third requirement will apply at the outset, but that the relevant fraction will rise to one half at some stage in the future. The Secretary of State is given power to implement this increase by s.243 of the Act.

8.7.6   The arrangements to be put in place may provide for a greater number of member-nominated trustees than one third/one half, but only if the employer so agrees.

8.7.7   There will no longer be a requirement that each scheme has at least two member-nominated trustees, or in the case of a scheme with less than 100 members, one member-nominated trustee.

8.7.8   A person wishing to be appointed as a member-nominated trustee need not be a member of the relevant scheme, but, in such circumstances, the employer must approve such person's nomination for selection.

8.7.9   To be elected, a member-nominated trustee must firstly be nominated by means of a process in which at least all of the active members of the scheme (or an organisation representing them) and all of the pensioner members of the scheme (or an organisation representing them) are eligible to participate. He must then be selected to act as a member-nominated trustee by some or all of the members of the scheme.

8.7.10   At the moment, it is possible to have in place arrangements whereby the employer has the final say in which members are elected as member-nominated trustees. This will no longer be possible under the new MNT provisions contained in the Act.

8.7.11   The removal of a member-nominated trustee will require the agreement of all of the other trustees. Furthermore, a member-nominated trustee will have an equal standing with those trustees who are not member-nominated, and may not be excluded from the exercise of any trustee functions by virtue only of the fact that he is a member-nominated trustee.

Implementing the MNT arrangements

8.7.12   The provisions currently in place relating to the procedures for appointing MNTs are set out in the Occupational Pension Schemes (Member-nominated Trustees and Directors) Regulations 1996, SI 1996/1216. These Regulations will be superseded by a Code of Practice, which will set out 'best practice' for implementing the new requirements to appoint MNTs. It is expected that the Code of Practice will simplify the provisions currently in place.

8.7.13   The Act provides that it is the trustees' responsibility to ensure that appropriate MNT arrangements are in place. The trustees of a scheme must implement appropriate arrangements within a 'reasonable' period of the new MNT provisions coming into force, and subsequently whenever any requirement arises under the arrangements to appoint an MNT. What would constitute a reasonable period has not been specified in the Act. However, it is likely that further guidance will be contained in a relevant Code of Practice issued by the Regulator. It is expected that existing MNT opt-outs will be allowed to run their course on the basis that, in many cases, this would allow a 'reasonable' period of time to pass.

8.7.14   Where a vacancy is not filled due to insufficient nominations, the new provisions provide that the nomination and selection process should be repeated at reasonable intervals until the vacancy is filled.

8.7.15   The new arrangements to be implemented by the trustees may provide that where the number of nominations received is equal to or less than the number of appointments required, all nominees shall be deemed to have been selected.

Member-nominated directors

8.7.16   If all of the trustees of a pension scheme to which the MNT provisions apply are companies, similar provisions to those in respect of member-nominated trustees will apply to each company in respect of its board of directors. There will be a requirement for at least one third (eventually rising to one half) of the directors of each trustee company to be member-nominated directors.

8.7.17   Under the 1995 Act, an independent trustee company is exempt from complying with the member-nominated director requirements in relation to the schemes for which it acts as independent trustee, as it is not associated with the employer of each scheme. However, under the new provisions, a corporate independent trustee should ensure, in relation to each scheme for which it acts as independent trustee, either that at least one trustee is an individual, or that, alternatively, it is appointed as a director to the board of a corporate trustee (i.e. does not act as a corporate trustee in its own right). Otherwise, it is likely that the new member-nominated director provisions would apply to the corporate independent trustee. The latter alternative (being appointed to the board of a corporate trustee) is less desirable than the former alternative, because the corporate independent trustee would then be liable to comply with directors' duties and responsibilities in respect of the corporate trustee.

8.7.18   Where a company is a trustee of more than one occupational pension scheme set up under trust, each of the schemes of which it is a trustee is to be treated as a single scheme for the purpose of the member-nominated director provisions. The trustee company may elect that this provision does not apply, or that it only applies in relation to certain schemes.

Implementation

8.7.19   The DWP has stated that the MNT provisions are likely to come into force in April 2006, and that the proportion of member-nominated trustees/directors is likely to be increased subsequently to one half by amending regulations some years after that, possibly in 2008.

Implications for trustees/employers

8.7.20   The trustees of a scheme will be responsible for ensuring compliance with the new MNT provisions. Failure to comply with the new MNT provisions will render the trustees of a relevant scheme liable to a fine under s.10 of the 1995 Act.

8.7.21   Trustees should consider now whether their schemes will comply with the new MNT provisions. If the arrangements currently in place do not comply, they may need to be modified or, upon the legislation coming into effect, completely replaced.

8.7.22   The requirement that at least one third, and eventually 50 per cent of the trustees are member-nominated trustees means that trustees should be communicating information to members as soon as possible about the role and responsibilities of trustees, and encouraging members to consider standing for nomination as a member-nominated trustees. Otherwise, it is anticipated that some schemes will not be able to fill all vacancies. If the trustees of a scheme are unable to fill a member-nominated trustee vacancy they will be required, at regular intervals, to repeat the election process. This may prove time-consuming and costly.

8.7.23   Once the new provisions are effective, a corporate independent trustee should ensure, in relation to each scheme for which it acts as independent trustee, either that at least one trustee is an individual, or that it is appointed as a director to the board of a corporate trustee (and does not act as a corporate trustee in its own right). Otherwise, it is likely that the new member-nominated director provisions would apply to the corporate independent trustee.

8.8   CONTRACTING OUT

Meaning of 'working life' in the 1993 Act

8.8.1   Section 282 changes the meaning of 'working life' in s.181 of the 1993 Act for the purposes of calculating GMPs. At present, 'working life' is defined for these purposes as having the same meaning as set out in para.5(8) of Sched.3 to the 1992 Act. Paragraph 5(8) defines 'working life' as the period beginning with (and including) the tax year in which a person reaches age 16 and ending with (and excluding) the tax year in which that person either attains pensionable age or dies, whichever is sooner.

8.8.2   Commencing in 2010, the 'pensionable age' referred to in that para.5(8) will rise for women from age 60 to 65 on a sliding scale set out in Sched.4 to the 1995 Act. However, 'pensionable age' for the purposes of GMPs will not be changed. The effect of s.282 of the Act is therefore to provide that 'working life' for the purposes of calculating GMP will end with the tax year before a man reaches age 65 or a woman reaches age 60, or the tax year before the person dies, whichever is sooner.

8.8.3   This change is expected to come into force on 6 April 2005.

Power to prescribe conditions by reference to Inland Revenue approval

8.8.4   Section 283 of the Act adds a new s.9(5A) to the 1993 Act. It enables regulations to be made in relation to contracted-out occupational or personal pension schemes, which may prescribe conditions by reference to the Inland Revenue's tax approval requirements for pension schemes.

Restriction on commutation and age at which benefits may be received

8.8.5   Section 284(1) of the Act amends s.21(1) of the 1993 Act (commutation of GMPs) so that where a scheme has to comply with s.13 (minimum pensions for earners) and s.17 (minimum pensions for widows or widowers), the scheme may provide for the payment of a lump sum instead of a pension, to the extent that regulations may allow.

8.8.6   Section 284(2) amends s.17 of the 1993 Act (minimum pensions for widows or widowers) so that where a person has received a lump sum instead of a GMP where regulations so permit, the person will be treated as not having received the lump sum for the purposes of calculating the minimum pension payable to the widow or widower.

8.8.7   Certain restrictions on protected rights built up in contracted-out money purchase schemes and appropriate personal pension schemes are removed, by means of s.284(3) to (7) which amends ss.28 and 29 of the 1993 Act. In particular, the changes enable protected rights to be paid as a lump sum subject to restrictions to be set out in regulations. The changes also remove the age-related restrictions on when a member's protected rights can come into effect, although in occupational schemes they will continue to have to be paid by age 65, unless the member agrees to a later date.

8.9   STAKEHOLDER PENSIONS

8.9.1   The definition of 'stakeholder pension scheme' in s.1 of the 1999 Act is amended in relation to the use of stakeholder funds to pay administrative expenses (s.285 of the Act). The amendment adds a reference to contributions paid 'by or on behalf or in respect of' a member, in order to cover contributions paid by an employer to the designated scheme of one of his employees or to cover contributions paid by another third party.

8.9.2   A new s.1(10) is also added to the 1999 Act to clarify that stakeholder pension schemes must be contracted-out, in order to be able to accept transfer payments which may included contracted-out rights.

8.10   ADDITIONAL VOLUNTARY CONTRIBUTIONS

8.10.1   The Act removes the 'voluntary contribution requirements' contained in the 1993 Act which currently require schemes to allow members to make AVCs. Section 111 of the 1993 Act is repealed by the Act (s.320 and Sched.13) with effect from a day to be appointed.

9 EMPLOYMENT-RELATED ASPECTS

9.1 FINANCIAL PLANNING

Introduction

9.1.1 The Act introduces new powers and obligations in respect of the Secretary of State, trustees/managers of occupational or personal pension schemes and employers regarding financial planning for retirement.

9.1.2 No commencement orders for these new provisions have yet been issued but the DWP has indicated that ss.234–236 will possibly come into force in June 2006 'if used', and, depending on what happens in relation to the above sections, s.237 may come into force in April 2007.

Secretary of State

9.1.3 Section 234 enables the Secretary of State to 'take action for the purpose of promoting or facilitating financial planning for retirement'. The action may include providing individuals with an estimate of the benefits that they are likely to receive in retirement, an estimate of the benefits that they are likely to need in retirement, and guidance on what action they can take to increase their benefits in retirement.

9.1.4 Sections 235, 236 and Sched.10 allow those holding information in relation to pensions and savings to release it to the Secretary of State for the purposes of s.234. There are limits on how the Secretary of State can use the information and to whom it can be disclosed.

Trustees and managers

9.1.5 Section 237 provides that trustees or managers of an occupational or personal pension scheme can be required by regulations to provide scheme members with combined pension forecasts (including their state, occupational and private pension benefits). The power to regulate in this area has been reserved for the Secretary of State, its use depending on the extent to which combined pension forecasts are issued by schemes on a voluntary basis. Section 298 facilitates the provision of state pension information to occupational and personal pension schemes for the purpose of producing combined pension forecasts.

Employers

9.1.6   Section 238 provides that employers may be required by regulations to facilitate access for their employees to information and advice about pensions and saving for retirement. Where they are so required, they will also have to inform the Regulator about what they have done to comply with the regulations. This system will be tested using pilot schemes conducted with employers on a voluntary basis.

Implications for trustees and employers

9.1.7   Trustees and managers should discuss with their advisers and/or administrators how they might introduce combined pension forecasts for their members. They may wish to consider introducing a pilot system by asking members to volunteer information about their other pension benefits.

9.1.8   Note that employers are already required to facilitate access to a stakeholder pension scheme, unless they fall within one of the exemptions in the Stakeholder Pension Schemes Regulations 2000, SI 2000/1403, and to provide information to members under the Occupational Pension Schemes (Disclosure of Information) Regulations 1996, SI 1996/1655.

9.1.9   However, employers should remain cautious when providing employees with advice about pensions and savings. At present, under the FSMA 2000, employers face criminal penalties if they promote financial products, including pensions, to their employees, unless they are authorised by the Financial Services Authority. Whilst this appears at odds with any obligations which may be imposed on an employer under s.238 of the Act, the Financial Services and Markets Act 2000 (Regulated Activities) (Amendment) (No. 2) Order 2004, SI 2004/2737, which comes into force on 6 April 2005 will exempt employers from the requirement to be authorised. As a result, companies should be more willing to communicate with their employees about their pension schemes, although they should still avoid providing individual financial advice.

9.1.10   The legislators were no doubt conscious in drafting these provisions that they raise issues under Arts.8 and/or 10 of the European Convention on Human Rights in allowing or requiring the provision of information about individuals. However, the Explanatory Notes stated that the measures were considered to be proportionate in order to meet the legitimate aim of furthering the economic wellbeing of the country and protecting the rights of individuals.

9.1.11   The information to be disclosed under the provisions may also constitute sensitive personal data for the purposes of the Data Protection Act 1998. However, it seems likely that, as the disclosures are required by law (see s.35 of the Data Protection Act), the transfer of data in this way will not be restricted by the Data Protection Act.

9.1.12 The Income Tax (Exemption of Minor Benefits) (Amendment) Regulations 2004, SI 2004/3087, which came into force on 14 December 2004, introduced a new tax exemption enabling employers to give pension information and advice to their employees without incurring a tax charge. The exemption only applies if the benefit is generally available to all employees and up to a limit of £150 for each employee in each year. If the cost to the employer is greater than £150, the whole amount will be subject to tax.

9.2 PENSION PROTECTION ON TRANSFERS OF EMPLOYMENT

Background

9.2.1 The Act contains provisions that extend the protection provided by the Transfer of Undertakings (Protection of Employment) Regulations 1981, SI 1981/1794 (TUPE) in respect of pension benefits.

9.2.2 Broadly, TUPE provides that an employee's contractual rights will transfer to the transferee company on a business transfer. However, reg.7 of TUPE contains an exemption in respect of so much of a contract of employment or collective agreement as relates to an occupational pension scheme, or any rights, powers, duties or liabilities arising from an occupational pension scheme in connection with the employee's employment.

9.2.3 This general exemption was qualified in 1993, because it appeared that the UK Government had not fully complied with the EU Acquired Rights Directive (Dir 77/187/EEC) in its drafting of TUPE. It was qualified so that 'any provisions of an occupational pension scheme which do not relate to benefits for old age, invalidity or survivors shall be treated as not being part of the scheme'.

9.2.4 As a result of the above wording, any provision of an occupational pension scheme that does not relate to old age, invalidity or survivors' benefits would potentially pass to a buyer on a business transfer under TUPE. However, it has not always been clear exactly what falls to be considered as being a benefit that is not for old age, invalidity or survivors, and there have been various high-profile cases on this point over recent years – see *Frankling* v. *BPS Public Sector* [1999] OPLR 295; *Beckmann* v. *Dynamco Whicheloe Macfarlane* (ECJ case C-164/00) [2002] OPLR 289; *Martin* v. *South Bank University* (ECJ Case C-4/01) [2004] 1 CMLR 15.

Changes in the Act

9.2.5   Section 257 of the Act sets out various conditions for pension protection on transfers of employment. In particular, there must be a transfer to which TUPE would generally apply. In addition, the transferring employee must have been:

(a) an active member of the transferor's occupational pension scheme at the date of transfer; or

(b) eligible (or in a waiting period for eligibility) to join the transferor's occupational pension scheme at the date of transfer.

9.2.6   If the transferor's scheme provided money purchase benefits, the employer must either have been required to contribute to it or has done so voluntarily.

9.2.7   Where the conditions of s.257 are satisfied, s.258 requires that the transferee must offer membership of either:

(a) a final salary scheme which meets the requirements of the reference scheme test or some other minimum standard specified by regulations; or

(b) a money purchase scheme or stakeholder pension scheme to which the transferee makes relevant contributions in respect of the employee.

9.2.8   Relevant contributions are to be prescribed by regulations but it is understood that employers will be required to match employee contributions to a maximum of 6 per cent.

9.2.9   Section 257(5) is intended to counter any attempts to avoid compliance. It provides that employees will still be deemed to qualify for protection even if their circumstances change due to measures that are 'by reason of the transfer'. These are likely to include measures such as the transferor closing its scheme or putting it into winding up. These provisions are similar to various parts of TUPE in respect of dismissal around the time of transfer.

9.2.10   It is important to note that employees can agree with the transferee to contract out of this protection (s.258(6)), whereas no such contracting out is permitted under TUPE.

9.2.11   The commencement orders for these provisions have yet to be issued, but it is expected that they will come into force on 6 April 2005.

Implications for employers

9.2.12   These provisions represent an attempt to keep both employees and employers happy by requiring that employers contribute to pension benefits for employees but not imposing on employers the burden of having to provide mirror image (or final salary) benefits.

9.2.13   Employers will need to consider these provisions for any transaction due to complete on or after 6 April 2005.

9.2.14 Depending upon the circumstances, some employers will find that the new protection provisions will increase their costs on transactions. There is also a concern that the new provisions may lead to a 'two-tier' system, with employers plumping for the cheaper option of a defined contribution arrangement for transferring employees acquired subsequent to a transaction, despite providing final salary benefits for all other employees. In such circumstances, questions of age and/or sex discrimination may arise.

9.2.15 Note that the provisions form a new implied contractual condition that will exist in addition to any other contractual rights an employee may have which transfer under TUPE as a result of the *Beckmann* and *Martin* cases (see above).

9.2.16 Also note that the requirement is to provide access to an 'occupational pension scheme'. There has long been debate as to whether a group personal pension scheme is or is not an occupational pension scheme. A narrowing of the gap between classic occupational pension schemes and other employer-sponsored arrangements has already begun in the recent Finance Act 2004; however it remains to be seen how this provision will be interpreted in practice.

9.3   CONSULTATION BY EMPLOYERS

Introduction

9.3.1 The Government recognised in its Green Paper *Simplicity, Security and Choice* (2002) the desirability of employers consulting employees and/or their representatives before making changes to their pension arrangements. As good practice in this area was not widespread, the Government indicated that it was considering the introduction of a requirement to consult employees and/or their representatives before making such changes.

9.3.2 Whilst pensions-related issues within a contractual context might fall within the remit of consultation obligations already imposed by other statutory provision, e.g. the Trade Union and Labour Relations (Consolidation) Act 1992 and the Information and Consultation of Employees Regulations 2004, SI 2004/3426 (2004 Regulations) (which come into force on 6 April 2005), ss.259–261 of the Act introduce the first pensions-specific consultation obligations. These will apply to the sponsoring employers of occupational pension schemes and to employers who operate direct payment arrangements for employees who are members of personal pension schemes. The Act makes it clear that these new consultation obligations are independent of and not a substitute for any other duty to consult.

Changes in the Act

9.3.3 On the coming into force of the Act and relevant secondary legislation, we will see the introduction of a new and separate obligation upon a 'prescribed person' who is the sponsoring employer of an occupational pension scheme to consult 'prescribed persons' in a 'prescribed manner' if it or the trustees or managers of its scheme are proposing to make a 'prescribed decision' about the scheme, before making that decision (s.259). Regulations may also require employers to inform trustees or managers of employees' responses to the consultation.

9.3.4   Similarly, a consultation obligation will be imposed upon an employer in relation to a personal pension scheme, where a direct payment arrangement is in place for one of more of its employees who are members of that scheme (s.260). The employer will be required to consult those employees if it is proposing to make a 'prescribed decision' which affects the direct payment arrangements.

9.3.5   Regulations are expected to flesh-out what and who is 'prescribed' and the form that the consultation should take. In relation to an occupational pension scheme, the Explanatory Notes suggest that regulations will impose the consultation duty upon employers where 'major or significant changes' are contemplated to the pension arrangements, such as:

(a) scheme wind up or closure to future accrual;
(b) closure of a scheme to new entrants;
(c) changing a scheme from defined benefit to defined contribution or hybrid;
(d) significantly reducing or ceasing an employer contribution to a defined contribution scheme.

9.3.6   In relation to a personal pension scheme, the Explanatory Notes suggest that a consultation obligation will be triggered by the removal or substantial reduction of an employer's contribution to the scheme.

9.3.7   Furthermore, the Explanatory Notes suggest that the employer may in certain circumstances be given some discretion in determining which employees to consult, although no further details are provided.

9.3.8   Regulations are also expected to specify:

(a) the information to be provided;
(b) the time allowed for the consultation;
(c) the persons who can act as representatives of persons to be consulted; and
(d) how the representatives might be selected.

9.3.9   In addition, regulations are expected to extend employment protections to consultation representatives (akin to those for trustees and trades union representatives). These protections would include the right to time off/remuneration and the right to present a complaint to an employment tribunal if representatives are subjected to a detriment or unfairly dismissed by reason of carrying out their duties.

9.3.10   The Regulator may also require employers, trustees or managers to provide it with information about the action taken to comply with the consultation provisions, and it may by order relax the consultation requirements.

9.3.11   No commencement orders for these new provisions have yet been issued, although the DWP has indicated that they will come into force on 6 April 2006.

Implications for employers and trustees

9.3.12   The Act provides that the validity of 'prescribed decisions' made by employers in relation to either an occupational pension scheme or a personal pension scheme will not be affected by a failure to follow the consultation requirements.

9.3.13   The position is somewhat different in relation to the trustees or managers of an occupational pension scheme. It is expected that they will be prevented by regulation from making a prescribed decision if the employer in relation to their scheme has not followed its consultation obligations.

9.3.14   It is possible that an employer's failure to comply with its consultation obligations might impact upon the ability of trustees or managers of an occupational pension scheme to make a prescribed decision themselves, for example exercising a joint power of amendment that closes their scheme to new entrants or changes the basis upon which the scheme provides benefits from defined benefit to defined contribution. The regulations might act as a shield for trustees, giving them the confidence and authority to resist pressure to make a prescribed decision until the employer has fulfilled its consultation obligations.

9.3.15   However, if the 'prescribed decision' is the employer's alone to make, it is not at liberty to ignore its obligations under the Act in the knowledge that its decision will not be overturned This is because s.314 of the Act imposes civil penalties in relation to any breach of regulations under the Act, and, if regulations so provide, s.116 of the 1995 Act will apply to the breach of any regulations made under the Act. Financial penalties of up to £5,000 in the case of individuals and £50,000 in the case of corporate bodies may therefore be imposed on an employer for contravention of its consultation obligations and, if regulations so stipulate, contravention may render individual employers or officers of a corporate employer liable to a summary (i.e. criminal) conviction.

Action required

9.3.16   Depending upon how widely the definition of 'prescribed decision' is drafted and whether there are any major or significant scheme changes on the horizon, these new obligations might not impact upon some employers at all.

9.3.17   Unlike other parts of the Act, the consultation provisions do not impose any requirement to amend a scheme's definitive documentation, its explanatory literature or to issue an announcement to members.

9.3.18   When the draft regulations are issued, employers might be well advised to consider whether the employee representation arrangements they currently have in place will satisfy the requirements of the Act. If not, they may wish to facilitate the appointment of employee consultation representatives, so that if they decide to take a 'prescribed decision' in the future, consultation is not delayed whilst appropriate structures are put in place.

Some final thoughts

9.3.19   We may not have heard the last word on what constitutes 'major and significant changes'. Whether regulations will set out a specific list of changes or whether there will be some form of quantitative measurement of the change is not yet certain. The former would seem preferable to the latter, or to the use of some form of actuarial test of significance. If a specified list is introduced, it may be that the list set out in the Explanatory Notes will be expanded to include such changes as:

(a) changing the definition of final pay in a defined benefit scheme or putting a cap on final pay;
(b) changing ill-health benefits;
(c) reducing the lump sum death-in-service benefit; and
(d) worsening the early retirement and/or lump sum commutation factors.

9.3.20   It is important to bear in mind that the Act only introduces a consultation obligation, rather than a consent requirement, and the ability of employees to influence 'prescribed decisions' may be limited.

9.3.21   It appears that the Government's intention behind the introduction of the consultation requirements was to complement the employment consultation requirements contained in the 2004 Regulations, which will be phased in (according to the size of the employer) from 6 April 2005. However if, as indeed they might, employees seek to extend the parameters of the 2004 Regulations to include decisions that affect their pension arrangements, it may mean that employers are required to consult via two separate processes on the same pension scheme changes, which will prove time consuming, costly and confusing. It may be that in such circumstances an employer could apply to the Regulator to relax the requirements for consultation under the Act.

9.4   MATERNITY, PATERNITY AND ADOPTION LEAVE

Changes in the Act

9.4.1   Section 265 inserts new paras.5A and 5B into Sched.5 (employment-related schemes for pensions or other benefits: equal treatment) of the Social Security Act 1989 after para.5 (unfair maternity provisions).

9.4.2   The purpose of para.5, Sched.5 of the Social Security Act 1989 was to safeguard pension rights during paid maternity leave. Paragraph 5 provided that employer pension contributions during periods of paid maternity leave should be made as if the employee was working normally, whilst member contributions would be based only on the actual salary received.

9.4.3   New paras.5A (unfair paternity leave provisions) and 5B (unfair adoption leave provisions) are intended to bring paid paternity leave and paid adoption leave into line with the existing legislation on paid maternity leave. Unsurprisingly then, these new provisions regarding paid paternity leave and paid adoption leave mirror the existing requirements for pension provision during paid maternity leave.

9.4.4   These new provisions, as with the existing para.5, relate to 'employment-related benefit schemes'. This term is defined in the 1989 Act as meaning schemes which provide service-related benefits.

9.4.5   No commencement orders for these new provisions have yet been issued, but the DWP has indicated that they will be brought into force in April 2005.

Content of paras.5A and 5B

9.4.6   For any period of paid paternity/adoption leave during which an employee receives contractual remuneration or statutory paternity/adoption pay, a member of an occupational pension scheme must be treated no less favourably than he would have been had he been working normally. The member, however, can only be required to pay contributions based on the remuneration he actually receives.

9.4.7   Under paras.5A and 5B any employment-related benefit scheme containing an 'unfair paternity/adoption leave provision' will breach the principle of equal treatment. A paternity/adoption leave provision is unfair if it either:

(a) relates to continuing membership of, or accrual of rights under, the scheme during any period of paid paternity/adoption leave, in the case of a member who is (or immediately before leave was) an employed earner, and it treats that person differently from the 'normal employment requirement' (the requirement that any period of paid paternity/adoption leave shall be treated as if it were a period throughout which the member works normally and receives the remuneration likely to be paid for doing so); or
(b) requires the amount of benefit provided by the scheme, to the extent that it falls to be determined by reference to earnings during paid paternity/adoption leave, to be determined contrary to the normal employment requirement.

9.4.8   If a scheme contains an 'unfair paternity/adoption leave provision' the provision will be overridden by Sched.5 to the effect that no less favourable treatment shall be accorded to the member than that which would be granted to him under the 'normal employment requirement'.

9.4.9   The provisions governing paternity leave and adoption leave are largely set out in the Paternity and Adoption Leave Regulations 2002, SI 2002/2788. Other provisions are contained in the Maternity and Parental Leave etc.

Regulations 1999, SI 1999/3312 (which introduced the right to unpaid leave for parents up to a maximum of 13 weeks), and the Paternity and Adoption Leave (Amendment) Regulations 2004, SI 2004/923 (which provided that all terms and conditions applying in relation to an employee returning from adoption leave (not just those relating to remuneration) are to be no less favourable than those which would have applied if the employee had not been absent).

Implications for employers and trustees

9.4.10   Trustees and employers of 'employment-related benefit schemes' will need to review their current practice in terms of pension provision for employees who are absent on paid paternity and adoption leave to ensure they will comply with these new requirements. Some schemes may already treat paid paternity and adoption leave in the same way as paid maternity leave and therefore already be compliant.

9.4.11   In practice, although these provisions will be overriding, employers will need to ensure that their treatment of those on paid paternity and adoption leave is compliant with the new requirements in terms of pension provision. Pension scheme trust deeds and rules should be reviewed and, if necessary, amended to reflect the new requirements. Employee handbooks and pension scheme booklets should also be reviewed and may need to be changed, as may other pieces of member literature. Members of pension and payroll departments and personnel teams will need to be trained to ensure that they are aware of the changes. Employers will also need to review their payroll systems to ensure that these are set up to calculate pension benefits correctly in these circumstances.

10 WINDING UP AND INSOLVENCY

10.1 INTRODUCTION

10.1.1 The Act makes a wide range of changes to the law relating to the calculation and treatment of employer debts due to a pension scheme where an employer becomes insolvent or where a scheme commences winding up. Sections 271 and 272 of the Act amend the existing s.75 of the 1995 Act (deficiencies in assets) and insert a new s.75A, which deals specifically with multi-employer schemes. The so-called 'moral hazard' provisions have received much publicity in the run-up to the implementation of the Act, and these are considered in detail below. In addition, the new Regulator is given broad powers to wind up pension schemes, impose freezing orders, and make restoration orders where schemes have suffered a transaction at an undervalue or a transaction to defraud creditors. Finally, the role of the insolvency practitioner has changed, particularly in relation to the appointment of independent trustees.

10.2 SECTION 75 OF THE 1995 ACT

10.2.1 Under the new version of s.75 of the 1995 Act, there will be two types of s.75 debt. Under s.75(2), a debt will arise in certain circumstances if a scheme goes into winding up (referred to here as 'wind-up debts'), and under s.75(4), in certain circumstances, a debt will arise where a 'relevant event' occurs in relation to the scheme employer (referred to here as 'relevant event debts').

10.2.2 Note that s.75 does not apply to money purchase schemes or certain prescribed schemes or schemes of a prescribed description (s.75(1)).

Section 75(2) – wind-up debts

10.2.3 A debt under s.75(2) of the 1995 Act will be treated as due from the employer to the trustees or managers of a scheme if:

(a) at any time between the commencement of a scheme's wind up and the occurrence of any relevant event in relation to the employer, the value of the assets of the scheme is less than the amount of its liabilities; and

(b) the trustees or managers of the scheme designate that time for the purposes of s.75(2) before a relevant event occurs in relation to the employer.

10.2.4   However, such a debt will not arise if a relevant event occurred during the period beginning with the 'appointed day' and ending with the commencement of the winding up of the scheme. The 'appointed day' is the day to be appointed by the Secretary of State under s.126(2) of the Act, following which date schemes which commence winding up may be eligible for the PPF, and is expected to be 6 April 2005. A relevant event is defined in new s.75(6A) as:

(a) an insolvency event in relation to the employer;
(b) the making of an application to the Board by the trustees under s.127 of the Act on the grounds that the employer is unlikely to continue as a going concern;
(c) receipt by the trustees of a notice from the Board under s.127(5)(a) of the Act following the Board becoming aware that the employer is unlikely to continue as a going concern, unless a cessation notice has been issued and become binding before the commencement of the winding up of the scheme; or
(d) the passing of a resolution for a members' voluntary winding up of the employer under s.89 of the Insolvency Act 1986.

10.2.5   If a debt does arise it will be an amount equal to the difference between the assets and the liabilities.

10.2.6   It remains to be seen exactly how trustees will be required to demonstrate that they have designated a time under s.75(2) which falls before the occurrence of a relevant event. Presumably, trustees should ensure that any such decision is recorded in a minute or is made by a written resolution which sets out the decision and confirms the date it was made. Trustees will need to monitor fluctuations in the potential debt during the period within which they are able to designate a time, bearing in mind the possibility of a relevant event occurring in relation to the employer. If a relevant event occurs (unless the event is a members' voluntary winding up), a relevant event debt under s.75(4) may arise instead and, unlike some relevant event debts, such a debt will not be contingent – see **Figure 10.1**.

Section 75(4) – relevant event debts

10.2.7   A debt arises under s.75(4) of the 1995 Act where, immediately before a relevant event occurs in relation to the employer, the value of the assets of the scheme is less than the amount of its liabilities at that time.

10.2.8   Note that the definition of an insolvency event used in the Act is much broader than the previous definition of insolvency used for s.75 purposes (see **para.10.2.22**).

10.2.9   The 'current relevant event' (i.e. the relevant event being considered) must have occurred after the appointed day (see **para.10.2.4**) and must not have occurred in yet to be prescribed circumstances.

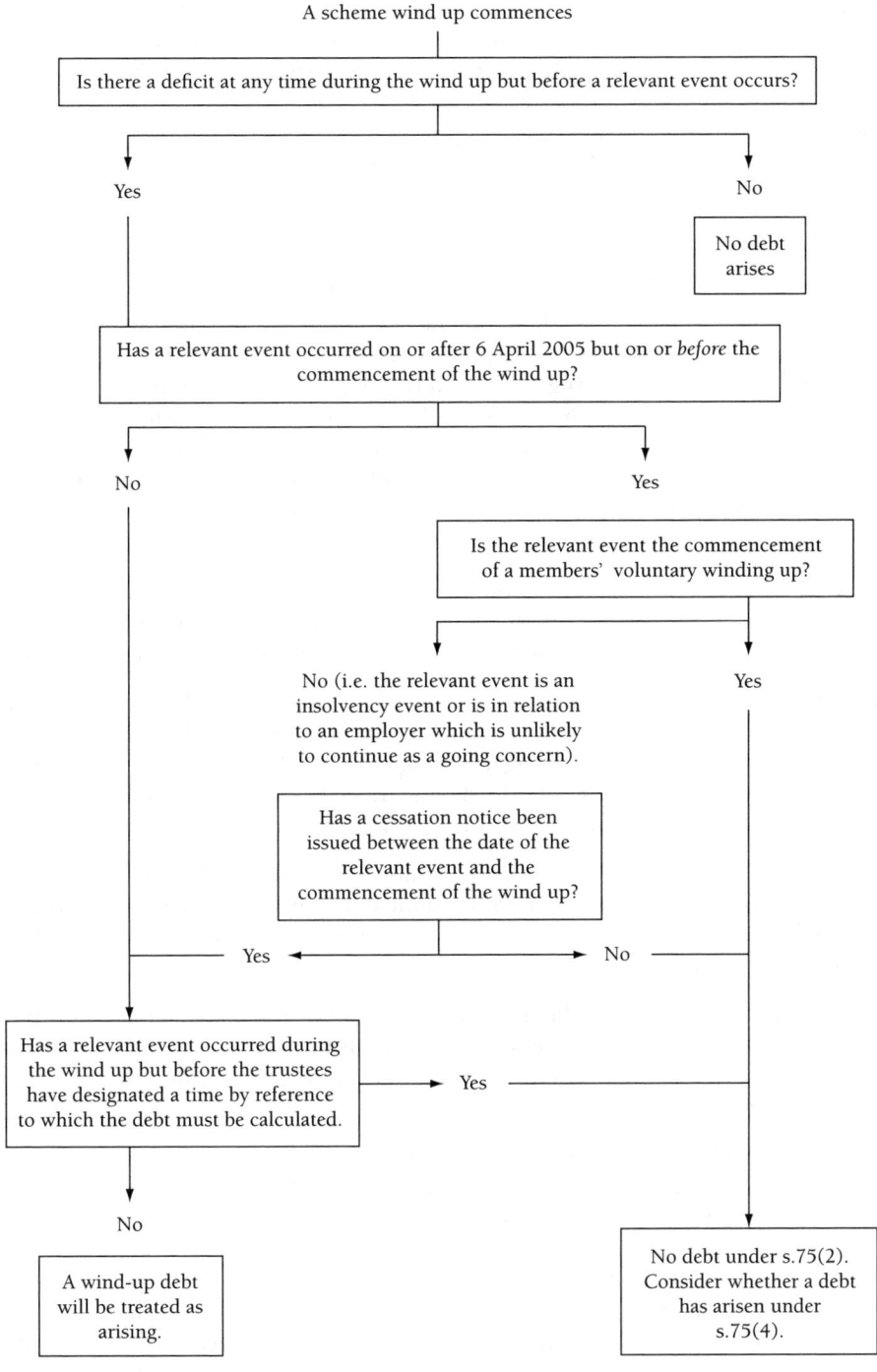

Figure 10.1 Flow chart for s.75(2) (wind-up debts)

10.2.10 If the scheme was being wound up immediately before that event, s.75(2) must not have applied in relation to the scheme to treat an amount as a debt due from the employer to the trustees or managers of the scheme. Section 75(2) would not apply in those circumstances if the trustees or managers did not designate a time for the determination of the debt before the qualifying relevant event occurred. If they did designate such a time, a debt may arise under s.75(2) instead.

10.2.11 If the current relevant event is not a members' voluntary winding up then either of the following must apply:

(a) no relevant event (other than a members' voluntary winding up) must have occurred in relation to the employer during the period beginning with the appointed day and ending immediately before the current relevant event; or
(b) a cessation event must have occurred in relation to the scheme in respect of a cessation notice issued during the period beginning with the occurrence of the last relevant event (other than a members' voluntary winding up) which occurred during the period referred to in (a) above and ending immediately before the current relevant event.

10.2.12 In addition, no resolution must have been passed for a members' voluntary winding up in relation to the employer within the period between the appointed day and ending immediately before the current relevant event.

10.2.13 In the above circumstances, an amount equal to the difference between the assets and liabilities of the scheme shall be treated as a debt due from the employer to the trustees or managers of the scheme. If the current event is not a members' voluntary winding up, the debt is treated as arising immediately before the occurrence of the current event for the purposes of insolvency law.

10.2.14 If the current relevant event is not a members' voluntary winding up and the scheme is not being wound up immediately before the current event, the debt will be contingent. It will be contingent upon the occurrence of either of the following:

(a) a scheme failure notice being issued in relation to the scheme for PPF purposes (by either an insolvency practitioner or the Board) after the occurrence of the current event, in circumstances where the following conditions are satisfied:

   (i)   the scheme failure notice is binding; and
   (ii) no resolution for a members' voluntary winding up occurred in relation to the employer before the failure notice became binding; and
   (iii) a cessation event has not occurred in relation to a cessation notice issued during the period beginning with the current event and ending immediately before the issuing of the scheme failure notice; and
   (iv) there is no possibility of a cessation event occurring in respect of a cessation notice issued during that period (see **para.10.2.20** for when a cessation event is treated as not being a possibility); or

(b) the commencement of the winding up of the scheme before a scheme failure notice or a cessation notice in relation to the scheme becomes binding, or the passing of a resolution for a members' voluntary winding up.

10.2.15   Presumably, whenever s.75(4) applies, the debt will be calculated as at a time immediately before the current relevant event occurs, whether or not the debt is contingent (see **Figure 10.2**). Regulations may provide further clarification.

Cessation events and cessation notices

10.2.16   A cessation event occurs when a cessation notice in relation to the scheme becomes binding under Part 2 of the Act (the PPF provisions). Generally, a cessation event occurs when the Board ceases to be involved in a scheme.

10.2.17   For the purposes of s.75 of the 1995 Act, cessation notices are:

(a) withdrawal notices issued under s.122(2)(b) of the Act (where an insolvency practitioner issues a withdrawal notice because he cannot confirm that a scheme rescue has occurred);
(b) notices issued by the Board under s.148 of the Act that no insolvency event has occurred or is likely to occur in the six months following the application of s.148;
(c) notices issued by an insolvency practitioner under s.122(4) of the Act (inability to confirm status of scheme) which have become binding in circumstances where s.148 of the Act does not apply.

10.2.18   A withdrawal notice issued under s.130(3) of the Act by the Board (scheme rescue has occurred) will be a cessation notice in cases where the relevant event is either the making by the trustees of an application under s.129(1) (the employer is unlikely to continue as a going concern) or the receipt by the trustees of notice from the Board under s.129(5)(a) (following the Board becoming aware that the employer is unlikely so to continue).

10.2.19   It should be noted that withdrawal notices issued under s.146 of the Act (where the Board determines that the scheme is not eligible for the PPF throughout the prescribed period) and s.147 (where the Board refuses to assume responsibility for a new scheme set up to obtain compensation from the PPF) are not cessation notices.

10.2.20   The occurrence of a cessation event is treated as a possibility until each of the following are no longer reviewable (s.75(6B)(d) of the 1995 Act):

(a) any cessation notice issued during the specified period;
(b) any failure to issue a cessation notice during the specified period;
(c) any notice issued by the Board under Chapter 2 or 3 of Part 2 of the Act which is relevant to the issue of a cessation notice during the relevant period; and
(d) any failure to issue a notice referred to in (c) above.

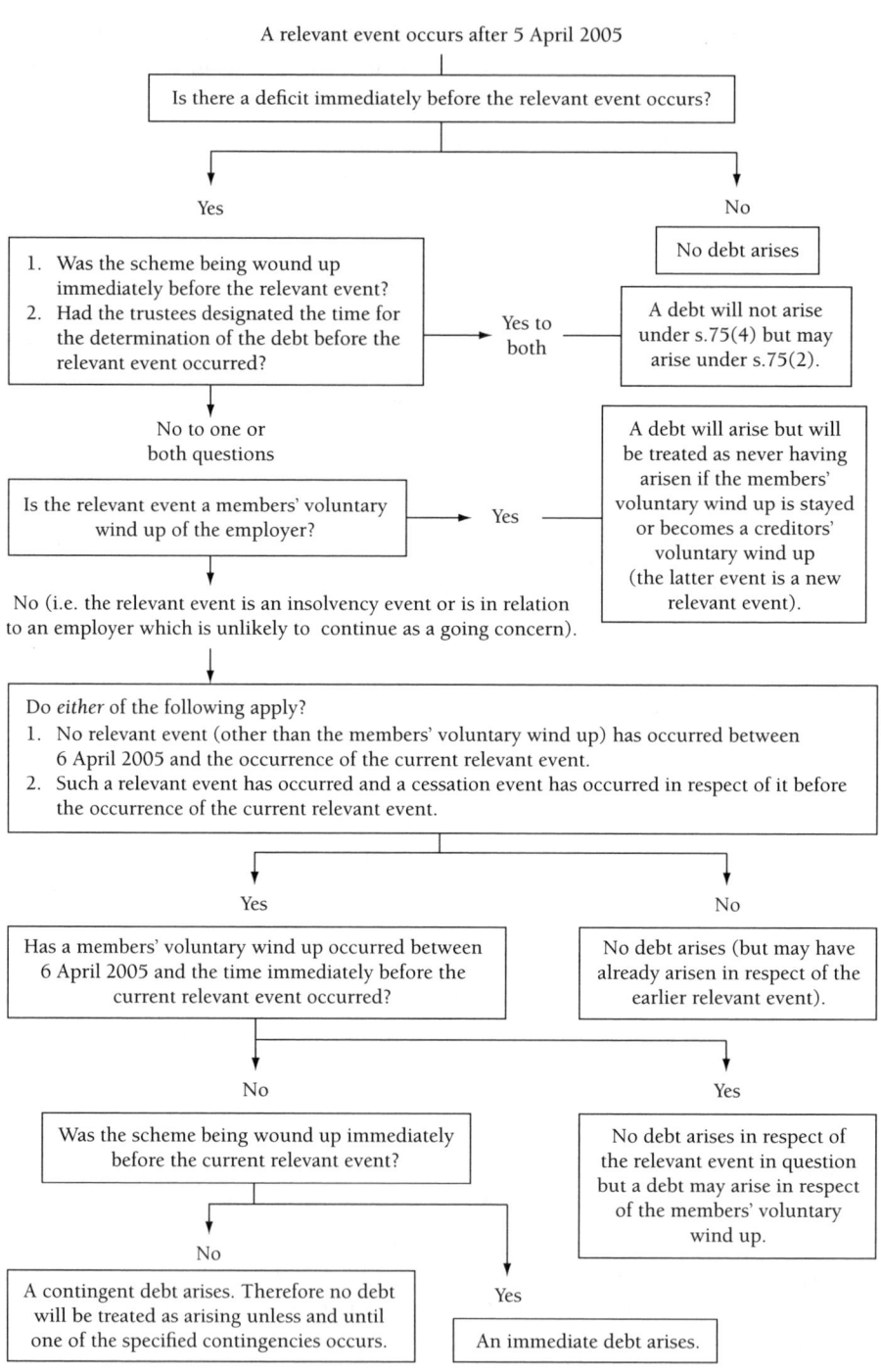

Figure 10.2 Flow chart for s.75(4) debts (relevant event debts)

10.2.21   The issue or failure to issue a notice referred to in **para.10.2.20** is to be regarded as reviewable during the period within which it may be reviewed under Chapter 6 of Part 2 of the Act (reviews, appeals and maladministration). If reviewed under that Chapter, such issue or failure to issue a notice will be reviewable until that review and any reconsideration, any reference to the PPF Ombudsman and any appeal against the PPF Ombudsman's directions or determinations have been finally disposed of.

Meaning of 'insolvency events'

10.2.22   As set out in s.121 of the Act, an 'insolvency event' for the purposes of s.75 of the 1995 Act in relation to a company occurs where:

(a) a nominee in relation to a proposal for a voluntary arrangement submits a report to the court stating that in his opinion meetings of the company and its creditors should be summoned to consider the proposal;
(b) the directors of a company file with the court documents and statements in relation to a moratorium where directors propose a voluntary arrangement;
(c) an administrative receiver is appointed;
(d) the company enters administration;
(e) a resolution is passed for a voluntary winding up without a declaration of solvency;
(f) a meeting of creditors is held converting a members' voluntary winding up into a creditors' voluntary winding up;
(g) a winding-up order is made by the court;
(h) an event occurs which is a prescribed event.

10.2.23   Section 121 of the Act sets out insolvency events which apply where the employer is an individual or a partnership.

Calculation of the debt

10.2.24   The liabilities and assets to be taken into account and their amount or value must be determined, calculated and verified by a person and in a manner to be prescribed. It is anticipated that all debts will be required to be calculated on an annuity buy out basis. Any scheme provision which limits the amount of its liabilities by reference to the amount of its assets is to be disregarded.

Member's voluntary winding up

10.2.25   If a resolution is passed for a members' voluntary winding up under s.89 of the Insolvency Act 1986 during the period beginning with the appointed day and ending with the commencement of the winding up of the scheme, a wind-up debt will not arise under s.75(2) of the 1995 Act.

10.2.26   The passing of such a resolution is, however, a relevant event which may give rise to a relevant event debt under s.75(4). Any such debt will not be contingent, but if the members' voluntary winding up is either stayed (other than in prescribed circumstances) or a meeting of creditors converts the members' voluntary winding up into a creditors' voluntary winding up, s.75 applies as if the resolution for the members' voluntary winding up had never been passed and any debt which arose by virtue of that resolution had never arisen (s.75(6D) of the 1995 Act).

10.2.27 If a meeting of creditors converts the members' voluntary winding up into creditors' voluntary winding up that conversion will be a relevant event that may give rise to a contingent debt under s.75(4).

10.2.28 It may be possible that, if a debt arises for a reason other than due to a members' voluntary winding up and ceases to be contingent, a later members' voluntary winding up could give rise to a second debt. In practice, however, this is unlikely to occur, given that the employer may not survive the first relevant event.

10.3 SECTION 75A: MULTI-EMPLOYER SCHEMES

10.3.1 Section 272 of the Act inserts a new s.75A into the 1995 Act relating to deficiencies in the assets of multi-employer schemes. The new s.75A enables the making of regulations to modify s.75 of the 1995 Act as it applies to multi-employer schemes, including the circumstances in which debts will become due under multi-employer schemes, how the debt will be calculated when only one employer is affected, how the debt will be divided between employers, and how the provisions apply to sectionalised schemes.

10.3.2 A multi-employer scheme is defined in s.75A(13) as a trust scheme which applies to earners in employments under different employers. This differs from the previous multi-employer provisions which applied to schemes where there was more than one employer, 'employer' being defined as the employer of persons in the description or category of employment to which the scheme relates. The new definition stresses that the scheme must apply to 'earners' but that term itself is not defined. There may therefore still be some uncertainty as to whether a scheme applies to earners in certain circumstances, for example if they have opted out of a scheme but are still eligible to join it, or if all of the earners of a particular employer are within a waiting period before they are eligible to join the scheme.

10.3.3 Regulations may set out the circumstances in which debts are treated as due in multi-employer schemes, which may include circumstances other than those that apply to single employer schemes, i.e. where the scheme is being wound up or where a relevant event occurs. The Explanatory Notes give the example of an additional trigger event, namely the withdrawal of an employer from a scheme in circumstances where other employers remain.

10.3.4 Regulations will also determine how a debt should be calculated where it only affects one employer amongst several (such as on its insolvency) or how a debt should be divided on winding up. Furthermore, regulations will contain provisions applying to sectionalised schemes, where each section is to be treated for the purposes of calculating any debt on the employer as separate schemes.

'Alternative manners'

10.3.5 The Explanatory Notes state that regulations will provide for the amount of a debt on the withdrawal of an employer from a multi-employer scheme generally to be calculated on a full buy-out basis, but provision will be made for a prescribed alternative (usually lower) basis to be used where approved arrangements are entered into with a view to ensuring that the scheme is supported in the future. Such alternative basis is referred to in s.75A(4) of the 1995 Act as 'alternative manners'.

10.3.6 For all approved arrangements other than transfers out of the scheme, the debt will be calculated on the same basis as the scheme-specific funding requirement introduced by the Act. Where the approved arrangement is a transfer of benefits out of the scheme, the liabilities transferred will be excluded from the debt calculation so as to reduce the debt. Therefore, the debt could be nil if all of the pension benefits in respect of the employer are transferred out. It appears that the employer will be able to make an application for the alternative manners to apply, and details of the application process will also be set out in regulations. It remains to be seen whether 'alternative manners' could be used in relation to any remaining debt or whether such liability will be calculated on the full buy-out basis.

10.3.7 Section 75A(5) says that regulations may make the application of each type of alternative manner depend on whether prescribed requirements are met, including that a prescribed arrangement is in place. It goes on to say that regulations may, in the case of each type of alternative manner, in prescribed circumstances allow the Regulator to issue a direction that any resulting multi-employer debt is unenforceable for such period as the Regulator may specify, and that the debt is to be recalculated applying a different manner. These powers are intended to enable an employer to apply for approval of arrangements after the debt has arisen.

10.3.8 Regulations may provide that a prescribed arrangement, the details of which are to be approved by the Regulator, must be in place and that the Regulator may not approve the details unless prescribed conditions are met. It is expected that the arrangements will be similar to those that may be required by financial support directions, i.e. joint and several liability of companies within a group, for the top holding company within the group to take on the liability for future debts, and the establishment of financial support for the scheme, such as bank guarantees. It will also be possible to agree that some or all of the liabilities of employees of the employer concerned are transferred out of the scheme into a new scheme.

10.3.9 The prescribed conditions referred to above may include a condition that the arrangement identifies one or more persons who are to be responsible for the arrangement and to whom the Regulator may issue a contribution notice if the arrangements are not properly maintained. Note that the person must consent to be identified in this way. The Regulator will then be able to issue a contribution notice requiring the person to pay a specified sum to the trustees or managers or to the Board if the prescribed arrangements cease to be in place, or if it considers that those arrangements are no longer appropriate and it considers that it is reasonable to impose liability on the person to pay the sum specified in the notice. The Regulations must also set out other relevant matters, such as how the amount of the contribution is determined and the contents of the contribution notice.

10.3.10 In the absence of regulations setting out the detail of how these 'alternative manners' will operate and the conditions upon which the Regulator may approve them, it is hard to know how useful these provisions will be in practice. A debt will still exist, albeit on a lower calculation basis, except in relation to liabilities for benefits that are transferred out. It may be possible to limit the debt arising on a company or business sale by transferring liabilities out of the scheme, but this may be of limited application and difficult to arrange in practice.

10.4   MORAL HAZARD PROVISIONS

10.4.1 There are two forms of moral hazard provision in the Act: contribution notices where there is avoidance of an employer debt, and financial support directions.

Contribution notices where avoidance of employer debt (ss.38–42)

10.4.2 A contribution notice may be issued by the Regulator to require the person to whom the notice is issued to pay an amount to a pension scheme.

10.4.3 The Regulator may only issue a contribution notice to a person if the following apply.

(a) The Regulator is of the opinion that the person was a party to an act or a deliberate failure to act (including persons who knowingly assist in the act or failure) and the main purpose or one of the main purposes of which was:

   (i) to prevent the recovery of the whole or any part of a debt (or prevent the occurrence of an event upon which a debt is contingent) which was, or might become, due from the employer in relation to the scheme under s.75 of the 1995 Act; or

   (ii) otherwise than in good faith, to prevent such a debt becoming due, to compromise or otherwise settle such a debt, or to reduce the amount of such a debt which would otherwise become due.

(b) The person was at any time in the relevant period (i.e. the period between the occurrence of the act or failure to act and the determination by the Regulator to issue the contribution notice) the employer in relation to the scheme, or a person connected with, or an associate of, the employer (see **para.10.4.4**).

(c) The Regulator is of the opinion that, in being a party to the act or failure, the person was not acting in accordance with his functions as an insolvency practitioner in relation to another person.

(d) The Regulator considers that it is reasonable to impose liability on the person to pay the sum specified in the notice.

10.4.4 'Connected persons' and 'associated persons' are defined in ss.249 and 435 of the Insolvency Act 1986 respectively. Where the employer is a company, a person is connected with the company if he is a director or shadow director of the company, or an associate of such a director or shadow director, or if he is an associate of the company. The definition of 'associate' covers a wide range of relationships, the main ones being: husband; wife; relative; relative-in-law; business partner (or a business partner's spouse or relative); employee; employer; trustee/beneficiary of a trust in certain circumstances; companies under the same control; and controlling shareholders, including individuals or companies who alone or with associates have one third or more of the voting power at general meetings or on whose instructions the directors are accustomed to act. Note that regulations may modify the above definitions (and others, such as 'subsidiary' and 'holding company') in relation to a partnership, a partner, a limited liability partnership or a member of such a partnership (s.57 of the Act).

10.4.5 The act or failure to act must have first occurred on or after 27 April 2004, and before any assumption of responsibility for the scheme by the Board. In addition, the act must have occurred during the period of six years ending with the determination by the Regulator to exercise the power to issue the contribution notice in question (and the failure to act must have first occurred during, or continued for the whole or part of, that period).

10.4.6 Contribution notices can be made in relation to occupational pension schemes other than money purchase schemes and any schemes that may be prescribed in regulations.

Determinations by the Regulator

10.4.7 Where the above conditions are fulfilled, the Regulator may issue a contribution notice but it is not bound to do so. Section 38(7) provides that in deciding whether it is reasonable to impose a liability on a person to pay the sum specified, the Regulator must take into account such matters as it considers relevant including the following.

(a) The degree of involvement of the person in the act or failure to act in question.

(b) The relationship which the person has or has had with the employer (including, where the employer is a company as defined in s.435(11) of the

Insolvency Act 1986, whether the person has or has had control of the employer within the meaning of s.435(10)).

(c) Any connection or involvement which the person has or has had with the scheme.

(d) If the act or failure to act was a notifiable event for the purposes of s.69 (duty to notify the Regulator of certain events), any failure by the person to comply with any obligation imposed on the person by s.69(1) to give the Regulator notice of the event.

(e) All the purposes of the act or failure to act (including whether a purpose of the act or failure was to prevent or limit loss of employment).

(f) The financial circumstances of the person.

(g) Any other prescribed matters.

The sum specified in a s.38 contribution notice

10.4.8   The contribution to be specified by the Regulator in a contribution notice may be the whole or part of the s.75 debt estimated by the Regulator as at the relevant time. If no debt was due at the relevant time the debt will be estimated by the Regulator as if a debt were due under s.75(2) of the 1995 Act (where a scheme is being wound up before a relevant insolvency event occurs in relation to the employer), and the relevant time will be the time designated by the trustees under s.75(2). For these purposes a debt includes a contingent debt due under s.75 of the 1995 Act.

10.4.9   The debt will be calculated as at the 'relevant time', being the time that the relevant act or failure occurred or, in the case of a continued failure, a time determined by the Regulator falling within the period during which the failure continued.

10.4.10   If the Regulator is satisfied that the act or failure has resulted in the estimated debt being less than it would otherwise have been, it may increase the amount of the debt as it thinks appropriate.

Content of contribution notices

10.4.11   A contribution notice must state the relevant act or failure being relied upon, the amount the person is required to pay and the notice must identify any other persons to whom contribution notices have been or are issued as a result of the act or failure to act in question and the sums specified in each of those notices.

Effect of contribution notices

10.4.12   A liability to pay a sum specified in a contribution notice is treated as a debt due from the person specified to the trustees or managers of the scheme. The Regulator may exercise the powers of the trustees to recover the amount.

10.4.13   During an assessment period for PPF purposes, the rights and powers of the trustees or managers to recover a debt due to them by virtue of a contribution notice are only exercisable by the Board and any amount recovered by the Board must be paid to the trustees or managers. Alternatively, the contribution notice may state that a sum is due to the Board, in which case the sum is treated as a debt due directly to the Board.

10.4.14   The Regulator may issue 'corresponding contribution notices' to persons who are jointly and severally liable for a debt resulting from the same act or failure to act. Such notices must be issued to all such persons and name all of the persons who are liable, they must specify that the liability is joint and several and each notice must specify the same sum.

10.4.15   Debts specified in contribution notices are not taken into account in ascertaining the amount or value of a debt for the purposes of the new s.75(2) and (4) of the 1995 Act.

Relationship between contribution notices and employer debts

10.4.16   Section 41 of the Act provides that the Regulator may issue a direction that the trustees or managers must not take any further steps to recover a s.75 debt (or contingent debt) pending the recovery of a debt due by virtue of a contribution notice. Failure to comply with this direction may lead to civil penalties being imposed under s.10 of the 1995 Act.

10.4.17   Such direction may be issued where a s.75 debt is due from the employer to the trustees or managers of the scheme or to the Board (if it has assumed responsibility for the scheme) at the time that the contribution notice is issued or if a debt becomes due under s.75 of the 1995 Act from the employer to the trustees or managers after the contribution notice has been issued but before the sum specified in it has been paid in full.

10.4.18   Any sums paid by virtue of a contribution notice to the trustees, managers or the Board will reduce the s.75 debt (or contingent debt) and the payer may apply to the Regulator for a reduction in the amount specified in the contribution notice. The Regulator may reduce the amount specified by an amount it considers reasonable and issue a revised contribution notice if it believes it is appropriate to do so, having regard to various matters set out in s.41(10) of the Act. Where the payer is jointly and severally liable for the debt with other persons and a revised contribution notice is issued, the Regulator must also issue revised notices to the other persons concerned.

Clearance statements (contribution notices)

10.4.19   An application may be made to the Regulator for a clearance statement under s.42 of the Act. A clearance statement is a statement by the Regulator that, in its opinion, and in the circumstances described in the application:

(a) the applicant would not be a party to an act or a deliberate failure to act falling within s.38(5)(a) of the Act;

(b) it would not be reasonable to impose any liability on the applicant by means of a contribution notice; or

(c) 'such requirements ... as may be prescribed' would not be satisfied in relation to the applicant.

10.4.20   The Regulator must decide whether or not to issue the clearance statement and, if it decides to do so, must issue the statement as soon as reasonably practicable. Once issued, a clearance statement binds the Regulator in relation to the exercise of the power to issue a contribution notice to the applicant unless there is a material difference between the circumstances in relation to which the exercise of the power under s.38 arises and the circumstances described in the application.

Implications for trustees, employers and others

10.4.21   As a result of the new provisions, a wide range of persons who are not participating employers could become liable to contribute to a pension scheme. Employers should be aware of when they and any connected and associated persons may be made liable under a contribution notice.

10.4.22   The provisions may apply to any arrangement to 'manage' a s.75 debt, including delaying a debt, reducing it, preventing it from arising or preventing it from being recovered. Any persons involved in such an arrangement might find themselves subject to a contribution notice if they are connected or associated with the employer.

10.4.23   The definition of connected or associated persons is broad and effectively 'pierces the corporate veil' by including individuals, even where the employers are companies.

10.4.24   There are also implications in relation to corporate transactions for purchasers of employers and employers' connected or associated persons. The possibility of being faced with a contribution notice is a fundamental concern in relation to company sales (note that a business cannot in itself be an associated or connected person) where there are final salary schemes.

10.4.25   Purchasers will have to investigate whether there have been any arrangements prior to completion of the transaction and since 27 April 2004, in respect of which a contribution notice could be made. Purchasers should also investigate whether there are any contribution notices in existence or whether circumstances are currently being investigated which may result in a contribution notice being made. In each such case, the Purchaser may wish to seek appropriate warranties. Indemnities may also be sought if investigations and/or disclosures raise concerns.

10.4.26   Some consideration of the possibility of contribution notices being imposed should be given in relation to company reconstructions where there is an element of s.75 debt management or avoidance.

Financial support directions

10.4.27   Financial support directions (FSDs) require the person to whom they are issued to secure financial support for the scheme. The Regulator has the power to issue an FSD if it determines that the value of the resources of the scheme employer are insufficient to meet a yet to be specified proportion of the estimated s.75 debt and there is an associated or connected person that could meet that percentage of the debt. An FSD can also be issued where the scheme employer is a service company i.e. a company that solely or principally provides the services of employees within its group of companies.

10.4.28   An FSD may be made in relation to occupational pension schemes other than money purchase schemes and any schemes that may be prescribed in regulations.

Effect of an FSD

10.4.29   An FSD requires the person(s) to whom it is issued to secure that:

(a) financial support is put in place within the period specified in the FSD;
(b) such financial support or other financial support remains in place while the scheme is in existence (i.e. until it is wound up); and
(c) the Regulator is notified in writing of events to be prescribed as soon as reasonably practicable after they occur. The events will include changes in the circumstances of the scheme or of the financial support. No duty of a person is to be regarded as contravened merely because of any information or opinion contained in any such notice.

The persons to whom an FSD may be issued

10.4.30   FSDs may be issued to one or more persons, provided, firstly, that the Regulator believes it is reasonable to impose an FSD on that person (bearing in mind the matters set out in s.43(7) of the Act) and, secondly, that the person is at the 'relevant time':

(a) the employer in relation to the scheme;
(b) an individual who is an associate of an individual who is the employer, but is not an associate of that individual by reason only of being employed by him; or
(c) a person, other than an individual, who is connected with or an associate of the employer.

10.4.31   'Relevant time' has the meaning set out below and 'connected' and 'associated' have the same meaning as in **para.10.4.4** relating to contribution notices.

Meaning of 'relevant time'

10.4.32   The 'relevant time' is a time determined by the Regulator within a period to be prescribed by regulations and which ends with the determination by the Regulator to exercise the power to issue the FSD. It is intended that the relevant time will be as close to the time of the Regulator's determination as possible.

Meaning of 'service company'

10.4.33   An employer is a service company if, at the relevant time, it is a member of a group of companies and its turnover as shown in its latest available accounts prepared in accordance with s.226 of the Companies Act 1985 is solely or principally derived from amounts charged for the provision of the services of its employees to other companies who are members of that group.

Meaning of 'insufficiently resourced'

10.4.34   The scheme employer is insufficiently resourced at the relevant time if:

(a) at that time, the value of the resources of the employer is less than the amount which is a percentage of the 'estimated s.75 debt' in relation to the scheme (this percentage is to be prescribed);

(b) there is at the relevant time a connected or associated person in relation to the scheme employer (under s.43(6)(b) or (c) of the Act) and the value of that person's resources is not less than the difference between the value of the resources of the employer and the amount which is the prescribed percentage of the estimated s.75 debt.

10.4.35   The estimated s.75 debt is the amount estimated by the Regulator as the debt which would be due from the employer if s.75(2) (debt on winding up before the employer's insolvency) applied and the trustees had decided to calculate the debt as at the relevant time. Any s.75 debt that is due from the employer at the relevant time will be disregarded.

Meaning of 'financial support'

10.4.36   'Financial support' means one or more of the following arrangements, the details of which are to be approved in a notice issued by the Regulator, if the Regulator is satisfied that the arrangement is reasonable in the circumstances:

(a) an arrangement whereby, at any time when the employer is a member of a group of companies, all the members of the group are jointly and severally liable for the whole or part of the 'employer's pension liabilities' in relation to the scheme;

(b) an arrangement whereby, at any time when the employer is a member of a group of companies, a company which meets prescribed requirements (including that the company must be located in the EU) and is the holding company of the group is liable for the whole or part of the 'employer's pension liabilities' in relation to the scheme;

(c) an arrangement which meets prescribed requirements (e.g. a bank guarantee) and whereby additional financial resources are provided to the scheme;

(d) other arrangements that may be prescribed.

10.4.37 In paras. (a) and (b) above the 'employer's pension liabilities' means liabilities for any amounts payable for or on behalf of the employer towards the scheme (whether on the employer's own account or otherwise) in accordance with a schedule of contributions under s.227 of the Act, and the liabilities for any debt which is or may become due to the trustees or managers of the scheme from the employer by virtue of s.75 or otherwise.

Clearance statements (FSDs)

10.4.38 Section 46 of the Act provides for the issue of clearance statements by the Regulator along similar lines to those set out in s.42 relating to contribution notices. Briefly, the Regulator may issue a clearance statement which states that:

(a) the employer would not be a service company for the purposes of s.44;

(b) the employer would not be 'insufficiently resourced'; or

(c) it would not be reasonable to impose an FSD on the applicant.

Contribution notices where an FSD is not complied with

10.4.39 The Regulator may issue a contribution notice to any one or more of the persons to whom the FSD was issued where there is non-compliance with an FSD (s.47). A contribution notice cannot be issued for this reason where the Board has assumed responsibility for a scheme (s.47(5)).

10.4.40 The contribution notice will state that the person is under a liability to pay the sum specified in the notice. It does not seem that the person to whom the notice is issued must necessarily be responsible for the non-compliance, although this is a factor that the Regulator must take into account.

10.4.41 The Regulator may only issue a contribution notice if it is of the opinion that it is reasonable to impose liability on the person to pay the sum specified. In deciding whether it is reasonable, the Regulator must have regard to such matters as it considers relevant including, where relevant:

(a) whether the person has taken reasonable steps to secure compliance with the FSD;

(b) the relationship which the person has or has had with the employer (including, where the employer is a company, whether the person has or has had control of the employer);

(c) the value of any benefits received directly or indirectly by the person, where that person falls within s.43(6)(b) or (c);

(d) the relationship which the person has or has had with the parties to any arrangements put in place in accordance with the direction (including, where any of those parties is a company, whether the person has or has had control of that company);

(e) any connection or involvement which the person has or has had with the scheme;

(f) the financial circumstances of the person; and

(g) any other prescribed matters.

10.4.42   For the purposes of the above 'control' has the meaning set out in s.435(10) of the Insolvency Act 1986.

10.4.43   The sum specified in the contribution notice may be the whole or a specified part of the shortfall sum in relation to the scheme. This sum is:

(a) if at the 'time of non-compliance' a s.75 debt is due from the employer to the trustees or managers, the amount that the Regulator estimates to be the amount of the debt at that time; or

(b) if at the 'time of non-compliance' a s.75 debt is not due from the employer to the trustees or managers then it is the amount estimated by the Regulator as the debt which would be due from the employer if s.75(2) of the 1995 Act (i.e. debt on winding up before the employer's insolvency) applied and the trustees had decided to calculate the debt as at the 'time of non-compliance'.

10.4.44   The 'time of non-compliance' is effectively the time that the non-compliance first occurs as set out in s.48(3). Where more than one such time occurs, the Regulator shall determine which such time is used.

10.4.45   The s.47 contribution notice must:

(a) contain a statement of the matters which it is asserted constitute the non-compliance with the FSD in respect of which the notice is issued;

(b) specify the sum which must be paid;

(c) identify any other persons to whom contribution notices have been or are issued in respect of the non-compliance in question and the sums specified in each of those notices;

(d) if the notice creates joint and several liability it must state this and comply with the requirements for corresponding contribution notices referred to in **para.10.4.49**.

Effect of a s.47 contribution notice

10.4.46   The sum specified is treated as a debt due from the person to the trustees or managers of the scheme.

10.4.47   The Regulator may, on behalf of the trustees or managers of the scheme, exercise such powers as the trustees or managers have to recover the debt.

10.4.48   During any assessment period in relation to the scheme, the rights and powers of the trustees or managers of the scheme in relation to any debt due to them by virtue of a contribution notice, are only exercisable by the Board. The Board must pay any amount recovered to the trustees or managers of the scheme.

10.4.49   Where the contribution notice so specifies, the person to whom the notice is issued ('P') is to be treated as jointly and severally liable for the debt with any persons specified in the notice who are persons to whom corresponding contribution notices are issued. A corresponding contribution notice is a notice which:

(a) is issued in respect of the same non-compliance with the FSD as the non-compliance in respect of which P's contribution notice is issued;
(b) specifies the same sum as is specified in P's contribution notice; and
(c) specifies that the person to whom the contribution notice is issued is jointly and severally liable with P, or with P and other persons, for that sum.

10.4.50   A debt due by virtue of a contribution notice is not to be taken into account for the purposes of s.75(2) and (4) of the 1995 Act (deficiencies in the scheme assets) when ascertaining the amount or value of the assets or liabilities of a scheme.

Relationship between s.47 contribution notices and employer debts.

10.4.51   If a s.75 debt is due from the employer at the time that the s.47 contribution notice is issued, or if such a debt becomes due before the whole of the amount payable under the contribution notice has been recovered, the Regulator may issue a direction to the trustees or managers not to recover the s.75 debt pending the recovery of all or part of the debt due under the contribution notice. Failure to comply with the direction may give rise to civil penalties under s.10 of the 1995 Act. Amounts paid under the contribution notice reduce the amount of s.75 debts.

10.4.52   As with the corresponding provisions relating to contribution notices under s.41 of the Act, the payer may apply to the Regulator to have the amount specified in the s.47 notice reduced.

Implications for employers and others

10.4.53   It will no longer be possible to rely on the corporate veil to contain pension scheme shortfalls by using service companies or employers that are not financially strong enough to support the scheme. Associated and connected persons could become subject to an FSD.

10.4.54   In relation to corporate transactions, the existence of FSDs should be investigated, as should the existence of any enquiries or investigations by the Regulator that could lead to an FSD. If the definition of 'relevant time' confines the potential recipients of FSDs to associated and connected persons at the time they are made (as it seems they will) a purchaser will not need to be worried about future FSDs. Appropriate investigations, warranties and indemnities will be essential in respect of all company purchases involving non-money purchase schemes.

10.5   SECTION 73: PREFERENTIAL LIABILITIES

10.5.1   Section 73 of the 1995 Act (preferential liabilities on winding up) contains what is commonly referred to as the 'statutory priority order'.

10.5.2   Section 73 was made subject to transitional provisions from 6 April 1997 to 5 April 2007. Since 6 April 1997, the transitional statutory priority order has itself been amended.

10.5.3   Currently, the statutory priority order is broadly as follows:

Priority	Description
1	Liabilities derived from the payment of additional voluntary contributions (AVCs).
2	Liabilities secured by pre-6 April 1997 contracts of insurance which are either not surrenderable or where the surrender value does not exceed the liabilities secured by the contract (excluding liability for increases to pensions).
3	Pensions in payment (excluding increases to them).
4	Deferred members' benefits (excluding increases to them), future benefits referable to pension credits (but excluding increases to pensions) and refunds of contributions to members with less than 2 years' pensionable service.
5	Increases to the pensions described at 2 and 3 above.
6	Increases to the benefits described at 4 above.

10.5.4   The priority status of any benefit is assessed by reference to the 'crystallisation date' which for most schemes will be the date the scheme starts to wind up. The financial effect of the statutory priority order for members is determined by the date the scheme starts to wind up and in some cases on the status of the company.

10.5.5   Section 270 of the Act replaces s.73 of the 1995 Act with three new sections (ss.73, 73A and 73B). The new provisions are expected to come into force on 6 April 2005.

10.5.6   The new s.73 applies to an occupational pension scheme other than a money purchase scheme, or a prescribed scheme, or a scheme of a prescribed description. The statutory priority order under the new s.73 will be as follows:

Priority   **Description**

1   Liabilities secured by pre-6 April 1997 contracts of insurance which are either not surrenderable or where the surrender value does not exceed the liabilities secured by the contract.

2   Pension and other benefit liabilities which correspond to the liability to secure pension and other benefits at the level of the PPF compensation.

3   Liability for benefits derived from AVCs.

4   Any other liabilities.

10.5.7   The priority of pre-6 April 1997 insured benefits is therefore maintained.

10.5.8   The relegation of liabilities derived from AVCs (previously top priority) is something of a surprise. However, the effect of this is only likely to be felt in schemes where AVCs are applied to purchase additional benefits within the scheme, for example added years. This is because s.73(10) of the 1995 Act makes it clear that, for the purposes of s.73, the assets and liabilities of a scheme do not include any assets or liabilities in respect of money purchase benefits under the scheme rules. It is anticipated that most additional contribution facilities will therefore fall within the exclusion from s.73.

10.5.9   Where the relegation of AVCs does have effect, s.73(8) provides that regulations may prescribe how it is to be determined whether benefits derived from AVCs fall within priority 1 or priority 2 outlined above. At a more general level, if member perception in relevant schemes is that AVCs are personal top-up arrangements, there may well be a challenge to the priority order on the grounds that it violates personal property under the Human Rights Act 1998.

10.5.10   The key change however is to bring the statutory priority order into line with the operation of the PPF by the Board. Where the Board assumes responsibility for a scheme, the statutory priority order will be irrelevant. Where the Board does not assume responsibility for a scheme, the statutory priority order will apply.

10.5.11   It is thought that, for these purposes, where the PPF has been involved in relation to a scheme the valuation obtained by the Board will, when it has become a binding valuation, be conclusive. If no such valuation is available, for instance, where a 'scheme rescue' occurs, but the scheme has to wind up in any event, it is assumed that the trustees will have to commission their own actuary to undertake such a valuation.

10.5.12   An important difference of the new statutory priority order is that no distinction is made between pensioner and non-pensioner liabilities. Confusingly, s.73B(6) of the 1995 Act arguably could maintain the priority of pensions in payment. The DWP's view is that priority is afforded to a particular instalment of a pension in payment rather than the pension in payment itself. It will be interesting to see how a court interprets this provision in due course.

10.5.13   The new statutory priority order replicates the old one in requiring schemes' assets to be applied first towards satisfying liabilities appearing in strict priority order. Where a priority cannot be satisfied in full, the relevant liabilities must be satisfied in the same proportions.

10.5.14   Under s.73B(4) and (5) of the 1995 Act, regulations may:

(a) describe how the assets and liabilities of the scheme to which s.73 applies are to be determined, calculated and verified. In this regard, it is thought that reference may well be made to binding valuations obtained by the Board;
(b) modify ss.73, 73A and 74 in relation to schemes where only part of the scheme is being wound up and, in particular, as they apply in relation to a multi-employer scheme.

10.5.15   Section 73(7) of the 1995 Act provides that regulations may modify the statutory priority order itself.

Operation of scheme during winding-up period

10.5.16   Section 73A of the 1995 Act introduces a number of amendments and clarifications which will be welcomed by those involved in the winding up of pension schemes. Section 73A applies when an occupational pension scheme to which s.73 applies is being wound up.

10.5.17   Some provisions are self-evident, such as s.73A(3), which provides that no benefits accrue and no new members can be admitted to a scheme when it is winding up. Section 73B(1) provides that any action taken in contravention of s.73A(3) is void.

10.5.18   Under s.73A(2), trustees must ensure that any pensions, or other benefits, paid to or in respect of a member are reduced, so far as necessary, to reflect the liabilities of the scheme to or in respect of the member which will be satisfied in accordance with s.73. In this regard the trustees may take such steps as they consider appropriate to recover overpayments or to top-up underpayments.

10.5.19   The mandatory requirement to reduce benefits in line with s.73 liabilities cautions against trustees establishing or securing benefits (including transfer values) on a full and final settlement basis before the end of the wind up. However, the discretionary provision allowing for adjustments to benefits, so as to enable trustees to achieve precise s.73 compliance, appears to continue to give trustees the ability to establish benefits on both an interim basis (with adjustments at the end of the wind up) or on a full and final settlement basis before the end of the wind up. It will be interesting to see how practice develops in due course.

10.5.20   Section 73A(7) also provides for regulations requiring the adjustment of certain discretionary and survivor benefits which arise during the winding-up period.

10.5.21   There is also a general provision to modify those sections as they apply to 'prescribed schemes or prescribed descriptions of schemes'.

10.5.22   Section 73B(6) allows for regulations to prescribe circumstances in which certain liabilities which crystallised prior to the commencement of the wind up are to be unaffected by ss.73, 73A and 74.

10.5.23   Section 73B also contains several provisions which help to clarify the situation for wind-up practitioners. In particular, regulations may prescribe that in the case of death, benefits arising during a winding up in respect of the death of a member prior to the commencement of winding up, the member's entitlement to payment of the benefit is to be treated as having arisen immediately before the commencement of the winding up period. It also clarifies (without reference to further regulations) that where a person who is entitled to payment of a benefit has postponed payment of it, he is not to be regarded as having become entitled to payment of the benefit prior to commencement of the winding up. Well-advised members of schemes at risk of wind up are therefore unlikely to seek to work beyond their normal retirement date. This is contrary to the developing policy of extending the working life of UK employees.

Discharge of liabilities by insurance, etc. on winding up

10.5.24   The Act also makes minor modifications to s.74 of the 1995 Act. The key change is to increase the ways in which trustees can be statutorily discharged by including a reference to payment of a cash sum in circumstances where prescribed requirements are met. This will be a welcome addition for trustees as the payment of trivial cash sums on winding up can be a practical way of securing benefits for a great number of members.

10.6   THE REGULATOR'S POWERS

10.6.1   In addition to the new powers to issue contribution notices and financial support directions under the so-called 'moral hazard' provisions of the Act referred to above, the Regulator is also given various powers in relation to the winding up of occupational pension schemes.

Powers to wind up occupational pension schemes

10.6.2   Under s.11 of the 1995 Act, OPRA (which is to be replaced by the Regulator) has the power to wind up an occupational pension scheme in certain circumstances. These are:

(a) if the scheme or any part of it ought to be replaced by a different scheme;
(b) if the scheme is no longer required; or
(c) if it is necessary in order to protect the interests of the generality of the members.

10.6.3   With the exception of the latter circumstance, OPRA could only wind up the scheme if requested to do so by either the trustees or managers of the scheme, any person other than the trustees or managers who has power to alter any of the rules of the scheme, or the employer.

10.6.4   Section 22 amends s.11 of the 1995 Act, so that if the Regulator thinks that the scheme or any part of it ought to be replaced by a different scheme or that the scheme is no longer required, it can order that it be wound up, whether or not it has received a request to do so.

10.6.5   Section 22 further amends s.11 of the 1995 Act by inserting new sub-sections (3A) and (3B). The new sub-sections give the Regulator power, during an assessment period, to wind up an occupational pension scheme if it is satisfied that it is necessary to do so in order to ensure that the scheme's protected liabilities do not exceed its assets or, if those liabilities do exceed its assets, to keep the excess to a minimum. The 'assessment period' begins with the insolvency of the employer and ends on the occurrence of one of several events – see **para.3.3**. 'Protected liabilities' are defined in s.131 of the Act, and broadly comprise the equivalent cost of securing members' benefits under the PPF, liabilities that do not relate to members, and the estimated cost of winding up the scheme (see **para.3.2.32**).

10.6.6   New s.11(6A) is inserted into the 1995 Act to make it clear that the Regulator may not exercise its powers to wind up an occupational pension scheme if to do so would breach the Human Rights Act 1998.

Freezing orders

10.6.7   Sections 23 to 32 of the Act give the Regulator power to make a freezing order in relation to an occupational pension scheme where the Regulator is considering making an order for the winding up of the scheme under s.11 of the 1995 Act.

10.6.8   A freezing order may only be made if the Regulator is satisfied that there is, or is likely to be, an immediate risk to the interests of the members under the scheme or the assets of the scheme, and that it is necessary to protect the interests of the generality of members of the scheme (s.23(2)(b)).

10.6.9   A freezing order will direct that, whilst the order applies, no benefits are to accrue to or in respect of members, and that the scheme cannot be wound up (except by order of the Regulator). A freezing order may also contain various other directions, such as that, whilst the order applies, no new members shall be admitted to the scheme, no further contributions shall be paid, no benefits or specified benefits shall be paid, benefits (and transfers out) shall only be paid on a reduced basis (s.23(4)).

10.6.10   A freezing order must specify the period for which it has effect. However, that period must generally not exceed three months (although it can be extended on one or more occasion, provided that the total period does not exceed six months).

10.6.11   No freezing order may be made during an assessment period in relation to the scheme, and a freezing order ceases to have effect when an assessment period begins.

10.6.12   The Regulator can make an order under s.30 containing directions (a post-freezing order direction) that if 'specified conditions' are met then 'specified benefits' will continue to accrue in respect of 'specified members'. The 'specified conditions' may also contain a requirement that a contribution of a 'specified amount' must be paid by the employer within a 'specified period'.

10.6.13   If a post-freezing order direction is made under s.30 the Regulator must notify the trustees, managers and employer of the scheme of the effects of the direction as soon as reasonably practicable.

10.6.14   Any action taken in contravention of a freezing order is void except to the extent that the action is validated by the Regulator under s.26, and employees who are directly affected by any action taken in contravention of a freezing order may apply to the Regulator for an order validating the action under s.26. A similar power is not conferred on the Regulator to validate any action in contravention of a post-freezing order direction.

10.6.15   Section 24(7) provides that regulations may modify the protection in the 1993 Act for early leavers where a freezing order contains a direction which restricts transfers or the refund of contributions.

10.6.16   The Regulator may order the trustees or managers of the scheme to inform the members that a freezing order or a post-freezing order is in effect and of the effects of the order. The period in which this notification must take place will be specified in the order.

10.6.17   If the employer does not pay the 'specified contribution' within the 'specified period', then except in prescribed circumstances, the trustees or managers must, within a prescribed period, give notice of such failure to the Regulator and to the member.

10.6.18   Section 32(1) provides that any order made under any of ss.23, 25, 26, 28, 30 and 31 will override any act, rule of law or any rule of the scheme, which would otherwise operate to prevent the order being made. However, the Regulator may not make an order which would breach the Human Rights Act 1998.

10.6.19   Freezing orders may not be made in respect of money purchase schemes (s.23(1)).

10.6.20   Section 23(4)(c) provides that a freezing order may contain a direction that any member contributions which have been deducted by the employer whilst a freezing order is in effect shall be repaid to the member by the employer. Civil penalties apply where an employer, without reasonable excuse, fails to comply with a direction to repay such contributions.

Implications for trustees, employers and others

10.6.21   A freezing order will operate in much the same way as an interim injunction made by a court. It will enable the Regulator to 'freeze' a scheme where it is considering making a winding-up order in respect of the scheme in circumstances where the Regulator is satisfied that there is an immediate risk to the interests of its members or assets if the order is not made.

10.6.22   A freezing order is likely to result in either the Regulator making a winding-up order in relation to the scheme, or the Regulator making a post-freezing order direction whereby the employer will be required to make a 'specified contribution' to the scheme within a 'specified period'. If the employer does not pay the 'specified contribution', then the employer may be subject to civil penalties under s.10 of the 1995 Act, and the amount which remains unpaid will be treated as a debt due from the employer to the trustees or managers of the scheme.

10.6.23   A post-freezing order direction may change the balance of power between the employer and the trustees in relation to the scheme, both whilst the order has effect and after it ceases to have effect. For example, an order which requires the employer to make a 'specified contribution' within a 'specified period' would override the scheme's contribution rule.

10.6.24   The section does not specify a time period in which such post-freezing order directions can be made. Presumably, the power would be exercised on or about the time that the freezing order ceased to have effect.

10.6.25   In relation to corporate transactions, the existence of a freezing order and/or post-freezing order direction in relation to a scheme should be considered. Purchasers should seek disclosure in relation to any freezing order and/or post-freezing order direction which has been made in relation to the scheme and to any related notification made to members of the scheme, together with confirmation that the employer has complied with any such freezing order and/or direction.

Transactions at an undervalue

10.6.26   Sections 52–57 of the Act give the Regulator powers similar to those given to insolvency practitioners by the Insolvency Act 1986 in relation to transactions at an undervalue.

10.6.27   A transaction is 'at an undervalue' if it is made by the trustees or managers of the scheme (or by some other person prescribed by regulations entitled to exercise powers in relation to the scheme) in favour of a third party either by way of gift or on terms that the consideration provided by the third party is significantly less than the value of the consideration provided by or on behalf of the trustees.

10.6.28   Under s.52 of the Act, the Regulator has power, in certain circumstances, to make a restoration order if assets to which that section applies are transferred out of the scheme at an undervalue. The purpose of the restoration order is to restore the position to what it would have been had the transaction not been entered into.

10.6.29   A 'relevant event' must have occurred in relation to the employer of the scheme, and the transaction at an undervalue must have occurred on or after 27 April 2004 but not more than two years before the occurrence of the 'relevant event'.

10.6.30   For these purposes, a 'relevant event' is:

(a) an insolvency event (as described elsewhere in this chapter) which occurs in relation to the employer on or after a date to be determined by regulations; or
(b) an application by the trustees of the scheme to the Board to take over responsibility for the scheme on or after a date to be determined by regulations; or
(c) receipt by the trustees of a notice from the Board that it has taken over responsibility for the scheme on or after a date to be determined by regulations.

10.6.31   The ability to make a restoration order will be affected if the current owner of the relevant property acquired the property in good faith for value (or subsequently acquired the property following its acquisition in good faith for value), in which case it would not be possible to make an effective restoration order in respect of that person. The Regulator could, however, make a restoration order requiring the payment of a sum of money in respect of the first person to enter into the transaction, if that person received a benefit as a result of the transaction otherwise than in good faith and for value.

10.6.32   If the person benefiting from a transaction at an undervalue is one of the trustees or managers or other prescribed persons entitled to exercise powers in relation to the scheme, there will be a rebuttable presumption that the benefit was not received in good faith. This also applies if the recipient of the benefit was a trustee or manager or employer of the scheme at the time of the acquisition or the recipient knew that the transaction was a transaction at an undervalue.

Persons connected or associated with a trustee or manager or employer, or other prescribed persons are also caught by this presumption. The definitions of 'connected' and 'associated' persons are those used in the Insolvency Act 1986 (ss.249 and 435 respectively). See **para.10.4.4** for the relevant definitions.

Meaning of 'property'

10.6.33   The types of property that might be the subject of a transaction at an undervalue include tangible and intangible assets, obligations and future and contingent property.

Effect of a restoration order

10.6.34   If the restoration order requires the payment of a sum of money, that sum is to be treated as a debt due from the person required to pay it. Consequently, the person to whom the debt is owed (usually the trustees/managers of the scheme) will be able to sue for recovery of the debt and will rank as an unsecured creditor, in respect of that debt, in the event of the insolvency of the debtor. The Regulator has certain powers to pursue the payment of the debt. If the scheme is in an assessment period, only the Board may pursue recovery of the debt.

Contribution notice on failure to comply with restoration order

10.6.35   If a restoration order is made for a non-monetary amount, and the person subject to the order fails to comply with it, the Regulator may issue a contribution notice to that person requiring that person to pay a specified amount to the trustees or managers (or, if appropriate, to the Board). The sum specified may be part or all of the amount by which the scheme's assets (as estimated by the Regulator) have decreased as a result of the transaction at an undervalue.

10.6.36   The sum specified in the contribution notice will constitute a debt due. The person to whom the debt is owed (either the trustees/managers of the scheme or the Board) will be able to sue for recovery of the debt and will rank as an unsecured creditor, in respect of that debt, in the event of the insolvency of the debtor.

Transaction by employer to defraud pension scheme

10.6.37   Under s.423 of the Insolvency Act 1986, if it can be established to the satisfaction of a court that a participating employer has entered into a transaction at an undervalue (for example by way of a group reorganisation) and that the aim of that transaction was to avoid its liabilities to its pension scheme, an application may be made to court for an order to restore the position to what it would have been had the transaction not been entered into. It is likely that the trustees of a scheme would be entitled to make such an application to the court. Section 58 of the Act extends this power to the Regulator if certain conditions are met. For the Regulator to be able to make such an application, either:

(a) an actuarial valuation under s.143 of the Act (and made by reference to a date falling after s.58 comes into force) indicates that the value of the assets of the scheme at the relevant time was less than the amount of the protected liabilities, or

(b) an actuarial valuation obtained by the trustees or managers of the scheme (and made by reference to a date falling after s.58 comes into force) indicates that the statutory funding objective in s.222 of the Act is not met.

10.6.38   The Regulator must apply for permission from the court before making an application where the participating employer is being wound up or where an administration order is in force in relation to that participating employer.

Implications for trustees and employers

10.6.39   The ability of the Regulator to issue restoration orders will, to some extent, focus the minds of trustees in ensuring that scheme assets are transferred at a fair value. Most trustees are, however, already well aware of their duties of good faith and to act in the best interests of the members of the scheme. Presumably, the new provisions are therefore intended to cover Maxwell-type scenarios, whilst well-run schemes should be unaffected by them.

10.6.40   Employers should ensure that, where it has an occupational pension scheme that is in deficit, or is likely to fall into deficit in the future, transactions into which it enters could not be interpreted as having as one of its objectives the avoidance of a debt on the employer. In particular, where group reorganisations take place in which assets are transferred from an employer to a holding, subsidiary or sister company, and where it is important for other reasons that the transaction is not set aside, the employer should ensure that the minutes of the directors' meeting at which the transaction is approved accurately record the reasons for the group reorganisation.

10.6.41   The provisions relating to the Regulator's power to wind up a scheme apply to all occupational pension schemes. The powers given to the Regulator in relation to transactions at an undervalue apply in relation to all occupational pension schemes except those schemes that are money purchase schemes, or prescribed schemes.

10.7   IMPLICATIONS FOR INSOLVENCY PRACTITIONERS

10.7.1   The Act both takes away and gives responsibilities to insolvency practitioners. The key provisions of the Act relevant to insolvency practitioners are the appointment of independent trustees (s.36) and the disclosure of information (ss.120–125).

Independent trustees

10.7.2   Prior to the implementation of the Act, insolvency practitioners had the duty, in certain circumstances, to appoint an independent trustee to an occupational pension scheme. Section 36 of the Act removes that duty from the insolvency practitioner and vests it in the Regulator instead.

10.7.3   The insolvency practitioner must, as soon as reasonably practicable, notify the Regulator, the Board and the trustees of the affected scheme when certain events occur. An example of such an event is where a practitioner begins to act in relation to an employer and immediately before that time the independent trustee provisions of the 1995 Act did not apply to the scheme. Similar provisions apply to the Official Receiver.

10.7.4   The Regulator has the power to appoint an independent trustee by order. Such a trustee must be a person whose name appears in a register to be compiled and maintained by the Regulator. The independence of such trustees will be measured against criteria contained in the new s.23 of the 1995 Act and which reflect the criteria used under the 1995 Act prior to the coming into force of the Act.

10.7.5   Section 25 of the 1995 Act is amended to the effect that, where an independent trustee has ceased to be an independent person, he must notify the Regulator in writing as soon as possible. Civil penalties under s.10 of the 1995 Act will apply if there is any failure to comply with these provisions without reasonable excuse.

10.7.6   The order appointing the independent trustee may provide for certain matters, such as how the fees and expense of the independent trustees are to be met. The order may provide for such fees and expenses to be borne by the employer and/or the scheme, or a combination of the two. The order may also provide for amounts paid from the scheme to be treated as a debt due from the employer. Any fees and expenses taken from the scheme will take priority over all other claims on the scheme.

Information relating to insolvency events

10.7.7   The Act imposes new obligations on an insolvency practitioner to provide information relating to an employer's insolvency (ss.120–125).

10.7.8   Section 120 imposes a duty upon the insolvency practitioner appointed to act in relation to an employer who has experienced an insolvency event (see above) to notify the Board, the Regulator and the scheme trustees of the occurrence of that event within the 'notification period'. The notification period is defined as the period beginning with the later of either the insolvency date, or the date on which the insolvency practitioner becomes aware that a scheme exists in relation to the employer (s.120(3)).

10.7.9   Under s.122, the insolvency practitioner is obliged to confirm the status of a scheme after the happening of an insolvency event in relation to the

employer. If an insolvency practitioner is able to confirm that either a scheme rescue is not possible or that a scheme rescue has occurred, the practitioner must
issue a notice to that effect. If the practitioner cannot decide whether or not a
scheme rescue is possible, the practitioner must issue a notice to that effect.
Whether or not the practitioner can issue a notice will depend on the matters to
be prescribed by regulations.

10.7.10   Notices issued under s.122 must be copied to the Board, the Regulator
and the scheme trustees. The notice requirements must be complied with as soon
as reasonably practicable.

10.7.11   Where the Board receives a s.122 notice from the insolvency practitioner, the Board must determine whether to approve the notice. The Board
must approve the notice only if it is satisfied that the notice was required to have
been issued and that the notice complies with the requirements of s.122. The
Board's subsequent 'determination notice' issued under s.123 must be copied to
the Regulator, the trustees or managers of the scheme, the insolvency practitioner
who issued the s.122 notice or any other insolvency practitioner in relation to the
employer, or, if there is no insolvency practitioner, the employer. A notice under
s.122 only becomes binding in the circumstances set out in s.125.

10.7.12   Where there is a failure to comply with s.122, the Board takes on the
obligations imposed on the insolvency practitioner with regard to issuing a
notice.

Conclusion

10.7.13   The new provisions relating to independent trustees should generally
make life simpler for insolvency practitioners. Once the insolvency practitioner
has issued a notice to the Regulator and others confirming his appointment or
confirming that his appointment has come to an end, it will be for the Regulator
to consider such matters as whether a trustee is needed, the independence of the
proposed trustee and the making of the appointment.

10.7.14   It should be noted that under the revised s.23 of the 1995 Act, the
Regulator merely has the *power* to appoint an independent trustee, rather than a
duty to do so. It remains to be seen how and in what circumstances the Regulator
will choose to exercise that power, and perhaps more importantly, in what circumstances the Regulator will choose not to exercise it, leaving a scheme in the
hands of a trusteeship with no 'independent' representation.

10.7.15   The insolvency practitioner will, however, be interested in the content
of the Regulator's order appointing the independent trustee, not least in relation
to the payment of the independent trustee's fees and expenses. If such fees and
expenses are ordered to be treated as a debt due from the employer, such a debt
would presumably rank alongside other unsecured creditors in the insolvency
and must be dealt with accordingly.

10.7.16   In relation to the new requirements for disclosure of information, the effect on the insolvency practitioner is likely to be minimal, with the practitioner's role effectively being limited to passing on information to the Regulator and others.

10.7.17   However, the provisions requiring the practitioner to form a view (or confirm that he cannot form a view) on whether a 'scheme rescue' can be achieved are currently somewhat sketchy. It is to be hoped that regulations will provide more guidance on what the notices required under this section will entail.

11 TRUSTEES' STANDARD OF CARE

11.1 INTRODUCTION

This chapter looks firstly at the events leading up to the introduction of the Act in order to understand more clearly why the changes have been introduced. It then considers the impact of the provisions of the Act in respect of the trustees' duties and their standard of care. Finally, it considers the practical implications of the new provisions for trustees.

11.2 THE RECENT BACKGROUND

The Myners Review of Institutional Investment in the UK

11.2.1 The Myners Review was instigated by the Government in 2000 in order to assess the effectiveness of institutional investment decision-making. Paul Myners was widely critical of trustees' behaviour and skill levels and proposed sets of principles to govern investment decision-making ('Myners Principles') for best practice in defined benefit and defined contribution schemes. When the Government set out its formal response to the Myners Principles in October 2001, it accepted the vast majority of Myners' original proposals. While it might be thought that the scope of the Myners Review was limited to one, albeit important, area of trustees' activities, it has nevertheless acted as a catalyst for change in trustee duties and the standard of care expected of trustees more generally.

11.2.2 The Government expected all occupational pension schemes (apart from insured schemes) to comply with the Myners Principles. For insured schemes it has proposed that the Myners Principles would not apply and, instead the recommendations of the Sandler Review of Medium and Long Term Retail Savings would apply. The corporate governance issues associated with product design and decision-making for such products have been addressed via Financial Services Act regulation and, most recently, in Treasury proposals for so-called 'stakeholder' savings and investment products (Treasury consultation issued in June 2004). The Myners Principles were published on the basis that compliance with them was voluntary, although the Government 'expects pension funds will publicly disclose' how they comply with the Myners Principles and therefore also expects (in a mandatory sense) trustees to explain to members how they have departed from the Myners Principles, and to justify why they have done so.

11.2.3   In itself, this requirement for justification of one's actions runs counter to one of the fundamental legal principles which support the concept of a private trust in English law, that where trustees are exercising a discretionary power they need not disclose why they have done so (*Re Beloved Wilkes's Charity* (1851) 3 Mac & G 440) and they may accordingly refuse to allow a beneficiary to inspect documents which reveal such information (*Re Londonderry's Settlement* [1965] 2 WLR 229).

11.2.4   The Government said originally that, if it was not satisfied by March 2003 that adoption of the Myners Principles across the pension fund industry as a whole had brought about 'effective change', it intended to legislate. The National Association of Pension Funds was asked to assist in the assessment of, both qualitatively and quantitatively, the take up of the Myners Principles, which were the subject of both detailed case studies of individual funds and a large sample survey which would differentiate between different sizes of funds. The Government originally expressed the measure of success which would obviate the need for legislation in absolute terms, so that it was looking for an 'increase towards 100% in the proportion of funds (defined benefit and defined contribution) which have produced a statement setting out, principle by principle, their compliance with the principles'. It also expected an 'increase towards 100% of funds which have sent their members this statement'.

11.2.5   In December 2004, the Government published its review of progress on the level of compliance with the Myners Principles by defined benefit schemes. The research revealed that, in a number of key areas, trustees had not taken sufficient action to demonstrate compliance with the Myners Principles. The Government review therefore contained revisions to a number of the Myners Principles, the detail of which is beyond the scope of this chapter. However, the most significant changes do concern some fundamental shifts in trustees' standard of care.

11.2.6   Firstly, the Government believes that the chairman of a board of trustees should assume the particular responsibility of ensuring that where trustees take investment decisions they should be familiar with investment issues and also that the board as a whole has sufficient trustees for that purpose. While this recommendation falls short of attempting to impose a power of appointment of investment experts as new trustees, it does represent a change in the role of the chairman. It imposes the type of duty one might expect in a corporate context but which does not sit happily with the fundamental principle of trust law of joint and several liability. For very large schemes (defined by the Government as those with over 5000 members), the Government suggested further increasing the chairman's responsibilities by stipulating that he and at least one third of the trustees should be familiar with investment issues, notwithstanding the fact that it is good practice to put an investment sub-committee in place to take investment decisions. Finally, the Government clarified the fact that not only should trustees report to members on the monitoring of their advisers' and fund managers' performance, but they should also report on their own performance.

11.2.7   Therefore, although compliance was always voluntary, trustees and their advisers have had to take the Myners Principles seriously. Simply ignoring the detail of the Myners Principles is likely to have a negative effect for regulation and how UK pension schemes are run generally in the longer term. In fact, the debate over voluntary compliance has to some extent been subsumed in wider legislative developments. However, at the time of writing, the Government has indicated that it will review compliance with the Myners Principles again in 2007, when it will decide whether 'policy action' will be necessary.

11.2.8   Notwithstanding the voluntary nature of compliance with the Myners Principles as a whole, the Government accepted that one recommendation of Myners would need to be enforced through legislation, namely that there should be a legal requirement that where trustees are taking a decision related to investments, the trustees should be able to do so with the skill and care of someone familiar with the issues concerned.

11.2.9   The formulation of the duty which was proposed by Myners is derived from s.404a(1)(B) of the US ERISA. This was that trustees should:

'act with the care, skill, prudence and diligence under the circumstances then prevailing that a prudent person acting in a like capacity and familiar with such matters would use in the conduct of an enterprise of like character and with like aims.'

11.2.10   In addition, where a pension scheme trustee has, or holds himself out as having, any special knowledge or experience, Myners proposed that he must exercise such care and skill as is reasonable in the circumstances. Similarly, where a pension scheme trustee acts in the course of a business or profession, he must exercise such skill as is reasonable in the circumstances, having regard to any special knowledge or experience that it is reasonable to expect of a person acting in the course of that kind of business or profession.

11.2.11   Myners also recommended that the US principles on shareholder activism should be incorporated into English law, making it a duty to intervene in the affairs of companies where it is in shareholders' and beneficiaries' interests. After consultation the Government instead endorsed a code which maintains the voluntary nature of compliance with the activism requirements but it recommended that trustees should ensure there is a contractual obligation, where relevant on their fund managers to comply with the code. For further discussions on shareholder activism see **para.6.2.20.**

11.3   A NEW STANDARD OF CARE?

11.3.1   To require familiarity with investment matters where trustees are taking investment decisions raises two key issues: what standard of care does the law currently expect of trustees generally and can trustees exclude liability for breach of that duty? Judged against the common law test of the level of expertise expected of trustees generally, which derives from Victorian cases such as *Re Whiteley* (1886) 33 Ch D 347, where the court held that a trustee must 'take such care as an ordinary prudent man would take if minded to make investments for the benefit of other people for whom he felt morally bound to provide', the new standard of familiarity does represent a significant advance. However, it would be misleading to think that the law in this area of trustees' duties of care has not advanced at all since the nineteenth century.

The Trustee Act 2000 – the statutory duty of care

11.3.2   The Trustee Act 2000 imposed a statutory duty of care as a default position 'unless it appears from the trust instrument that the duty is not meant to apply'. This duty, as set out in s.1(1) is as follows:

'Whenever the duty under this subsection applies to a trustee, he must exercise such skill and care as is reasonable in the circumstances, having regard in particular–

(a) to any special knowledge or experience that he has or holds himself out as having; and
(b) if he acts as trustee in the course of a business or profession, to any special knowledge or experience that it is reasonable to expect of a person acting in the course of that kind of business or profession.'

11.3.3   However, paras.1 and 3 of Sched.1 to the Trustee Act 2000 exclude the application of that Act to pension scheme trustees when exercising their powers of investment or when they are using custodians or nominees.

The current law – the 1995 Act

11.3.4   So what does the law currently expect of pension trustees? The Act does contain some guidance for pension scheme trustees on the duty of care which is expected in relation to investment matters, which is presumably why s.1 of the Trustee Act 2000 does not apply in that situation. Section 33(1) of the 1995 Act (investment powers: duty of care) provides:

'Liability for breach of an obligation under any rule of law to take care or exercise skill in the performance of any investment functions, where the function is exercisable:

(a) by a trustee of a trust scheme or,
(b) by a person to whom the function has been delegated under s.34 [an authorised fund manager]

cannot be excluded or restricted by any instrument or agreement.'

11.3.5   The fact that trustees (and fund managers for that matter) cannot *exclude* liability for any breach of their investment duties to members of a scheme does not, of itself, imply a particular duty of skill, care, knowledge or expertise. However, there are other provisions of the 1995 Act which do help in defining the way in which investment powers must be exercised. These are as follows.

(a) Subject to any restriction imposed by the scheme, trustees have as wide a power of investment as they would have if they were the absolute beneficial owners of the assets of the scheme (s.34(1)).

(b) Trustees must prepare, maintain and from time to time revise a written Statement of Investment Principles ('SIP') governing decisions about investments (s.35(1)).

(c) Trustees and fund managers must have regard to the need for diversification of investments and the suitability to the scheme of investments generally and specifically (s.36(2)) (this duty was previously imposed by s.6(1) of the Trustee Investment Act 1961).

(d) Trustees must take 'proper advice' before investing in any manner, and, if the advice relates to investments regulated under the Financial Services and Markets Act 2000 (FSMA 2000), such proper advice being obtained from a person who is authorised under the FSMA 2000 to give investment advice (s.36(3)) (a 'proper advice' requirement was imposed by s.6(2) of the Trustee Investment Act 1961).

11.3.6   If the new Myners standards had been confined to investment decisions alone, it might have been implied that trustees would be under a higher standard of care in relation to investment matters than they were in respect of non-investment matters. This would hardly have been a desirable outcome for trustees, if so, and might, presumably, have led to a separate breed of investment specialist trustees. However, the Government said that it was not its intention that trustees should need to become investment experts and it accepted representations that in fact a new duty should apply across the board where trustees exercise any function. This is covered by the Act.

11.4   CHANGES TO TRUSTEES' DUTY AND STANDARDS OF CARE

New trustee obligations under the Act

11.4.1   Sections 247 and 248 of the Act will implement Myners' original recommendations in an expanded form, by introducing new statutory obligations on, respectively, individual trustees and corporate trustees to be 'conversant with' certain scheme documents and have 'knowledge and understanding' of certain matters. The DWP has indicated that these provisions will come into force in April 2006.

Two standards of care

11.4.2   There are two standards imposed by the Act. The first is in relation to scheme specific matters, such as the trust deed and rules, the SIP, the most recent statement of funding principles and any other document recording policy on the administration of the scheme, where the trustee in question must be 'conversant with' those specific documents. Under the second standard, trustees must have 'knowledge and understanding of' the following matters:

(a) the law relating to pensions and trusts;
(b) the principles of funding of occupational pension schemes and the investment of such scheme's assets, and any other matters to be prescribed.

11.4.3   The Regulator will issue guidance under a Code of Practice as to the degree of knowledge, training, experience or qualifications regarded as necessary to fulfil the above requirements, although it should be noted that the yardstick by which the requirements will be measured is whether or not the individual possesses the requisite knowledge and understanding in order to exercise his functions properly as a trustee. If, therefore, the individual is not exercising a given function because, for example, he is not a member of a particular sub-committee, it could be argued that he has no need to acquire the relevant knowledge. (However, this argument would not apply to the chairman of a trustee board in relation to investment matters under the latest revisions of the Myners Principles, see **para.11.2.5**.) Although ease of administration may require schemes to structure themselves in this way, there are dangers in such a course of action, given that, as a matter of trust law, each trustee is liable for the actions and omissions of his fellow trustees and one would, therefore, expect trustees to want to be able to evaluate critically what they are doing as a whole (in line with one of Myners' other recommendations).

11.4.4   It is not yet clear what is meant by 'documents recording the policy of trustees in relation to scheme administration', but, presumably, this would extend beyond scheme booklets and announcements to members (with which trustees would be expected to be familiar in any event) to contractual arrangements entered into by the trustees with third parties. This could include investment management agreements, scheme administration agreements and operating guidelines for administrators and actuarial appointment letters.

11.4.5   The use of two different terms in ss.247 and 248 ('conversant with' and 'knowledge and understanding') raises some interesting questions as to the standard of care expected of trustees. We will have to wait for the Regulator to issue its code of practice and possibly the courts to interpret these terms, although it would seem rather unfair, for instance, to expect an encyclopaedic knowledge of pensions and trust law to be acquired by every trustee. On the other hand, it would seem more reasonable to expect a trustee to know and understand the scheme documents. At the very least, the trustee should know enough to know what he does *not* know and where there are areas of doubt in the documents.

11.4.6   The documents which are likely to fall under the category of 'scheme documents' is for the trustees themselves to determine but the authors envisage that at least the following will be included:

(a) scheme booklet, announcements and other communications;
(b) the most recent actuarial valuation and subsequent actuarial advice;
(c) minutes of meetings (for relevant previous decisions);

(d) schedule of contributions or payment schedule;
(e) annual report and accounts;
(f) documents from any pension provider and any relevant insurance policy;
(g) any agreement or contract to which the trustees are a party;
(h) matters relating to the trustee bank account (e.g. signatories' obligations etc.);
(i) the procedures manual (including the internal disputes resolution (IDR) procedure and the member nominated trustee (MNT) arrangements);
(j) any control reports relating to administration and service level agreements with scheme administration providers.

Supplementary provisions under the Act

11.4.7   Section 249 contains some supplementary provisions and states that the application of the new duties does not affect any other rule of law affecting trustees' knowledge or expertise. This is no doubt a nod to the judgment in *Bartlett v. Barclays Bank Trust Co. Ltd (No. 1)* [1980] 2 WLR 430, which established that the law expected a higher degree of knowledge of professional trustees who hold out that they have a particular expertise which non-professional trustees would not claim to have. It may also refer to the provisions of s.33(1) of the 1995 Act quoted above, which prevents trustees from excluding liability for breaches of their investment functions.

11.4.8   It is anticipated that regulations made under s.247 will either not apply (or may apply with modifications) to newly appointed trustees until a reasonable 'period of grace' has passed, to trustees who are sole members of a scheme, or to trustees of a small self-administered scheme.

'Conversant with'

11.4.9   The Act provides that each individual who is a trustee of an occupational pension scheme (s.247(3)) or a director of a corporate trustee (s.248(4)) must, in respect of the scheme to which the individual is a trustee, be conversant with the following:

(a) the trust deed and rules;
(b) the SIP (maintained under s.35 of the 1995 Act);
(c) the statement of funding principles (if applicable);
(d) the policy documents.

11.4.10   OPRA has produced a helpful 'scope document', which although at the time of writing was still a work in progress, is useful in providing guidance as to some of the items of knowledge, understanding and conversance which trustees might be expected to cover to comply with the requirements of the Act. OPRA's guidance indicates that 'conversant with' is intended to mean 'familiar with' and, whilst there are undoubtedly legal precedents dealing with the meaning of this phrase it seems likely that the Regulator will adopt this common sense approach.

11.4.11   The typical areas in respect of the trust deed and rules that trustees should be 'familiar with' are likely to include:

(a) the duties and responsibilities of trustees under their own trust deed and scheme rules;
(b) the key powers within the trust deed and the balance of those powers between employer and trustees including powers relating to the setting of contributions, amendment, transfers, and powers in response to specific events or corporate activity;
(c) classes of beneficiaries (i.e. members) in their scheme including eligibility for membership, the benefits payable to all members, and how those benefits are paid;
(d) insurance policies and any other documents governing the scheme or its benefits.

'Knowledge and understanding'

11.4.12   Sections 247(4) (for an individual trustee) and 248(5) (for a corporate trustee) provide that individuals who are individual trustees or directors of a corporate trustee of an occupational pension scheme must have knowledge and understanding of:

(a) the law relating to pensions and trusts;
(b) the principles relating to the funding of occupational pension schemes; and
(c) such matters as may be prescribed.

11.4.13   According to ss.247(5) and 248(6) of the Act, the degree of knowledge and understanding is subjective, being the degree appropriate for the purposes of enabling the individual to properly exercise the function in question. The Regulator is expected to issue guidance on the standards required.

11.5   CODES OF PRACTICE

11.5.1   In June 2002 the Trustee Code of Practice Group chaired by Brian Holden MBE launched the first independently produced set of guidelines for trustees called 'A Code of Practice for Pension Scheme Trustees'. The Code summarises trustees' responsibilities and sets out an overall picture of what being a trustee means, the roles trustees play, the framework within which they work, and how to find information and advice. This has been seen as 'best practice' for trustees, but compliance has been purely voluntary.

Role of OPRA

11.5.2   One of OPRA's current means of communicating with trustees is to issue memoranda (OPRA notes) on topics of interest or concern for the industry. This practice will continue but be given a statutory footing under the Act via the Regulator issuing Codes of Practice under s.90. The Codes may be of two types:

(a) they may give practice guidance in relation to the exercise of functions under pensions legislation (defined as the 1993 Act, the 1995 Act (excluding any rules relating to equal treatment), Part 1 and s.33 of the 1999 Act (stakeholder pensions and pension credits arising on divorce) and the Act); or

(b) they may represent the Regulator's interpretation of 'the standards of conduct and practice expected from those who exercise such functions'.

Mandatory codes of practice

11.5.3 While the Act gives the Regulator a general power to issue Codes of Practice in relation to 'pensions legislation' as defined above, it is subject to a statutory requirement to issue Codes of Practice on the subjects set out in the table included in the Appendix to this Chapter. In addition, the Regulator must issue Codes of Practice on:

(a) what constitutes a 'reasonable' period for the purposes of any provision of pensions legislation (other than anything related to the PPF) which requires any action to be taken within such a period; and

(b) such other matters as are prescribed.

11.6   IMPLICATIONS FOR TRUSTEES

Exercise of trustees' functions by committee

11.6.1   Under s.247(5) the degree of knowledge and understanding by which a trustee would be judged is that which is 'appropriate for the purposes of enabling the individual properly to exercise his functions as trustee of any relevant scheme' (s.248(6) contains a comparable provision in relation to directors of a corporate trustee).

11.6.2   Section 249(1) goes on to elaborate on the word 'functions' by specifying that for the purposes of ss.247 and 248, a person's:

> 'functions as trustee of a relevant scheme are any functions which he has by virtue of being such a trustee and include, in particular –
>
> (a) any functions which he has as one of the trustees authorised under section 34(5)(a) of the Pensions Act 1995 (c.26) (delegation of investment discretions) in the case of the scheme, and
>
> (b) any functions which he otherwise has as a member of the committee of the trustees of the scheme.'

11.6.3   The Act does not address the question of whether, because these sections link the standard of care expected of a given trustee as an individual to the functions exercised, a trustee who does not exercise those functions could be held liable for the actions or omissions of his fellow trustee.

11.6.4   As a general principle, if an individual has had nothing to do with the exercise of a particular function which, it turns out, was made without regard to the expected standard of knowledge and understanding which applied to that particular function, it would seem unfair to punish him. In a criminal prosecution by OPRA in July 1999 (*Biltons Tableware Limited (in receivership)*, reported only in OPRA Bulletin 11), the Crown Court found a managing director not guilty after he had claimed that he had no knowledge of the failure to pay employees' contributions to the scheme, since this was a matter that he had delegated to the finance director (who had pleaded guilty to the offence). The judge directed the jury in that case that:

> 'a company director was entitled under company law principles to delegate to a fellow director the responsibility for matters falling within that director's area of management . . . While the managing director's lack of understanding of the company's financial position might reflect on his abilities as a director, it did not amount to consent, neglect or connivance in relation to offences under the Pensions Act 1995.'

11.6.5   Despite this ruling, the trust law rule that trustees are jointly and severally liable is likely to take precedence. The principle of joint and several liability of trustees is a long-standing one and there are numerous early authorities supporting it (see, for example, *Fletcher* v. *Green* (1864) 33 Beav 426). Until the introduction of the Civil Liability (Contribution) Act 1978, the courts required that the joint liability of trustees meant that there would be an equal sharing of the liability, regardless of fault. However, under that Act, the court has a discretion in relation to the amount to be recovered against two or more defendants who are liable in respect of damage. This is an equitable jurisdiction and includes breach of trust as one of the forms of liability to which the Act applies (s.6(1)). However, the Civil Liability (Contribution) Act 1978 does not apply to situations in which one trustee is entitled to an indemnity (s.7(3)).

11.6.6   It would be unusual to find a trust deed and rules or the terms of reference of a sub-committee which expressly dealt with the liability of the members of that particular committee. As a practical point, it would seem to be unworkable to fix particular trustees who agree to act on a particular committee with liability for the actions of that committee and one would expect trustees as a whole to want to be able to evaluate what the committee was doing (in line with Myners' recommendations on trustees' self-assessment). However, the latest amendments to the Myners Principles in relation to the position of trustee chairmen (see **para.11.2.5**) run counter to this argument.

11.6.7   As far as investment sub-committees are concerned, s.34(5) of the 1995 Act makes it clear that, even where the authority to take investment decisions has been delegated to a sub-committee of two or more trustees, 'the trustees are liable for any acts or defaults in the exercise of the discretion if they would be so liable if they were the actual default of the trustees as a whole'. Because of the way in which s.34(5)(a) is drafted, investment sub-committees should not give any powers to take investment decisions to non-trustees if such people are permitted to be members of the committee.

Differences in treatment for corporate trustee and individual trustees

11.6.8   It is notoriously difficult to make directors of a limited trustee company personally liable. In *HR & Others* v. *JAPT & Others* [1997] PLR 1999 the individual directors were also officers of the principal employer and made certain decisions in relation to the affairs of the scheme that clearly favoured the interests of the employer to the detriment of members' interests. In respect of a potential claim against the individual directors, Mr Justice Lindsay decided that directors did not have a direct fiduciary duty to scheme members and for a court to 'pierce the corporate veil' and render a trustee director personally liable, it would be necessary to establish concealment of facts and/or some element of dishonesty on the part of the individual director.

11.6.9   There are limited circumstances where claims could be brought against individual trustee directors of pension schemes, but these are beyond the ambit of this text.

11.6.10   Under s.248 of the Act, the onus is on the trustee company itself to comply with the requirements for knowledge and understanding. In the event that individual trustee directors were to fail to discharge their duties to do so, the trustee company would be liable to pay any regulatory fine arising (note the absence of any express sanction under the section itself), and would also be exposed in respect of a claim for damages for breach of trust or maladministration. However, unless there is an express requirement for the director to discharge the specific trustee duties in the memorandum and articles of the trustee company (or in a service contract between the company and each individual director) the trustee company is likely to be unable to enforce performance of the trustee duties. Nor will it have any way to recover against the director for non-performance of the duties.

11.6.11   As the trustee company's exposure is limited to its paid up capital, it is questionable whether additional precautions should be taken by corporate trustees to ensure they have a right of action against directors in respect of the performance of their trustee duties. However, it may be useful in future to double check the governing documentation of a corporate trustee to confirm that appropriate steps have been taken to reduce potential liability.

11.7   SOME PRACTICAL POINTS

Decisions and records

11.7.1   Currently, s.49(2) of the 1995 Act only requires trustees formally to maintain records of their meetings (including sub-committee meetings) and any books and records relating to 'prescribed transactions'. The Act does not enlarge upon this list of specific record-keeping requirements. However, the issue of codes of practice by the Regulator (and the accompanying expectation that trustees will adhere to those codes unless they have good reason not to do so), together with the increasingly litigious environment in which trustees operate, mean that it is good practice to establish records of how and when decisions were reached and on what basis (although there would be no claim for a breach of a statutory duty in not adhering to a code of practice).

11.7.2   Under trust law trustees are not required to provide reasons for their decisions neither can they be required by the courts to do so. The Pensions Ombudsman has however indicated that pension scheme trustees should provide members with reasons for their decisions and, where appropriate, copies of minutes of trustee meetings and other relevant documents.

11.7.3   The Data Protection Act 1998 has also increased the likelihood of the trustees having to disclose reasons for their decisions. A beneficiary of a scheme may make a 'subject access' request under that Act. This request may include a request for sight of trustee minutes. If those minutes are in computer or auto-mated form then any personal data in those minutes which relates to that indi-vidual would normally have to be disclosed (without disclosing data relating to another individual).

11.7.4   A balance should be struck when compiling scheme minutes relating to the exercise of a discretion to demonstrate good practice, review of appropriate documents, consideration of relevant factors and powers, with a sufficient audit trail to assist the trustees to defend any decision. It would be sensible for the scheme's legal adviser to review the format of the minutes to check that the trustees comply with good practice.

Trustee training

11.7.5   The Act requires trustees to be conversant with their scheme documents and to have knowledge and understanding of the law relating to pensions and trusts and the principles relating to funding of occupational pension schemes and investments. This is a substantial amount of information, much of which is of a complex nature, and this points to a need for increased trustee training. This is not a new concept, however. Myners recommended that trustee training be improved, but even so such training does not appear to be commonplace amongst all schemes. An OPRA survey in 2003 looked into the type of training being pro-vided to pension scheme trustees. It found that introductory level training was the most common course and for newly appointed trustees the only distinct form of training. Amongst established trustees, scheme bespoke training, investment training and advanced level training were popular.

11.7.6   Whilst recognising the importance of trustee training to ensure higher standards of trusteeship there is a danger that it will add to the already increasing pressures on occupational pension schemes. Although training may sound like a simple concept it could be difficult to implement in practice. Trustees have very different backgrounds and experiences, whilst schemes are also varied. As a result, the same training would not be appropriate to all trustees/schemes.

11.7.7 The training needs to be tailored and effective, it is not acceptable just to pay lip service to the concept. Ensuring that training is in fact provided and attended would be difficult to police. There is also the issue of accrediting the training provided. There will presumably need to be a mechanism for trustees to show that they had reached a certain level of knowledge or competency at the end of the training. Knowledge will have to be kept up-to-date, as training is an on-going requirement, it is not simply a process to be undertaken on first becoming a trustee.

11.7.8 The cost of the training and the cost of setting up and running an approval system could be material: who should pay, the fund or the employer? It must be remembered that employers are not obliged to provide pension funds, it is simply good practice to do so.

Increased claims to the Pensions Ombudsman

11.7.9 It could be argued that these new duties go no further than the existing common law standard of care that trustees should exercise in the performance of their functions. In practice, however, formalising trustee duties in this way may mean that more members will bring challenges before the Pensions Ombudsman, claiming that statutory duties have not been met. Trustees are likely to see increased claims.

Make up of trustee boards

11.7.10 It is foreseeable that these increased standards and responsibilities on trustees will discourage individuals from standing for selection as trustees. More professional trustees are likely to be appointed, either because no individuals offer to act as trustees or because the appointment of professional trustees is likely to improve standards and reduce the likelihood of claims. This would of course have cost implications, and does not fit easily with the obligation to increase MNT representation.

11.7.11 Employers should take care over the selection of trustees to ensure that those with the greatest aptitude for the task are appointed. These may, of course, not be the same people who have the greatest understanding of and relationship with the membership, thereby potentially weakening a valuable connection between the trustees and the members.

11.8   CONCLUSION

11.8.1 The new statutory obligations on individual and corporate trustees to be 'conversant with' and have 'knowledge and understanding' of certain matters can be interpreted as going beyond the standards of care which currently apply. The Act incorporates specific standards for trustees which supplement the current mix of statutory and best practice and which will be supplemented by codes of practice. There is a need for transparency, independence and proper governance in relation to trustee decisions, so that the trustees can demonstrate compliance with the standard of care requirements, if required. These additional requirements add to the continuing risk that over-regulation and increasing costs will encourage employers to abandon pension funds altogether, which is clearly not the Government's intention.

ANNEXE 11A: SUMMARY

Section of the Act	Requirement/Duty	Applicable to/ responsibility for	Comment
s.69	Give notice in writing to the Regulator of a notifiable event as soon as reasonably practicable after becoming aware of the notifiable event	■ Trustees/Managers of occupational schemes, if the event relates to the scheme ■ Employers, if the event relates to the employer	Obligations apply also to 'prescribed pensions'. A scheme is only eligible if not in winding up and not a money purchase scheme.
s.70	Report breaches of the law to the Regulator in writing, based on reasonable belief of actual non-compliance or non-compliance in past (but not anticipated breaches in future)	■ Trustees/managers of occupational or personal schemes ■ Administrator ■ Employer ■ Professional adviser ■ Other advisers to trustees or managers	Applies more widely than s.69. Breach must be of material significance.
Part 3	Scheme Funding duties to obtain:		
s.222(4)	■ Statutory Funding Objective, including methods and assumption for calculating scheme's technical provisions	■ Trustees or managers	Applies to occupational schemes (except money purchase schemes) only, but each item must be agreed by the employer, and actuary must advise on each item.
s.223	■ Statement of Funding Principles		
s.224	■ Actuarial valuations and reports		
s.226	■ Recovery plan		
s.227	■ Schedule of contributions		
s.228	■ Notification to the Regulator of a failure to make payments under the schedule of contributions		

Section of the Act	Requirement/Duty	Applicable to/ responsibility for	Comment
ss.241–243	Member nominated trustee directors arrangements	Trustees	Not applicable to prescribed schemes or schemes where all members are trustees.
ss.247–249	To be conversant with: ■ statement of investment principles; ■ statement of funding principles; ■ any documents regarding policy relating to administration of the scheme Knowledge and understanding of: ■ law relating to pensions and trusts ■ principles of funding of occupational schemes and investment of assets ■ any other prescribed matters	Trustees and directors of corporate trustees	Code of Practice not obliged to cover s.249 (supplemental provisions).
s.49(9)(b), 1995 Act	Reporting material failures to pay employee contributions on time; such reports to be made to the Regulator and the member(s) concerned.	Trustees or Managers	Section 49(9)(b) of the 1995 Act is amended by s.269 to include a materiality. threshold
s.67 to s.67I 1995 Act	Ensuring modifications to 'subsisting rights' are made in accordance with correct procedures, i.e. consent requirements in respect of protected modifications and actuarial equivalence requirements in all other cases. Trustee approval and reporting requirements also apply.	Trustees/Actuary	Code may also cover powers of the Regulator in s.67G–H.

Section of the Act	Requirement/Duty	Applicable to/ responsibility for	Comment
s.88(1), 1995 Act	Reporting material failures to the Regulator and the members regarding any payments due to a money purchase scheme in accordance with payment schedule.	Trustees or managers	Section 88 of the 1995 Act is amended by s.269(2).
s.111A(7A), 1993 Act	Reporting material failures by employer to pay contributions due to a personal pension scheme on time; report must be made to the Regulator and the employee within a reasonable period after the due date.	Trustees or managers of a personal pension scheme (or stakeholder scheme)	Sub-section (7A) is inserted by s.268(2) of the 2004 Act. Currently s.111A(8) of the 1993 Act only imposes civil liability on the employer: there is no reporting requirement.

12 THE IORP DIRECTIVE

12.1 INTRODUCTION

12.1.1 The IORP Directive on the Activities and Supervision of Institutions for Occupational Retirement Provision 2003/41/EC, was approved by the European Parliament in March 2003, ratified by the European Council of Economic and Finance Ministers in May 2003 and officially published in the European Union's *Official Journal* in September 2003. Each Member State now has until 23 September 2005 to implement the IORP Directive into its national legislation. Member States may delay the application of certain Articles to schemes operating within their own jurisdiction until 23 September 2010. These cover limits on self-investment and a requirement for schemes which themselves (rather than the sponsoring employer) guarantee the liabilities to retain a safe buffer (rather akin to the capital reserve requirements imposed on life offices).

12.1.2 Although individual Member States will continue to be responsible for setting their own rules, they must abide by the constraints laid down by the Directive.

12.1.3 The IORP Directive's long-term objective is to facilitate cross-border pension schemes within the EU as part of a general objective of completing the single market in financial services. In order to make that possible, it establishes a framework in which minimum standards for schemes within the Directive's ambit (see below) are prescribed. This chapter will concentrate on the impact on existing UK schemes, briefly touching on the opportunities for cross-border schemes which have been opened up by the Directive.

12.2 APPLICATION OF THE DIRECTIVE

12.2.1 The IORP Directive does not cover all existing EU pension schemes. It excludes:

(a) state pension arrangements;
(b) 'pay-as-you-go' schemes;
(c) book reserve schemes;
(d) schemes where employees have no legal rights to benefits; and
(e) schemes covered by other EU Directives.

12.2.2   The effect is therefore to include all the UK funded schemes which do not fall in any of these categories.

12.2.3   As noted above, the IORP Directive is required to be implemented in Member States by 23 September 2005. As a result, where the Act implements provisions from the Directive, any underlying regulations should be in force by that deadline.

12.3   SCOPE OF THE DIRECTIVE: UK DOMESTIC SCHEMES

12.3.1   As noted above, the IORP Directive aims for minimum (although not uniform) standards. The key areas that it covers are:

(a) funding;
(b) supervision and administration;
(c) disclosure; and
(d) investment.

12.3.2   Although the Government felt that existing pensions law broadly complied with the Directive, there are some differences. The Act therefore changes some existing law to comply.

Funding

12.3.3   The Act's detailed provisions on funding are considered elsewhere (see **Chapter 5**). However, it is worth tracing the link with some of those provisions to the Directive.

12.3.4   Article 16 of the IORP Directive requires pension schemes to comply with a funding requirement. This differs depending upon whether the scheme operates only on a domestic basis, or whether it operates on a cross-border basis. A domestic scheme (i.e. for these purposes one operating only within the UK) is required under Art.16(1) to have 'at all times sufficient and appropriate assets to cover the technical provisions in respect of the total range of pension schemes operated'. If a scheme accepts employees from another Member State, there is a more onerous requirement that it must 'at all times be fully funded' in respect of the total range of pension schemes operated (Art.16(3) – such cross-border schemes are discussed at **para.12.4**).

12.3.5   The scheme specific funding requirements are introduced by Part 3 of the Act. Although part of a wider policy objective, the provisions are also intended to comply with the IORP Directive, hence the use of terminology, such as 'technical provisions' which is unfamiliar to UK ears and which is borrowed directly from the Directive. 'Technical provisions' are not defined in the Directive itself, but the Act (s.222(2)) defines the expression as 'the amount required on an actuarial calculation to make provision for the scheme's liabilities'. Section 222 of the Act provides that every scheme (other than a money purchase scheme or a prescribed scheme (see s.221)) is subject to a requirement that it must have sufficient and appropriate assets to cover its technical provisions ('the statutory funding objective').

12.3.6   Much detail is to be fleshed out in regulations. However, a new requirement is that trustees must prepare a 'Statement of Funding Principles' which sets out their policy for ensuring that the statutory funding objective is met and the circumstances in which they would consider commissioning additional valuations (see s.223 of the Act).

12.3.7   If after obtaining an actuarial valuation, it appears to the trustees or managers that the statutory funding objective was not met on the effective date of the valuation, they must prepare a 'recovery plan' (see s.226 of the Act). The recovery plan is to be available to members on request and information from it will be disclosed in the annual statement provided to members. In addition, a copy of the recovery plan must be sent to the Regulator. (This reflects the requirements set out in Art.16(2) of the IORP Directive which accepts that funding is not an exact science and that there may not always be sufficient assets to cover the technical provisions. However, it requires a 'concrete and realisable plan'.)

12.3.8   With regard to cross-border schemes, which must be 'fully funded' at all times, no specific provision appears in the Act, even although this is a more rigorous standard. It is likely that the new Regulator will be required to ensure that a stricter regime (perhaps more frequent funding checks and more immediate cash injection in the event of underfunding) exists for those schemes. Certainly the Regulator has sufficient powers to enable this to be done.

Supervision and administration

12.3.9   Aside from the more eye-catching provisions on funding, investment and cross-border pensions discussed further below, the IORP Directive contains numerous provisions of a more administrative nature. These provisions include the regulation, registration and supervision of pension schemes, the information to be disclosed to scheme members and beneficiaries, the requirements for trustees to have appropriate qualifications and experience and the requirement for pension schemes to have adequate internal control mechanisms. As is apparent from what follows, the Act picks up on many of these points to the extent that corresponding provisions did not already exist in UK pensions law.

Regulatory provisions

12.3.10   The competent authorities in each EU Member State have a significant role to play under the IORP Directive. Indeed, one of the main aims of the Directive as stated in the preamble is to ensure that the competent authorities have adequate rights to information and powers of intervention with respect to schemes and those who run them.

12.3.11   The 'competent authorities' are defined as the national authorities designated to carry out the duties prescribed in the Directive. In the UK, this means the new Pensions Regulator.

Information-gathering powers

12.3.12   Article 13 of the IORP Directive requires the competent authorities to have various powers in respect of any pension scheme located in their territory. In particular, the competent authority must have the power:

(a) to require schemes to supply it with information and documentation;

(b) to supervise outsourcing relationships;

(c) to obtain regularly statements of investment policy principles, annual reports and accounts and all documents necessary for the purposes of supervision (such as internal interim reports, actuarial valuations and assumptions, asset-liability studies, evidence of consistency with the investment policy principles, evidence of proper payment of contributions and auditors' reports); and

(d) to carry out on-site inspections at the scheme's premises or premises relating to outsourced functions, to check if activities are being carried out in accordance with the supervisory rules.

12.3.13   Where necessary, the UK Government has extended the powers of the Regulator beyond those available to its precursor, OPRA, to ensure that the UK complies with the Directive. The provisions in the Act relating to the Regulator are stated to have been specifically drafted to comply with the relevant provisions of the Directive.

12.3.14   The existing power vested in OPRA to require the production of documents relevant to the discharge of its functions (see s.98 of the 1995 Act) has been extended in s.72 of the Act to give the Regulator a more general power to request by notice in writing any information or documentation from a trustee or manager, a professional adviser, an employer and others that is relevant to the exercise of the Regulator's functions.

12.3.15   In addition, the Regulator is given power in s.63 to issue scheme return notices. A scheme return notice will require production of all registrable information as defined in s.60 of the Act, such as the name and address of the scheme and its trustees, the status of the scheme etc. It may also require the production of other information which the Regulator reasonably requires for the purposes of the exercise of its functions in relation to the scheme in question.

12.3.16   On-site inspections are already a reality in the UK pursuant to ss.99–101 of the 1995 Act, but the Act widens the existing inspection provisions (see ss.73–79). So, for example, s.73 contains a power for an inspector to enter premises liable to inspection at any reasonable time to investigate whether the 'occupational scheme provisions' are being or have been complied with. The 'occupational scheme provisions' are similar to, but wider than, the 'regulatory provisions' referred to in s.99 of the 1995 Act. Section 74 of the Act permits inspection to investigate whether an employer is complying with the duty to facilitate access to stakeholder pension schemes.

Supervisory powers

12.3.17   The IORP Directive envisages that the competent authorities will adopt a pro-active role in the supervision of schemes within their territory, and requires them to be granted various powers to intervene in the running of pension schemes (Art.14).

12.3.18   In particular, the competent authorities must require all schemes within their territory to have sound administrative and accounting procedures and adequate internal control mechanisms. This is reflected in the statutory objectives of the Regulator set out in the Act, one of which is to promote the good administration of work-based pension schemes (s.5(1)(d) of the Act). Although the existing requirements for professional advisers, the whistle blowing requirements and the Regulator's information-gathering powers probably satisfy this requirement, it is likely that either via regulations or via a Code of Practice to be issued by the Regulator in due course, more detail of the internal control mechanisms which pension schemes will be required to have in place will follow.

12.3.19   In order to prevent or remedy any irregularities prejudicial to the interests of members, the IORP Directive requires the competent authorities to have power to take such measures as they consider appropriate and necessary. This includes measures of an administrative or financial nature, either with regard to the scheme in question or against those running the scheme. It also includes power to restrict or prohibit the free disposal of scheme assets in certain circumstances. Corresponding provisions appear in the Act. See, for example, the power of the Regulator to issue improvement notices (s.13), the power to issue third-party notices (s.14), the power to apply for an injunction (or interdict in Scotland) or an order of restitution from the court (ss.15 and 16 respectively) and the powers to freeze or wind up a scheme (ss.22–32).

12.3.20   In order to safeguard the interests of members and beneficiaries, the competent authorities may transfer powers relating to the running of a scheme to a 'special representative who is fit to exercise those powers' (Art.14(3)). In its consultation paper on the implementation of the IORP Directive, the DWP expressed the view that this requirement is satisfied by existing powers to appoint an independent trustee with exclusive powers referring to s.7(2) of the 1995 Act.

12.3.21   The competent authorities may prohibit or restrict a scheme's activities, particularly if the interests of members and beneficiaries are at risk or where the scheme 'fails seriously in its obligations under the rules to which it is subject'. Corresponding powers are vested in the Regulator under the Act, namely the powers to freeze, modify or wind up a scheme where the Regulator believes the members' interests are at risk.

12.3.22   According to the Directive, any decision to prohibit a scheme's activities must be supported by precise reasons and be notified to the relevant scheme. Furthermore, decisions taken in relation to a scheme pursuant to laws, regulations and provisions adopted under the Directive's provisions must be subject to the right of appeal to the courts.

Miscellaneous points

12.3.23   Many of the IORP Directive's 'miscellaneous' provisions are largely uncontroversial as far as the UK is concerned, because similar provisions already appear in UK pensions legislation and/or procedure. A typical example of this is the requirement (Art.8 of the Directive) to ensure that there is legal separation between a sponsoring employer and the pension scheme operated by it, in order to safeguard scheme assets in the event of the employer's insolvency. This is a basic principle of UK trust law and current Inland Revenue tax approval, and as such it is a familiar concept to those involved in the UK pensions industry. In any event, the principle is now reinforced by s.252 of the Act which says that, except where regulations so provide, in order to operate as a funded scheme, UK-based occupational pension schemes must be established under irrevocable trust.

12.3.24   Another general requirement of the IORP Directive is that all pension schemes within the EU are registered in a national register. Again, this is a familiar concept to the UK pensions industry, but the requirement to set up and maintain a register has been restated in ss. 59–65 of the Act.

12.3.25   More controversially, the IORP Directive requires each Member State to ensure that all schemes are run by 'persons of good repute who must themselves have appropriate professional qualifications and experience or employ advisers with appropriate professional qualifications and experience' (Art.9(1)(b)). Partly as a result of this provision, the Act contains a requirement (see ss.247–249) for trustees of occupational schemes (whether individual or corporate trustees) to be conversant with and have knowledge and understanding of specified documents and matters relating to the performance of their functions.

12.3.26   The Regulator is required to issue a Code of Practice on this point under s.90(2)(f) of the Act, and the Code of Practice will give more details of the kinds of knowledge, training, experience or qualifications regarded as necessary to meet the requirements of the relevant Sections. See **Chapter 11** for more on the new standard of care applying to trustees under the Act.

12.3.27   Occupational pension schemes are required by Art.7 of the IORP Directive to limit their activities to retirement benefit-related operations. This provision is incorporated into the Act at s.255(1), and at s.255(5) 'retirement benefits' are defined as benefits related to reaching or the expectation of reaching retirement, and benefits which supplement such benefits such as those relating to death, disability, termination of employment, sickness or poverty. There is a potential exemption from this restriction in s.255(2) for prescribed schemes or schemes of a prescribed description. It may be that the UK will take advantage of the small pension scheme and statutory scheme exclusions in Art.5 to exclude such schemes from the ambit of s.255.

Disclosure

12.3.28   The IORP Directive imposes its own set of disclosure (or 'information') requirements on schemes (Art.11). More particularly, it requires the annual report and accounts, the statement of investment policy principles and details of changes to scheme rules to be made available to members and beneficiaries. Furthermore, members are entitled to receive on request 'detailed and substantial' information on the target level of benefits (if any), benefits on leaving service, where the member bears the investment risk, the range of investment options, if applicable, and the arrangements relating to the transfer of pension rights to another scheme on leaving service. The UK is already largely compliant with these disclosure requirements, due to the Occupational Pension Schemes (Disclosure of Information) Regulations 1996, SI 1996/1655 (as amended). However, the Directive also requires members to receive every year 'brief particulars of the situation of the institution as well as the current level of financing of their accrued individual entitlements', and this is a new provision so far as the UK is concerned. While this is not addressed directly in the Act, there appear to be powers in s.237 to implement this, should the Government wish to incorporate the Directive provisions via combined pension forecasts. Otherwise, further amendment of the Disclosure Regulations can be anticipated.

Investment

12.3.29   The IORP Directive is the first step to an internal market for occupational retirement provision organised on a European scale and by establishing the 'prudent person' rule as the underlying principle for capital investment, the Directive makes it possible for institutions to operate across borders. Article 18 sets out the investment rules with which schemes must comply and codifies the 'prudent man' principle which already exists in UK law and the duty to invest assets in the best interests of members (*Cowan v. Scargill* [1984] 2 All ER 750).

12.3.30   The investment provisions of the Directive largely move the rest of Europe towards the so-called 'Anglo-Saxon' schemes approach, and major changes to UK law are therefore unnecessary. However, ss.244–246 of the Act specifically incorporate provisions not found elsewhere in existing legislation (see **Chapter 6** for a detailed discussion on the changes made by the Act to ss.35 and 36 of the 1995 Act).

12.3.31   For completeness, the relevant provisions of the Directive dealing with investment are: Article 12 – Statement of investment policy principles; Article 18 – Investment rules; and Article 19 – Management and custody.

12.3.32   Article 18 of the IORP Directive deals with investment rules and provides that Member States must require institutions to invest in accordance with the 'prudent person' rule (Art.18(1)) and in particular, in accordance with the following.

(a) The assets must be invested in the best interests of members and beneficiaries (Art.18(1)(a)).
(b) The assets must be invested in such a way as to ensure the security, quality, liquidity and profitability of the portfolio as a whole (Art.18(1)(b)).
(c) Assets held to cover the technical provisions must be invested in a manner appropriate to the nature and duration of the expected future retirement benefits (Art.18(1)(b)).
(d) The assets must be predominantly invested on regulated markets (Art.18(1)(c)).
(e) Restrictions on investments in derivatives. Investment in derivative instruments will be possible if they contribute to a reduction of investment risk or facilitate efficient portfolio management (Art.18(1)(d)).
(f) The assets must be properly diversified so as to avoid over-reliance on any particular asset, issuer or group of undertakings and accumulations of risk in the portfolio as a whole (Art.18(1)(e)).
(g) Investment in the employer must be no more than 5 per cent of the portfolio and where the employer belongs to a group, investment in the undertakings of the group must not exceed 10 per cent of the portfolio (Art.18(1)(f)).

12.3.33　All of these rules are based on the premise that a pension fund will be managed on the principle of the 'prudent person' who is required to invest in the best interests of the beneficiaries of the fund. This principle corresponds to the duty of care currently applied in the UK to trustees at common law, and which is reinforced by the provisions of ss.35 and 36 of the 1995 Act, which prevent trustees or their appointed investment managers from excluding or limiting their duty of care to scheme members in respect of their investment functions.

12.3.34　It has been suggested that a narrow interpretation of this might prevent trustees from considering the interests of the scheme sponsor (where for example trustees might decide to remain mis-matched, or not to buy out liabilities with an insurer).

12.3.35　However, the prudent person is also required under Art.18.1(b) to invest the assets of the fund so as to 'ensure the security, quality, liquidity and profitability of the portfolio as a whole' and 'in a manner appropriate to the nature and duration' of the expected future benefits. So long as this principle is interpreted on a global rather than on an individual investment basis, it is in keeping with the way in which the UK Courts have interpreted the standard of care expected of trustees when exercising their investment functions.

'Appropriate' assets

12.3.36　In a funding context, the Act has applied these general principles by requiring that 'every scheme is subject to a requirement ('the statutory funding objective') that it must have sufficient and *appropriate* assets to cover its technical provisions' (emphasis added). The word 'appropriate' is not defined although the Explanatory Notes to the Act assist by referring to other provisions of Art.18. However, Art.18(1)(c) requires pension schemes to be invested 'predominantly on regulated markets'. Because a significant number of UK pension schemes, especially at the smaller end of the market (and in particular money purchase schemes that are not subject to the statutory funding objective) are wholly or largely invested through life assurance policies which are not themselves traded on such markets (even if the underlying securities held by such funds may be so invested), a concern was raised with the UK Government that such funds might be in breach of this requirement. However, the UK Government has stated that it will apply a 'look through' policy to this provision, so the underlying investments, rather than the life policy itself, would be considered.

Derivatives

12.3.37   Article 18(1)(d) of the IORP Directive requires that the use of derivative instruments is restricted to the 'reduction of investment risks or for the purposes of efficient portfolio management'. This language is derived from the Directives which govern the investment rules applicable to insurance companies (as are other requirements relating to aggregations of risk by counterparty and currency matching elsewhere in Art.18). Because of the lack of supply of index-linked gilts in the UK, synthetic securities which have similar characteristics to such gilts (created via a swap with an investment bank whereby the coupon on a corporate bond is exchanged for an income flow provided by the bank) have come to be used by larger defined benefits schemes in order to match their longer-term liabilities. It has been suggested that such instruments cannot easily be characterised as either risk reducing or efficient portfolio management. Such transactions have, however, been countenanced by the Inland Revenue, which in August 2003 issued guidance (Tax Bulletin 66) on the ways in which schemes could enter into derivatives without falling foul of the principle that such schemes must not be trading in investments.

Self-investment and borrowing

12.3.38   Another aspect of the diversification rules set out in Art.18 of the IORP Directive is that a scheme must neither hold more than 5 per cent of its assets in investments in the sponsoring employer, nor more than 10 per cent of its portfolio in the same group as the sponsoring employer. The first part of this rule is in keeping with the provisions of s.40 of the 1995 Act, but there is no corresponding provision to allow a 10 per cent group holding limit (although for a multi-employer industry-wide schemes there is currently a 20 per cent limit). The UK Government has already announced that it will relax the rules in this area, although it remains to be seen whether many schemes will take advantage of such a relaxation, especially given the overriding prudent person principle. Draft regulations are expected to be issued for consultation on these provisions.

12.3.39   Article 18(2) prevents pension schemes from borrowing or providing guarantees for third parties, although borrowing for liquidity purposes and on a temporary basis will be permitted. The Act already contains, at s.246, a new s.36A of the 1995 Act which will mirror the provisions of the Directive, although the Government has confirmed that it will allow 'conditional borrowing' and also provide exemptions from this provision for unapproved schemes and small self-administered pension schemes (i.e. those with 12 or fewer members, all of whom are trustees). It has been suggested that the requirement might also need to be relaxed in circumstances where pension schemes are involved in bulk transfers but it is not yet clear whether this would qualify as being on a 'temporary basis'.

12.3.40   Articles 18(3)–18(6) contain provisions which prevent Member States from imposing certain localisation and quantitative limits on investments, but since there are no such restrictions in the UK there is no change in the law in this area. For a discussion on ring-fencing under cross-border arrangements see below.

Custody of investments

12.3.41   Article 19 of the IORP Directive ensures that pension schemes do not restrict the appointment of investment managers and custodians from other Member States. Therefore there could be significant opportunities for UK investment managers and custodians to expand their business.

Statement of investment policy principles

12.3.42   Article 12 of the IORP Directive formalises the requirement for pension funds to have a written statement of investment policy principles. Currently, s.35 of the 1995 Act satisfies most of the requirements of Art.12, although the requirement that this must be reviewed every three years and after a significant change in the investment policy of the fund does not appear in s.35. Section 244 of the Act will amend s.35 of the 1995 Act.

12.3.43   The Article also includes a requirement for a statement of investment policy to cover 'investment risk measurement methods' and 'risk-management process'. Amendments will need to be made to the regulations under s.35 of the 1995 Act to accommodate the fact that trustees of UK pension schemes are only currently required to set out in general terms their policy in relation to 'risk' (which is not defined), whereas the Directive requires information to be given as to investment risk measurement methods used and the risk management processes which are implemented by trustees.

12.4   CROSS-BORDER ACTIVITIES

12.4.1   Article 20 of the IORP Directive (Cross-border activities) provides that, subject to certain conditions, each Member State shall allow:

(a) domestic employers to sponsor foreign pension schemes; and

(b) foreign employers to sponsor domestic pension schemes.

12.4.2 Sections 287–295 of the Act ('Cross-Border Activities Within European Union') essentially mirror the requirements of Art.20 of the Directive. Sections 287–292 deal with the situation where the pension scheme in question is located in the UK, and s.293 deals with the converse situation where the pension scheme is located in another Member State.

12.4.3 Sections 288–292 of the Act set out the conditions that a UK occupational pension scheme must satisfy (on pain of a civil penalty being imposed under s.10 of the 1995 Act) in order to operate as a cross-border scheme. The scheme must:

(a) apply to and be authorised by the Regulator to engage in such cross-border activity and to receive contributions from the particular overseas employer in question (ss.288 and 289);

(b) be notified by the Regulator as to the foreign Member State's social and labour law requirements – following the receipt by the Regulator of the necessary information from the authorities of the foreign Member State (s.290).

12.4.4 Section 291 of the Act obliges the trustees of the UK occupational pension scheme to operate the scheme in accordance with the social and labour laws of the relevant foreign Member State, insofar as the scheme relates to members who are or have been employed by the foreign employer in question.

12.4.5 For example, consider a Dutch employer that wants to participate in a UK pension scheme. The conditions are basically as follows:

(a) the UK pension scheme must notify (and provide certain information to) the UK authorities (who must then pass this information on to the Dutch authorities);

(b) the UK authorities must issue the UK pension scheme with prior authorisation; and

(c) the Dutch authorities must inform the UK authorities of the requirements of 'social and labour law' relevant to the field of occupational pensions under which a pension scheme sponsored by an employer in the Netherlands must be operated, and the UK authorities must then pass this information on to the UK scheme (which must comply with these requirements).

12.4.6 Section 292 of the Act allows the Regulator, in such circumstances as may subsequently be prescribed by regulations, to issue a notice to the trustees of the UK occupational pension scheme directing them to ensure that some or all of the assets and/or liabilities of the scheme are ring-fenced (i.e. enabling the UK and other country sections of the scheme to be funded separately).

12.4.7 Section 293 of the Act sets out certain duties that the Regulator has where a UK employer is participating in a pension scheme administered in another Member State. The Regulator must:

(a) inform the overseas authorities of the relevant UK 'social and labour law' requirements;

(b) notify the overseas authorities from time to time of any significant change in the relevant UK legal requirements; and

(c) monitor the scheme's activities and notify the overseas authorities of any breaches of relevant UK legal requirements that it detects (the Regulator also has power, in the case of any such breach, to notify the UK employer in question to cease participating in the scheme).

12.4.8   What is 'social and labour law'? Section 295 of the Act (Interpretation) simply refers back to Art.20 of the IORP Directive. The Directive does not define the term either, although it is clear from Art.20(5) and reproduced in the Act that it is the requirements of social and labour law 'relevant to the field of occupational pensions' which are in issue. Those commentators who have suggested that almost anything could comprise 'social or labour law' are perhaps too pessimistic. There is some guidance in the Directive.

(a) Preamble 37 states that social and labour law includes 'for example the definition and payment of retirement benefits and the conditions for transferability of pension rights'.

(b) Article 20(1) provides that cross-border activities are without prejudice to national social and labour law on the organisation of pension systems, including 'compulsory membership and the outcomes of collective bargaining agreements'.

12.4.9   The interpretation of 'social and labour law' is crucial. It has been suggested that some Member States may use this provision to prevent non-domestic schemes being a viable proposition for employees within their jurisdiction. Given that the thrust of the Directive is to ensure the freedom of provision of services, it is to be hoped that the Commission will apply any pressure needed to ensure that freedom is not frustrated under the guise of excessive (rather than legitimate) member protection.

12.4.10   Another change to the law in the UK was required by Art.19.3, which allows for the possibility of a pension scheme's assets held by a custodian or a depository to be frozen where a supervising regulator in the home Member State feels it is necessary to do so in order to protect the security of the benefits of the members of the fund. UK legislation does not currently give either OPRA or the Financial Services Authority such a power but the Act does confer this right on the new Regulator. Section 294 of the Act provides that, if the Regulator receives a request from a competent authority of a Member State for assistance in prohibiting the free disposal of UK-held assets of a European pensions institution that has its main administration in that Member State, the court may grant an injunction restraining a defendant, or in Scotland an interdict prohibiting a defendant, from disposing or otherwise dealing with the assets. Unlike the other sections discussed above, s.294 could impact even on a foreign pension scheme that has no UK members.

12.4.11   Neither the Directive nor the Act requires that contributions to a foreign pension scheme be treated in the same way for tax purposes as contributions to a domestic pension scheme (which has been the practical bar to cross-border pension activity in the past). It should be pointed out that tax changes do not form the purpose of either the Directive or the Act. The Directive does however show that the EU authorities are determined to facilitate the formation of genuine cross-border pension arrangements (rather than merely the traditionally more common 'ad hoc' arrangements whereby seconded ex-pats continue to participate in their home country pension scheme). In light of recent decisions by the European Court of Justice (e.g. *Danner* v. *Finland* Case C-136/00 (3 October 2002) and *Skandia* v. *Ramstedt* Case C-422/01 (26 June 2003)), it seems clear that, notwithstanding the absence of anti-tax discrimination provisions in the Directive, tax discrimination is not regarded as permissible under EU law deriving from Treaties. The EU authorities are likely to take the view that, provided the requirements of ss.287 to 295 of the Act are complied with, tax discrimination by the Inland Revenue in relation to cross-border pension arrangements is not permissible. It should also be noted that there is other relevant legislation in this area. The Finance Act 2004 for example makes express provision for:

(a) persons worldwide to be allowed to join UK registered pension schemes; and
(b) persons based in the UK to be members of overseas pension schemes.

However, the Finance Act contains only limited provisions for tax relief in relation to (a) and (b) above. In particular, only 'relevant UK individuals' will be able to obtain tax relief on their contributions to UK registered pension schemes. It remains to be seen to what extent these provisions will be challenged in the future as being too restrictive.

12.4.12   Although the regulations are still awaited, they are likely to be relatively 'light-touch' in order to facilitate efficiencies and other benefits which could be achieved by cross-border schemes.

13 FINANCIAL ASSISTANCE SCHEME

13.1 INTRODUCTION

13.1.1   On 14 May 2004 the Government announced that £400 million of public money would be made available to fund a Financial Assistance Scheme (FAS) to benefit individuals who have suffered as a result of their pension scheme winding up underfunded. The FAS has been included in the Act at s.286 which provides, amongst other things, that the Secretary of State will 'make provision by regulations for a scheme for making payments to, or in respect of, qualifying members of qualifying pension schemes' (s.286(1)).

13.1.2   The FAS was the Government's attempt to head off a backbench revolt in Parliament which threatened to scupper the entire Act. The backbenchers' main concern was that, since the PPF would apply only to schemes which began to wind up after its introduction, it failed to protect members whose benefits had been curtailed because their schemes had already started to (or finished) wind up in an underfunded state. The scale of this concern has been reinforced by DWP research (published on its website on 30 June 2004) under the heading 'Insolvent pension wind ups – research into numbers affected'. This research indicates that approximately 65,000 pension scheme members have already lost significant proportions of their expected pension benefits.

13.1.3   The detail of the FAS – for example, who will benefit, the level of benefits to be provided, and how it will operate – is not yet known. Section 286 of the Act is very high level: it defines 'qualifying members' and 'qualifying pension schemes' for the FAS purposes (see s.286(2)), but otherwise leaves the detail to be fleshed out in regulations. The DWP has indicated that it aims to have the FAS up and running by April 2005.

13.1.4   The Pensions Minister, Malcolm Wicks, stated to the House of Commons on 2 December 2004 that formal regulatory consultation would begin in Spring 2005, and regulations would be laid before Parliament once this procedure was concluded. According to the Minister's statement, the body to administer the FAS will be set up in April 2005 and payments will commence as soon as practicable thereafter. Until the regulations are published, we can only speculate as to what they will contain.

13.1.5   At the time of writing, the DWP is consulting with stakeholders to develop the structure and parameters of the FAS. An Industry Working Group meets regularly to guide and inform the Government's thinking, and trustees, administrators and actuaries have been asked to provide details, via online questionnaires, of schemes that have wound up or are in the process of winding up unable to meet their liabilities in full.

13.1.6   This data collection exercise will help to create a database of potentially eligible schemes, as well as to establish the scale and nature of the problem, and define the parameters of the FAS.

13.2   WHO WILL BENEFIT FROM THE FAS?

13.2.1   The FAS will apply to 'qualifying pension schemes', i.e. non-money purchase schemes that have either completed wind up or are in the process of winding up with insufficient assets 'to satisfy in full' their liabilities 'calculated in the prescribed manner' (s.286(2)). At the time of writing, it is unclear whether a 'qualifying pension scheme' will have to have an insolvent sponsoring employer, although the Government has hinted that solvent employers may be excluded. The strongest indication of this to date was given on 2 December 2004 when the Pensions Minister, Malcolm Wicks, in a statement to the House of Commons stated that:

> 'Solvent employers have a duty to support their schemes and provide benefits that members were expecting. So it is right that the FAS focuses on insolvent employers. Nevertheless, issues concerning the definition of "employer solvency" remain under active consideration.'

Clearly, as there is only a finite (and relatively limited) fund available it would not be realistic to expect the FAS to be available to all schemes which have ever wound up underfunded. Given the limited money available and Malcolm Wicks' comments it is likely that employer insolvency will be a prerequisite for a scheme's eligibility for the FAS. It is not yet clear how this likely requirement would work in a multi-employer scheme.

13.2.2   'Qualifying pension schemes' will be restricted for FAS purposes by reference to the date when they began to wind up. The Government faced the problem of choosing a cut-off date which was not seen to be arbitrary. Early suggestions in the pensions industry were that the FAS would only be available to members of schemes which began to wind up between 5 April 1997 (the date the 1995 Act came into force) and 6 April 2005 (when the PPF is expected to come into effect). The Government finally announced on 2 December 2004 that the qualifying period would be from 1 January 1997 to 6 April 2005. The Government stated that information they had gathered showed that the vast majority of schemes which commenced winding up with significant shortfalls did so after January 1997, and so chose this date as the starting point of the qualifying period.

13.2.3   While the starting date is perhaps arbitrary in that it does not relate to any legislative or common law anniversary, in our opinion it is not unreasonable, particularly given that it dates back prior to the implementation of the 1995 Act. The overall effect of the qualifying period is that the FAS and the PPF will provide seamless coverage (subject to their rules and funding) for underfunded scheme wind ups.

13.3   ELIGIBILITY

13.3.1   The Act states that the FAS will award payments to 'qualifying members' of 'qualifying schemes' (s.286(1)); it will be members of schemes, rather than the schemes themselves, that will qualify for assistance. The qualification process is likely to consist of two parts: scheme qualification followed by member qualification.

13.3.2   At the time of writing, other than the online questionnaires on the DWP website by which schemes can register initial interest in the FAS, there is little concrete information on the likely qualification process. Malcolm Wicks' statement to the House of Commons of 2 December 2004 confirmed that the Government's intention was to announce its proposals in early 2005 'by way of indicative assistance levels to those facing the most urgent difficulties, as well as an indicative list of schemes that are likely to be eligible for assistance if those schemes are subsequently shown to comply with the FAS rules' (whatever these transpire to be).

13.3.3   The DWP has indicated that a process for dealing with disputes arising during this process will be developed. Inevitably, natural justice will require some kind of appeals procedure.

13.4   SAFEGUARDS AGAINST FRAUDULENT APPLICATIONS

13.4.1   It is anticipated that the FAS body will be given powers similar to those of the PPF to take action against any scheme professional or individual who provides fraudulent information. It is likely that it would seek to recover assistance already paid out or reduce assistance levels promised. What action it would take where the members themselves are not responsible for the fraud is, however, not clear. The FAS body may feel that it would not be reasonable to recover assistance already paid out or reduce assistance levels promised.

13.5   FUNDING

13.5.1   All we know at this stage is that the Government has pledged £400 million of public money to the FAS, spread over 20 years. Exactly how the money will be paid, however, is not clear. There could, for example, be 20 equal annual payments of £20 million, although it would be sensible to 'front load' the instalments. A graduated scale of initial higher payments would help to deal with the likelihood of initial significant activity to deal with the most serious cases. There are numerous possibilities but, as yet, we have no indication of the Government's intention. Whether the £400 million figure is fixed or linked to inflation is also unclear. The method of funding adopted is likely to impact significantly on the effectiveness of the FAS, and may well also impact on its overall structure (see **para.13.7**).

13.5.2   The Act provides in s.286(5) that 'Regulations . . . may not make provision for the imposition of a levy or charge on any person for the purpose of funding, directly or indirectly, the financial assistance scheme.' The Government had previously expressed the hope that additional contributions might be forthcoming from industry, but the inclusion of s.286(5) reflects the opposition of industry to providing financial support for the FAS, and the Government's acceptance of this.

13.5.3   It is of no surprise that the private sector's unwillingness to contribute to the FAS led to the amendment to the Act. There is no incentive for companies to contribute, other than the fact that the FAS is likely to improve public confidence in the pensions system. Bearing in mind the already escalating costs of pension provision and the imminent PPF levy, this is not considered to be a strong enough incentive.

13.5.4   The other possible sources of additional FAS funding are all equally problematic. Drawing on insurers' orphan assets (reported to amount to around £3 billion) gives rise to potential human rights difficulties; whilst increasing taxes or introducing a retrospective levy are both unlikely to be politically acceptable.

13.6   EXPECTED LEVELS OF PAYMENT

13.6.1   The level of benefit available will depend on the number and size of claims submitted, the final size of the fund and the method of delivering assistance, none of which is yet known. It is, however, inevitable that the levels of benefits paid out by the FAS will be lower than those to be paid by the PPF. Indeed, it appears to be agreed across the industry that the £400 million set aside by the Government will fall far short of the amount needed to provide assistance to all scheme members who have lost out.

13.6.2   With regard to the maximum payments that can be made to members under the FAS, Malcolm Wicks stated on 2 December 2004 that the Government was actively considering a benefit cap, which would be set at a lower level than that of the PPF (which is currently expected to be a cap on pension of £25,000 p.a.). He also indicated that, to save on bureaucracy and focus resources on the hardest hit, the FAS will only cover those individuals who would receive at least £10 a week 'or equivalent' from it.

13.6.3   The likelihood is that the FAS will focus first on helping the worst affected scheme members. FAS payments will not be means tested, in the sense that s.286(6) provides that regulations:

> 'may not require any income or capital of a qualifying member of a qualifying scheme (other than income or capital which derives, directly or indirectly, from that scheme) to be taken into account when assessing whether the member is entitled to a payment under the financial assistance scheme or the amount of payment to which the member is entitled.'

13.6.4   One issue made clear in Malcolm Wicks' statement of 2 December 2004 is that younger members, who theoretically have a longer time to work and replace a pension wholly or partially lost, are unlikely to receive the same level of assistance as older members nearer retirement: assistance will probably be 'geared' by reference to the number of years a claimant is from retirement.

13.6.5   Depending on the payment structure adopted by the Government, it may be that in the early years a few of the hardest-hit schemes will absorb all of that year's (and possibly future years') funds, leaving little or nothing for less severely affected schemes.

13.7   STRUCTURE OF THE FAS

13.7.1   The Government indicated in December 2004 that the FAS is likely to operate by way of a top-up arrangement, which is likely to prove the easiest way to administer benefits. A top-up arrangement has a number of advantages over a pooled arrangement (which was considered to be the only other practical way in which the FAS could operate). A top-up arrangement carries no funding (and therefore also no underfunding) risk, and is also likely to be easier to establish in the time available.

13.7.2   Payments will be made to individuals, regardless of gender, once they reach the age of 65, and are likely to be by way of a top-up pension, cash lump sum, or purchase of an annuity.

13.8   WHO WILL BE RESPONSIBLE FOR RUNNING THE FAS?

13.8.1   Again, this is not yet known. The Act allows for regulations to specify whether the FAS will be managed by the Secretary of State or by a different body (s.286(3)(a)). It also allows for regulations to give the Regulator or Board of the PPF certain functions in relation to the FAS, so there may ultimately end up being some cross-over between the FAS and the PPF (s.286(3)(h)). At present, however, we understand that the two schemes are intended to operate separately as no public funds are to be used for the PPF.

13.9   RELATIONSHIP TO DEEMED BUYBACK

13.9.1   Trustees of under-funded contracted-out schemes which began winding up after 5 April 1997 should also consider whether the deemed buyback procedure might assist their members (see the 1993 Act, ss.46–48 and Sched.2; Occupational Pension Schemes (Contracting Out) (Amount Required for Restoring State Scheme Rights and Miscellaneous Amendment) Regulations 1998, SI 1998/1397). In essence, deemed buyback provides a mechanism by which members can be reinstated into the State Earnings Related Pension Scheme/State Second Pension (SERPS/S2P). There are a number of preconditions which have to be satisfied (see the Revenue's 'Cessation of Contracted Out Pension Schemes' Manual (CA15), sections 6 and 7), and also a number of complexities to overcome. One of these is that the original regulations governing deemed buyback calculations do not cover calculations beyond the end of the 2001/02 tax year, new regulations to bring the position up to date are currently in preparation. Professional advice on deemed buyback will be essential.

13.10   WHEN WILL THE FAS BECOME EFFECTIVE?

13.10.1   The FAS is expected to commence from April 2005, with the first payments following as soon as possible thereafter. The Government indicated in the debates in Parliament on 19 and 20 May that it intends to review the scheme every three years.

13.11   PRACTICAL IMPLICATIONS FOR SCHEMES NOT YET IN WIND UP

13.11.1   The FAS will have limited relevance to most schemes which are not already in winding up. With the PPF due to be in place by 6 April 2005, many severely underfunded schemes will hope to continue to avoid wind up until that date, given that the FAS is likely to provide much lower benefits for members than can be expected under the PPF.

13.11.2   The only circumstances in which the trustees of a continuing scheme might feel that the FAS would be of help could be where a severely underfunded scheme is holding out for the introduction of the PPF, and the trustees consider that their scheme's eligibility for the PPF could be a problem. In this instance, it is possible that the members might be better off if the trustees wind up the scheme and claim under the FAS. This is, however, unlikely in practice given the low expected levels of FAS benefit.

13.12   IMPLICATIONS FOR SCHEMES CURRENTLY WINDING UP

13.12.1   There are a number of FAS related issues facing trustees of schemes currently winding up. These include how the wind up should be progressed, and the view taken by OPRA of the winding up process in the light of the FAS.

How should trustees progress winding up in light of the FAS?

13.12.2   Initially, there was some confusion over how the introduction of the FAS affected schemes in wind up, especially where those schemes were close to finalising the winding up or annuitising benefits under the scheme. There was a concern among trustees that a scheme which completed winding up before the FAS was implemented might exclude itself from assistance. Conversely, trustees were wary of delaying the winding up of schemes in anticipation of a benefit under the FAS for which their members might ultimately not qualify.

OPRA's guidance

13.12.3   To assist trustees in the decision making progress, OPRA issued guidance by way of an update in August 2004, explaining OPRA's expectations in respect of schemes which were winding up (see OPRA Update 9, August 2004).

13.12.4   OPRA stated that trustees should continue actively to progress wind ups, and should identify liabilities and member shortfalls as soon as possible to enable FAS entitlements to be calculated more easily. OPRA suggested that trustees should ideally postpone buying out benefits until entitlements for members eligible for assistance under the FAS could be calculated. However, OPRA also specifically confirmed that:

(a) where trustees considered it was in the best interests of members to buy out benefits, or for example where individual members were likely to fall outside the parameters for FAS assistance (such as those members near the top of the priority order), then they should go ahead and buy out benefits; and

(b) members would not be excluded from the FAS simply because their trustees had completed the winding up or bought out members' annuities.

Government statement on 2 December 2004

13.12.5   The Government stated in December 2004 that the FAS was most likely to operate by means of a top up to the occupational pensions which individuals would otherwise receive, and 'Trustees should therefore fulfil their duty to wind-up schemes in an expeditious manner (including annuitisation if appropriate)'.

Problems associated with buying out benefits

13.12.6   The market for buying bulk deferred annuity policies has shrunk to the extent that, at the time of writing, only two insurance companies on the open market offer appropriate products. The advice in the Government statement issued on 2 December 2004 is reinforced by the fact that the bulk annuity buy out market is not competitive and delays in buying out benefits can see the terms available for members worsen. In addition, once buy-out quotes have been obtained, these may only be honoured by the insurance companies concerned for a limited period. It would therefore be unwise for trustees to obtain quotes, and then seek to rely on these indefinitely while waiting for FAS eligibility and benefits to be assessed.

13.12.7   Bearing in mind the associated difficulties with buying out benefits and the potential dangers of delaying the process, trustees should consider seeking the advice of the scheme actuary and their other advisers at every stage of the process.

Ongoing responsibilities of trustees and advisers to schemes in wind-up

13.12.8   It is anticipated that the FAS will be up and running by April 2005. Trustees have a continuing fiduciary duty to their members up to the point at which the wind up concludes and their scheme ceases to exist. Trustees should therefore at least investigate the FAS, and consider whether it is likely to benefit their members. If a scheme wind up is likely to be completed before the date the FAS is implemented, the trustees should not rescind their position until they have properly completed the procedures for seeking assistance under the FAS for their members.

13.12.9   Advisers to schemes in winding up have a duty to ensure that trustees are aware of the FAS, and of the procedures which need to be completed to qualify for assistance. Early registration via the online questionnaires on the DWP website closed on 10 December 2004, although schemes will have an opportunity to register themselves formally with the FAS once it opens for business. Advisers will also need to provide guidance on the appropriateness of buying out benefits, and assist trustees generally in how they should approach issues associated with the FAS.

13.12.10   Given the short period of time before the FAS is expected to be in place, regulations and guidelines concerning formal registration, implementation, and the design of the FAS can be expected to arrive thick and fast over the coming months. Trustees must work closely with their advisers over this period to ensure that they keep abreast of developments, and realise whatever assistance may be available for their members, keeping within the Government's timetables.

13.13   IMPLICATIONS FOR SCHEMES WHICH HAVE BEEN WOUND UP

13.13.1   The law in this area is not clear, but it is our view that there are no continuing obligations faced by either professional or lay trustees to pursue the FAS in relation to a pension scheme which has already completed winding up. It seems that the fiduciary duties of the trustees will cease when the trust is dissolved at the conclusion of the wind up process.

13.13.2   In theory, it might be possible to interpret the law as imposing on a trustee a duty beyond this point to act in the best interests of the scheme's members. On this analysis, the trustee would be under a continuing obligation to pursue the FAS on behalf of the scheme's members, even if this were several years after the conclusion of the wind up. In practical terms, however, this is a questionable expectation. If trustees remained liable to the members of schemes that had been wound up, any new legislation could theoretically impose on them new duties of which they might well be unaware, and with which they might well be unable to comply.

13.13.3   With regards to professional advisers to schemes which have completed winding up, there is probably no obligation on their part to inform the former trustees of the availability of the FAS. Save for an ongoing obligation of confidentiality, the duties owed by a legal adviser to trustees of a pension scheme come to an end upon the termination of the retainer. Where a scheme has completed winding up, the client would normally cease to be a trustee (see **para.13.13.1**), and the retainer would therefore be terminated. Ideally, written confirmation of this termination and the termination of the trustees' fiduciary duties should be obtained.

13.13.4   As things stand, it would therefore appear that, at most, only a moral duty would be imposed on a legal adviser or on professional/lay trustees with regards to advising on, and pursuing, the FAS in relation to schemes which have already completed wind up. Nonetheless, some trustees and advisers with knowledge of recently completed wind ups where the FAS might prove of benefit will doubtless want to assist in whatever ways they can.

14 THE IMPACT OF THE ACT

14.1 INTRODUCTION

14.1.1 At the beginning of this book, we considered the last previous major piece of pensions legislation, the 1995 Act, and contrasted the impact that it was expected to have at the time that it was introduced with what actually happened. We concluded that outside events, from investment markets to tax and accounting changes, were the main drivers towards the reduction in the scope and security of employer-sponsored pension arrangements. Although the 1995 Act contributed to the complexity and cost of administering company schemes and led to major changes in the relationship of companies, trustees and members, it would not have had the same impact had economic and financial conditions for funded pension schemes remained benign.

14.2 THE IMPACT OF THE ACT

What is likely to be the impact of the Act?

14.2.1 Will the Act reverse the trend and improve security? Will pensions law be simpler and clearer? Even on the face of the Act as it stands, without the accompanying regulations and explanatory codes, material changes to existing law are obvious. It is also clear that the new law will be at least as complex as existing provisions, and will have a much more general impact on commercial life. The introduction of the PPF, for example, has prompted the need for contribution notices, financial support directions and clearance procedures, which will undoubtedly have an impact on corporate transactions and reorganisations.

14.2.2 The law in this area, and its relationship with existing concepts such as the 'debt on the employer' obligation, is difficult, attempting as it does to strike a reasonable balance between the interests of scheme members and the available resources. There can be uncomfortable choices between using resources to support pensions or maintain jobs in some enterprises. Scheme members are not the only category of stakeholders that employers must consider. The complexity of the law does not make it easy to communicate. The fact that pensions are becoming a major political issue is unlikely to help. The PPF has undoubtedly raised greater expectations of member security than it actually affords, and the prospect of further changes cannot be ruled out when the gap between member expectations and reality hits home. The difficulty of even drawing a line to determine when the protection begins, seen in the introduction of the FAS, illustrates the problem.

14.2.3   The new Regulator has been given increased powers, and in the light of member concern it can be expected to be more proactive than its predecessor. Whether the resources allocated to the Regulator are sufficient to allow it to do the job that the public expects is another matter.

14.2.4   We can expect trustees also to take a much more proactive stance as they try to gauge the strength of the company's ability to fund its pension promise. Many of the situations in which they will be expected to act are unlikely to be clear-cut – in corporate deals for example or simply trying to agree an appropriate contribution rate. It will be difficult for trustees to take a common sense approach given the duties and expectations that they have to satisfy unless the eventual Codes of Practice live up to their original promise to guide rather than prescribe.

14.2.5   The increased duties on trustees, for example to demonstrate 'knowledge and experience', may well deter individuals from wishing to stand. If company appointed trustees also find themselves in difficulty because of conflict, the trend towards professional trustees is likely to increase. This is not necessarily a bad thing, although there are perhaps insufficient numbers of appropriately experienced individuals to offer schemes a real choice. However it will be a marked change both from the way in which most schemes are run now and from the role originally envisaged for trustees, i.e. as knowledgeable laymen.

14.2.6   Furthermore, some of the major changes in schemes are outside the ambit of the legislation altogether (e.g. the discussions currently taking place about the role and duties of actuaries for example).

14.3   THE FUTURE

14.3.1   In the authors' view the Act is a very considerable change in the legal basis of company sponsored schemes and it does not appear that any simplification of the law has been achieved. Some pensioners and future pensioners may well be better off than they would otherwise have been, but there are also likely to be losers as well as winners. The costs of the PPF levy are a concern.

14.3.2   Perhaps the most obvious point is that, as ever, company pensions depend on the willingness and, crucially, the *ability* of companies to pay. The expense attaching to traditional defined benefit schemes mean they are a thing of the past for most private sector employees not already in such schemes. This in turn causes human resource problems for a 'two-tier' workforce, and there is anecdotal evidence of a disincentive to labour mobility. The Act will not increase

the overall number of employees covered by company schemes, and may accelerate the decline in existing coverage. If this suggests that company pensions
remain under something of a cloud, the silver lining may be in the possible
reinvigoration of the stakeholder pension, if only as an escape from Pensions Act
regulation.

Appendix
PENSIONS ACT 2004

2004 CHAPTER 35

CONTENTS

PART 1   THE PENSIONS REGULATOR

PART 2   THE BOARD OF THE PENSION PROTECTION FUND

CHAPTER 1   THE BOARD

CHAPTER 2   INFORMATION RELATING TO EMPLOYER'S INSOLVENCY ETC

CHAPTER 3   PENSION PROTECTION

CHAPTER 4   FRAUD COMPENSATION

CHAPTER 5   GATHERING INFORMATION

PART 4   FINANCIAL PLANNING FOR RETIREMENT

PART 5   OCCUPATIONAL AND PERSONAL PENSION SCHEMES: MISCELLANEOUS PROVISIONS

PART 6   FINANCIAL ASSISTANCE SCHEME FOR MEMBERS OF CERTAIN PENSION SCHEMES

PART 7   CROSS-BORDER ACTIVITIES WITHIN EUROPEAN UNION

PART 8   STATE PENSIONS

PART 9   MISCELLANEOUS AND SUPPLEMENTARY

PENSIONS ACT 2004

2004 CHAPTER 35

An Act to make provision relating to pensions and financial planning for retirement and
provision relating to entitlement to bereavement payments, and for connected purposes.
                                                                    [18 November 2004]

BE IT ENACTED by the Queen's most Excellent Majesty, by and with the advice and
consent of the Lords Spiritual and Temporal, and Commons, in this present Parliament
assembled, and by the authority of the same, as follows:–

PART 1   THE PENSIONS REGULATOR

Establishment

1 The Pensions Regulator

There shall be a body corporate called the Pensions Regulator (in this Act referred to as 'the Regulator').

2 Membership of the Regulator

(1)   The Regulator is to consist of the following members –

    (a)   a chairman appointed by the Secretary of State,

    (b)   the Chief Executive of the Regulator, and

    (c)   at least five other persons appointed by the Secretary of State after consulting the chairman.

(2)   The chairman must not be appointed from the staff of the Regulator or be the chairman of the Board of the Pension Protection Fund (see section 108).

(3)   At least two of the members appointed under subsection (1)(c) must be appointed from the staff of the Regulator.

(4)   In appointing persons under subsection (1)(c) the Secretary of State must secure that a majority of the members of the Regulator are non-executive members.

(5)   No member of the staff of the Board of the Pension Protection Fund is eligible for appointment as a member of the Regulator.

(6)   In this Part –

    (a)   references to executive members of the Regulator are to –

        (i)   the Chief Executive, and

        (ii)   the members appointed under subsection (1)(c) from the staff of the Regulator, and

    (b)   references to non-executive members of the Regulator are to members who are not executive members.

3 Further provision about the Regulator

Schedule 1 makes further provision about the Regulator, including provision as to –

the terms of appointment, tenure and remuneration of members,
the appointment of the Chief Executive and other staff,
the proceedings of the Regulator,
its funding and accounts, and
the status and liability of the Regulator, its members and staff.

General provisions about functions

4 Regulator's functions

(1)   The Regulator has –

    (a)   the functions transferred to it from the Occupational Pensions Regulatory Authority by virtue of this Act or any provisions in force in Northern Ireland corresponding to this Act, and

    (b)   any other functions conferred by, or by virtue of, this or any other enactment.

(2)   As regards the exercise of the Regulator's functions –

    (a)   the non-executive functions listed in subsection (4) of section 8 must, by virtue of subsection (2) of that section, be discharged by the committee established under that section,

(b)   the functions mentioned in the following provisions are exercisable only by the Determinations Panel –

   (i)   section 10(1) (the power in certain circumstances to determine whether to exercise the functions listed in Schedule 2 and to exercise them), and

   (ii)   section 99(10) (the functions concerning the compulsory review of certain determinations), and

(c)   the exercise of other functions of the Regulator may be delegated by the Regulator under paragraph 20 of Schedule 1.

(3)   Subsection (2) is subject to any regulations made by the Secretary of State under paragraph 21 of Schedule 1 (power to limit or permit delegation of functions).

5 Regulator's objectives

(1)   The main objectives of the Regulator in exercising its functions are –

(a)   to protect the benefits under occupational pension schemes of, or in respect of, members of such schemes,

(b)   to protect the benefits under personal pension schemes of, or in respect of, members of such schemes within subsection (2),

(c)   to reduce the risk of situations arising which may lead to compensation being payable from the Pension Protection Fund (see Part 2), and

(d)   to promote, and to improve understanding of, the good administration of work-based pension schemes.

(2)   For the purposes of subsection (1)(b) the members of personal pension schemes within this subsection are –

(a)   the members who are employees in respect of whom direct payment arrangements exist, and

(b)   where the scheme is a stakeholder pension scheme, any other members.

(3)   In this section –

'stakeholder pension scheme' means a personal pension scheme which is or has been registered under section 2 of the Welfare Reform and Pensions Act 1999 (c. 30) (register of stakeholder schemes);

'work-based pension scheme' means –

   (a)   an occupational pension scheme,

   (b)   a personal pension scheme where direct payment arrangements exist in respect of one or more members of the scheme who are employees, or

   (c)   a stakeholder pension scheme.

6 Supplementary powers

The Regulator may do anything (except borrow money) which –

(a)   is calculated to facilitate the exercise of its functions, or

(b)   is incidental or conducive to their exercise.

7 Transfer of OPRA's functions to the Regulator

(1)   Subject to the provisions of this Act, the functions of the Occupational Pensions Regulatory Authority ('OPRA') conferred by or by virtue of –

(a)   the Pension Schemes Act 1993 (c. 48),

(b)   the Pensions Act 1995 (c. 26), and

(c)   the Welfare Reform and Pensions Act 1999,

are hereby transferred to the Regulator.

(2) Accordingly –

    (a)   in section 181(1) of the Pension Schemes Act 1993 (which defines 'the Regulatory Authority' to mean OPRA), for the definition of 'the Regulatory Authority' substitute –

        '"the Regulatory Authority" means the Pensions Regulator;',

    (b)   in section 124(1) of the Pensions Act 1995 (which defines 'the Authority', in Part 1 of that Act, to mean OPRA), for the definition of 'the Authority' substitute –

        '"the Authority" means the Pensions Regulator,',

    (c)   in section 8(1) of the Welfare Reform and Pensions Act 1999 (c. 30) (which defines 'the Authority', in Part 1 of that Act to mean OPRA), for the definition of 'the Authority' substitute –

        '"the Authority" means the Pensions Regulator;', and

    (d)   in section 33 of that Act (time for discharge of pension credit liability), in subsection (5) for 'the Occupational Pensions Regulatory Authority' substitute 'the Pensions Regulator'.

Non-executive functions

8 Non-executive functions

(1) The functions listed in subsection (4) (in this Part referred to as 'the non-executive functions') are functions of the Regulator.

(2) The Regulator must establish a committee to discharge the non-executive functions on its behalf.

(3) Only non-executive members of the Regulator may be members of the committee.

(4) The non-executive functions are –

    (a)   the duty to keep under review the question whether the Regulator's internal financial controls secure the proper conduct of its financial affairs;

    (b)   the duty to determine under paragraph 8(4)(b) of Schedule 1, subject to the approval of the Secretary of State, the terms and conditions as to remuneration of any Chief Executive appointed under paragraph 8(4)(a) of that Schedule.

(5) The committee established under this section must prepare a report on the discharge of the non-executive functions for inclusion in the Regulator's annual report to the Secretary of State under section 11.

(6) The committee's report must relate to the same period as that covered by the Regulator's report.

(7) The committee may establish sub-committees, and the members of any such sub-committee –

    (a)   may include persons who are not members of the committee or of the Regulator, but

    (b)   must not include persons who are executive members or other staff of the Regulator.

(8) The committee may authorise any of its members or any of its sub-committees to discharge on its behalf –

    (a)   any of the non-executive functions;

    (b)   the duty to prepare a report under subsection (5).

(9) The committee (or any of its sub-committees) may be authorised under paragraph 20(1) of Schedule 1 to exercise further functions of the Regulator.

(10) This section is subject to any regulations made by the Secretary of State under paragraph 21 of Schedule 1 (power to limit or permit delegation of functions).

The Determinations Panel

9 The Determinations Panel

(1) The Regulator must establish and maintain a committee consisting of –

(a) a chairman, and
(b) at least six other persons,

(in this Part referred to as 'the Determinations Panel').

(2) The Regulator must appoint as the chairman of the Panel the person nominated in accordance with paragraph 11 of Schedule 1 (nomination by a committee established by the chairman of the Regulator).

(3) The chairman of the Panel must –

(a) decide the number of persons to be appointed as the other members of the Panel, and
(b) nominate a person suitable for each of those appointments.

(4) The Regulator must then appoint as the other members of the Panel the persons nominated by the chairman of the Panel.

(5) The following are ineligible for appointment as members of the Panel –

(a) any member of the Regulator;
(b) any member of the staff of the Regulator;
(c) any member of the Board of the Pension Protection Fund;
(d) any member of the staff of that Board.

(6) The Panel may establish sub-committees consisting of members of the Panel.

(7) Further provision about the Panel is made in Schedule 1, including provision as to the terms of appointment, tenure and remuneration of members and as to its procedure.

10 Functions exercisable by the Determinations Panel

(1) The Determinations Panel is to exercise on behalf of the Regulator –

(a) the power to determine, in the circumstances described in subsection (2), whether to exercise a reserved regulatory function, and
(b) where it so determines to exercise a reserved regulatory function, the power to exercise the function in question.

(2) Those circumstances are –

(a) where the Regulator considers that the exercise of the reserved regulatory function may be appropriate, or
(b) where an application is made under, or by virtue of, any of the provisions listed in subsection (6) for the Regulator to exercise the reserved regulatory function.

(3) Where subsection (1) applies, the powers mentioned in that subsection are not otherwise exercisable by or on behalf of the Regulator.

(4) For the purposes of this Part, a function of the Regulator is a 'reserved regulatory function' if it is a function listed in Schedule 2.

(5) Regulations may amend Schedule 2 by –

(a) adding any function of the Regulator conferred by, or by virtue of, this or any other enactment,
(b) omitting any such function, or
(c) altering the description of any such function contained in that Schedule.

(6) The provisions referred to in subsection (2)(b) are –

(a) section 20(10) (application to permit payments out of an account that is subject to a restraining order);
(b) section 26(2) (application for order validating action taken in contravention of freezing order);

(c) section 41(7) (application for the issue of a revised contribution notice under section 41(9));

(d) section 50(7) (application for the issue of a revised contribution notice under section 50(9));

(e) section 3(3) of the Pensions Act 1995 (c. 26) (application for revocation of prohibition order);

(f) section 4(5) of that Act (application for revocation of a suspension order);

(g) section 7(5A) of that Act (application for appointment of a trustee under section 7(3)(a) or (c) of that Act);

(h) section 29(5) of that Act (application for waiver of disqualification);

(i) section 69(1) of that Act (application for order authorising modification or modifying a scheme);

(j) section 71A(2) of that Act (application for modifying a scheme to secure winding up);

(k) section 99(4A) of the Pension Schemes Act 1993 (c. 48) (application for extension under section 99(4) of that Act of a period for compliance);

(l) section 101J(6)(a) of that Act (application for extension under section 101J(2) of that Act of a period for compliance).

(7) Regulations may amend subsection (6) by –

(a) adding any provision of this or any other enactment to the list in that subsection, or

(b) omitting or altering the description of any provision mentioned in that list.

(8) The Panel may be authorised under paragraph 20(4) or (6) of Schedule 1 to exercise further functions of the Regulator on behalf of the Regulator.

(9) The Panel may authorise any of its members or any of its sub-committees to exercise on its behalf –

(a) any of the functions of the Regulator which are exercisable by the Panel on behalf of the Regulator, or

(b) any of the functions of the Panel under section 93(3), section 99(11) and paragraph 18(2) of Schedule 1 (procedure).

(10) This section is subject to any regulations made by the Secretary of State under paragraph 21 of Schedule 1 (power to limit or permit delegation of functions).

Annual report

11 Annual reports to Secretary of State

(1) The Regulator must prepare a report for each financial year.

(2) Each report –

(a) must deal with the activities of the Regulator in the financial year for which it is prepared, including the matters mentioned in subsection (3), and

(b) must include the report prepared under subsection (5) of section 8 by the committee established under that section.

(3) The matters referred to in subsection (2)(a) are –

(a) the strategic direction of the Regulator and the manner in which it has been kept under review;

(b) the steps taken to scrutinise the performance of the Chief Executive in securing that the Regulator's functions are exercised efficiently and effectively;

(c) the Regulator's objectives and targets (including its main objectives as set out in section 5 or in any corresponding provision in force in Northern Ireland) and the steps taken to monitor the extent to which they are being met.

(4) The Regulator must send each report to the Secretary of State as soon as practicable after the end of the financial year for which it is prepared.

(5) The Secretary of State must lay before each House of Parliament a copy of every report received by him under this section.

(6) In this section 'financial year' means –

    (a) the period beginning with the date on which the Regulator is established and ending with the next following 31st March, and

    (b) each successive period of 12 months.

Provision of information, education and assistance

12 Provision of information, education and assistance

(1) The Regulator may provide such information, education and assistance as it considers appropriate to those involved in –

    (a) the administration of work-based pension schemes, or

    (b) advising the trustees or managers in relation to such schemes as to their operation.

(2) To the extent that it is not authorised to do so under subsection (1), the Regulator may also provide such information, education and assistance as it considers appropriate to –

    (a) employers in relation to work-based pension schemes,

    (b) persons involved in advising such employers as to the operation of such schemes, or

    (c) persons upon whom duties are imposed by or by virtue of section 238 (information and advice to employees).

(3) For the purposes of subsection (2), 'employers in relation to work-based pension schemes' means, in the case of stakeholder pension schemes, the persons upon whom duties are imposed by or by virtue of section 3 of the Welfare Reform and Pensions Act 1999 (c. 30) (duty of employers to facilitate access to stakeholder pension schemes).

(4) In this section –

'assistance' does not include financial assistance;

'stakeholder pension scheme' and 'work-based pension scheme' have the same meaning as in section 5 (Regulator's objectives).

New powers in respect of occupational and personal pension schemes

13 Improvement notices

(1) If the Regulator is of the opinion that a person –

    (a) is contravening one or more provisions of the pensions legislation, or

    (b) has contravened one or more of those provisions in circumstances that make it likely that the contravention will continue or be repeated,

it may issue a notice (an 'improvement notice') to that person directing him to take, or refrain from taking, such steps as are specified in the notice in order to remedy or prevent a recurrence of the contravention.

(2) An improvement notice must –

    (a) state that the Regulator is of that opinion and specify the provision or provisions of the pensions legislation in question,

    (b) contain a statement of the matters which it is asserted constitute the contravention and of the evidence on which that opinion is based, and

    (c)   in respect of each step specified in the notice, state the period (being a period of not less than 21 days beginning with the date of the notice) within which it must be complied with.

(3) Directions in an improvement notice –

    (a)   may be framed to any extent by reference to a code of practice issued by the Regulator under section 90, and

    (b)   may be framed so as to afford the person to whom the notice is issued a choice between different ways of remedying or preventing the recurrence of the contravention.

(4) Directions in an improvement notice may be expressed to be conditional on compliance by a third party with a specified direction, or specified directions, contained in a notice under section 14 (third party notices).

(5) An improvement notice may direct the person to whom it is issued to inform the Regulator, within such period as may be specified in the notice, of how he has complied, or is complying, with the notice.

(6) Where a contravention of a provision of the pensions legislation consists of a failure to take action within a time limit, for the purposes of this section the contravention continues until such time as the action is taken.

(7) In this section 'pensions legislation' means any enactment contained in or made by virtue of –

    (a)   the Pension Schemes Act 1993 (c. 48),

    (b)   Part 1 of the Pensions Act 1995 (c. 26), other than sections 62 to 66A of that Act (equal treatment),

    (c)   Part 1 or section 33 of the Welfare Reform and Pensions Act 1999 (c. 30), or

    (d)   this Act.

(8) If the trustees or managers of an occupational or personal pension scheme fail to comply with an improvement notice issued to them, section 10 of the Pensions Act 1995 (civil penalties) applies to any trustee or manager who has failed to take all reasonable steps to secure compliance.

(9) That section also applies to any other person who, without reasonable excuse, fails to comply with an improvement notice issued to him.

14 Third party notices

(1) Where the Regulator is of the opinion that –

    (a)   a person –

        (i)   is contravening one or more provisions of the pensions legislation, or

        (ii) has contravened one or more of those provisions in circumstances that make it likely that the contravention will continue or be repeated,

    (b)   the contravention is or was, wholly or partly, a result of a failure of another person ('the third party') to do any thing, and

    (c)   that failure is not itself a contravention of the pensions legislation,

the Regulator may issue a notice (a 'third party notice') directing the third party to take, or refrain from taking, such steps as are specified in the notice in order to remedy or prevent a recurrence of his failure.

(2) A third party notice must –

    (a)   state that the Regulator is of that opinion and specify the provision or provisions of the pensions legislation in question,

    (b)   contain a statement of –

        (i)   the matters which it is asserted constitute the contravention of the provision or provisions, and

(ii)   the matters which it is asserted constitute the failure by the third party,

and the evidence on which that opinion is based, and

(c)   in respect of each step specified in the notice, state the period (being a period of not less than 21 days beginning with the date of the notice) within which it must be complied with.

(3)   Directions in a third party notice may be framed so as to afford the third party a choice between different ways of remedying or preventing the recurrence of his failure.

(4)   A third party notice may direct the third party to inform the Regulator, within such period as may be specified in the notice, of how he has complied, or is complying, with the notice.

(5   Where a contravention of a provision of the pensions legislation consists of a failure to take action within a time limit, for the purposes of this section the contravention continues until such time as the action is taken.

(6)   Section 10 of the Pensions Act 1995 (c. 26) (civil penalties) applies to a person who, without reasonable excuse, fails to comply with a third party notice issued to him.

(7)   No duty to which a person is subject is to be regarded as contravened merely because of anything required to be done in compliance with a third party notice. This is subject to section 311 (protected items).

(8)   In this section 'pensions legislation' has the same meaning as in section 13.

15   Injunctions and interdicts

(1)   If, on the application of the Regulator, the court is satisfied that –

(a)   there is a reasonable likelihood that a particular person will do any act which constitutes a misuse or misappropriation of any of the assets of an occupational or personal pension scheme, or

(b)   a particular person has done any such act and there is a reasonable likelihood that he will continue or repeat the act in question or do a similar act,

the court may grant an injunction restraining him from doing so or, in Scotland, an interdict prohibiting him from doing so.

(2)   The jurisdiction conferred by this section is exercisable by the High Court or the Court of Session.

16   Restitution

(1)   If, on the application of the Regulator, the court is satisfied that there has been a misuse or misappropriation of any of the assets of an occupational or personal pension scheme, it may order any person involved to take such steps as the court may direct for restoring the parties to the position in which they were before the misuse or misappropriation occurred.

(2)   For this purpose a person is 'involved' if he appears to the court to have been knowingly concerned in the misuse or misappropriation of the assets.

(3)   The jurisdiction conferred by this section is exercisable by the High Court or the Court of Session.

17   Power of the Regulator to recover unpaid contributions

(1)   Where any employer contribution payable towards an occupational or personal pension scheme is not paid on or before its due date, the Regulator may, on behalf of the trustees or managers of the scheme, exercise such powers as the trustees or managers have to recover that contribution.

(2)   For the purposes of subsection (1), any employer contribution payable towards a personal pension scheme which is not paid on or before its due date is, if not a debt due from the employer to the trustees or managers apart from this subsection, to be treated as if it were such a debt.

(3)   In this section –

'due date' –

- (a) in relation to employer contributions payable towards an occupational pension scheme in accordance with a schedule of contributions under section 227, has the same meaning as in section 228,
- (b) in relation to employer contributions payable in accordance with a payment schedule under section 87 of the Pensions Act 1995 (c. 26) (schedules of payments to money purchase schemes), has the meaning given by subsection (2)(c) of that section, and
- (c) in relation to employer contributions payable towards a personal pension scheme, has the same meaning as in section 111A of the Pension Schemes Act 1993 (c. 48) (monitoring of employer payments to personal pension schemes);

'employer contribution' –

- (a) in relation to an occupational pension scheme, means any contribution payable by or on behalf of the employer towards the scheme in accordance with a schedule of contributions under section 227 of this Act or a payment schedule under section 87 of the Pensions Act 1995 (c. 26) (schedules of payments to money purchase schemes) whether –
  - (i) on the employer's own account (but in respect of one or more employees), or
  - (ii) on behalf of an employee out of deductions from the employee's earnings, and
- (b) in relation to a personal pension scheme, means any contribution payable towards the scheme under direct payment arrangements.

18 Pension liberation: interpretation

(1) In this section and sections 19 to 21 –

- (a) 'pension scheme' means an occupational pension scheme or a personal pension scheme,
- (b) 'deposit-taker' has the meaning given by subsections (8A) and (8B) of section 49 of the Pensions Act 1995, except that, for the purposes of this definition, subsection (8A)(c) of that section has effect with the omission of the words from 'or' to the end,
- (c) references to money liberated from a pension scheme are to be read in accordance with subsection (2),
- (d) 'liberated member', in relation to money liberated from a pension scheme, means the member of the pension scheme who is referred to in subsection (2)(a), and
- (e) 'restraining order' means a restraining order under section 20.

(2) Money is to be taken to have been liberated from a pension scheme if –

- (a) the money directly or indirectly represents an amount that, in respect of accrued rights of a member of a pension scheme, has been transferred out of the scheme in pursuance of –
  - (i) a relevant statutory provision, or
  - (ii) a provision of the applicable rules, other than a relevant statutory provision,
- (b) the trustees or managers of the scheme transferred the amount out of the scheme on the basis that a third party ('the liberator') would secure that the amount was used in an authorised way,
- (c) the amount has not been used in an authorised way, and
- (d) the liberator has not secured, and is not likely to secure, that the amount will be used in an authorised way.

(3) The following are 'relevant statutory provisions' for the purposes of subsection (2) –

    (a) section 94(1)(a), (aa) or (b) of the Pension Schemes Act 1993 (c. 48) (right to cash equivalent under Chapter 4 of Part 4 of that Act);

    (b) section 101AB(1)(a) of that Act (right to cash transfer sum under Chapter 5 of Part 4 of that Act);

    (c) section 101F(1) of that Act (right to cash equivalent of pension credit benefit).

(4) In subsection (2) 'authorised way' means –

    (a) where the amount concerned is transferred out of the scheme in pursuance of a provision mentioned in subsection (3)(a), a way specified in subsection (2) or, as the case may be, subsection (3) of section 95 of the Pension Schemes Act 1993;

    (b) where that amount is transferred out in pursuance of the provision mentioned in subsection (3)(b), a way specified in section 101AE(2) of that Act;

    (c) where that amount is transferred out in pursuance of the provision mentioned in subsection (3)(c), a way specified in subsection (2) or, as the case may be, subsection (3) of section 101F of that Act;

    (d) where that amount is transferred out in pursuance of a provision of the kind mentioned in subsection (2)(a)(ii), a way that is authorised by the applicable rules for amounts transferred out in pursuance of that provision.

(5) In this section 'the applicable rules' has the same meaning as, in the case of the pension scheme concerned, that expression has in section 94 of the Pension Schemes Act 1993.

19 Pension liberation: court's power to order restitution

(1) This section applies where money has been liberated from a pension scheme.

(2) In this section 'recoverable property' means (subject to subsection (3)) –

    (a) the money or any of it, or

    (b) property (of any kind and wherever situated) that, directly or indirectly, represents any of the money.

(3) Where a person acquires the beneficial interest in recoverable property in good faith, for value and without notice that the property is, or (as the case may be) represents, money liberated from a pension scheme –

    (a) the property ceases to be recoverable property, and

    (b) no property that subsequently represents it is recoverable property.

(4) The court, on the application of the Regulator, may make such order as the court thinks just and convenient for the purpose of securing that recoverable property, or money representing its value or proceeds of its sale, is transferred –

    (a) towards a pension scheme,

    (b) towards an annuity or insurance policy, or

    (c) to the liberated member.

(5) An order under subsection (4) may (in particular) direct a person who holds recoverable property, or has any degree of control over recoverable property, to take steps for the purpose mentioned in that subsection.

(6) Where the court makes an order under paragraph (a) of subsection (4), it may by order direct the trustees or managers of the scheme referred to in that paragraph –

    (a) to take steps for the purpose mentioned in that subsection;

    (b) to apply the property or money transferred, in such manner as the court may direct, for the purpose of providing benefits under that scheme to or in respect of the liberated member.

(7) Regulations may modify any of the provisions of the Pension Schemes Act 1993 (c. 48) as it applies in relation to cases where an order is made under subsection (6).

(8) The jurisdiction conferred by this section is exercisable by the High Court or the Court of Session.

(9) The generality of the jurisdiction conferred by section 16 is not to be taken to be prejudiced by this section.

(10) The generality of the jurisdiction conferred by this section is not to be taken to be prejudiced by section 21.

20 Pension liberation: restraining orders

(1) The Regulator may make a restraining order in relation to an account with a deposit-taker if –

    (a)   it is satisfied that the account contains money which has been liberated from a pension scheme,

    (b)   it is satisfied that the account is held by or on behalf of –

        (i)   the liberator, or

        (ii) a person who has to, or in practice is likely to, ensure that the account is operated in accordance with the liberator's directions, and

    (c)   the order is made pending consideration being given to the making of one or more repatriation orders in relation to the account under section 21.

(2) A restraining order is an order directing that no credit or debit of any amount may be made to the account concerned ('the restrained account') during the period for which the order has effect.

(3) A restraining order must –

    (a)   specify the name of the deposit-taker in respect of which it is made,

    (b)   identify the account in respect of which it is made, and

    (c)   contain such other information as may be prescribed.

(4) A restraining order –

    (a)   takes effect when the deposit-taker concerned is notified by the Regulator of the making of the order, and

    (b)   (subject to subsection (7)) ceases to have effect through expiry of time at the end of the six months beginning with the day when it is made.

(5) The Regulator may, at a time when a restraining order has effect, make an order extending (or further extending) the restraining order.

(6) An order under subsection (5) (an 'extension order') takes effect –

    (a)   when the deposit-taker concerned is notified by the Regulator of the making of the order, but

    (b)   only if notification under paragraph (a) occurs at a time when the restraining order concerned has effect.

(7) Where an extension order takes effect –

    (a)   the restraining order concerned does not cease to have effect through expiry of time until the end of the six months beginning with the time when it would have ceased to have effect through expiry of time had it not been extended, but

    (b)   for so long as the extension order has effect, no further extension order can take effect before that time in relation to the restraining order.

(8) A restraining order does not prevent the crediting to the restrained account of an amount representing interest payable by the deposit-taker on any amount which is, or has been, in the account.

(9) Where a restraining order has effect, the deposit-taker must return to the payer any money credited to the restrained account in breach of the order.

(10) Where a restraining order has effect, the Regulator may, on an application made by or with the consent of the person by whom the restrained account is held, by order

permit a payment specified in the order to be made out of the account if the Regulator is satisfied –

    (a)   that the payment will be made for the purpose of enabling –

        (i)   any individual to meet his reasonable living expenses, or

        (ii) any person to carry on a trade, business, profession or occupation,

    (b)   that the beneficial interest in the money out of which the payment will be made belongs –

        (i)   to the individual, or person, concerned, or

        (ii) to a person who consents to the making of the payment, and

    (c)   that the money out of which the payment will be made is not money liberated from a pension scheme.

(11) Section 10 of the Pensions Act 1995 (c. 26) (civil penalties) applies to a deposit-taker who, without reasonable excuse, fails to comply with any obligation imposed by a restraining order or by this section.

21 Pension liberation: repatriation orders

(1) Subsections (2) and (3) apply where –

    (a)   a restraining order has effect, and

    (b)   the Regulator is satisfied that the restrained account contains an amount of money liberated from a pension scheme.

(2) The Regulator may by order –

    (a)   direct the deposit-taker concerned to pay from the account a sum not exceeding that amount –

        (i)   towards a pension scheme,

        (ii) towards an annuity or insurance policy, or

        (iii) to the liberated member, and

    (b)   where it makes an order under paragraph (a)(i), direct the trustees or managers of the scheme to apply the sum, in such manner as the Regulator may direct, for the purpose of providing benefits under the scheme to or in respect of the liberated member.

(3) If it appears to the Regulator, on taking an overall view of transactions taking place before the restraining order was made, that there are two or more individuals each of whom is a person who is or may be the liberated member in relation to some of the money, the Regulator may determine the sums to be paid from the restrained account under subsection (2) on any basis that appears to the Regulator to be just and reasonable.

(4) Regulations may modify any of the provisions of the Pension Schemes Act 1993 (c. 48) as it applies in relation to cases where an order is made under subsection (2)(b).

(5) Section 10 of the Pensions Act 1995 (c. 26) (civil penalties) applies to a deposit-taker who, without reasonable excuse, fails to comply with a direction given to him under subsection (2)(a).

(6) If the trustees or managers of a pension scheme fail to comply with a direction given to them under subsection (2)(b), that section applies to any trustee or manager who has failed to take all reasonable steps to secure compliance.

(7) In this section 'restrained account' has the meaning given by section 20.

Powers in relation to winding up of occupational pension schemes

22 Powers to wind up occupational pension schemes

In section 11 of the Pensions Act 1995 (powers to wind up occupational pension schemes) –

(a) omit subsection (3),

(b) before subsection (4) insert –

'(3A) The Authority may, during an assessment period (within the meaning of section 132 of the Pensions Act 2004 (meaning of "assessment period" for the purposes of Part 2 of that Act)) in relation to an occupational pension scheme, by order direct the scheme to be wound up if they are satisfied that it is necessary to do so in order –

(a) to ensure that the scheme's protected liabilities do not exceed its assets, or

(b) if those liabilities do exceed its assets, to keep the excess to a minimum.

(3B) In subsection (3A) –

(a) "protected liabilities" has the meaning given by section 131 of the Pensions Act 2004, and

(b) references to the assets of the scheme are references to those assets excluding any assets representing the value of any rights in respect of money purchase benefits (within the meaning of that Act) under the scheme.',

(c) at the end of subsection (4) insert –

'This subsection is subject to sections 28, 135 and 219 of the Pensions Act 2004 (winding up order made when freezing order has effect in relation to scheme, during assessment period under Part 2 of that Act etc).', and

(d) after subsection (6) insert –

'(6A) Subsection (6) does not have effect to authorise the Authority to make an order as mentioned in paragraph (a) or (b) of that subsection, if their doing so would be unlawful as a result of section 6(1) of the Human Rights Act 1998 (unlawful for public authority to act in contravention of a Convention right).'

23 Freezing orders

(1) This section applies to an occupational pension scheme which is not a money purchase scheme.

(2) The Regulator may make a freezing order in relation to such a scheme if and only if –

(a) the order is made pending consideration being given to the making of an order in relation to the scheme under section 11(1)(c) of the Pensions Act 1995 (c. 26) (power to wind up schemes where necessary to protect the generality of members), and

(b) the Regulator is satisfied that –

(i) there is, or is likely to be if the order is not made, an immediate risk to the interests of members under the scheme or the assets of the scheme, and

(ii) it is necessary to make the freezing order to protect the interests of the generality of the members of the scheme.

But no freezing order may be made in relation to a scheme during an assessment period (within the meaning of section 132) in relation to the scheme (see section 135(11)).

(3) A freezing order is an order directing that during the period for which it has effect –

(a) no benefits are to accrue under the scheme rules to, or in respect of, members of the scheme, and

(b) winding up of the scheme may not begin.

(4) A freezing order may also contain one or more of the following directions which have effect during the period for which the order has effect –

(a) a direction that no new members, or no specified classes of new member, are to be admitted to the scheme;

(b) a direction that –

(i)   no further contributions or payments, or

(ii) no further specified contributions or payments,

are to be paid towards the scheme by or on behalf of the employer, any members or any specified members of the scheme;

(c) a direction that any amount or any specified amount which –

(i)   corresponds to any contribution which would be due to be paid towards the scheme on behalf of a member but for a direction under paragraph (b), and

(ii) has been deducted from a payment of any earnings in respect of an employment,

is to be repaid to the member in question by the employer;

(d) a direction that no benefits, or no specified benefits, are to be paid to or in respect of any members or any specified members under the scheme rules;

(e) a direction that payments of all benefits or specified benefits under the scheme rules to or in respect of all the members or specified members may only be made from the scheme if they are reduced in a specified manner or by a specified amount;

(f) a direction that –

(i)   no transfers or no specified transfers of, or no transfer payments or no specified transfer payments in respect of, any member's rights under the scheme rules are to be made from the scheme, or

(ii) no other steps or no specified other steps are to be taken to discharge any liability of the scheme to or in respect of a member of the scheme in respect of pensions or other benefits;

(g) a direction that no statements of entitlement are to be provided to members of the scheme under section 93A of the Pension Schemes Act 1993 (c. 48) (salary related schemes: right to statement of entitlement);

(h) a direction that –

(i)   no refunds of, or no specified refunds of, or in respect of, contributions paid by or in respect of a member towards the scheme are to be made from the scheme, or

(ii) refunds or specified refunds of, or in respect of, contributions paid by or in respect of a member towards the scheme may only be made from the scheme if they are determined in a specified manner and satisfy such other conditions as may be specified.

(5) In subsection (4)(b) –

(a) the references to contributions do not include contributions due to be paid before the order takes effect, and

(b) the references to payments towards a scheme include payments in respect of pension credits where the person entitled to the credit is a member of the scheme.

(6) A freezing order may not contain a direction under subsection (4)(d) or (e) which reduces the benefits payable to or in respect of a member, for the period during which the order has effect, below the level to which the trustees or managers of the scheme

would have power to reduce them if a winding up of the scheme had begun at the time when the freezing order took effect.

(7) A direction under subsection (4)(f) may, in particular, provide that transfers or specified transfers of, or transfer payments or specified transfer payments in respect of, any member's rights under the scheme rules may not be made from the scheme unless the amounts paid out from the scheme in respect of the transfers or transfer payments are determined in a specified manner and the transfer or transfer payments satisfy such other conditions as may be specified.

(8) A freezing order may also require the trustees or managers of the scheme to obtain an actuarial valuation within a specified period.

(9) A freezing order containing such a requirement must specify –

(a) the date by reference to which the assets and liabilities are to be valued,
(b) the assets and liabilities which are to be taken into account,
(c) the manner in which the valuation must be prepared,
(d) the information and statements which it must contain, and
(e) any other requirements that the valuation must satisfy.

(10) For the purposes of subsection (8) –

'an actuarial valuation' means a written valuation of the scheme's assets and liabilities prepared and signed by the actuary;
'the actuary' means –

(a)   the actuary appointed under section 47(1)(b) of the Pensions Act 1995 (c. 26) (professional advisers) in relation to the scheme, or
(b)   if no such actuary has been appointed –

(i) a person with prescribed qualifications or experience, or
(ii) a person approved by the Secretary of State.

(11) In this section 'specified' means specified in the freezing order.

24 Consequences of freezing order

(1) If a freezing order is made in relation to a scheme any action taken in contravention of the order is void except to the extent that the action is validated by an order under section 26.

(2) A freezing order in relation to a scheme does not prevent any increase in a benefit which is an increase which would otherwise accrue in accordance with the scheme or any enactment during the period for which the order has effect, unless the order contains a direction to the contrary.

(3) A freezing order in relation to a scheme does not prevent the scheme being wound up in pursuance of an order under section 11 of the Pensions Act 1995 (power to wind up occupational pension schemes).

(4) If a freezing order contains a direction under section 23(4)(b) that no further contributions, or no further specified contributions, are to be paid towards a scheme during the period for which the order has effect –

(a)   any contributions which are the subject of the direction and which would otherwise be due to be paid towards the scheme during that period are to be treated as if they do not fall due, and
(b)   any obligation to pay those contributions (including any obligation under section 49(8) of the Pensions Act 1995 to pay amounts deducted corresponding to such contributions) is to be treated as if it does not arise.

(5) If a freezing order contains a direction under section 23(4)(f) (no transfers or discharge of member's rights) it does not prevent –

(a)   giving effect to a pension sharing order or provision, or
(b)   giving effect to a pension earmarking order in a case where –

(i) the order requires a payment to be made if a payment in respect of any benefits under the scheme becomes due to a person, and

(ii) a direction under section 23(4)(d) or (e) does not prevent the payment becoming due.

(6) For the purposes of subsection (5) –

'pension sharing order or provision' means an order or provision falling within section 28(1) of the Welfare Reform and Pensions Act 1999 (c. 30) (activation of pension sharing);

'pension earmarking order' means –

(a) an order under section 23 of the Matrimonial Causes Act 1973 (c. 18) (financial provision orders in connection with divorce etc) so far as it includes provision made by virtue of section 25B or 25C of that Act (powers to include provision about pensions),

(b) an order under section 12A(2) or (3) of the Family Law (Scotland) Act 1985 (c. 37) (powers in relation to pension lump sums when making a capital sum order), or

(c) an order under Article 25 of the Matrimonial Causes (Northern Ireland) Order 1978 (S.I. 1978/1045 (N.I.15)) so far as it includes provision made by virtue of Article 27B or 27C of that Order (Northern Ireland powers corresponding to those mentioned in paragraph (a)).

(7) Regulations may modify any provisions of –

(a) Chapter 4 of Part 4 of the Pension Schemes Act 1993 (c. 48) (protection for early leavers: transfer values), or

(b) Chapter 5 of that Part (protection for early leavers: cash transfer sums and contribution refunds),

in their application to an occupational pension scheme in relation to which a freezing order is made containing a direction under section 23(4)(f), (g) or (h) (no transfers etc in respect of member's rights or refunds of contributions etc from the scheme).

(8 Disregarding subsection (1), if a freezing order made in relation to a scheme is not complied with, section 10 of the Pensions Act 1995 (c. 26) (civil penalties) applies to any trustee or manager of the scheme who has failed to take all reasonable steps to secure compliance.

(9) Subsection (8) does not apply in the case of non-compliance with a direction under section 23(4)(c) (direction that certain deducted contributions are to be repaid by the employer).

(10) In such a case, section 10 of the Pensions Act 1995 (civil penalties) applies to an employer who, without reasonable excuse, fails to repay an amount as required by the direction.

25 Period of effect etc of freezing order

(1) A freezing order must specify the period for which it has effect.

(2) The period specified must not exceed three months.

(3) The Regulator may on one or more occasions by order extend the period for which the order has effect.

(4) But the total period for which the order has effect must not exceed six months.

(5) This section is subject to sections 27, 28 and 29 (effect of winding up and assessment period on freezing orders).

26 Validation of action in contravention of freezing order

(1) If a freezing order is made in relation to a scheme, the Regulator may by order validate action taken in contravention of the order.

(2) Any of the following persons may apply to the Regulator for an order under this section validating particular action –

    (a) the trustees or managers of the scheme;

    (b) any person directly affected by the action.

27 Effect of determination to wind up scheme on freezing order

(1) This section applies where –

    (a) the Regulator determines to make an order under section 11 of the Pensions Act 1995 (c. 26) (power to wind up occupational pension schemes) in relation to a scheme ('a winding up order'),

    (b) that determination is made during the period for which a freezing order has effect in relation to the scheme,

    (c) the case is not one to which the special procedure in section 98 applies (immediate exercise of powers where immediate risk to assets etc), and

    (d) the winding up order accordingly cannot be made until the expiry of the period specified in section 96(5) (no exercise during period of referral to the Tribunal etc).

(2) In such a case the freezing order is to continue to have effect until –

    (a) where the winding up order is made, it ceases to have effect under section 28 from the time when that order is made, or

    (b) the determination to make the winding up order is revoked.

(3) Subsection (2) is subject to the Regulator's power under section 101 to revoke the freezing order at any time.

28 Effect of winding up order on freezing order

(1) This section applies where –

    (a) an order is made under section 11 of the Pensions Act 1995 ('the 1995 Act') (power to wind up occupational pension schemes) in relation to a scheme, and

    (b) the order is made during the period for which a freezing order has effect in relation to the scheme.

(2) In such a case –

    (a) the winding up of the scheme in pursuance of the order under section 11 of the 1995 Act is to be taken as beginning at the time when the freezing order took effect, and

    (b) the freezing order ceases to have effect from the time when the order under section 11 of the 1995 Act is made.

(3) The Regulator may by order direct any specified person –

    (a) to take such specified steps as it considers are necessary as a result of the winding up of the scheme being deemed under subsection (2)(a) to have begun at the time when the freezing order took effect, and

    (b) to take those steps within a specified period.

(4) If the trustees or managers of a scheme fail to comply with a direction to them contained in an order under this section, section 10 of the 1995 Act (civil penalties) applies to any trustee or manager who has failed to take all reasonable steps to secure compliance.

(5) That section also applies to any other person who, without reasonable excuse, fails to comply with a direction to him contained in an order under this section.

(6) In this section 'specified' means specified in an order under this section.

29 Effect of assessment period under Part 2 on freezing order

Where an assessment period (within the meaning of section 132) begins in relation to a scheme, any freezing order in relation to the scheme ceases to have effect when the assessment period begins.

30 Power to give a direction where freezing order ceases to have effect

(1) This section applies where –

    (a) the Regulator revokes a freezing order in relation to a scheme or it otherwise ceases to have effect, and

    (b) at the time when the freezing order ceases to have effect, the Regulator has not made an order under section 11 of the Pensions Act 1995 (c. 26) ('the 1995 Act') in relation to the scheme.

(2) In such a case the Regulator may make an order under this section in relation to the scheme containing a direction that, if specified conditions are met, specified benefits are to accrue under the scheme rules to, or in respect of, specified members of the scheme in respect of specified periods of service being service in employment which but for the freezing order would have qualified the member in question for those benefits under the scheme rules.

(3) The conditions mentioned in subsection (2) may include –

    (a) a requirement that specified benefits do not accrue to, or in respect of, a member or a specified member unless a contribution of a specified amount is paid by or on behalf of the member towards the scheme within a specified period;

    (b) a requirement that a contribution of a specified amount must be paid by or on behalf of the employer within a specified period;

    (c) a requirement that such contributions as are specified under paragraph (a) or (b) are to be accepted for the period for which the freezing order had effect or any part of that period.

(4) Where the freezing order contained a direction under section 23(4)(d) or (e) and any amount of any benefit under the scheme rules was not paid as a result of the direction –

    (a) the direction does not affect any entitlement to that benefit, and

    (b) any benefit to which a member, or a person in respect of a member, remains entitled at the end of the period for which the freezing order had effect is an amount which falls due to the member or, as the case may be, the person at the end of that period.

(5) If an order made under this section in relation to a scheme is not complied with, section 10 of the 1995 Act (civil penalties) applies to a trustee or a manager of the scheme who has failed to take all reasonable steps to secure compliance.

(6) Subsection (7) applies if –

    (a) an order is made under this section in relation to a scheme,

    (b) the order contains a requirement as described in subsection (3)(b) that a contribution of a specified amount must be paid by or on behalf of the employer within a specified period, and

    (c) the contribution is not paid within that period.

(7) In such a case –

    (a) section 10 of the 1995 Act applies to the employer if he has failed, without reasonable excuse, to secure compliance,

    (b) the amount which for the time being remains unpaid after the end of the specified period is to be treated as a debt due from the employer to the trustees or managers of the scheme, and

    (c) except in prescribed circumstances, the trustees or managers must, within a prescribed period, give notice of the failure to pay to the Regulator and to the member.

(8) If in any case subsection (7)(c) is not complied with, section 10 of the 1995 Act applies to any trustee or manager who has failed to take all reasonable steps to secure compliance.

(9) In this section 'specified' means specified in an order under this section.

31 Notification of trustees, managers, employers and members

(1) This section applies where –

(a) a freezing order is made in relation to a scheme,

(b) an order is made under section 26 validating action taken in contravention of a freezing order made in relation to a scheme,

(c) an order is made under section 28 directing specified steps to be taken following the winding up of a scheme, or

(d) an order is made under section 30 in relation to a scheme where a freezing order ceases to have effect.

(2) The Regulator must, as soon as reasonably practicable after the order has been made, notify –

(a) the trustees or managers of the scheme, and

(b) the employer in relation to the scheme,

of the fact that the order has been made and of its effect.

(3) The Regulator may by order direct the trustees or managers of the scheme to notify –

(a) all the members of the scheme, or

(b) the members of the scheme specified in the order,

of the fact that the order mentioned in subsection (1) has been made and of its effect.

(4) Notification is to be within the period and in the manner specified in the order under subsection (3).

(5) If the trustees or managers of a scheme fail to comply with a direction to them contained in an order made under subsection (3), section 10 of the Pensions Act 1995 (c. 26) (civil penalties) applies to any trustee or manager who has failed to take all reasonable steps to secure compliance.

32 Sections 23 to 31: supplementary

(1) An order may be made in relation to a scheme under any of sections 23, 25, 26, 28, 30 and 31 –

(a) in spite of any enactment or rule of law, or any rule of the scheme, which would otherwise operate to prevent the order being made, and

(b) without regard to any such enactment, rule of law or rule of the scheme as would otherwise require, or might otherwise be taken to require, the implementation of any procedure or the obtaining of any consent, with a view to the making of the order.

(2) Subsection (1) does not have effect to authorise the Regulator to make an order as mentioned in that subsection if its doing so would be unlawful as a result of section 6(1) of the Human Rights Act 1998 (c. 42) (unlawful for public authority to act in contravention of a Convention right).

Trustees of occupational pension schemes

33 Prohibition orders

For section 3 of the Pensions Act 1995 (c. 26) (prohibition orders) substitute –

'3 Prohibition orders

(1) The Authority may by order prohibit a person from being a trustee of –

    (a)   a particular trust scheme,

    (b)   a particular description of trust schemes, or

    (c)   trust schemes in general,

    if they are satisfied that he is not a fit and proper person to be a trustee of the scheme or schemes to which the order relates.

(2) Where a prohibition order is made under subsection (1) against a person in respect of one or more schemes of which he is a trustee, the order has the effect of removing him.

(3) The Authority may, on the application of any person prohibited under this section, by order revoke the order either generally or in relation to a particular scheme or description of schemes.

(4) An application under subsection (3) may not be made –

    (a)   during the period within which the determination to exercise the power to make the prohibition order may be referred to the Tribunal under section 96(3) or 99(7) of the Pensions Act 2004, and

    (b)   if the determination is so referred, until the reference, and any appeal against the Tribunal's determination, has been finally disposed of.

(5) A revocation made at any time under this section cannot affect anything done before that time.

(6) The Authority must prepare and publish a statement of the policies they intend to adopt in relation to the exercise of their powers under this section.

(7) The Authority may revise any statement published under subsection (6) and must publish any revised statement.

(8) In this section "the Tribunal" means the Pensions Regulator Tribunal established under section 102 of the Pensions Act 2004.'

34 Suspension orders

In section 4 of the Pensions Act 1995 (c. 26) (suspension orders) –

    (a) after subsection (1)(a) insert –

        '(aa) pending consideration being given to the institution of proceedings against him for an offence involving dishonesty or deception,',

    (b) in subsection (2) –

        (i)   in paragraph (a) after 'paragraph (a)' insert 'or (aa)',

        (ii)   after 'have effect' insert 'in relation to a trust scheme', and

        (iii) after 'section 3(1)' insert 'in relation to that scheme',

    (c) after subsection (5) insert –

        '(5A) An application under subsection (5) may not be made –

            (a)   during the period within which the determination to exercise the power to make an order under subsection (1) may be referred to the Tribunal under section 96(3) or 99(7) of the Pensions Act 2004, and

            (b)   if the determination is so referred, until the reference, and any appeal against the Tribunal's determination, has been finally disposed of.'; and

    (d) after subsection (6) insert –

        '(7) In this section "the Tribunal" means the Pensions Regulator Tribunal established under section 102 of the Pensions Act 2004.'

35 Appointments of trustees by the Regulator

(1) In section 7 of the Pensions Act 1995 (appointment of trustees) –

    (a) omit subsection (4), and

    (b) after subsection (5) insert –

        '(5A) An application may be made to the Authority in relation to a trust scheme by –

            (a) the trustees of the scheme,

            (b) the employer, or

            (c) any member of the scheme,

        for the appointment of a trustee of the scheme under subsection (3)(a) or (c).'

(2) In section 8 of that Act (consequences of appointment of trustees under section 7), for subsections (1) and (2) substitute –

        '(1) An order under section 7 appointing a trustee may provide for any fees and expenses of trustees appointed under the order to be paid –

            (a) by the employer,

            (b) out of the resources of the scheme, or

            (c) partly by the employer and partly out of those resources.

        (2) Such an order may also provide that an amount equal to the amount (if any) paid out of the resources of the scheme by virtue of subsection (1)(b) or (c) is to be treated for all purposes as a debt due from the employer to the trustees of the scheme.'

36 Independent trustees

(1) Part 1 of the Pensions Act 1995 (c. 26) (occupational pension schemes) is amended as follows.

(2) In section 22 (circumstances in which provisions relating to independent trustees apply) –

    (a) in subsection (1)(b) omit 'or' at the end of sub-paragraph (i) and after that sub-paragraph insert –

        '(ia) the interim receiver of the property of a person who is the employer in relation to the scheme, or',

    (b) in subsection (2), after 'a scheme' insert 'by virtue of subsection (1)',

    (c) after subsection (2) insert –

        '(2A) To the extent that it does not already apply by virtue of subsection (1), this section also applies in relation to a trust scheme –

            (a) at any time during an assessment period (within the meaning of section 132 of the Pensions Act 2004) in relation to the scheme, and

            (b) at any time, not within paragraph (a), when the scheme is authorised under section 153 of that Act (closed schemes) to continue as a closed scheme.', and

    (d) after subsection (2A) (inserted by paragraph (c) above) insert –

        '(2B) The responsible person must, as soon as reasonably practicable, give notice of an event within subsection (2C) to –

            (a) the Authority,

            (b) the Board of the Pension Protection Fund, and

            (c) the trustees of the scheme.

        (2C) The events are –

(a)   the practitioner beginning to act as mentioned in subsection (1)(a), if immediately before he does so this section does not apply in relation to the scheme;

(b)   the practitioner ceasing to so act, if immediately after he does so this section does not apply in relation to the scheme;

(c)   the official receiver beginning to act in a capacity mentioned in subsection (1)(b)(i), (ia) or (ii), if immediately before he does so this section does not apply in relation to the scheme;

(d)   the official receiver ceasing to act in such a capacity, if immediately after he does so this section does not apply in relation to the scheme.

(2D) For the purposes of subsection (2B) "the responsible person" means –

(a)   in the case of an event within subsection (2C)(a) or (b) the practitioner, and

(b)   in the case of an event within subsection (2C)(c) or (d), the official receiver.

(2E) Regulations may require prescribed persons in prescribed circumstances where this section begins or ceases to apply in relation to a trust scheme by virtue of subsection (2A) to give a notice to that effect to –

(a)   the Authority,

(b)   the Board of the Pension Protection Fund, and

(c)   the trustees of the scheme.

(2F) A notice under subsection (2B), or regulations under subsection (2E), must be in writing and contain such information as may be prescribed.'

(3)   For sections 23 and 24 (appointment of independent trustees) substitute –

'23 Power to appoint independent trustees

(1)   While section 22 applies in relation to a trust scheme, the Authority may by order appoint as a trustee of the scheme a person who –

(a)   is an independent person in relation to the scheme, and

(b)   is registered in the register maintained by the Authority in accordance with regulations under subsection (4).

(2)   In relation to a particular trust scheme, no more than one trustee may at any time be an independent trustee appointed under subsection (1).

(3)   For the purposes of this section a person is independent in relation to a trust scheme only if –

(a)   he has no interest in the assets of the employer or of the scheme otherwise than as trustee of the scheme,

(b)   he is neither connected with, nor an associate of –

(i)   the employer,

(ii)   any person for the time being acting as an insolvency practitioner in relation to the employer, or

(iii) the official receiver acting in any of the capacities mentioned in section 22(1)(b) in relation to the employer, and

(c)   he satisfies any prescribed requirements;

and any reference in this Part to an independent trustee is to be construed accordingly.

(4)   Regulations must provide for the Authority to compile and maintain a register of persons who satisfy the prescribed conditions for registration.

(5)   Regulations under subsection (4) may provide –

          (a)   for copies of the register or of extracts from it to be provided to prescribed persons in prescribed circumstances;

          (b)   for the inspection of the register by prescribed persons in prescribed circumstances.

    (6)   The circumstances which may be prescribed under subsection (5)(a) or (b) include the payment by the person to whom the copy is to be provided, or by whom the register is to be inspected, of such reasonable fee as may be determined by the Authority.

    (7)   This section is without prejudice to the powers conferred by section 7.'

(4) In section 25 (appointment and powers of independent trustees: further provisions) –

    (a) for subsection (4)(a) substitute –

      '(a) he must as soon as reasonably practicable give written notice of that fact to the Authority, and',

    (b) after subsection (5) insert –

      '(5A) Section 10 applies to any person who, without reasonable excuse, fails to comply with subsection (4)(a).', and

    (c) for subsection (6) substitute –

      '(6) An order under section 23(1) may provide for any fees and expenses of the trustee appointed under the order to be paid –

          (a) by the employer,

          (b) out of the resources of the scheme, or

          (c) partly by the employer and partly out of those resources.

      (7) Such an order may also provide that an amount equal to the amount (if any) paid out of the resources of the scheme by virtue of subsection (6)(b) or (c) is to be treated for all purposes as a debt due from the employer to the trustees of the scheme.

      (8) Where, by virtue of subsection (6)(b) or (c), an order makes provision for any fees or expenses of the trustee appointed under the order to be paid out of the resources of the scheme, the trustee is entitled to be so paid in priority to all other claims falling to be met out of the scheme's resources.'

37 Disqualification

In section 30 of the Pensions Act 1995 (c. 26) (consequences of disqualification under section 29), for subsection (1) substitute –

    '(1) Where a person who is a trustee of a trust scheme becomes disqualified under section 29 in relation to the scheme, his becoming so disqualified has the effect of removing him as a trustee.'

Contribution notices where avoidance of employer debt

38 Contribution notices where avoidance of employer debt

(1) This section applies in relation to an occupational pension scheme other than –

    (a) a money purchase scheme, or

    (b) a prescribed scheme or a scheme of a prescribed description.

(2) The Regulator may issue a notice to a person stating that the person is under a liability to pay the sum specified in the notice (a 'contribution notice') –

(a) to the trustees or managers of the scheme, or

(b) where the Board of the Pension Protection Fund has assumed responsibility for the scheme in accordance with Chapter 3 of Part 2 (pension protection), to the Board.

(3) The Regulator may issue a contribution notice to a person only if –

(a) the Regulator is of the opinion that the person was a party to an act or a deliberate failure to act which falls within subsection (5),

(b) the person was at any time in the relevant period –

    (i) the employer in relation to the scheme, or

    (ii) a person connected with, or an associate of, the employer,

(c) the Regulator is of the opinion that the person, in being a party to the act or failure, was not acting in accordance with his functions as an insolvency practitioner in relation to another person, and

(d) the Regulator is of the opinion that it is reasonable to impose liability on the person to pay the sum specified in the notice.

(4) But the Regulator may not issue a contribution notice, in such circumstances as may be prescribed, to a person of a prescribed description.

(5) An act or a failure to act falls within this subsection if –

(a) the Regulator is of the opinion that the main purpose or one of the main purposes of the act or failure was –

    (i) to prevent the recovery of the whole or any part of a debt which was, or might become, due from the employer in relation to the scheme under section 75 of the Pensions Act 1995 (c. 26) (deficiencies in the scheme assets), or

    (ii) otherwise than in good faith, to prevent such a debt becoming due, to compromise or otherwise settle such a debt, or to reduce the amount of such a debt which would otherwise become due,

(b) it is an act which occurred, or a failure to act which first occurred –

    (i) on or after 27th April 2004, and

    (ii) before any assumption of responsibility for the scheme by the Board in accordance with Chapter 3 of Part 2, and

(c) it is either –

    (i) an act which occurred during the period of six years ending with the determination by the Regulator to exercise the power to issue the contribution notice in question, or

    (ii) a failure which first occurred during, or continued for the whole or part of, that period.

(6) For the purposes of subsection (3) –

(a) the parties to an act or a deliberate failure include those persons who knowingly assist in the act or failure, and

(b) 'the relevant period' means the period which –

    (i) begins with the time when the act falling within subsection (5) occurs or the failure to act falling within that subsection first occurs, and

    (ii) ends with the determination by the Regulator to exercise the power to issue the contribution notice in question.

(7) The Regulator, when deciding for the purposes of subsection (3)(d) whether it is reasonable to impose liability on a particular person to pay the sum specified in the notice, must have regard to such matters as the Regulator considers relevant including, where relevant, the following matters –

(a) the degree of involvement of the person in the act or failure to act which falls within subsection (5),

(b) the relationship which the person has or has had with the employer (including, where the employer is a company within the meaning of subsection (11) of section 435 of the Insolvency Act 1986 (c. 45), whether the person has or has had control of the employer within the meaning of subsection (10) of that section),

(c) any connection or involvement which the person has or has had with the scheme,

(d) if the act or failure to act was a notifiable event for the purposes of section 69 (duty to notify the Regulator of certain events), any failure by the person to comply with any obligation imposed on the person by subsection (1) of that section to give the Regulator notice of the event,

(e) all the purposes of the act or failure to act (including whether a purpose of the act or failure was to prevent or limit loss of employment),

(f) the financial circumstances of the person, and

(g) such other matters as may be prescribed.

(8) For the purposes of this section references to a debt due under section 75 of the Pensions Act 1995 (c. 26) include a contingent debt under that section.

(9) Accordingly, in the case of such a contingent debt, the reference in subsection (5)(a)(ii) to preventing a debt becoming due is to be read as including a reference to preventing the occurrence of any of the events specified in section 75(4C)(a) or (b) of that Act upon which the debt is contingent.

(10) For the purposes of this section –

(a) section 249 of the Insolvency Act 1986 (connected persons) applies as it applies for the purposes of any provision of the first Group of Parts of that Act,

(b) section 435 of that Act (associated persons) applies as it applies for the purposes of that Act, and

(c) section 74 of the Bankruptcy (Scotland) Act 1985 (c. 66) (associated persons) applies as it applies for the purposes of that Act.

(11) For the purposes of this section 'insolvency practitioner', in relation to a person, means –

(a) a person acting as an insolvency practitioner, in relation to that person, in accordance with section 388 of the Insolvency Act 1986, or

(b) an insolvency practitioner within the meaning of section 121(9)(b) (persons of a prescribed description).

39 The sum specified in a section 38 contribution notice

(1) The sum specified by the Regulator in a contribution notice under section 38 may be either the whole or a specified part of the shortfall sum in relation to the scheme.

(2) Subject to subsection (3), the shortfall sum in relation to a scheme is –

(a) in a case where, at the relevant time, a debt was due from the employer to the trustees or managers of the scheme under section 75 of the Pensions Act 1995 (c. 26) ('the 1995 Act') (deficiencies in the scheme assets), the amount which the Regulator estimates to be the amount of that debt at that time, and

(b) in a case where, at the relevant time, no such debt was due, the amount which the Regulator estimates to be the amount of the debt under section 75 of the 1995 Act which would become due if –

(i) subsection (2) of that section applied, and

(ii) the time designated by the trustees or managers of the scheme for the purposes of that subsection were the relevant time.

(3) Where the Regulator is satisfied that the act or failure to act falling within section 38(5) resulted –

(a) in a case falling within paragraph (a) of subsection (2), in the amount of the debt which became due under section 75 of the 1995 Act being less than it would otherwise have been, or

(b) in a case falling within paragraph (b) of subsection (2), in the amount of any such debt calculated for the purposes of that paragraph being less than it would otherwise have been,

the Regulator may increase the amounts calculated under subsection (2)(a) or (b) by such amount as the Regulator considers appropriate.

(4) For the purposes of this section 'the relevant time' means –

(a) in the case of an act falling within subsection (5) of section 38, the time of the act, or

(b) in the case of a failure to act falling within that subsection –

(i) the time when the failure occurred, or

(ii) where the failure continued for a period of time, the time which the Regulator determines and which falls within that period.

(5) For the purposes of this section –

(a) references to a debt due under section 75 of the 1995 Act include a contingent debt under that section, and

(b) references to the amount of such a debt include the amount of such a contingent debt.

40   Content and effect of a section 38 contribution notice

(1) This section applies where a contribution notice is issued to a person under section 38.

(2) The contribution notice must –

(a) contain a statement of the matters which it is asserted constitute the act or failure to act which falls within subsection (5) of section 38,

(b) specify the sum which the person is stated to be under a liability to pay, and

(c) identify any other persons to whom contribution notices have been or are issued as a result of the act or failure to act in question and the sums specified in each of those notices.

(3) Where the contribution notice states that the person is under a liability to pay the sum specified in the notice to the trustees or managers of the scheme, the sum is to be treated as a debt due from the person to the trustees or managers of the scheme.

(4) In such a case, the Regulator may, on behalf of the trustees or managers of the scheme, exercise such powers as the trustees or managers have to recover the debt.

(5) But during any assessment period (within the meaning of section 132) in relation to the scheme, the rights and powers of the trustees or managers of the scheme in relation to any debt due to them by virtue of a contribution notice are exercisable by the Board of the Pension Protection Fund to the exclusion of the trustees or managers and the Regulator.

(6) Where, by virtue of subsection (5), any amount is paid to the Board in respect of a debt due by virtue of a contribution notice, the Board must pay the amount to the trustees or managers of the scheme.

(7) Where the contribution notice states that the person is under a liability to pay the sum specified in the notice to the Board, the sum is to be treated as a debt due from the person to the Board.

(8) Where the contribution notice so specifies, the person to whom the notice is issued ('P') is to be treated as jointly and severally liable for the debt with any persons specified in the notice who are persons to whom corresponding contribution notices are issued.

(9) For the purposes of subsection (8), a corresponding contribution notice is a notice which –

    (a) is issued as a result of the same act or failure to act falling within subsection (5) of section 38 as the act or failure as a result of which P's contribution notice is issued,

    (b) specifies the same sum as is specified in P's contribution notice, and

    (c) specifies that the person to whom the contribution notice is issued is jointly and severally liable with P, or with P and other persons, for the debt in respect of that sum.

(10) A debt due by virtue of a contribution notice is not to be taken into account for the purposes of section 75(2) and (4) of the Pensions Act 1995 (c. 26) (deficiencies in the scheme assets) when ascertaining the amount or value of the assets or liabilities of a scheme.

41 Section 38 contribution notice: relationship with employer debt

(1) This section applies where a contribution notice is issued to a person ('P') under section 38 and condition A or B is met.

(2) Condition A is met if, at the time at which the contribution notice is issued, there is a debt due under section 75 of the Pensions Act 1995 ('the 1995 Act') (deficiencies in the scheme assets) from the employer –

    (a) to the trustees or managers of the scheme, or

    (b) where the Board of the Pension Protection Fund has assumed responsibility for the scheme in accordance with Chapter 3 of Part 2 (pension protection), to the Board.

(3) Condition B is met if, after the contribution notice is issued but before the whole of the debt due by virtue of the notice is recovered, a debt becomes due from the employer to the trustees or managers of the scheme under section 75 of the 1995 Act.

(4) The Regulator may issue a direction to the trustees or managers of the scheme not to take any or any further steps to recover the debt due to them under section 75 of the 1995 Act pending the recovery of all or a specified part of the debt due to them by virtue of the contribution notice.

(5) If the trustees or managers fail to comply with a direction issued to them under subsection (4), section 10 of the 1995 Act (civil penalties) applies to any trustee or manager who has failed to take all reasonable steps to secure compliance.

(6) Any sums paid –

    (a) to the trustees or managers of the scheme in respect of any debt due to them by virtue of the contribution notice, or

    (b) to the Board in respect of any debt due to it by virtue of the contribution notice,

are to be treated as reducing the amount of the debt due to the trustees or managers or, as the case may be, to the Board under section 75 of the 1995 Act.

(7) Where a sum is paid to the trustees or managers of the scheme or, as the case may be, to the Board in respect of the debt due under section 75 of the 1995 Act, P may make an application under this subsection to the Regulator for a reduction in the amount of the sum specified in P's contribution notice.

(8) An application under subsection (7) must be made as soon as reasonably practicable after the sum is paid to the trustees or managers or, as the case may be, to the Board in respect of the debt due under section 75 of the 1995 Act.

(9) Where such an application is made to the Regulator, the Regulator may, if it is of the opinion that it is appropriate to do so –

    (a) reduce the amount of the sum specified in P's contribution notice by an amount which it considers reasonable, and

    (b) issue a revised contribution notice specifying the revised sum.

(10) For the purposes of subsection (9), the Regulator must have regard to such matters as the Regulator considers relevant including, where relevant, the following matters –

 (a) the amount paid in respect of the debt due under section 75 of the 1995 Act since the contribution notice was issued,
 (b) any amounts paid in respect of the debt due by virtue of that contribution notice,
 (c) whether contribution notices have been issued to other persons as a result of the same act or failure to act falling within subsection (5) of section 38 as the act or failure as a result of which P's contribution notice was issued,
 (d) where such contribution notices have been issued, the sums specified in each of those notices and any amounts paid in respect of the debt due by virtue of those notices,
 (e) whether P's contribution notice specifies that P is jointly and severally liable for the debt with other persons, and
 (f) such other matters as may be prescribed.

(11) Where –

 (a) P's contribution notice specifies that P is jointly and severally liable for the debt with other persons, and
 (b) a revised contribution notice is issued to P under subsection (9) specifying a revised sum,

the Regulator must also issue revised contribution notices to those other persons specifying the revised sum and their joint and several liability with P for the debt in respect of that sum.

(12) For the purposes of this section –

 (a) references to a debt due under section 75 of the 1995 Act include a contingent debt under that section, and
 (b) references to the amount of such a debt include the amount of such a contingent debt.

42 Section 38 contribution notice: clearance statements

(1) An application may be made to the Regulator under this section for the issue of a clearance statement within paragraph (a), (b) or (c) of subsection (2) in relation to circumstances described in the application.

(2) A clearance statement is a statement, made by the Regulator, that in its opinion in the circumstances described in the application –

 (a) the applicant would not be, for the purposes of subsection (3)(a) of section 38, a party to an act or a deliberate failure to act falling within subsection (5)(a) of that section,
 (b) it would not be reasonable to impose any liability on the applicant under a contribution notice issued under section 38, or
 (c) such requirements of that section as may be prescribed would not be satisfied in relation to the applicant.

(3) Where an application is made under this section, the Regulator –

 (a) may request further information from the applicant;
 (b) may invite the applicant to amend the application to modify the circumstances described.

(4) Where an application is made under this section, the Regulator must as soon as reasonably practicable –

 (a) determine whether to issue the clearance statement, and
 (b) where it determines to do so, issue the statement.

(5) A clearance statement issued under this section binds the Regulator in relation to the exercise of the power to issue a contribution notice under section 38 to the applicant unless –

(a) the circumstances in relation to which the exercise of the power under that section arises are not the same as the circumstances described in the application, and

(b) the difference in those circumstances is material to the exercise of the power.

Financial support directions

43 Financial support directions

(1) This section applies in relation to an occupational pension scheme other than –

(a) a money purchase scheme, or

(b) a prescribed scheme or a scheme of a prescribed description.

(2) The Regulator may issue a financial support direction under this section in relation to such a scheme if the Regulator is of the opinion that the employer in relation to the scheme –

(a) is a service company, or

(b) is insufficiently resourced,

at a time determined by the Regulator which falls within subsection (9) ('the relevant time').

(3) A financial support direction in relation to a scheme is a direction which requires the person or persons to whom it is issued to secure –

(a) that financial support for the scheme is put in place within the period specified in the direction,

(b) that thereafter that financial support or other financial support remains in place while the scheme is in existence, and

(c) that the Regulator is notified in writing of prescribed events in respect of the financial support as soon as reasonably practicable after the event occurs.

(4) A financial support direction in relation to a scheme may be issued to one or more persons.

(5) But the Regulator may issue such a direction to a person only if –

(a) the person is at the relevant time a person falling within subsection (6), and

(b) the Regulator is of the opinion that it is reasonable to impose the requirements of the direction on that person.

(6) A person falls within this subsection if the person is –

(a) the employer in relation to the scheme,

(b) an individual who –

(i) is an associate of an individual who is the employer, but

(ii) is not an associate of that individual by reason only of being employed by him, or

(c) a person, other than an individual, who is connected with or an associate of the employer.

(7) The Regulator, when deciding for the purposes of subsection (5)(b) whether it is reasonable to impose the requirements of a financial support direction on a particular person, must have regard to such matters as the Regulator considers relevant including, where relevant, the following matters –

(a) the relationship which the person has or has had with the employer (including, where the employer is a company within the meaning of subsection (11) of section 435 of the Insolvency Act 1986 (c. 45), whether the person has or has had control of the employer within the meaning of subsection (10) of that section),

(b) in the case of a person falling within subsection (6)(b) or (c), the value of any benefits received directly or indirectly by that person from the employer,

(c) any connection or involvement which the person has or has had with the scheme,

(d) the financial circumstances of the person, and

(e) such other matters as may be prescribed.

(8) A financial support direction must identify all the persons to whom the direction is issued.

(9) A time falls within this subsection if it is a time which falls within a prescribed period which ends with the determination by the Regulator to exercise the power to issue the financial support direction in question.

(10) For the purposes of subsection (3), a scheme is in existence until it is wound up.

(11) No duty to which a person is subject is to be regarded as contravened merely because of any information or opinion contained in a notice given by virtue of subsection (3)(c).

This is subject to section 311 (protected items).

44 Meaning of 'service company' and 'insufficiently resourced'

(1) This section applies for the purposes of section 43 (financial support directions).

(2) An employer ('E') is a 'service company' at the relevant time if –

(a) E is a company within the meaning given by section 735(1) of the Companies Act 1985 (c. 6),

(b) E is a member of a group of companies, and

(c) E's turnover, as shown in the latest available accounts for E prepared in accordance with section 226 of that Act, is solely or principally derived from amounts charged for the provision of the services of employees of E to other members of that group.

(3) The employer in relation to a scheme is insufficiently resourced at the relevant time if –

(a) at that time the value of the resources of the employer is less than the amount which is a prescribed percentage of the estimated section 75 debt in relation to the scheme, and

(b) there is at that time a person who falls within subsection (6)(b) or (c) of section 43 and the value at that time of that person's resources is not less than the amount which is the difference between –

(i) the value of the resources of the employer, and

(ii) the amount which is the prescribed percentage of the estimated section 75 debt.

(4) For the purposes of subsection (3) –

(a) what constitutes the resources of a person is to be determined in accordance with regulations, and

(b) the value of a person's resources is to be determined, calculated and verified in a prescribed manner.

(5) In this section the 'estimated section 75 debt', in relation to a scheme, means the amount which the Regulator estimates to be the amount of the debt which would

become due from the employer to the trustees or managers of the scheme under section 75 of the Pensions Act 1995 (c. 26) (deficiencies in the scheme assets) if –

(a) subsection (2) of that section applied, and

(b) the time designated by the trustees or managers of the scheme for the purposes of that subsection were the relevant time.

(6) When calculating the estimated section 75 debt in relation to a scheme under subsection (5), the amount of any debt due at the relevant time from the employer under section 75 of the Pensions Act 1995 (c. 26) is to be disregarded.

(7) In this section 'the relevant time' has the same meaning as in section 43.

45 Meaning of 'financial support'

(1) For the purposes of section 43 (financial support directions), 'financial support' for a scheme means one or more of the arrangements falling within subsection (2) the details of which are approved in a notice issued by the Regulator.

(2) The arrangements falling within this subsection are –

(a) an arrangement whereby, at any time when the employer is a member of a group of companies, all the members of the group are jointly and severally liable for the whole or part of the employer's pension liabilities in relation to the scheme;

(b) an arrangement whereby, at any time when the employer is a member of a group of companies, a company (within the meaning given in section 736 of the Companies Act 1985 (c. 6)) which meets prescribed requirements and is the holding company of the group is liable for the whole or part of the employer's pension liabilities in relation to the scheme;

(c) an arrangement which meets prescribed requirements and whereby additional financial resources are provided to the scheme;

(d) such other arrangements as may be prescribed.

(3) The Regulator may not issue a notice under subsection (1) approving the details of one or more arrangements falling within subsection (2) unless it is satisfied that the arrangement is, or the arrangements are, reasonable in the circumstances.

(4) In subsection (2), 'the employer's pension liabilities' in relation to a scheme means –

(a) the liabilities for any amounts payable by or on behalf of the employer towards the scheme (whether on his own account or otherwise) in accordance with a schedule of contributions under section 227, and

(b) the liabilities for any debt which is or may become due to the trustees or managers of the scheme from the employer whether by virtue of section 75 of the Pensions Act 1995 (deficiencies in the scheme assets) or otherwise.

46 Financial support directions: clearance statements

(1) An application may be made to the Regulator under this section for the issue of a clearance statement within paragraph (a), (b) or (c) of subsection (2) in relation to circumstances described in the application and relating to an occupational pension scheme.

(2) A clearance statement is a statement, made by the Regulator, that in its opinion in the circumstances described in the application –

(a) the employer in relation to the scheme would not be a service company for the purposes of section 43,

(b) the employer in relation to the scheme would not be insufficiently resourced for the purposes of that section, or

(c) it would not be reasonable to impose the requirements of a financial support direction, in relation to the scheme, on the applicant.

(3) Where an application is made under this section, the Regulator –

   (a) may request further information from the applicant;
   (b) may invite the applicant to amend the application to modify the circumstances described.

(4) Where an application is made under this section, the Regulator must as soon as reasonably practicable –

   (a) determine whether to issue the clearance statement, and
   (b) where it determines to do so, issue the statement.

(5) A clearance statement issued under this section binds the Regulator in relation to the exercise of the power to issue a financial support direction under section 43 in relation to the scheme to the applicant unless –

   (a) the circumstances in relation to which the exercise of the power under that section arises are not the same as the circumstances described in the application, and
   (b) the difference in those circumstances is material to the exercise of the power.

47 Contribution notices where non-compliance with financial support direction

(1) This section applies where there is non-compliance with a financial support direction issued in relation to a scheme under section 43.

(2) The Regulator may issue a notice to any one or more of the persons to whom the direction was issued stating that the person is under a liability to pay to the trustees or managers of the scheme the sum specified in the notice (a 'contribution notice').

(3) The Regulator may issue a contribution notice to a person only if the Regulator is of the opinion that it is reasonable to impose liability on the person to pay the sum specified in the notice.

(4) The Regulator, when deciding for the purposes of subsection (3) whether it is reasonable to impose liability on a particular person to pay the sum specified in the notice, must have regard to such matters as the Regulator considers relevant including, where relevant, the following matters –

   (a) whether the person has taken reasonable steps to secure compliance with the financial support direction,
   (b) the relationship which the person has or has had with the employer (including, where the employer is a company within the meaning of subsection (11) of section 435 of the Insolvency Act 1986 (c. 45), whether the person has or has had control of the employer within the meaning of subsection (10) of that section),
   (c) in the case of a person to whom the financial support direction was issued as a person falling within section 43(6)(b) or (c), the value of any benefits received directly or indirectly by that person from the employer,
   (d) the relationship which the person has or has had with the parties to any arrangements put in place in accordance with the direction (including, where any of those parties is a company within the meaning of subsection (11) of section 435 of the Insolvency Act 1986, whether the person has or has had control of that company within the meaning of subsection (10) of that section),
   (e) any connection or involvement which the person has or has had with the scheme,
   (f) the financial circumstances of the person, and
   (g) such other matters as may be prescribed.

(5) A contribution notice may not be issued under this section in respect of non-compliance with a financial support direction in relation to a scheme where the Board of the Pension Protection Fund has assumed responsibility for the scheme in accordance with Chapter 3 of Part 2 (pension protection).

48 The sum specified in a section 47 contribution notice

(1) The sum specified by the Regulator in a contribution notice under section 47 may be either the whole or a specified part of the shortfall sum in relation to the scheme.

(2) The shortfall sum in relation to a scheme is –

  (a) in a case where, at the time of non-compliance, a debt was due from the employer to the trustees or managers of the scheme under section 75 of the Pensions Act 1995 (c. 26) ('the 1995 Act') (deficiencies in the scheme assets), the amount which the Regulator estimates to be the amount of that debt at that time, and

  (b) in a case where, at the time of non-compliance, no such debt was due, the amount which the Regulator estimates to be the amount of the debt under section 75 of the 1995 Act which would become due if –

    (i) subsection (2) of that section applied, and

    (ii) the time designated by the trustees or managers of the scheme for the purposes of that subsection were the time of non-compliance.

(3) For the purposes of this section 'the time of non-compliance' means –

  (a) in the case of non-compliance with paragraph (a) of subsection (3) of section 43 (financial support directions), the time immediately after the expiry of the period specified in the financial support direction for putting in place the financial support,

  (b) in the case of non-compliance with paragraph (b) of that subsection, the time when financial support for the scheme ceased to be in place,

  (c) in the case of non-compliance with paragraph (c) of that subsection, the time when the prescribed event occurred in relation to which there was the failure to notify the Regulator, or

  (d) where more than one of paragraphs (a) to (c) above apply, whichever of the times specified in the applicable paragraphs the Regulator determines.

49 Content and effect of a section 47 contribution notice

(1) This section applies where a contribution notice is issued to a person under section 47.

(2) The contribution notice must –

  (a) contain a statement of the matters which it is asserted constitute the non-compliance with the financial support direction in respect of which the notice is issued, and

  (b) specify the sum which the person is stated to be under a liability to pay.

(3) The sum specified in the notice is to be treated as a debt due from the person to the trustees or managers of the scheme.

(4) The Regulator may, on behalf of the trustees or managers of the scheme, exercise such powers as the trustees or managers have to recover the debt.

(5) But during any assessment period (within the meaning of section 132) in relation to the scheme, the rights and powers of the trustees or managers of the scheme in relation to any debt due to them by virtue of a contribution notice, are exercisable by the Board of the Pension Protection Fund to the exclusion of the trustees or managers and the Regulator.

(6) Where, by virtue of subsection (5), any amount is paid to the Board in respect of a debt due by virtue of a contribution notice, the Board must pay the amount to the trustees or managers of the scheme.

(7) The contribution notice must identify any other persons to whom contribution notices have been or are issued in respect of the non-compliance in question and the sums specified in each of those notices.

(8) Where the contribution notice so specifies, the person to whom the notice is issued ('P') is to be treated as jointly and severally liable for the debt with any persons specified in the notice who are persons to whom corresponding contribution notices are issued.

(9) For the purposes of subsection (8), a corresponding contribution notice is a notice which –

    (a) is issued in respect of the same non-compliance with the financial support direction as the non-compliance in respect of which P's contribution notice is issued,

    (b) specifies the same sum as is specified in P's contribution notice, and

    (c) specifies that the person to whom the contribution notice is issued is jointly and severally liable with P, or with P and other persons, for the debt in respect of that sum.

(10) A debt due by virtue of a contribution notice is not to be taken into account for the purposes of section 75(2) and (4) of the Pensions Act 1995 (c. 26) (deficiencies in the scheme assets) when ascertaining the amount or value of the assets or liabilities of a scheme.

50 Section 47 contribution notice: relationship with employer debt

(1) This section applies where a contribution notice is issued to a person ('P') under section 47 and condition A or B is met.

(2) Condition A is met if, at the time at which the contribution notice is issued, there is a debt due from the employer to the trustees or managers of the scheme under section 75 of the Pensions Act 1995 ('the 1995 Act') (deficiencies in the scheme assets).

(3) Condition B is met if, after the contribution notice is issued but before the whole of the debt due by virtue of the notice is recovered, a debt becomes due from the employer to the trustees or managers of the scheme under section 75 of the 1995 Act.

(4) The Regulator may issue a direction to the trustees or managers of the scheme not to take any or any further steps to recover the debt due to them under section 75 of the 1995 Act pending the recovery of all or a specified part of the debt due to them by virtue of the contribution notice.

(5) If the trustees or managers fail to comply with a direction issued to them under subsection (4), section 10 of the 1995 Act (civil penalties) applies to any trustee or manager who has failed to take all reasonable steps to secure compliance.

(6) Any sums paid –

    (a) to the trustees or managers of the scheme in respect of any debt due to them by virtue of the contribution notice, or

    (b) to the Board of the Pension Protection Fund in respect of any debt due to it by virtue of the contribution notice (where it has assumed responsibility for the scheme in accordance with Chapter 3 of Part 2 (pension protection)),

are to be treated as reducing the amount of the debt due to the trustees or managers or, as the case may be, to the Board under section 75 of the 1995 Act.

(7) Where a sum is paid to the trustees or managers of the scheme or, as the case may be, to the Board in respect of the debt due under section 75 of the 1995 Act, P may make an application under this subsection to the Regulator for a reduction in the amount of the sum specified in P's contribution notice.

(8) An application under subsection (7) must be made as soon as reasonably practicable after the sum is paid to the trustees or managers or, as the case may be, to the Board in respect of the debt due under section 75 of the 1995 Act.

(9) Where such an application is made to the Regulator, the Regulator may, if it is of the opinion that it is appropriate to do so –

(a) reduce the amount of the sum specified in P's contribution notice by an amount which it considers reasonable, and

(b) issue a revised contribution notice specifying the revised sum.

(10) For the purposes of subsection (9), the Regulator must have regard to such matters as the Regulator considers relevant including, where relevant, the following matters –

(a) the amount paid in respect of the debt due under section 75 of the 1995 Act since the contribution notice was issued,

(b) any amounts paid in respect of the debt due by virtue of that contribution notice,

(c) whether contribution notices have been issued to other persons in respect of the same non-compliance with the financial support direction in question as the non-compliance in respect of which P's contribution notice was issued,

(d) where such contribution notices have been issued, the sums specified in each of those notices and any amounts paid in respect of the debt due by virtue of those notices,

(e) whether P's contribution notice specifies that P is jointly and severally liable for the debt with other persons, and

(f) such other matters as may be prescribed.

(11) Where –

(a) P's contribution notice specifies that P is jointly and severally liable for the debt with other persons, and

(b) a revised contribution notice is issued to P under subsection (9) specifying a revised sum,

the Regulator must also issue revised contribution notices to those other persons specifying the revised sum and their joint and several liability with P for the debt in respect of that sum.

51 Sections 43 to 50: interpretation

(1) In sections 43 to 50 –

'group of companies' means a holding company and its subsidiaries within the meaning given by section 736(1) of the Companies Act 1985 (c. 6) and 'member' in relation to such a group is to be construed accordingly;
'holding company' has the meaning given by section 736(1) of that Act.

(2) For the purposes of those sections –

(a) references to a debt due under section 75 of the Pensions Act 1995 (c. 26) include a contingent debt under that section, and

(b) references to the amount of such a debt include the amount of such a contingent debt.

(3) For the purposes of those sections –

(a) section 249 of the Insolvency Act 1986 (c. 45) (connected persons) applies as it applies for the purposes of any provision of the first Group of Parts of that Act,

(b) section 435 of that Act (associated persons) applies as it applies for the purposes of that Act, and

(c) section 74 of the Bankruptcy (Scotland) Act 1985 (c. 66) (associated persons) applies as it applies for the purposes of that Act.

Transactions at an undervalue

52 Restoration orders where transactions at an undervalue

(1) This section applies in relation to an occupational pension scheme other than –

    (a) a money purchase scheme, or

    (b) a prescribed scheme or a scheme of a prescribed description.

(2) The Regulator may make a restoration order in respect of a transaction involving assets of the scheme if –

    (a) a relevant event has occurred in relation to the employer in relation to the scheme, and

    (b) the transaction is a transaction at an undervalue entered into with a person at a time which –

        (i)   is on or after 27th April 2004, but

        (ii) is not more than two years before the occurrence of the relevant event in relation to the employer.

(3) A restoration order in respect of a transaction involving assets of a scheme is such an order as the Regulator thinks fit for restoring the position to what it would have been if the transaction had not been entered into.

(4) For the purposes of this section a relevant event occurs in relation to the employer in relation to a scheme if and when on or after the appointed day –

    (a) an insolvency event occurs in relation to the employer, or

    (b) the trustees or managers of the scheme make an application under subsection (1) of section 129 or receive a notice from the Board of the Pension Protection Fund under subsection (5)(a) of that section (applications and notifications prior to the Board assuming responsibility for a scheme).

(5) For the purposes of subsection (4) –

    (a) the 'appointed day' means the day appointed under section 126(2) (no pension protection under Chapter 3 of Part 2 if the scheme begins winding up before the day appointed by the Secretary of State),

    (b) section 121 (meaning of 'insolvency event') applies for the purposes of determining if and when an insolvency event has occurred in relation to the employer, and

    (c) the reference to an insolvency event in relation to the employer does not include an insolvency event which occurred in relation to him before he became the employer in relation to the scheme.

(6) For the purposes of this section and section 53, a transaction involving assets of a scheme is a transaction at an undervalue entered into with a person ('P') if the trustees or managers of the scheme or appropriate persons in relation to the scheme –

    (a) make a gift to P or otherwise enter into a transaction with P on terms that provide for no consideration to be provided towards the scheme, or

    (b) enter into a transaction with P for a consideration the value of which, in money or money's worth, is significantly less than the value, in money or money's worth, of the consideration provided by or on behalf of the trustees or managers of the scheme.

(7) In subsection (6) 'appropriate persons' in relation to a scheme means a person who, or several persons each of whom is a person who, at the time at which the transaction in question is entered into, is –

    (a) a person of a prescribed description, and

    (b) entitled to exercise powers in relation to the scheme.

(8) For the purposes of this section and section 53 –

'assets' includes future assets;

'transaction' includes a gift, agreement or arrangement and references to entering into a transaction are to be construed accordingly.

(9) The provisions of this section apply without prejudice to the availability of any other remedy, even in relation to a transaction where the trustees or managers of the scheme or appropriate persons in question had no power to enter into the transaction.

53 Restoration orders: supplementary

(1) This section applies in relation to a restoration order under section 52 in respect of a transaction involving assets of a scheme ('the transaction').

(2) The restoration order may in particular –

(a) require any assets of the scheme (whether money or other property) which were transferred as part of the transaction to be transferred back –

    (i) to the trustees or managers of the scheme, or

    (ii) where the Board of the Pension Protection Fund has assumed responsibility for the scheme, to the Board;

(b) require any property to be transferred to the trustees or managers of the scheme or, where the Board has assumed responsibility for the scheme, to the Board if it represents in any person's hands –

    (i) any of the assets of the scheme which were transferred as part of the transaction, or

    (ii) property derived from any such assets so transferred;

(c) require such property as the Regulator may specify in the order, in respect of any consideration for the transaction received by the trustees or managers of the scheme, to be transferred –

    (i) by the trustees or managers of the scheme, or

    (ii) where the Board has assumed responsibility for the scheme, by the Board,

to such persons as the Regulator may specify in the order;

(d) require any person to pay, in respect of benefits received by him as a result of the transaction, such sums (not exceeding the value of the benefits received by him) as the Regulator may specify in the order –

    (i) to the trustees or managers of the scheme, or

    (ii) where the Board has assumed responsibility for the scheme, to the Board.

(3) A restoration order is of no effect to the extent that it prejudices any interest in property which was acquired in good faith and for value or any interest deriving from such an interest.

(4) Nothing in subsection (3) prevents a restoration order requiring a person to pay a sum of money if the person received a benefit as a result of the transaction otherwise than in good faith and for value.

(5) Where a person has acquired an interest in property from a person or has received a benefit as a result of the transaction and –

(a) he is one of the trustees or managers or appropriate persons who entered into the transaction as mentioned in subsection (6) of section 52, or

(b) at the time of the acquisition or receipt –

    (i) he has notice of the fact that the transaction was a transaction at an under-value,

    (ii) he is a trustee or manager, or the employer, in relation to the scheme, or

    (iii) he is connected with, or an associate of, any of the persons mentioned in paragraph (a) or (b)(ii), then, unless the contrary is shown, it is to be presumed for the purposes of subsections (3) and (4) that the interest was acquired or the benefit was received otherwise than in good faith.

(6) For the purposes of this section –

    (a) section 249 of the Insolvency Act 1986 (c. 45) (connected persons) applies as it applies for the purposes of any provision of the first Group of Parts of that Act,

    (b) section 435 of that Act (associated persons) applies as it applies for the purposes of that Act, and

    (c) section 74 of the Bankruptcy (Scotland) Act 1985 (c. 66) (associated persons) applies as it applies for the purposes of that Act.

(7) For the purposes of this section 'property' includes –

    (a) money, goods, things in action, land and every description of property wherever situated, and

    (b) obligations and every description of interest, whether present or future or vested or contingent, arising out of, or incidental to, property.

(8) References in this section to where the Board has assumed responsibility for a scheme are to where the Board has assumed responsibility for the scheme in accordance with Chapter 3 of Part 2 (pension protection).

54 Content and effect of a restoration order

(1) This section applies where a restoration order is made under section 52 in respect of a transaction involving assets of a scheme.

(2) Where the restoration order imposes an obligation on a person to do something, the order must specify the period within which the obligation must be complied with.

(3) Where the restoration order imposes an obligation on a person ('A') to transfer or pay a sum of money to a person specified in the order ('B'), the sum is to be treated as a debt due from A to B.

(4) Where the trustees or managers of the scheme are the persons to whom the debt is due, the Regulator may on their behalf, exercise such powers as the trustees or managers have to recover the debt.

(5) But during any assessment period (within the meaning of section 132) in relation to the scheme, the rights and powers of the trustees or managers of the scheme in relation to any debt due to them by virtue of a restoration order are exercisable by the Board of the Pension Protection Fund to the exclusion of the trustees or managers and the Regulator.

(6) Where, by virtue of subsection (5), any amount is transferred or paid to the Board in respect of a debt due by virtue of a restoration order, the Board must pay the amount to the trustees or managers of the scheme.

55 Contribution notice where failure to comply with restoration order

(1) This section applies where –

    (a) a restoration order is made under section 52 in respect of a transaction involving assets of a scheme ('the transaction'), and

    (b) a person fails to comply with an obligation imposed on him by the order which is not an obligation to transfer or pay a sum of money.

(2) The Regulator may issue a notice to the person stating that the person is under a liability to pay the sum specified in the notice (a 'contribution notice') –

    (a) to the trustees or managers of the scheme, or

    (b) where the Board of the Pension Protection Fund has assumed responsibility for the scheme in accordance with Chapter 3 of Part 2 (pension protection), to the Board.

(3) The sum specified by the Regulator in a contribution notice may be either the whole or a specified part of the shortfall sum in relation to the scheme.

(4) The shortfall sum in relation to the scheme is the amount which the Regulator estimates to be the amount of the decrease in the value of the assets of the scheme as a result of the transaction having been entered into.

56 Content and effect of a section 55 contribution notice

(1) This section applies where a contribution notice is issued to a person under section 55.

(2) The contribution notice must –

   (a) contain a statement of the matters which it is asserted constitute the failure to comply with the restoration order under section 52 in respect of which the notice is issued, and

   (b) specify the sum which the person is stated to be under a liability to pay.

(3) Where the contribution notice states that the person is under a liability to pay the sum specified in the notice to the trustees or managers of the scheme, the sum is to be treated as a debt due from the person to the trustees or managers of the scheme.

(4) In such a case, the Regulator may, on behalf of the trustees or managers of the scheme, exercise such powers as the trustees or managers have to recover the debt.

(5) But during any assessment period (within the meaning of section 132) in relation to the scheme, the rights and powers of the trustees or managers of the scheme in relation to any debt due to them by virtue of a contribution notice, are exercisable by the Board of the Pension Protection Fund to the exclusion of the trustees or managers and the Regulator.

(6) Where, by virtue of subsection (5), any amount is paid to the Board in respect of a debt due by virtue of a contribution notice, the Board must pay the amount to the trustees or managers of the scheme.

(7) Where the contribution notice states that the person is under a liability to pay the sum specified in the notice to the Board, the sum is to be treated as a debt due from the person to the Board.

Sections 38 to 56: partnerships and limited liability partnerships

57 Sections 38 to 56: partnerships and limited liability partnerships

(1) For the purposes of any of sections 38 to 56, regulations may modify any of the definitions mentioned in subsection (2) (as applied by any of those sections) in relation to –

   (a) a partnership or a partner in a partnership;

   (b) a limited liability partnership or a member of such a partnership.

(2) The definitions mentioned in subsection (1) are –

   (a) section 249 of the Insolvency Act 1986 (c. 45) (connected persons),

   (b) section 435 of that Act (associated persons),

   (c) section 74 of the Bankruptcy (Scotland) Act 1985 (c. 66) (associated persons), and

   (d) section 736 of the Companies Act 1985 (c. 6) (meaning of 'subsidiary' and 'holding company' etc).

(3) Regulations may also provide that any provision of sections 38 to 51 applies with such modifications as may be prescribed in relation to –

   (a) any case where a partnership is or was –

     (i) the employer in relation to an occupational pension scheme, or

     (ii) for the purposes of any of those sections, connected with or an associate of the employer;

    (b) any case where a limited liability partnership is –

        (i)   the employer in relation to an occupational pension scheme, or

        (ii)   for the purposes of any of those sections, connected with or an associate of the employer.

(4) Regulations may also provide that any provision of sections 52 to 56 applies with such modifications as may be prescribed in relation to a partnership or a limited liability partnership.

(5) For the purposes of this section –

    (a) 'partnership' includes a firm or entity of a similar character formed under the law of a country or territory outside the United Kingdom, and

    (b) references to a partner are to be construed accordingly.

(6) For the purposes of this section, 'limited liability partnership' means –

    (a) a limited liability partnership formed under the Limited Liability Partnerships Act 2000 (c. 12) or the Limited Liability Partnerships Act (Northern Ireland) 2002 (c. 12 (N.I.)), or

    (b) an entity which is of a similar character to such a limited liability partnership and which is formed under the law of a country or territory outside the United Kingdom,

and references to a member of a limited liability partnership are to be construed accordingly.

(7) This section is without prejudice to –

    (a) section 307 (power to modify this Act in relation to certain categories of scheme), and

    (b) section 318(4) (power to extend the meaning of 'employer').

Applications under the Insolvency Act 1986

58 Regulator's right to apply under section 423 of Insolvency Act 1986

(1) In this section 'section 423' means section 423 of the Insolvency Act 1986 (transactions defrauding creditors).

(2) The Regulator may apply for an order under section 423 in relation to a debtor if –

    (a) the debtor is the employer in relation to an occupational pension scheme, and

    (b) condition A or condition B is met in relation to the scheme.

(3) Condition A is that an actuarial valuation under section 143 obtained by the Board of the Pension Protection Fund in respect of the scheme indicates that the value of the assets of the scheme at the relevant time, as defined by that section, was less than the amount of the protected liabilities, as defined by section 131, at that time.

(4) Condition B is that an actuarial valuation, as defined by section 224(2), obtained by the trustees or managers of the scheme indicates that the statutory funding objective in section 222 is not met.

(5) In a case where the debtor –

    (a) has been adjudged bankrupt,

    (b) is a body corporate which is being wound up or is in administration, or

    (c) is a partnership which is being wound up or is in administration,

subsection (2) does not enable an application to be made under section 423 except with the permission of the court.

(6) An application made under this section is to be treated as made on behalf of every victim of the transaction who is –

    (a) a trustee or member of the scheme, or

    (b) the Board.

(7) This section does not apply where the valuation mentioned in subsection (3) or (4) is made by reference to a date that falls before the commencement of this section.

(8) Expressions which are defined by section 423 for the purposes of that section have the same meaning when used in this section.

Register of schemes

59 Register of occupational and personal pension schemes

(1) The Regulator must compile and maintain a register of occupational pension schemes and personal pension schemes which are, or have been, registrable schemes (referred to in this Act as 'the register').

(2) In this section and sections 62 to 65 'registrable scheme' means an occupational pension scheme, or a personal pension scheme, of a prescribed description.

(3) In respect of each registrable scheme, the Regulator must record in the register –

    (a) the registrable information most recently provided to it in respect of the scheme, and

    (b) if the Regulator has received –

        (i) a notice under section 62(5) (scheme which is wound up or ceases to be registrable),

        (ii) a copy of a notice under section 160 (transfer notice), or

        (iii) any notice, or copy of a notice, under any provision in force in Northern Ireland corresponding to a provision mentioned in sub-paragraph (i) or (ii),

    that fact.

(4) In respect of each scheme which has been a registrable scheme, but

    (a) has been, or is treated as having been, wound up, or

    (b) has ceased to be a registrable scheme,

the Regulator must maintain in the register the registrable information last provided to it in respect of the scheme.

(5) Information recorded in the register must be so recorded in such manner as the Regulator considers appropriate.

(6) In particular, the register may consist of more than one part.

(7) In this section references to 'registrable information', in relation to a scheme to which any provision in force in Northern Ireland corresponding to section 60(2) ('the corresponding Northern Ireland provision') applies, are to information of any description within the corresponding Northern Ireland provision.

60 Registrable information

(1) For the purposes of sections 59 to 65 'registrable information', in relation to an occupational or personal pension scheme, means information within subsection (2).

(2) That information is –

    (a) the name of the scheme;

    (b) the address of the scheme;

    (c) the full names and addresses of each of the trustees or managers of the scheme;

    (d) the status of the scheme with respect to the following matters –

        (i) whether new members may be admitted to the scheme;

        (ii) whether further benefits may accrue to, or in respect of, members under the scheme;

        (iii) whether further contributions may be paid towards the scheme;

        (iv) whether any members of the scheme are active members;

(e) the categories of benefits under the scheme;

(f) in the case of an occupational pension scheme –

  (i)   the name and address of each relevant employer, and

  (ii) any other name by which any relevant employer has been known at any time on or after the relevant date;

(g) in the case of an occupational pension scheme, the number of members of the scheme on the later of –

  (i)   the last day of the scheme year which ended most recently, and

  (ii) the day on which the scheme became a registrable scheme; and

(h) such other information as may be prescribed.

(3) Regulations may make provision about the interpretation of any of the descriptions in subsection (2).

(4) For the purposes of subsection (2)(f) –

'relevant employer' means any person –

  (a) who is, or

  (b) who, at any time on or after 6th April 1975, has been,

the employer in relation to the scheme;

'relevant date', in relation to a relevant employer, means –

  (a) 6th April 1975, or

  (b) if later, the date on which the relevant employer first became the employer in relation to the scheme.

61 The register: inspection, provision of information and reports etc

(1) Regulations may provide –

  (a) for –

    (i)   information recorded in the register,

    (ii)   extracts from the register, or

    (iii) copies of the register or of extracts from it,

   to be provided to prescribed persons in prescribed circumstances, and

  (b) for the inspection of –

    (i)   the register,

    (ii)   extracts from the register, or

    (iii) copies of the register or of extracts from it,

   by prescribed persons in prescribed circumstances.

(2) Regulations under subsection (1) may, in particular –

  (a) confer functions on –

    (i)   the Secretary of State, or

    (ii) a person authorised by him for the purposes of the regulations;

  (b) make provision with respect to the disclosure of information obtained by virtue of the regulations.

(3) Regulations which contain any provision made by virtue of subsection (2)(b) may, in particular, modify section 82 (restricted information).

(4) The Secretary of State may direct the Regulator to submit to him statistical and other reports concerning –

  (a) information recorded in the register, and

  (b) the operation of the Regulator's functions in relation to the register.

(5) A direction under subsection (4) may specify –

(a) the form in which, and

(b) the times at which,

reports required by the direction are to be submitted.

(6) The Secretary of State may publish any report submitted to him by virtue of a direction under subsection (4) in such manner as he considers appropriate.

62 The register: duties of trustees or managers

(1) Subsection (2) applies where –

(a) a registrable scheme is established, or

(b) an occupational or personal pension scheme otherwise becomes a registrable scheme.

(2) The trustees or managers of the scheme must, before the end of the initial notification period –

(a) notify the Regulator that the scheme is a registrable scheme, and

(b) provide to the Regulator all the registrable information with respect to the scheme.

(3) In subsection (2), the 'initial notification period' means the period of three months beginning with –

(a) the date on which the scheme is established, or

(b) if later, the date on which it becomes a registrable scheme.

(4) Where there is a change in any registrable information in respect of a registrable scheme, the trustees or managers of the scheme must as soon as reasonably practicable, notify the Regulator –

(a) of that fact, and

(b) of the new registrable information.

(5) Where a registrable scheme –

(a) ceases to be a registrable scheme, or

(b) is wound up (otherwise than under section 161(2) (effect of Board assuming responsibility for scheme)),

the trustees or managers of the scheme must as soon as reasonably practicable, notify the Regulator of that fact.

(6) If subsection (2), (4) or (5) is not complied with, section 10 of the Pensions Act 1995 (c. 26) (civil penalties) applies to any trustee or manager who has failed to take all reasonable steps to secure compliance.

63 Duty of the Regulator to issue scheme return notices

(1) The Regulator must issue scheme return notices in accordance with this section requiring scheme returns to be provided in respect of registrable schemes.

(2) In respect of each registrable scheme, the Regulator –

(a) must issue the first scheme return notice in accordance with subsection (3), and

(b) must issue subsequent scheme return notices in accordance with subsection (4).

(3) The return date specified in a scheme return notice issued in respect of a scheme under subsection (2)(a) –

(a) must fall within the period of three years beginning with –

(i) the date on which the Regulator receives a notice under section 62(2)(a) in respect of the scheme, or

(ii) if earlier, the date on which the Regulator first becomes aware that the scheme is a registrable scheme, and

(b) if the trustees or managers have complied with paragraph (b) of section 62(2), must fall after the end of the period of one year beginning with the date on which they provided the information required by that paragraph to the Regulator.

(4) The return date specified in a scheme return notice issued in respect of a scheme under subsection (2)(b) must fall –

(a) within the period of three years, but
(b) after the end of the period of one year,

beginning with the return date specified in the previous scheme return notice issued in respect of the scheme.

64 Duty of trustees or managers to provide scheme return

(1) The trustees or managers of a registrable scheme in respect of which a scheme return notice is issued must, on or before the return date, provide a scheme return to the Regulator.
(2) If a scheme return in respect of a scheme is not provided in compliance with subsection (1), section 10 of the Pensions Act 1995 (c. 26) (civil penalties) applies to any trustee or manager of the scheme who has failed to take all reasonable steps to secure compliance.

65 Scheme returns: supplementary

(1) This section has effect for the purposes of sections 63 and 64.
(2) In those sections and this section, in relation to a scheme return notice –

'return date' means the date specified under subsection (3)(b) in the scheme return notice;
'scheme return' means a document in the form (if any) specified in the scheme return notice, containing the information required by the notice.

(3) A scheme return notice must specify –

(a) the descriptions of information required by it, and
(b) the return date,

and may specify the form in which that information is to be provided.
(4) A scheme return notice in respect of a registrable scheme –

(a) must require all registrable information in relation to the scheme, and
(b) may require other information which the Regulator reasonably requires for the purposes of the exercise of its functions in relation to the scheme.

(5) The return date specified in a scheme return notice must fall after the end of the period of 28 days beginning with the date on which the notice is issued.
(6) A scheme return notice must be in writing and is treated as issued in respect of a registrable scheme when it is sent to the trustees or managers of the scheme.

Register of prohibited trustees

66 Register of prohibited trustees

(1) The Regulator must keep in such manner as it thinks fit a register of all persons who are prohibited under section 3 of the Pensions Act 1995 ('the prohibition register').
(2) Arrangements made by the Regulator for the prohibition register must secure that the contents of the register are not disclosed or otherwise made available to members of the public except in accordance with section 67.
(3) Nothing in subsection (2) requires the Regulator to exclude any matter from a report published under section 89 (reports of Regulator's consideration of cases).

67 Accessibility of register of prohibited trustees

(1) The Regulator must make arrangements to secure that the prohibition register is open, during its normal working hours, for inspection in person and without notice at –

    (a) the principal office used by it for the carrying out of its functions, and

    (b) such other of its offices (if any) as it considers to be places where it would be reasonable for a copy of the register to be kept open for inspection.

(2) If a request is made to the Regulator –

    (a) to state whether a particular person identified in the request is a person appearing in the prohibition register as prohibited in respect of an occupational trust scheme specified in the request,

    (b) to state whether a particular person so identified is a person appearing in that register as prohibited in respect of a particular description of occupational trust schemes so specified, or

    (c) to state whether a particular person so identified is a person appearing in that register as prohibited in respect of all occupational trust schemes,

the Regulator must promptly comply with the request in such manner as it considers reasonable.

(3) The Regulator may, in such manner as it considers appropriate, publish a summary of the prohibition register if (subject to subsections (6) to (8)) the summary –

    (a) contains all the information described in subsection (4),

    (b) arranges that information in the manner described in subsection (5),

    (c) does not (except by identifying a person as prohibited in respect of all occupational trust schemes, in respect of a particular description of such schemes or in respect of a particular such scheme) identify any of the schemes in respect of which persons named in the summary are prohibited, and

    (d) does not disclose any other information contained in the register.

(4) That information is –

    (a) the full names and titles, so far as the Regulator has a record of them, of all the persons appearing in the register as persons who are prohibited,

    (b) the dates of birth of such of those persons as are persons whose dates of birth are matters of which the Regulator has a record, and

    (c) in the case of each person whose name is included in the published summary, whether that person appears in the register –

        (i) as prohibited in respect of only one occupational trust scheme,

        (ii) as prohibited in respect of one or more particular descriptions of such schemes, but not in respect of all such schemes, or

        (iii) as prohibited in respect of all such schemes.

(5) For the purposes of paragraph (c) of subsection (4), the information in the published register must be arranged in three separate lists, one for each of the descriptions of prohibition specified in the sub-paragraphs of that paragraph.

(6) The Regulator must ensure, in the case of any published summary, that a person is not identified in the summary as a prohibited person if it appears to the Regulator that the determination by virtue of which that person appears in the register –

    (a) is the subject of any pending reference, review, appeal or legal proceedings which could result in that person's removal from the register, or

    (b) is a determination which might still become the subject of any such reference, review, appeal or proceedings.

(7) The Regulator must ensure, in the case of any published summary, that the particulars relating to a person do not appear in a particular list mentioned in subsection (5) if it

appears to the Regulator that a determination by virtue of which that person's particulars would appear in that list –

    (a) is the subject of any pending reference, review, appeal or legal proceedings which could result in such a revocation or other overturning of a prohibition of that person as would require his particulars to appear in a different list, or

    (b) is a determination which might still become the subject of any such reference, review, appeal or proceedings.

(8) Where subsection (7) prevents a person's particulars from being included in a particular list in the published summary, they must be included, instead, in the list (if any) in which they would have been included if the prohibition to which the reference, review, appeal or proceedings relate or might relate had already been revoked or otherwise overturned.

(9) For the purposes of this section a determination is one which might still become the subject of a reference, review, appeal or proceedings if, and only if, in the case of that determination –

    (a) the time for the making of an application for a review or reference, or for the bringing of an appeal or other proceedings, has not expired, and

    (b) there is a reasonable likelihood that such an application might yet be made, or that such an appeal or such proceedings might yet be brought.

(10) In this section –

    'name', in relation to a person any of whose names is recorded by the Regulator as an initial, means that initial;

    'occupational trust scheme' means an occupational pension scheme established under a trust.

Collecting information relevant to the Board of the Pension Protection Fund

68 Information relevant to the Board

The Regulator may collect any information which appears to it to be relevant to the exercise of the functions of the Board of the Pension Protection Fund.

69 Duty to notify the Regulator of certain events

(1) Except where the Regulator otherwise directs, the appropriate person must give notice of any notifiable event to the Regulator.

(2) In subsection (1) 'notifiable event' means –

    (a) a prescribed event in respect of an eligible scheme, or

    (b) a prescribed event in respect of the employer in relation to an eligible scheme.

(3) For the purposes of subsection (1) –

    (a) in the case of an event within subsection (2)(a), each of the following is 'the appropriate person' –

        (i) the trustees or managers of the scheme,

        (ii) a person of a prescribed description, and

    (b) in relation to an event within subsection (2)(b), each of the following is 'the appropriate person' –

        (i) the employer in relation to the scheme,

        (ii) a person of a prescribed description.

(4) A notice under subsection (1) –

    (a) must be in writin...

    (b) subject to subsect... ...ably practicable after the person giving it ... ...nt.

(5) Regulations may require ... ... (1) to be given before the beginning of the prescribe... ... ...ie notifiable event in question.

(6) No duty to which a person ... ...be regarded as contravened merely because of any information or opinio... ...ined in a notice under this section.

This is subject to section 311 (protected items).

(7) Where the trustees or managers of a scheme fail to comply with an obligation imposed on them by subsection (1), section 10 of the Pensions Act 1995 (c. 26) (civil penalties) applies in relation to any trustee or manager who has failed to take all reasonable steps to secure compliance with that subsection.

(8) That section also applies to any other person who, without reasonable excuse, fails to comply with an obligation imposed on him by subsection (1).

(9) In this section –

'eligible scheme' has the meaning given by section 126;
'event' includes a failure to act.

Reporting breaches of the law

70 Duty to report breaches of the law

(1) Subsection (2) imposes a reporting requirement on the following persons –

    (a) a trustee or manager of an occupational or personal pension scheme;

    (b) a person who is otherwise involved in the administration of such a scheme;

    (c) the employer in relation to an occupational pension scheme;

    (d) a professional adviser in relation to such a scheme;

    (e) a person who is otherwise involved in advising the trustees or managers of an occupational or personal pension scheme in relation to the scheme.

(2) Where the person has reasonable cause to believe that –

    (a) a duty which is relevant to the administration of the scheme in question, and is imposed by or by virtue of an enactment or rule of law, has not been or is not being complied with, and

    (b) the failure to comply is likely to be of material significance to the Regulator in the exercise of any of its functions,

he must give a written report of the matter to the Regulator as soon as reasonably practicable.

(3) No duty to which a person is subject is to be regarded as contravened merely because of any information or opinion contained in a written report under this section.

This is subject to section 311 (protected items).

(4) Section 10 of the Pensions Act 1995 (c. 26) (civil penalties) applies to any person who, without reasonable excuse, fails to comply with an obligation imposed on him by this section.

Reports by skilled persons

71 Reports by skilled persons

(1) The Regulator may issue a notice (a 'report notice') to –

(a) the trustees or managers of a work-based pension scheme,

(b) any employer in relation to such a scheme, or

(c) any person who is otherwise involved in the administration of such a scheme,

requiring them or, as the case may be, him to provide the Regulator with a report on one or more specified matters which are relevant to the exercise of any of the Regulator's functions.

(2) A report notice must require the person appointed to make the report to be a person –

(a) nominated or approved by the Regulator, and

(b) appearing to the Regulator to have the skills necessary to make a report on the matter or matters concerned.

(3) A report notice may require the report to be provided to the Regulator –

(a) in a specified form;

(b) before a specified date.

(4) The costs of providing a report in accordance with a report notice must be met by the person to whom the notice is issued ('the notified person').

(5) But a report notice may require a specified person (other than the Regulator) to reimburse to the notified person the whole or any part of the costs of providing the report.

(6) Where, by virtue of subsection (5), an amount is required to be reimbursed by a specified person to the notified person, that amount is to be treated as a debt due from the specified person to the notified person.

(7) If the trustees or managers of a work-based pension scheme fail to comply with a report notice issued to them, section 10 of the Pensions Act 1995 (civil penalties) applies to any trustee or manager who has failed to take all reasonable steps to secure compliance.

(8) That section also applies to any other person who, without reasonable excuse, fails to comply with a report notice issued to him.

(9) Where a report notice is issued, any person who is providing (or who at any time has provided) services to the notified person in relation to a matter on which the report is required must give the person appointed to make the report such assistance as he may reasonably require.

(10) The duty imposed by subsection (9) is enforceable, on the application of the Regulator, by an injunction or, in Scotland, by an order for specific performance under section 45 of the Court of Session Act 1988 (c. 36).

(11) In this section –

'specified', in relation to a report notice, means specified in the notice;

'work-based pension scheme' has the same meaning as in section 5 (Regulator's objectives).

Gathering information

72 Provision of information

(1) The Regulator may, by notice in writing, require any person to whom subsection (2) applies to produce any document, or provide any other information, which is –

(a) of a description specified in the notice, and

(b) relevant to the exercise of the Regulator's functions.

(2) This subsection applies to –

(a) a trustee or manager of an occupational or personal pension scheme,

(b) a professional adviser in relation to an occupational pension scheme,

(c) the employer in relation to –

> (i) an occupational pension scheme, or
> (ii) a personal pension scheme where direct payment arrangements exist in respect of one or more members of the scheme who are employees, and

(d) any other person appearing to the Regulator to be a person who holds, or is likely to hold, information relevant to the exercise of the Regulator's functions.

(3) Where the production of a document, or the provision of information, is required by a notice given under subsection (1), the document must be produced, or information must be provided, in such a manner, at such a place and within such a period as may be specified in the notice.

73 Inspection of premises

(1) An inspector may, for the purposes of investigating whether, in the case of any occupational pension scheme, the occupational scheme provisions are being, or have been, complied with, at any reasonable time enter premises liable to inspection.

(2) In subsection (1), the 'occupational scheme provisions' means provisions contained in or made by virtue of –

(a) any of the following provisions of this Act –

this Part;
Part 3 (scheme funding);
sections 241 to 243 (member-nominated trustees and directors);
sections 247 to 249 (requirement for knowledge and understanding);
section 252 (UK-based scheme to be trust with effective rules);
section 253 (non-European scheme to be trust with UK-resident trustee);
section 255 (activities of occupational pension schemes);
section 256 (no indemnification for fines or civil penalties);
sections 259 and 261 (consultation by employers);
Part 7 (cross-border activities within European Union);
Part 9 (miscellaneous and supplementary);

(b) either of the following provisions of the Welfare Reform and Pensions Act 1999 (c. 30) –

section 33 (time for discharge of pension credit liability);
section 45 (information);

(c) any of the provisions of Part 1 of the Pensions Act 1995 (c. 26) (occupational pension schemes), other than –

> (i) sections 51 to 54 (indexation), and
> (ii) sections 62 to 65 (equal treatment)

(d) any of the following provisions of the Pension Schemes Act 1993 (c. 48) –

Chapter 4 of Part 4 (transfer values);
Chapter 5 of Part 4 (early leavers: cash transfer sums and contribution refunds);
Chapter 2 of Part 4A (pension credit transfer values);
section 113 (information);
section 175 (levy);

(e) any provisions in force in Northern Ireland corresponding to any provisions within paragraphs (a) to (d).

(3) An inspector may, for the purposes of investigating whether, in the case of a stakeholder scheme –

(a) sections 1 and 2(4) of the Welfare Reform and Pensions Act 1999 (stakeholder pension schemes: registration etc), or
(b) any corresponding provisions in force in Northern Ireland,

are being, or have been, complied with, at any reasonable time enter premises liable to inspection.

(4) An inspector may, for the purposes of investigating whether, in the case of any trust-based personal stakeholder scheme, the trust-based scheme provisions are being, or have been, complied with, at any reasonable time enter premises liable to inspection.

(5) In subsection (4) –

'trust-based personal stakeholder scheme' means a personal pension scheme which –

   (a)   is a stakeholder scheme, and
   (b)   is established under a trust;

the 'trust-based scheme provisions' means any provisions contained in or made by virtue of –

   (a)   any provision which applies in relation to trust-based personal stakeholder schemes by virtue of paragraph 1 of Schedule 1 to the Welfare Reform and Pensions Act 1999 (c. 30), as the provision applies by virtue of that paragraph, or
   (b)   any corresponding provision in force in Northern Ireland.

(6) Premises are liable to inspection for the purposes of this section if the inspector has reasonable grounds to believe that –

   (a)   members of the scheme are employed there,
   (b)   documents relevant to the administration of the scheme are being kept there, or
   (c)   the administration of the scheme, or work connected with that administration, is being carried out there.

(7) In this section, 'stakeholder scheme' means an occupational pension scheme or a personal pension scheme which is or has been registered under –

   (a)   section 2 of the Welfare Reform and Pensions Act 1999 (register of stakeholder schemes), or
   (b)   any corresponding provision in force in Northern Ireland.

74 Inspection of premises in respect of employers' obligations

(1) An inspector may, for the purposes of investigating whether an employer is complying, or has complied, with the requirements under –

   (a)   section 3 of the Welfare Reform and Pensions Act 1999 (duty of employers to facilitate access to stakeholder pension schemes), or
   (b)   any corresponding provision in force in Northern Ireland,

at any reasonable time enter premises liable to inspection.

(2) Premises are liable to inspection for the purposes of subsection (1) if the inspector has reasonable grounds to believe that –

   (a)   employees of the employer are employed there,
   (b)   documents relevant to the administration of the employer's business are being kept there, or
   (c)   the administration of the employer's business, or work connected with that administration, is being carried out there.

(3) In subsections (1) and (2), 'employer' has the meaning given by section 3(9) of the Welfare Reform and Pensions Act 1999 (or, where subsection (1)(b) applies, by any corresponding provision in force in Northern Ireland).

(4) An inspector may, for the purposes of investigating whether, in the case of any direct payment arrangements relating to a personal pension scheme, any of the following provisions –

(a) regulations made by virtue of sections 260 and 261 (consultation by employers),

(b) section 111A of the Pension Schemes Act 1993 (c. 48) (monitoring of employers' payments to personal pension schemes), or

(c) any corresponding provisions in force in Northern Ireland,

is being, or has been, complied with, at any reasonable time enter premises liable to inspection.

(5) Premises are liable to inspection for the purposes of subsection (4) if the inspector has reasonable grounds to believe that –

(a) employees of the employer are employed there,

(b) documents relevant to the administration of –

    (i) the employer's business,

    (ii) the direct payment arrangements, or

    (iii) the scheme to which those arrangements relate,

are being kept there, or

(c) either of the following is being carried out there –

    (i) the administration of the employer's business, the arrangements or the scheme;

    (ii) work connected with that administration.

(6) In the application of subsections (4) and (5) in relation to any provision mentioned in subsection (4)(c) (a 'corresponding Northern Ireland provision'), references in those subsections to –

direct payment arrangements,

a personal pension scheme,

the employer, or

employees of the employer

are to be read as having the meanings that they have for the purposes of the corresponding Northern Ireland provision.

75 Inspection of premises: powers of inspectors

(1) Subsection (2) applies where, for a purpose mentioned in subsection (1), (3) or (4) of section 73 or subsection (1) or (4) of section 74, an inspector enters premises which are liable to inspection for the purposes of that provision.

(2) While there, the inspector –

(a) may make such examination and inquiry as may be necessary for the purpose for which he entered the premises,

(b) may require any person on the premises to produce, or secure the production of, any document relevant to compliance with the regulatory provisions for his inspection,

(c) may take copies of any such document,

(d) may take possession of any document appearing to be a document relevant to compliance with the regulatory provisions or take in relation to any such document any other steps which appear necessary for preserving it or preventing interference with it,

(e) may, in the case of any such document which consists of information which is stored in electronic form and is on, or accessible from, the premises, require the information to be produced in a form –

    (i) in which it can be taken away, and

    (ii) in which it is legible or from which it can readily be produced in a legible form, and

(f)   may, as to any matter relevant to compliance with the regulatory provisions, examine, or require to be examined, either alone or in the presence of another person, any person on the premises whom he has reasonable cause to believe to be able to give information relevant to that matter.

76 Inspection of premises: supplementary

(1)   This section applies for the purposes of sections 73 to 75.

(2)   Premises which are a private dwelling-house not used by, or by permission of, the occupier for the purposes of a trade or business are not liable to inspection.

(3)   Any question whether –

(a)   anything is being or has been done or omitted which might by virtue of any of the regulatory provisions give rise to a liability for a civil penalty under or by virtue of section 10 of the Pensions Act 1995 (c. 26) or section 168(4) of the Pension Schemes Act 1993 (c. 48) (or under or by virtue of any provision in force in Northern Ireland corresponding to either of them), or

(b)   an offence is being or has been committed under any of the regulatory provisions,

is to be treated as a question whether the regulatory provision is being, or has been, complied with.

(4)   An inspector applying for admission to any premises for the purposes of section 73 or 74 must, if so required, produce his certificate of appointment.

(5)   When exercising a power under section 73, 74 or 75 an inspector may be accompanied by such persons as he considers appropriate.

(6)   Any document of which possession is taken under section 75 may be retained –

(a)   if the document is relevant to proceedings against any person for any offence which are commenced before the end of the retention period, until the conclusion of those proceedings, and

(b)   otherwise, until the end of the retention period.

(7)   In subsection (6), 'the retention period' means the period comprising –

(a)   the period of 12 months beginning with the date on which possession was taken of the document, and

(b)   any extension of that period under subsection (8).

(8)   The Regulator may, by a direction made before the end of the retention period (including any extension of it under this subsection), extend it by such period not exceeding 12 months as the Regulator considers appropriate.

(9)   'The regulatory provisions', in relation to an inspection under subsection (1), (3) or (4) of section 73 or subsection (1) or (4) of section 74, means the provision or provisions referred to in that subsection.

77 Penalties relating to sections 72 to 75

(1)   A person who, without reasonable excuse, neglects or refuses to provide information or produce a document when required to do so under section 72 is guilty of an offence.

(2)   A person who without reasonable excuse –

(a)   intentionally delays or obstructs an inspector exercising any power under section 73, 74 or 75,

(b)   neglects or refuses to produce, or secure the production of, any document when required to do so under section 75, or

(c)   neglects or refuses to answer a question or to provide information when so required,

is guilty of an offence.

(3) A person guilty of an offence under subsection (1) or (2) is liable on summary conviction to a fine not exceeding level 5 on the standard scale.

(4) An offence under subsection (1) or (2)(b) or (c) may be charged by reference to any day or longer period of time; and a person may be convicted of a second or subsequent offence by reference to any period of time following the preceding conviction of the offence.

(5) Any person who intentionally and without reasonable excuse alters, suppresses, conceals or destroys any document which he is or is liable to be required to produce under section 72 or 75 is guilty of an offence.

(6) Any person guilty of an offence under subsection (5) is liable –

    (a) on summary conviction, to a fine not exceeding the statutory maximum;

    (b) on conviction on indictment, to a fine or imprisonment for a term not exceeding two years, or both.

78 Warrants

(1) A justice of the peace may issue a warrant under this section if satisfied on information on oath given by or on behalf of the Regulator that there are reasonable grounds for believing –

    (a) that there is on, or accessible from, any premises any document –

        (i) whose production has been required under section 72 or 75, or any corresponding provision in force in Northern Ireland, and

        (ii) which has not been produced in compliance with that requirement,

    (b) that there is on, or accessible from, any premises any document whose production could be so required and, if its production were so required, the document –

        (i) would not be produced, but

        (ii) would be removed, or made inaccessible, from the premises, hidden, tampered with or destroyed, or

    (c) that –

        (i) an offence has been committed,

        (ii) a person will do any act which constitutes a misuse or misappropriation of the assets of an occupational pension scheme or a personal pension scheme,

        (iii) a person is liable to pay a penalty under or by virtue of section 10 of the Pensions Act 1995 (c. 26) (civil penalties) or section 168(4) of the Pension Schemes Act 1993 (c. 48) (civil penalties for breach of regulations), or under or by virtue of any provision in force in Northern Ireland corresponding to either of them, or

        (iv) a person is liable to be prohibited from being a trustee of an occupational or personal pension scheme under section 3 of the Pensions Act 1995 (prohibition orders), including that section as it applies by virtue of paragraph 1 of Schedule 1 to the Welfare Reform and Pensions Act 1999 (c. 30) (stakeholder schemes), or under or by virtue of any corresponding provisions in force in Northern Ireland,

    and that there is on, or accessible from, any premises any document which relates to whether the offence has been committed, whether the act will be done or whether the person is so liable, and whose production could be required under section 72 or 75 or any corresponding provision in force in Northern Ireland.

(2) A warrant under this section shall authorise an inspector –

    (a) to enter the premises specified in the information, using such force as is reasonably necessary for the purpose,

(b) to search the premises and –

    (i)   take possession of any document appearing to be such a document as is mentioned in subsection (1), or

    (ii) take in relation to such a document any other steps which appear necessary for preserving it or preventing interference with it,

(c) to take copies of any such document,

(d) to require any person named in the warrant to provide an explanation of any such document or to state where it may be found or how access to it may be obtained, and

(e) in the case of any such document which consists of information which is stored in electronic form and is on, or accessible from, the premises, to require the information to be produced in a form –

    (i)   in which it can be taken away, and

    (ii) in which it is legible or from which it can readily be produced in a legible form.

(3) In subsection (1), any reference in paragraph (a) or (b) to a document does not include any document which is relevant to whether a person has complied with –

(a) subsection (3) of section 238 (information and advice to employees) or regulations under subsection (4) of that section, or

(b) any provision in force in Northern Ireland which corresponds to that subsection (3) or is made under provision corresponding to that subsection (4),

and is not relevant to the exercise of the Regulator's functions for any other reason.

(4) For the purposes of subsection (1)(c)(iii), any liability to pay a penalty under –

(a) section 10 of the Pensions Act 1995 (c. 26), or

(b) any corresponding provision in force in Northern Ireland,

which might arise out of a failure to comply with any provision within subsection (3)(a) or (b) is to be disregarded.

(5) References in subsection (2) to such a document as is mentioned in subsection (1) are to be read in accordance with subsections (3) and (4).

(6) When executing a warrant under this section, an inspector may be accompanied by such persons as he considers appropriate.

(7) A warrant under this section continues in force until the end of the period of one month beginning with the day on which it is issued.

(8) Any document of which possession is taken under this section may be retained –

(a) if the document is relevant to proceedings against any person for any offence which are commenced before the end of the retention period, until the conclusion of those proceedings, and

(b) otherwise, until the end of the retention period.

(9) In subsection (8), 'the retention period' means the period comprising –

(a) the period of 12 months beginning with the date on which possession was taken of the document, and

(b) any extension of that period under subsection (10).

(10) The Regulator may, by a direction made before the end of the retention period (including any extension of it under this subsection), extend it by such period not exceeding 12 months as the Regulator considers appropriate.

(11) In the application of this section in Scotland –

(a) the reference to a justice of the peace is to be read as a reference to the sheriff, and

(b) the references in subsections (1) and (2)(a) to information are to be read as references to evidence.

79 Sections 72 to 78: interpretation

(1) This section applies for the purposes of sections 72 to 78.

(2) 'Document' includes information recorded in any form, and any reference to production of a document, in relation to information recorded otherwise than in a legible form, is to producing a copy of the information –

(a) in a legible form, or

(b) in a form from which it can readily be produced in a legible form.

(3) 'Inspector' means a person appointed by the Regulator as an inspector.

Provision of false or misleading information

80 Offences of providing false or misleading information

(1) Any person who knowingly or recklessly provides the Regulator with information which is false or misleading in a material particular is guilty of an offence if the information –

(a) is provided in purported compliance with a requirement under –

(i)   section 62 (the register: duties of trustees or managers),

(ii) section 64 (duty of trustees or managers to provide scheme return),

(iii) section 72 (provision of information), or

(iv) section 75 (inspection of premises: powers of inspectors),

(b) is provided in applying for registration of a pension scheme under section 2 of the Welfare Reform and Pensions Act 1999 (c. 30) (registration of stakeholder pension schemes), or

(c) is provided otherwise than as mentioned in paragraph (a) or (b) but in circumstances in which the person providing the information intends, or could reasonably be expected to know, that it would be used by the Regulator for the purpose of exercising its functions under this Act or the Pensions Act 1995 (c. 26).

(2) Any person guilty of an offence under subsection (1) is liable –

(a) on summary conviction, to a fine not exceeding the statutory maximum;

(b) on conviction on indictment, to a fine or imprisonment for a term not exceeding two years, or both.

Use of information

81 Use of information

Information –

(a) contained in the register, or

(b) otherwise held by the Regulator in the exercise of any of its functions,

may be used by the Regulator for the purposes of, or for any purpose connected with or incidental to, the exercise of its functions.

Disclosure of information

82 Restricted information

(1) Restricted information must not be disclosed –

(a) by the Regulator, or

(b) by any person who receives the information directly or indirectly from the Regulator.

(2) Subsection (1) is subject to –

    (a) subsection (3), and

    (b) sections 71(9), 83 to 88 and 235.

(3) Subject to section 88(4), restricted information may be disclosed with the consent of the person to whom it relates and (if different) the person from whom the Regulator obtained it.

(4) For the purposes of this section and sections 83 to 87, 'restricted information' means any information obtained by the Regulator in the exercise of its functions which relates to the business or other affairs of any person, except for information –

    (a) which at the time of the disclosure is or has already been made available to the public from other sources, or

    (b) which is in the form of a summary or collection of information so framed as not to enable information relating to any particular person to be ascertained from it.

(5) Any person who discloses information in contravention of this section is guilty of an offence and liable –

    (a) on summary conviction, to a fine not exceeding the statutory maximum;

    (b) on conviction on indictment, to a fine or imprisonment for a term not exceeding two years, or both.

83 Information supplied to the Regulator by corresponding overseas authorities

(1) Subject to subsection (2), for the purposes of section 82, 'restricted information' includes information which has been supplied to the Regulator, for the purposes of its functions, by an authority which exercises functions corresponding to the functions of the Regulator in a country or territory outside the United Kingdom.

(2) Sections 84 to 87 do not apply to such information as is mentioned in subsection (1), and such information must not be disclosed except –

    (a) as provided in section 82(3),

    (b) for the purpose of enabling or assisting the Regulator to discharge its functions, or

    (c) by or on behalf of –

        (i) the Regulator, or

        (ii) any public authority (within the meaning of section 6 of the Human Rights Act 1998 (c. 42)) which receives the information directly or indirectly from the Regulator,

    for any of the purposes specified in section 17(2)(a) to (d) of the Anti-terrorism, Crime and Security Act 2001 (c. 24) (criminal proceedings and investigations).

(3) Section 18 of the Anti-terrorism, Crime and Security Act 2001 (restriction on disclosure of information for overseas purposes) has effect in relation to a disclosure authorised by subsection (2) as it has effect in relation to a disclosure authorised by any of the provisions to which section 17 of that Act applies.

84 Disclosure for facilitating exercise of functions by the Regulator

(1) Section 82 does not preclude the disclosure of restricted information in any case in which disclosure is for the purpose of enabling or assisting the Regulator to exercise its functions.

(2) Subsection (3) applies where, in order to enable or assist the Regulator properly to exercise any of its functions, the Regulator considers it necessary to seek advice from any qualified person on any matter of law, accountancy, valuation or other matter requiring the exercise of professional skill.

(3) Section 82 does not preclude the disclosure by the Regulator to a person qualified to provide that advice of such information as appears to the Regulator to be necessary to ensure that he is properly informed with respect to the matters on which his advice is sought.

85 Disclosure for facilitating exercise of functions by the Board

Section 82 does not preclude the disclosure of restricted information in any case in which disclosure is for the purpose of enabling or assisting the Board of the Pension Protection Fund to exercise its functions.

86 Disclosure for facilitating exercise of functions by other supervisory authorities

(1) Section 82 does not preclude the disclosure by the Regulator of restricted information to any person specified in the first column of Schedule 3 if the Regulator considers that the disclosure would enable or assist that person to exercise the functions specified in relation to him in the second column of that Schedule.

(2) The Secretary of State may after consultation with the Regulator –

    (a) by order amend Schedule 3 by –

        (i) adding any person exercising regulatory functions and specifying functions in relation to that person,

        (ii) removing any person for the time being specified in the Schedule, or

        (iii) altering the functions for the time being specified in the Schedule in relation to any person, or

    (b) by order restrict the circumstances in which, or impose conditions subject to which, disclosure may be made to any person for the time being specified in the Schedule.

87 Other permitted disclosures

(1) Section 82 does not preclude the disclosure by the Regulator of restricted information to –

    (a) the Secretary of State,

    (b) the Commissioners of Inland Revenue or their officers, or

    (c) the Department for Social Development in Northern Ireland,

if the disclosure appears to the Regulator to be desirable or expedient in the interests of members of occupational pension schemes or personal pension schemes or in the public interest.

(2) Section 82 does not preclude the disclosure of restricted information –

    (a) by or on behalf of –

        (i) the Regulator, or

        (ii) any public authority (within the meaning of section 6 of the Human Rights Act 1998 (c. 42)) which receives the information directly or indirectly from the Regulator,

    for any of the purposes specified in section 17(2)(a) to (d) of the Anti-terrorism, Crime and Security Act 2001 (c. 24) (criminal proceedings and investigations),

    (b) in connection with any proceedings arising out of –

        (i) this Act,

        (ii) the Welfare Reform and Pensions Act 1999 (c. 30),

        (iii) the Pensions Act 1995 (c. 26), or

        (iv) the Pension Schemes Act 1993 (c. 48),

    or any corresponding enactment in force in Northern Ireland, or any proceedings for breach of trust in relation to an occupational pension scheme,

    (c) with a view to the institution of, or otherwise for the purposes of, proceedings under –

        (i) section 7 or 8 of the Company Directors Disqualification Act 1986 (c. 46), or

      (ii)   Article 10 or 11 of the Companies (Northern Ireland) Order 1989 (S.I. 1989/2404 (N.I. 18)) or of the Company Directors Disqualification (Northern Ireland) Order 2002 (S.I. 2002/3150 (N.I. 4)),

   (d) in connection with any proceedings under –

      (i)   the Insolvency Act 1986 (c. 45), or

      (ii)   the Insolvency (Northern Ireland) Order 1989 (S.I. 1989/2405 (N.I. 19)),

      which the Regulator has instituted or in which it has a right to be heard,

   (e) with a view to the institution of, or otherwise for the purposes of, any disciplinary proceedings relating to the exercise of his professional duties by a solicitor, an actuary, an accountant or an insolvency practitioner,

   (f) with a view to the institution of, or otherwise for the purposes of, any disciplinary proceedings relating to the exercise by a public servant of his functions,

   (g) for the purpose of enabling or assisting an authority in a country outside the United Kingdom to exercise functions corresponding to those of the Regulator under this Act, the Welfare Reform and Pensions Act 1999 (c. 30), the Pensions Act 1995 (c. 26) or the Pension Schemes Act 1993 (c. 48), or

   (h) in pursuance of a Community obligation.

(3) In subsection (2)(f), 'public servant' means an officer or servant of the Crown or of any prescribed authority.

(4) Section 82 does not preclude the disclosure by the Regulator of restricted information to –

   (a) the Director of Public Prosecutions,

   (b) the Director of Public Prosecutions for Northern Ireland,

   (c) the Lord Advocate,

   (d) a procurator fiscal, or

   (e) a constable.

(5) Section 82 does not preclude the disclosure of restricted information in any case where the disclosure is required by or by virtue of an enactment.

(6) Section 82 does not preclude the disclosure of restricted information in any case where the disclosure is to a Regulator-appointed trustee of an occupational pension scheme for the purpose of enabling or assisting him to exercise his functions in relation to the scheme.

(7) In subsection (6), 'Regulator-appointed trustee' means a trustee appointed by the Regulator under section 7 or 23(1) of the Pensions Act 1995 or any corresponding provision in force in Northern Ireland.

(8) Section 82 does not preclude the disclosure by any person mentioned in subsection (1) or (4) of restricted information obtained by the person by virtue of that subsection, if the disclosure is made with the consent of the Regulator.

(9) Section 82 does not preclude the disclosure by any person specified in the first column of Schedule 3 of restricted information obtained by the person by virtue of section 86(1), if the disclosure is made –

   (a) with the consent of the Regulator, and

   (b) for the purpose of enabling or assisting the person to exercise any functions specified in relation to him in the second column of the Schedule.

(10) Before deciding whether to give its consent to such a disclosure as is mentioned in subsection (8) or (9), the Regulator must take account of any representations made to it, by the person seeking to make the disclosure, as to the desirability of the disclosure or the necessity for it.

(11) Section 18 of the Anti-terrorism, Crime and Security Act 2001 (c. 24) (restriction on disclosure of information for overseas purposes) has effect in relation to a disclosure authorised by subsection (2) as it has effect in relation to a disclosure authorised by any of the provisions to which section 17 of that Act applies.

88 Tax information

(1) This section applies to information held by any person in the exercise of tax functions about any matter which is relevant, for the purposes of those functions, to tax or duty in the case of an identifiable person (in this section referred to as 'tax information').

(2) No obligation as to secrecy imposed by section 182 of the Finance Act 1989 (c. 26) or otherwise shall prevent the disclosure of tax information to the Regulator for the purpose of enabling or assisting the Regulator to discharge its functions.

(3) Where tax information is disclosed to the Regulator by virtue of subsection (2) above or section 19 of the Anti-terrorism, Crime and Security Act 2001 (disclosure of information held by revenue departments), it must, subject to subsection (4), be treated for the purposes of section 82 as restricted information.

(4) Sections 82(3), 83 to 87 and 235 do not apply to tax information which is disclosed to the Regulator as mentioned in subsection (3), and such information may not be disclosed by the Regulator or any person who receives the information directly or indirectly from the Regulator except –

   (a) to, or in accordance with authority given by, the Commissioners of Inland Revenue or the Commissioners of Customs and Excise, or

   (b) with a view to the institution of, or otherwise for the purposes of, any criminal proceedings.

(5) In this section 'tax functions' has the same meaning as in section 182 of the Finance Act 1989.

Reports

89 Publishing reports etc

(1) The Regulator may, if it considers it appropriate to do so in any particular case, publish a report of the consideration given by it to the exercise of its functions in relation to that case and the results of that consideration.

(2) The publication of a report under subsection (1) may be in such form and manner as the Regulator considers appropriate.

(3) For the purposes of the law of defamation, the publication of any matter by the Regulator is privileged unless the publication is shown to be made with malice.

Codes of practice

90 Codes of practice

(1) The Regulator may issue codes of practice –

   (a) containing practical guidance in relation to the exercise of functions under the pensions legislation, and

   (b) regarding the standards of conduct and practice expected from those who exercise such functions.

(2) The Regulator must issue one or more such codes of practice relating to the following matters –

   (a) what constitutes a 'reasonable' period for the purposes of any provision of the pensions legislation (other than any enactment contained in or made by virtue of Part 2) which requires any action to be taken within such a period;

   (b) the discharge of the duty imposed by section 69 (duty to notify Regulator of certain events);

   (c) the discharge of the duty imposed by section 70 (duty to report breaches of the law);

(d) the discharge of duties imposed on trustees or managers of occupational pension schemes by, or by virtue of, Part 3 (scheme funding);

(e) the discharge of the duties imposed by sections 241 and 242 (member-nominated trustees and directors);

(f) the obligations imposed by sections 247 and 248 (requirements for knowledge and understanding: individual and corporate trustees);

(g) the discharge of the duty imposed by section 49(9)(b) of the Pensions Act 1995 (c. 26) (duty of trustees or managers of occupational pension schemes to report material failures by employers to pay contributions deducted from employee's earnings timeously);

(h) the discharge of the duties imposed by sections 67 to 67I of that Act (the subsisting rights provisions);

(i) the discharge of the duty imposed by section 88(1) of that Act (duties of trustees and managers of money purchase schemes to report failures to pay employer contributions etc timeously);

(j) the discharge of the duty imposed by section 111A(7A) of the Pension Schemes Act 1993 (c. 48) (duty of trustees or managers of personal pension schemes to report material failures to pay employer contributions timeously);

(k) such other matters as are prescribed for the purposes of this section.

(3) The Regulator may from time to time revise the whole or any part of a code of practice issued under this section and issue that revised code.

(4) A failure on the part of any person to observe any provision of a code of practice does not of itself render that person liable to any legal proceedings.

This is subject to section 13(3)(a) and (8) (power for improvement notice to direct that person complies with code of practice and civil penalties for failure to comply).

(5) A code of practice issued under this section is admissible in evidence in any legal proceedings and, if any provision of such a code appears to the court or tribunal concerned to be relevant to any question arising in the proceedings, it must be taken into account in determining that question.

(6) In this section –

'legal proceedings' includes proceedings of the Pensions Ombudsman, proceedings of the Ombudsman for the Board of the Pension Protection Fund and proceedings of the Board of the Pension Protection Fund under section 207 or 208; and

'the pensions legislation' means any enactment contained in or made by virtue of –

(a) the Pension Schemes Act 1993 (c. 48),

(b) Part 1 of the Pensions Act 1995 (c. 26), other than sections 62 to 66A of that Act (equal treatment),

(c) Part 1 or section 33 of the Welfare Reform and Pensions Act 1999 (c. 30), or

(d) this Act.

(7) Sections 91 and 92 make provision about the procedure to be followed when a code of practice is issued or revoked.

91 Procedure for issue and publication of codes of practice

(1) Where the Regulator proposes to issue a code of practice it must prepare and publish a draft of the code.

(2) Where the Regulator publishes a draft under subsection (1), it must consult –

(a) such persons as it considers appropriate, and

(b) any other persons the Secretary of State requires it to consult.

(3) Having considered any representations made on the draft, the Regulator must make such modifications to it as it considers appropriate.

(4) Subsections (2) and (3) do not apply –

(a) to a code made for the purpose only of consolidating other codes issued under section 90, or

(b) to a code if the Secretary of State considers consultation inexpedient by reason of urgency.

(5) If the Regulator determines to proceed with a draft, it must send it to the Secretary of State who –

(a) if he approves of it, must lay it before Parliament, and

(b) if he does not approve of it, must publish details of his reasons for withholding approval.

(6) Where a draft is laid before Parliament under subsection (5)(a) –

(a) if within the period mentioned in subsection (7) either House so resolves, no further proceedings may be taken on the draft code;

(b) if no such resolution is passed, the Regulator must issue the code in the form of the draft.

(7) The period referred to in subsection (6)(a) is the period of 40 days –

(a) beginning with the day on which the draft is laid before Parliament (or, if it is laid before the two Houses on different days, with the later of the two days), and

(b) ignoring any period during which Parliament is dissolved or prorogued or during which both Houses are adjourned for more than four days.

(8) The fact that no further proceedings may be taken on a draft code in accordance with subsection (6)(a) does not prevent the laying of a new draft.

(9) A code issued in accordance with subsection (6)(b) shall come into effect on such day as the Secretary of State may by order appoint.

Without prejudice to section 315, such an order may contain such transitional provisions or savings as appear to the Secretary of State to be necessary or expedient in connection with the code of practice brought into operation.

(10) The Regulator must arrange for any code issued by it under section 90 to be published in the way appearing to it to be appropriate.

(11) The Regulator may charge a reasonable fee for providing a person with a copy of a code published under this section.

(12) This section applies to a revised code as it applies to the first issue of a code.

92 Revocation of codes of practice

(1) A code of practice may be revoked by the Secretary of State by order.

(2) An order under this section may be made only with the consent of the Regulator.

(3) Without prejudice to section 315, an order under this section may contain such savings as appear to the Secretary of State to be necessary or expedient in connection with the revocation of the code.

Exercise of regulatory functions

93 The Regulator's procedure in relation to its regulatory functions

(1) The Regulator must determine the procedure that it proposes to follow in relation to the exercise of its regulatory functions.

(2) For the purposes of this Part the 'regulatory functions' of the Regulator are –

(a) the power to issue an improvement notice under section 13,

(b) the power to issue a third party notice under section 14,

(c) the reserved regulatory functions (see Schedule 2),

(d) the power to issue a clearance statement under section 42,

(e) the power to issue a notice under section 45(1) approving the details of arrangements,

(f)   the power to issue a clearance statement under section 46,

(g)   the power to vary or revoke under section 101 (to the extent that it does not fall within paragraph (c)),

(h)   the power to make an order under section 154(8),

(i)   the power to make an order under section 219(4),

(j)   the power to grant or revoke authorisation under section 288,

(k)   the power to grant or revoke approval under section 289,

(l)   the power to issue a notice under section 293(5),

(m)   the power by direction under section 2(3)(a) of the Welfare Reform and Pensions Act 1999 (c. 30) to refuse to register a scheme under section 2 of that Act,

(n)   the power to make an order under section 7 of the Pensions Act 1995 (c. 26) appointing a trustee (to the extent that it does not fall within paragraph (c)),

(o)   the power to make an order under section 23 of that Act appointing an independent trustee,

(p)   the power to give directions under section 72B of that Act (directions facilitating winding up), and

(q)   such other functions of the Regulator as may be prescribed.

(3)   The Determinations Panel must determine the procedure to be followed by it in relation to any exercise by it on behalf of the Regulator of –

(a)   the power to determine whether to exercise a regulatory function, and

(b)   where the Panel so determines to exercise a regulatory function, the power to exercise the function in question.

(4)   The procedure determined under this section –

(a)   must provide for the procedure required under –

(i)   section 96 (standard procedure), and

(ii)   section 98 (special procedure), and

(b)   may include such other procedural requirements as the Regulator or, as the case may be, the Panel considers appropriate.

(5)   This section is subject to –

(a)   sections 99 to 104 (the remaining provisions concerning the procedure in relation to the regulatory functions), and

(b)   any regulations made by the Secretary of State under paragraph 19 of Schedule 1.

94   Publication of procedure in relation to regulatory functions

(1)   The Regulator must issue a statement of the procedure determined under section 93.

(2)   The Regulator must arrange for the statement to be published in the way appearing to it to be appropriate.

(3)   The Regulator may charge a reasonable fee for providing a person with a copy of the statement.

(4)   If the procedure determined under section 93 is changed in a material way, the Regulator must publish a revised statement.

(5)   The Regulator must, without delay, give the Secretary of State a copy of any statement which it issues under this section.

95   Application of standard and special procedure

(1)   The Regulator must comply with the standard procedure (see section 96) or, where section 97 applies, the special procedure (see section 98) in a case where –

(a)   the Regulator considers that the exercise of one or more of the regulatory functions may be appropriate, or

(b)   an application is made under or by virtue of –

(i)   any of the provisions listed in section 10(6), or

(ii)   any prescribed provision of this or any other enactment,

for the Regulator to exercise a regulatory function.

(2)   For the purposes of section 96, references to the regulatory action under consideration in a particular case are –

(a)   in a case falling within subsection (1)(a), references to the exercise of the one or more regulatory functions which the Regulator considers that it may be appropriate to exercise, and

(b)   in a case falling within subsection (1)(b), references to the exercise of the regulatory function which is the subject-matter of the application.

(3)   Neither section 96 (standard procedure) nor section 98 (special procedure) apply in relation to a determination whether to exercise a regulatory function on a review under section 99 (compulsory review of regulatory action).

96 Standard procedure

(1)   The procedure determined under section 93 must make provision for the standard procedure.

(2)   The 'standard procedure' is a procedure which provides for –

(a)   the giving of notice to such persons as it appears to the Regulator would be directly affected by the regulatory action under consideration (a 'warning notice'),

(b)   those persons to have an opportunity to make representations,

(c)   the consideration of any such representations and the determination whether to take the regulatory action under consideration,

(d)   the giving of notice of the determination to such persons as appear to the Regulator to be directly affected by it (a 'determination notice'),

(e)   the determination notice to contain details of the right of referral to the Tribunal under subsection (3),

(f)   the form and further content of warning notices and determination notices and the manner in which they are to be given, and

(g)   the time limits to be applied at any stage of the procedure.

(3)   Where the standard procedure applies, the determination which is the subject-matter of the determination notice may be referred to the Tribunal (see section 102) by –

(a)   any person to whom the determination notice is given as required under subsection (2)(d), and

(b)   any other person who appears to the Tribunal to be directly affected by the determination.

(4)   Subsection (3) does not apply where the determination which is the subject-matter of the determination notice is a determination to issue a clearance statement under section 42 or 46.

(5)   Where the determination which is the subject-matter of the determination notice is a determination to exercise a regulatory function and subsection (3) applies, the Regulator must not exercise the function –

(a)   during the period within which the determination may be referred to the Tribunal (see section 103(1)), and

(b)   if the determination is so referred, until the reference, and any appeal against the Tribunal's determination, has been finally disposed of.

(6)   Subsection (5) does not apply where the determination is a determination to exercise any of the following functions –

(a)   the power to make a direction under section 76(8) extending the retention period for documents taken into possession under section 75;

(b)   the power to make a direction under section 78(10) extending the retention period for documents taken into possession under that section;

(c)   the power to make an order under section 154(8);

(d)   the power to make an order under section 219(4);

(e)   the power to grant or revoke authorisation under section 288;

(f)   the power to grant or revoke approval under section 289;

(g)   the power to issue a notice under section 293(5);

(h)   the power to make an order under section 3(1) of the Pensions Act 1995 (c. 26) prohibiting a person from being a trustee;

(i)   the power to make an order under section 3(3) of that Act revoking such an order;

(j)   the power to make an order under section 4(1) of that Act suspending a trustee;

(k)   the power to make an order under section 4(2) of that Act extending the period for which an order under section 4(1) of that Act has effect;

(l)   the power to make an order under section 4(5) of that Act revoking an order under section 4(1) of that Act suspending a trustee;

(m)   the power to make an order under section 7 of that Act appointing a trustee;

(n)   the power under section 9 of that Act to exercise by order the same jurisdiction and powers as the High Court or the Court of Session for vesting property in, or transferring property to, trustees in consequence of the appointment or removal of a trustee;

(o)   the power to make an order under section 23 of that Act appointing an independent trustee;

(p)   the power under section 29(5) of that Act to give a notice waiving a disqualification under section 29 of that Act;

(q)   the power under section 30(2) of that Act to exercise by order the same jurisdiction and powers as the High Court or the Court of Session for vesting property in, or transferring property to, the trustees where a trustee becomes disqualified under section 29 of that Act;

(r)   the power to give directions under section 72B of that Act facilitating a winding up;

(s)   the power by direction under section 99(4) of the Pension Schemes Act 1993 (c. 48) to grant an extension of the period within which the trustees or managers of a scheme are to carry out certain duties;

(t)   the power by direction under section 101J(2) of that Act to extend the period for compliance with a transfer notice;

(u)   such other regulatory functions as may be prescribed;

(v)   the power under section 101(1)(b) to vary or revoke in relation to the exercise of any of the regulatory functions mentioned in paragraphs (a) to (u) other than those mentioned in paragraph (i) or (l).

97 Special procedure: applicable cases

(1)   The special procedure in section 98 (and not the standard procedure) applies to –

(a)   a case falling within subsection (2),

(b)   a case falling within subsection (3), and

(c)   a case falling within subsection (4).

(2)   A case falls within this subsection if –

(a)   the Regulator considers that it may be necessary to exercise a regulatory function listed in subsection (5) immediately because there is, or the Regulator considers it likely that if a warning notice were to be given there would be, an immediate risk to –

(i)   the interests of members under an occupational or personal pension scheme, or

(ii)   the assets of such a scheme,

(b) the Regulator accordingly dispenses with the giving of a warning notice and an opportunity to make representations as described in section 96(2)(a) and (b), and

(c) the Regulator determines to exercise the function immediately on the basis that it is necessary to do so because there is, or the Regulator considers it likely that if the function were not exercised immediately there would be, an immediate risk to –

　(i)   the interests of members under an occupational or personal pension scheme, or

　(ii) the assets of such a scheme.

(3) A case falls within this subsection if –

(a) the Regulator gives a warning notice as described in section 96(2)(a) in relation to a determination whether to exercise a regulatory function listed in subsection (5), and

(b) before it has considered the representations of those persons to whom the warning notice is given, the Regulator determines to exercise the function immediately on the basis that it is necessary to do so because there is, or the Regulator considers it likely that if the function were not exercised immediately there would be, an immediate risk to –

　(i)   the interests of members under an occupational or personal pension scheme, or

　(ii) the assets of such a scheme.

(4) A case falls within this subsection if the Regulator –

(a) gives a warning notice as described in section 96(2)(a) in relation to a determination whether to exercise a regulatory function which –

　(i)   is listed in subsection (5), and

　(ii) is not a function listed in section 96(6) (functions which may be exercised immediately under the standard procedure),

(b) considers the representations of those persons to whom the warning notice is given, and

(c) determines to exercise the function immediately on the basis that it is necessary to do so because there is, or the Regulator considers it likely that if the function were not exercised immediately there would be, an immediate risk to –

　(i)   the interests of members under an occupational or personal pension scheme, or

　(ii) the assets of such a scheme.

(5) The regulatory functions referred to in subsections (2), (3) and (4) are –

(a) the power to make or extend a restraining order under section 20;

(b) the power to make a freezing order under section 23;

(c) the power to make an order under section 25(3) extending the period for which a freezing order has effect;

(d) the power to make an order under section 26 validating action taken in contravention of a freezing order;

(e) the power to make an order under section 28 directing that specified steps are taken;

(f) the power to make an order under section 30 giving a direction where a freezing order ceases to have effect;

(g) the power to make an order under section 31(3) directing the notification of members;

(h) the power to make an order under section 231 modifying a scheme, giving directions or imposing a schedule of contributions;

(i) the power to make an order under section 3(1) of the Pensions Act 1995 (c. 26) prohibiting a person from being a trustee;

(j) the power to make an order under section 3(3) of that Act revoking such an order;

(k) the power to make an order under section 4(1) of that Act suspending a trustee;

(l) the power to make an order under section 4(5) of that Act revoking such an order;

(m) the power to make an order under section 7 of that Act appointing a trustee;

(n) the power under section 9 of that Act to exercise by order the same jurisdiction and powers as the High Court or the Court of Session for vesting property in, or transferring property to, trustees in consequence of the appointment or removal of a trustee;

(o) the power to make an order under section 11 of that Act directing or authorising an occupational pension scheme to be wound up;

(p) the power to make an order under section 23 of that Act appointing an independent trustee;

(q) the power under section 29(5) of that Act to give a notice waiving a disqualification under section 29 of that Act;

(r) the power under section 30(2) of that Act to exercise by order the same jurisdiction and powers as the High Court or the Court of Session for vesting property in, or transferring property to, the trustees where a trustee becomes disqualified under section 29 of that Act;

(s) the power to make an order under section 67G(2) of that Act by virtue of which any modification of, or grant of rights under, an occupational pension scheme is void to any extent;

(t) the power to make an order under section 67H(2) of that Act prohibiting, or specifying steps to be taken in relation to, the exercise of a power to modify an occupational pension scheme;

(u) such other regulatory functions as may be prescribed;

(v) the power under section 101(1)(b) to vary or revoke in relation to the exercise of any of the regulatory functions mentioned in paragraphs (a) to (u) other than those mentioned in paragraph (j) or (l).

98 Special procedure

(1) The procedure determined under section 93 must make provision for the special procedure.

(2) The 'special procedure' is a procedure which provides for –

(a) the giving of notice of the determination to exercise the regulatory function to such persons as appear to the Regulator to be directly affected by it (a 'determination notice'),

(b) the determination notice to contain details of the requirement for the Regulator to review the determination under section 99(1) and of any subsequent right of referral to the Tribunal under section 99(7),

(c) the persons to whom the determination notice was given (as required under paragraph (a)) to have an opportunity to make representations in relation to the determination before it is reviewed under section 99(1),

(d) the consideration of any such representations before the determination on the review,

(e) the giving of a notice in accordance with section 99(4) of the determination on the review (a 'final notice'),

(f) the final notice to contain details of the right of referral to the Tribunal under section 99(7),

(g) the form and further content of determination notices and final notices and the manner in which they are to be given, and

(h) the time limits to be applied at any stage of the procedure.

99 Compulsory review

(1) In a case where the special procedure applies, the Regulator must review the determination to exercise the regulatory function.

(2) The review must be determined as soon as reasonably practicable.

(3) The Regulator's powers on a review under this section include power to –

   (a) confirm, vary or revoke the determination,

   (b) confirm, vary or revoke any order, notice or direction made, issued or given as a result of the determination,

   (c) substitute a different determination, order, notice or direction,

   (d) deal with the matters arising on the review as if they had arisen on the original determination, and

   (e) make savings and transitional provision.

(4) When the Regulator has completed a review under this section a notice of its determination on the review must be given to such persons as appear to it to be directly affected by its determination on the review.

(5) If the final notice contains a determination to exercise a different regulatory function to the function which was the subject-matter of the determination notice, then the final notice may not be given unless –

   (a) such persons as appear to the Regulator to be directly affected by the exercise of the regulatory function have been given an opportunity to make representations, and

   (b) the Regulator has considered any such representations before it makes its determination on the review.

(6) Subsection (5) does not apply if the regulatory function is listed in section 97(5) and the Regulator determines to exercise it immediately on the basis that it is necessary to do so because there is, or the Regulator considers it likely that if the function were not exercised immediately there would be, an immediate risk to –

   (a) the interests of members under an occupational or personal pension scheme, or

   (b) the assets of such a scheme.

(7) The determination which is the subject-matter of a final notice may be referred to the Tribunal (see section 102) by –

   (a) any person to whom the final notice is given as required under subsection (4), and

   (b) any other person who appears to the Tribunal to be directly affected by the determination.

(8) Where that determination is a determination to exercise a different regulatory function to the function which was the subject-matter of the determination notice, the Regulator must not exercise the regulatory function –

   (a) during the period within which the determination may be referred to the Tribunal (see section 103(1)), and

   (b) if the determination is so referred, until the reference, and any appeal against the Tribunal's determination, has been finally disposed of.

(9) Subsection (8) does not apply where –

   (a) the regulatory function in question is a function listed in section 96(6) (functions which may be exercised immediately under the standard procedure), or

   (b) the regulatory function in question is a function listed in section 97(5) (functions which may be exercised immediately under the special procedure) and the Regulator determines to exercise it immediately on the basis described in subsection (6).

(10) The functions of the Regulator under this section are exercisable on behalf of the Regulator by the Determinations Panel (and are not otherwise exercisable by or on behalf of the Regulator).

(11) The Panel must determine the procedure that it proposes to follow in relation to the exercise of those functions.

(12) Section 94 (publication of Regulator's procedure) applies in relation to the procedure determined under subsection (11) as it applies to the procedure determined under section 93 (procedure in relation to the regulatory functions).

100 Duty to have regard to the interests of members etc

(1) The Regulator must have regard to the matters mentioned in subsection (2) –

    (a) when determining whether to exercise a regulatory function –

        (i)   in a case where the requirements of the standard or special procedure apply, or

        (ii) on a review under section 99, and

    (b) when exercising the regulatory function in question.

(2) Those matters are –

    (a) the interests of the generality of the members of the scheme to which the exercise of the function relates, and

    (b) the interests of such persons as appear to the Regulator to be directly affected by the exercise.

101 Powers to vary or revoke orders, notices or directions etc

(1) The Regulator may vary or revoke –

    (a) any determination by the Regulator whether to exercise a regulatory function, or

    (b) any order, notice or direction made, issued or given by the Regulator in the exercise of a regulatory function.

(2) Subsection (1)(b) does not apply to –

    (a) an order under section 3(3) of the Pensions Act 1995 (c. 26) revoking a prohibition order under that section,

    (b) an order under section 4(5) of that Act revoking a suspension order under that section,

    (c) a direction under section 2(3) of the Welfare Reform and Pensions Act 1999 (c. 30) refusing to register a scheme under section 2 of that Act or removing a scheme from the register of stakeholder pension schemes, or

    (d) such other orders, notices or directions made, issued or given by the Regulator, in the exercise of a regulatory function, as may be prescribed.

(3) A variation or revocation of an order, a notice or a direction must be made by an order, a notice or a direction (as the case may be).

(4) A variation or revocation made under this section must take effect from a specified time which must not be a time earlier than the time when the variation or revocation is made.

(5) The power to vary or revoke under this section –

    (a) is not to be treated for the purposes of subsection (1) as a regulatory function, and

    (b) is in addition to any such power which is conferred on the Regulator by, or by virtue of, this or any other enactment.

The Pensions Regulator Tribunal

102   The Pensions Regulator Tribunal

(1) There shall be a tribunal to be known as the Pensions Regulator Tribunal (in this Act referred to as 'the Tribunal').

(2) The Tribunal is to have the functions conferred on it by this Act or any provisions in force in Northern Ireland corresponding to this Act.

(3) The Lord Chancellor may by rules make such provision as appears to him to be necessary or expedient in respect of the conduct of proceedings before the Tribunal.

(4) Schedule 4 (which makes provision as respects the Tribunal and its proceedings) has effect.

(5) But that Schedule does not limit the Lord Chancellor's powers under this section.

103   References to the Tribunal

(1) A reference to the Tribunal under this Act must be made –

    (a) in the case of a reference under section 96(3) (referral following determination under standard procedure), during the period of 28 days beginning with the day on which the determination notice in question is given,

    (b) in the case of a reference under section 99(7) (referral following determination under special procedure), during the period of 28 days beginning with the day on which the final notice in question is given, or

    (c) in either case, during such other period as may be specified in rules made under section 102.

(2) Subject to rules made under section 102, the Tribunal may allow a reference to be made after the end of the relevant period specified in or under subsection (1).

(3) On a reference, the Tribunal may consider any evidence relating to the subject-matter of the reference, whether or not it was available to the Regulator at the material time.

(4) On a reference, the Tribunal must determine what (if any) is the appropriate action for the Regulator to take in relation to the matter referred to the Tribunal.

(5) On determining a reference, the Tribunal must remit the matter to the Regulator with such directions (if any) as the Tribunal considers appropriate for giving effect to its determination.

(6) Those directions may include directions to the Regulator –

    (a) confirming the Regulator's determination and any order, notice or direction made, issued or given as a result of it;

    (b) to vary or revoke the Regulator's determination, and any order, notice or direction made, issued or given as a result of it;

    (c) to substitute a different determination, order, notice or direction;

    (d) to make such savings and transitional provision as the Tribunal considers appropriate.

(7) The Regulator must act in accordance with the determination of, and any direction given by, the Tribunal (and accordingly sections 96 to 99 (standard and special procedure) do not apply).

(8) The Tribunal may, on determining a reference, make recommendations as to the procedure followed by the Regulator or the Determinations Panel.

(9) An order of the Tribunal may be enforced –

    (a) as if it were an order of a county court, or

    (b) in Scotland, as if it were an order of the Court of Session.

104 Appeal on a point of law

(1) A party to a reference to the Tribunal may with permission appeal –

   (a) to the Court of Appeal, or
   (b) in Scotland, to the Court of Session,

   on a point of law arising from a decision of the Tribunal disposing of the reference.

(2) 'Permission' means permission given by –

   (a) the Tribunal, or
   (b) if it is refused by the Tribunal, by the Court of Appeal or, in Scotland, the Court of Session.

(3) If, on an appeal under subsection (1), the court considers that the decision of the Tribunal was wrong in law, it may –

   (a) remit the matter to the Tribunal for rehearing and determination by it under section 103, or
   (b) itself make a determination.

(4) An appeal may not be brought from a decision of the Court of Appeal under subsection (3) except with the leave of –

   (a) the Court of Appeal, or
   (b) the House of Lords.

(5) An appeal lies, with the leave of the Court of Session or the House of Lords, from any decision of the Court of Session under this section, and such leave may be given on such terms as to costs, expenses or otherwise as the Court of Session or the House of Lords may determine.

(6) Rules made under section 102 may make provision for regulating or prescribing any matters incidental to or consequential on an appeal under this section.

105 Redetermination etc by the Tribunal

(1) This section applies where an application is made to the Tribunal for permission under section 104(2)(a) to appeal from a decision of the Tribunal disposing of a reference.

(2) If the person who constitutes, or is the chairman of, the Tribunal for the purposes of dealing with that application considers that the decision of the Tribunal disposing of the reference was wrong in law, he may set aside the decision and refer the matter –

   (a) for rehearing and redetermination by the Tribunal under section 103, or
   (b) for rehearing and determination under that section by a differently constituted Tribunal.

106 Legal assistance scheme

(1) The Lord Chancellor may by regulations establish a scheme governing the provision of legal assistance in connection with proceedings before the Tribunal.

(2) The legal assistance scheme may, in particular, make provision as to –

   (a) the kinds of legal assistance that may be provided;
   (b) the persons by whom legal assistance may be provided;
   (c) the manner in which applications for legal assistance are to be made;
   (d) the criteria on which eligibility for legal assistance is to be determined;
   (e) the persons or bodies by whom applications are to be determined;
   (f) appeals against refusals of applications;
   (g) the revocation or variation of decisions;
   (h) its administration and the enforcement of its provisions.

(3) Legal assistance under the scheme may be provided subject to conditions or restrictions.

(4) Those conditions may include conditions as to the making of contributions by the person to whom the assistance is provided.

(5) The Lord Chancellor must fund, out of money provided by Parliament, the costs of the scheme including the costs of legal assistance provided under it.

(6) In this Part 'the legal assistance scheme' means any scheme in force by virtue of subsection (1).

PART 2   THE BOARD OF THE PENSION PROTECTION FUND

CHAPTER 1   THE BOARD

Establishment

107 The Board of the Pension Protection Fund

There shall be a body corporate called the Board of the Pension Protection Fund (in this Act referred to as 'the Board').

108 Membership of the Board

(1) The Board is to consist of the following members –

    (a) a chairman,

    (b) the Chief Executive of the Board, and

    (c) at least five other persons ('ordinary members').

(2) The chairman must not be appointed from the staff of the Board or be the chairman of the Regulator.

(3) The number of ordinary members must not exceed any maximum number which may be prescribed.

(4) At least two ordinary members must be appointed from the staff of the Board.

(5) No member of the Determinations Panel established by the Regulator under section 9, or member of the staff of the Regulator, is eligible for appointment as a member of the Board.

(6) Any power to appoint ordinary members must be exercised so as to secure that a majority of the members of the Board are non-executive members.

(7) In this Part –

    (a) references to executive members of the Board are to –

        (i) the Chief Executive, and

        (ii) the ordinary members appointed from the staff of the Board, and

    (b) references to non-executive members of the Board are to members who are not executive members.

109 Further provision about the Board

Schedule 5 makes further provision about the Board, including provision as to –

the appointment of members,

the terms of appointment, tenure and remuneration of members,

the appointment of the Chief Executive and other staff,

the proceedings of the Board,

its accounts, and

the status and liability of the Board, its members and staff.

General provision about functions

110 Board's functions

(1) The Board must hold, manage and apply, in accordance with this Part and any provision in force in Northern Ireland corresponding to it –

(a) a fund to be known as the Pension Protection Fund, and

(b) a fund to be known as the Fraud Compensation Fund.

(2) Sections 175 and 189 make provision for contributions to those funds to be levied by the Board.

(3) The Board also has such other functions as are conferred on it by, or by virtue of, this or any other enactment.

111 Supplementary powers

The Board may do anything which –

(a) is calculated to facilitate the exercise of its functions, or

(b) is incidental or conducive to their exercise.

Non-executive functions

112 Non-executive functions

(1) The functions listed in subsection (4) (in this Part referred to as 'the non-executive functions') are functions of the Board.

(2) The Board must establish a committee to discharge the non-executive functions on its behalf.

(3) Only non-executive members of the Board may be members of that committee.

(4) The non-executive functions are –

(a) the duty to keep under review the question whether the Board's internal financial controls secure the proper conduct of its financial affairs;

(b) the duty to determine under sub-paragraph (5)(a) of paragraph 12 of Schedule 5, subject to the approval of the Secretary of State, the terms and conditions as to remuneration of any Chief Executive appointed under sub-paragraph (4) of that paragraph;

(c) the duty to determine under paragraph 13(3)(a) of that Schedule, subject to the approval of the Secretary of State, the terms and conditions as to remuneration of any member of the staff who is also to be an executive member of the Board;

(d) the duty to determine under paragraph 13(3)(b) of that Schedule, the terms and conditions as to remuneration of any member of the staff of a description prescribed for the purposes of that provision.

(5) The committee established under this section must prepare a report on the discharge of the non-executive functions for inclusion in the Board's annual report to the Secretary of State under section 119.

(6) The committee's report must relate to the same period as that covered by the Board's report.

(7) The members of any sub-committee of the committee (established by virtue of paragraph 15(2) of Schedule 5) –

(a) may include persons who are not members of the committee, but

(b) must not include persons who are executive members or other staff of the Board.

(8) The committee may authorise any of its sub-committees to discharge on its behalf –

(a) any of the non-executive functions;

(b) the duty to prepare a report under subsection (5).

Financial matters

113 Investment of funds

(1) The Board may invest for the purposes of the prudent management of its financial affairs.

(2) When exercising the power conferred by subsection (1) in relation to the Pension Protection Fund, the Board must have regard to –

(a) the interests of persons who are or may become entitled to compensation under the pension compensation provisions (see section 162) or any corresponding provisions in force in Northern Ireland, and

(b) the effect of the exercise of the power on the rate of any levy which may be imposed under section 174 or 175 or any corresponding provision in force in Northern Ireland and the interests which persons have in the rate of any such levy.

(3) When exercising the power conferred by subsection (1) in relation to the Fraud Compensation Fund, the Board must have regard to –

(a) the interests of members of occupational pension schemes in relation to which section 189(1), or any corresponding provision in force in Northern Ireland, applies, and

(b) the effect of the exercise of the power on the level of any levy which may be imposed under section 189 or any corresponding provision in force in Northern Ireland and the interests which persons have in the rate of any such levy.

(4) For the purposes of subsection (1) there must be at least two fund managers.

(5) For this purpose 'fund manager' means an individual who or firm which is appointed by the Board to manage the fund maintained under section 173 (the Pension Protection Fund).

(6) The Board must not appoint an individual or firm as a fund manager unless it is satisfied –

(a) in the case of an individual, that the individual has the appropriate knowledge and experience for managing the investments of the Pension Protection Fund, or

(b) in the case of a firm, that arrangements are in place to secure that any individual who will exercise functions which the firm has as fund manager will, at the time he exercises those functions, have the appropriate knowledge and experience for managing the investments of that Fund.

114 Investment principles

(1) The Board must secure –

(a) that a statement of investment principles is prepared and maintained, and

(b) that the statement is reviewed at such intervals, and on such occasions, as may be prescribed and, if necessary, revised.

(2) In this section 'statement of investment principles' means a written statement of the investment principles governing determinations about investments made by or on behalf of the Board.

(3) Before preparing or revising a statement of investment principles, the Board must comply with any prescribed requirements.

(4) A statement of investment principles must be in the prescribed form and cover, amongst other things, the prescribed matters.

115 Borrowing

(1) The Board may –

(a) borrow from a deposit-taker such sums as it may from time to time require for exercising any of its functions;

(b) give security for any money borrowed by it.

(2) The Board may not borrow if the effect would be –

(a) to take the aggregate amount outstanding in respect of the principal of sums borrowed by it over its borrowing limit, or

(b) to increase the amount by which the aggregate amount so outstanding exceeds that limit.

(3) In this section –

'borrowing limit' means such limit as the Secretary of State may specify by order;

'deposit-taker' means –

(a) a person who has permission under Part 4 of the Financial Services and Markets Act 2000 (c. 8) to accept deposits, or

(b) an EEA firm of the kind mentioned in paragraph 5(b) of Schedule 3 to that Act which has permission under paragraph 15 of that Schedule (as a result of qualifying for authorisation under paragraph 12 of that Schedule) to accept deposits.

(4) The definition of 'deposit-taker' in subsection (3) must be read with –

(a) section 22 of the Financial Services and Markets Act 2000,

(b) any relevant order under that section, and

(c) Schedule 2 to that Act.

116 Grants

The Secretary of State may pay the Board out of money provided by Parliament such sums as he may determine towards any of its expenses, other than expenditure which by virtue of section 173(3) or 188(3) is payable out of –

(a) the Pension Protection Fund, or

(b) the Fraud Compensation Fund.

117 Administration levy

(1) Regulations may provide for the imposition of a levy ('administration levy') in respect of eligible schemes (see section 126) for the purpose of meeting –

(a) expenditure of the Secretary of State relating to the establishment of the Board;

(b) any expenditure of the Secretary of State under section 116.

(2) An administration levy is payable to the Secretary of State by or on behalf of –

(a) the trustees or managers of an eligible scheme, or

(b) any other prescribed person.

(3) An administration levy is payable at the prescribed rate and at prescribed times.

(4) Before prescribing a rate under subsection (3), the Secretary of State must consult the Board.

(5) An amount payable by a person on account of an administration levy is a debt due from him to the Secretary of State.

(6) An amount so payable is recoverable by the Secretary of State or, if he so determines, by the Regulator on his behalf.

(7) Without prejudice to the generality of subsections (1), (5) and (6), regulations under this section may include provision relating to –

(a) the collection and recovery of amounts payable by way of levy under this section;

(b) the circumstances in which any such amount may be waived.

118 Fees

(1) Regulations may authorise the Board –

(a) to charge prescribed fees;

(b) to charge fees sufficient to meet prescribed costs.

(2) Regulations under subsection (1) may prescribe, or authorise the Board to determine, the time at which any fee is due.

(3) Any fee which is owed to the Board by virtue of regulations under this section may be recovered as a debt due to the Board.

Annual reports

119 Annual reports to Secretary of State

(1) The Board must prepare a report for each financial year.

(2) Each report –

  (a) must deal with the activities of the Board in the financial year for which it is prepared, including the matters mentioned in subsection (3), and

  (b) must include the report prepared under subsection (5) of section 112 by the committee established under that section.

(3) The matters referred to in subsection (2)(a) are –

  (a) the strategic direction of the Board and the manner in which it has been kept under review;

  (b) the steps taken to scrutinise the performance of the Chief Executive in securing that the Board's functions are exercised efficiently and effectively;

  (c) the Board's objectives and targets and the steps taken to monitor the extent to which they are being met.

(4) The Board must send each report to the Secretary of State as soon as practicable after the end of the financial year for which it is prepared.

(5) The Secretary of State must lay before each House of Parliament a copy of every report received by him under this section.

(6) In this section 'financial year' means –

  (a) the period beginning with the date on which the Board is established and ending with the next following 31st March, and

  (b) each successive period of 12 months.

CHAPTER 2   INFORMATION RELATING TO EMPLOYER'S INSOLVENCY ETC

Insolvency events

120 Duty to notify insolvency events in respect of employers

(1) This section applies where, in the case of an occupational pension scheme, an insolvency event occurs in relation to the employer.

(2) The insolvency practitioner in relation to the employer must give a notice to that effect within the notification period to –

  (a) the Board,

  (b) the Regulator, and

  (c) the trustees or managers of the scheme.

(3) For the purposes of subsection (2) the 'notification period' is the prescribed period beginning with the later of –

  (a) the insolvency date, and

  (b) the date the insolvency practitioner becomes aware of the existence of the scheme.

(4) A notice under this section must be in such form and contain such information as may be prescribed.

121 Insolvency event, insolvency date and insolvency practitioner

(1) In this Part each of the following expressions has the meaning given to it by this section –

    'insolvency event'
    'insolvency date'
    'insolvency practitioner'.

(2) An insolvency event occurs in relation to an individual where –

    (a) he is adjudged bankrupt or sequestration of his estate has been awarded;

    (b) the nominee in relation to a proposal for a voluntary arrangement under Part 8 of the Insolvency Act 1986 (c. 45) submits a report to the court under section 256(1) or 256A(3) of that Act which states that in his opinion a meeting of the individual's creditors should be summoned to consider the debtor's proposal;

    (c) a deed of arrangement made by or in respect of the affairs of the individual is registered in accordance with the Deeds of Arrangement Act 1914 (c. 47);

    (d) he executes a trust deed for his creditors or enters into a composition contract;

    (e) he has died and –

        (i)   an insolvency administration order is made in respect of his estate in accordance with an order under section 421 of the Insolvency Act 1986, or

        (ii) a judicial factor appointed under section 11A of the Judicial Factors (Scotland) Act 1889 (c. 39) is required by that section to divide the individual's estate among his creditors.

(3) An insolvency event occurs in relation to a company where –

    (a) the nominee in relation to a proposal for a voluntary arrangement under Part 1 of the Insolvency Act 1986 submits a report to the court under section 2 of that Act (procedure where nominee is not the liquidator or administrator) which states that in his opinion meetings of the company and its creditors should be summoned to consider the proposal;

    (b) the directors of the company file (or in Scotland lodge) with the court documents and statements in accordance with paragraph 7(1) of Schedule A1 to that Act (moratorium where directors propose voluntary arrangement);

    (c) an administrative receiver within the meaning of section 251 of that Act is appointed in relation to the company;

    (d) the company enters administration within the meaning of paragraph 1(2)(b) of Schedule B1 to that Act;

    (e) a resolution is passed for a voluntary winding up of the company without a declaration of solvency under section 89 of that Act;

    (f) a meeting of creditors is held in relation to the company under section 95 of that Act (creditors' meeting which has the effect of converting a members' voluntary winding up into a creditors' voluntary winding up);

    (g) an order for the winding up of the company is made by the court under Part 4 or 5 of that Act.

(4) An insolvency event occurs in relation to a partnership where –

    (a) an order for the winding up of the partnership is made by the court under any provision of the Insolvency Act 1986 (c. 45) (as applied by an order under section 420 of that Act (insolvent partnerships));

    (b) sequestration is awarded on the estate of the partnership under section 12 of the Bankruptcy (Scotland) Act 1985 (c. 66) or the partnership grants a trust deed for its creditors;

    (c) the nominee in relation to a proposal for a voluntary arrangement under Part 1 of the Insolvency Act 1986 (as applied by an order under section 420 of that Act) submits a report to the court under section 2 of that Act (procedure where nominee is not the liquidator or administrator) which states that in his opinion meetings of the members of the partnership and the partnership's creditors should be summoned to consider the proposal;

 (d) the members of the partnership file with the court documents and statements in accordance with paragraph 7(1) of Schedule A1 to that Act (moratorium where directors propose voluntary arrangement) (as applied by an order under section 420 of that Act);

 (e) an administration order under Part 2 of that Act (as applied by section 420 of that Act) is made in relation to the partnership.

(5) An insolvency event also occurs in relation to a person where an event occurs which is a prescribed event in relation to such a person.

(6) Except as provided by subsections (2) to (5), for the purposes of this Part an event is not to be regarded as an insolvency event in relation to a person.

(7) The Secretary of State may by order amend subsection (4)(e) to make provision consequential upon any order under section 420 of the Insolvency Act 1986 (insolvent partnerships) applying the provisions of Part 2 of that Act (administration) as amended by the Enterprise Act 2002 (c. 40).

(8) 'Insolvency date', in relation to an insolvency event, means the date on which the event occurs.

(9) 'Insolvency practitioner', in relation to a person, means –

 (a) a person acting as an insolvency practitioner, in relation to that person, in accordance with section 388 of the Insolvency Act 1986;

 (b) in such circumstances as may be prescribed, a person of a prescribed description.

(10) In this section –

 'company' means a company within the meaning given by section 735(1) of the Companies Act 1985 (c. 6) or a company which may be wound up under Part 5 of the Insolvency Act 1986 (c. 45) (unregistered companies);

 'person acting as an insolvency practitioner', in relation to a person, includes the official receiver acting as receiver or manager of any property of that person.

(11) In applying section 388 of the Insolvency Act 1986 under subsection (9) above –

 (a) the reference in section 388(2)(a) to a permanent or interim trustee in sequestration must be taken to include a reference to a trustee in sequestration, and

 (b) section 388(5) (which includes provision that nothing in the section applies to anything done by the official receiver or the Accountant in Bankruptcy) must be ignored.

Status of scheme

122 Insolvency practitioner's duty to issue notices confirming status of scheme

(1) This section applies where an insolvency event has occurred in relation to the employer in relation to an occupational pension scheme.

(2) An insolvency practitioner in relation to the employer must –

 (a) if he is able to confirm that a scheme rescue is not possible, issue a notice to that effect (a 'scheme failure notice'), or

 (b) if he is able to confirm that a scheme rescue has occurred, issue a notice to that effect (a 'withdrawal notice').

(3) Subsection (4) applies where –

 (a) in prescribed circumstances, insolvency proceedings in relation to the employer are stayed or come to an end, or

 (b) a prescribed event occurs.

(4) If a person who was acting as an insolvency practitioner in relation to the employer immediately before this subsection applies has not been able to confirm in relation to the scheme –

(a) that a scheme rescue is not possible, or

(b) that a scheme rescue has occurred,

he must issue a notice to that effect.

(5) For the purposes of this section –

(a) a person is able to confirm that a scheme rescue has occurred in relation to an occupational pension scheme if, and only if, he is able to confirm such matters as are prescribed for the purposes of this paragraph, and

(b) a person is able to confirm that a scheme rescue is not possible, in relation to such a scheme if, and only if, he is able to confirm such matters as are prescribed for the purposes of this paragraph.

(6) Where an insolvency practitioner or former insolvency practitioner in relation to the employer issues a notice under this section, he must give a copy of that notice to –

(a) the Board,

(b) the Regulator, and

(c) the trustees or managers of the scheme.

(7) A person must comply with an obligation imposed on him by subsection (2), (4) or (6) as soon as reasonably practicable.

(8) Regulations may require notices issued under this section –

(a) to be in a prescribed form;

(b) to contain prescribed information.

123 Approval of notices issued under section 122

(1) This section applies where the Board receives a notice under section 122(6) ('the section 122 notice').

(2) The Board must determine whether to approve the section 122 notice.

(3) The Board must approve the section 122 notice if, and only if, it is satisfied –

(a) that the insolvency practitioner or former insolvency practitioner who issued the notice was required to issue it under that section, and

(b) that the notice complies with any requirements imposed by virtue of subsection (8) of that section.

(4) Where the Board makes a determination for the purposes of subsection (2), it must issue a determination notice and give a copy of that notice to –

(a) the Regulator,

(b) the trustees or managers of the scheme,

(c) the insolvency practitioner or the former insolvency practitioner who issued the section 122 notice,

(d) any insolvency practitioner in relation to the employer (who does not fall within paragraph (c)), and

(e) if there is no insolvency practitioner in relation to the employer, the employer.

(5) In subsection (4) 'determination notice' means a notice which is in the prescribed form and contains such information about the determination as may be prescribed.

Board's duties

124 Board's duty where there is a failure to comply with section 122

(1) This section applies where in relation to an occupational pension scheme –

    (a) the Board determines under section 123 not to approve a notice issued under section 122 by an insolvency practitioner or former insolvency practitioner in relation to the employer, or

    (b) an insolvency practitioner or former insolvency practitioner in relation to the employer fails to issue a notice under section 122 and the Board is satisfied that such a notice ought to have been issued under that section.

(2) The obligations on the insolvency practitioner or former insolvency practitioner imposed by subsections (2) and (4) of section 122 are to be treated as obligations imposed on the Board and the Board must accordingly issue a notice as required under that section.

(3) Subject to subsections (4) and (5), where a notice is issued under section 122 by the Board by virtue of this section, it has effect as if it were a notice issued under section 122 by an insolvency practitioner or, as the case may be, former insolvency practitioner in relation to the employer.

(4) Where a notice is issued under section 122 by virtue of this section, section 122(6) does not apply and the Board must, as soon as reasonably practicable, give a copy of the notice to –

    (a) the Regulator,

    (b) the trustees or managers of the scheme,

    (c) the insolvency practitioner or former insolvency practitioner mentioned in subsection (1),

    (d) any insolvency practitioner in relation to the employer (who does not fall within paragraph (c)), and

    (e) if there is no insolvency practitioner in relation to the employer, the employer.

(5) Where the Board –

    (a) is required to issue a notice under section 122 by virtue of this section, and

    (b) is satisfied that the notice ought to have been issued at an earlier time,

it must specify that time in the notice and the notice is to have effect as if it had been issued at that time.

125 Binding notices confirming status of scheme

(1) Subject to subsection (2), for the purposes of this Part, a notice issued under section 122 is not binding until –

    (a) the Board issues a determination notice under section 123 approving the notice,

    (b) the period within which the issue of the determination notice under that section may be reviewed by virtue of Chapter 6 has expired, and

    (c) if the issue of the determination notice is so reviewed –

        (i) the review and any reconsideration,

        (ii) any reference to the PPF Ombudsman in respect of the issue of the notice, and

        (iii) any appeal against his determination or directions,

    has been finally disposed of and the determination notice has not been revoked, varied or substituted.

(2) Where a notice is issued under section 122 by the Board by virtue of section 124, the notice is not binding until –

    (a) the period within which the issue of the notice may be reviewed by virtue of Chapter 6 has expired, and

    (b) if the issue of the notice is so reviewed –

(i)   the review and any reconsideration,

(ii) any reference to the PPF Ombudsman in respect of the issue of the notice, and

(iii) any appeal against his determination or directions,

has been finally disposed of and the notice has not been revoked, varied or substituted.

(3) Where a notice issued under section 122 becomes binding, the Board must as soon as reasonably practicable give a notice to that effect together with a copy of the binding notice to –

(a) the Regulator,

(b) the trustees or managers of the scheme,

(c) the insolvency practitioner or former insolvency practitioner who issued the notice under section 122 or, where that notice was issued by the Board by virtue of section 124, the insolvency practitioner or former insolvency practitioner mentioned in subsection (1) of that section,

(d) any insolvency practitioner in relation to the employer (who does not fall within paragraph (c)), and

(e) if there is no insolvency practitioner in relation to the employer, the employer.

(4) A notice under subsection (3) –

(a) must be in the prescribed form and contain such information as may be prescribed, and

(b) where it is given in relation to a withdrawal notice issued under section 122(2)(b) which has become binding, must state the time from which the Board ceases to be involved with the scheme (see section 149).

CHAPTER 3   PENSION PROTECTION

Eligible schemes

126 Eligible schemes

(1) Subject to the following provisions of this section, in this Part references to an 'eligible scheme' are to an occupational pension scheme which –

(a) is not a money purchase scheme, and

(b) is not a prescribed scheme or a scheme of a prescribed description.

(2) A scheme is not an eligible scheme if it is being wound up immediately before the day appointed by the Secretary of State by order for the purposes of this subsection.

(3) Regulations may provide that where –

(a) an assessment period begins in relation to an eligible scheme (see section 132), and

(b) after the beginning of that period, the scheme ceases to be an eligible scheme,

the scheme is, in such circumstances as may be prescribed, to be treated as remaining an eligible scheme for the purposes of such of the provisions mentioned in subsection (4) as may be prescribed.

(4) Those provisions are –

(a) any provision of this Part, and

(b) any other provision of this Act in which 'eligible scheme' has the meaning given by this section.

(5) Regulations may also provide that a scheme which would be an eligible scheme in the absence of this subsection is not an eligible scheme in such circumstances as may be prescribed.

Circumstances in which Board assumes responsibility for eligible schemes

127 Duty to assume responsibility for schemes following insolvency event

(1) This section applies where a qualifying insolvency event has occurred in relation to the employer in relation to an eligible scheme.

(2) The Board must assume responsibility for the scheme in accordance with this Chapter if –

    (a) the value of the assets of the scheme at the relevant time was less than the amount of the protected liabilities at that time (see sections 131 and 143),

    (b) after the relevant time a scheme failure notice is issued under section 122(2)(a) in relation to the scheme and that notice becomes binding, and

    (c) a withdrawal event has not occurred in relation to the scheme in respect of a withdrawal notice which has been issued during the period –

        (i) beginning with the occurrence of the qualifying insolvency event, and

        (ii) ending immediately before the issuing of the scheme failure notice under section 122(2)(a),

    and the occurrence of such a withdrawal event in respect of a withdrawal notice issued during that period is not a possibility (see section 149).

(3) For the purposes of this section, in relation to an eligible scheme an insolvency event ('the current event') in relation to the employer is a qualifying insolvency event if –

    (a) it occurs on or after the day appointed under section 126(2), and

    (b) it –

        (i) is the first insolvency event to occur in relation to the employer on or after that day, or

        (ii) does not occur within an assessment period (see section 132) in relation to the scheme which began before the occurrence of the current event.

(4) For the purposes of this section –

    (a) the reference in subsection (2)(a) to the assets of the scheme is a reference to those assets excluding any assets representing the value of any rights in respect of money purchase benefits under the scheme rules, and

    (b) 'the relevant time' means the time immediately before the qualifying insolvency event occurs.

(5) This section is subject to sections 146 and 147 (cases where Board must refuse to assume responsibility for a scheme).

128 Duty to assume responsibility for schemes following application or notification

(1) This section applies where, in relation to an eligible scheme, the trustees or managers of the scheme –

    (a) make an application under subsection (1) of section 129 (a 'section 129 application'), or

    (b) receive a notice from the Board under subsection (5)(a) of that section (a 'section 129 notification').

(2) The Board must assume responsibility for the scheme in accordance with this Chapter if –

    (a) the value of the assets of the scheme at the relevant time was less than the amount of the protected liabilities at that time (see sections 131 and 143),

    (b) after the relevant time the Board issues a scheme failure notice under section 130(2) in relation to the scheme and that notice becomes binding, and

    (c) a withdrawal event has not occurred in relation to the scheme in respect of a withdrawal notice which has been issued during the period –

(i)   beginning with the making of the section 129 application or, as the case may be, the receipt of the section 129 notification, and

(ii)   ending immediately before the issuing of the scheme failure notice under section 130(2),

and the occurrence of such a withdrawal event in respect of a withdrawal notice issued during that period is not a possibility (see section 149).

(3)   In subsection (2) –

(a)   the reference in paragraph (a) to the assets of the scheme is a reference to those assets excluding any assets representing the value of any rights in respect of money purchase benefits under the scheme rules, and

(b)   'the relevant time' means the time immediately before the section 129 application was made or, as the case may be, the section 129 notification was received.

(4)   An application under section 129(1) or notification under section 129(5)(a) is to be disregarded for the purposes of subsection (1) if it is made or given during an assessment period (see section 132) in relation to the scheme which began before the application was made or notification was given.

(5)   This section is subject to sections 146 and 147 (cases where Board must refuse to assume responsibility for a scheme).

129   Applications and notifications for the purposes of section 128

(1)   Where the trustees or managers of an eligible scheme become aware that –

(a)   the employer in relation to the scheme is unlikely to continue as a going concern, and

(b)   the prescribed requirements are met in relation to the employer,

they must make an application to the Board for it to assume responsibility for the scheme under section 128.

(2)   Where the Board receives an application under subsection (1), it must give a copy of the application to –

(a)   the Regulator, and

(b)   the employer.

(3)   An application under subsection (1) must –

(a)   be in the prescribed form and contain the prescribed information, and

(b)   be made within the prescribed period.

(4)   Where the Regulator becomes aware that –

(a)   the employer in relation to an eligible scheme is unlikely to continue as a going concern, and

(b)   the requirements mentioned in subsection (1)(b) are met in relation to the employer,

it must give the Board a notice to that effect.

(5)   Where the Board receives a notice under subsection (4), it must –

(a)   give the trustees or managers of the scheme a notice to that effect, and

(b)   give the employer a copy of that notice.

(6)   The duty imposed by subsection (1) does not apply where the trustees or managers of an eligible scheme become aware as mentioned in that subsection by reason of a notice given to them under subsection (5).

(7)   The duty imposed by subsection (4) does not apply where the Regulator becomes aware as mentioned in that subsection by reason of a copy of an application made by the trustees or managers of the eligible scheme in question given to the Regulator under subsection (2).

(8) Regulations may require notices under this section to be in the prescribed form and contain the prescribed information.

130 Board's duty where application or notification received under section 129

(1) This section applies where the Board –

    (a) receives an application under subsection (1) of section 129 and is satisfied that paragraphs (a) and (b) of that subsection are satisfied in relation to the application, or

    (b) is notified by the Regulator under section 129(4).

(2) If the Board is able to confirm that a scheme rescue is not possible, it must as soon as reasonably practicable issue a notice to that effect (a 'scheme failure notice').

(3) If the Board is able to confirm that a scheme rescue has occurred, it must as soon as reasonably practicable issue a notice to that effect (a 'withdrawal notice').

(4) The Board must, as soon as reasonably practicable, give a copy of any notice issued under subsection (2) or (3) to –

    (a) the Regulator,

    (b) the trustees or managers of the scheme, and

    (c) the employer.

(5) For the purposes of this section –

    (a) the Board is able to confirm that a scheme rescue has occurred in relation to an occupational pension scheme if, and only if, it is able to confirm such matters as are prescribed for the purposes of this paragraph, and

    (b) the Board is able to confirm that a scheme rescue is not possible in relation to such a scheme if, and only if, it is able to confirm such matters as are prescribed for the purposes of this paragraph.

(6) For the purposes of this Part a notice issued under subsection (2) or (3) is not binding until –

    (a) the period within which the issue of the notice may be reviewed by virtue of Chapter 6 has expired, and

    (b) if the issue of the notice is so reviewed –

        (i) the review and any reconsideration,

        (ii) any reference to the PPF Ombudsman in respect of the issue of the notice, and

        (iii) any appeal against his determination or directions,

    has been finally disposed of and the notice has not been revoked, varied or substituted.

(7) Where a notice issued under subsection (2) or (3) becomes binding, the Board must as soon as reasonably practicable give a notice to that effect together with a copy of the binding notice to –

    (a) the Regulator,

    (b) the trustees or managers of the scheme, and

    (c) the employer.

(8) Notices under this section must be in the prescribed form and contain such information as may be prescribed.

(9) A notice given under subsection (7) in relation to a withdrawal notice under subsection (3) which has become binding must state the time from which the Board ceases to be involved with the scheme (see section 149).

131 Protected liabilities

(1) For the purposes of this Chapter the protected liabilities, in relation to an eligible scheme, at a particular time ('the relevant time') are –

(a) the cost of securing benefits for and in respect of members of the scheme which correspond to the compensation which would be payable, in relation to the scheme, in accordance with the pension compensation provisions (see section 162) if the Board assumed responsibility for the scheme in accordance with this Chapter,

(b) liabilities of the scheme which are not liabilities to, or in respect of, its members, and

(c) the estimated cost of winding up the scheme.

(2) For the purposes of determining the cost of securing benefits within subsection (1)(a), references in sections 140 to 142 and Schedule 7 (pension compensation provisions) to the assessment date are to be read as references to the date on which the time immediately after the relevant time falls.

Restrictions on schemes during the assessment period

132 Assessment periods

(1) In this Part references to an assessment period are to be construed in accordance with this section.

(2) Where, in relation to an eligible scheme, a qualifying insolvency event occurs in relation to the employer, an assessment period –

(a) begins with the occurrence of that event, and

(b) ends when –

    (i) the Board ceases to be involved with the scheme (see section 149),

    (ii) the trustees or managers of the scheme receive a transfer notice under section 160, or

    (iii) the conditions in section 154(2) (no scheme rescue but sufficient assets to meet protected liabilities etc) are satisfied in relation to the scheme,

whichever first occurs.

(3) In subsection (2) 'qualifying insolvency event' has the meaning given by section 127(3).

(4) Where, in relation to an eligible scheme, an application is made under section 129(1) or a notification is received under section 129(5)(a), an assessment period –

(a) begins when the application is made or the notification is received, and

(b) ends when –

    (i) the Board ceases to be involved with the scheme (see section 149),

    (ii) the trustees or managers of the scheme receive a transfer notice under section 160, or

    (iii) the conditions in section 154(2) (no scheme rescue but sufficient assets to meet protected liabilities etc) are satisfied in relation to the scheme,

whichever first occurs.

(5) For the purposes of subsection (4) an application under section 129(1) or notification under section 129(5)(a) is to be disregarded if it is made or given during an assessment period in relation to the scheme which began before the application was made or notification was given.

(6) This section is subject to section 159 (which provides for further assessment periods to begin in certain circumstances where schemes are required to wind up or continue winding up under section 154).

133 Admission of new members, payment of contributions etc

(1) This section applies where there is an assessment period in relation to an eligible scheme.

(2) No new members of any class may be admitted to the scheme during the assessment period.

(3) Except in prescribed circumstances and subject to prescribed conditions, no further contributions (other than those due to be paid before the beginning of the assessment period) may be paid towards the scheme during the assessment period.

(4) Any obligation to pay contributions towards the scheme during the assessment period (including any obligation under section 49(8) of the Pensions Act 1995 (c. 26) to pay amounts deducted corresponding to such contributions) is to be read subject to subsection (3) and section 150 (obligation to pay contributions when assessment period ends).

(5) No benefits may accrue under the scheme rules to, or in respect of, members of the scheme during the assessment period.

(6) Subsection (5) does not prevent any increase, in a benefit, which would otherwise accrue in accordance with the scheme or any enactment.

This subsection is subject to section 138 (which limits the scheme benefits payable during an assessment period).

(7) Subsection (5) does not prevent the accrual of money purchase benefits to the extent that they are derived from income or capital gains arising from the investment of payments which are made by, or in respect of, a member of the scheme.

(8) Where a person is entitled to a pension credit derived from another person's shareable rights under the scheme, nothing in this section prevents the trustees or managers of the scheme discharging their liability in respect of the credit under Chapter 1 of Part 4 of the Welfare Reform and Pensions Act 1999 (c. 30) (sharing of rights under pension arrangements) by conferring appropriate rights under the scheme on that person.

(9) In subsection (8) –

'appropriate rights' has the same meaning as in paragraph 5 of Schedule 5 to that Act (pension credits: mode of discharge);
'shareable rights' has the same meaning as in Chapter 1 of Part 4 of that Act (sharing of rights under pension arrangements).

(10) Any action taken in contravention of this section is void.

(11) Disregarding subsection (10), section 10 of the Pensions Act 1995 (civil penalties) applies to any trustee or manager of a scheme who fails to take all reasonable steps to secure compliance with this section.

134 Directions

(1) This section applies where there is an assessment period in relation to an eligible scheme.

(2) With a view to ensuring that the scheme's protected liabilities do not exceed its assets or, if they do exceed its assets, that the excess is kept to a minimum, the Board may give a relevant person in relation to the scheme directions regarding the exercise during that period of his powers in respect of –

(a) the investment of the scheme's assets,
(b) the incurring of expenditure,
(c) the instigation or conduct of legal proceedings, and
(d) such other matters as may be prescribed.

(3) In subsection (2) –

(a) 'relevant person' in relation to a scheme means –

(i) the trustees or managers of the scheme,
(ii) the employer in relation to the scheme, or
(iii) such other persons as may be prescribed, and

(b) the reference to the assets of the scheme is a reference to those assets excluding any assets representing the value of any rights in respect of money purchase benefits under the scheme rules.

(4) The Board may revoke or vary any direction under this section.

(5) Where a direction under this section given to the trustees or managers of a scheme is not complied with, section 10 of the Pensions Act 1995 (c. 26) (civil penalties) applies to any such trustee or manager who has failed to take all reasonable steps to secure compliance with the direction.

(6) That section also applies to any other person who, without reasonable excuse, fails to comply with a direction given to him under this section.

135 Restrictions on winding up, discharge of liabilities etc

(1) This section applies where there is an assessment period in relation to an eligible scheme.

(2) Subject to subsection (3), the winding up of the scheme must not begin during the assessment period.

(3) Subsection (2) does not apply to the winding up of the scheme in pursuance of an order by the Regulator under section 11(3A) of the Pensions Act 1995 (Regulator's powers to wind up occupational pension schemes to protect Pension Protection Fund) directing the scheme to be wound up (and section 219 makes provision for the backdating of the winding up).

(4) During the assessment period, except in prescribed circumstances and subject to prescribed conditions –

(a) no transfers of, or transfer payments in respect of, any member's rights under the scheme rules are to be made from the scheme, and

(b) no other steps may be taken to discharge any liability of the scheme to or in respect of a member of the scheme in respect of –

(i) pensions or other benefits, or

(ii) such other liabilities as may be prescribed.

(5) Subsection (4) –

(a) is subject to section 138, and

(b) applies whether or not the scheme was being wound up immediately before the assessment period or began winding up by virtue of subsection (3).

(6) Subsection (7) applies where, on the commencement of the assessment period –

(a) a member's pensionable service terminates, and

(b) he becomes a person to whom Chapter 5 of Part 4 of the Pension Schemes Act 1993 (c. 48) (early leavers: cash transfer sums and contribution refunds) applies.

Section 150(5) (retrospective accrual of benefits in certain circumstances) is to be disregarded for the purposes of determining whether a member falls within paragraph (a) or (b).

(7) Where this subsection applies, during the assessment period –

(a) no right or power conferred by that Chapter may be exercised, and

(b) no duty imposed by that Chapter may be discharged.

(8) Where a person is entitled to a pension credit derived from another person's shareable rights (within the meaning of Chapter 1 of Part 4 under of the Welfare Reform and Pensions Act 1999 (c. 30) (sharing of rights under pension arrangements)) under the scheme, nothing in subsection (4) prevents the trustees or managers of the scheme discharging their liability in respect of the credit in accordance with that Chapter.

(9) Any action taken in contravention of this section is void, except to the extent that the Board validates the action (see section 136).

(10) Disregarding subsection (9), where there is a contravention of this section, section 10 of the Pensions Act 1995 (c. 26) (civil penalties) applies to any trustee or manager who has failed to take all reasonable steps to secure compliance with this section.

(11) The Regulator may not make a freezing order (see section 23) in relation to the scheme during the assessment period.

136 Power to validate contraventions of section 135

(1) The Board may validate an action for the purposes of section 135(9) only if it is satisfied that to do so is consistent with the objective of ensuring that the scheme's protected liabilities do not exceed its assets or, if they do exceed its assets, that the excess is kept to a minimum.

(2) Where the Board determines to validate, or not to validate, any action of the trustees or managers for those purposes, it must issue a notice to that effect and give a copy of that notice to –

   (a) the Regulator,
   (b) the trustees or managers of the scheme,
   (c) any insolvency practitioner in relation to the employer or, if there is no such insolvency practitioner, the employer, and
   (d) any other person who appears to the Board to be directly affected by the determination.

(3) A notice under subsection (2) must contain a statement of the Board's reasons for the determination.

(4) The validation of an action does not take effect –

   (a) until –
      (i) the Board has issued a notice under subsection (2) relating to the determination, and
      (ii) the period within which the issue of that notice may be reviewed by virtue of Chapter 6 has expired, and
   (b) if the issue of the notice is so reviewed, until –
      (i) the review and any reconsideration,
      (ii) any reference to the PPF Ombudsman in respect of the issue of the notice, and
      (iii) any appeal against his determination or directions,

   has been finally disposed of.

(5) In subsection (1) the reference to the assets of the scheme is a reference to those assets excluding any assets representing the value of any rights in respect of money purchase benefits under the scheme rules.

137 Board to act as creditor of the employer

(1) Subsection (2) applies where there is an assessment period in relation to an eligible scheme.

(2) During the assessment period, the rights and powers of the trustees or managers of the scheme in relation to any debt (including any contingent debt) due to them by the employer, whether by virtue of section 75 of the Pensions Act 1995 (c. 26) (deficiencies in the scheme assets) or otherwise, are exercisable by the Board to the exclusion of the trustees or managers.

(3) Where, by virtue of subsection (2), any amount is paid to the Board in respect of such a debt, the Board must pay that amount to the trustees or managers of the scheme.

138 Payment of scheme benefits

(1) Subsections (2) and (3) apply where there is an assessment period in relation to an eligible scheme.

(2) The benefits payable to or in respect of any member under the scheme rules during the assessment period must be reduced to the extent necessary to ensure that they do not exceed the compensation which would be payable to or in respect of the member in accordance with this Chapter if –

    (a) the Board assumed responsibility for the scheme in accordance with this Chapter, and

    (b) the assessment date referred to in Schedule 7 were the date on which the assessment period began.

(3) But where, on the commencement of the assessment period –

    (a) a member's pensionable service terminates, and

    (b) he becomes a person to whom Chapter 5 of Part 4 of the Pension Schemes Act 1993 (c. 48) (early leavers: cash transfer sums and contribution refunds) applies,

no benefits are payable to or in respect of him under the scheme during the assessment period.

(4) Section 150(5) (retrospective accrual of benefits in certain circumstances) is to be disregarded for the purposes of determining whether a member falls within paragraph (a) or (b) of subsection (3).

(5) Nothing in subsection (3) prevents the payment of benefits attributable (directly or indirectly) to a pension credit, during the assessment period, in accordance with subsection (2).

(6) Where at any time during the assessment period the scheme is being wound up, subject to any reduction required under subsection (2) and to subsection (3), the benefits payable to or in respect of any member under the scheme rules during that period are the benefits that would have been so payable in the absence of the winding up of the scheme.

(7) Subsections (2), (3) and (6) are subject to sections 150(1) to (3) and 154(13) (which provide for the adjustment of amounts paid during an assessment period when that period ends other than as a result of the Board assuming responsibility for the scheme).

(8) For the purposes of subsections (2) and (3) the trustees or managers of the scheme may take such steps as they consider appropriate (including steps adjusting future payments under the scheme rules) to recover any overpayment or pay any shortfall.

(9) Section 10 of the Pensions Act 1995 (c. 26) (civil penalties) applies to a trustee or manager of a scheme who fails to take all reasonable steps to secure compliance with subsections (2) and (3).

(10) Regulations may provide that, where there is an assessment period in relation to an eligible scheme –

    (a) in such circumstances as may be prescribed subsection (2) does not operate to require the reduction of benefits payable to or in respect of any member;

    (b) the commencement of a member's pension or payment of a member's lump sum or other benefits is, in such circumstances and on such terms and conditions as may be prescribed, to be postponed for the whole or any part of the assessment period for which he continues in employment after attaining normal pension age.

(11) For the purposes of subsection (10) –

    (a) 'normal pension age', in relation to an eligible scheme and any pension or other benefit under it, means the age specified in the scheme rules as the earliest age at which the pension or other benefit becomes payable without actuarial adjustment (disregarding any scheme rule making special provision as to early payment on the grounds of ill health), and

    (b) where different ages are so specified in relation to different parts of a pension or other benefit –

> (i) subsection (10) has effect as if those parts were separate pensions or, as the case may be, benefits, and
>
> (ii) in relation to a part of a pension or other benefit, the reference in that subsection to normal pension age is to be read as a reference to the age specified in the scheme rules as the earliest age at which that part becomes so payable.

(12) Regulations may provide that, in prescribed circumstances, where –

> (a) a member of the scheme died before the commencement of the assessment period, and
>
> (b) during the assessment period, a person becomes entitled under the scheme rules to a benefit of a prescribed description in respect of the member,

the benefit, or any part of it, is, for the purposes of subsection (2), to be treated as having become payable before the commencement of the assessment period.

(13) Nothing in subsection (2) or (3) applies to money purchase benefits.

139 Loans to pay scheme benefits

(1) Subsection (2) applies where section 138(2) applies in relation to an eligible scheme.

(2) Where the Board is satisfied that the trustees or managers of the scheme are not able to pay benefits under the scheme rules (reduced in accordance with section 138(2)) as they fall due, it may, on an application by the trustees or managers, lend to them such amounts as the Board considers appropriate for the purpose of enabling them to pay those benefits.

(3) Where an amount lent to the trustees or managers of a scheme under subsection (2) is outstanding at –

> (a) the time the Board ceases to be involved with the scheme, or
>
> (b) if earlier –
>
> > (i) the time during the assessment period when an order is made under section 11(3A) of the Pensions Act 1995 (c. 26) directing the winding up of the scheme, or
> >
> > (ii) where no such order is made during that period, the time when the assessment period ends because the conditions in section 154(2) or (5) are satisfied,

that amount, together with the appropriate interest on it, falls to be repaid by the trustees or managers of the scheme to the Board at that time.

(4) No loan may be made under subsection (2) after the time mentioned in subsection (3)(b)(i).

(5) In subsection (2) the reference to 'benefits' does not include money purchase benefits.

(6) In subsection (3) 'the appropriate interest' on an amount lent under subsection (2) means interest at the prescribed rate from the time the amount was so lent until repayment.

(7) Subject to this section, the Board may make a loan under subsection (2) on such terms as it thinks fit.

Ill health pensions

140 Reviewable ill health pensions

(1) This section applies where there is an assessment period in relation to an eligible scheme.

(2) The Board may review a reviewable ill health pension in respect of a member if –

     (a) disregarding section 141, the member would be entitled to compensation under paragraph 3 of Schedule 7 in respect of the pension if the Board assumed responsibility for the scheme,

     (b) the member did not attain normal pension age in respect of the pension before the assessment date, and

     (c) the pension is attributable to the member's pensionable service.

(3) An ill health pension in respect of a member is reviewable for the purposes of subsection (2) if the member is entitled to the pension by reason of an award under the scheme rules ('the award') which was made –

     (a) in the period of three years ending immediately before the assessment date, or

     (b) before the end of the prescribed period beginning with the assessment date, in response to an application made before that date.

(4) Where –

     (a) before the assessment date, an application was made under the scheme for the award of a pension before normal pension age by virtue of any provision of the scheme rules making special provision as to early payment of pension on grounds of ill health, and

     (b) the trustees or managers of the scheme failed to decide the application before the end of the period mentioned in subsection (3)(b),

section 10 of the Pensions Act 1995 (c. 26) (civil penalties) applies to any trustee or manager who has failed to take all reasonable steps to secure that the application was decided before the end of that period.

(5) Where –

     (a) the award was made in response to an application which –

          (i) was made on or after the assessment date, or

          (ii) was made before that date but not decided by the trustees or managers of the scheme before the end of the period mentioned in subsection (3)(b), and

     (b) in the absence of this subsection, the award would take effect before the assessment date,

the award is, for the purposes of determining the compensation payable under this Chapter in a case where the Board assumes responsibility for the scheme, to be treated as taking effect after the date on which the decision to make the award was made.

(6) Regulations must prescribe the procedure to be followed in relation to the review of a pension under this section and any subsequent decision under section 141.

141 Effect of a review

(1) This section applies where, during an assessment period in relation to an eligible scheme, the Board reviews an ill health pension by virtue of section 140.

(2) Where the conditions of subsection (3) are satisfied, the Board may determine that the compensation payable in respect of the pension, in a case where the Board assumes responsibility for the scheme, is to be determined in the prescribed manner on and after the relevant date.

(3) The conditions are –

     (a) that the annual rate of compensation which would be payable under this Part in respect of the pension at the assessment date, if the Board assumed responsibility for the scheme, exceeds the notional reviewed rate of compensation in respect of the pension,

     (b) that the Board is satisfied –

(i) that the decision to make the award was made in ignorance of, or was based upon a mistake as to, a material fact relevant to the decision,

(ii) that, at the time that decision was made, the member knew or could reasonably have been expected to know of that fact and that it was relevant to the decision, and

(iii) that, had the trustees or managers known about, or not been mistaken as to, that fact, they could not reasonably have decided to make the award, and

(c) that the Board is not satisfied that the criteria in the admissible rules governing entitlement to early payment of pension on grounds of ill health were satisfied in respect of the member at any time after that decision but before the assessment date.

(4) For the purposes of subsection (2) 'the relevant date' means the date during the assessment period on which a scheme valuation in relation to the scheme becomes binding.

(5) The power to make a decision in respect of the pension under subsection (2) may only be exercised at a time which falls –

(a) during the assessment period but before the time the Board first approves a scheme valuation under section 144 in relation to the scheme, and

(b) within a reasonable period beginning with the assessment date or, where the decision to make the award was made at a later date, that date.

(6) Regulations made for the purposes of subsection (2) may, in particular, include provision applying any provision of Schedule 7 with such modifications as may be prescribed.

142 Sections 140 and 141: interpretation

(1) For the purposes of sections 140 and 141 –

'admissible rules' is to be construed in accordance with Schedule 7;

'assessment date' means the date on which the assessment period begins;

'ill health pension', in relation to a scheme, means a pension which, immediately before the assessment date, is a pension to which a person is entitled under the admissible rules in circumstances where that entitlement arose before normal pension age by virtue of any provision of the admissible rules making special provision as to early payment of pension on grounds of ill health;

'normal pension age', in relation to a scheme and any pension under it, means the age specified in the admissible rules as the earliest age at which the pension becomes payable without actuarial adjustment (disregarding any admissible rule making special provision as to early payment on the grounds of ill health) and sub-paragraphs (2) and (3) of paragraph 34 of Schedule 7 apply in relation to this section as they apply in relation to that Schedule;

'notional reviewed rate of compensation', in respect of an ill health pension, means –

(a) the annual rate of compensation which would be payable in respect of the pension at the assessment date, if the Board assumed responsibility for the scheme and the compensation so payable at that date was determined in accordance with regulations under section 141(2), or

(b) if no such compensation would have been so payable at that date, nil;

'pensionable service' is to be construed in accordance with Schedule 7;

'scheme valuation', in relation to a scheme, means a valuation under section 143 of the assets and protected liabilities of the scheme as at the time immediately before the assessment period begins.

(2) For the purposes of section 140(4) –

(a) the definition of 'normal pension age' in subsection (1), and

(b) sub-paragraphs (2) and (3) of paragraph 34 of Schedule 7 as they apply by virtue of that definition,

have effect as if the references in those provisions to the admissible rules were references to the scheme rules.

(3) Paragraph 37(4) of Schedule 7 (references to 'ill health' to be construed in accordance with regulations) applies in relation to sections 140 and 141 and this section as if, in that provision, the reference to that Schedule included a reference to those sections and this section.

(4) In those sections references to the Board assuming responsibility for the scheme are to the Board assuming responsibility for the scheme in accordance with this Chapter at the time the assessment period in question comes to an end.

Valuation of assets and liabilities

143 Board's obligation to obtain valuation of assets and protected liabilities

(1) This section applies in a case within subsection (1) of section 127 or 128.

(2) For the purposes of determining whether the condition in subsection (2)(a) of the section in question is satisfied, the Board must, as soon as reasonably practicable, obtain an actuarial valuation of the scheme as at the relevant time.

(3) For those purposes, regulations may provide that any of the following are to be regarded as assets or protected liabilities of the scheme at the relevant time if prescribed requirements are met –

(a) a debt due to the trustees or managers of the scheme by virtue of a contribution notice issued under section 38, 47 or 55 during the pre-approval period;

(b) an obligation arising under financial support for the scheme (within the meaning of section 45) put in place during the pre-approval period in accordance with a financial support direction issued under section 43;

(c) an obligation imposed by a restoration order made under section 52 during the pre-approval period in respect of a transaction involving assets of the scheme.

(4) For the purposes of this section, regulations may prescribe how –

(a) the assets and the protected liabilities of eligible schemes, and

(b) their amount or value,

are to be determined, calculated and verified.

(5) Regulations under subsection (4) may provide, in particular, that when calculating the amount or value of assets or protected liabilities of an eligible scheme at the relevant time which consist of any of the following –

(a) a debt (including any contingent debt) due to the trustees or managers of the scheme from the employer under section 75 of the Pensions Act 1995 (c. 26) (deficiencies in the scheme assets),

(b) a debt due to the trustees or managers of the scheme by virtue of a contribution notice issued under section 38, 47 or 55,

(c) an obligation arising under financial support for the scheme (within the meaning of section 45) put in place in accordance with a financial support direction issued under section 43, or

(d) an obligation imposed by a restoration order made under section 52 in respect of a transaction involving assets of the scheme,

account must be taken in the prescribed manner of prescribed events which occur during the pre-approval period.

(6) Subject to any provision made under subsection (4), the matters mentioned in paragraphs (a) and (b) of that subsection are to be determined, calculated and verified in accordance with guidance issued by the Board.

(7) In calculating the amount of any liabilities for the purposes of this section, a provision of the scheme rules which limits the amount of the scheme's liabilities by reference to the value of its assets is to be disregarded.

(8) The duty imposed by subsection (2) ceases to apply if and when the Board ceases to be involved with the scheme.

(9) Nothing in subsection (2) requires the actuarial valuation to be obtained during any period when the Board considers that an event may occur which, by virtue of regulations under subsection (3) or (4), may affect the value of the assets or the amount of the protected liabilities of the scheme for the purposes of the valuation.

(10) In a case where there are one or more reviewable ill health pensions (within the meaning of section 140), nothing in subsection (2) requires the actuarial valuation to be obtained during the period mentioned in section 141(5)(b) (period during which Board may exercise its power to make a decision following a review) relating to any such pension.

(11) For the purposes of this section –

    (a) 'actuarial valuation', in relation to the scheme, means a written valuation of the assets and protected liabilities of the scheme which –

        (i)   is in the prescribed form and contains the prescribed information, and

        (ii) is prepared and signed by –

            (a)   a person with prescribed qualifications or experience, or

            (b)   a person approved by the Secretary of State,

    (b) 'the pre-approval period', in relation to the scheme, means the period which –

        (i)   begins immediately after the relevant time, and

        (ii) ends immediately before the time the Board first approves a valuation of the scheme under section 144 after the relevant time,

    (c) 'the relevant time' –

        (i)   in a case within subsection (1) of section 127, has the meaning given in subsection (4)(b) of that section, and

        (ii) in a case within subsection (1) of section 128, has the meaning given in subsection (3)(b) of that section, and

    (d) references to 'assets' do not include assets representing the value of any rights in respect of money purchase benefits under the scheme rules.

144 Approval of valuation

(1) This section applies where the Board obtains a valuation in respect of a scheme under section 143.

(2) Where the Board is satisfied that the valuation has been prepared in accordance with that section, it must –

    (a) approve the valuation, and

    (b) give a copy of the valuation to –

        (i)   the Regulator,

        (ii) the trustees or managers of the scheme, and

        (iii) any insolvency practitioner in relation to the employer or, if there is no such insolvency practitioner, the employer.

(3) Where the Board is not so satisfied, it must obtain another valuation under that section.

145 Binding valuations

(1) For the purposes of this Chapter a valuation obtained under section 143 is not binding until –

   (a) it is approved under section 144,
   (b) the period within which the approval may be reviewed by virtue of Chapter 6 has expired, and
   (c) if the approval is so reviewed –

    (i)   the review and any reconsideration,
    (ii) any reference to the PPF Ombudsman in respect of the approval, and
    (iii) any appeal against his determination or directions,

   has been finally disposed of.

(2) For the purposes of determining whether or not the condition in section 127(2)(a) or, as the case may be, section 128(2)(a) (condition that scheme assets are less than protected liabilities) is satisfied in relation to a scheme, a binding valuation is conclusive.

   This subsection is subject to section 172(3) and (4) (treatment of fraud compensation payments).

(3) Where a valuation becomes binding under this section the Board must as soon as reasonably practicable give a notice to that effect together with a copy of the binding valuation to –

   (a) the Regulator,
   (b) the trustees or managers of the scheme, and
   (c) any insolvency practitioner in relation to the employer or, if there is no such insolvency practitioner, the employer.

(4) A notice under subsection (3) must be in the prescribed form and contain the prescribed information.

Refusal to assume responsibility

146 Schemes which become eligible schemes

(1) Regulations may provide that where the Board is satisfied that an eligible scheme was not such a scheme throughout such period as may be prescribed, the Board must refuse to assume responsibility for the scheme under this Chapter.

(2) Where, by virtue of subsection (1), the Board is required to refuse to assume responsibility for a scheme, it –

   (a) must issue a notice to that effect (a 'withdrawal notice'), and
   (b) give a copy of that notice to –

    (i)   the Regulator,
    (ii) the trustees or managers of the scheme, and
    (iii) any insolvency practitioner in relation to the employer or, if there is no such insolvency practitioner, the employer.

(3) For the purposes of this Part a withdrawal notice issued by virtue of this section is not binding until –

   (a) the period within which the issue of the notice may be reviewed by virtue of Chapter 6 has expired, and
   (b) if the issue of the notice is so reviewed –

    (i)   the review and any reconsideration,
    (ii) any reference to the PPF Ombudsman in respect of the issue of the notice, and
    (iii) any appeal against his determination or directions,

has been finally disposed of and the notice has not been revoked, varied or substituted.

(4) Where a withdrawal notice issued by virtue of this section becomes binding, the Board must as soon as reasonably practicable give a notice to that effect together with a copy of the binding notice to –

(a) the Regulator,

(b) the trustees or managers of the scheme, and

(c) any insolvency practitioner in relation to the employer or, if there is no such insolvency practitioner, the employer.

(5) Notices under this section must be in the prescribed form and contain such information as may be prescribed.

(6) A notice given under subsection (4) must state the time from which the Board ceases to be involved with the scheme (see section 149).

147 New schemes created to replace existing schemes

(1) The Board must refuse to assume responsibility for a scheme ('the new scheme') under this Chapter where it is satisfied that –

(a) the new scheme was established during such period as may be prescribed,

(b) the employer in relation to the new scheme was, at the date of establishment of that scheme, also the employer in relation to a scheme established before the new scheme (the 'old scheme'),

(c) a transfer or transfers of, or a transfer payment or transfer payments in respect of, any rights of members under the old scheme has or have been made to the new scheme, and

(d) the main purpose or one of the main purposes of establishing the new scheme and making the transfer or transfers, or transfer payment or transfer payments, was to enable those members to receive compensation under the pension compensation provisions in respect of their rights under the new scheme in circumstances where, in the absence of the transfer or transfers, regulations under section 146 would have operated to prevent such payments in respect of their rights under the old scheme.

(2) Where, under subsection (1), the Board is required to refuse to assume responsibility for a scheme, it –

(a) must issue a notice to that effect (a 'withdrawal notice'), and

(b) give a copy of that notice to –

(i) the Regulator,

(ii) the trustees or managers of the scheme, and

(iii) any insolvency practitioner in relation to the employer or, if there is no such insolvency practitioner, the employer.

(3) For the purposes of this Part a withdrawal notice issued under this section is not binding until –

(a) the period within which the issue of the notice may be reviewed by virtue of Chapter 6 has expired, and

(b) if the issue of the notice is so reviewed –

(i) the review and any reconsideration,

(ii) any reference to the PPF Ombudsman in respect of the issue of the notice, and

(iii) any appeal against his determination or directions,

has been finally disposed of and the notice has not been revoked, varied or substituted.

(4) Where a withdrawal notice issued under this section becomes binding, the Board must as soon as reasonably practicable give a notice to that effect together with a copy of the binding notice to –

(a) the Regulator,

(b) the trustees or managers of the scheme, and

(c) any insolvency practitioner in relation to the employer or, if there is no such insolvency practitioner, the employer.

(5) Notices under this section must be in the prescribed form and contain such information as may be prescribed.

(6) A notice given under subsection (4) must state the time from which the Board ceases to be involved with the scheme (see section 149).

148 Withdrawal following issue of section 122(4) notice

(1) This section applies where –

(a) a notice under section 122(4) (inability to confirm status of scheme) is issued in relation to an eligible scheme and becomes binding, and

(b) a withdrawal event has not occurred in relation to the scheme in respect of a withdrawal notice which has been issued during the period –

(i) beginning with the occurrence of the last insolvency event in relation to the employer, and

(ii) ending immediately before the notice under section 122(4) becomes binding,

and the occurrence of such a withdrawal event in respect of a withdrawal notice issued during that period is not a possibility (see section 149).

(2) The Board must determine whether any insolvency event –

(a) has occurred in relation to the employer since the issue of the notice under section 122(4), or

(b) is likely to so occur before the end of the period of six months beginning with the date on which this section applies.

(3) If the Board determines under subsection (2) that no insolvency event has occurred or is likely to occur as mentioned in that subsection, it must issue a notice to that effect (a 'withdrawal notice').

(4) Where –

(a) no withdrawal notice is issued under subsection (3) before the end of the period mentioned in subsection (2)(b), and

(b) no further insolvency event occurs in relation to the employer during that period,

the Board must issue a notice to that effect (a 'withdrawal notice').

(5) Where the Board is required to issue a withdrawal notice under this section, it must give a copy of the notice to –

(a) the Regulator,

(b) the trustees or managers of the scheme, and

(c) the employer.

(6) For the purposes of this Part, a withdrawal notice issued under this section is not binding until –

(a) the period within which the issue of the notice may be reviewed by virtue of Chapter 6 has expired, and

(b) if the issue of the notice is so reviewed –

>   (i)   the review and any reconsideration,
>   (ii) any reference to the PPF Ombudsman in respect of the issue of the notice,
>   and
>   (iii) any appeal against his determination or directions,
>
>   has been finally disposed of and the notice has not been revoked, varied or
>   substituted.

(7) Where a withdrawal notice issued under this section becomes binding, the Board
    must as soon as reasonably practicable give a notice to that effect together with a copy
    of the binding notice to –

    (a) the Regulator,
    (b) the trustees or managers of the scheme, and
    (c) the employer.

(8) Notices under this section must be in the prescribed form and contain such
    information as may be prescribed.

(9) A notice given under subsection (7) must state the time from which the Board ceases
    to be involved with the scheme (see section 149).

Cessation of involvement with a scheme

149 Circumstances in which Board ceases to be involved with an eligible scheme

(1) Where an assessment period begins in relation to an eligible scheme, the Board ceases
    to be involved with the scheme, for the purposes of this Part, on the occurrence of the
    first withdrawal event after the beginning of that period.

(2) For this purpose the following are withdrawal events in relation to a scheme –

    (a) a withdrawal notice issued under section 122(2)(b) (scheme rescue has
         occurred) becoming binding;
    (b) a withdrawal notice issued under section 130(3) (scheme rescue has occurred)
         becoming binding;
    (c) a withdrawal notice issued under or by virtue of section 146 or 147 (refusal to
         assume responsibility) becoming binding;
    (d) a withdrawal notice issued under section 148 (no insolvency event has occurred
         or is likely to occur) becoming binding;

    and references in this Chapter to a 'withdrawal event' are to be construed accordingly.

(3) Subsection (4) applies where a withdrawal notice mentioned in subsection (2) is
    issued in relation to a scheme and becomes binding and –

    (a) an insolvency event in relation to the employer occurs during the interim period
         and, if subsection (4) did not apply, the event would not be a qualifying insol-
         vency event within the meaning given by subsection (3) of section 127 solely
         because the condition in sub-paragraph (ii) of paragraph (b) of that subsection
         would not be satisfied, or
    (b) an application under section 129(1) is made, or a notification under section
         129(5)(a) is given, in relation to the scheme during the interim period and, if
         subsection (4) did not apply, the application or notification would be disregarded
         for the purposes of –

        (i)   subsection (1) of section 128 by virtue of subsection (4) of that section,
              and
        (ii) subsection (4) of section 132 by virtue of subsection (5) of that section.

(4) In such a case, the withdrawal notice is to be treated for the purposes of subsections
    (1) and (2), as if the time when it became binding was the time immediately before –

(a) in a case falling within subsection (3)(a), the occurrence of the insolvency event, and

(b) in a case falling within subsection (3)(b), the making of the application under section 129(1) or, as the case may be, the giving of the notification under section 129(5)(a).

(5) For the purposes of subsection (3), the 'interim period' in relation to a scheme means the period beginning with the issuing of the withdrawal notice in relation to the scheme and ending with that notice becoming binding.

(6) For the purposes of this Chapter –

(a) the occurrence of a withdrawal event in relation to a scheme in respect of a withdrawal notice issued during a particular period ('the specified period') is a possibility until each of the following are no longer reviewable –

　(i) any withdrawal notice which has been issued in relation to the scheme during the specified period,

　(ii) any failure to issue such a withdrawal notice during the specified period,

　(iii) any notice which has been issued by the Board under Chapter 2 or this Chapter which is relevant to the issue of a withdrawal notice in relation to the scheme during the specified period or to such a withdrawal notice which has been issued during that period becoming binding,

　(iv) any failure to issue such a notice as is mentioned in sub-paragraph (iii), and

(b) the issue of, or failure to issue, a notice is to be regarded as reviewable –

　(i) during the period within which it may be reviewed by virtue of Chapter 6, and

　(ii) if the matter is so reviewed, until –

　　(a) the review and any reconsideration,

　　(b) any reference to the PPF Ombudsman in respect of the matter, and

　　(c) any appeal against his determination or directions,

　　has been finally disposed of.

150 Consequences of the Board ceasing to be involved with a scheme

(1) Where –

(a) an assessment period comes to an end by virtue of the Board ceasing to be involved with an eligible scheme, and

(b) during the assessment period any amount of any benefit payable to a member, or to a person in respect of a member, under the scheme rules was not paid by reason of section 138 (requirement to pay benefits in accordance with the pension compensation provisions),

that amount falls due to the member, or as the case may be, person at the end of that period.

(2) Where the winding up of the scheme began before the end of the assessment period (whether by virtue of section 219 (backdating the winding up of eligible schemes) or otherwise), the reference in subsection (1)(b) to the amount of any benefit payable to a member, or to a person in respect of a member, under the scheme rules is a reference to the amount so payable taking account of any reduction required by virtue of sections 73 to 73B of the Pensions Act 1995 (c. 26) (provisions relating to the winding up of certain schemes).

(3) Where –

(a) an assessment period comes to an end by virtue of the Board ceasing to be involved with an eligible scheme, and

(b) during the assessment period the amount of benefit paid to a member, or to a person in respect of a member, under the scheme rules exceeded the amount that would have been payable in the absence of section 138(6) (requirement to disregard winding up when paying benefits during assessment period),

the trustees or managers of the scheme must, at the end of that period, take such steps as they consider appropriate (including steps to adjust future payments under the scheme rules) to recover an amount equal to the excess from the person to whom it was paid.

(4) Subsections (1) to (3) are without prejudice to section 73A(2)(b) of the Pensions Act 1995 (c. 26) (requirement to adjust benefits paid to reflect liabilities which can be met on winding up).

(5) Regulations may provide that, in cases within paragraph (a) of subsection (1), benefits are to accrue under the scheme rules, in such circumstances as may be prescribed, to or in respect of members of the scheme in respect of any specified period of service being service in employment which, but for section 133(5), would have qualified the member in question for those benefits under the scheme rules.

(6) Regulations under subsection (5) may in particular make provision –

(a) for benefits not to accrue to, or in respect of, a member unless contributions are paid by or on behalf of the member towards the scheme within a prescribed period;

(b) for contributions towards the scheme which, but for section 133, would have been payable by or on behalf of the employer (otherwise than on behalf of an employee) during the assessment period, to fall due;

(c) requiring that such contributions as are mentioned in paragraph (a) or (b) are accepted for the assessment period or any part of that period;

(d) modifying section 31 of the Welfare Reform and Pensions Act 1999 (c. 30) (reduction of benefit where a person's shareable rights are subject to a pension debit), in its application in relation to cases where benefits accrue under the scheme by virtue of regulations under subsection (5).

(7) In this section 'contributions' means, in relation to an eligible scheme, contributions payable towards the scheme by or on behalf of the employer or the active members of the scheme in accordance with the schedule of contributions maintained under section 227 in respect of the scheme.

Reconsideration

151 Application for reconsideration

(1) Where subsection (2) or (3) applies in relation to an eligible scheme, the trustees or managers of the scheme may make an application to the Board under this section for it to assume responsibility for the scheme in accordance with this Chapter.

(2) This subsection applies where –

(a) a scheme failure notice has been issued under section 122(2)(a) in relation to the scheme, that notice has become binding and the trustees or managers have received a copy of the binding notice under section 125(3),

(b) the valuation obtained by the Board under section 143 in respect of the scheme has become binding, and

(c) the Board would have been required to assume responsibility for the scheme under section 127 but for the fact that the condition in subsection (2)(a) of that section was not satisfied.

(3) This subsection applies where –

(a) the Board has issued a scheme failure notice under subsection (2) of section 130 in relation to the scheme, that notice has become binding and the trustees or managers have received a copy of the binding notice under subsection (7) of that section,

(b) the valuation obtained by the Board under section 143 in respect of the scheme has become binding, and

(c) the Board would have been required to assume responsibility for the scheme under section 128 but for the fact that the condition in subsection (2)(a) of that section was not satisfied.

(4) An application under this section must be in the prescribed form, contain the prescribed information and be accompanied by –

(a) a protected benefits quotation in the prescribed form, and

(b) audited scheme accounts for a period which –

   (i) begins with such date as may be determined in accordance with regulations, and

   (ii) ends with a date which falls within the prescribed period ending with the day on which the application is made.

(5) An application under this section must be made within the authorised period.

(6) In this section 'the authorised period' means the prescribed period which begins –

(a) where subsection (2) applies, with the later of –

   (i) the day on which the trustees or managers received the copy of the binding notice mentioned in paragraph (a) of that subsection, and

   (ii) the day on which they received a copy of the binding valuation mentioned in paragraph (b) of that section, and

(b) where subsection (3) applies, with the later of –

   (i) the day on which the trustees or managers received the copy of the binding notice mentioned in paragraph (a) of that subsection, and

   (ii) the day on which they received a copy of the binding valuation mentioned in paragraph (b) of that subsection.

(7) Where the Board receives an application under subsection (1), it must give a copy of the application to the Regulator.

(8) For the purposes of this section –

'audited scheme accounts', in relation to a scheme, means –

   (a) accounts obtained by the trustees or managers of the scheme ('the scheme accounts') which are prepared in accordance with subsections (9) to (11) and audited by the auditor in relation to the scheme, and

   (b) a report by the auditor, in the prescribed form, as to whether or not such requirements as may be prescribed are satisfied in relation to the scheme accounts;

'auditor', in relation to a scheme, has the meaning given by section 47 of the Pensions Act 1995 (c. 26);

'protected benefits quotation', in relation to a scheme, means a quotation for one or more annuities from one or more insurers, being companies willing to accept payment in respect of the members from the trustees or managers of the scheme, which would provide in respect of each member of the scheme from the reconsideration time –

   (a) benefits for or in respect of the member corresponding to the compensation which would be payable to or in respect of the member in accordance with the pension compensation provisions if the Board assumed responsibility for the scheme by virtue of this section, or

    (b)   benefits in accordance with the member's entitlement or accrued rights (including pension credit rights within the meaning of section 124(1) of the Pensions Act 1995 (c. 26)) under the scheme rules (other than his entitlement or rights in respect of money purchase benefits),

whichever benefits can, in the case of that member, be secured at the lower cost;

'the reconsideration time', in relation to an application under this section, means the time immediately before the end of the period to which the audited scheme accounts mentioned in subsection (4)(b) relate.

(9) The scheme accounts are prepared in accordance with this subsection if, subject to subsections (10) and (11), they –

    (a)   include a statement of the assets of the scheme (excluding any assets representing the value of any rights in respect of money purchase benefits under the scheme rules) as at the reconsideration time, and

    (b)   are prepared in accordance with such other requirements as may be prescribed.

(10) Subject to subsection (11), regulations under subsection (4) of section 143 (other than regulations made by virtue of subsection (5) of that section), and guidance under subsection (6) of that section, apply to the scheme accounts as they apply for the purposes of a valuation under that section.

(11) Regulations may provide that, where an asset of a prescribed description has been acquired during the assessment period, the value assigned to the asset as at the reconsideration time is to be determined, for the purposes of the scheme accounts, in the prescribed manner.

(12) For the purposes of this section –

    (a)   regulations may prescribe how the cost of securing the benefits mentioned in paragraph (a) of the definition of 'protected benefits quotation' in subsection (8) is to be determined, calculated and verified, and

    (b)   subject to any provision made under paragraph (a), that cost is to be determined, calculated and verified in accordance with guidance issued by the Board.

(13) Where the scheme is being wound up, for the purposes of determining the benefits which fall within paragraph (b) of the definition of 'protected benefits quotation' in subsection (8) no account is to be taken of the winding up of the scheme.

152 Duty to assume responsibility following reconsideration

(1) This section applies where an application is made in respect of a scheme in accordance with section 151.

(2) The Board must assume responsibility for the scheme in accordance with this Chapter if it is satisfied that the value of the assets of the scheme at the reconsideration time is less than the aggregate of –

    (a)   the amount quoted in the protected benefits quotation accompanying the application,

    (b)   the amount at that time of the liabilities of the scheme which are not liabilities to, or in respect of, members of the scheme, and

    (c)   the estimated costs of winding up the scheme at that time.

(3) Where the Board makes a determination for the purposes of subsection (2), it must issue a determination notice and give a copy of that notice to –

    (a)   the trustees or managers of the scheme, and

    (b)   the Regulator.

(4) In subsection (3) 'determination notice' means a notice which is in the prescribed form and contains such information about the determination as may be prescribed.

(5) But where the Board is satisfied of the matters mentioned in subsection (2), it is not required to assume responsibility for the scheme under subsection (2) until the determination notice issued under subsection (3) becomes binding.

(6) For the purposes of subsection (5) a determination notice is not binding until –

    (a) the period within which the issue of the notice may be reviewed by virtue of Chapter 6 has expired, and

    (b) if the issue of the notice is so reviewed –

        (i) the review and any reconsideration,

        (ii) any reference to the PPF Ombudsman in respect of the issue of the notice, and

        (iii) any appeal against his determination or directions,

    has been finally disposed of and the notice has not been revoked, varied or substituted.

(7) Where a determination notice issued under subsection (3) becomes binding, the Board must as soon as reasonably practicable give a notice to that effect together with a copy of the binding notice to –

    (a) the trustees or managers of the scheme, and

    (b) the Regulator.

(8) A notice under subsection (7) must be in the prescribed form and contain such information as may be prescribed.

(9) The Board may –

    (a) for the purposes of subsection (2), obtain its own valuation of the assets of the scheme as at the reconsideration time (within the meaning of section 151), and

    (b) for the purposes of subsection (2)(b), obtain its own valuation of the liabilities of the scheme as at that time;

    and where it does so, subsections (9)(b), (10) and (11) of section 151 apply in relation to the valuation as they apply in relation to the scheme accounts (within the meaning of that section).

(10) Regulations under subsection (4) of section 143, and guidance under subsection (6) of that section, apply for the purposes of this section in relation to the estimated costs within subsection (2)(c) as they apply for the purposes of section 143 in relation to protected liabilities within section 131(1)(c).

(11) In this section references to the assets of the scheme do not include assets representing the value of any rights in respect of money purchase benefits under the scheme rules.

(12) This section is subject to sections 146 and 147 (refusal to assume responsibility for a scheme).

Closed schemes

153 Closed schemes

(1) This section applies where section 151(2) or (3) (scheme rescue not possible but scheme has sufficient assets to meet the protected liabilities) applies in relation to an eligible scheme.

(2) If the trustees or managers of the scheme are unable to obtain a full buy-out quotation, they must, within the authorised period, apply to the Board for authority to continue as a closed scheme.

(3) For the purposes of determining whether they must make an application under subsection (2), the trustees or managers of the scheme must take all reasonable steps to obtain a full buy-out quotation in respect of the scheme.

(4) An application under subsection (2) must –

    (a) be in the prescribed form and contain the prescribed information, and

    (b) be accompanied by evidence in the prescribed form which shows that the trustees or managers of the scheme have complied with the obligation under subsection (3) but were unable to obtain a full buy-out quotation.

(5)   Where the Board receives an application under subsection (2), if it is satisfied that the trustees or managers have complied with the obligation under subsection (3) but were unable to obtain a full buy-out quotation, it must authorise the scheme to continue as a closed scheme.

(6)   Where the Board determines an application in respect of a scheme under this section, it must issue a determination notice and give a copy of that notice to –

(a)   the trustees or managers of the scheme, and

(b)   the Regulator.

(7)   In this section –

'authorised period' has the same meaning as in section 151;

'determination notice' means a notice which is in the prescribed form and contains such information about the determination as may be prescribed;

'full buy-out quotation', in relation to a scheme, means a quotation for one or more annuities from one or more insurers (being companies willing to accept payment in respect of the members from the trustees or managers of the scheme) which would provide in respect of each member of the scheme, from a relevant date, benefits in accordance with the member's entitlement or accrued rights, including pension credit rights, under the scheme rules (other than his entitlement or rights in respect of money purchase benefits);

'pension credit rights' has the meaning given by section 124(1) of the Pensions Act 1995 (c. 26);

'relevant date' means a date within the authorised period.

(8)   If the trustees or managers of the scheme fail to comply with subsection (2) or (3), section 10 of the Pensions Act 1995 (civil penalties) applies to any trustee or manager who has failed to take all reasonable steps to secure compliance.

Winding up

154   Requirement to wind up schemes with sufficient assets to meet protected liabilities

(1)   Where, in relation to an eligible scheme, an assessment period within section 132(2) or (4) comes to an end because the conditions in subsection (2) of this section are satisfied, the trustees or managers of the scheme must –

(a)   wind up the scheme, or

(b)   where the winding up of the scheme began before the assessment period (whether by virtue of section 219 or otherwise), continue the winding up of the scheme.

(2)   The conditions are –

(a)   that subsection (2) or (3) of section 151 (scheme rescue not possible but scheme has sufficient assets to meet the protected liabilities) applies in relation to the scheme,

(b)   that –

(i)   the trustees or managers did not make an application under that section or section 153(2) within the authorised period (within the meaning of section 151(6)) (or any such application has been withdrawn), or

(ii)   if such an application was made, it has been finally determined, and

(c)   that, if an application was made under section 151, the Board is not required to assume responsibility for the scheme by virtue of section 152(2).

(3)   For the purposes of subsection (2)(b)(ii) an application is not finally determined until –

    (a) the Board has issued a determination notice in respect of the application under section 152 or, as the case may be, section 153,

    (b) the period within which the issue of the notice may be reviewed by virtue of Chapter 6 has expired, and

    (c) if the issue of the notice is so reviewed –

        (i) the review and any reconsideration,

        (ii) any reference to the PPF Ombudsman in respect of the issue of the notice, and

        (iii) any appeal against his determination or directions,

    has been finally disposed of.

(4) Where, in relation to an eligible scheme, an assessment period within section 159(3) comes to an end because the conditions in subsection (5) of this section are satisfied, the trustees or managers of the scheme must continue the winding up of the scheme begun (whether in accordance with this section or otherwise) before that assessment period.

(5) The conditions are –

    (a) that an application is made by, or notice is given to, the trustees or managers of the scheme under section 157 (applications and notifications where closed schemes have insufficient assets),

    (b) that the valuation obtained by the Board in respect of the scheme under section 158(3) has become binding, and

    (c) that the Board is not required to assume responsibility for the scheme by virtue of section 158(1) (duty to assume responsibility for closed scheme).

(6) Where a scheme is wound up in accordance with subsection (1)(a), the winding up is to be taken as beginning immediately before the assessment period.

(7) Without prejudice to the power to give directions under section 134, but subject to any order made under subsection (8), the Board may give the trustees or managers of the scheme directions relating to the manner of the winding up of the scheme under this section (and may vary or revoke any such direction given by it).

(8) The Regulator may by order direct any person specified in the order –

    (a) to take such steps as are so specified as it considers are necessary as a result of –

        (i) the winding up of the scheme beginning, by virtue of subsection (6), immediately before the assessment period, or

        (ii) the winding up of the scheme being continued under subsection (1)(b), and

    (b) to take those steps within a period specified in the order.

(9) If the trustees or managers of a scheme fail to comply with a direction to them under subsection (7), or contained in an order under subsection (8), section 10 of the Pensions Act 1995 (c. 26) (civil penalties) applies to any trustee or manager who has failed to take all reasonable steps to secure compliance.

(10) That section also applies to any other person who, without reasonable excuse, fails to comply with a direction to him contained in an order under subsection (8).

(11) The winding up of a scheme under this section is as effective in law as if it had been made under powers conferred by or under the scheme.

(12) This section must be complied with in relation to a scheme –

    (a) in spite of any enactment or rule of law, or any rule of the scheme, which would otherwise operate to prevent the winding up, and

    (b) without regard to any such enactment, rule of law or rule of the scheme as would otherwise require or might otherwise be taken to require the implementation of any procedure or the obtaining of any consent with a view to the winding up.

(13) Where an assessment period in relation to an eligible scheme comes to an end by virtue of the conditions in subsection (2) or (5) being satisfied, subsections (1) to (4) of section 150 apply as they apply where an assessment period comes to an end by virtue of the Board ceasing to be involved with the scheme, except that in subsection (2) of that section the reference to section 219 is to be read as a reference to subsection (6) of this section.

(14) Where a public service pension scheme is required to be wound up under this section, the appropriate authority may by order make provision modifying any enactment in which the scheme is contained or under which it is made.

(15) In subsection (14) 'the appropriate authority', in relation to a scheme, means such Minister of the Crown or government department as may be designated by the Treasury as having responsibility for the particular scheme.

Provisions applying to closed schemes

155 Treatment of closed schemes

(1) In this section 'closed scheme' means an eligible scheme which is authorised under section 153 to continue as a closed scheme.

(2) The provisions mentioned in subsection (3) apply in relation to a closed scheme at any time when the trustees or managers of the scheme are required to wind up or continue winding up the scheme under section 154 as if that time fell within an assessment period in relation to the scheme.

(3) The provisions are –

    (a) section 40(5) and (6) (Board to act as creditor for debt due by virtue of a contribution notice under section 38);

    (b) section 49(5) and (6) (Board to act as creditor for debt due by virtue of a contribution notice under section 47);

    (c) section 54(5) and (6) (Board to act as creditor for debt due by virtue of a restoration order under section 52);

    (d) section 56(5) and (6) (Board to act as creditor for debt due by virtue of a contribution notice under section 55);

    (e) section 133 (admission of new members, payment of contributions etc);

    (f) section 134 (directions);

    (g) section 137 (Board to act as creditor of the employer).

(4) Regulations may require the trustees or managers of a closed scheme in relation to which the provisions mentioned in subsection (3) apply to comply with such requirements as may be prescribed when providing for the discharge of any liability to, or in respect of, a member of the scheme for pensions or other benefits.

156 Valuations of closed schemes

(1) Regulations may make provision requiring the trustees or managers of closed schemes to obtain actuarial valuations of the scheme at such intervals as may be prescribed for the purposes of enabling them to determine –

    (a) the benefits payable under the scheme rules;

    (b) whether to make an application under section 157.

(2) Regulations under this section may prescribe how –

    (a) the assets, the full scheme liabilities and the protected liabilities in relation to closed schemes, and

    (b) their amount or value,

are to be determined, calculated and verified.

(3) Subject to any provision made under subsection (2), those matters are to be determined, calculated and verified in accordance with guidance issued by the Board.

(4) In calculating the amount of any liabilities for the purposes of a valuation required by virtue of this section, a provision of the scheme rules which limits the amount of the scheme's liabilities by reference to the value of its assets is to be disregarded.

(5) Nothing in regulations under this section may require the trustees or managers of a closed scheme to obtain an actuarial valuation of the scheme until –

  (a) the period within which the issue of the determination notice, under section 153(6), in respect of the Board's determination to authorise the scheme to continue as a closed scheme, may be reviewed by virtue of Chapter 6 has expired, and

  (b) if the issue of the notice is so reviewed –

    (i)   the review and any reconsideration,

    (ii) any reference to the PPF Ombudsman in respect of the issue of the notice, and

    (iii) any appeal against his determination or directions,

  has been finally disposed of and the notice has not been revoked, varied or substituted.

(6) In this section, in relation to a scheme –

  'actuarial valuation' means a written valuation of –

    (a) the scheme's assets,

    (b) the full scheme liabilities, and

    (c) the protected liabilities in relation to the scheme, prepared and signed by the actuary;

  'the actuary' means –

    (a) the actuary appointed under section 47(1)(b) of the Pensions Act 1995 (c. 26) (professional advisers) in relation to the scheme, or

    (b) if no such actuary has been appointed –

      (i) a person with prescribed qualifications or experience, or

      (ii) a person approved by the Secretary of State;

  'assets' do not include assets representing the value of any rights in respect of money purchase benefits under the scheme rules;

  'closed scheme' has the same meaning as in section 155;

  'full scheme liabilities' means –

    (a) the liabilities under the scheme rules to or in respect of members of the scheme,

    (b) other liabilities of the scheme, and

    (c) the estimated cost of winding up the scheme;

  'liabilities' does not include liabilities in respect of money purchase benefits under the scheme rules.

Reconsideration of closed schemes

157 Applications and notifications where closed schemes have insufficient assets

(1) If at any time the trustees or managers of a closed scheme become aware that the value of the assets of the scheme is less than the amount of the protected liabilities in relation to the scheme, they must, before the end of the prescribed period beginning with that time, make an application to the Board for it to assume responsibility for the scheme.

(2) Where the Board receives an application under subsection (1), it must give a copy of the application to the Regulator.

(3) If at any time the Regulator becomes aware that the value of the assets of the scheme is less than the amount of the protected liabilities in relation to the scheme, it must give the Board a notice to that effect.

(4) Where the Board receives a notice under subsection (3), it must give the trustees or managers of the scheme a notice to that effect.

(5) The duty imposed by subsection (1) does not apply where the trustees or managers of a closed scheme become aware as mentioned in that subsection by reason of a notice given to them under subsection (4).

(6) The duty imposed by subsection (3) does not apply where the Regulator becomes aware as mentioned in that subsection by reason of a copy of an application made by the trustees or managers of the closed scheme being given to it under subsection (2).

(7) Regulations may require notices and applications under this section to be in the prescribed form and contain the prescribed information.

(8) If the trustees or managers of a closed scheme fail to comply with subsection (1), section 10 of the Pensions Act 1995 (c. 26) (civil penalties) applies to any trustee or manager who has failed to take all reasonable steps to secure compliance.

(9) In this section –

'assets', in relation to a scheme, do not include assets representing the value of any rights in respect of money purchase benefits under the scheme rules;
'closed scheme' has the same meaning as in section 155.

158 Duty to assume responsibility for closed schemes

(1) Where the trustees or managers of a closed scheme –

(a) make an application under subsection (1) of section 157, or
(b) receive a notice from the Board under subsection (4) of that section,

the Board must assume responsibility for the scheme in accordance with this Chapter if the value of the assets of the scheme at the relevant time was less than the amount of the protected liabilities at that time.

(2) In subsection (1) the reference to the assets of the scheme is a reference to those assets excluding any assets representing the value of any rights in respect of money purchase benefits under the scheme rules.

(3) For the purposes of determining whether the condition in subsection (1) is satisfied, the Board must, as soon as reasonably practicable, obtain an actuarial valuation (within the meaning of section 143) of the scheme as at the relevant time.

(4) Subject to subsection (6), subsection (3) of section 143 applies for those purposes as it applies for the purposes mentioned in subsection (2) of that section (and the definitions contained in paragraphs (b) and (d) of subsection (11) of that section apply accordingly).

(5) Subject to subsection (6), the following provisions apply in relation to a valuation obtained under subsection (3) as they apply in relation to a valuation obtained under section 143 –

(a) subsections (4) to (7) and (11)(b) and (d) of that section;
(b) section 144 (approval of valuation), other than subsection (2)(b)(iii) (duty to give copy of approved valuation to employer's insolvency practitioner);
(c) section 145 (binding valuations), other than subsection (3)(c) (duty to give copy of binding valuation to employer's insolvency practitioner).

(6) In the application of sections 143 and 145 by virtue of subsection (4) or (5) –

(a) subsections (3), (5) and (11)(b) and (d) of section 143 apply as if the references to 'the relevant time' were references to that term as defined in subsection (8) below, and
(b) subsection (2) of section 145 applies as if the reference to section 128(2)(a) included a reference to subsection (1) of this section.

(7) An application under subsection (1) of section 157, or notification under subsection (4) of that section, is to be disregarded for the purposes of subsection (1) if it is made or given during an assessment period (see sections 132 and 159) in relation to the scheme which began before the application was made or notification was given.

(8) In this section –

'closed scheme' has the same meaning as in section 155;

'the relevant time' means the time immediately before the application mentioned in subsection (1)(a) was made, or (as the case may be) the notice mentioned in subsection (1)(b) was received, by the trustees or managers of the scheme.

159 Closed schemes: further assessment periods

(1) Subsection (3) applies where –

(a) an application is made under subsection (1) of section 157 in relation to a closed scheme, or

(b) the trustees or managers of the scheme receive a notice under subsection (4) of that section.

(2) For the purposes of subsection (1) an application under subsection (1) of section 157, or notification under subsection (4) of that section, is to be disregarded if it is made or given during an assessment period (see section 132 and this section) in relation to the scheme which began before the application was made or notification was given.

(3) An assessment period –

(a) begins when the application is made or the notice is received by the trustees or managers of the scheme, and

(b) ends when –

(i) the trustees or managers receive a transfer notice under section 160, or

(ii) the conditions in section 154(5) (closed scheme with sufficient assets to meet protected liabilities etc) are satisfied in relation to the scheme,

whichever first occurs.

(4) In this section 'closed scheme' has the same meaning as in section 155.

Assumption of responsibility for a scheme

160 Transfer notice

(1) This section applies where the Board is required to assume responsibility for a scheme under section 127, 128, 152 or 158.

(2) The Board must give the trustees or managers a notice (a 'transfer notice').

(3) In a case to which section 127 or 128 applies, a transfer notice may not be given until the valuation obtained under section 143 is binding.

(4) In a case to which section 158 applies, a transfer notice may not be given until the valuation obtained under subsection (3) of that section is binding.

(5) A transfer notice may not be given in relation to a scheme during any period when the issue of, or failure to issue, a withdrawal notice under or by virtue of section 146 or 147 (refusal to assume responsibility) is reviewable (see section 149(6)(b)).

(6) The Board must give a copy of any notice given under subsection (2) to –

(a) the Regulator, and

(b) any insolvency practitioner in relation to the employer or, if there is no such insolvency practitioner, the employer.

(7) This section is subject to section 172(1) and (2) (no transfer notice within first 12 months of assessment period or when fraud compensation application is pending).

161 Effect of Board assuming responsibility for a scheme

(1) Where a transfer notice is given to the trustees or managers of an eligible scheme, the Board assumes responsibility for the scheme in accordance with this Chapter.

(2) The effect of the Board assuming responsibility for a scheme is that –

(a) the property, rights and liabilities of the scheme are transferred to the Board, without further assurance, with effect from the time the trustees or managers receive the transfer notice,

(b) the trustees or managers of the scheme are discharged from their pension obligations from that time, and

(c) from that time the Board is responsible for securing that compensation is (and has been) paid in accordance with the pension compensation provisions,

and, accordingly, the scheme is to be treated as having been wound up immediately after that time.

(3) In subsection (2)(a) the reference to liabilities of the scheme does not include any liability to, or in respect of, any member of the scheme, other than –

(a) liabilities in respect of money purchase benefits, and

(b) such other liabilities as may be prescribed.

(4) In subsection (2)(b) 'pension obligations' in relation to the trustees or managers of the scheme means –

(a) their obligations to provide pensions or other benefits to or in respect of persons (including any obligation to provide guaranteed minimum pensions within the meaning of the Pension Schemes Act 1993 (c. 48)), and

(b) their obligations to administer the scheme in accordance with the scheme rules and this or any other enactment.

(5) Schedule 6 makes provision in respect of the transfer of the property, rights and liabilities of a scheme under subsection (2)(a).

(6) Regulations may make further provision regarding such transfers.

(7) Without prejudice to the generality of subsection (6), regulations may authorise the Board to modify a term of a relevant contract of insurance if –

(a) any rights or liabilities under the contract are transferred to the Board by virtue of subsection (2)(a), and

(b) as a result of the transfer, the Board is required, by reason of that term, to pay a specified amount or specified amounts to a specified person who, immediately before the time mentioned in subsection (2)(a), was a member of the scheme or a person entitled to benefits in respect of such a member.

(8) In subsection (7) –

'relevant contract of insurance' means a contract of insurance which –

(a) is entered with a view to securing the whole or part of the scheme's liability for –

(i) any pension or other benefit payable to or in respect of one particular person whose entitlement to payment of a pension or other benefit has arisen, and

(ii) any benefit which will be payable in respect of that person on his death, and

(b) is a contract –

(i) which may not be surrendered, or

(ii) in respect of which the amount payable on surrender does not exceed the liability secured;

'specified' means specified in, or determined in accordance with, the contract of insurance.

162   The pension compensation provisions

(1)   Schedule 7 makes provision for compensation to be paid in relation to a scheme for which the Board assumes responsibility in accordance with this Chapter, including provision for –

  (a)   periodic compensation to be paid to or in respect of members,
  (b)   lump sum compensation to be paid to members,
  (c)   a cap to be imposed on the periodic compensation and lump sum compensation payable, and
  (d)   annual increases to be made to periodic compensation.

(2)   In this Part references to the pension compensation provisions are to the provisions of, and the provisions made by virtue of, this section, sections 140 to 142, 161(2)(c), 164 and 168 and Schedule 7.

(Those references do not include any provision of, or made by virtue of, section 170 (discharge of liabilities in respect of money purchase benefits).)

163   Adjustments to be made where the Board assumes responsibility for a scheme

(1)   This section applies where the Board assumes responsibility for an eligible scheme in accordance with this Chapter.

(2)   Any benefits (other than money purchase benefits) which –

  (a)   were payable under the scheme rules to any member, or to any person in respect of any member, during the period beginning with the assessment date and ending with the receipt by the trustees or managers of the transfer notice, and
  (b)   have been paid before the trustees or managers receive the transfer notice,

are to be regarded as going towards discharging any liability of the Board to pay compensation to the member or, as the case may be, person in accordance with the pension compensation provisions.

(3)   Regulations may provide that, in prescribed circumstances, where –

  (a)   a member of the scheme died before the commencement of the assessment period, and
  (b)   during the period mentioned in subsection (2)(a), a person became entitled under the scheme rules to a benefit of a prescribed description in respect of the member,

the benefit, or any part of it, is, for the purposes of subsection (2), to be treated as having become payable before the assessment date.

(4)   The Board must –

  (a)   if any amount paid, during the period mentioned in subsection (2)(a), by the trustees or managers of the scheme to a member, or to a person in respect of a member, exceeded the entitlement of that member or person under the pension compensation provisions, take such steps as it considers appropriate (including adjusting future compensation payments made in accordance with those provisions) to recover an amount equal to the aggregate of –

    (i)   the amount of the excess, and
    (ii)   interest on that amount, at the prescribed rate, for the period which begins when the excess was paid by the trustees or managers and ends with the recovery of the excess, and

  (b)   if any amount so paid was less than that entitlement (or no amount was paid in respect of that entitlement), pay an amount to the member or person concerned equal to the aggregate of –

(i)   the amount of the shortfall, and

(ii)   interest on that amount, at the prescribed rate, for the period which begins when the shortfall ought to have been paid by the trustees or managers and ends with the payment of the shortfall by the Board.

(5) In subsection (4) references to an amount paid do not include –

(a)   an amount paid in respect of any money purchase benefit, or

(b)   any other amount of a prescribed description.

(6) Nothing in subsection (4) requires the Board –

(a)   to recover any amount from a person in such circumstances as may be prescribed, or

(b)   to recover from any person any amount which it considers to be trivial.

(7) In this section 'assessment date' is to be construed in accordance with Schedule 7.

164 Postponement of compensation entitlement for the assessment period

(1) Regulations may provide that, where the Board assumes responsibility for an eligible scheme, the entitlement of any member of the scheme to compensation under this Chapter is, in such circumstances as may be prescribed, postponed for the whole or any part of the assessment period for which he continued in employment after attaining normal pension age.

(2) Regulations under subsection (1) may provide that the postponement is on such terms and conditions (including those relating to increments) as may be prescribed.

(3) In subsection (1) the reference to 'normal pension age' is to normal pension age, within the meaning of paragraph 34 of Schedule 7, in relation to the pension or lump sum in respect of which the entitlement to compensation arises.

165 Guaranteed minimum pensions

(1) The Board must notify the Commissioners of Inland Revenue where, by reason of it assuming responsibility for an eligible scheme in accordance with this Chapter, the trustees or managers of the scheme are discharged from their liability to provide a guaranteed minimum pension (within the meaning of the Pension Schemes Act 1993 (c. 48)) to or in respect of a member of the scheme.

(2) Notification under subsection (1) must be given as soon as reasonably practicable.

(3) In section 47 of the Pension Schemes Act 1993 (further provision concerning entitlement to a guaranteed minimum pension for the purposes of section 46), after subsection (7) insert –

'(8) For the purposes of section 46, a person shall be treated as entitled to a guaranteed minimum pension to which he would have been entitled but for the fact that the trustees or managers were discharged from their liability to provide that pension on the Board of the Pension Protection Fund assuming responsibility for the scheme.'

166 Duty to pay scheme benefits unpaid at assessment date etc

(1) This section applies where the Board assumes responsibility for a scheme in accordance with this Chapter.

(2) Subject to subsection (4), the Board must pay any amount by way of pensions or other benefits which a person had become entitled to payment of under the scheme rules before the assessment date but which remained unpaid at the time the transfer notice was received by the trustees or managers of the scheme.

(3) If, immediately before the assessment date, the person is entitled to the amount but has postponed payment of it, subsection (2) does not apply.

(4) Subsection (2) does not apply in relation to the amount of –

(a) any transfer payment, or

(b) any payment in respect of a refund of contributions.

(5) Regulations may provide that, in prescribed circumstances, where –

(a) a member of the scheme died before the commencement of the assessment period, and

(b) during the period beginning with the assessment date and ending with the receipt by the trustees or managers of the transfer notice, a person became entitled under the scheme rules to a benefit of a prescribed description in respect of the member,

that person's entitlement to the benefit, or to any part of it, is, for the purposes of subsection (2), to be treated as having arisen before the assessment date.

(6) Regulations may make provision requiring the Board, in such circumstances as may be prescribed, to take such steps (including making payments) as may be prescribed in respect of rights of prescribed descriptions to which members of the scheme were entitled immediately before the commencement of the assessment period.

(7) For the purposes of regulations made under subsection (6) –

(a) this Chapter (other than this subsection), and

(b) the scheme rules (including any relevant legislative provision within the meaning of section 318(3)),

are to have effect subject to such modifications as may be prescribed.

(8) In this section 'assessment date' is to be construed in accordance with Schedule 7.

167 Modification of Chapter where liabilities discharged during assessment period

(1) Regulations may modify any of the provisions of this Chapter as it applies to cases –

(a) where any liability to provide pensions or other benefits to or in respect of any member or members under a scheme is discharged during an assessment period in relation to the scheme by virtue of –

(i) regulations under section 135(4), or

(ii) the Board validating any action mentioned in section 135(9), or

(b) where, in prescribed circumstances, any such liability of a prescribed description is discharged on the assessment date but before the commencement of the assessment period.

(2) In this section 'assessment date' is to be construed in accordance with Schedule 7.

168 Administration of compensation

(1) Regulations may make further provision regarding the operation and administration of this Chapter.

(2) Regulations under subsection (1) may, in particular, make provision –

(a) prescribing the manner in which and time when compensation is to be paid including provision requiring periodic compensation to be paid by instalments);

(b) for calculating the amounts of compensation according to a prescribed scale or otherwise adjusting them to avoid fractional amounts or facilitate computation;

(c) prescribing the circumstances and manner in which compensation to which a person ('the beneficiary') is entitled may be made to another person on behalf of the beneficiary for any purpose (including the discharge in whole or in part of an obligation of the beneficiary or any other person);

(d) for the payment or distribution of compensation to or among persons claiming to be entitled on the death of any person and for dispensing with strict proof of their title;

(e) for the recovery of amounts of compensation paid by the Board in excess of entitlement (together with interest on such amounts for the period from payment until recovery);

(f) specifying the circumstances in which payment of compensation can be suspended.

(3) In this section 'compensation' means compensation payable under Schedule 7 or under section 141(2).

Discharge of Board's liabilities

169 Discharge of liabilities in respect of compensation

(1) This section applies where the Board assumes responsibility for an eligible scheme in accordance with this Chapter.

(2) The Board may provide for the discharge of any liability imposed by this Chapter to provide compensation –

(a) by the taking out of a policy of insurance or a number of such policies;

(b) by the entry into an annuity contract or a number of such contracts;

(c) by the transfer of the benefit of such a policy or policies or such a contract or contracts;

(d) in prescribed circumstances, by the payment of a cash sum calculated in the prescribed manner.

170 Discharge of liabilities in respect of money purchase benefits

(1) This subsection applies where –

(a) the Board assumes responsibility for an eligible scheme in accordance with this Chapter, and

(b) one or more members are entitled, or have accrued rights, under the scheme rules to money purchase benefits.

(2) Regulations must make provision in respect of cases to which subsection (1) applies requiring the Board to secure that liabilities in respect of such benefits transferred to the Board under section 161 are discharged by it in the prescribed manner.

(3) The provision made under subsection (2) must include provision prescribing the manner in which protected rights are to be given effect to.

(4) In this section –

'accrued rights', under the scheme rules of a scheme, include pension credit rights within the meaning of section 124(1) of the Pensions Act 1995 (c. 26);

'protected rights' has the meaning given by section 10 of the Pension Schemes Act 1993 (c. 48) (protected rights and money purchase benefits).

Equal treatment

171 Equal treatment

(1) This section applies where –

(a) a woman has been employed on like work with a man in the same employment,

(b) a woman has been employed on work rated as equivalent with that of a man in the same employment, or

(c) a woman has been employed on work which, not being work in relation to which paragraph (a) or (b) applies, was, in terms of the demands made on her (for instance under such headings as effort, skill and decision), of equal value to that of a man in the same employment, and service in that employment was pensionable service under an occupational pension scheme.

(2)   If, apart from this subsection, any of the payment functions so far as it relates (directly or indirectly) to that pensionable service –

(a)   is or becomes less favourable to the woman than it is to the man, or

(b)   is or becomes less favourable to the man than it is to the woman,

that function has effect with such modifications as are necessary to ensure that the provision is not less favourable.

(3)   Subsection (2) does not operate in relation to any difference as between a woman and a man in the operation of any of the payment functions if the Board proves that the difference is genuinely due to a material factor which –

(a)   is not the difference of sex, but

(b)   is a material difference between the woman's case and the man's case.

(4)   Subsection (2) does not apply in such circumstances as may be prescribed.

(5)   This section has effect in relation to the exercise of any payment function in so far as it relates (directly or indirectly) to any pensionable service on or after 17th May 1990.

(6)   In this section –

'payment function' means any function conferred on the Board by or by virtue of this Chapter which relates to a person's entitlement to or the payment of any amount under or by virtue of –

(a)   the pension compensation provisions,

(b)   section 166 (duty to pay scheme benefits unpaid at assessment date etc),

(c)   section 169 (discharge of liabilities in respect of compensation), or

(d)   section 170 (discharge of liabilities in respect of money purchase benefits);

'pensionable service' has the meaning given by section 124(1) of the Pensions Act 1995 (c. 26).

Relationship with fraud compensation regime

172 Relationship with fraud compensation regime

(1)   No transfer notice may be given in respect of a scheme within the first 12 months of an assessment period in relation to the scheme.

(2)   Where an application has been made under section 182 (application for fraud compensation payment), no transfer notice may be given until –

(a)   the Board has determined the application,

(b)   the period within which the Board's determination may be reviewed by virtue of Chapter 6 has expired, and

(c)   if the determination is so reviewed –

(i)   the review and any reconsideration,

(ii)   any reference to the PPF Ombudsman in respect of the determination, and

(iii)   any appeal against his determination or directions, has been finally disposed of.

(3)   Subsection (4) applies where during an assessment period in relation to a scheme the Board determines to make one or more fraud compensation payments ('the fraud compensation') to the trustees or managers of the scheme under Chapter 4 of this Part.

(4)   For the purposes of determining whether the condition in section 127(2)(a), 128(2)(a), 152(2) or 158(1) is satisfied, any fraud compensation payment which becomes payable after the relevant time is, to the extent that it relates to a loss incurred by the scheme before that time, to be regarded as an asset of the scheme at that time.

(5) For the purposes of subsection (4) 'the relevant time' –

(a) in the case of section 127(2)(a), has the same meaning as in that provision,

(b) in the case of section 128(2)(a), has the same meaning as in that provision,

(c) in the case of section 152(2) means the reconsideration time (within the meaning of section 151), and

(d) in the case of section 158(1), has the same meaning as in that provision.

(6) Subsection (4) does not apply to the extent that the fraud compensation is payable in respect of a reduction in the value of money purchase assets of the scheme.

For this purpose 'money purchase assets' means assets representing the value of any rights in respect of money purchase benefits under the scheme rules.

The fund

173 Pension Protection Fund

(1) The Pension Protection Fund shall consist of –

(a) property and rights transferred to the Board under section 161(2)(a),

(b) contributions levied under section 174 or 175 (initial and pension protection levies),

(c) money borrowed by the Board under section 115 for the purposes of this Chapter,

(d) any income or capital gain credited under subsection (2),

(e) any amount paid to the Board by virtue of section 139 (repayment of loans to trustees or managers and payment of interest),

(f) amounts recovered under section 163(4)(a) or by virtue of section 168(2)(e) (overpayments),

(g) any amount paid to the Board in respect of a debt due to the Board under section 40(7) by virtue of a contribution notice under section 38,

(h) any property transferred or amounts paid to the Board as required by a restoration order under section 52,

(i) any amount paid to the Board in respect of a debt due to the Board under section 56(7) by virtue of a contribution notice under section 55,

(j) amounts transferred from the Fraud Compensation Fund under section 187 (fraud compensation transfer payments), and

(k) amounts of a prescribed description (other than amounts paid, directly or indirectly, to the Board by the Crown).

(2) The Board must credit to the Pension Protection Fund any income or capital gain arising from the assets in the Fund.

(3) The following are to be paid or transferred out of the Pension Protection Fund –

(a) any sums required to meet liabilities transferred to the Board under section 161(2)(a),

(b) any sums required to make payments in accordance with the pension compensation provisions,

(c) any sums required for the repayment of, and the payment of interest on, money within subsection (1)(c),

(d) any sums required to make loans under section 139 (loans to trustees or managers),

(e) any sums required to make payments under section 163(4)(b) (underpayments during the assessment period),

(f) any sums required to make payments under section 166 (payment of unpaid scheme benefits etc),

(g) any sums required to discharge liabilities under section 169 or 170 (discharge of liabilities in respect of compensation or money purchase benefits),

(h)   any sums required to meet any liabilities arising from obligations imposed on the Board by a restoration order under section 52,

(i)   any property (other than sums) required to meet any liabilities –

(i)   transferred to the Board as mentioned in paragraph (a) and arising from obligations imposed by a restoration order under section 52, or

(ii)   arising from obligations imposed on the Board by such an order,

(j)   any sums required to meet expenditure incurred by virtue of section 161(5) and paragraph 7 of Schedule 6 (expenditure associated with transfer of property, rights and liabilities to the Board), and

(k)   sums required for prescribed purposes.

(4)   No other amounts are to be paid or transferred out of the Pension Protection Fund.

(5)   In subsection (1) (other than paragraph (d)) and subsection (3) (other than paragraph (c)) any reference to a provision of this Act is to be read as including a reference to any provision in force in Northern Ireland corresponding to that provision.

The levies

174 Initial levy

(1)   Regulations must make provision for imposing a levy ('the initial levy') in respect of eligible schemes for the period ('the initial period') which –

(a)   begins with the day appointed for this purpose by the regulations, and

(b)   ends on the following 31st March or, if the regulations so provide, 12 months after the day referred to in paragraph (a).

(2)   The regulations must prescribe –

(a)   the factors by reference to which the initial levy is to be assessed,

(b)   the rate of the levy, and

(c)   the time or times during the initial period when the levy, or any instalment of the levy, becomes payable.

(3)   Regulations under this section may only be made with the approval of the Treasury.

175 Pension protection levies

(1)   For each financial year falling after the initial period, the Board must impose both of the following –

(a)   a risk-based pension protection levy in respect of all eligible schemes;

(b)   a scheme-based pension protection levy in respect of eligible schemes.

In this Chapter 'pension protection levy' means a levy imposed in accordance with this section.

(2)   For the purposes of this section –

(a)   a risk-based pension protection levy is a levy assessed by reference to –

(i)   the difference between the value of a scheme's assets (disregarding any assets representing the value of any rights in respect of money purchase benefits under the scheme rules) and the amount of its protected liabilities,

(ii)   except in relation to any prescribed scheme or scheme of a prescribed description, the likelihood of an insolvency event occurring in relation to the employer in relation to a scheme, and

(iii)   if the Board considers it appropriate, one or more other risk factors mentioned in subsection (3), and

(b)   a scheme-based pension protection levy is a levy assessed by reference to –

      (i)   the amount of a scheme's liabilities to or in respect of members (other than liabilities in respect of money purchase benefits), and

      (ii) if the Board considers it appropriate, one or more other scheme factors mentioned in subsection (4).

(3) The other risk factors referred to in subsection (2)(a)(iii) are factors which the Board considers indicate one or more of the following –

    (a) the risks associated with the nature of a scheme's investments when compared with the nature of its liabilities;

    (b) such other matters as may be prescribed.

(4) The other scheme factors referred to in subsection (2)(b)(ii) are –

    (a) the number of persons who are members, or fall within any description of member, of a scheme;

    (b) the total annual amount of pensionable earnings of active members of a scheme;

    (c) such other factors as may be prescribed.

(5) The Board must, before the beginning of each financial year, determine in respect of that year –

    (a) the factors by reference to which the pension protection levies are to be assessed,

    (b) the time or times by reference to which those factors are to be assessed,

    (c) the rate of the levies, and

    (d) the time or times during the year when the levies, or any instalment of levy, becomes payable.

(6) Different risk factors, scheme factors or rates may be determined in respect of different descriptions of scheme.

(7) The rate determined in respect of a description of scheme may be nil.

(8) In this section –

'initial period' is to be construed in accordance with section 174;

'pensionable earnings', in relation to an active member under a scheme, means the earnings by reference to which a member's entitlement to benefits would be calculated under the scheme rules if he ceased to be an active member at the time by reference to which the factor within subsection (4)(b) is to be assessed.

(9) In this section and sections 176 to 181 'financial year' means a period of 12 months ending with 31st March.

(10) The Board's duty to impose pension protection levies in respect of any financial year is subject to –

    (a) section 177 (amounts to be raised by the pension protection levies), and

    (b) section 180 (transitional provision).

176 Supplementary provisions about pension protection levies

(1) The Board must consult such persons as it considers appropriate in the prescribed manner before making a determination under section 175(5) in respect of a financial year if –

    (a) that year is the first financial year for which the Board is required to impose levies under section 175,

    (b) any of the proposed levy factors or levy rates is different, or applies to a different description of scheme, from the levy factors and levy rates in respect of the pension protection levies imposed in the previous financial year, or

    (c) no consultation has been required under this subsection in relation to the pension protection levies imposed for either of the previous two financial years.

(2) The Board must publish details of any determination under section 175(5) in the prescribed manner.

177 Amounts to be raised by the pension protection levies

(1) Before determining the pension protection levies to be imposed for a financial year, the Board must estimate the amount which will be raised by the levies it proposes to impose.

(2) The Board must impose levies for a financial year in a form which it estimates will raise an amount not exceeding the levy ceiling for the financial year.

(3) The pension protection levies imposed for a financial year must be in a form which the Board estimates will result in at least 80% of the amount raised by the levies for that year being raised by the risk-based pension protection levy.

(4) For the first financial year after the transitional period, regulations may modify subsection (2) so as to provide that the reference to the levy ceiling for the financial year is to be read as a reference to such lower amount as is prescribed.

(5) For the second financial year after the transitional period and for any subsequent financial year, the Board must impose pension protection levies in a form which it estimates will raise an amount which does not exceed by more than 25% the amount estimated under subsection (1) in respect of the pension protection levies imposed for the previous financial year.

(6) The Secretary of State may by order substitute a different percentage for the percentage for the time being specified in subsection (5).

(7) Before making an order under subsection (6), the Secretary of State must consult such persons as he considers appropriate.

(8) Regulations under subsection (4), or an order under subsection (6), may be made only with the approval of the Treasury.

(9) In this section –

    (a) 'risk-based pension protection levy' and 'scheme-based pension protection levy' are to be construed in accordance with section 175, and

    (b) 'transitional period' has the meaning given by section 180(3).

178 The levy ceiling

(1) The Secretary of State must, before the beginning of each financial year for which levies are required to be imposed under section 175, specify by order the amount which is to be the levy ceiling for that year for the purposes of section 177.

(2) An order under subsection (1) in respect of the first financial year for which levies are imposed under section 175 may be made only with the approval of the Treasury.

(3) Subject to subsection (8), the amount specified under subsection (1) for a financial year ('the current year') after the first year for which levies are imposed under section 175 must be –

    (a) where it appears to the Secretary of State that the level of earnings in the review period has increased, the amount specified under subsection (1) for the previous financial year increased by the earnings percentage for that review period specified under subsection (6), and

    (b) in any other case, the amount specified under subsection (1) for the previous financial year.

(4) In subsection (3) –

'level of earnings' means the general level of earnings obtaining in Great Britain;
'review period' in relation to the current year means the period of 12 months ending with the prescribed date in the previous financial year.

(5) For the purposes of subsection (3), the Secretary of State must, in respect of each review period, review the general level of earnings obtaining in Great Britain and any changes in that level; and for the purposes of such a review the Secretary of State may estimate the general level of earnings in such manner as he thinks appropriate.

(6) Where it appears to the Secretary of State that the general level of earnings has increased during the review period, he must by order specify the percentage by which that level has so increased ('the earnings percentage').

(7) The Secretary of State must discharge the duties imposed by subsections (5) and (6) in respect of a review period before the beginning of the prescribed period which ends at the time the first financial year after the review period begins.

(8) The Secretary of State may, on the recommendation of the Board and with the approval of the Treasury, make an order under subsection (1) in respect of a financial year which specifies an amount exceeding the amount required to be specified under subsection (3).

(9) Before making a recommendation for the purposes of subsection (8), the Board must consult such persons as it considers appropriate in the prescribed manner.

179 Valuations to determine scheme underfunding

(1) For the purposes of enabling risk-based pension protection levies (within the meaning of section 175) to be calculated in respect of eligible schemes, regulations may make provision requiring the trustees or managers of each such scheme to provide the Board or the Regulator on the Board's behalf –

(a) with an actuarial valuation of the scheme at such intervals as may be prescribed, and

(b) with such other information as the Board may require in respect of the assets and protected liabilities of the scheme at such times as may be prescribed.

(2) For the purposes of this section, in relation to a scheme –

'an actuarial valuation' means a written valuation of the scheme's assets and protected liabilities prepared and signed by the actuary;

'the actuary' means –

(a) the actuary appointed under section 47(1)(b) of the Pensions Act 1995 (c. 26) (professional advisers) in relation to the scheme, or

(b) if no such actuary has been appointed –

(i) a person with prescribed qualifications or experience, or

(ii) a person approved by the Secretary of State.

(3) Regulations under this section may prescribe how –

(a) the assets and the protected liabilities of schemes, and

(b) their amount or value,

are to be determined, calculated and verified.

(4) Subject to any provision made under subsection (3), those matters are to be determined, calculated and verified in accordance with guidance issued by the Board.

(5) In calculating the amount of any liabilities for the purposes of a valuation required by virtue of this section, a provision of the scheme rules which limits the amount of the scheme's liabilities by reference to the value of its assets is to be disregarded.

(6) In this section references to 'assets' do not include assets representing the value of any rights in respect of money purchase benefits under the scheme rules.

180 Pension protection levies during the transitional period

(1) Regulations may provide that in respect of any financial year during the transitional period –

(a) sections 175 and 177(3) are to apply with such modifications as may be prescribed;

(b) section 177(2) is to apply as if the reference to the levy ceiling for the financial year were a reference to such lower amount as is specified in the regulations.

(2) Regulations which contain provision made by virtue of subsection (1)(b) may only be made with the approval of the Treasury.

(3) For the purposes of this section 'the transitional period' means the prescribed period beginning immediately after the initial period (within the meaning of section 174).

(4) If the transitional period begins with a date other than 1st April, regulations may provide that any provision of this section or of sections 175 to 179 applies, with such modifications as may be prescribed, in relation to –

    (a) the period beginning at the same time as the transitional period and ending with the following 31st March, and

    (b) the financial year which begins immediately after that period.

181 Calculation, collection and recovery of levies

(1) This section applies in relation to –

    (a) the initial levy imposed under section 174 in respect of a scheme, and

    (b) any pension protection levy imposed under section 175 in respect of a scheme.

(2) The levy is payable to the Board by or on behalf of –

    (a) the trustees or managers of the scheme, or

    (b) any other prescribed person.

(3) The Board must in respect of the levy –

    (a) determine the schemes in respect of which it is imposed,

    (b) calculate the amount of the levy in respect of each of those schemes, and

    (c) notify any person liable to pay the levy in respect of the scheme of the amount of the levy in respect of the scheme and the date or dates on which it becomes payable.

(4) The Board may require the Regulator to discharge, on the Board's behalf, its functions under subsection (3) in respect of the levy.

(5) Where a scheme is an eligible scheme for only part of the period for which the levy is imposed, except in prescribed circumstances, the amount of the levy payable in respect of the scheme for that period is such proportion of the full amount as that part bears to that period.

(6) An amount payable by a person on account of the levy is a debt due from him to the Board.

(7) An amount so payable may be recovered –

    (a) by the Board, or

    (b) if the Board so determines, by the Regulator on its behalf.

(8) Regulations may make provision relating to –

    (a) the collection and recovery of amounts payable by way of any levy in relation to which this section applies;

    (b) the circumstances in which any such amount may be waived.

CHAPTER 4   FRAUD COMPENSATION

Entitlement to fraud compensation

182 Cases where fraud compensation payments can be made

(1) The Board shall, in accordance with this section, make one or more payments (in this Part referred to as 'fraud compensation payments') in respect of an occupational pension scheme if –

    (a)   the scheme is not a prescribed scheme or a scheme of a prescribed description,

    (b)   the value of the assets of the scheme has been reduced since the relevant date and the Board considers that there are reasonable grounds for believing that the reduction was attributable to an act or omission constituting a prescribed offence,

    (c)   subsection (2), (3) or (4) applies,

    (d)   an application is made which meets the requirements of subsection (5), and

    (e)   the application is made within the authorised period.

(2)   This subsection applies where –

    (a)   a qualifying insolvency event has occurred in relation to the employer in relation to the scheme,

    (b)   after that event, a scheme failure notice has been issued under section 122(2)(a) in relation to the scheme and that notice has become binding, and

    (c)   a cessation event has not occurred in relation to the scheme in respect of a cessation notice which has been issued during the period –

        (i)   beginning with the occurrence of the insolvency event, and

        (ii) ending immediately before the issuing of the scheme failure notice under section 122(2)(a),

    and the occurrence of such a cessation event in respect of a cessation notice issued during that period is not a possibility.

(3)   This subsection applies where –

    (a)   in relation to the scheme, an application has been made under subsection (1), or a notification has been given under subsection (5)(a), of section 129, and

    (b)   in response to that application, or the notice given by the Regulator under subsection (4) of that section, the Board has issued a scheme failure notice under section 130(2) in relation to the scheme and that notice has become binding.

(4)   This subsection applies where –

    (a)   the scheme is not an eligible scheme,

    (b)   the employer in relation to the scheme is unlikely to continue as a going concern,

    (c)   the prescribed requirements are met in relation to the employer,

    (d)   the application under this section states that the case is one in relation to which paragraphs (b) and (c) apply, and

    (e)   in response to that application the Board has issued a notice under section 183(2) confirming that a scheme rescue is not possible in relation to the scheme and that notice has become binding.

(5)   An application meets the requirements of this subsection if –

    (a)   it is made by a prescribed person, and

    (b)   it is made in the prescribed manner and contains the prescribed information.

(6)   Subject to subsection (7), an application is made within the authorised period if it is made within the period of 12 months beginning with the later of –

    (a)   the time of the relevant event, or

    (b)   the time when the auditor or actuary of the scheme, or the trustees or managers, knew or ought reasonably to have known that a reduction of value falling within subsection (1)(b) had occurred,

    or within such longer period as the Board may determine in any case.

(7)   No application for fraud compensation may be made under this section in respect of a scheme once a transfer notice is given in relation to the scheme under section 160.

(8)   For the purposes of this section, an insolvency event ('the current event') in relation to the employer is a qualifying insolvency event if –

(a)   it occurs on or after the day appointed under section 126(2), and

(b)   either –

    (i)   it is the first insolvency event to occur in relation to the employer on or after that day, or

    (ii)   a cessation event has occurred in relation to the scheme in respect of a cessation notice issued during the period –

        (a)   beginning with the occurrence of the last insolvency event which occurred before the current event, and

        (b)   ending with the occurrence of the current event.

(9) For the purposes of this section –

(a)   a cessation event in relation to a scheme occurs when a cessation notice in relation to the scheme becomes binding,

(b)   a 'cessation notice' means –

    (i)   a withdrawal notice issued in relation to the scheme under section 122(2)(b) (scheme rescue has occurred),

    (ii)   a withdrawal notice issued in relation to the scheme under section 130(3) (scheme rescue has occurred),

    (iii)   a withdrawal notice issued in relation to the scheme under section 148 (no insolvency event has occurred or is likely to occur),

    (iv)   a notice issued in relation to the scheme under section 183(2)(b) (scheme rescue has occurred), or

    (v)   a notice issued under section 122(4) (inability to confirm status of scheme) in a case where the notice has become binding and section 148 does not apply,

(c)   the occurrence of a cessation event in relation to a scheme in respect of a cessation notice issued during a particular period ('the specified period') is a possibility until each of the following are no longer reviewable –

    (i)   any cessation notice which has been issued in relation to the scheme during the specified period,

    (ii)   any failure to issue such a cessation notice during the specified period,

    (iii)   any notice which has been issued by the Board under Chapter 2 or 3 which is relevant to the issue of a cessation notice in relation to the scheme during the specified period or to such a cessation notice which has been issued during that period becoming binding,

    (iv)   any failure to issue such a notice as is mentioned in sub-paragraph (iii), and

(d)   the issue of, or failure to issue, a notice is to be regarded as reviewable –

    (i)   during the period within which it may be reviewed by virtue of Chapter 6, and

    (ii)   if the matter is so reviewed, until –

        (a)   the review and any reconsideration,

        (b)   any reference to the PPF Ombudsman in respect of the matter, and

        (c)   any appeal against his determination or directions, has been finally disposed of.

(10) In this section –

'auditor' and 'actuary', in relation to an occupational pension scheme, have the meaning given by section 47 of the Pensions Act 1995 (c. 26);

'the relevant event' means –

    (a)   in a case where subsection (2) applies in relation to an eligible scheme, the event within paragraph (a) of that subsection,

    (b)   in any other case where subsection (2) applies, the issue of the scheme failure notice under section 122(2)(a) mentioned in paragraph (b) of that subsection,

    (c)   in a case where subsection (3) applies, the event within paragraph (a) of that subsection, and

    (d)   in a case where subsection (4) applies, the trustees or managers becoming aware that paragraphs (b) and (c) of that subsection apply in relation to the scheme;

'the relevant date' means –

    (a)   in the case of an occupational pension scheme established under a trust, 6th April 1997, and

    (b)   in any other case, the day appointed by the Secretary of State by order for the purposes of this section.

(11) This section is subject to section 184(2) (no fraud compensation payments to be made until settlement date determined).

183 Board's duties in respect of certain applications under section 182

(1) This section applies where, in a case to which paragraphs (a) to (c) of subsection (4) of section 182 apply (employer not likely to continue as going concern etc), the Board receives an application within paragraph (d) of that subsection.

(2) If the Board is able to confirm –

    (a)   that a scheme rescue is not possible, or

    (b)   that a scheme rescue has occurred,

it must, as soon as reasonably practicable, issue a notice to that effect.

(3) Where the Board issues a notice under subsection (2), it must, as soon as reasonably practicable, give a copy of the notice to –

    (a)   the Regulator,

    (b)   the trustees or managers of the scheme,

    (c)   if the trustees or managers did not make the application mentioned in subsection (1), the person who made that application, and

    (d)   any insolvency practitioner in relation to the employer or, if there is no such insolvency practitioner, the employer.

(4) For the purposes of this Chapter a notice issued under subsection (2) is not binding until –

    (a)   the period within which the issue of the notice may be reviewed by virtue of Chapter 6 has expired, and

    (b)   if the issue of the notice is so reviewed –

        (i)   the review and any reconsideration,

        (ii)   any reference to the PPF Ombudsman in respect of the issue of the notice, and

        (iii)   any appeal against his determination or directions,

has been finally disposed of and the notice has not been revoked, varied or substituted.

(5) Where a notice issued under subsection (2) becomes binding, the Board must as soon as reasonably practicable give a notice to that effect together with a copy of the binding notice to the persons to whom it is required to give a copy notice under subsection (3).

(6) A notice under subsection (5) must be in the prescribed form and contain such information as may be prescribed.

(7) Section 130(5) (circumstances in which scheme rescue can or cannot be confirmed) applies for the purposes of this section.

184 Recovery of value

(1) Where an application for a fraud compensation payment is made, the trustees or managers must obtain any recoveries of value, to the extent that they may do so without disproportionate cost and within a reasonable time.

(2) No fraud compensation payment may be made until the date ('the settlement date') determined by the Board, after consulting the trustees or managers of the scheme in question, as the date after which further recoveries of value are unlikely to be obtained without disproportionate cost or within a reasonable time.

(3) In this section 'recovery of value' means any increase in the value of the assets of the scheme, being an increase attributable to any payment received (otherwise than from the Board) by the trustees or managers of the scheme in respect of any act or omission –

    (a) which there are reasonable grounds for believing constituted an offence prescribed for the purposes of paragraph (b) of section 182(1), and

    (b) to which any reduction in value falling within that paragraph was attributable.

(4) It is for the Board to determine whether anything received by the trustees or managers of the scheme is to be treated as a payment received in respect of any such act or omission.

For this purpose 'payment' includes any money or money's worth.

185 Fraud compensation payments

(1) Where the Board determines to make one or more fraud compensation payments, it must make the payment or payments to the trustees or managers of the scheme in accordance with this section.

(2) A fraud compensation payment may be made on such terms (including terms requiring repayment in whole or in part) and on such conditions as the Board considers appropriate.

(3) The amount of the payment (or, if there is more than one, the aggregate) must not exceed the difference between –

    (a) the amount of the reduction (or, if more than one, the aggregate amount of the reductions) within section 182(1)(b), and

    (b) the amount of any recoveries of value obtained before the settlement date (within the meaning of section 184(2)).

(4) Subject to subsection (3), the Board –

    (a) must determine the amount of any fraud compensation payment in accordance with regulations made for the purposes of this subsection, and

    (b) must take account of any interim payment already made under section 186.

(5) The Board must give written notice of its determination under subsection (4) to –

    (a) the Regulator,

    (b) the trustees or managers of the scheme,

    (c) if the trustees or managers did not make the application under section 182 (fraud compensation payments), the person who made that application, and

    (d) any insolvency practitioner in relation to the employer or, if there is no such insolvency practitioner, the employer.

186 Interim payments

(1) The Board may, on an application under section 182, make a payment or payments to the trustees or managers of an occupational pension scheme if –

    (a) it is of the opinion that –

> (i)   the case is one to which subsection (1) of that section applies or may apply, and
>
> (ii)   the trustees or managers would not otherwise be able to meet liabilities of a prescribed description, but
>
> (b)   it has not determined the settlement date under section 184.

(2)   Amounts payable under this section must not exceed the amounts determined in accordance with regulations.

(3)   The Board may, except in prescribed circumstances, recover so much of any payment made under subsection (1) as it considers appropriate if, after the payment is made, it determines –

> (a)   that the case is not one to which section 182(1) applies, or
>
> (b)   that the amount of the payment was excessive.

(4)   Subject to that, a payment under subsection (1) may be made on such terms (including terms requiring repayment in whole or in part) and on such conditions as the Board considers appropriate.

187   Board's powers to make fraud compensation transfer payments

(1)   This section applies where –

> (a)   the Board assumes responsibility for a scheme in accordance with Chapter 3,
>
> (b)   the value of the assets of the scheme was reduced after the relevant date but before the transfer notice (within the meaning of section 160) was received by the trustees or managers of the scheme and there are reasonable grounds for believing that the reduction was attributable to an act or omission constituting an offence prescribed for the purposes of section 182(1)(b), and
>
> (c)   no application was made under section 182 in respect of that reduction (or any such application was withdrawn before it was determined).

(2)   The Board may transfer an amount from the Fraud Compensation Fund to the Pension Protection Fund ('fraud compensation transfer payment') in respect of the reduction in value, subject to the provisions of this section.

(3)   The Board must obtain any recoveries of value, to the extent that it may do so without disproportionate cost and within a reasonable time.

(4)   No fraud compensation transfer payment may be made until the date determined by the Board as the date after which further recoveries of value are unlikely to be obtained without disproportionate cost and within a reasonable time.

(5)   In this section 'recovery of value' means any increase in the value of the Pension Protection Fund, being an increase attributable to any payment received (otherwise than under this section) by the Board in respect of any act or omission –

> (a)   which there are reasonable grounds for believing constituted an offence prescribed for the purposes of section 182(1)(b), and
>
> (b)   to which any reduction in value falling within subsection (1)(b) above was attributable.

(6)   It is for the Board to determine whether anything received by it is to be treated as a payment received in respect of any such act or omission.

For this purpose 'payment' includes any money or money's worth.

(7)   The amount of any fraud compensation transfer payment (or, if there is more than one, the aggregate) must not exceed the difference between –

> (a)   the amount of the reduction (or, if more than one, the aggregate amount of the reductions) within subsection (1)(b), and
>
> (b)   the amount of any recoveries of value obtained by the Board before the date determined by the Board under subsection (4).

(8) Subject to subsection (7), the Board must determine the amount of any fraud compensation transfer payment in accordance with regulations made for the purposes of this subsection.

(9) In this section 'the relevant date' has the meaning given by section 182(10).

The fund

188 Fraud Compensation Fund

(1) The Fraud Compensation Fund shall consist of –

    (a) any property and rights transferred under section 302 (dissolution of the Pensions Compensation Board) which the Board designates as assets of the Fund,

    (b) contributions levied under section 189 (fraud compensation levy),

    (c) money borrowed by the Board under section 115 for the purposes of this Chapter,

    (d) amounts recovered under section 186 (recovery of interim payments), and

    (e) any income or capital gain credited under subsection (2).

(2) The Board must credit to the Fraud Compensation Fund any income or capital gain arising from the assets in the Fund.

(3) The following are payable out of the Fraud Compensation Fund –

    (a) sums required to meet liabilities transferred to the Board under section 302 (dissolution of the Pensions Compensation Board), which the Board designates as liabilities of the Fund,

    (b) payments under section 185 (fraud compensation payments),

    (c) payments under section 186(1) (interim payments),

    (d) amounts required to be transferred to the Pension Protection Fund under section 187 (fraud compensation transfer payments),

    (e) money required for the repayment of, and the payment of interest on, money within subsection (1)(c).

(4) No other amounts are payable out of the Fraud Compensation Fund.

(5) In subsection (1) (other than paragraphs (a) and (e)) and subsection (3) (other than paragraphs (a) and (e)) any reference to a provision of this Act is to be read as including a reference to any provision in force in Northern Ireland corresponding to that provision.

The levy

189 Fraud compensation levy

(1) For the purposes of meeting expenditure payable out of the Fraud Compensation Fund, regulations may provide for the imposition of a levy ('fraud compensation levy') in respect of occupational pension schemes.

(2) Subsection (1) does not apply in relation to any scheme which is prescribed or of a description prescribed under section 182(1)(a) (schemes not eligible for fraud compensation).

(3) A fraud compensation levy imposed in respect of a scheme is payable to the Board by or on behalf of –

    (a) the trustees or managers of the scheme, or

    (b) any other prescribed person.

(4) A fraud compensation levy is so payable at prescribed times and at a rate, not exceeding the prescribed rate, determined by the Board.

(5) In determining the amount of expenditure in respect of which a fraud compensation levy is to be imposed, the Board may take one year with another (and, in doing so,

must have regard to expenditure estimated to be incurred in current or future periods and to actual expenditure incurred in previous periods).

(6) Notice of the rates determined by the Board under subsection (4) must be given to prescribed persons in the prescribed manner.

(7) The Board must in respect of any fraud compensation levy imposed under this section –

(a)   determine the schemes in respect of which it is imposed,

(b)   calculate the amount of the levy in respect of each of those schemes, and

(c)   notify any person liable to pay the levy in respect of the scheme of the amount of the levy in respect of the scheme and the date or dates on which it becomes payable.

(8) The Board may require the Regulator to discharge, on the Board's behalf, its functions under subsection (7) in respect of the levy.

(9) An amount payable by a person on account of a fraud compensation levy is a debt due from him to the Board.

(10) An amount so payable may be recovered –

(a)   by the Board, or

(b)   if the Board so determines, by the Regulator on its behalf.

(11) Without prejudice to the generality of subsection (1), (9) or (10), regulations under this section may include provision relating to –

(a)   the collection and recovery of amounts payable by way of levy under this section;

(b)   the circumstances in which any such amount may be waived.

CHAPTER 5   GATHERING INFORMATION

190   Information to be provided to the Board etc

(1) Regulations may require such persons as may be prescribed to provide –

(a)   to the Board, or

(b)   to a person –

(i)   with whom the Board has made arrangements under paragraph 18 of Schedule 5, and

(ii)   who is authorised by the Board for the purposes of the regulations,

information of a prescribed description at such times, or in such circumstances, as may be prescribed.

(2) Regulations under subsection (1) may in particular make provision for requiring such persons as may be prescribed to provide any information or evidence needed for a determination of entitlement to compensation under Chapter 3 of this Part.

(3) Regulations made by virtue of paragraph (b) of that subsection must make provision regarding the manner in which the persons required to provide information are to be notified of the identity of the person authorised as mentioned in sub-paragraph (ii) of that paragraph.

191   Notices requiring provision of information

(1) Any person to whom subsection (3) applies may be required by a notice in writing to produce any document, or provide any other information, which is –

(a)   of a description specified in the notice, and

(b)   relevant to the exercise of the Board's functions in relation to an occupational pension scheme.

(2) A notice under subsection (1) may be given by –

(a)   the Board, or

(b)   a person authorised by the Board for the purposes of this section in relation to the scheme.

(3)   This subsection applies to –

(a)   a trustee or manager of the scheme,

(b)   a professional adviser in relation to the scheme,

(c)   the employer in relation to the scheme,

(d)   an insolvency practitioner in relation to the employer, and

(e)   any other person appearing to the Board, or person giving the notice, to be a person who holds, or is likely to hold, information relevant to the discharge of the Board's functions in relation to the scheme.

(4)   Where the production of a document, or the provision of information, is required by a notice given under subsection (1), the document must be produced, or information must be provided, in such a manner, at such a place and within such a period as may be specified in the notice.

192   Entry of premises

(1)   An appointed person may, for the purpose of enabling or facilitating the performance of any function of the Board in relation to an occupational pension scheme, at any reasonable time enter scheme premises and, while there –

(a)   may make such examination and inquiry as may be necessary for such purpose,

(b)   may require any person on the premises to produce, or secure the production of, any document relevant to that purpose for inspection by the appointed person,

(c)   may take copies of any such document,

(d)   may take possession of any document appearing to be such a document or take in relation to any such document any other steps which appear necessary for preserving it or preventing interference with it,

(e)   may, in the case of any such document which consists of information which is stored in electronic form and is on, or accessible from, the premises, require the information to be produced in a form –

(i)   in which it can be taken away, and

(ii)   in which it is legible or from which it can readily be produced in a legible form, and

(f)   may, as to any matter relevant to the exercise of the Board's functions in relation to the scheme, examine, or require to be examined, either alone or in the presence of another person, any person on the premises whom he has reasonable cause to believe to be able to give information relevant to that matter.

(2)   Premises are scheme premises for the purposes of subsection (1) if the appointed person has reasonable grounds to believe that –

(a)   they are being used for the business of the employer,

(b)   an insolvency practitioner in relation to the employer is acting there in that capacity,

(c)   documents relevant to –

(i)   the administration of the scheme, or

(ii)   the employer,

are being kept there, or

(d)   the administration of the scheme, or work connected with the administration of the scheme, is being carried out there,

unless the premises are a private dwelling-house not used by, or by permission of, the occupier for the purposes of a trade or business.

(3) An appointed person applying for admission to any premises for the purposes of this section must, if so required, produce his certificate of appointment.

(4) When exercising a power under this section an appointed person may be accompanied by such persons as he considers appropriate.

(5) Any document of which possession is taken under this section may be retained until the end of the period comprising –

    (a) the period of 12 months beginning with the date on which possession was taken of the document, and

    (b) any extension of that period under subsection (6).

(6) The Board may before the end of the period mentioned in subsection (5) (including any extension of it under this subsection) extend it by such period not exceeding 12 months as the Board considers appropriate.

(7) In this section 'appointed person' means a person appointed by the Board for the purposes of this section in relation to the scheme.

193 Penalties relating to sections 191 and 192

(1) A person who, without reasonable excuse, neglects or refuses to provide information or produce a document when required to do so under section 191 is guilty of an offence.

(2) A person who without reasonable excuse –

    (a) intentionally delays or obstructs an appointed person exercising any power under section 192,

    (b) neglects or refuses to produce, or secure the production of, any document when required to do so under that section, or

    (c) neglects or refuses to answer a question or to provide information when so required,

is guilty of an offence.

(3) In subsection (2)(a) 'appointed person' has the same meaning as it has in section 192.

(4) A person guilty of an offence under subsection (1) or (2) is liable on summary conviction to a fine not exceeding level 5 on the standard scale.

(5) An offence under subsection (1) or (2)(b) or (c) may be charged by reference to any day or longer period of time; and a person may be convicted of a second or subsequent offence by reference to any period of time following the preceding conviction of the offence.

(6) Any person who intentionally and without reasonable excuse alters, suppresses, conceals or destroys any document which he is or is liable to be required to produce under section 191 or 192 is guilty of an offence.

(7) Any person guilty of an offence under subsection (6) is liable –

    (a) on summary conviction, to a fine not exceeding the statutory maximum;

    (b) on conviction on indictment, to a fine or imprisonment for a term not exceeding two years, or both.

194 Warrants

(1) A justice of the peace may issue a warrant under this section if satisfied on information on oath given by or on behalf of the Board that there are reasonable grounds for believing –

    (a) that there is on, or accessible from, any premises any document –

        (i) whose production has been required under section 191 or 192, or any corresponding provision in force in Northern Ireland, and

        (ii) which has not been produced in compliance with that requirement,

    (b) that there is on, or accessible from, any premises any document relevant to the exercise of the Board's functions in relation to an occupational pension scheme whose production could be so required and, if its production were so required, the document –

(i)   would not be produced, but

(ii) would be removed, or made inaccessible, from the premises, hidden, tampered with or destroyed, or

(c) that a person will do any act which constitutes a misuse or misappropriation of the assets of an occupational pension scheme and that there is on, or accessible from, any premises any document –

(i)   which relates to whether the act will be done, and

(ii) whose production could be required under section 191 or 192, or any corresponding provision in force in Northern Ireland.

(2) A warrant under this section shall authorise an inspector –

(a) to enter the premises specified in the information, using such force as is reasonably necessary for the purpose,

(b) to search the premises and –

(i)   take possession of any document appearing to be such a document as is mentioned in subsection (1), or

(ii) take in relation to such a document any other steps which appear necessary for preserving it or preventing interference with it,

(c) to take copies of any such document,

(d) to require any person named in the warrant to provide an explanation of any such document or to state where it may be found or how access to it may be obtained, and

(e) in the case of any such document which consists of information which is stored in electronic form and is on, or accessible from, the premises, to require the information to be produced in a form –

(i)   in which it can be taken away, and

(ii) in which it is legible or from which it can readily be produced in a legible form.

(3) When executing a warrant under this section, an inspector may be accompanied by such persons as he considers appropriate.

(4) A warrant under this section continues in force until the end of the period of one month beginning with the day on which it is issued.

(5) Any document of which possession is taken under this section may be retained until the end of the period comprising –

(a) the period of 12 months beginning with the date on which possession was taken of the document, and

(b) any extension of that period under subsection (6).

(6) The Board may before the end of the period mentioned in subsection (5) (including any extension of it under this subsection) extend it by such period not exceeding 12 months as the Board considers appropriate.

(7) In this section 'inspector' means a person appointed by the Board as an inspector.

(8) In the application of this section in Scotland –

(a) the reference to a justice of the peace is to be read as a reference to the sheriff, and

(b) the references in subsections (1) and (2)(a) to information are to be read as references to evidence.

Provision of false or misleading information

195 Offence of providing false or misleading information to the Board

(1) Any person who knowingly or recklessly provides information which is false or misleading in a material particular is guilty of an offence if the information –

    (a) is provided in purported compliance with a requirement under –

        (i) section 190 (information to be provided to the Board etc),

        (ii) section 191 (notices requiring provision of information), or

        (iii) section 192 (entry of premises), or

    (b) is provided otherwise than as mentioned in paragraph (a) but in circumstances in which the person providing the information intends, or could reasonably be expected to know, that it would be used by the Board for the purposes of exercising its functions under this Act.

(2) Any person guilty of an offence under subsection (1) is liable –

    (a) on summary conviction, to a fine not exceeding the statutory maximum;

    (b) on conviction on indictment, to a fine or imprisonment for a term not exceeding two years, or both.

Use of information

196 Use of information

Information held by the Board in the exercise of any of its functions may be used by the Board for the purposes of, or for any purpose connected with or incidental to, the exercise of its functions.

Disclosure of information

197 Restricted information

(1) Restricted information must not be disclosed –

    (a) by the Board, or

    (b) by any person who receives the information directly or indirectly from the Board.

(2) Subsection (1) is subject to –

    (a) subsection (3), and

    (b) sections 198 to 203 and 235.

(3) Subject to section 202(4), restricted information may be disclosed with the consent of the person to whom it relates and (if different) the person from whom the Board obtained it.

(4) For the purposes of this section and sections 198 to 203, 'restricted information' means any information obtained by the Board in the exercise of its functions which relates to the business or other affairs of any person, except for information –

    (a) which at the time of the disclosure is or has already been made available to the public from other sources, or

    (b) which is in the form of a summary or collection of information so framed as not to enable information relating to any particular person to be ascertained from it.

(5) Any person who discloses information in contravention of this section is guilty of an offence and liable –

    (a) on summary conviction, to a fine not exceeding the statutory maximum;

    (b) on conviction on indictment, to a fine or imprisonment for a term not exceeding two years, or both.

(6)   Information which –

(a)   is obtained under section 191 by a person authorised under subsection (2)(b) of that section, but

(b)   if obtained by the Board, would be restricted information,

is treated for the purposes of subsections (1) and (3) and sections 198 to 203 as restricted information which the person has received from the Board.

198   Disclosure for facilitating exercise of functions by the Board

(1)   Section 197 does not preclude the disclosure of restricted information in any case in which disclosure is for the purpose of enabling or assisting the Board to exercise its functions.

(2)   Subsection (3) applies where, in order to enable or assist the Board properly to exercise any of its functions, the Board considers it necessary to seek advice from any qualified person on any matter of law, accountancy, valuation or other matter requiring the exercise of professional skill.

(3)   Section 197 does not preclude the disclosure by the Board to a person qualified to provide that advice of such information as appears to the Board to be necessary to ensure that he is properly informed with respect to the matters on which his advice is sought.

199   Disclosure for facilitating exercise of functions by the Regulator

Section 197 does not preclude the disclosure of restricted information in any case in which disclosure is for the purpose of enabling or assisting the Regulator to exercise its functions.

200   Disclosure for facilitating exercise of functions by other supervisory authorities

(1)   Section 197 does not preclude the disclosure by the Board of restricted information to any person specified in the first column of Schedule 8 if the Board considers that the disclosure would enable or assist that person to exercise the functions specified in relation to him in the second column of that Schedule.

(2)   The Secretary of State may after consultation with the Board –

(a)   by order amend Schedule 8 by –

(i)   adding any person exercising regulatory functions and specifying functions in relation to that person,

(ii)   removing any person for the time being specified in the Schedule, or

(iii)   altering the functions for the time being specified in the Schedule in relation to any person, or

(b)   by order restrict the circumstances in which, or impose conditions subject to which, disclosure may be made to any person for the time being specified in the Schedule.

201   Other permitted disclosures

(1)   Section 197 does not preclude the disclosure by the Board of restricted information to –

(a)   the Secretary of State,

(b)   the Commissioners of Inland Revenue or their officers, or

(c)   the Department for Social Development in Northern Ireland,

if the disclosure appears to the Board to be desirable or expedient in the interests of members of occupational pension schemes or in the public interest.

(2)   Section 197 does not preclude the disclosure of restricted information –

(a)   by or on behalf of –

(i)   the Board, or

(ii)   any public authority (within the meaning of section 6 of the Human Rights

Act 1998 (c. 42)) which receives the information directly or indirectly from the Board,

for any of the purposes specified in section 17(2)(a) to (d) of the Anti-terrorism, Crime and Security Act 2001 (c. 24) (criminal proceedings and investigations),

(b) in connection with any proceedings arising out of –

  (i) this Act,
  (ii) the Welfare Reform and Pensions Act 1999 (c. 30),
  (iii) the Pensions Act 1995 (c. 26), or
  (iv) the Pension Schemes Act 1993 (c. 48),

or any corresponding enactment in force in Northern Ireland, or any proceedings for breach of trust in relation to an occupational pension scheme,

(c) with a view to the institution of, or otherwise for the purposes of, proceedings under –

  (i) section 7 or 8 of the Company Directors Disqualification Act 1986 (c. 46), or
  (ii) Article 10 or 11 of the Companies (Northern Ireland) Order 1989 (S.I. 1989/2404 (N.I. 18)) or of the Company Directors Disqualification (Northern Ireland) Order 2002 (S.I. 2002/3150 (N.I. 4)),

(d) in connection with any proceedings under –

  (i) the Insolvency Act 1986 (c. 45), or
  (ii) the Insolvency (Northern Ireland) Order 1989 (S.I. 1989/2405 (N.I. 19)),

which the Board has instituted or in which it has a right to be heard,

(e) with a view to the institution of, or otherwise for the purposes of, any disciplinary proceedings relating to the exercise of his professional duties by a solicitor, an actuary, an accountant or an insolvency practitioner,

(f) with a view to the institution of, or otherwise for the purpose of, any disciplinary proceedings relating to the exercise by a public servant of his functions, or

(g) in pursuance of a Community obligation.

(3) In subsection (2)(f), 'public servant' means an officer or servant of the Crown or of any prescribed authority.

(4) Section 197 does not preclude the disclosure by the Board of restricted information to –

(a) the Director of Public Prosecutions,
(b) the Director of Public Prosecutions for Northern Ireland,
(c) the Lord Advocate,
(d) a procurator fiscal, or
(e) a constable.

(5) Section 197 does not preclude the disclosure of restricted information in any case where the disclosure is required by or by virtue of an enactment.

(6) Section 197 does not preclude the disclosure of restricted information in any case where the disclosure is to a Regulator-appointed trustee of an occupational pension scheme for the purpose of enabling or assisting him to exercise his functions in relation to the scheme.

(7) In subsection (6), 'Regulator-appointed trustee' means a trustee appointed by the Regulator under section 7 or 23(1) of the Pensions Act 1995 (c. 26) or any corresponding provision in force in Northern Ireland.

(8) Section 197 does not preclude the disclosure by any person mentioned in subsection (1) or (4) of restricted information obtained by the person by virtue of that subsection, if the disclosure is made with the consent of the Board.

(9) Section 197 does not preclude the disclosure by any person specified in the first column of Schedule 8 of restricted information obtained by the person by virtue of section 200(1), if the disclosure is made –

(a) with the consent of the Board, and

(b) for the purpose of enabling or assisting the person to exercise any functions specified in relation to him in the second column of the Schedule.

(10) Before deciding whether to give its consent to such a disclosure as is mentioned in subsection (8) or (9), the Board must take account of any representations made to it, by the person seeking to make the disclosure, as to the desirability of the disclosure or the necessity for it.

(11) Section 18 of the Anti-terrorism, Crime and Security Act 2001 (c. 24) (restriction on disclosure of information for overseas purposes) has effect in relation to a disclosure authorised by subsection (2) as it has effect in relation to a disclosure authorised by any of the provisions to which section 17 of that Act applies.

202 Tax information

(1) This section applies to information held by any person in the exercise of tax functions about any matter which is relevant, for the purposes of those functions, to tax or duty in the case of an identifiable person (in this section referred to as 'tax information').

(2) No obligation as to secrecy imposed by section 182 of the Finance Act 1989 (c. 26) or otherwise shall prevent the disclosure of tax information to the Board for the purpose of enabling or assisting the Board to discharge its functions.

(3) Where tax information is disclosed to the Board by virtue of subsection (2) above or section 19 of the Anti-terrorism, Crime and Security Act 2001 (disclosure of information held by revenue departments), it must, subject to subsection (4), be treated for the purposes of section 197 as restricted information.

(4) Sections 197(3), 198 to 201, 203 and 235 do not apply to tax information which is disclosed to the Board as mentioned in subsection (3), and such information may not be disclosed by the Board or any person who receives the information directly or indirectly from the Board except –

(a) to, or in accordance with authority given by, the Commissioners of Inland Revenue or the Commissioners of Customs and Excise, or

(b) with a view to the institution of, or otherwise for the purposes of, any criminal proceedings.

(5) In this section 'tax functions' has the same meaning as in section 182 of the Finance Act 1989 (c. 26).

Provision of information to members of schemes etc

203 Provision of information to members of schemes etc

(1) Regulations may –

(a) require the Board to provide information of prescribed descriptions to such persons as may be prescribed at prescribed times, or

(b) require trustees or managers of occupational pension schemes to provide such information –

(i) relating to the exercise of the Board's functions in relation to any scheme of which they are trustees or managers,

(ii) relating to any notice issued or application or determination made under Chapter 2, 3 or 4 which relates to any such scheme, or

(iii) otherwise relating to the Board's involvement with any such scheme,

as may be prescribed to prescribed persons at prescribed times or in prescribed circumstances.

(2) Section 197 does not preclude the disclosure of restricted information by the Board which relates to the entitlement of a particular individual to compensation under

Chapter 3 if the disclosure is made to that individual or to a person authorised by him.

(3) Section 197 does not preclude the disclosure of restricted information by the Board if –

    (a) the information relates to the exercise of the Board's functions in relation to an occupational pension scheme,

    (b) the disclosure is made to –

        (i) all affected persons, or

        (ii) all affected persons of a particular description, and

    (c) the Board is satisfied that, in all the circumstances, it is reasonable to make the disclosure.

(4) In subsection (3) 'affected person', in relation to an occupational pension scheme, means a person –

    (a) who is a member of the scheme, or

    (b) who is for the time being nominated by a member of the scheme for the purposes of that subsection.

(5) A nomination by a member of the scheme under subsection (4)(b) –

    (a) may be made by notice in writing given by the member,

    (b) becomes effective when the notice is received by the Board, and

    (c) ceases to be effective when the Board receives a further notice from the member withdrawing the nomination.

(6) In the case of an occupational pension scheme, section 197 does not preclude the disclosure of restricted information by the Board if –

    (a) the disclosure is made to any of the following in relation to the scheme –

        (i) a trustee or manager,

        (ii) any professional adviser,

        (iii) the employer,

        (iv) the insolvency practitioner in relation to the employer,

    (b) the information is relevant to the exercise of that person's functions in relation to the scheme, and

    (c) the Board considers that it is reasonable in all the circumstances to make the disclosure for the purpose of facilitating the exercise of those functions.

Interpretation

204 Sections 190 to 203: interpretation

(1) This section applies for the purposes of sections 190 to 203.

(2) 'Document' includes information recorded in any form, and any reference to production of a document, in relation to information recorded otherwise than in a legible form, is to producing a copy of the information –

    (a) in a legible form, or

    (b) in a form from which it can readily be produced in a legible form.

(3) Where the Board has assumed responsibility for a scheme –

    (a) any reference to the Board's functions in relation to the scheme includes a reference to the functions which it has by virtue of having assumed responsibility for the scheme, and

    (b) any reference to a trustee, manager, professional adviser or employer in relation to the scheme is to be read as a reference to a person who held that position in relation to the scheme before the Board assumed responsibility for it.

Reports

205 Publishing reports etc

(1) The Board may, if it considers it appropriate to do so in any particular case, publish a report of the exercise of, or any matter arising out of or connected with the exercise of, any of its functions in that case.

(2) The publication of a report under subsection (1) may be in such form and manner as the Board considers appropriate.

(3) For the purposes of the law of defamation, the publication of any matter by the Board is privileged unless the publication is shown to be made with malice.

CHAPTER 6   REVIEWS, APPEALS AND MALADMINISTRATION

Review etc by the Board

206 Meaning of 'reviewable matters'

(1) For the purposes of this Chapter, 'reviewable matter' means a matter mentioned in Schedule 9.

(2) Regulations may provide, in relation to any reference in that Schedule to a failure by the Board to do any act or make any determination, that –

(a) the reference is to be construed as a reference to a failure by the Board to do the act or make the determination within a prescribed period, and

(b) the reference is to be construed as not including a failure to do the act or make the determination which first occurs after a prescribed time.

(3) Regulations may make provision suspending the effect of any determination, direction or other act of the Board, or any notice given or issued by it, which relates to a reviewable matter until –

(a) the period within which the matter may be reviewed by virtue of this Chapter has expired, and

(b) if the matter is so reviewed –

(i) the review and any reconsideration,

(ii) any reference to the PPF Ombudsman in respect of the matter, and

(iii) any appeal against his determination or directions,

has been finally disposed of.

(4) Regulations may amend Schedule 9 by –

(a) adding to it any other description of determination, act or failure of, or matter determined or for determination by, the Board, or

(b) removing from it any such determination, act, failure or matter for the time being mentioned in it.

(5) Regulations under subsection (4) may also modify any provision of this Part in consequence of provision made by virtue of paragraph (a) or (b) of that subsection.

207 Review and reconsideration by the Board of reviewable matters

(1) Regulations must –

(a) provide for the Board, on the written application of an interested person, to give a decision ('a review decision') on any reviewable matter, and

(b) require a committee of the Board constituted for the purposes of this section (the 'Reconsideration Committee'), on the written application of an interested person following a review decision, to reconsider the reviewable matter and give a decision ('a reconsideration decision').

(2) In subsection (1), 'interested person' in relation to a reviewable matter, means a person of a description prescribed in relation to reviewable matters of that description.

(3) Regulations under subsection (1) may –

(a) permit a review decision in respect of a reviewable matter of a prescribed description to be made otherwise than on an application, and

(b) permit a reconsideration decision in respect of such a matter to be made otherwise than on an application.

(4) Regulations under subsection (1) must provide for the Board's powers on making a review decision or reconsideration decision to include power –

(a) to vary or revoke the determination, direction or other decision already made by the Board in respect of the reviewable matter,

(b) to substitute a different determination, direction or decision,

(c) to provide for such variations, revocations or substitutions, or any determinations, directions or other decisions made as a result of the review decision or reconsideration decision, to be treated as if they were made at such time (which may be a time prior to the making of the review decision or reconsideration decision) as the Board considers appropriate,

(d) to provide for any notice varied, substituted, issued or given by the Board as a result of the review decision or reconsideration decision, to be treated as if it were issued or given at such time (which may be a time prior to the making of the review decision or reconsideration decision) as the Board considers appropriate,

(e) generally to deal with the matters arising on the review decision or reconsideration decision as if they had arisen on the original determination, direction or decision,

(f) to pay such compensation as the Board considers appropriate to such persons as it may determine, and

(g) to make savings and transitional provision.

(5) Regulations under subsection (1) must include provision –

(a) about applications under the regulations for a review decision or reconsideration decision in respect of a reviewable matter, including the times by which they are to be made,

(b) requiring notice –

(i) of such applications, or

(ii) of a decision of the Board or the Reconsideration Committee by virtue of subsection (3) to give a review decision or reconsider a reviewable matter otherwise than on such an application,

to be given to interested persons in relation to the matter,

(c) with a view to securing that individuals concerned in giving a reconsideration decision were not concerned in the reviewable matter in respect of which the decision is to be made,

(d) as to the procedure for reaching and giving decisions under the regulations, including –

(i) rights of interested persons to make representations to the Reconsideration Committee on a reconsideration under regulations made under subsection (1)(b), and

(ii) the times by which decisions are to be given, and

(e) requiring notice of the review decision or the reconsideration decision in respect of a reviewable matter to be given to interested persons in relation to the matter.

(6) Provision required by subsection (5)(c) may modify paragraphs 15 and 16 of Schedule 5 (membership and procedure of committees of the Board).

208 Investigation by the Board of complaints of maladministration

(1) Regulations must make provision for dealing with relevant complaints.

(2) For the purposes of this Chapter, 'relevant complaint' means a complaint –

   (a) by a person who is or might become entitled to compensation under the pension compensation provisions, or

   (b) by a person who has or may make an application under section 182 (fraud compensation),

   alleging that he has sustained injustice in consequence of maladministration in connection with any act or omission by the Board or any person exercising functions on its behalf.

(3) Regulations under subsection (1) must –

   (a) provide for the Board to investigate and give decisions on matters complained of in relevant complaints, and

   (b) provide for a committee of the Board, on applications following such decisions, to investigate matters complained of and give decisions on them.

(4) Such regulations may, in particular, make provision –

   (a) about the making of relevant complaints and applications under the regulations, including the times by which they are to be made,

   (b) with a view to securing that individuals concerned in giving a decision were not concerned in the matter which is the subject of the relevant complaint in question,

   (c) as to the procedure for reaching and giving decisions under the regulations, including –

      (i) rights of prescribed persons to make representations to the Board, on an investigation under regulations made under subsection (3)(b), and

      (ii) the times by which decisions are to be given, and

   (d) requiring notice –

      (i) of a relevant complaint under the regulations, or

      (ii) of a decision under the regulations in respect of the complaint,

   to be given to prescribed persons in relation to the matter.

(5) Regulations under subsection (1) may confer power on the Board to pay such compensation as it considers appropriate to such persons as it considers have sustained injustice in consequence of the matters complained of.

(6) The power conferred by subsection (4)(b) includes power to modify paragraphs 15 and 16 of Schedule 5 (membership and procedure of committees of the Board).

The PPF Ombudsman

209 The Ombudsman for the Board of the Pension Protection Fund

(1) There is to be a commissioner to be known as the Ombudsman for the Board of the Pension Protection Fund (in this Act referred to as 'the PPF Ombudsman').

(2) The PPF Ombudsman is to be appointed by the Secretary of State on such terms and conditions as are determined by the Secretary of State.

(3) The PPF Ombudsman –

   (a) is to hold and vacate office in accordance with the terms and conditions of his appointment, and

   (b) may resign or be removed from office in accordance with those terms and conditions.

(4) The Secretary of State may by order make provision –

(a) about the payment, or provision for payment, of remuneration, compensation for loss of office, pension, allowances or gratuities to or in respect of the PPF Ombudsman;

(b) about the reimbursement of the PPF Ombudsman in respect of any expenses incurred by him in the performance of his functions;

(c) about the staff of the PPF Ombudsman and the provision of facilities (including additional staff) to him;

(d) about the delegation of the functions of the PPF Ombudsman to his staff or to any such additional staff;

(e) authorising the PPF Ombudsman –

(i) to charge such fees as are specified in the order;

(ii) to charge fees sufficient to meet such costs as are specified in the order;

(f) conferring powers to enable the PPF Ombudsman to obtain such information and documents as he may require for the performance of his functions;

(g) about restrictions on the disclosure of information held by him.

(5) An order under subsection (4)(e) –

(a) may prescribe, or authorise the PPF Ombudsman to determine, the time at which any fee is due, and

(b) provide that any fee which is owed to the PPF Ombudsman by virtue of an order under subsection (4)(e) may be recovered as a debt due to the PPF Ombudsman.

(6) The Secretary of State must pay to the PPF Ombudsman out of money provided by Parliament such sums as may be required to be paid by the Secretary of State to or in respect of the PPF Ombudsman by virtue of an order under subsection (4).

(7) Regulations may provide for the imposition of a levy in respect of eligible schemes for the purpose of meeting expenditure of the Secretary of State under subsection (6).

(8) Where regulations make such provision, subsections (2), (3), (5), (6) and (7) of section 117 (administration levy) apply in relation to the levy as they apply in relation to an administration levy (within the meaning of that section), except that in subsection (7) the reference to subsection (1) of that section is to be read as a reference to subsection (7) of this section.

210 Deputy PPF Ombudsmen

(1) The Secretary of State may appoint one or more persons to act as a deputy to the PPF Ombudsman (in this Chapter referred to as 'a Deputy PPF Ombudsman').

(2) Any such appointment is to be on such terms and conditions as the Secretary of State determines.

(3) A Deputy PPF Ombudsman –

(a) is to hold and vacate office in accordance with the terms and conditions of his appointment, and

(b) may resign or be removed from office in accordance with those terms and conditions.

(4) A Deputy PPF Ombudsman may perform the functions of the PPF Ombudsman –

(a) during any vacancy in that office,

(b) at any time when the PPF Ombudsman is for any reason unable to discharge his functions, or

(c) at any other time, with the consent of the Secretary of State.

(5) References to the PPF Ombudsman in relation to the performance of his functions are accordingly to be construed as including references to a Deputy PPF Ombudsman in relation to the performance of those functions.

(6) An order by the Secretary of State under section 209(4) may make provision –

(a) about the payment, or provision for payment, of remuneration, compensation for loss of office, pension, allowances or gratuities to or in respect of a Deputy PPF Ombudsman;

(b) about the reimbursement of any expenses incurred by a Deputy PPF Ombudsman in the performance of any of the PPF Ombudsman's functions.

211 Status etc of the PPF Ombudsman and deputies

(1) In Part 3 of Schedule 1 to the House of Commons Disqualification Act 1975 (c. 24) (other disqualifying offices), at the appropriate place insert –

'Ombudsman for the Board of the Pension Protection Fund and any deputy to that Ombudsman appointed under section 210 of the Pensions Act 2004.'

(2) In Part 3 of Schedule 1 to the Northern Ireland Assembly Disqualification Act 1975 (c. 25) (other disqualifying offices), at the appropriate place insert –

'Ombudsman for the Board of the Pension Protection Fund and any deputy to that Ombudsman appointed under section 210 of the Pensions Act 2004.'

(3) The persons to whom section 1 of the Superannuation Act 1972 (c. 11) (persons to or in respect of whom benefits may be provided by schemes under that section) applies are to include –

the PPF Ombudsman
a Deputy PPF Ombudsman
the employees of the PPF Ombudsman.

(4) The PPF Ombudsman must pay to the Minister for the Civil Service, at such times as he may direct, such sums as he may determine in respect of the increase attributable to subsection (3) in the sums payable out of money provided by Parliament under that Act.

(5) In Schedule 4 to the Parliamentary Commissioner Act 1967 (c. 13) (relevant tribunals for the purposes of section 5(7) of that Act), at the appropriate place insert –

'The Ombudsman for the Board of the Pension Protection Fund established under section 209 of the Pensions Act 2004.'

212 Annual reports to Secretary of State

(1) The PPF Ombudsman must prepare a report on the discharge of his functions for each financial year.

(2) The PPF Ombudsman must send each report to the Secretary of State as soon as practicable after the end of the financial year for which it is prepared.

(3) The Secretary of State must arrange for the publication of each report sent to him under subsection (2).

(4) In this section 'financial year' means –

(a) the period beginning with the date on which the PPF Ombudsman is established and ending with the next following 31st March, and

(b) each successive period of 12 months.

References to the PPF Ombudsman

213 Reference of reviewable matter to the PPF Ombudsman

(1) Regulations must make provision –

(a) for a reviewable matter to be referred to the PPF Ombudsman following a reconsideration decision under regulations made under subsection (1)(b) or by virtue of subsection (3)(b) of section 207 in respect of the matter, and

(b) for the PPF Ombudsman –

(i) to investigate and determine what (if any) is the appropriate action for the Board to take in relation to the matter, and

(ii) to remit the matter to the Board with directions for the purpose of giving effect to his determination.

(2) Regulations under subsection (1) must make provision about the making of references to the PPF Ombudsman, including provision –

(a) about the descriptions of persons who may make them,

(b) about the manner of making such references, including the times by which they are to be made, and

(c) for prescribed persons to be notified of –

(i) references made under the regulations, and

(ii) determinations and directions given under the regulations.

(3) Regulations under subsection (1) must –

(a) require the PPF Ombudsman to conduct an oral hearing in relation to any reviewable matter referred to him under the regulations or to dispose of the matter on the basis of written representations,

(b) enable the PPF Ombudsman to consider evidence relating to the matter which was not available to the Board or the Reconsideration Committee, and

(c) make other provision about the procedure for conducting investigations, and reaching and giving determinations, under the regulations, including the times by which determinations are to be given.

(4) The provision that may be made by virtue of subsection (3)(c) includes provision –

(a) conferring rights on prescribed persons –

(i) to make representations to the PPF Ombudsman in relation to a reviewable matter referred to him by virtue of this section,

(ii) to be heard or represented at any oral hearing by the PPF Ombudsman in relation to such a matter,

(b) about the consideration of evidence by the PPF Ombudsman, including –

(i) production of documents,

(ii) oral hearings,

(iii) expert evidence,

(iv) attendance of witnesses,

(c) conferring rights on prescribed persons to continue a reference made by a person who has died or is otherwise unable to act for himself,

(d) as to the costs or expenses of prescribed persons,

(e) conferring rights on prescribed persons to apply for a stay (or in Scotland, for a sist) in relation to prescribed legal proceedings which begin after the reference is made and conferring power on the relevant court to make an order staying (or sisting) the proceedings if it is satisfied of prescribed matters, and

(f) for securing that any determination or direction of the PPF Ombudsman under the regulations is binding on prescribed persons.

(5) Regulations under subsection (1) may include provision –

(a) conferring power on the PPF Ombudsman to direct the Board to pay such compensation as he considers appropriate to such persons as he may direct,

(b) conferring power on the Board to make such payments,

(c) conferring power on the PPF Ombudsman to direct that –

(i) any determinations, directions or other decisions which are made by the Board in accordance with any determination or direction given by him, or

(ii) any variations, revocations or substitutions of its determinations, directions or other decisions which are made by the Board in accordance with any determination or direction given by him, are to be treated as if they were made at such time (which may be a time prior to his determination or direction) as he considers appropriate,

(d) conferring power on the PPF Ombudsman to direct that any notice varied, substituted, issued or given by the Board in accordance with any determination or direction given by him is to be treated –

(i) as if it were issued or given at such time (which may be a time prior to his determination or direction) as he considers appropriate;

(ii) as if it became binding for the purposes of this Part at the time at which he gives his determination or direction or at such later time as he considers appropriate,

(e) prescribing the circumstances in which any determination or other act of the Board in accordance with any determination or direction given by the PPF Ombudsman, is not to be treated as being a reviewable matter for the purposes of this Chapter, and

(f) conferring such other powers on the Board as may be required when a matter is remitted to it (including such powers as the Board may have on making a review decision or a reconsideration decision under regulations made under section 207(1)).

214 Investigation by PPF Ombudsman of complaints of maladministration

(1) Regulations must provide for the investigation and determination by the PPF Ombudsman of such matters as may be prescribed following decisions on relevant complaints given by the Board or the committee of the Board referred to in section 208(3)(b) under regulations made under that section.

(2) Regulations under this section must make provision –

(a) prescribing the descriptions of person who may refer matters to the PPF Ombudsman under the regulations,

(b) about the manner in which such references may be made, including the times by which they are to be made,

(c) about the procedure for conducting investigations, and reaching and giving determinations, on such references, including the times by which the determinations are to be given,

(d) about the powers of the PPF Ombudsman on making such determinations, including –

(i) the power to direct the Board to pay such compensation as he considers appropriate to such persons as he considers have sustained injustice in consequence of the matters complained of, and

(ii) the power to direct the Board to take or refrain from taking such other steps as he may specify,

(e) conferring such powers on the Board as are necessary to comply with such requirements,

(f) for prescribed persons to be notified of –

(i) references to the PPF Ombudsman under the regulations, and

(ii) determinations and directions by the PPF Ombudsman under the regulations,

(g) conferring rights on prescribed persons –

(i) to make representations to the PPF Ombudsman in relation to a matter referred to him by virtue of this section,

(ii) to be heard or represented at any oral hearing by the PPF Ombudsman in relation to such a matter,

(h) about the consideration of evidence by the PPF Ombudsman, including –

      (i)   production of documents,
      (ii) oral hearings,
      (iii) expert evidence,
      (iv) attendance of witnesses,

(i)   conferring rights on prescribed persons to continue a reference made by a person who has died or is otherwise unable to act for himself,

(j)   as to the costs or expenses of prescribed persons,

(k) conferring rights on prescribed persons to apply for a stay (or in Scotland, for a sist) in relation to prescribed legal proceedings which begin after the reference is made and conferring power on the relevant court to make an order staying (or sisting) the proceedings if it is satisfied of prescribed matters, and

(l)   for securing that any determination or direction of the PPF Ombudsman under the regulations is binding on prescribed persons.

215 Referral of questions of law

The PPF Ombudsman may refer any question of law arising for determination in connection with –

(a) a reviewable matter referred to him by virtue of regulations under section 213, or

(b) a matter referred to him by virtue of regulations under section 214,

to, in England and Wales, the High Court or, in Scotland, the Court of Session.

216 Publishing reports etc

(1) If the PPF Ombudsman considers it appropriate to do so in any particular case, he may publish in such form and manner as he considers appropriate a report of any investigation carried out by virtue of regulations under section 213 or 214 and of the result of that investigation.

(2) For the purposes of the law of defamation, the publication of any matter by the PPF Ombudsman under or by virtue of any provision of this Chapter shall be absolutely privileged.

217 Determinations of the PPF Ombudsman

(1) A person bound by a determination or direction by the PPF Ombudsman by virtue of regulations made under section 213 or 214 may appeal on a point of law arising from the determination or direction –

(a) in England and Wales, to the High Court, or

(b) in Scotland, to the Court of Session.

(2) Any determination or direction of the PPF Ombudsman is enforceable –

(a) in England and Wales, in a county court as if it were a judgment or order of that court, and

(b) in Scotland, in like manner as an extract registered decree arbitral bearing warrant for execution issued by the sheriff court of any sheriffdom in Scotland.

218 Obstruction etc of the PPF Ombudsman

(1) This section applies if any person –

(a) without lawful excuse obstructs the PPF Ombudsman in the performance of his functions, or

(b) is guilty of any act or omission in relation to an investigation by the PPF Ombudsman under regulations made under section 213 or 214, which, if that investigation were a proceeding in the court, would constitute contempt of court.

(2) The PPF Ombudsman may certify the offence to the court.

(3) Where an offence is certified under subsection (2), the court may –

(a) inquire into the matter,

(b) hear any witnesses who may be produced against or on behalf of the person charged with the offence and any statement that may be offered in defence, and

(c) deal with him in any manner in which the court could deal with him if he had committed the like offence in relation to the court.

(4) This section is to be construed, in its application to Scotland, as if contempt of court were categorised as an offence in Scots law.

(5) In this section 'the court' means –

(a) in England and Wales, a county court;

(b) in Scotland, the sheriff.

CHAPTER 7   MISCELLANEOUS

Backdating the winding up of eligible schemes

219 Backdating the winding up of eligible schemes

(1) Subsection (3) applies where –

(a) a qualifying insolvency event occurs in relation to the employer in relation to an eligible scheme, and

(b) the winding up of the scheme begins at or after the time of that event but not later than the first of the following events in relation to the scheme –

(i) a scheme failure notice or a withdrawal notice issued under section 122(2) in relation to the scheme becoming binding,

(ii) a withdrawal notice issued under section 148 in relation to the scheme becoming binding, or

(iii) a notice issued under section 122(4) becoming binding in a case where section 148 does not apply.

(2) Subsection (3) also applies where –

(a) the trustees or managers of an eligible scheme –

(i) make an application to the Board under subsection (1) of section 129, or

(ii) receive a notice from the Board under subsection (5)(a) of that section, and

(b) the winding up of the scheme begins –

(i) at or after the time the application is made or notice is received, but

(ii) not later than a scheme failure notice or a withdrawal notice issued under section 130(2) or (3) in relation to the scheme becoming binding.

(3) The winding up of the scheme is to be taken as beginning immediately before the event within subsection (1)(a) or, as the case may be, subsection (2)(a) if –

(a) the winding up is in pursuance of an order of the Regulator under section 11 of the Pensions Act 1995 (c. 26) directing the winding up of the scheme, or

(b) in any other case, the trustees or managers of the scheme so determine.

(4) In a case where subsection (3) applies, the Regulator may by order direct any person specified in the order –

(a) to take such steps as are so specified as it considers are necessary as a result of the winding up of the scheme beginning in accordance with that subsection, and

(b) to take those steps within a period specified in the order.

(5) If the trustees or managers of a scheme fail to comply with a direction to them contained in an order under subsection (4), section 10 of the Pensions Act 1995 (civil penalties) applies to any trustee or manager who has failed to take all reasonable steps to secure compliance.

(6) That section also applies to any other person who, without reasonable excuse, fails to comply with a direction to him contained in an order under subsection (4).

(7) For the purposes of this section 'qualifying insolvency event' has the same meaning as in section 127.

(8) Subsection (4) of section 128 applies for the purposes of subsection (2) of this section as it applies for the purposes of subsection (1) of that section.

(9) This section is to be read subject to section 135 (which restricts the winding up of an eligible scheme during an assessment period).

Pension sharing

220 Pension sharing

(1) Regulations may modify any of the provisions of this Part as it applies in relation to –

   (a) cases where a person's shareable rights under an eligible scheme have (at any time) become subject to a pension debit;

   (b) cases where –

      (i) a pension sharing order or provision in respect of such rights is made before the time a transfer notice under section 160 is received by the trustees or managers of the eligible scheme, and

      (ii) that order or provision takes effect on or after the receipt by them of the notice.

(2) Regulations may also modify any of the provisions of Chapter 1 of Part 4 of the Welfare Reform and Pensions Act 1999 (c. 30) (pension sharing) as it applies in relation to –

   (a) cases within subsection (1)(a) where any liability of the trustees or managers of the eligible scheme in respect of a pension credit was not discharged before the time a transfer notice under section 160 was received by the trustees or managers of the eligible scheme;

   (b) cases within subsection (1)(b).

(3) In this section –

   'pension debit' and 'shareable rights' have the same meaning as in Chapter 1 of Part 4 of the Welfare Reform and Pensions Act 1999 (c. 30) (pension sharing);

   'pension sharing order or provision' means an order or provision falling within section 28(1) of that Act (activation of pension sharing).

PART 3   SCHEME FUNDING

Introductory

221 Pension schemes to which this Part applies

(1) The provisions of this Part apply to every occupational pension scheme other than –

   (a) a money purchase scheme, or

   (b) a prescribed scheme or a scheme of a prescribed description.

(2) Regulations under subsection (1)(b) may provide for exemptions from all or any of the provisions of this Part.

Scheme funding

222 The statutory funding objective

(1) Every scheme is subject to a requirement ('the statutory funding objective') that it must have sufficient and appropriate assets to cover its technical provisions.

(2) A scheme's 'technical provisions' means the amount required, on an actuarial calculation, to make provision for the scheme's liabilities.

(3) For the purposes of this Part –

(a) the assets to be taken into account and their value shall be determined, calculated and verified in a prescribed manner, and

(b) the liabilities to be taken into account shall be determined in a prescribed manner and the scheme's technical provisions shall be calculated in accordance with any prescribed methods and assumptions.

(4) Regulations may –

(a) provide for alternative prescribed methods and assumptions,

(b) provide that it is for the trustees or managers to determine which methods and assumptions are to be used in calculating a scheme's technical provisions, and

(c) require the trustees or managers, in making their determination, to take into account prescribed matters and follow prescribed principles.

(5) Any provision of the scheme rules that limits the amount of the scheme's liabilities by reference to the value of its assets shall be disregarded.

223 Statement of funding principles

(1) The trustees or managers must prepare, and from time to time review and if necessary revise, a written statement of –

(a) their policy for securing that the statutory funding objective is met, and

(b) such other matters as may be prescribed.

This is referred to in this Part as a 'statement of funding principles'.

(2) The statement must, in particular, record any decisions by the trustees or managers as to –

(a) the methods and assumptions to be used in calculating the scheme's technical provisions, and

(b) the period within which, and manner in which, any failure to meet the statutory funding objective is to be remedied.

(3) Provision may be made by regulations –

(a) as to the period within which a statement of funding principles must be prepared, and

(b) requiring it to be reviewed, and if necessary revised, at such intervals, and on such occasions, as may be prescribed.

(4) Where any requirement of this section is not complied with, section 10 of the Pensions Act 1995 (c. 26) (civil penalties) applies to a trustee or manager who has failed to take all reasonable steps to secure compliance.

224 Actuarial valuations and reports

(1) The trustees or managers must obtain actuarial valuations –

(a) at intervals of not more than one year or, if they obtain actuarial reports for the intervening years, at intervals of not more than three years, and

(b) in such circumstances and on such other occasions as may be prescribed.

(2) In this Part –

(a) an 'actuarial valuation' means a written report, prepared and signed by the actuary, valuing the scheme's assets and calculating its technical provisions,

(b)   the effective date of an actuarial valuation is the date by reference to which the assets are valued and the technical provisions calculated,

(c)   an 'actuarial report' means a written report, prepared and signed by the actuary, on developments affecting the scheme's technical provisions since the last actuarial valuation was prepared, and

(d)   the effective date of an actuarial report is the date by reference to which the information in the report is stated.

(3)   The intervals referred to in subsection (1)(a) are between effective dates of the valuations, and –

(a)   the effective date of the first actuarial valuation must be not more than one year after the establishment of the scheme, and

(b)   the effective date of any actuarial report must be not more than one year after the effective date of the last actuarial valuation, or, if more recent, the last actuarial report.

(4)   The trustees or managers must ensure that a valuation or report obtained by them is received by them within the prescribed period after its effective date.

(5)   Nothing in this section affects any power or duty of the trustees or managers to obtain actuarial valuations or reports at more frequent intervals or in other circumstances or on other occasions.

(6)   An actuarial valuation or report (whether obtained under this section or in pursuance of any other power or duty) must be prepared in such a manner, give such information, contain such statements and satisfy such other requirements as may be prescribed.

(7)   The trustees or managers must secure that any actuarial valuation or report obtained by them (whether obtained under this section or in pursuance of any other power or duty) is made available to the employer within seven days of their receiving it.

(8)   Where subsection (1), (4) or (7) is not complied with, section 10 of the Pensions Act 1995 (c. 26) (civil penalties) applies to a trustee or manager who has failed to take all reasonable steps to secure compliance.

225   Certification of technical provisions

(1)   When an actuarial valuation is carried out, the calculation of the technical provisions must be certified by the actuary.

(2)   The certificate must state that in the opinion of the actuary the calculation is made in accordance with regulations under section 222.

(3)   If the actuary cannot give the certificate required by subsection (2) he must report the matter in writing to the Regulator within a reasonable period after the end of the period within which the valuation must be received by the trustees or managers.

Section 10 of the Pensions Act 1995 (civil penalties) applies to the actuary if he fails without reasonable excuse to comply with this subsection.

226   Recovery plan

(1)   If having obtained an actuarial valuation it appears to the trustees or managers of a scheme that the statutory funding objective was not met on the effective date of the valuation, they must, within the prescribed time –

(a)   if there is no existing recovery plan in force, prepare a recovery plan;

(b)   if there is an existing recovery plan in force, review and if necessary revise it.

(2)   A recovery plan must set out –

(a)   the steps to be taken to meet the statutory funding objective, and

(b)   the period within which that is to be achieved.

(3)   A recovery plan must comply with any prescribed requirements and must be appropriate having regard to the nature and circumstances of the scheme.

(4) In preparing or revising a recovery plan the trustees or managers must take account of prescribed matters.

(5) Provision may be made by regulations as to other circumstances in which a recovery plan may or must be reviewed and if necessary revised.

(6) The trustees or managers must, except in prescribed circumstances, send a copy of any recovery plan to the Regulator within a reasonable period after it is prepared or, as the case may be, revised.

The copy of any recovery plan sent to the Regulator must be accompanied by the prescribed information.

(7) Where any requirement of this section is not complied with, section 10 of the Pensions Act 1995 (c. 26) (civil penalties) applies to a trustee or manager who has failed to take all reasonable steps to secure compliance.

227 Schedule of contributions

(1) The trustees or managers must prepare, and from time to time review and if necessary revise, a schedule of contributions.

(2) A 'schedule of contributions' means a statement showing –

   (a) the rates of contributions payable towards the scheme by or on behalf of the employer and the active members of the scheme, and

   (b) the dates on or before which such contributions are to be paid.

(3) Provision may be made by regulations –

   (a) as to the period within which, after the establishment of a scheme, a schedule of contributions must be prepared,

   (b) requiring the schedule of contributions to be reviewed, and if necessary revised, at such intervals, and on such occasions, as may be prescribed, and

   (c) as to the period for which a schedule of contributions is to be in force.

(4) The schedule of contributions must satisfy prescribed requirements.

(5) The schedule of contributions must be certified by the actuary and –

   (a) the duty to prepare or revise the schedule is not fulfilled, and

   (b) the schedule shall not come into force,

   until it has been so certified.

(6) The certificate must state that, in the opinion of the actuary –

   (a) the schedule of contributions is consistent with the statement of funding principles, and

   (b) the rates shown in the schedule are such that –

      (i)   where the statutory funding objective was not met on the effective date of the last actuarial valuation, the statutory funding objective can be expected to be met by the end of the period specified in the recovery plan, or

      (ii) where the statutory funding objective was met on the effective date of the last actuarial valuation, the statutory funding objective can be expected to continue to be met for the period for which the schedule is to be in force.

(7) Where the statutory funding objective was not met on the effective date of the last actuarial valuation, the trustees or managers must send a copy of the schedule of contributions to the Regulator within a reasonable period after it is prepared or, as the case may be, revised.

(8) Where any requirement of the preceding provisions of this section is not complied with, section 10 of the Pensions Act 1995 (civil penalties) applies to a trustee or manager who has failed to take all reasonable steps to secure compliance.

(9) If the actuary is unable to give the certificate required by subsection (6), he must report the matter in writing to the Regulator within a reasonable period after the end of the period within which the schedule is required to be prepared or, as the case may be, revised.

Section 10 of the Pensions Act 1995 (c. 26) (civil penalties) applies to the actuary if he fails without reasonable excuse to comply with this subsection.

(10) The provisions of subsections (1), (3) and (5) to (9) above do not apply in relation to a schedule of contributions imposed by the Regulator under section 231 or, as the case may be, where such a schedule of contributions is in force.

228 Failure to make payments

(1) This section applies where an amount payable in accordance with the schedule of contributions by or on behalf of the employer or an active member of a scheme is not paid on or before the due date.

(2) If the trustees or managers have reasonable cause to believe that the failure is likely to be of material significance in the exercise by the Regulator of any of its functions, they must, except in prescribed circumstances, give notice of the failure to the Regulator and to the members within a reasonable period.

(3) The amount unpaid (whether payable by the employer or not), if not a debt due from the employer to the trustees or managers apart from this subsection, shall be treated as such a debt.

(4) Section 10 of the Pensions Act 1995 (civil penalties) applies –

   (a) where subsection (2) above is not complied with, to a trustee or manager who has failed to take all reasonable steps to secure compliance with that subsection;

   (b) to the employer if he fails without reasonable excuse to make a payment required of him –

      (i) in accordance with the schedule of contributions, or

      (ii) by virtue of subsection (3) above.

(5) This section applies in relation to a schedule of contributions imposed by the Regulator under section 231 as in relation to one agreed between the trustees or managers and the employer.

229 Matters requiring agreement of the employer

(1) The trustees or managers must obtain the agreement of the employer to –

   (a) any decision as to the methods and assumptions to be used in calculating the scheme's technical provisions (see section 222(4));

   (b) any matter to be included in the statement of funding principles (see section 223);

   (c) any provisions of a recovery plan (see section 226);

   (d) any matter to be included in the schedule of contributions (see section 227).

(2) If it appears to the trustees or managers that it is not otherwise possible to obtain the employer's agreement within the prescribed time to any such matter, they may (if the employer agrees) by resolution modify the scheme as regards the future accrual of benefits.

(3) No modification may be made under subsection (2) that on taking effect would or might adversely affect any subsisting right of –

   (a) any member of the scheme, or

   (b) any survivor of a member of the scheme.

For this purpose 'subsisting right' and 'survivor' have the meanings given by section 67A of the Pensions Act 1995 (c. 26).

(4) Any such modification must be –

   (a) recorded in writing by the trustees or managers, and

   (b) notified to the active members within one month of the modification taking effect.

(5) If the trustees or managers are unable to reach agreement with the employer within the prescribed time on any such matter as is mentioned in subsection (1), they must report the failure in writing to the Regulator within a reasonable period.

(6) Where subsection (1), (4) or (5) is not complied with, section 10 of the Pensions Act 1995 (civil penalties) applies to a trustee or manager who has failed to take all reasonable steps to secure compliance.

230 Matters on which advice of actuary must be obtained

(1) The trustees or managers must obtain the advice of the actuary before doing any of the following –

   (a) making any decision as to the methods and assumptions to be used in calculating the scheme's technical provisions (see section 222(4));
   (b) preparing or revising the statement of funding principles (see section 223);
   (c) preparing or revising a recovery plan (see section 226);
   (d) preparing or revising the schedule of contributions (see section 227);
   (e) modifying the scheme as regards the future accrual of benefits under section 229(2).

(2) Regulations may require the actuary to comply with any prescribed requirements when advising the trustees or managers of a scheme on any such matter.

(3) The regulations may require the actuary to have regard to prescribed guidance.

   'Prescribed guidance' means guidance that is prepared and from time to time revised by a prescribed body and, if the regulations so provide, is approved by the Secretary of State.

(4) Where subsection (1) is not complied with, section 10 of the Pensions Act 1995 (civil penalties) applies to a trustee or manager who has failed to take all reasonable steps to secure compliance.

231 Powers of the Regulator

(1) The powers conferred by this section are exercisable where it appears to the Regulator with respect to a scheme (as a result of a report made to it or otherwise) –

   (a) that the trustees or managers have failed to comply with the requirements of section 223 with respect to the preparation or revision of a statement of funding principles;
   (b) that the trustees or managers have failed to obtain an actuarial valuation as required by section 224(1);
   (c) that the actuary is unable, on an actuarial valuation required by section 224(1), to certify the calculation of the scheme's technical provisions;
   (d) that the trustees or managers have failed to comply with the requirements of section 226 with respect to the preparation or revision of a recovery plan;
   (e) that the trustees or managers have failed to comply with the requirements of section 227 with respect to the preparation or revision of a schedule of contributions;
   (f) that the actuary is unable to certify a schedule of contributions (see section 227(6));
   (g) that the employer has failed to make payments in accordance with the schedule of contributions, or that are required of him by virtue of section 228(3), and the failure is of material significance;
   (h) that the trustees or managers have been unable to reach agreement with the employer within the prescribed time as to a matter in relation to which such agreement is required (see section 229(5)).

(2) In any of those circumstances the Regulator may by order exercise all or any of the following powers –

(a) it may modify the scheme as regards the future accrual of benefits;

(b) it may give directions as to –

    (i) the manner in which the scheme's technical provisions are to be calculated, including the methods and assumptions to be used in calculating the scheme's technical provisions, or

    (ii) the period within which, and manner in which, any failure to meet the statutory funding objective is to be remedied;

(c) it may impose a schedule of contributions specifying –

    (i) the rates of contributions payable towards the scheme by or on behalf of the employer and the active members of the scheme, and

    (ii) the dates on or before which such contributions are to be paid.

(3) No modification may be made under subsection (2)(a) that on taking effect would or might adversely affect any subsisting right of –

(a) any member of the scheme, or

(b) any survivor of a member of the scheme.

For this purpose 'subsisting right' and 'survivor' have the meanings given by section 67A of the Pensions Act 1995.

(4) In exercising any of the powers conferred by this section the Regulator must comply with any prescribed requirements.

(5) The powers conferred by this section are in addition to any other powers exercisable by the Regulator under this Act or the Pensions Act 1995 (c. 26).

Supplementary provisions

232 Power to modify provisions of this Part

Regulations may modify the provisions of this Part as they apply in prescribed circumstances.

233 Construction as one with the Pensions Act 1995

This Part shall be construed as one with Part 1 of the Pensions Act 1995 (c. 26).

PART 4   FINANCIAL PLANNING FOR RETIREMENT

Retirement planning

234 Promoting and facilitating financial planning for retirement

(1) The Secretary of State and the Northern Ireland Department may take action for the purpose of promoting or facilitating financial planning for retirement.

(2) The action may in particular include the provision of facilities for the purpose of enabling or assisting an individual or a person authorised by him –

(a) to estimate the financial resources the individual is likely to need after his retirement;

(b) to estimate the financial resources that are likely to be available to the individual after his retirement, from pensions and other sources;

(c) to ascertain what action might be taken with a view to increasing the financial resources available to the individual after his retirement.

(3) This section does not authorise the Secretary of State or the Northern Ireland Department to take action which the Secretary of State or the Northern Ireland Department would otherwise be prohibited from taking under section 21 of the Financial Services and Markets Act 2000 (c. 8) (restrictions on financial promotion).

(4) In this section 'the Northern Ireland Department' means the Department for Social Development in Northern Ireland.

235 Supply of information for purposes of section 234

(1) This section applies to –
  (a) information which is relevant for determining the pensions and other benefits that may become payable to or in respect of an individual;
  (b) information which relates to the financial resources of, or available to, an individual;
  (c) information which relates to action taken in connection with –
      (i) providing facilities for saving (for retirement or otherwise) by individuals, or
      (ii) promoting or facilitating saving (for retirement or otherwise) by individuals.
(2) A person who holds information to which this section applies may supply it to –
  (a) the Secretary of State or the Northern Ireland Department, or
  (b) a person providing services to the Secretary of State or the Northern Ireland Department,
  for use for the purposes of functions under section 234(1).
(3) Information supplied under subsection (2) must not be supplied by the recipient except –
  (a) if the information relates to an individual –
      (i) to the individual or a person authorised by him;
      (ii) to another person, with the consent of the individual;
  (b) in any case –
      (i) to a person to whom it could be supplied under subsection (2);
      (ii) to any person with a view to the institution of relevant criminal proceedings or otherwise for the purposes of relevant criminal proceedings.
(4) In subsection (3) 'relevant criminal proceedings' means criminal proceedings under –
  (a) the Pension Schemes Act 1993 (c. 48);
  (b) the Pensions Act 1995 (c. 26);
  (c) this Act;
  (d) any enactment in force in Northern Ireland corresponding to an Act mentioned in any of paragraphs (a) to (c).
(5) In this section 'the Northern Ireland Department' means the Department for Social Development in Northern Ireland.
(6) This section is subject to sections 88 and 202 (tax information disclosed to the Regulator or the Board).

236 Use and supply of information: private pensions policy and retirement planning

Schedule 10 (which makes provision about the use and supply of information for purposes relating to private pensions policy and retirement planning) has effect.

237 Combined pension forecasts

(1) Regulations may require the trustees or managers of an occupational or personal pension scheme to provide any member of the scheme with –
  (a) the information specified in subsection (2), together with
  (b) the information specified in subsection (3).
(2) The information referred to in subsection (1)(a) is information relating to the member which –

    (a) is state pension information for the purposes of section 42 of the Child Support, Pensions and Social Security Act 2000 (c. 19),

    (b) has been disclosed to the trustees or managers under that section (or, by virtue of that section, is treated as having been so disclosed), and

    (c) is of a description specified in the regulations.

(3) The information referred to in subsection (1)(b) is information which –

    (a) relates to the pensions and other benefits likely to accrue to the member, or capable of being secured by him, under the scheme, and

    (b) is of a description specified in the regulations.

(4) Regulations under subsection (1) may require information referred to in that subsection to be provided at a time or times specified in the regulations.

Employee information and advice

238 Information and advice to employees

(1) Regulations may require employers to take action for the purpose of enabling employees to obtain information and advice about pensions and saving for retirement.

(2) Regulations under subsection (1) may in particular –

    (a) provide that they are to apply in relation to employers of a prescribed description and employees of a prescribed description;

    (b) make different provision for different descriptions of employers and employees;

    (c) make provision as to the action to be taken by employers (including the frequency at which, and the time and place at which, action is to be taken);

    (d) make provision as to the description of information and advice in relation to which requirements apply;

    (e) make provision about the description of person authorised to provide any such information and advice.

(3) Employers to whom regulations under subsection (1) apply must provide information to the Regulator about the action taken by them for the purpose of complying with the regulations.

(4) Regulations may make provision as to –

    (a) the information to be provided under subsection (3);

    (b) the form and manner in which the information is to be provided;

    (c) the period within which the information is to be provided.

(5) Section 10 of the Pensions Act 1995 (c. 26) (civil penalties) applies to any person who, without reasonable excuse, fails to comply with subsection (3).

(6) In this section 'employer' means any employer, whether or not resident or incorporated in any part of the United Kingdom.

PART 5   OCCUPATIONAL AND PERSONAL PENSION SCHEMES: MISCELLANEOUS PROVISIONS

Categories of pension scheme

239 Categories of pension scheme

(1) Section 1 of the Pension Schemes Act 1993 (c. 48) (categories of pension scheme) is amended as follows.

(2) The provisions of the section shall become subsection (1) of the section.

(3) In that subsection, for the definitions of 'occupational pension scheme' and 'personal pension scheme' substitute –

'"occupational pension scheme" means a pension scheme –

   (a)   that –

        (i)   for the purpose of providing benefits to, or in respect of, people with service in employments of a description, or

       (ii)   for that purpose and also for the purpose of providing benefits to, or in respect of, other people,

        is established by, or by persons who include, a person to whom subsection (2) applies when the scheme is established or (as the case may be) to whom that subsection would have applied when the scheme was established had that subsection then been in force, and

   (b)   that has its main administration in the United Kingdom or outside the member States,

or a pension scheme that is prescribed or is of a prescribed description;

"personal pension scheme" means a pension scheme that –

   (a)   is not an occupational pension scheme, and

   (b)   is established by a person within any of the paragraphs of section 154(1) of the Finance Act 2004;'.

(4) After that subsection insert –

'(2) This subsection applies –

   (a)   where people in employments of the description concerned are employed by someone, to a person who employs such people,

   (b)   to a person in an employment of that description, and

   (c)   to a person representing interests of a description framed so as to include –

        (i)   interests of persons who employ people in employments of the description mentioned in paragraph (a), or

       (ii)   interests of people in employments of that description.

(3) For the purposes of subsection (2), if a person is in an employment of the description concerned by reason of holding an office (including an elective office) and is entitled to remuneration for holding it, the person responsible for paying the remuneration shall be taken to employ the office-holder.

(4) In the definition in subsection (1) of "occupational pension scheme", the reference to a description includes a description framed by reference to an employment being of any of two or more kinds.

(5) In subsection (1) "pension scheme" (except in the phrases "occupational pension scheme", "personal pension scheme" and "public service pension scheme") means a scheme or other arrangements, comprised in one or more instruments or agreements, having or capable of having effect so as to provide benefits to or in respect of people –

   (a)   on retirement,

   (b)   on having reached a particular age, or

   (c)   on termination of service in an employment.

(6) The power of the Treasury under section 154(4) of the Finance Act 2004 (power to amend sections 154 and 155) includes power consequentially to amend –

   (a)   paragraph (a) of the definition in subsection (1) of "personal pension scheme", and

   (b)   any provision in force in Northern Ireland corresponding to that paragraph.'

240 Meaning of 'employer' in Part 1 of the Pensions Act 1995

(1) In section 125 of the Pensions Act 1995 (c. 26) (supplementary provision relating to interpretation), in subsection (3) (extension of meaning of 'employer') –

> (a)   after 'include' insert ' –
>
> > (a)' , and
>
> (b)   after 'scheme' insert ';
>
> > (b)   such other persons as may be prescribed'.

(2) In section 175 of that Act (parliamentary control of orders and regulations), in subsection (2) (instruments subject to affirmative resolution procedure), omit 'or' at end of paragraph (c) and after that paragraph insert –

> '(ca) section 125(3)(b), or'.

Requirements for member-nominated trustees and directors

241 Requirement for member-nominated trustees

(1) The trustees of an occupational trust scheme must secure –

> (a)   that, within a reasonable period of the commencement date, arrangements are in place which provide for at least one-third of the total number of trustees to be member-nominated trustees, and
>
> (b)   that those arrangements are implemented.

(2) 'Member-nominated trustees' are trustees of an occupational trust scheme who –

> (a)   are nominated as the result of a process in which at least the following are eligible to participate –
>
> > (i)   all the active members of the scheme or an organisation which adequately represents the active members, and
> >
> > (ii) all the pensioner members of the scheme or an organisation which adequately represents the pensioner members, and
>
> (b)   are selected as a result of a process which involves some or all of the members of the scheme.

(3) The 'commencement date', in relation to a scheme, is –

> (a)   the date upon which this section first applies in relation to the scheme, or
>
> (b)   in the case of a scheme to which this section has ceased to apply and then reapplies, the date on which the section reapplies to it.

(4) The arrangements may provide for a greater number of member-nominated trustees than that required to satisfy the one-third minimum mentioned in subsection (1)(a) only if the employer has approved the greater number.

(5) The arrangements –

> (a)   must provide for the nomination and selection process to take place within a reasonable period of any requirement arising under the arrangements to appoint a member-nominated trustee,
>
> (b)   must provide, where a vacancy is not filled because insufficient nominations are received, for the nomination and selection process to be repeated at reasonable intervals until the vacancy is filled,
>
> (c)   must provide that where the employer so requires, a person who is not a member of the scheme must have the employer's approval to qualify for selection as a member-nominated trustee, and
>
> (d)   subject to paragraph (c), may provide that, where the number of nominations received is equal to or less than the number of appointments required, the nominees are deemed to be selected.

(6)   The arrangements must provide that the removal of a member-nominated trustee requires the agreement of all the other trustees.

(7)   Nothing in the arrangements or in the provisions of the scheme may exclude member-nominated trustees from the exercise of functions exercisable by other trustees by reason only of the fact that they are member-nominated trustees.

(8)   This section does not apply in relation to an occupational trust scheme if –

(a)   every member of the scheme is a trustee of the scheme and no other person is such a trustee,

(b)   every trustee of the scheme is a company, or

(c)   the scheme is of a prescribed description.

(9)   If, in the case of an occupational trust scheme, the arrangements required by subsection (1) –

(a)   are not in place as required by subsection (1)(a), or

(b)   are not being implemented,

section 10 of the Pensions Act 1995 (c. 26) (civil penalties) applies to any trustee who has failed to take all reasonable steps to secure compliance.

242   Requirement for member-nominated directors of corporate trustees

(1)   Where a company is a trustee of an occupational trust scheme and every trustee of the scheme is a company, the company must secure –

(a)   that, within a reasonable period of the commencement date, arrangements are in place which provide for at least one-third of the total number of directors of the company to be member-nominated directors, and

(b)   that those arrangements are implemented.

(2)   'Member-nominated directors' are directors of the company in question who –

(a)   are nominated as the result of a process in which at least the following are eligible to participate –

(i)   all the active members of the occupational trust scheme or an organisation which adequately represents the active members, and

(ii)   all the pensioner members of the occupational trust scheme or an organisation which adequately represents the pensioner members, and

(b)   are selected as a result of a process which involves some or all of the members of that scheme.

(3)   The 'commencement date', in relation to a company, is –

(a)   the date upon which this section first applies in relation to the company, or

(b)   in the case of a company to which this section has ceased to apply and then reapplies, the date on which the section reapplies to it.

(4)   The arrangements may provide for a greater number of member-nominated directors than that required to satisfy the one-third minimum mentioned in subsection (1)(a) only if the employer has approved the greater number.

(5)   The arrangements –

(a)   must provide for the nomination and selection process to take place within a reasonable period of any requirement arising under the arrangements to appoint a member-nominated director,

(b)   must provide, where a vacancy is not filled because insufficient nominations are received, for the nomination and selection process to be repeated at reasonable intervals until the vacancy is filled,

(c)   must provide that where the employer so requires, a person who is not a member of the scheme must have the employer's approval to qualify for selection as a member-nominated director, and

(d) subject to paragraph (c), may provide that, where the number of nominations received is equal to or less than the number of appointments required, the nominees are deemed to be selected.

(6) The arrangements must provide that the removal of a member-nominated director requires the agreement of all the other directors.

(7) Nothing in the arrangements may exclude member-nominated directors from the exercise of functions exercisable by other directors by reason only of the fact that they are member-nominated directors.

(8) Where the same company is a trustee of two or more occupational trust schemes by reference to each of which this section applies to the company, then, subject to subsection (9), the preceding provisions of this section have effect as if –

(a) the schemes were a single scheme,

(b) the members of each of the schemes were members of that single scheme, and

(c) the references to 'the employer' were references to all the employers in relation to the schemes.

(9) Where, apart from this subsection, subsection (8) would apply in relation to a company, the company may elect that subsection (8) –

(a) is not to apply as mentioned in that subsection, or

(b) is to apply but only in relation to some of the schemes to which it would otherwise apply.

(10) This section does not apply in relation to an occupational trust scheme if the scheme is of a prescribed description.

(11) If, in the case of a company which is a trustee of an occupational trust scheme, the arrangements required by subsection (1) –

(a) are not in place as required by subsection (1)(a), or

(b) are not being implemented,

section 10 of the Pensions Act 1995 (c. 26) (civil penalties) applies to the company.

243 Member-nominated trustees and directors: supplementary

(1) The Secretary of State may, by order, amend sections 241(1)(a) and (4) and 242(1)(a) and (4) by substituting, in each of those provisions, 'one-half' for 'one-third'.

(2) Regulations may modify sections 241 and 242 (including any of the provisions mentioned in subsection (1)) in their application to prescribed cases.

(3) In sections 241 and 242 –

'company' means a company within the meaning given by section 735(1) of the Companies Act 1985 (c. 6) or a company which may be wound up under Part 5 of the Insolvency Act 1986 (c. 45) (unregistered companies);

'occupational trust scheme' means an occupational pension scheme established under a trust.

Obligations of trustees of occupational pension schemes

244 Investment principles

For section 35 of the Pensions Act 1995 (investment principles) substitute –

'35 Investment principles

(1) The trustees of a trust scheme must secure –

(a) that a statement of investment principles is prepared and maintained for the scheme, and

(b) that the statement is reviewed at such intervals, and on such occasions, as may be prescribed and, if necessary, revised.

(2)   In this section "statement of investment principles", in relation to a trust scheme, means a written statement of the investment principles governing decisions about investments for the purposes of the scheme.

(3)   Before preparing or revising a statement of investment principles, the trustees of a trust scheme must comply with any prescribed requirements.

(4)   A statement of investment principles must be in the prescribed form and cover, amongst other things, the prescribed matters.

(5)   Neither a trust scheme nor a statement of investment principles may impose restrictions (however expressed) on any power to make investments by reference to the consent of the employer.

(6)   If in the case of a trust scheme –

(a)   a statement of investment principles has not been prepared, is not being maintained or has not been reviewed or revised, as required by this section, or

(b)   the trustees have not complied with the obligation imposed on them by subsection (3),

section 10 applies to any trustee who has failed to take all reasonable steps to secure compliance.

(7)   Regulations may provide that this section is not to apply to any scheme which is of a prescribed description.'

245 Power to make regulations governing investment by trustees

(1)   Section 36 of the Pensions Act 1995 (c. 26) (choosing investments) is amended as follows.

(2)   For subsection (1) substitute –

'(1)   The trustees of a trust scheme must exercise their powers of investment in accordance with regulations and in accordance with subsections (3) and (4), and any fund manager to whom any discretion has been delegated under section 34 must exercise the discretion in accordance with regulations.

(1A) Regulations under subsection (1) may, in particular –

(a)   specify criteria to be applied in choosing investments, and

(b)   require diversification of investments.'

(3)   Omit subsection (2).

(4)   In subsection (3) for 'the matters mentioned in subsection (2) and' substitute 'the requirements of regulations under subsection (1), so far as relating to the suitability of investments, and to'.

(5)   For subsection (8) substitute –

'(8)   If the trustees of a trust scheme –

(a)   fail to comply with regulations under subsection (1), or

(b)   do not obtain and consider advice in accordance with this section,

section 10 applies to any trustee who has failed to take all reasonable steps to secure compliance.'

(6)   After subsection (8) insert –

'(9)   Regulations may exclude the application of any of the preceding provisions of this section to any scheme which is of a prescribed description.'

246 Borrowing by trustees

After section 36 of the Pensions Act 1995 insert –

'36A Restriction on borrowing by trustees

Regulations may prohibit the trustees of a trust scheme, or the fund manager to whom any discretion has been delegated under section 34, from borrowing money or acting as a guarantor, except in prescribed cases.'

247 Requirement for knowledge and understanding: individual trustees

(1) This section applies to every individual who is a trustee of an occupational pension scheme.

(2) In this section, 'relevant scheme', in relation to an individual, means any occupational pension scheme of which he is a trustee.

(3) An individual to whom this section applies must, in relation to each relevant scheme, be conversant with –

    (a)   the trust deed and rules of the scheme,

    (b)   any statement of investment principles for the time being maintained under section 35 of the Pensions Act 1995 (c. 26),

    (c)   in the case of a relevant scheme to which Part 3 (scheme funding) applies, the statement of funding principles most recently prepared or revised under section 223, and

    (d)   any other document recording policy for the time being adopted by the trustees relating to the administration of the scheme generally.

(4) An individual to whom this section applies must have knowledge and understanding of –

    (a)   the law relating to pensions and trusts,

    (b)   the principles relating to –

        (i)   the funding of occupational pension schemes, and

        (ii) investment of the assets of such schemes, and

    (c)   such other matters as may be prescribed.

(5) The degree of knowledge and understanding required by subsection (4) is that appropriate for the purposes of enabling the individual properly to exercise his functions as trustee of any relevant scheme.

248 Requirement for knowledge and understanding: corporate trustees

(1) This section applies to any company which is a trustee of an occupational pension scheme.

(2) In this section, 'relevant scheme', in relation to a company, means any occupational pension scheme of which it is a trustee.

(3) A company to which this section applies must, in relation to each relevant scheme, secure that each individual who exercises any function which the company has as trustee of the scheme is conversant with each of the documents mentioned in subsection (4) so far as it is relevant to the exercise of the function.

(4) Those documents are –

    (a)   the trust deed and rules of the scheme,

    (b)   any statement of investment principles for the time being maintained under section 35 of the Pensions Act 1995,

    (c)   in the case of a relevant scheme to which Part 3 (scheme funding) applies, the statement of funding principles most recently prepared or revised under section 223, and

    (d)   any other document recording policy for the time being adopted by the trustees relating to the administration of the scheme generally.

(5) A company to which this section applies must secure that any individual who exercises any function which the company has as trustee of any relevant scheme has knowledge and understanding of –

(a) the law relating to pensions and trusts,

(b) the principles relating to –

    (i) the funding of occupational pension schemes, and

    (ii) investment of the assets of such schemes, and

(c) such other matters as may be prescribed.

(6) The degree of knowledge and understanding required by subsection (5) is that appropriate for the purposes of enabling the individual properly to exercise the function in question.

(7) References in this section to the exercise by an individual of any function of a company are to anything done by the individual on behalf of the company which constitutes the exercise of the function by the company.

(8) In this section 'company' means a company within the meaning given by section 735(1) of the Companies Act 1985 (c. 6) or a company which may be wound up under Part 5 of the Insolvency Act 1986 (c. 45) (unregistered companies).

249 Requirement for knowledge and understanding: supplementary

(1) For the purposes of sections 247 and 248, a person's functions as trustee of a relevant scheme are any functions which he has by virtue of being such a trustee and include, in particular –

(a) any functions which he has as one of the trustees authorised under section 34(5)(a) of the Pensions Act 1995 (c. 26) (delegation of investment discretions) in the case of the scheme, and

(b) any functions which he otherwise has as a member of a committee of the trustees of the scheme.

(2) Regulations may provide for any provision in section 247 or 248 –

(a) not to apply, or

(b) to apply with modifications,

to a trustee in prescribed circumstances.

(3) Nothing in either of those sections affects any rule of law requiring a trustee to have knowledge of, or expertise in, any matter.

Payment of surplus to employer

250 Payment of surplus to employer

For section 37 of the Pensions Act 1995 (payment of surplus to employer) substitute –

'37 Payment of surplus to employer

(1) This section applies to a trust scheme if –

(a) apart from this section power is conferred on the employer or any other person to make payments to the employer out of funds held for the purposes of the scheme, and

(b) the scheme is not being wound up.

(2) Where the power referred to in subsection (1)(a) is conferred by the scheme on a person other than the trustees –

(a) it cannot be exercised by that person but may instead be exercised by the trustees, and

(b) any restriction imposed by the scheme on the exercise of the power shall, so far as capable of doing so, apply to its exercise by the trustees.

(3) The power referred to in subsection (1)(a) may only be exercised if –

(a)   the trustees have obtained a written valuation of the scheme's assets and liabilities prepared and signed by a prescribed person;

(b)   there is a certificate in force –

   (i)   stating that in the opinion of that person the prescribed requirements are met as at the date by reference to which the assets are valued and the liabilities are calculated, and

   (ii)   specifying what in the opinion of that person is the maximum amount of payment that may be made to the employer;

(c)   the payment does not exceed the maximum amount specified in the certificate;

(d)   the trustees are satisfied that it is in the interests of the members that the power is exercised in the manner proposed;

(e)   where the power is conferred by the scheme on the employer, the employer has asked for the power to be exercised, or consented to its being exercised, in the manner proposed;

(f)   there is no freezing order in force in relation to the scheme under section 23 of the Pensions Act 2004; and

(g)   notice of the proposal to exercise the power has been given, in accordance with prescribed requirements, to the members of the scheme.

(4)   Provision may be made by regulations as to –

(a)   the requirements (which may be alternative requirements) that must be met, in relation to any proposed payment to the employer out of funds held for the purposes of a scheme, with respect to the value of the scheme's assets and the amount of its liabilities;

(b)   the assets and liabilities to be taken into account for that purpose and the manner in which their value or amount is to be determined, calculated and verified;

(c)   the maximum amount of the payment that may be made to the employer, having regard to the value of the scheme's assets and the amount of its liabilities;

(d)   the giving of a certificate as to the matters mentioned in paragraphs (a) and (c); and

(e)   the period for which such a certificate is to be in force.

(5)   The trustees must also comply with any other prescribed requirements in connection with the making of a payment under this section.

(6)   If the trustees –

(a)   purport to exercise the power referred to in subsection (1)(a) without complying with the requirements of this section, or

(b)   fail to comply with any requirement of regulations under subsection (5),

section 10 applies to any of them who has failed to take all reasonable steps to secure compliance.

(7)   If a person other than the trustees purports to exercise the power referred to in subsection (1)(a), section 10 applies to him.

(8)   Regulations may provide that in prescribed circumstances this section does not apply, or applies with prescribed modifications, to schemes of a prescribed description.'

251 Payment of surplus to employer: transitional power to amend scheme

(1)   This section applies to a scheme which immediately before the commencement of section 250 was one to which section 37 of the Pensions Act 1995 (c. 26) applied (see subsection (1) of that section, as it then had effect).

(2) No payment to the employer may be made out of funds held for the purposes of the scheme except by virtue of a resolution of the trustees under this section.

This applies even if the payment is one proposed to be made in fulfilment of an agreement or arrangement entered into before the commencement of this section.

(3) Where the scheme was so expressed as (apart from section 37, as it then applied) to confer power to make payments to the employer out of funds held for the purposes of the scheme otherwise than in pursuance of proposals approved under paragraph 6(1) of Schedule 22 to the Income and Corporation Taxes Act 1988 (c. 1), the trustees may resolve that the power –

(a) shall become exercisable according to its terms, or

(b) shall become so exercisable, but only in such circumstances and subject to such conditions as may be specified in the resolution.

(4) Where the scheme was so expressed as to confer power to make payments to the employer out of funds held for the purposes of the scheme only in pursuance of proposals approved under paragraph 6(1) of Schedule 22 to the Income and Corporation Taxes Act 1988, the trustees may resolve that the power shall instead be exercisable in such circumstances and subject to such conditions as may be specified in the resolution.

(5) In either case the trustees must be satisfied that it is in the interests of the members of the scheme that the power is exercised in the manner proposed.

(6) The power conferred by subsection (3) or (4) –

(a) may not be exercised unless notice of the proposal to exercise it has been given, in accordance with prescribed requirements, to the employer and to the members of the scheme,

(b) may only be exercised once, and

(c) ceases to be exercisable five years after the commencement of this section.

(7) The exercise of any power to make payments to the employer by virtue of a resolution under this section is subject to section 37 of the Pensions Act 1995 (c. 26) as substituted by section 250.

Restrictions on payment into occupational pension schemes

252 UK-based scheme to be trust with effective rules

(1) Subsections (2) and (3) apply to an occupational pension scheme that has its main administration in the United Kingdom.

(2) If the scheme is not established under irrevocable trusts, the trustees or managers of the scheme must secure that no funding payment is accepted.

(3) If the rules stipulating –

(a) the benefits under the scheme, and

(b) any conditions subject to which benefits under the scheme accrue,

are not in force, or if those rules are not set out in writing, the trustees or managers of the scheme must secure that no funding payment is accepted.

(4) Subsection (2) or (3) does not apply to an occupational pension scheme if it is a prescribed scheme or a scheme of a prescribed description.

(5) Section 10 of the Pensions Act 1995 (civil penalties) applies to a trustee or manager of an occupational pension scheme that has its main administration in the United Kingdom if –

(a) subsection (2) or (3) requires the trustees or managers of the scheme to secure that no funding payment is accepted,

(b) a funding payment is accepted, and

(c) the trustee or manager has failed to take all reasonable steps to secure that no funding payment is accepted.

(6) In this section 'funding payment', in relation to a scheme, means a payment made to the scheme to fund benefits for, or in respect of, any or all of the members.

253 Non-European scheme to be trust with UK-resident trustee

(1) Subsections (2) and (3) apply to an occupational pension scheme that has its main administration outside the member States.

(2) An employer based in any part of the United Kingdom may cause a contribution to be paid to the scheme in respect of an employee (whether or not employed in the United Kingdom) only if the conditions in subsection (4) are satisfied at the time of payment.

(3) An employer based outside the United Kingdom may cause a contribution to be paid to the scheme in respect of an employee employed in the United Kingdom only if the conditions in subsection (4) are satisfied at the time of payment.

(4) Those conditions are –

(a) that the scheme is established under irrevocable trusts, and

(b) that a trustee of the scheme is resident in the United Kingdom.

(5) Subsection (2) or (3) does not apply to an occupational pension scheme if it is a prescribed scheme or a scheme of a prescribed description.

(6) Section 10 of the Pensions Act 1995 (c. 26) (civil penalties) applies to an employer who causes a contribution to be paid to an occupational pension scheme that has its main administration outside the member States if –

(a) subsection (2) or (3) applies in relation to the payment of the contribution,

(b) the conditions in subsection (4) are not satisfied at the time of payment, and

(c) the employer does not have a reasonable excuse for causing payment to occur at a time when those conditions are not satisfied.

(7) In this section 'based' –

(a) in relation to an employer who is a body corporate, means incorporated, and

(b) in relation to any other employer, means resident.

254 Representative of non-European scheme to be treated as trustee

(1) In the case of an occupational pension scheme that has its main administration outside the member States, a reference in pensions legislation to the trustees, or a trustee, of the scheme includes a person who is for the time being appointed by the trustees of the scheme to be a representative of the scheme for the purposes of this section.

(2) Subsection (1) does not apply to a prescribed reference.

(3) In subsection (1) 'pensions legislation' means any enactment contained in or made by virtue of –

(a) the Pension Schemes Act 1993 (c. 48),

(b) the Pensions Act 1995,

(c) Parts 1 to 4 of the Welfare Reform and Pensions Act 1999 (c. 30), or

(d) this Act.

Activities of occupational pension schemes

255 Activities of occupational pension schemes

(1) If an occupational pension scheme has its main administration in the United Kingdom, the trustees or managers of the scheme must secure that the activities of the scheme are limited to retirement-benefit activities.

(2) Subsection (1) does not apply to a scheme if it is a prescribed scheme or a scheme of a prescribed description.

(3) Section 10 of the Pensions Act 1995 (civil penalties) applies to a trustee or manager of a scheme to which subsection (1) applies if –

   (a) the scheme has activities that are not retirement-benefit activities, and

   (b) the trustee or manager has failed to take all reasonable steps to secure that the activities of the scheme are limited to retirement-benefit activities.

(4) In this section 'retirement-benefit activities' means –

   (a) operations related to retirement benefits, and

   (b) activities arising from operations related to retirement benefits.

(5) In subsection (4) 'retirement benefits' means –

   (a) benefits paid by reference to reaching, or expecting to reach, retirement, and

   (b) benefits that are supplementary to benefits within paragraph (a) and that are provided on an ancillary basis –

      (i) in the form of payments on death, disability or termination of employment, or

     (ii) in the form of support payments or services in the case of sickness, poverty or need, or death.

No indemnification for fines or civil penalties

256 No indemnification for fines or civil penalties

(1) No amount may be paid out of the assets of an occupational or personal pension scheme for the purpose of reimbursing, or providing for the reimbursement of, any trustee or manager of the scheme in respect of –

   (a) a fine imposed by way of penalty for an offence of which he is convicted, or

   (b) a penalty which he is required to pay under or by virtue of section 10 of the Pensions Act 1995 (c. 26) or section 168(4) of the Pension Schemes Act 1993 (c. 48) (civil penalties).

(2) For the purposes of subsection (1), providing for the reimbursement of a trustee or manager in respect of a fine or penalty includes (among other things) providing for the payment of premiums in respect of a policy of insurance where the risk is or includes the imposition of such a fine or the requirement to pay such a penalty.

(3) Where any amount is paid out of the assets of an occupational or personal pension scheme in contravention of this section, section 10 of the Pensions Act 1995 (civil penalties) applies to any trustee or manager who fails to take all reasonable steps to secure compliance.

(4) Where a trustee or manager of an occupational or personal pension scheme –

   (a) is reimbursed, out of the assets of the scheme or in consequence of provision for his reimbursement made out of those assets, in respect of any of the matters mentioned in subsection (1)(a) or (b), and

   (b) knows, or has reasonable grounds to believe, that he has been reimbursed as mentioned in paragraph (a),

then, unless he has taken all reasonable steps to secure that he is not so reimbursed, he is guilty of an offence.

(5) A person guilty of an offence under subsection (4) is liable –

   (a) on summary conviction, to a fine not exceeding the statutory maximum, and

   (b) on conviction on indictment, to imprisonment for a term not exceeding two years, or a fine, or both.

Pension protection on transfer of employment

257 Conditions for pension protection

(1) This section applies in relation to a person ('the employee') where –

    (a) there is a transfer of an undertaking, or part of an undertaking, to which the TUPE Regulations apply,

    (b) by virtue of the transfer the employee ceases to be employed by the transferor and becomes employed by the transferee, and

    (c) at the time immediately before the employee becomes employed by the transferee –

        (i) there is an occupational pension scheme ('the scheme') in relation to which the transferor is the employer, and

        (ii) one of subsections (2), (3) and (4) applies.

(2) This subsection applies where –

    (a) the employee is an active member of the scheme, and

    (b) if any of the benefits that may be provided under the scheme are money purchase benefits –

        (i) the transferor is required to make contributions to the scheme in respect of the employee, or

        (ii) the transferor is not so required but has made one or more such contributions.

(3) This subsection applies where –

    (a) the employee is not an active member of the scheme but is eligible to be such a member, and

    (b) if any of the benefits that may be provided under the scheme are money purchase benefits, the transferor would have been required to make contributions to the scheme in respect of the employee if the employee had been an active member of it.

(4) This subsection applies where –

    (a) the employee is not an active member of the scheme, nor eligible to be such a member, but would have been an active member of the scheme or eligible to be such a member if, after the date on which he became employed by the transferor, he had been employed by the transferor for a longer period, and

    (b) if any of the benefits that may be provided under the scheme are money purchase benefits, the transferor would have been required to make contributions to the scheme in respect of the employee if the employee had been an active member of it.

(5) For the purposes of this section, the condition in subsection (1)(c) is to be regarded as satisfied in any case where it would have been satisfied but for any action taken by the transferor by reason of the transfer.

(6) In subsection (1)(a), the reference to an undertaking, or part of an undertaking, has the same meaning as in the TUPE Regulations.

(7) In the case of a scheme which is contracted-out by virtue of section 9 of the Pension Schemes Act 1993 (c. 48), the references in subsections (2)(b), (3)(b) and (4)(b) to contributions mean contributions other than minimum payments (within the meaning of that Act).

(8) In this section –

    the 'TUPE Regulations' means the Transfer of Undertakings (Protection of Employment) Regulations 1981 (S.I. 1981/1794);

    references to the transferor include any associate of the transferor, and section 435 of the Insolvency Act 1986 (c. 45) applies for the purposes of this section as it applies for the purposes of that Act.

258 Form of protection

(1) In a case where section 257 applies, it is a condition of the employee's contract of employment with the transferee that the requirements in subsection (2) or the requirement in subsection (3) are complied with.

(2) The requirements in this subsection are that –

    (a) the transferee secures that, as from the relevant time, the employee is, or is eligible to be, an active member of an occupational pension scheme in relation to which the transferee is the employer, and

    (b) in a case where the scheme is a money purchase scheme, as from the relevant time –

        (i) the transferee makes relevant contributions to the scheme in respect of the employee, or

        (ii) if the employee is not an active member of the scheme but is eligible to be such a member, the transferee would be required to make such contributions if the employee were an active member, and

    (c) in a case where the scheme is not a money purchase scheme, as from the relevant time the scheme –

        (i) satisfies the statutory standard referred to in section 12A of the Pension Schemes Act 1993 (c. 48), or

        (ii) if regulations so provide, complies with such other requirements as may be prescribed.

(3) The requirement in this subsection is that, as from the relevant time, the transferee makes relevant contributions to a stakeholder pension scheme of which the employee is a member.

(4) The requirement in subsection (3) is for the purposes of this section to be regarded as complied with by the transferee during any period in relation to which the condition in subsection (5) is satisfied.

(5) The condition in this subsection is that the transferee has offered to make relevant contributions to a stakeholder pension scheme of which the employee is eligible to be a member (and the transferee has not withdrawn the offer).

(6) Subsection (1) does not apply in relation to a contract if or to the extent that the employee and the transferee so agree at any time after the time when the employee becomes employed by the transferee.

(7) In this section –

'the relevant time' means –

    (a) in a case where section 257 applies by virtue of the application of subsection (2) or (3) of that section, the time when the employee becomes employed by the transferee;

    (b) in a case where that section applies by virtue of the application of subsection (4) of that section, the time at which the employee would have been a member of the scheme referred to in subsection (1)(c)(i) of that section or (if earlier) would have been eligible to be such a member;

'relevant contributions' means such contributions in respect of such period or periods as may be prescribed;

'stakeholder pension scheme' means a pension scheme which is registered under section 2 of the Welfare Reform and Pensions Act 1999 (c. 30).

Consultation by employers

259 Consultation by employers: occupational pension schemes

(1) Regulations may require any prescribed person who is the employer in relation to an occupational pension scheme and who –

(a) proposes to make a prescribed decision in relation to the scheme, or

(b) has been notified by the trustees or managers of the scheme that they propose to make a prescribed decision in relation to the scheme,

to consult prescribed persons in the prescribed manner before the decision is made.

(2) Regulations may require the trustees or managers of an occupational pension scheme not to make a prescribed decision in relation to the scheme unless –

(a) they have notified the employer of the proposed decision, and

(b) they are satisfied that the employer has undertaken any consultation required by virtue of subsection (1).

(3) The validity of any decision made in relation to an occupational pension scheme is not affected by any failure to comply with regulations under this section.

(4) Section 261 contains further provisions about regulations under this section.

260 Consultation by employers: personal pension schemes

(1) Regulations may require any prescribed person who –

(a) is the employer in relation to a personal pension scheme where direct payment arrangements exist in respect of one or more members of the scheme who are his employees, and

(b) proposes to make a prescribed decision affecting the application of the direct payment arrangements in relation to those employees,

to consult prescribed persons in the prescribed manner before he makes the decision.

(2) The validity of any decision prescribed for the purposes of subsection (1)(b) is not affected by any failure to comply with regulations under this section.

(3) Section 261 contains further provisions about regulations under this section.

261 Further provisions about regulations relating to consultation

(1) In this section 'consultation regulations' means regulations under section 259 or 260.

(2) Consultation regulations may –

(a) make provision about the time to be allowed for consultation;

(b) prescribe the information which must be provided to the persons who are required to be consulted;

(c) confer a discretion on the employer in prescribed cases as to the persons who are to be consulted;

(d) make provision about the representatives the employees may have for the purposes of the regulations and the methods by which those representatives are to be selected;

(e) require or authorise the holding of ballots;

(f) amend, apply with or without modifications, or make provision similar to, any provision of the Employment Rights Act 1996 (c. 18) (including, in particular, Parts 5, 10 and 13), the Employment Tribunals Act 1996 (c. 17) or the Trade Union and Labour Relations (Consolidation) Act 1992 (c. 52);

(g) enable any requirement for consultation imposed by the regulations to be waived or relaxed by order of the Regulator;

(h) require the employer to communicate to the trustees and managers of the scheme any representations received by the employer in response to any consultation required by the regulations.

(3) Persons on whom obligations are imposed by consultation regulations, either as employers or as the trustees or managers of occupational pension schemes, must, if so required by the Regulator, provide information to the Regulator about the action taken by them for the purpose of complying with the regulations.

(4) Consultation regulations may make provision as to –

    (a) the information to be provided under subsection (3);

    (b) the form and manner in which the information is to be provided;

    (c) the period within which the information is to be provided.

(5) Nothing in consultation regulations is to be regarded as affecting any duty to consult arising otherwise than under the regulations.

Modification of pension rights

262 Modification of subsisting rights

For section 67 of the Pensions Act 1995 (c. 26) substitute –

'67 The subsisting rights provisions

(1) The subsisting rights provisions apply to any power conferred on any person by an occupational pension scheme to modify the scheme, other than a power conferred by –

    (a) a public service pension scheme, or

    (b) a prescribed scheme or a scheme of a prescribed description.

(2) Any exercise of such a power to make a regulated modification is voidable in accordance with section 67G unless the following are satisfied in respect of the modification –

    (a) in the case of each affected member –

        (i) if the modification is a protected modification, the consent requirements (see section 67B),

        (ii) if it is not, either the consent requirements or the actuarial equivalence requirements (see section 67C),

    (b) the trustee approval requirement (see section 67E), and

    (c) the reporting requirement (see section 67F).

(3) The subsisting rights provisions do not apply in relation to the exercise of a power –

    (a) for a purpose connected with debits under section 29(1) of the Welfare Reform and Pensions Act 1999, or

    (b) in a prescribed manner.

(4) References in this section and sections 67A to 67I to "the subsisting rights provisions" are to this section and those sections.

(5) Subsection (6) applies in relation to the exercise of a power to which the subsisting rights provisions apply to make a regulated modification where a member of the scheme dies before the requirements mentioned in subsection (2), so far as they apply in his case, have been complied with in respect of the modification if –

    (a) before he died he had given his consent to the modification in accordance with section 67B(4)(b), or

    (b) before he died, or before the trustees of the scheme had become aware that he had died, the trustees had complied with section 67C(4)(a), (b) and (d) in respect of the modification in his case.

(6) Any of the requirements mentioned in subsection (2), as it applies in respect of the modification –

(a) which is satisfied in the case of the member, or

(b) which would have been satisfied in his case had he not died before it was satisfied,

is to be taken to be satisfied in the case of any survivor of the member in respect of the modification.

67A The subsisting rights provisions: interpretation

(1) In the subsisting rights provisions, each of the following expressions has the meaning given to it by the following provisions of this section –

"regulated modification"

"protected modification"

"detrimental modification"

"affected member"

"subsisting right'"

"scheme rules".

(2) "Regulated modification" means a modification which is –

(a) a protected modification, or

(b) a detrimental modification,

or is both.

(3) "Protected modification" means a modification of an occupational pension scheme which –

(a) on taking effect would or might result in any subsisting right of –

(i) a member of the scheme, or

(ii) a survivor of a member of the scheme,

which is not a right or entitlement to money purchase benefits becoming, or being replaced with, a right or entitlement to money purchase benefits under the scheme rules,

(b) would or might result in a reduction in the prevailing rate of any pension in payment under the scheme rules, or

(c) is of a prescribed description.

For the purposes of paragraph (a), the reference in the definition of "money purchase benefits" in section 181(1) of the Pension Schemes Act 1993 to the widow or widower of a member of an occupational pension scheme is to be read as including any other survivor of the member.

(4) "Detrimental modification" means a modification of an occupational pension scheme which on taking effect would or might adversely affect any subsisting right of –

(a) any member of the scheme, or

(b) any survivor of a member of the scheme.

(5) A person is an "affected member" –

(a) in relation to a protected modification within paragraph (a) or (b) of subsection (3), if, at the time the modification takes effect, he is –

(i) a member of the scheme, or

(ii) a survivor of a member of the scheme,

and, on taking effect, the modification would or might affect any of his subsisting rights as mentioned in that paragraph,

    (b)   in relation to a protected modification within paragraph (c) of that subsection, if he is of a prescribed description, and

    (c)   in relation to a detrimental modification which is not a protected modification if, at the time the modification takes effect, he is –

        (i)   a member of the scheme, or

        (ii)   a survivor of a member of the scheme,

        and, on taking effect, the modification would or might adversely affect any of his subsisting rights.

(6)   "Subsisting right" means –

    (a)   in relation to a member of an occupational pension scheme, at any time –

        (i)   any right which at that time has accrued to or in respect of him to future benefits under the scheme rules, or

        (ii)   any entitlement to the present payment of a pension or other benefit which he has at that time, under the scheme rules, and

    (b)   in relation to the survivor of a member of an occupational pension scheme, at any time, any entitlement to benefits, or right to future benefits, which he has at that time under the scheme rules in respect of the member.

    For this purpose, "right" includes a pension credit right.

(7)   At any time when the pensionable service of a member of an occupational pension scheme is continuing, his subsisting rights are to be determined as if he had opted, immediately before that time, to terminate that service.

(8)   "Scheme rules", in relation to a scheme, means –

    (a)   the rules of the scheme, except so far as overridden by a relevant legislative provision,

    (b)   the relevant legislative provisions, to the extent that they have effect in relation to the scheme and are not reflected in the rules of the scheme, and

    (c)   any provision which the rules of the scheme do not contain but which the scheme must contain if it is to conform with the requirements of Chapter 1 of Part 4 of the Pension Schemes Act 1993 (preservation of benefit under occupational pension schemes).

(9)   For the purposes of subsection (8) –

    (a)   "relevant legislative provision" means any provision contained in any of the following provisions –

        (i)   Schedule 5 to the Social Security Act 1989 (equal treatment for men and women);

        (ii)   Chapters 2 to 5 of Part 4 of the Pension Schemes Act 1993 (certain protection for early leavers) or regulations made under any of those Chapters;

        (iii)   Part 4A of that Act (requirements relating to pension credit benefit) or regulations made under that Part;

        (iv)   section 110(1) of that Act (requirement as to resources for annual increase of guaranteed minimum pensions);

        (v)   this Part of this Act (occupational pensions) or subordinate legislation made or having effect as if made under this Part;

        (vi)   section 31 of the Welfare Reform and Pensions Act 1999 (pension debits: reduction of benefit);

        (vii)   any provision mentioned in section 306(2) of the Pensions Act 2004;

    (b)   a relevant legislative provision is to be taken to override any of the provisions of the scheme if, and only if, it does so by virtue of any of the following provisions –

       (i) paragraph 3 of Schedule 5 to the Social Security Act 1989;

      (ii) section 129(1) of the Pension Schemes Act 1993;

    (iii) section 117(1) of this Act;

    (iv) section 31(4) of the Welfare Reform and Pensions Act 1999;

     (v) section 306(1) of the Pensions Act 2004.

(10) For the purposes of this section –

    (a) "survivor", in relation to a member of an occupational pension scheme, means a person who –

       (i) is the widow or widower of the member, or

      (ii) has survived the member and has any entitlement to benefit, or right to future benefits, under the scheme rules in respect of the member, and

    (b) a modification would or might adversely affect a person's subsisting right if it would alter the nature or extent of the entitlement or right so that the benefits, or future benefits, to which the entitlement or right relates would or might be less generous.

(11) In the subsisting rights provisions, in relation to –

    (a) the exercise of a power to modify an occupational pension scheme to which the subsisting rights provisions apply, or

    (b) a modification made, or to be made, in exercise of such a power,

references to 'the scheme' are to be read as references to the scheme mentioned in paragraph (a).

67B The consent requirements

(1) References in the subsisting rights provisions to the consent requirements, in respect of a regulated modification, are to be read in accordance with this section.

(2) The consent requirements apply in the case of an affected member –

    (a) if the modification is a protected modification;

    (b) if it is not a protected modification, unless the actuarial equivalence requirements apply in his case.

(3) The consent requirements consist of –

    (a) the informed consent requirement (see subsection (4)), and

    (b) the timing requirement (see subsection (6)).

(4) The informed consent requirement is satisfied in the case of an affected member if before the modification is made –

    (a) the trustees have –

       (i) given him information in writing adequate to explain the nature of the modification and its effect on him,

      (ii) notified him in writing that he may make representations to the trustees about the modification,

    (iii) afforded him a reasonable opportunity to make such representations, and

    (iv) notified him in writing that the consent requirements apply in his case in respect of the modification, and

    (b) after the trustees have complied with paragraph (a)(i), (ii) and (iv), the affected member has given his consent in writing to the modification.

(5) If –

    (a) the modification is not a protected modification, and

    (b)   before the modification is made the trustees notify an affected member in writing that –

        (i)   if he gives his consent to the modification for the purposes of the consent requirements, those requirements apply in his case in respect of the modification, but

        (ii) otherwise, the actuarial equivalence requirements apply in his case in respect of the modification,

the trustees are to be taken to have complied with subsection (4)(a)(iv) in respect of him.

(6)   The timing requirement is satisfied in the case of an affected member if the modification takes effect within a reasonable period after the member has given his consent to the modification in accordance with subsection (4)(b).

67C The actuarial equivalence requirements

(1)   References in the subsisting rights provisions to the actuarial equivalence requirements, in respect of a detrimental modification which is not a protected modification, are to be read in accordance with this section and section 67D.

(2)   The actuarial equivalence requirements apply in the case of an affected member only if –

    (a)   the modification is not a protected modification, and

    (b)   the trustees of the scheme determine that they are to apply in his case.

(3)   The actuarial equivalence requirements consist of –

    (a)   the information requirement (see subsection (4)),

    (b)   the actuarial value requirement (see subsection (5)), and

    (c)   the actuarial equivalence statement requirement (see subsection (6)).

(4)   The information requirement is satisfied in the case of an affected member if before the modification is made the trustees have taken all reasonable steps to –

    (a)   give him information in writing adequate to explain the nature of the modification and its effect on him,

    (b)   notify him in writing that he may make representations to the trustees about the modification,

    (c)   afford him a reasonable opportunity to make such representations, and

    (d)   notify him in writing that the actuarial equivalence requirements apply in his case in respect of the modification.

(5)   The actuarial value requirement is satisfied in the case of an affected member if before the modification is made the trustees have made such arrangements, or taken such steps, as are adequate to secure that actuarial value will be maintained.

(6)   The actuarial equivalence statement requirement is satisfied in the case of an affected member if the trustees have, within a reasonable period beginning with the date on which the modification takes effect, obtained an actuarial equivalence statement relating to the affected member in respect of the modification.

(7)   For the purposes of subsection (6) "actuarial equivalence statement" means a statement in writing which –

    (a)   is given by –

        (i)   the actuary appointed in relation to the scheme under section 47(1)(b), or

        (ii) a person with prescribed qualifications or experience or who is approved by the Secretary of State, and

    (b)   certifies that actuarial value has been maintained.

(8) For the purposes of subsections (5) and (7) as they apply in relation to an affected member, actuarial value is maintained if the actuarial value, immediately after the time at which the modification takes effect, of the affected member's subsisting rights is equal to or greater than the actuarial value of his subsisting rights immediately before that time.

67D The actuarial equivalence requirements: further provisions

(1) This section applies for the purposes of section 67C.

(2) Where –

   (a) the information requirement has been satisfied in the case of an affected member in respect of a proposed modification ("the original modification"),

   (b) before the trustees have made a determination, or given their consent, for the purposes of section 67E(1) in relation to the original modification, the original modification has been revised, and

   (c) the modification as so revised ("the revised modification") does not differ from the original modification in any material respect,

   the information requirement is to be taken to have been satisfied in relation to the revised modification.

(3) The trustees are to be regarded as having taken all reasonable steps to notify an affected member as mentioned in section 67C(4)(d) in respect of a modification if they have taken all reasonable steps to notify him in writing that –

   (a) if he gives his consent to the modification for the purposes of the consent requirements, those requirements apply in his case in respect of the modification, but

   (b) otherwise, the actuarial equivalence requirements apply in his case in respect of the modification.

(4) Any calculation for the purposes of section 67C of the actuarial value of an affected member's subsisting rights at any time must conform with such requirements as may be prescribed.

(5) Requirements prescribed by regulations under subsection (4) may include requirements for any such calculation to be made in accordance with guidance that –

   (a) is prepared and from time to time revised by a prescribed body, and

   (b) if the regulations so provide, is approved by the Secretary of State.

(6) Nothing in subsections (6) and (7) of section 67C precludes actuarial equivalence statements relating to –

   (a) two or more affected members, or

   (b) affected members of any particular description,

   in respect of a modification being given in a single document.

67E The trustee approval requirement

(1) For the purposes of section 67(2)(b), the trustee approval requirement is satisfied in relation to the exercise of a power to make a regulated modification if –

   (a) the trustees of the scheme have determined to exercise the power to make the modification, or

   (b) if the power is exercised by another person, the trustees have consented to the exercise of the power to make the modification,

   and the making of the determination, or giving of consent, complies with subsections (2) and (3).

(2) The trustees must not make a determination, or give their consent, for the purposes of subsection (1) unless, in the case of each affected member –

(a)   if the modification is a protected modification, the informed consent requirement is satisfied (within the meaning of section 67B), or

(b)   if it is not a protected modification –

(i)   the informed consent requirement is satisfied, or

(ii)   the information and actuarial value requirements are satisfied (within the meaning of section 67C),

in respect of the modification.

(3)   The trustees must not make a determination, or give their consent, for the purposes of subsection (1) more than a reasonable period after the first consent given by an affected member under section 67B(4)(b) in respect of the modification was given.

67F   The reporting requirement

(1)   For the purposes of section 67(2)(c), the reporting requirement is satisfied in relation to the exercise of a power to which the subsisting rights provisions apply to make a regulated modification if the trustees have, in accordance with subsection (2) –

(a)   notified each affected member in whose case the consent requirements apply in respect of the modification, and

(b)   taken all reasonable steps to notify each affected member in whose case the actuarial equivalence requirements apply in respect of the modification,

that they have made a determination, or given their consent, for the purposes of section 67E(1) in relation to the exercise of the power to make the modification.

(2)   The trustees must give (or, where the actuarial equivalence requirements apply, take all reasonable steps to give) the notification –

(a)   within a reasonable period beginning with the date of the determination or giving of consent mentioned in subsection (1), and

(b)   before the date on which the modification takes effect.

67G   Powers of the Authority: voidable modifications

(1)   Subsection (2) applies in relation to a regulated modification made in exercise of a power to which the subsisting rights provisions apply which is voidable by virtue of –

(a)   section 67(2), or

(b)   section 67H(3).

(2)   The Authority may make an order declaring that subsection (6) applies in relation to the regulated modification.

(3)   An order under subsection (2) relating to a regulated modification may also declare that subsection (6) applies in relation to –

(a)   any other modification of the scheme made by the exercise of the power mentioned in subsection (1), or

(b)   the grant of any rights under the scheme (whether by virtue of the attribution of notional periods as pensionable service or otherwise) in connection with the regulated modification.

(4)   An order under subsection (2) relating to a regulated modification must specify the affected member or affected members or description of affected members in respect of whom subsection (6) applies ("the specified persons").

(5)   An order under subsection (2) relating to a regulated modification may also –

(a)   require the trustees to take, within the time specified in the order, such steps as are so specified for the purpose of giving effect to the order;

    (b)   declare that subsection (7) applies in relation to anything done by the trustees after the time at which the modification would, disregarding the order, have taken effect which –

        (i)   would not have contravened any provision of the scheme rules if the modification had taken effect at that time, but

        (ii) as a result of the modification being void to any extent by virtue of the order, would (but for that subsection) contravene such a provision.

This is without prejudice to section 174(3).

(6)   Where the Authority make an order declaring that this subsection applies in relation to a modification of a scheme, or the grant of any rights under the scheme, the modification or grant is void to the extent specified in the order, and in respect of the specified persons, as from the time when it would, disregarding the order, have taken effect.

(7)   Where, by virtue of subsection (5)(b), the Authority make an order under subsection (2) declaring that this subsection applies in relation to anything done by the trustees, that thing is to be taken, for such purposes as are specified in the order, not to have contravened any provision of the trust deed or scheme rules.

(8)   An order under subsection (2) relating to a regulated modification, or other modification, of a scheme or the grant of any rights under the scheme may be made before or after the time at which the modification or grant would, disregarding the order, have taken effect.

67H Powers of the Authority to intervene

(1)   Subsection (2) applies where the Authority have reasonable grounds to believe that a power to which the subsisting rights provisions apply –

    (a)   will be exercised, or

    (b)   has been exercised,

to make a regulated modification in circumstances where the modification will be voidable by virtue of section 67(2).

(2)   The Authority may by order –

    (a)   in a case within subsection (1)(a), direct the person on whom the power is conferred not to exercise the power to make the regulated modification;

    (b)   require the trustees to take, within the time specified in the order, such steps as are so specified for the purpose of securing that any of the requirements mentioned in section 67(2) is satisfied.

(3)   A regulated modification made in exercise of a power to which the subsisting rights provisions apply is voidable in accordance with section 67G if –

    (a)   the exercise of the power contravened an order under paragraph (a) of subsection (2), or

    (b)   the trustees fail to comply with a requirement imposed by an order under paragraph (b) of that subsection relating to any exercise of the power to make the modification.

67I Subsisting rights provisions: civil penalties

(1)   Subsections (2) and (3) apply where a regulated modification is voidable by virtue of section 67(2).

(2)   Where the modification was made by the exercise of a power –

    (a)   by the trustees of the scheme, or

    (b)   by any other person in circumstances which do not fall within subsection (3),

section 10 applies to any trustee who has failed to take all reasonable steps to secure that the modification is not so voidable.

(3) Section 10 applies to any person other than the trustees of the scheme who, without reasonable excuse, exercises a power to make the modification if –

    (a) the trustees have not given their consent, for the purposes of section 67E(1), to the exercise of the power to make the modification, or

    (b) in the case of any affected member, the timing requirement is not satisfied (within the meaning of section 67B) in respect of the modification.

(4) Where the trustees fail to comply with any requirement imposed, by virtue of subsection (5)(a) of section 67G, by an order under subsection (2) of that section, section 10 applies to any trustee who has failed to take all reasonable steps to secure such compliance.

(5) Where a regulated modification is made by the exercise of a power in contravention of an order under section 67H(2)(a) –

    (a) if the power is exercised by the trustees, section 10 applies to any trustee who has failed to take all reasonable steps to secure that the order was not contravened;

    (b) section 10 applies to any other person who without reasonable excuse exercises the power in contravention of the order.

(6) Where the trustees fail to comply with any requirement specified in an order under section 67H(2)(b), section 10 applies to any trustee who has failed to take all reasonable steps to secure such compliance.'

Short service benefit

263 Increase in age at which short service benefit must be payable

(1) In section 71 of the Pension Schemes Act 1993 (c. 48) (basic principle as to short service benefit), for subsection (3) substitute –

'(3) Subject to subsection (4), short service benefit must be made payable as from an age which is no greater than –

    (a) the age of 65, or

    (b) if in the member's case normal pension age is greater than 65, normal pension age.'

(2) In section 72 of that Act (no discrimination between short service and long service beneficiaries), at the end add –

'(4) This section is subject to subsections (3) and (6) of section 71 (age at which short service benefit is to be payable).'

Early leavers

264 Early leavers: cash transfer sums and contribution refunds

After section 101 of the Pension Schemes Act 1993 insert –

'CHAPTER 5   EARLY LEAVERS: CASH TRANSFER SUMS AND CONTRIBUTION REFUNDS

101AA Scope of Chapter 5

(1) This Chapter applies to any member of an occupational pension scheme to which Chapter 1 applies (see section 69(3)) if –

(a) his pensionable service terminates before he attains normal pension age, and

(b) on the date on which his pensionable service terminates –

(i) the three month condition is satisfied, but

(ii) he does not have relevant accrued rights to benefit under the scheme.

(2) For the purposes of subsection (1), the three month condition is that the period of the member's pensionable service under the scheme, taken together with –

(a) any previous period of his pensionable service under the scheme, and

(b) any period throughout which he was employed in linked qualifying service under another scheme,

amounts to at least three months.

(3) A period counts for the purposes of paragraph (a) or (b) of subsection (2) only so far as it counts towards qualification for long service benefit within the meaning of Chapter 1.

(4) For the purposes of subsection (1), "relevant accrued rights to benefit under the scheme", in relation to a member of a scheme, means rights which –

(a) have accrued to or in respect of him under the scheme, and

(b) entitle him to the relevant benefits which would have accrued to or in respect of him under the applicable rules if paragraphs (a) and (b) of section 71(1) (and the word "and" immediately preceding them) did not have effect.

(5) References in the following provisions of this Chapter to a member, in relation to an occupational pension scheme, are to a member of the scheme to whom this Chapter applies.

101AB Right to cash transfer sum and contribution refund

(1) On the termination of his pensionable service, a member of an occupational pension scheme acquires a right to whichever one he elects of the following options –

(a) a cash transfer sum;

(b) a contribution refund.

(2) Subsection (1) is subject to the following provisions of this Chapter.

(3) In this Chapter "cash transfer sum" means, in relation to a member of an occupational pension scheme, the cash equivalent, at the date on which his pensionable service terminates, of the benefits mentioned in section 101AA(4)(b).

(4) In this Chapter, "contribution refund" means, in relation to a member of an occupational pension scheme, a sum representing the aggregate of –

(a) the member's employee contributions to the scheme, and

(b) where transfer credits have been allowed to the member under the scheme by virtue of a payment ("the transfer payment") made by the trustees or managers of another occupational pension scheme, the member's employee contributions to that other scheme, so far as they –

(i) relate to the transfer payment, and

(ii) do not, in aggregate, exceed the amount of the transfer payment.

(5) In subsection (4), "employee contributions" means, in relation to a member of an occupational pension scheme, contributions made to the scheme by or on behalf of the member on his own account, but does not include –

(a) a transfer payment by virtue of which transfer credits have been allowed to the member under the scheme, or

(b) any pension credit or amount paid to the scheme which is attributable (directly or indirectly) to a pension credit.

101AC Notification of right to cash transfer sum or contribution refund

(1) This section applies where the pensionable service of a member of an occupational pension scheme has terminated.

(2) The trustees or managers of the scheme must –

(a) within a reasonable period after the termination give the member a statement in writing containing information adequate to explain –

(i) the nature of the right acquired by him under section 101AB, and

(ii) how he may exercise the right,

and such other information as may be prescribed, and

(b) afford the member a reasonable period after giving him that statement within which to exercise the right.

(3) The statement given under subsection (2)(a) must specify, in particular –

(a) in relation to the cash transfer sum to which the member acquires a right under section 101AB, its amount and the permitted ways in which the member can use it,

(b) the amount of the contribution refund to which the member so acquires a right, and

(c) the last day on which the member may, disregarding section 101AI(2), exercise the right ("the reply date").

(4) Information which may be prescribed under subsection (2)(a) includes, in particular –

(a) information about any tax liability in respect of, or deduction required or permitted to be made from, the cash transfer sum or contribution refund, and

(b) information about the effect on other rights of the member (whether under the applicable rules or otherwise) of exercising the right.

(5) The trustees or managers may notify the member that, if he does not exercise the right mentioned in subsection (2)(a)(i) on or before the reply date, the trustees or managers will be entitled to pay the contribution refund to him.

(6) Where the trustees or managers of the scheme fail to comply with subsection (2), section 10 of the Pensions Act 1995 (civil penalties) applies to any trustee or manager who has failed to take all reasonable steps to secure compliance.

101AD Exercise of right under section 101AB

(1) This section applies where a member of an occupational pension scheme acquires a right under section 101AB.

(2) The member may exercise the right by giving a notice in writing to that effect to the trustees or managers stating –

(a) which of the options under section 101AB(1) he elects, and

(b) if he elects for the cash transfer sum, the permitted way in which he requires that sum to be used.

(3) The notice under subsection (2) must be given on or before –

(a) the reply date, or

(b) such later date as the trustees or managers may allow in his case under section 101AI(2).

101AE Permitted ways of using cash transfer sum

(1) This section applies in relation to a cash transfer sum to which a member of an occupational pension scheme acquires a right under section 101AB.

(2) The ways in which the cash transfer sum may be used are –

(a) for acquiring transfer credits allowed under the rules of another occupational pension scheme –

 (i) whose trustees or managers are able and willing to accept the cash transfer sum, and

 (ii) which satisfies prescribed requirements,

(b) for acquiring rights allowed under the rules of a personal pension scheme –

 (i) whose trustees or managers are able and willing to accept the cash transfer sum, and

 (ii) which satisfies prescribed requirements,

(c) for purchasing one or more appropriate annuities,

(d) in such circumstances as may be prescribed, for subscribing to other pension arrangements which satisfy prescribed requirements.

(3) For the purposes of subsection (2), "appropriate annuity" means an annuity which satisfies prescribed requirements and is purchased from an insurer who –

(a) falls within section 19(4)(a),

(b) is chosen by the member, and

(c) is willing to accept payment on account of the member from the trustees or managers of the scheme.

101AF Calculation of cash transfer sum and contribution refund

(1) Cash transfer sums are to be calculated and verified in the prescribed manner.

(2) Any calculation of a contribution refund must conform with such requirements as may be prescribed.

(3) Regulations may provide –

(a) for amounts to be deducted in respect of administrative costs in calculating cash transfer sums;

(b) for a cash transfer sum or contribution refund to be increased or reduced in prescribed circumstances.

(4) The circumstances that may be prescribed under subsection (3)(b) include in particular –

(a) a failure by the trustees or managers of the scheme to comply with section 101AG(2) or (4) in relation to the cash transfer sum or contribution refund, and

(b) the state of funding of the scheme.

(5) Regulations under subsection (3)(b) may provide –

(a) for a cash transfer sum to be reduced so that the member has no right to have any amount paid by way of cash transfer sum in respect of him;

(b) for a contribution refund to be reduced so that the member has no right to receive any amount by way of contribution refund under this Chapter.

101AG Duties of trustees or managers following exercise of right

(1) This section applies where a member of an occupational pension scheme has exercised a right under section 101AB in accordance with section 101AD.

(2) Where the member has elected for the cash transfer sum, the trustees or managers of the scheme must, within a reasonable period beginning with the date on which the right was exercised, do what is needed to carry out the requirement specified in the member's notice under section 101AD(2)(b).

(3) When the trustees or managers have done what is needed to carry out that requirement, they are discharged from any obligation –

(a)   in respect of any rights (including conditional rights) of, or in respect of, the member to relevant benefits under the applicable rules, and

(b)   to make any other payment by way of refund to or in respect of the member of, or in respect of –

(i)   the contributions, or any payment, mentioned in section 101AB(4), or

(ii)   any other contributions made to the scheme, or any other scheme, in respect of the member (other than any pension credit or amount attributable (directly or indirectly) to a pension credit).

(4)   Where the member has elected for the contribution refund, the trustees or managers of the scheme must, within a reasonable period beginning with the date on which the right was exercised, do what is needed to secure that the amount of the contribution refund is paid to the member or as he directs.

(5)   When the trustees or managers have done what is needed to secure the payment of the contribution refund as mentioned in subsection (4) –

(a)   they are discharged from any obligation in respect of any rights (including conditional rights) of, or in respect of, the member to relevant benefits under the applicable rules, and

(b)   if they are required under the applicable rules, or determine in accordance with those rules, to make any payment ("the refund payment") by way of refund to or in respect of the member of, or in respect of –

(i)   the contributions, or any payment, mentioned in section 101AB(4), or

(ii)   any other contributions made to the scheme, or any other scheme, in respect of the member (other than any pension credit or amount attributable (directly or indirectly) to a pension credit),

the amount of the contribution refund may be set off against the refund payment.

(6)   Where the trustees or managers fail to comply with subsection (2) or (4), section 10 of the Pensions Act 1995 (civil penalties) applies to any trustee or manager who has failed to take all reasonable steps to secure compliance.

101AH Powers of trustees or managers where right not exercised

(1)   This section applies where –

(a)   a member of an occupational pension scheme does not exercise a right acquired by him under section 101AB on or before the reply date or such later date as the trustees or managers of the scheme allow in his case under section 101AI(2), and

(b)   the trustees or managers of the scheme have notified the member as mentioned in section 101AC(5).

(2)   The trustees or managers may within a reasonable period beginning with –

(a)   the reply date, or

(b)   if a later date has been allowed as mentioned in subsection (1), that later date,

pay the contribution refund to the member.

(3)   When the trustees or managers have paid the contribution refund to the member –

(a)   they are discharged from any obligation in respect of any rights (including conditional rights) of, or in respect of, the member to relevant benefits under the applicable rules, and

(b)   if they are required under the applicable rules, or determine in accordance with those rules, to make any payment ("the refund payment") by way of refund to or in respect of the member of, or in respect of –

(i)   the contributions, or any payment, mentioned in section 101AB(4), or

(ii) any other contributions made to the scheme, or any other scheme, in respect of the member (other than any pension credit or amount attributable (directly or indirectly) to a pension credit),

the amount of the contribution refund may be set off against the refund payment.

101AI   Rights under section 101AB: further provision

(1) A member of an occupational pension scheme loses any right acquired by him under section 101AB –

(a)   if the scheme is wound up, or

(b)   subject to subsection (2), if he fails to exercise the right on or before the reply date.

(2) If the member has failed to exercise any such right on or before the reply date, the trustees or managers of the scheme may allow him to exercise it on or before such later date as they may determine on the application of the member.

(3) Where the trustees or managers determine a later date under subsection (2) –

(a)   they must give a notice in writing to that effect to the member, and

(b)   subsection (1)(b) applies in relation to the member as if the reference to the reply date were a reference to the later date.

(4) For the purposes of subsection (3) and sections 101AC(2) and 101AD(2), a document or notice may be given to a person –

(a)   by delivering it to him,

(b)   by leaving it at his proper address, or

(c)   by sending it by post to him at that address.

(5) For the purposes of subsection (4), and section 7 of the Interpretation Act 1978 (service of documents by post) in its application to that subsection, the proper address of a person is –

(a)   in the case of a body corporate, the address of the registered or principal office of the body, and

(b)   in any other case, the last known address of the person.

(6) This Chapter is subject to any provision made by or under section 61 (deduction of contributions equivalent premium from refund of scheme contributions) –

(a)   permitting any amount to be deducted from any payment of a contribution refund, or

(b)   requiring the payment of a contribution refund to be delayed.

(7) In this Chapter, except where the context otherwise requires, the following expressions have the following meanings –

"the applicable rules" means –

(a)   the rules of the scheme, except so far as overridden by a relevant legislative provision,

(b)   the relevant legislative provisions, to the extent that they have effect in relation to the scheme and are not reflected in the rules of the scheme, and

(c)   any provision which the rules of the scheme do not contain but which the scheme must contain if it is to conform with the requirements of Chapter 1 of this Part;

"member" has the meaning given in section 101AA(5);

"permitted way", in relation to a cash transfer sum, means any of the ways specified in section 101AE(2) in which the sum may be used;

"relevant benefits" means benefits which are not attributable (directly or indirectly) to a pension credit;

"reply date" in relation to a member whose pensionable service has terminated, has the meaning given in section 101AC(3)(c).

(8) For the purposes of subsection (7) –

(a) "relevant legislative provision" means any provision contained in any of the following provisions –

(i) Schedule 5 to the Social Security Act 1989 (equal treatment for men and women);

(ii) this Chapter or Chapter 2, 3 or 4 of this Part of this Act or regulations made under this Chapter or any of those Chapters;

(iii) Part 4A of this Act or regulations made under that Part;

(iv) section 110(1) of this Act;

(v) Part 1 of the Pensions Act 1995 (occupational pensions) or subordinate legislation made or having effect as if made under that Part;

(vi) section 31 of the Welfare Reform and Pensions Act 1999 (pension debits: reduction of benefit);

(vii) any provision mentioned in section 306(2) of the Pensions Act 2004;

(b) a relevant legislative provision is to be taken to override any of the provisions of the scheme if, and only if, it does so by virtue of any of the following provisions –

(i) paragraph 3 of Schedule 5 to the Social Security Act 1989;

(ii) section 129(1) of this Act;

(iii) section 117(1) of the Pensions Act 1995;

(iv) section 31(4) of the Welfare Reform and Pensions Act 1999;

(v) section 306(1) of the Pensions Act 2004.'

Safeguarding pension rights

265 Paternity leave and adoption leave

(1) In Schedule 5 to the Social Security Act 1989 (c. 24) (employment-related schemes for pensions or other benefits: equal treatment), after paragraph 5 insert –

'5A Unfair paternity leave provisions

(1) Where an employment-related benefit scheme includes any unfair paternity leave provisions (irrespective of any differences on the basis of sex in the treatment accorded to members under those provisions), then –

(a) the scheme shall be regarded to that extent as not complying with the principle of equal treatment; and

(b) subject to sub-paragraph (3), this Schedule shall apply accordingly.

(2) In this paragraph "unfair paternity leave provisions", in relation to an employment-related benefit scheme, means any provision –

(a) which relates to continuing membership of, or the accrual of rights under, the scheme during any period of paid paternity leave in the case of any member who is (or who, immediately before the commencement of such a period, was) an employed earner and which treats such a member otherwise than in accordance with the normal employment requirement; or

(b) which requires the amount of any benefit payable under the scheme to or in respect of any such member, to the extent that it falls to be determined by reference to earnings during a period which included a period of paid paternity leave, to be determined otherwise than in accordance with the normal employment requirement.

(3) In the case of any unfair paternity leave provision –

    (a)   the more favourable treatment required by paragraph 3(1) is treatment no less favourable than would be accorded to the member in accordance with the normal employment requirement; and

    (b)   paragraph 3(2) does not authorise the making of any such election as is there mentioned;

but, in respect of any period of paid paternity leave, a member shall only be required to pay contributions on the amount of contractual remuneration or statutory paternity pay actually paid to or for him in respect of that period.

(4) In this paragraph –

"period of paid paternity leave", in the case of a member, means a period –

    (a)   throughout which the member is absent from work in circumstances where sub-paragraph (5), (6) or (7) applies, and

    (b)   for which the employer (or if he is no longer in his employment, his former employer) pays him any contractual remuneration or statutory paternity pay; and

"the normal employment requirement" is the requirement that any period of paid paternity leave shall be treated as if it were a period throughout which the member in question works normally and receives the remuneration likely to be paid for doing so.

(5) This sub-paragraph applies if –

    (a)   the member's absence from work is due to the birth or expected birth of a child, and

    (b)   the member satisfies the conditions prescribed under section 171ZA(2)(a)(i) and (ii) of the Social Security Contributions and Benefits Act 1992 in relation to that child.

(6) This sub-paragraph applies if –

    (a)   the member's absence from work is due to the placement or expected placement of a child for adoption under the law of any part of the United Kingdom, and

    (b)   the member satisfies the conditions prescribed under section 171ZB(2)(a)(i) and (ii) of that Act in relation to that child.

(7) This sub-paragraph applies if –

    (a)   the member's absence from work is due to the adoption or expected adoption of a child who has entered the United Kingdom in connection with or for the purposes of adoption which does not involve the placement of the child for adoption under the law of any part of the United Kingdom, and

    (b)   the member satisfies the conditions prescribed under section 171ZB(2)(a)(i) and (ii) of that Act (as applied by virtue of section 171ZK of that Act (adoption cases not involving placement under the law of the United Kingdom)) in relation to that child.

5B Unfair adoption leave provisions

(1) Where an employment-related benefit scheme includes any unfair adoption leave provisions (irrespective of any differences on the basis of sex in the treatment accorded to members under those provisions), then –

    (a)   the scheme shall be regarded to that extent as not complying with the principle of equal treatment; and

     (b)   subject to sub-paragraph (3), this Schedule shall apply accordingly.

(2) In this paragraph "unfair adoption leave provisions", in relation to an employment-related benefit scheme, means any provision –

     (a)   which relates to continuing membership of, or the accrual of rights under, the scheme during any period of paid adoption leave in the case of any member who is (or who, immediately before the commencement of such a period, was) an employed earner and which treats such a member otherwise than in accordance with the normal employment requirement; or

     (b)   which requires the amount of any benefit payable under the scheme to or in respect of any such member, to the extent that it falls to be determined by reference to earnings during a period which included a period of paid adoption leave, to be determined otherwise than in accordance with the normal employment requirement.

(3) In the case of any unfair adoption leave provision –

     (a)   the more favourable treatment required by paragraph 3(1) is treatment no less favourable than would be accorded to the member in accordance with the normal employment requirement; and

     (b)   paragraph 3(2) does not authorise the making of any such election as is there mentioned;

but, in respect of any period of paid adoption leave, a member shall only be required to pay contributions on the amount of contractual remuneration or statutory adoption pay actually paid to or for him in respect of that period.

(4) In this paragraph –

"period of paid adoption leave", in the case of a member, means a period –

     (a)   throughout which the member is absent from work in circumstances where sub-paragraph (5) or (6) applies, and

     (b)   for which the employer (or, if he is no longer in his employment, his former employer) pays him any contractual remuneration or statutory adoption pay; and

"the normal employment requirement" is the requirement that any period of paid adoption leave shall be treated as if it were a period throughout which the member in question works normally and receives the remuneration likely to be paid for doing so.

(5) This sub-paragraph applies if –

     (a)   the member's absence from work is due to the placement, or expected placement, of a child for adoption under the law of any part of the United Kingdom, and

     (b)   the member is a person with whom the child is, or is expected to be, placed for such adoption.

(6) This sub-paragraph applies if –

     (a)   the member's absence from work is due to the adoption or expected adoption of a child who has entered the United Kingdom in connection with or for the purposes of adoption which does not involve the placement of the child for adoption under the law of any part of the United Kingdom, and

     (b)   the member is a person by whom the child has been or is expected to be adopted.'

(2) The provision that may be made under section 142(1) of the Adoption and Children Act 2002 (c. 38) (power to make consequential etc provision to give full effect to any provision of that Act) includes provision modifying paragraph 5A or 5B of Schedule 5 to the Social Security Act 1989 (c. 24) (as inserted by subsection (1) above).

266 Inalienability of occupational pension

(1) Section 91 of the Pensions Act 1995 (c. 26) (inalienability of occupational pension) is amended as follows.

(2) In subsection (5) (exceptions to the rule of inalienability) at the end insert –

'(f) subject to subsection (6), a charge or lien on, or set-off against, the person in question's entitlement, or right, for the purpose of discharging some monetary obligation due from the person in question to the scheme arising out of a payment made in error in respect of the pension.'

(3) In subsection (6) (limits on the charge, lien or set-off under subsection (5)(d) or (e)) for 'or (e)' substitute ', (e) or (f)'.

Voluntary contributions

267 Voluntary contributions

(1) Omit section 111 of the Pension Schemes Act 1993 (c. 48) (requirements for schemes to provide facilities for members to pay voluntary contributions, and relating to any such contributions).

(2) In section 132 of that Act (duty to bring schemes into conformity with indirectly-applying requirements) omit from 'or the voluntary' to third 'requirements'.

(3) In section 181(1) of that Act (general interpretation) omit the definition of 'voluntary contributions requirements'.

Payments by employers

268 Payments made by employers to personal pension schemes

(1) Section 111A of the Pension Schemes Act 1993 (c. 48) (monitoring of employers' payments to personal pension schemes) is amended as follows.

(2) For subsections (3) to (7) substitute –

'(3) The trustees or managers of the scheme must monitor the payment of contributions by or on behalf of the employer under the direct payment arrangements.

(4) The trustees or managers may request the employer to provide them, (or arrange for them to be provided) with the payment information specified in the request.

(5) For the purposes of subsection (4) "payment information" is information required by the trustees or managers to enable them to discharge the duty imposed by subsection (3).

(6) The employer must comply with a request under subsection (4) within a reasonable period.

(7) Where, as a result of the employer's failure to so comply, the trustees or managers are unable to discharge the duty imposed by subsection (3), they must give notice to that effect to the Regulatory Authority within a reasonable period.

(7A) Where –

(a) a contribution payable under the direct payment arrangements has not been paid on or before its due date, and

(b) the trustees or managers have reasonable cause to believe that the failure to pay the contribution is likely to be of material significance in the exercise by the Regulatory Authority of any of their functions,

they must give notice to that effect to the Regulatory Authority and the employee within a reasonable period after the due date.'

(3) In subsection (8) (employer's liability for civil penalties) for 'subsection (3) or (5)' substitute 'subsection (6) and as a result the trustees or managers of the scheme are unable to discharge the duty imposed by subsection (3)'.

(4) In subsection (9) (liability of trustees or managers for civil penalties) for 'subsection (6) or (7)' substitute 'subsection (7) or (7A)'.

269 Payments made by employers and members to occupational pension schemes

(1) In section 49 of the Pensions Act 1995 (c. 26) (other responsibilities of trustees, employers, etc), in subsection (9) (duty of trustee etc to report a failure by employer to pay contributions deducted from earnings on time) for paragraph (b) substitute –

'(b) if the trustees or managers have reasonable cause to believe that the failure is likely to be of material significance in the exercise by the Authority of any of their functions, they must, except in prescribed circumstances, give notice of the failure to the Authority and the member within a reasonable period after the end of the prescribed period under subsection (8).'

(2) In section 88 of that Act (schedules of payments to money purchase schemes), for subsection (1) (duty of trustees or managers to report a failure to pay amounts on time) substitute –

'(1) Where, in the case of an occupational pension scheme to which section 87 applies –

(a) there is a failure to pay on or before the due date any amounts payable in accordance with the payment schedule, and

(b) the trustees or managers have reasonable cause to believe that the failure is likely to be of material significance in the exercise by the Authority of any of their functions,

they must, except in prescribed circumstances, give notice of the failure to the Authority and to the members of the scheme within a reasonable period after the due date.'

Winding up

270 Winding up

(1) For section 73 of the Pensions Act 1995 (c. 26) (preferential liabilities on winding up) substitute –

'73 Preferential liabilities on winding up

(1) This section applies where an occupational pension scheme to which this section applies is being wound up to determine the order in which the assets of the scheme are to be applied towards satisfying the liabilities of the scheme in respect of pensions and other benefits.

(2) This section applies to an occupational pension scheme other than a scheme which is –

(a) a money purchase scheme, or

(b) a prescribed scheme or a scheme of a prescribed description.

(3) The assets of the scheme must be applied first towards satisfying the amounts of the liabilities mentioned in subsection (4) and, if the assets are insufficient to satisfy those amounts in full, then –

(a) the assets must be applied first towards satisfying the amounts of the liabilities mentioned in earlier paragraphs of subsection (4) before the amounts of the liabilities mentioned in later paragraphs, and

(b) where the amounts of the liabilities mentioned in one of those paragraphs cannot be satisfied in full, those amounts must be satisfied in the same proportions.

(4) The liabilities referred to in subsection (3) are –

    (a)   where –

        (i)   the trustees or managers of the scheme are entitled to benefits under a relevant pre-1997 contract of insurance entered into in relation to the scheme, and

        (ii) either that contract may not be surrendered or the amount payable on surrender does not exceed the liability secured by the contract,

        the liability so secured;

    (b)   any liability for pensions or other benefits to the extent that the amount of the liability does not exceed the corresponding PPF liability, other than a liability within paragraph (a);

    (c)   any liability for pensions or other benefits which, in the opinion of the trustees or managers, are derived from the payment by any member of voluntary contributions, other than a liability within paragraph (a) or (b);

    (d)   any other liability in respect of pensions or other benefits.

(5)   For the purposes of subsection (4) –

"corresponding PPF liability" in relation to any liability for pensions or other benefits means –

    (a)   where the liability is to a member of the scheme, the cost of securing benefits for or in respect of the member corresponding to the compensation which would be payable to or in respect of the member in accordance with the pension compensation provisions if the Board of the Pension Protection Fund assumed responsibility for the scheme in accordance with Chapter 3 of Part 2 of the Pensions Act 2004 (pension protection), and

    (b)   where the liability is to another person in respect of a member of the scheme, the cost of securing benefits for that person corresponding to the compensation which would be payable to that person in respect of the member in accordance with the pension compensation provisions if the Board assumed responsibility for the scheme in accordance with that Chapter;

"relevant pre-1997 contract of insurance" means a contract of insurance which was entered into before 6th April 1997 with a view to securing the whole or part of the scheme's liability for –

    (a)   any pension or other benefit payable to or in respect of one particular person whose entitlement to payment of a pension or other benefit has arisen, and

    (b)   any benefit which will be payable in respect of that person on his death.

(6)   For the purposes of this section, when determining the corresponding PPF liability in relation to any liability of a scheme to, or in respect of, a member for pensions or other benefits, the pension compensation provisions apply with such modifications as may be prescribed.

(7)   Regulations may modify subsection (4).

(8)   For the purposes of that subsection –

    (a)   regulations may prescribe how it is to be determined whether a liability for pensions or other benefits which, in the opinion of the trustees or managers of the scheme, are derived from the payment by any member of voluntary contributions falls within paragraph (a) or (b) of that subsection;

    (b)   no pension or other benefit which is attributable (directly or indirectly) to a pension credit is to be regarded for the purposes of paragraph (c) of that subsection as derived from the payment of voluntary contributions.

(9)   Where, on the commencement of the winding up period, a member becomes a person to whom Chapter 5 of Part 4 of the Pension Schemes Act 1993 (early

leavers: cash transfer sums and contribution refunds) applies, that Chapter applies in relation to him with such modifications as may be prescribed.

(10) For the purposes of this section –

"assets" of a scheme to which this section applies do not include any assets representing the value of any rights in respect of money purchase benefits under the scheme rules;

"liabilities" of such a scheme do not include any liabilities in respect of money purchase benefits under the scheme rules;

"the pension compensation provisions" has the same meaning as in Part 2 of the Pensions Act 2004 (see section 162 of that Act);

"scheme rules" has the same meaning as in the Pensions Act 2004 (see section 318 of that Act);

"winding up period", in relation to an occupational pension scheme to which this section applies, means the period which –

(a) begins with the day on which the time immediately after the beginning of the winding up of the scheme falls, and

(b) ends when the winding up of the scheme is completed.

73A Operation of scheme during winding up period

(1) This section applies where an occupational pension scheme to which section 73 applies is being wound up.

(2) During the winding up period, the trustees or managers of the scheme –

(a) must secure that any pensions or other benefits (other than money purchase benefits) paid to or in respect of a member are reduced, so far as necessary, to reflect the liabilities of the scheme to or in respect of the member which will be satisfied in accordance with section 73, and

(b) may, for the purposes of paragraph (a), take such steps as they consider appropriate (including steps adjusting future payments) to recover any overpayment or pay any shortfall.

(3) During the winding up period –

(a) no benefits may accrue under the scheme rules to, or in respect of, members of the scheme, and

(b) no new members of any class may be admitted to the scheme.

(4) Subsection (3) does not prevent any increase, in a benefit, which would otherwise accrue in accordance with the scheme or any enactment.

(5) Subsection (3) does not prevent the accrual of money purchase benefits to the extent that they are derived from income or capital gains arising from the investment of payments which are made by, or in respect of, a member of the scheme.

(6) Where a person is entitled to a pension credit derived from another person's shareable rights under the scheme, subsection (3) does not prevent the trustees or managers of the scheme discharging their liability in respect of the credit under Chapter 1 of Part 4 of the Welfare Reform and Pensions Act 1999 (sharing of rights under pension arrangements) by conferring appropriate rights under the scheme on that person.

(7) Regulations may require the trustees or managers of the scheme, in prescribed circumstances –

(a) to adjust the entitlement of a person to a pension or other benefit under the scheme rules where the entitlement arises as a result of a discretionary award which takes effect during the winding up period;

(b) to adjust the entitlement of a person ("the survivor") to a pension or other benefit under the scheme rules where –

> (i)   a member of the scheme, or a person who was (or might have become) entitled to a pension or other benefit in respect of a member, dies during the winding up period, and
>
> (ii) the survivor's entitlement is to a pension or other benefit in respect of the member (whether arising on the date of that death or subsequently).

(8) Regulations under subsection (7) may, in particular –

> (a)   prescribe how the required adjustments to entitlement are to be determined and the manner in which they are to be made;
>
> (b)   in a case where the commencement of the winding up of the scheme is backdated (whether in accordance with section 154 of the Pensions Act 2004 (requirement to wind up schemes with sufficient assets to meet protected liabilities) or otherwise), require any adjustment to a person's entitlement to be made with effect from the time the award takes effect;
>
> (c)   without prejudice to sections 10(3) to (9), 73B(2) and 116, make provision about the consequences of breaching the requirements of the regulations.

(9) If the scheme confers power on any person other than the trustees or managers of the scheme to apply the assets of the scheme in respect of pensions or other benefits (including increases in pensions or benefits), it cannot be exercised by that person but may, subject to the provisions made by or by virtue of this section and sections 73 and 73B, be exercised instead by the trustees or managers.

(10) For the purposes of this section –

> "appropriate rights" has the same meaning as in paragraph 5 of Schedule 5 to the Welfare Reform and Pensions Act 1999 (pension credits: mode of discharge);
>
> "discretionary award" means an award of a prescribed description;
>
> "shareable rights" has the same meaning as in Chapter 1 of Part 4 of the Welfare Reform and Pensions Act 1999 (sharing of rights under pension arrangements);

and subsection (10) of section 73 applies as it applies for the purposes of that section.

73B   Sections 73 and 73A: supplementary

(1) Any action taken in contravention of section 73A(3) is void.

(2) If any provision made by or by virtue of the winding up provisions is not complied with in relation to a scheme to which section 73 applies, section 10 applies to any trustee or manager of the scheme who has failed to take all reasonable steps to secure compliance.

(3) For the purposes of subsection (2), when determining whether section 73A(3) has been complied with subsection (1) of this section is to be disregarded.

(4) Regulations may –

> (a)   prescribe how, for the purposes of the winding up provisions –
>
> > (i)   the assets and liabilities of a scheme to which section 73 applies, and
> >
> > (ii) their value or amount,
>
> are to be determined, calculated and verified;
>
> (b)   modify any of the winding up provisions as it applies –
>
> > (i)   to prescribed schemes or prescribed descriptions of schemes;
> >
> > (ii) in relation to a scheme where only part of the scheme is being wound up;
> >
> > (iii) in relation to a case where any liability of the scheme in respect of a member has been discharged by virtue of regulations under section 135(4) of the Pensions Act 2004 (power to make regulations permitting discharge of scheme's liabilities during an assessment period).

(5) Without prejudice to the generality of subsection (4), regulations under paragraph (b)(i) of that subsection may, in particular, modify any of the winding up provisions as it applies in relation to a scheme in relation to which there is more than one employer.

(6) The winding up provisions do not apply –

    (a)   in relation to any liability for an amount by way of pensions or other benefits which a person became entitled to payment of, under the scheme rules, before commencement of the winding up period,

    (b)   in prescribed circumstances, in relation to any liability in respect of rights of a prescribed description to which a member of the scheme became entitled under the scheme rules by reason of his pensionable service under the scheme terminating before the commencement of the winding up period,

    (c)   in relation to any liability in respect of rights of prescribed descriptions to which a member of the scheme had become entitled under the scheme rules before the commencement of the winding up period, or

    (d)   in relation to any liability the discharge of which is validated under section 136 of the Pensions Act 2004 (power to validate actions taken during an assessment period to discharge liabilities of a scheme).

(7) But nothing in subsection (6) prevents the winding up provisions applying in relation to a liability under Chapter 4 of Part 4 of the Pension Schemes Act 1993 (transfer values) which –

    (a)   arose before the commencement of the winding up of the scheme, and

    (b)   was not discharged before the commencement of the winding up period.

(8) Regulations may provide that, in prescribed circumstances, where –

    (a)   an occupational pension scheme to which section 73 applies is being wound up,

    (b)   a member of the scheme died before the winding up began, and

    (c)   during the winding up period a person becomes entitled under the scheme rules to a benefit of a prescribed description in respect of the member,

his entitlement to payment of all or part of the benefit is, for the purposes of subsection (6), to be treated as having arisen immediately before the commencement of the winding up period.

(9) If, immediately before the winding up period in relation to an occupational pension scheme to which section 73 applies, a person is entitled to an amount but has postponed payment of it, he is not, for the purposes of subsection (6), to be regarded as having become entitled to payment of the amount before that period.

(10) For the purposes of this section –

    (a)   "winding up provisions" means this section and sections 73, 73A and 74, and

    (b)   subsection (10) of section 73 applies as it applies for the purposes of that section.'

(2) In section 74 of the Pensions Act 1995 (c. 26) (discharge of liabilities by insurance, etc on winding up) –

    (a) for subsection (1) substitute –

        '(1) This section applies where an occupational pension scheme to which section 73 applies is being wound up.',

    (b) in subsection (2) omit '(including increases in pensions)',

    (c) in subsection (3), after paragraph (d) insert –

        '(e) by the payment of a cash sum in circumstances where prescribed requirements are met.',

    (d) in subsection (4) –

      (i)   for 'rules of the scheme' substitute 'scheme rules', and

      (ii) omit '(including increases in pensions)',

(e) omit subsection (5)(b) and the word 'or' immediately preceding it, and

(f)   after subsection (5) insert –

    '(6) For the purposes of this section –

        (a) references to assets of the scheme do not include any assets representing the value of any rights in respect of money purchase benefits under the scheme rules, and

        (b) references to liabilities of the scheme do not include any liabilities in respect of money purchase benefits under the scheme rules;

     and 'scheme rules' has the same meaning as in the Pensions Act 2004 (see section 318 of that Act).'

Deficiency in assets of certain occupational pension schemes

271 Debt due from the employer when assets insufficient

(1) Section 75 of the Pensions Act 1995 (c. 26) (deficiencies in the assets) is amended as follows.

(2) For subsections (1) to (4) substitute –

    '(1) This section applies in relation to an occupational pension scheme other than a scheme which is –

        (a) a money purchase scheme, or

        (b) a prescribed scheme or a scheme of a prescribed description.

    (2) If –

        (a) at any time which falls –

            (i) when a scheme is being wound up, but

            (ii) before any relevant event in relation to the employer which occurs while the scheme is being wound up,

        the value of the assets of the scheme is less than the amount at that time of the liabilities of the scheme, and

        (b) the trustees or managers of the scheme designate that time for the purposes of this subsection (before the occurrence of an event within paragraph (a)(ii)),

        an amount equal to the difference shall be treated as a debt due from the employer to the trustees or managers of the scheme.

        This is subject to subsection (3).

    (3) Subsection (2) applies only if –

        (a) either –

            (i) no relevant event within subsection (6A)(a) or (b) occurred in relation to the employer during the period beginning with the appointed day and ending with the commencement of the winding up of the scheme, or

            (ii) during the period –

                 (a) beginning with the occurrence of the last such relevant event which occurred during the period mentioned in sub-paragraph (i), and

                 (b) ending with the commencement of the winding up of the scheme, a cessation notice was issued in relation to the scheme and became binding, and

(b) no relevant event within subsection (6A)(c) has occurred in relation to the employer during the period mentioned in paragraph (a)(i).

(4) Where –

(a) immediately before a relevant event ("the current event") occurs in relation to the employer the value of the assets of the scheme is less than the amount at that time of the liabilities of the scheme,

(b) the current event –

(i) occurred on or after the appointed day, and
(ii) did not occur in prescribed circumstances,

(c) if the scheme was being wound up immediately before that event, subsection (2) has not applied in relation to the scheme to treat an amount as a debt due from the employer to the trustees or managers of the scheme,

(d) if the current event is within subsection (6A)(a) or (b), either –

(i) no relevant event within subsection (6A)(a) or (b) occurred in relation to the employer during the period beginning with the appointed day and ending immediately before the current event, or
(ii) a cessation event has occurred in relation to the scheme in respect of a cessation notice issued during the period –

(a) beginning with the occurrence of the last such relevant event which occurred during the period mentioned in sub-paragraph (i), and
(b) ending immediately before the current event, and

(e) no relevant event within subsection (6A)(c) has occurred in relation to the employer during the period mentioned in paragraph (d)(i),

an amount equal to the difference shall be treated as a debt due from the employer to the trustees or managers of the scheme.

(4A) Where the current event is within subsection (6A)(a) or (b), the debt under subsection (4) is to be taken, for the purposes of the law relating to insolvency as it applies to the employer, to arise immediately before the occurrence of the current event.

(4B) Subsection (4C) applies if, in a case within subsection (4) –

(a) the current event is within subsection (6A)(a) or (b), and
(b) the scheme was not being wound up immediately before that event.

(4C) Where this subsection applies, the debt due from the employer under subsection (4) is contingent upon –

(a) a scheme failure notice being issued in relation to the scheme after the current event and the following conditions being satisfied –

(i) the scheme failure notice is binding,
(ii) no relevant event within subsection (6A)(c) has occurred in relation to the employer before the scheme failure notice became binding, and
(iii) a cessation event has not occurred in relation to the scheme in respect of a cessation notice issued during the period –

(a) beginning with the occurrence of the current event, and
(b) ending immediately before the issuing of the scheme failure notice,

and the occurrence of such a cessation event in respect of a cessation notice issued during that period is not a possibility, or

      (b)   the commencement of the winding up of the scheme before –

          (i)   any scheme failure notice or cessation notice issued in relation to the scheme becomes binding, or

         (ii)   any relevant event within subsection (6A)(c) occurs in relation to the employer.'

(3) In subsection (5) for 'subsection (1)' substitute 'subsections (2) and (4)'.

(4) In subsection (6) –

    (a)   after 'scheme' insert 'rules', and

    (b)   at the end insert –

    'In this subsection "scheme rules" has the same meaning as in the Pensions Act 2004 ("the 2004 Act") (see section 318 of that Act).'

(5) After subsection (6) insert –

    '(6A) For the purposes of this section, a relevant event occurs in relation to the employer in relation to an occupational pension scheme if and when –

      (a)   an insolvency event occurs in relation to the employer,

      (b)   the trustees or managers of the scheme make an application under subsection (1) of section 129 of the 2004 Act or receive a notice from the Board of the Pension Protection Fund under subsection (5)(a) of that section, or

      (c)   a resolution is passed for a voluntary winding up of the employer in a case where a declaration of solvency has been made under section 89 of the Insolvency Act 1986 (members' voluntary winding up).

    (6B) For the purposes of this section –

      (a)   a "cessation notice", in the case of a relevant event within subsection (6A)(a), means –

         (i)   a withdrawal notice issued under section 122(2)(b) of the 2004 Act (scheme rescue has occurred),

        (ii)   a withdrawal notice issued under section 148 of that Act (no insolvency event has occurred or is likely to occur),

       (iii)   a notice issued under section 122(4) of that Act (inability to confirm status of scheme) in a case where the notice has become binding and section 148 of that Act does not apply,

      (b)   a "cessation notice" in the case of a relevant event within subsection (6A)(b), means a withdrawal notice issued under section 130(3) of the 2004 Act (scheme rescue has occurred),

      (c)   a cessation event occurs in relation to a scheme when a cessation notice in relation to the scheme becomes binding,

      (d)   the occurrence of a cessation event in relation to a scheme in respect of a cessation notice issued during a particular period ("the specified period") is a possibility until each of the following are no longer reviewable –

         (i)   any cessation notice which has been issued in relation to the scheme during the specified period,

        (ii)   any failure to issue such a cessation notice during the specified period,

       (iii)   any notice which has been issued by the Board under Chapter 2 or 3 of Part 2 of the 2004 Act which is relevant to the issue of a cessation notice in relation to the scheme during the specified period or to such a cessation notice which has been issued during that period becoming binding,

(iv) any failure to issue such a notice as is mentioned in sub-paragraph (iii),

(e) the issue or failure to issue a notice is to be regarded as reviewable –

(i) during the period within which it may be reviewed by virtue of Chapter 6 of Part 2 of the 2004 Act, and

(ii) if the matter is so reviewed, until –

(a) the review and any reconsideration,

(b) any reference to the Ombudsman for the Board of the Pension Protection Fund in respect of the matter, and

(c) any appeal against his determination or directions,

has been finally disposed of, and

(f) a 'scheme failure notice' means a scheme failure notice issued under section 122(2)(a) or 130(2) of the 2004 Act (scheme rescue not possible).

(6C) For the purposes of this section –

(a) section 121 of the 2004 Act applies for the purposes of determining if and when an insolvency event has occurred in relation to the employer,

(b) "appointed day" means the day appointed under section 126(2) of the 2004 Act (no pension protection under Chapter 3 of Part 2 of that Act if the scheme begins winding up before the day appointed by the Secretary of State),

(c) references to a relevant event in relation to an employer do not include a relevant event which occurred in relation to him before he became the employer in relation to the scheme,

(d) references to a cessation notice becoming binding are to the notice in question mentioned in subsection (6B)(a) or (b) and issued under Part 2 of the 2004 Act becoming binding within the meaning given by that Part of that Act, and

(e) references to a scheme failure notice becoming binding are to the notice in question mentioned in subsection (6B)(f) and issued under Part 2 of the 2004 Act becoming binding within the meaning given by that Part of that Act.

(6D) Where –

(a) a resolution is passed for a voluntary winding up of the employer in a case where a declaration of solvency has been made under section 89 of the Insolvency Act 1986 (members' voluntary winding up), and

(b) either –

(i) the voluntary winding up of the employer is stayed other than in prescribed circumstances, or

(ii) a meeting of creditors is held in relation to the employer under section 95 of that Act (creditors' meeting which has the effect of con-verting a members' voluntary winding up into a creditors' voluntary winding up),

this section has effect as if that resolution had never been passed and any debt which arose under this section by virtue of the passing of that resolution shall be treated as if it had never arisen.'

(6) Omit subsection (9).

272 Debt due from the employer in the case of multi-employer schemes

After section 75 of the Pensions Act 1995 (c. 26) (deficiencies in the assets) insert –

'75A Deficiencies in the assets: multi-employer schemes

(1) Regulations may modify section 75 (deficiencies in the assets) as it applies in relation to multi-employer schemes.

(2) The regulations may in particular provide for the circumstances in which a debt is to be treated as due under section 75 from an employer in relation to a multi-employer scheme (a "multi-employer debt").

(3) Those circumstances may include circumstances other than those in which the scheme is being wound up or a relevant event occurs (within the meaning of section 75).

(4) For the purposes of regulations under this section, regulations under section 75(5) may prescribe alternative manners for determining, calculating and verifying –

   (a)   the liabilities and assets of the scheme to be taken into account, and

   (b)   their amount or value.

(5) The regulations under this section may in particular –

   (a)   provide for the application of each of the prescribed alternative manners under section 75(5) to depend upon whether prescribed requirements are met;

   (b)   provide that, where in a particular case a prescribed alternative manner under section 75(5) is applied, the Authority may in prescribed circumstances issue a direction –

      (i)   that any resulting multi-employer debt is to be unenforceable for such a period as the Authority may specify, and

      (ii)   that the amount of the debt is to be re-calculated applying a different prescribed manner under section 75(5) if prescribed requirements are met within that period.

(6) The prescribed requirements mentioned in subsection (5) may include a requirement that a prescribed arrangement, the details of which are approved in a notice issued by the Authority, is in place.

(7) The regulations may provide that the Authority may not approve the details of such an arrangement unless prescribed conditions are met.

(8) Those prescribed conditions may include a requirement that –

   (a)   the arrangement identifies one or more persons to whom the Authority may issue a contribution notice under the regulations, and

   (b)   the Authority are satisfied of prescribed matters in respect of each of those persons.

(9) For the purposes of subsection (8) a 'contribution notice' is a notice stating that the person to whom it is issued is under a liability to pay the sum specified in the notice –

   (a)   to the trustees of the multi-employer scheme in question, or

   (b)   where the Board of the Pension Protection Fund has assumed responsibility for the scheme in accordance with Chapter 3 of Part 2 of the Pensions Act 2004 (pension protection), to the Board.

(10) The regulations may provide for the Authority to have power to issue a contribution notice to a person identified in an arrangement as mentioned in subsection (8) if –

   (a)   the arrangement ceases to be in place or the Authority consider that the arrangement is no longer appropriate, and

(b)   the Authority are of the opinion that it is reasonable to impose liability on the person to pay the sum specified in the notice.

(11) Where a contribution notice is issued to a person under the regulations as mentioned in subsection (8), the sum specified in the notice is to be treated as a debt due from that person to the person to whom it is to be paid as specified in the notice.

(12) Where the regulations provide for the issuing of a contribution notice by the Authority as mentioned in subsection (8) –

    (a)   the regulations must –

        (i)   provide for how the sum specified by the Authority in a contribution notice is to be determined,

        (ii) provide for the circumstances (if any) in which a person to whom a contribution notice is issued is jointly and severally liable for the debt,

        (iii) provide for the matters which the notice must contain, and

        (iv) provide for who may exercise the powers to recover the debt due by virtue of the contribution notice, and

    (b)   the regulations may apply with or without modifications some or all of the provisions of sections 47 to 51 of the Pensions Act 2004 (contribution notices where non-compliance with financial support direction) in relation to contribution notices issued under the regulations.

(13) In this section "multi-employer scheme" means a trust scheme which applies to earners in employments under different employers.

(14) This section is without prejudice to the powers conferred by –

section 75(5) (power to prescribe the manner of determining, calculating and verifying assets and liabilities etc),

section 75(10) (power to modify section 75 as it applies in prescribed circumstances),

section 118(1)(a) (power to modify any provisions of this Part in their application to multi-employer trust schemes), and

section 125(3) (power to extend for the purposes of this Part the meaning of "employer").'

Pension disputes

273 Resolution of disputes

For section 50 of the Pensions Act 1995 (c. 26) (resolution of disputes) substitute –

'50 Requirement for dispute resolution arrangements

(1) The trustees or managers of an occupational pension scheme must secure that dispute resolution arrangements are made and implemented.

(2) Dispute resolution arrangements are such arrangements as are required by this section for the resolution of pension disputes.

(3) For this purpose a pension dispute is a dispute which –

    (a)   is between –

        (i)   the trustees or managers of a scheme, and

        (ii) one or more persons with an interest in the scheme (see section 50A),

    (b)   is about matters relating to the scheme, and

    (c)   is not an exempted dispute (see subsection (9)).

(4) The dispute resolution arrangements must provide a procedure –

    (a)   for any of the parties to the dispute mentioned in subsection (3)(a)(ii) to make an application for a decision to be taken on the matters in dispute ("an application for the resolution of a pension dispute"), and

    (b)   for the trustees or managers to take that decision.

(5) Where an application for the resolution of a pension dispute is made in accordance with the dispute resolution arrangements, the trustees or managers must –

    (a)   take the decision required on the matters in dispute within a reasonable period of the receipt of the application by them, and

    (b)   notify the applicant of the decision within a reasonable period of it having been taken.

(6) The procedure provided for by the dispute resolution arrangements must include the provision required by section 50B.

(7) Dispute resolution arrangements under subsection (1) must, in the case of existing schemes, have effect on and after the date of commencement of this section in relation to applications made on or after that date.

(8) This section does not apply in relation to an occupational pension scheme if –

    (a)   every member of the scheme is a trustee of the scheme,

    (b)   the scheme has no more than one member, or

    (c)   the scheme is of a prescribed description.

(9) For the purposes of this section a dispute is an exempted dispute if –

    (a)   proceedings in respect of it have been commenced in any court or tribunal,

    (b)   the Pensions Ombudsman has commenced an investigation in respect of it as a result of a complaint made or a dispute referred to him, or

    (c)   it is of a prescribed description.

(10) If, in the case of an occupational pension scheme, the dispute resolution arrangements required by this section to be made –

    (a)   have not been made, or

    (b)   are not being implemented,

section 10 applies to any of the trustees or managers who have failed to take all reasonable steps to secure that such arrangements are made or implemented.

50A Meaning of "person with an interest in the scheme"

(1) For the purposes of section 50 a person is a person with an interest in an occupational pension scheme if –

    (a)   he is a member of the scheme,

    (b)   he is a widow, widower or surviving dependant of a deceased member of the scheme,

    (c)   he is a surviving non-dependant beneficiary of a deceased member of the scheme,

    (d)   he is a prospective member of the scheme,

    (e)   he has ceased to be within any of the categories of persons referred to in paragraphs (a) to (d), or

    (f)   he claims to be such a person as is mentioned in paragraphs (a) to (e) and the dispute relates to whether he is such a person.

(2) In subsection (1)(c) a "non-dependant beneficiary", in relation to a deceased member of an occupational pension scheme, means a person who, on the death of the member, is entitled to the payment of benefits under the scheme.

(3) In subsection (1)(d) a "prospective member" means any person who, under the terms of his contract of service or the rules of the scheme –

    (a)   is able, at his own option, to become a member of the scheme,

(b) will become so able if he continues in the same employment for a sufficiently long period,

(c) will be admitted to the scheme automatically unless he makes an election not to become a member, or

(d) may be admitted to it subject to the consent of his employer.

50B The dispute resolution procedure

(1) The procedure provided for by the dispute resolution arrangements under section 50 must include the following provision.

(2) The procedure must provide that an application for the resolution of a pension dispute under section 50(4) may be made or continued on behalf of a person who is a party to the dispute mentioned in section 50(3)(a)(ii) –

(a) where the person dies, by his personal representative,

(b) where the person is a minor or is otherwise incapable of acting for himself, by a member of his family or some other person suitable to represent him, and

(c) in any other case, by a representative nominated by him.

(3) The procedure may include provision about the time limits for making an application for the resolution of a pension dispute but it must require that –

(a) in the case of a person with an interest in a scheme as mentioned in section 50A(1)(e), the time limit for making an application is the end of the period of six months beginning immediately after the date upon which he ceased to be a person with an interest as mentioned in section 50A(1)(a), (b), (c) or (d), and

(b) in the case of a person with an interest in a scheme as mentioned in section 50A(1)(f) who is claiming to be such a person as is mentioned in section 50A(1)(e), the time limit for making an application is the end of the period of six months beginning immediately after the date upon which he claims that he ceased to be a person with an interest as mentioned in section 50A(1)(a), (b), (c) or (d).

(4) The procedure must include provision about –

(a) the manner in which an application for the resolution of a pension dispute is to be made,

(b) the particulars which must be included in such an application, and

(c) the manner in which any decisions required are to be reached and given.

(5) The procedure must provide that if, after an application for the resolution of a pension dispute has been made, the dispute becomes an exempted dispute within the meaning of section 50(9)(a) or (b), the resolution of the dispute under the procedure ceases.'

The Pensions Ombudsman

274 The Pensions Ombudsman and Deputy Pensions Ombudsmen

(1) In subsection (2) of section 145 of the Pension Schemes Act 1993 (c. 48) (the Pensions Ombudsman) after 'hold' insert 'and vacate'.

(2) For subsection (3) of that section substitute –

'(3) The Pensions Ombudsman may resign or be removed from office in accordance with those terms and conditions.'

(3) After that section insert –

'145A Deputy Pensions Ombudsmen

(1) The Secretary of State may appoint one or more persons to act as a deputy to the Pensions Ombudsman ("a Deputy Pensions Ombudsman").

(2) Any such appointment is to be upon such terms and conditions as the Secretary of State thinks fit.

(3) A Deputy Pensions Ombudsman –

  (a) is to hold and vacate office in accordance with the terms and conditions of his appointment, and

  (b) may resign or be removed from office in accordance with those terms and conditions.

(4) A Deputy Pensions Ombudsman may perform the functions of the Pensions Ombudsman –

  (a) during any vacancy in that office,

  (b) at any time when the Pensions Ombudsman is for any reason unable to discharge his functions, or

  (c) at any other time, with the consent of the Secretary of State.

(5) References to the Pensions Ombudsman in relation to the performance of his functions are accordingly to be construed as including references to a Deputy Pensions Ombudsman in relation to the performance of those functions.

(6) The Secretary of State may –

  (a) pay to or in respect of a Deputy Pensions Ombudsman such amounts –

    (i) by way of remuneration, compensation for loss of office, pension, allowances and gratuities, or

    (ii) by way of provision for any such benefits,

    as the Secretary of State may determine, and

  (b) reimburse the Pensions Ombudsman in respect of any expenses incurred by a Deputy Pensions Ombudsman in the performance of any of the Pensions Ombudsman's functions.'

(4) In Part 3 of Schedule 1 to the House of Commons Disqualification Act 1975 (c. 24) (other disqualifying offices), after 'Pensions Ombudsman' insert 'and any deputy to that Ombudsman appointed under section 145A of the Pension Schemes Act 1993'.

(5) In Part 3 of Schedule 1 to the Northern Ireland Assembly Disqualification Act 1975 (c. 25)(other disqualifying offices), at the appropriate place insert –

'Pensions Ombudsman and any deputy to that Ombudsman appointed under section 145A of the Pension Schemes Act 1993.'

(6) The persons to whom section 1 of the Superannuation Act 1972 (c. 11) (persons to or in respect of whom benefits may be provided by schemes under that section) applies are to include a deputy to the Pensions Ombudsman.

(7) The Pensions Ombudsman must pay to the Minister for the Civil Service, at such times as he may direct, such sums as he may determine in respect of the increase attributable to subsection (6) in the sums payable out of money provided by Parliament under that Act.

(8) The Pensions Ombudsman must also pay to the Minister for the Civil Service, at such times as he may direct, such sums as he may determine in respect of the amount payable out of money provided by Parliament under that Act which is attributable to the following persons being persons to whom section 1 of that Act applies –

  (a) the Pensions Ombudsman;

  (b) the employees of the Pensions Ombudsman.

275 Jurisdiction

(1) After section 146(4) of the Pension Schemes Act 1993 (c. 48) (power to apply Part 10 of that Act to those concerned with the administration of a scheme) insert –

'(4A) For the purposes of subsection (4) a person or body of persons is concerned with the administration of an occupational or personal pension scheme where the person or body is responsible for carrying out an act of administration concerned with the scheme.'

(2) The amendment made by this section has effect in relation to the making of any provision under section 146(4) of the Pension Schemes Act 1993 applying Part 10 of that Act in relation to a complaint or a dispute in so far as it relates to a matter which arises on or after the day on which this section comes into force.

(3) For the purposes of subsection (2), a question falling within section 146(1)(g) of the Pension Schemes Act 1993 is to be treated as a dispute.

276 Investigations

(1) Omit section 54 of the Child Support, Pensions and Social Security Act 2000 (c. 19) ('the 2000 Act') (which amends sections 148, 149 and 151 of the Pension Schemes Act 1993 and which has not been brought into force except for the purpose of making regulations and rules).

(2) Omit the following provisions of the Pension Schemes Act 1993 –

   (a) section 148(5)(ba) and (bb) as inserted by section 54(2) of the 2000 Act,
   (b) section 149(1), (1A) and (1B) as substituted by section 54(3) of the 2000 Act,
   (c) section 149(3)(ba) as substituted by section 54(4) of the 2000 Act,
   (d) section 149(3)(d) and the word 'and' immediately preceding it as inserted by section 54(5) of the 2000 Act,
   (e) section 149(8) as inserted by section 54(6) of the 2000 Act,
   (f) section 151(1)(c) and the word 'and' immediately preceding it as inserted by section 54(7) of the 2000 Act,
   (g) section 151(3)(ba) and (bb) as substituted by section 54(8) of the 2000 Act, and
   (h) in section 151(3)(c) the words 'any of paragraphs (a) to (bb)' as inserted by section 54(8) of the 2000 Act,

to the extent that those amendments made by section 54 of the 2000 Act have been brought into force for the purpose of making regulations and rules.

Pension compensation

277 Amendments relating to the Pensions Compensation Board

(1) The Pensions Act 1995 (c. 26) is amended as follows.

(2) In section 80 (review of decisions of the Pensions Compensation Board) –

   (a) after subsection (2) insert –

      '(2A) The Compensation Board may also review such a determination without an application being made.', and

   (b) for subsections (4) and (5) substitute –

      '(4) Regulations may make provision –

         (a) with respect to reviews under this section (or any corresponding provision in force in Northern Ireland);
         (b) with respect to applications under subsection (2) (or any corresponding provision in force in Northern Ireland) and the procedure to be adopted on any such application.'

(3) In section 81 (cases where compensation provisions apply), omit subsections (1)(d), (2A) and (7).

(4) In section 83 (amount of compensation) for subsections (3) and (4) substitute –

      '(3) The amount of the payment, or (if there is more than one) the aggregate, must not exceed the aggregate of –

(a)   the amount (if any) by which the shortfall at the application date exceeds the recoveries of value made between the application date and the settlement date, and

(b)   interest at the prescribed rate for the prescribed period on the amount of that excess (if any).'

Annual increases in rate of pensions

278 Annual increase in rate of certain occupational pensions

(1)   Section 51 of the Pensions Act 1995 (annual increase in rate of certain occupational pensions) is amended in accordance with subsections (2) to (6).

(2)   In subsection (1) –

(a)   omit 'and' at the end of sub-paragraph (i) of paragraph (a),

(b)   at the end of sub-paragraph (ii) of that paragraph insert –

'(iii) in the case where the pension becomes a pension in payment on or after the commencement day, is not a money purchase scheme, and',

and

(c)   for paragraph (b) substitute –

'(b)   the whole, or any part of, the pension is attributable –

(i)   to pensionable service on or after the appointed day, or

(ii)   in the case of money purchase benefits where the pension is in payment before the commencement day, to payments in respect of employment carried on on or after the appointed day, and

(c)   apart from this section –

(i)   the annual rate of the pension, or

(ii)   if only part of the pension is attributable as described in paragraph (b), so much of the annual rate as is attributable to that part,

would not be increased each year by at least the appropriate percentage of that rate.'

(3)   In subsection (2) after 'money purchase benefits' insert 'where the pension is in payment before the commencement day'.

(4)   In subsection (4)(b) for '5 per cent per annum' substitute '–

(i)   in the case of a category X pension, 5% per annum, and

(ii)   in the case of a category Y pension, 2.5% per annum.'

(5)   After subsection (4) insert –

'(4A) For the purposes of this section, a pension is a category X pension if it is –

(a)   a pension which became a pension in payment before the commencement day, or

(b)   a pension –

(i)   which becomes a pension in payment on or after the commencement day, and

(ii)   the whole of which is attributable to pensionable service before that day.

(4B) For the purposes of this section, a pension is a category Y pension if it is a pension –

(a)   which becomes a pension in payment on or after the commencement day, and

(b)   the whole of which is attributable to pensionable service on or after the commencement day.

(4C) For the purposes of applying this section in the case of a pension –

(a) which becomes a pension in payment on or after the commencement day,

(b) part of which is attributable to pensionable service before the commencement day, and

(c) part of which is attributable to pensionable service on or after that day,

each of those parts of the pension is to be treated as if it were a separate pension.'

(6) In subsection (5) –

(a) for 'the provisions of subsections (2) and (3)' substitute 'any of the provisions of this section', and

(b) in paragraph (a), after 'appointed day' insert 'or the commencement day'.

(7) After that section insert –

'51Z Meaning of "the appropriate percentage"

(1) For the purposes of section 51(1)(c) and (2), "the appropriate percentage" in relation to an increase in the whole or part of the annual rate of a pension –

(a) in the case of a category X pension, means the revaluation percentage for the latest revaluation period specified in the order under paragraph 2 of Schedule 3 to the Pension Schemes Act 1993 (revaluation of accrued pension benefits) which is in force at the time of the increase, and

(b) in the case of a category Y pension, means whichever is the lesser of –

(i) the revaluation percentage for the latest revaluation period specified in the order under paragraph 2 of Schedule 3 to the Pension Schemes Act 1993 which is in force at the time of the increase, and

(ii) 2.5%.

(2) In this section "the revaluation percentage" and "the revaluation period" have the same meaning as in paragraph 2 of Schedule 3 to the Pension Schemes Act 1993.'

(8) In section 54(3) of that Act (sections 51 to 53: supplementary), at the appropriate place insert –

'"the commencement day" means the day appointed for the coming into force of section 278 of the Pensions Act 2004 (amendments to section 51),'.

279 Annual increase in rate of certain personal pensions

(1) Section 162 of the Pensions Act 1995 (c. 26) (annual increase in rate of certain personal pensions) is amended in accordance with subsection (2).

(2) In subsection (1) omit 'and' at the end of paragraph (a) and for paragraph (b) substitute –

'(b) the pension became a pension in payment before the commencement day,

(c) the whole, or any part of, the pension is attributable to contributions in respect of employment carried on or after the appointed day, and

(d) apart from this section –

(i) the annual rate of the pension, or

(ii) if only part of the pension is attributable as described in paragraph (c), so much of the annual rate as is attributable to that part,

would not be increased each year by at least the appropriate percentage of that rate.'

(3) In section 163(3) of that Act (section 162: supplementary) –

(a) in the definition of 'appropriate percentage', for the words from 'revaluation period' to the end substitute 'latest revaluation period specified in the order under paragraph 2 of Schedule 3 to the Pension Schemes Act 1993 (revaluation of accrued pension benefits) which is in force at the time of the increase (expressions used in this definition having the same meaning as in that paragraph of that Schedule)', and

(b) at the appropriate place insert –

'"the commencement day" means the day appointed for the coming into force of section 279 of the Pensions Act 2004 (amendments to section 162),'.

280 Power to increase pensions giving effect to pension credits etc

(1) Section 40 of the Welfare Reform and Pensions Act 1999 (c. 30) (power of the Secretary of State to increase pensions provided to give effect to certain rights) is amended as follows.

(2) In subsection (1), for '5%' substitute 'the maximum percentage'.

(3) In subsection (2), for 'This' substitute 'Subject to subsection (2A), this'.

(4) After subsection (2) insert –

'(2A) Subsection (2) does not apply to pensions which –

    (a)   are money purchase benefits, and
    (b)   become pensions in payment on or after the commencement day.

(2B) For the purposes of subsection (1) the "maximum percentage" means –

    (a)   5% in a case where –

        (i)   the pension is in payment before the commencement day, or
        (ii) the pension is not in payment before the commencement day but the entitlement to the relevant pension credit arose before that day, and

    (b)   2.5% in a case where the entitlement to the relevant pension credit arises on or after the commencement day.'

(5) In subsection (3), at the appropriate places insert –

'"commencement day" means the day appointed for the coming into force of section 280 of the Pensions Act 2004 (amendments to section 40);'
'"money purchase benefit" has the meaning given by section 181(1) of the Pension Schemes Act 1993;'
'"relevant pension credit" means the pension credit to which the eligible pension credit rights or, as the case may be, the safeguarded rights are (directly or indirectly) attributable;'.

Revaluation

281 Exemption from statutory revaluation requirement

(1) Section 84 of the Pension Schemes Act 1993 (c. 48) (basis of revaluation) is amended as follows.

(2) In subsection (5), after paragraph (a) insert 'or

    (b)   under any arrangement which maintains the value of the pension or other benefit by reference to the rise in the retail prices index during that period,'.

(3) After that subsection add –

'(6) In subsection (5)(b), "retail prices index" means –

    (a)   the general index of retail prices (for all items) published by the Office for National Statistics, or
    (b)   where that index is not published for a month, any substituted index or figures published by that Office.'

Contracting out

282 Meaning of 'working life' in Pension Schemes Act 1993

In section 181 of the Pension Schemes Act 1993 (c. 48) (general interpretation), in subsection (1) for the definition of 'working life' substitute –

"working life", in relation to a person, means the period beginning with the tax year in which the person attains the age of 16 and ending with –

(a) the tax year before the one in which the person attains the age of 65 in the case of a man or 60 in the case of a woman, or

(b) if earlier, the tax year before the one in which the person dies.'

283 Power to prescribe conditions by reference to Inland Revenue approval

In section 9 of the Pension Schemes Act 1993 (requirements for certification of schemes: general), after subsection (5) insert –

'(5A) Regulations about pension schemes made under this Chapter may contain provisions framed by reference to whether or not a scheme –

(a) is approved under Chapter 1 (retirement benefit schemes) of Part 14 of the Income and Corporation Taxes Act 1988, or is a relevant statutory scheme within the meaning of that Chapter, or

(b) is approved under Chapter 4 (personal pension schemes) of that Part.'

284 Restrictions on commutation and age at which benefits may be received

(1) For section 21(1) of the Pension Schemes Act 1993 (commutation of guaranteed minimum pensions) substitute –

'(1) A scheme may, in such circumstances and subject to such restrictions and conditions as may be prescribed, provide for the payment of a lump sum instead of a pension required to be provided by the scheme in accordance with section 13 or 17.'

(2) In section 17 of that Act (minimum pensions for widows and widowers), at the end insert –

'(8) Where –

(a) a lump sum is paid to an earner under provisions included in a scheme by virtue of section 21(1), and

(b) those provisions are of a prescribed description,

the earner shall be treated for the purposes of this section as having any guaranteed minimum under section 14 that he would have had but for that payment.'

(3) In section 28 of that Act (ways of giving effect to protected rights), in subsection (4) (provision of a lump sum) –

(a) after 'provision of a lump sum' insert ', subject to such restrictions as may be prescribed,',

(b) omit paragraphs (a) and (b), and (c) at the end insert '; and (e) such other conditions as may be prescribed are satisfied.'

(4) Omit subsections (4A) and (4B) of that section.

(5) In subsections (3) and (5) of that section, for ', (4) or (4A)' substitute 'or (4)'.

(6) In subsection (8) of that section, in the definition of 'the starting date' omit ', which must not be earlier than the member's 60th birthday,'.

(7) In section 29(1) of that Act (how a pension may comply with 'the pension requirements' for the purposes of section 28) –

(a) in paragraph (a), for the words from 'date' to 'or on' substitute 'date that is not later than the member's 65th birthday, or on', and

(b) in paragraph (aa)(ii) omit the words from 'and is not' to '75th birthday,'.

Stakeholder pensions

285 Meaning of 'stakeholder pension scheme'

(1) Section 1 of the Welfare Reform and Pensions Act 1999 (c. 30) (meaning of 'stakeholder pension scheme') is amended in accordance with subsections (2) to (4).

(2) In subsection (1) (requirements to be met by stakeholder pension schemes), in paragraph (a) for 'to (9)' substitute 'to (10)'.

(3) In subsection (5) (prescribed requirements relating to administrative expenses of scheme), in paragraph (a) for 'by or on behalf of' substitute 'by, or on behalf or in respect of,'.

(4) After subsection (9) insert –

'(10) The ninth condition is that –

    (a) if the scheme is an occupational pension scheme, it is specified in a contracting-out certificate in relation to all categories of employment to which the scheme relates, and

    (b) if the scheme is a personal pension scheme, it is an appropriate scheme within the meaning of section 7(4) of the 1993 Act.'

(5) In section 2 of that Act (registration of stakeholder pension), in subsection (2)(b)(i) for 'to (9)' substitute 'to (10)'.

PART 6   FINANCIAL ASSISTANCE SCHEME FOR MEMBERS OF CERTAIN PENSION SCHEMES

286 Financial assistance scheme for members of certain pension schemes

(1) The Secretary of State must make provision, by regulations, for a scheme for making payments to, or in respect of, qualifying members of qualifying pension schemes ('the financial assistance scheme').

(2) For the purposes of this section –

'qualifying member', in relation to a qualifying pension scheme, means a person –

    (a) who, at such time as may be prescribed, is a member of the scheme in respect of whom the scheme's pension liabilities are unlikely to be satisfied in full because the scheme has insufficient assets, or

    (b) who, at such time as may be prescribed, had ceased to be a member of the scheme and in respect of whom the scheme's pension liabilities were not satisfied in full, before he ceased to be such a member, because the scheme had insufficient assets,

and in respect of whom prescribed conditions are satisfied at such time as may be prescribed;

'qualifying pension scheme' means an occupational pension scheme (including such a scheme which has been fully wound up) –

    (a) which, at such time as may be prescribed, is not –

        (i) a money purchase scheme, or

        (ii) a scheme of a prescribed description,

    (b) the winding up of which began during the prescribed period ending immediately before the day appointed under section 126(2),

(c) the employer in relation to which satisfies such conditions as may be prescribed at such time as may be prescribed, and

(d) prescribed details of which have been notified to such person as may be prescribed by a person of a prescribed description –

(i) in the prescribed form and manner, and

(ii) before the prescribed date;

'scheme's pension liabilities', in respect of a member of a qualifying pension scheme, means the liabilities of the scheme to, or in respect of, the member in respect of pensions or other benefits (including increases in pensions);

and a qualifying pension scheme has, or had, insufficient assets if the assets of the scheme are, or were, insufficient to satisfy in full the liabilities of the scheme calculated in the prescribed manner.

(3) Regulations under subsection (1) may, in particular, make provision –

(a) for the financial assistance scheme to be managed by the Secretary of State, a body established by or for the purposes of the regulations or such other person as may be prescribed;

(b) for the person who manages the financial assistance scheme ('the scheme manager') to hold (whether on trust or otherwise), manage and apply a fund in accordance with the regulations or, where the fund is held on trust, the deed of trust;

(c) for the property, rights and liabilities of qualifying pension schemes to be transferred to the scheme manager in prescribed circumstances and for the trustees or managers of a qualifying pension scheme in respect of which such a transfer has occurred to be discharged from prescribed liabilities;

(d) prescribing the circumstances in which payments are to be made by the scheme manager to, or in respect of, qualifying members of qualifying pension schemes and the manner in which the amount of any payment is to be determined, and, where the fund is held by the fund manager on trust, the circumstances and manner may be prescribed by reference to the deed of trust;

(e) authorising the Secretary of State –

(i) where he is not the scheme manager, to pay grants to the scheme manager;

(ii) where he is the scheme manager, to pay amounts into the fund held by him in accordance with the regulations;

(iii) to pay grants to other prescribed persons in connection with the financial assistance scheme;

(f) prescribing the circumstances in which amounts are to be paid into or out of the fund held by the scheme manager;

(g) for or in connection with –

(i) the review of, or appeals against, any determination, or failure to make a determination, in connection with the financial assistance scheme, or

(ii) the investigation of complaints relating to the financial assistance scheme,

and for the establishment of a body or the appointment of a person or persons to hear such appeals or conduct such investigations;

(h) conferring functions in relation to the financial assistance scheme on the Pensions Regulator or the Board of the Pension Protection Fund;

(i) providing for a person to exercise a discretion in dealing with any matter in relation to the financial assistance scheme;

(j) applying any provision of Part 1 or 2 with such modifications as may be prescribed;

and such regulations may make different provision for different cases or descriptions of case and include such incidental, supplementary, consequential or transitional provision as appears to the Secretary of State to be expedient.

(4) Any amount which, by virtue of subsection (3)(e), the Secretary of State pays under regulations under subsection (1) is to be to paid out of money provided by Parliament.

(5) Regulations under subsection (1) may not make provision for the imposition of a levy or charge on any person for the purpose of funding, directly or indirectly, the financial assistance scheme.

(6) Regulations under subsection (1) may not require any income or capital of a qualifying member of a qualifying pension scheme (other than income or capital which derives, directly or indirectly, from that scheme) to be taken into account when determining whether the member is entitled to a payment under the financial assistance scheme or the amount of any payment to which the member is entitled.

(7) For the purposes of subsection (6), regulations may prescribe the circumstances in which a qualifying member of a qualifying pension scheme is to be regarded as having income or capital which derives, directly or indirectly, from that scheme.

(8) A time or period prescribed under subsection (2) may fall (or, in the case of a period, wholly or partly fall) at a time before the passing of this Act.

(9) Nothing in this section prejudices the operation of section 315 (subordinate legislation (general provisions)).

PART 7   CROSS-BORDER ACTIVITIES WITHIN EUROPEAN UNION

UK occupational pension scheme receiving contributions from European employer

287 Occupational pension scheme receiving contributions from European employer

(1) The trustees or managers of an occupational pension scheme must not accept any contribution to the scheme from a European employer unless all the following conditions are met.

(2) Condition A is that the trustees or managers of the scheme are authorised by the Regulator under section 288.

(3) Condition B is that the trustees or managers of the scheme are approved by the Regulator under section 289 in relation to the European employer.

(4) Condition C is that either –

(a) the period of two months beginning with the date on which the Regulator notified the trustees or managers of the scheme under section 289(2)(a)(ii) has expired, or

(b) before the end of that period, the trustees or managers have received information forwarded to them by the Regulator in accordance with section 290(1).

(5) If the trustees or managers of a scheme fail to comply with subsection (1), section 10 of the Pensions Act 1995 (c. 26) (civil penalties) applies to any trustee or manager who has failed to take all reasonable steps to secure compliance.

(6) In this Part –

'European employer' has the prescribed meaning;
'host member State', in relation to a European employer, means a member State determined in accordance with regulations.

288 General authorisation to accept contributions from European employers

(1) An application by the trustees or managers of an occupational pension scheme for authorisation under this section must be made to the Regulator in the prescribed form and in the prescribed manner.

(2) On receipt of the application, the Regulator must –

(a) where the Regulator is satisfied that the applicant meets prescribed conditions, grant the authorisation, and

(b) in any other case, refuse the authorisation.

(3) Regulations may make provision as to –

(a) the revocation by the Regulator of authorisation under this section, and

(b) the criteria to be applied by the Regulator in reaching any decision relating to the revocation of authorisation.

289 Approval in relation to particular European employer

(1) An application by the trustees or managers of an occupational pension scheme for approval under this section in relation to a European employer is made by the trustees or managers of the scheme giving the Regulator in the prescribed manner a notice ('the notice of intention') in the prescribed form which –

(a) specifies the European employer ('the specified employer'),

(b) states their intention, subject to approval under this section, to accept contributions from the specified employer,

(c) specifies the host member State, and

(d) contains other prescribed information.

(2) On receipt of the notice of intention, the Regulator must within three months –

(a) where the Regulator is satisfied that the persons giving the notice of intention meet prescribed conditions –

(i) notify the competent authority of the host member State of the receipt by the Regulator of the notice of intention and of the contents of the notice, and

(ii) notify the persons who gave the notice of intention that they are approved for the purposes of this section in relation to the specified employer, or

(b) in any other case, notify the persons who gave the notification that they are not so approved.

(3) If the Regulator does not act under subsection (2)(a) or (b) within the period of three months beginning with the day on which the notice of intention was received, the persons who gave the notice of intention are to be taken to have been approved for the purposes of this section in relation to the specified employer at the end of the period.

(4) Regulations may make provision as to –

(a) the revocation by the Regulator of approval under this section, and

(b) the criteria to be applied by the Regulator in reaching any decision relating to the revocation of approval.

290 Notification of legal requirements of host member State outside United Kingdom

(1) Where –

(a) the Regulator has notified the competent authority of the host member State under subsection (2)(a)(i) of section 289, and

(b) in pursuance of Article 20(5) of the Directive, the Regulator receives information from the competent authority as to requirements of the social and labour law of the host member State and as to the other matters referred to in Article 20(5),

the Regulator must as soon as reasonably practicable forward that information to the person who gave the notice of intention under section 289.

(2) Where –

(a) the trustees or managers of an occupational pension scheme are approved under section 289 in relation to a European employer, and

(b) in pursuance of Article 20(8) of the Directive the Regulator receives information ('the new information') from the competent authority of the host member State as to changes affecting any information previously forwarded under subsection (1),

the Regulator must as soon as reasonably practicable forward the new information to the trustees or managers.

291 Duty of trustees or managers to act consistently with law of host member State

(1) Where the trustees or managers of an occupational pension scheme receive contributions to the scheme from a European employer, the trustees or managers must ensure that the scheme, so far as it relates to members who are or have been employed by the employer, is operated in a way which is consistent with the requirements of the social and labour law of the host member State.

(2) Regulations may modify any provision of pensions legislation in its application to members of an occupational pension scheme in respect of which the employer is a European employer.

(3) If the trustees or managers of a scheme fail to comply with subsection (1), section 10 of the Pensions Act 1995 (c. 26) (civil penalties) applies to any trustee or manager who has failed to take all reasonable steps to secure compliance.

(4) In this section 'pensions legislation' means –

(a) the Pension Schemes Act 1993 (c. 48),

(b) Part 1 of the Pensions Act 1995, other than sections 62 to 66A of that Act (equal treatment),

(c) Part 1 or section 33 of the Welfare Reform and Pensions Act 1999 (c. 30), or

(d) this Act.

292 Power of Regulator to require ring-fencing of assets

(1) Where the trustees or managers of an occupational pension scheme receive contributions to the scheme from a European employer, the Regulator may in prescribed circumstances issue a notice ('a ring-fencing notice') to the trustees or managers of the scheme directing them to take, or refrain from taking, such steps of a prescribed description as are specified in the notice for the purpose of ring-fencing some or all of the assets or liabilities (or both) of the scheme.

(2) In subsection (1), 'ring-fencing' has the same meaning as in the Directive.

(3) If the trustees or managers of an occupational pension scheme fail to comply with a ring-fencing notice given to them, section 10 of the Pensions Act 1995 (civil penalties) applies to any trustee or manager who has failed to take all reasonable steps to secure compliance.

European occupational pension scheme receiving contributions from UK employer

293 Functions of Regulator in relation to institutions administered in other member States

(1) Where a UK employer makes (or proposes to make) contributions to a European pensions institution, any function which Article 20 of the Directive requires or authorises to be exercised by the competent authorities of the host member State is exercisable by the Regulator.

(2) If the Regulator receives a notification in pursuance of Article 20(4) of the Directive from the competent authority in another member State, the Regulator must within two months inform that authority of any relevant legal requirements.

(3) Where there is a significant change in any relevant legal requirements, the Regulator must as soon as reasonably practicable inform any competent authority in relation to which it has provided information under subsection (2) of that change.

(4) Where a UK employer makes contributions to a European pensions institution, the Regulator must –

   (a) monitor the compliance of that institution with the relevant legal requirements, and

   (b) if the Regulator becomes aware of any contravention by the institution of any relevant legal requirements, inform the competent authority of the member State in which the institution has its main administration of the failure.

(5) If the Regulator is satisfied that a European pensions institution which receives contributions from a UK employer is contravening any relevant legal requirements, the Regulator may issue a notice to the UK employer directing him –

   (a) to take or refrain from taking such steps as are specified in the notice in order to remedy the failure by the institution, or

   (b) to cease to make further contributions to the institution.

(6) Regulations may make further provision about the effect of a notice under subsection (5)(b), including provision conferring functions on the Regulator.

(7) Section 10 of the Pensions Act 1995 (civil penalties) applies to any UK employer who, without reasonable excuse, fails to comply with a notice under subsection (5).

(8) In this section –

   'European pensions institution' means an institution for occupational retirement provision, as defined by Article 6(a) of the Directive, that has its main administration in a member State other than the United Kingdom;

   'relevant legal requirements' means such requirements of the law relating to occupational pension schemes, as it applies in any part of the United Kingdom, as may be prescribed;

   'UK employer' means an employer who –

   (a) in the case of a body corporate, is incorporated under the law of the United Kingdom or any part of the United Kingdom, or

   (b) in any other case, is resident in the United Kingdom.

Assistance for other European regulators

294 Stopping disposal of assets of institutions administered in other member States

(1) This section applies if the Regulator receives a request from the competent authority of a member State for assistance in prohibiting the free disposal of UK-held assets of a European pensions institution that has its main administration in that member State.

(2) The court may on an application made by the Regulator with respect to UK-held assets of the institution grant –

   (a) an injunction restraining a defendant, or

   (b) in Scotland, an interdict prohibiting a defender (or, in proceedings by petition, a respondent),

   from disposing of, or otherwise dealing with, assets to which the application relates.

(3) If the court grants an injunction or interdict under subsection (2), it may by subsequent orders make provision for such incidental, consequential and supplementary matters as it considers necessary to enable the competent authority that sent the request to perform any of its functions in relation to assets subject to the injunction or interdict.

(4) If the institution is not a party to proceedings under subsection (2) or (3), the institution –

(a) has the same rights to notice of the proceedings as a defendant (or, in Scotland, as a defender or, as the case may be, as a respondent), and

(b) may take part as a party in the proceedings.

(5) In deciding any question as to costs or expenses, a court before which any proceedings take place –

(a) may take account of any additional expense which it considers that any party to the proceedings has incurred as a result of the participation of the institution in pursuance of subsection (4)(b), and

(b) may award the whole or part of the additional expense as costs or (as the case may be) expenses to the party who incurred it (whatever the outcome of the Regulator's application).

(6) For the purposes of this section –

'European pensions institution' has the meaning given by section 293;

'UK-held assets' of a European pensions institution are assets of the institution held by a depositary or custodian located in the United Kingdom, and here 'assets', 'depositary', 'custodian' and 'located' have the same meaning as in Article 19(3) of the Directive.

(7) The jurisdiction conferred by subsections (2) and (3) is exercisable by the High Court or the Court of Session.

Interpretation

295 Interpretation of Part

In this Part –

'competent authority', in relation to a member State other than the United Kingdom, means a national authority designated in accordance with the law of that State to carry out the duties provided for in the Directive;

'the Directive' means Directive 2003/41/EC of the European Parliament and of the Council on the activities and supervision of institutions for occupational retirement provision;

'European employer' has the meaning given by section 287(6);

'host member State', in relation to a European employer, has the meaning given by section 287(6);

'social and labour law', in relation to a member State other than the United Kingdom, means the social and labour law (within the meaning of Article 20 of the Directive) of that State relevant to occupational pension schemes (within the meaning of that Article).

PART 8   STATE PENSIONS

Entitlement to more than one pension

296 Persons entitled to more than one Category B retirement pension

In section 43(3) of the Social Security Contributions and Benefits Act 1992 (c. 4) (persons entitled to more than one retirement pension) –

(a) for paragraph (a) substitute –

'(a) to both a Category A retirement pension and one or more Category B retirement pensions under this Part for the same period,

(aa) to more than one Category B retirement pension (but not a Category A retirement pension) under this Part for the same period, or', and

(b)   for the words from 'paragraph (a)' to 'above' substitute 'paragraph (a), (aa) or (b) (as the case may be)'.

Deferral of state pension

297 Deferral of retirement pensions and shared additional pensions

(1)   For section 55 of the Social Security Contributions and Benefits Act 1992 (increase of retirement pension where entitlement is deferred) substitute –

'55 Pension increase or lump sum where entitlement to retirement pension is deferred

(1)   Where a person's entitlement to a Category A or Category B retirement pension is deferred, Schedule 5 to this Act has effect.

(2)   In that Schedule –

paragraph A1 makes provision enabling an election to be made where the pensioner's entitlement is deferred

paragraphs 1 to 3 make provision about increasing pension where the pensioner's entitlement is deferred

paragraphs 3A and 3B make provision about lump sum payments where the pensioner's entitlement is deferred

paragraph 3C makes provision enabling an election to be made where the pensioner's deceased spouse has deferred entitlement

paragraphs 4 to 7 make provision about increasing pension where the pensioner's deceased spouse has deferred entitlement

paragraphs 7A and 7B make provision about lump sum payments where the pensioner's deceased spouse has deferred entitlement

paragraphs 7C to 9 make supplementary provision.

(3)   For the purposes of this Act a person's entitlement to a Category A or Category B retirement pension is deferred if and so long as that person –

(a)   does not become entitled to that pension by reason only –

(i)   of not satisfying the conditions of section 1 of the Administration Act (entitlement to benefit dependent on claim), or

(ii)   in the case of a Category B retirement pension payable by virtue of a spouse's contributions, of the spouse not satisfying those conditions with respect to his Category A retirement pension, or

(b)   in consequence of an election under section 54(1), falls to be treated as not having become entitled to that pension,

and, in relation to any such pension, "period of deferment" shall be construed accordingly.'

(2)   For section 55C of that Act (increase of shared additional pension where entitlement is deferred) substitute –

'55C Pension increase or lump sum where entitlement to shared additional pension is deferred

(1)   Where a person's entitlement to a shared additional pension is deferred, Schedule 5A to this Act has effect.

(2)   In that Schedule –

paragraph 1 makes provision enabling an election to be made where the person's entitlement is deferred paragraphs 2 and 3 make provision about increasing pension where the person's entitlement is deferred

paragraphs 4 and 5 make provision about lump sum payments where the person's entitlement is deferred.

(3)   For the purposes of this Act, a person's entitlement to a shared additional pension is deferred –

(a)   where he would be entitled to a Category A or Category B retirement pension but for the fact that his entitlement is deferred, if and so long as his entitlement to such a pension is deferred, and

(b)   otherwise, if and so long as he does not become entitled to the shared additional pension by reason only of not satisfying the conditions of section 1 of the Administration Act (entitlement to benefit dependent on claim),

and, in relation to a shared additional pension, "period of deferment" shall be construed accordingly.'

(3)   In paragraph 6 of Schedule 4 to the Pensions Act 1995 (c. 26) (which, with effect from 6th April 2010, amends the existing law regarding the deferment of pensions), for sub-paragraph (5) (commencement) substitute –

'(5)   The preceding sub-paragraphs shall come into force as follows –

(a)   sub-paragraphs (1) and (4) shall come into force on 6th April 2005;

(b)   sub-paragraphs (2) and (3) shall have effect in relation to incremental periods (within the meaning of Schedule 5 to the Social Security Contributions and Benefits Act 1992 (c. 4)) beginning on or after that date.'

(4)   Schedule 11 (which contains further amendments relating to the deferral of retirement pensions and shared additional pensions) has effect.

Miscellaneous

298   Disclosure of state pension information

(1)   Section 42 of the Child Support, Pensions and Social Security Act 2000 (c. 19) (disclosure of state pension information) is amended as follows.

(2)   In subsection (2), for the words from the beginning to 'information', substitute, 'The Secretary of State may, in the prescribed manner, disclose or authorise the disclosure of any information'.

(3)   After subsection (3) insert –

'(3A)   For the purposes of this section and of any regulations made under it, anything done by or in relation to a person who –

(a)   provides, or proposes to provide, relevant services to a person falling within subsection (3) ("the qualifying person"), and

(b)   is authorised in writing by the qualifying person to act for the purposes of this section,

is treated as done by or in relation to the qualifying person.

In paragraph (a) "relevant services" means services that may involve the giving of advice or forecasts to which information to which this section applies may be relevant.'

(4)   In subsection (7) –

(a)   omit the 'and' at the end of paragraph (c), and

(b)   after paragraph (d) insert – ', and (e) a projection of the amount of any lump sum to which that individual is likely to become entitled, or might become entitled in particular circumstances.'

(5) In subsection (11) –

    (a) for the definitions of 'basic retirement pension' and 'additional retirement pension', substitute –

        '"additional retirement pension" means any additional pension or shared additional pension under the Social Security Contributions and Benefits Act 1992, or any graduated retirement benefit under sections 36 and 37 of the National Insurance Act 1965;

        '"basic retirement pension' means any basic pension under the Social Security Contributions and Benefits Act 1992;',

    (b) after the definition of 'employer', insert –

        '"lump sum" means a lump sum under Schedule 5 or 5A to the Social Security Contributions and Benefits Act 1992;', and

    (c) for the definitions of 'trustee' and 'manager', substitute –

        '"trustee or manager', in relation to an occupational or personal pension scheme, means –

            (a) in the case of a scheme established under a trust, the trustee or trustees of the scheme, and

            (b) in any other case, the person or persons responsible for the management of the scheme.'

299 Claims for certain benefits following termination of reciprocal agreement with Australia

(1) This section applies to claims for –

    (a) retirement pension,
    (b) bereavement benefit, or
    (c) widow's benefit,

made on or after 1st March 2001 (the date from which the termination of the reciprocal agreement with Australia had effect).

(2) This section also applies to claims for retirement pension or widow's benefit made before 1st March 2001 if the claimant only became entitled to the pension or benefit on or after that date.

(3) For the purposes of such claims –

    (a) the relevant provisions of the reciprocal agreement with Australia shall be treated as continuing in force as provided by this section; and
    (b) the relevant UK legislation shall have effect as if modified to the extent required to give effect to those provisions (as they continue in force by virtue of this section).

(4) The relevant provisions of that agreement are treated as continuing in force as follows –

    (a) references to periods during which a person was resident in Australia are only to periods spent in Australia before 6th April 2001 and forming part of a period of residence in Australia which began before 1st March 2001;
    (b) Articles 3(3) and 5(2) (entitlement by virtue of previous receipt of pension in Australia) apply only to persons who were last in Australia during a period falling within paragraph (a) above;
    (c) references to the territory of the United Kingdom do not include the islands of Jersey, Guernsey, Alderney, Herm or Jethou;
    (d) references to widow's benefit, widow's payment, widow's pension and widowed mother's allowance include, respectively, bereavement benefit, bereavement payment, bereavement allowance and widowed parent's allowance;
    (e) for the purposes of claims by a widower –

(i)   for retirement pension by virtue of his wife's insurance, or

(ii) for bereavement benefit,

references to widows and husbands include, respectively, widowers and wives.

(5) An order made under –

(a) section 179 of the Social Security Administration Act 1992 (c. 5), or

(b) section 155 of the Social Security Administration (Northern Ireland) Act 1992 (c. 8),

may, in consequence of a change in the law of Great Britain or, as the case may be, Northern Ireland, modify the relevant provisions of the reciprocal agreement with Australia as they are treated as continuing in force for the purposes of claims to which this section applies.

(6) For the purposes of this section –

(a) 'the reciprocal agreement with Australia' means the agreement set out in Schedule 1 to the Social Security (Australia) Order 1992 (S.I. 1992/ 1312) and the Social Security (Australia) Order (Northern Ireland) 1992 (S.R. 1992 No. 269) (as amended by the exchange of notes set out in Schedule 3 to those Orders);

(b) 'the relevant provisions' of that agreement are the provisions of Articles 1, 3, 5, 8, 18, 20 and 24, so far as they relate to the United Kingdom;

(c) 'the relevant UK legislation' is –

(i)   the Social Security Contributions and Benefits Act 1992 (c. 4);

(ii) the Social Security Administration Act 1992;

(iii) the Social Security Contributions and Benefits (Northern Ireland) Act 1992 (c. 7); and

(iv) the Social Security Administration (Northern Ireland) Act 1992;

and, for the purposes of subsection (5), a change in the law of Great Britain or Northern Ireland includes any change made after the date of the reciprocal agreement with Australia.

(7) In this section –

'retirement pension' has the meaning given by the reciprocal agreement with Australia;

'bereavement benefit' means bereavement payment, widowed parent's allowance or bereavement allowance payable under the Social Security Contributions and Benefits Act 1992 or the Social Security Contributions and Benefits (Northern Ireland) Act 1992;

'widow's benefit' means widow's payment, widowed mother's allowance or widow's pension payable under either of those Acts.

(8) This section shall be deemed to have had effect at all times on and after 1st March 2001.

(9) Nothing in this section affects Article 2(2) of the Social Security (Australia) Order 2000 (S.I. 2000/3255) or Article 2(2) of the Social Security (Australia) Order (Northern Ireland) 2000 (S.R. 2000 No. 407) (which provide for cases where a person was in receipt of benefit on 28th February 2001 or had claimed a benefit to which he was entitled on or before that date).

PART 9   MISCELLANEOUS AND SUPPLEMENTARY

Dissolution of existing bodies

300   Dissolution of OPRA

(1)   The Occupational Pensions Regulatory Authority ('OPRA') is hereby dissolved.

(2)   An order under section 322 which appoints the day on which subsection (1) comes into force may provide –

    (a)   for all property, rights and liabilities to which OPRA is entitled or subject immediately before that day to become the property, rights and liabilities of the Regulator or the Secretary of State, and

    (b)   for any function of OPRA falling to be exercised on or after that day, or which fell to be exercised before that day but has not been exercised, to be exercised by the Regulator, the Secretary of State or the Department for Social Development in Northern Ireland.

(3)   Subject to subsection (4), information obtained by the Regulator by virtue of subsection (2) is to be treated for the purposes of sections 82 to 87 (disclosure of information) as having been obtained by the Regulator in the exercise of its functions from the person from whom OPRA obtained it.

(4)   Information obtained by the Regulator by virtue of subsection (2) which was supplied to OPRA for the purposes of its functions by an authority exercising functions corresponding to the functions of OPRA in a country or territory outside the United Kingdom (the 'overseas authority') is to be treated for the purposes mentioned in subsection (3) as having been supplied to the Regulator for the purposes of its functions by the overseas authority.

(5)   Where tax information disclosed to OPRA is obtained by the Regulator by virtue of subsection (2), subsection (3) does not apply and subsections (3) and (4) of section 88 apply as if that information had been disclosed to the Regulator by virtue of subsection (2) of that section.

For this purpose 'tax information' has the same meaning as in that section.

301   Transfer of employees from OPRA to the Regulator

(1)   For the purposes of the Transfer of Undertakings (Protection of Employment) Regulations 1981 (S.I. 1981/1794) ('TUPE'), the transfer of functions from OPRA to the Regulator ('the transfer') is to be treated as a transfer of an undertaking.

(2)   The provisions of Regulation 7 of TUPE (exclusion of occupational pension schemes) shall not apply in relation to the transfer.

302   Dissolution of the Pensions Compensation Board

(1)   The Pensions Compensation Board is hereby dissolved.

(2)   An order under section 322 appointing the day on which subsection (1) is to come into force may provide –

    (a)   for all property, rights and liabilities to which the Pensions Compensation Board is entitled or subject immediately before that day to become property, rights and liabilities of the Board, and

    (b)   for any function of the Pensions Compensation Board falling to be exercised on or after that day, or which fell to be exercised before that day but has not been exercised, to be exercised by the Board.

(3)   Information obtained by the Board by virtue of subsection (2) is to be treated for the purposes of sections 197 to 201 and 203 (disclosure of information) as having been obtained by the Board in the exercise of its functions from the person from whom the Pensions Compensation Board obtained it.

(4)   Where tax information disclosed to the Pensions Compensation Board is obtained by the Board by virtue of subsection (2), subsection (3) does not apply, and subsections (3) and (4) of section 202 apply as if that information had been disclosed to the Board by virtue of subsection (2) of that section.

For this purpose 'tax information' has the same meaning as in that section.

(5)   Where the Pensions Compensation Board's disclosure under section 114(3) of the Pensions Act 1995 (c. 26) of information to which subsection (3) applies was subject to any express restriction, the Board's powers of disclosure under sections 198 to 201 and 203, in relation to that information, are subject to the same restriction.

Service of notifications etc and electronic working

303 Service of notifications and other documents

(1)   This section applies where provision made (in whatever terms) by or under this Act authorises or requires –

(a)   a notification to be given to a person, or

(b)   a document of any other description (including a copy of a document) to be sent to a person.

(2)   The notification or document may be given to the person in question –

(a)   by delivering it to him,

(b)   by leaving it at his proper address, or

(c)   by sending it by post to him at that address.

(3)   The notification or document may be given or sent to a body corporate by being given or sent to the secretary or clerk of that body.

(4)   The notification or document may be given or sent to a firm by being given or sent to –

(a)   a partner in the firm, or

(b)   a person having the control or management of the partnership business.

(5)   The notification or document may be given or sent to an unincorporated body or association by being given or sent to a member of the governing body of the body or association.

(6)   For the purposes of this section and section 7 of the Interpretation Act 1978 (c. 30) (service of documents by post) in its application to this section, the proper address of a person is –

(a)   in the case of a body corporate, the address of the registered or principal office of the body,

(b)   in the case of a firm, or an unincorporated body or association, the address of the principal office of the firm, body or association,

(c)   in the case of any person to whom the notification or other document is given or sent in reliance on any of subsections (3) to (5), the proper address of the body corporate, firm or (as the case may be) other body or association in question, and

(d)   in any other case, the last known address of the person in question.

(7)   In the case of –

(a)   a company registered outside the United Kingdom,

(b)   a firm carrying on business outside the United Kingdom, or

(c)   an unincorporated body or association with offices outside the United Kingdom,

the references in subsection (6) to its principal office include references to its principal office within the United Kingdom (if any).

(8)   In this section 'notification' includes notice; and references in this section to sending a document to a person include references to making an application to him.

(9)   This section has effect subject to section 304.

304 Notification and documents in electronic form

(1) This section applies where –

    (a) section 303 authorises the giving or sending of a notification or other document by its delivery to a particular person ('the recipient'), and

    (b) the notification or other document is transmitted to the recipient –

        (i) by means of an electronic communications network, or

        (ii) by other means but in a form that nevertheless requires the use of apparatus by the recipient to render it intelligible.

(2) The transmission has effect for the purposes of this Act as a delivery of the notification or other document to the recipient, but only if the requirements imposed by or under this section are complied with.

(3) Where the recipient is a relevant authority –

    (a) it must have indicated its willingness to receive the notification or other document in a manner mentioned in subsection (1)(b),

    (b) the transmission must be made in such manner, and satisfy such other conditions, as it may require, and

    (c) the notification or other document must take such form as it may require.

(4) Where the person making the transmission is a relevant authority, it may (subject to subsection (5)) determine –

    (a) the manner in which the transmission is made, and

    (b) the form in which the notification or other document is transmitted.

(5) Where the recipient is a person other than a relevant authority –

    (a) the recipient, or

    (b) the person on whose behalf the recipient receives the notification or other document,

must have indicated to the person making the transmission the recipient's willingness to receive notifications or documents transmitted in the form and manner used.

(6) An indication given to any person for the purposes of subsection (5) –

    (a) must be given to that person in such manner as he may require,

    (b) may be a general indication or one that is limited to notifications or documents of a particular description,

    (c) must state the address to be used and must be accompanied by such other information as that person requires for the making of the transmission, and

    (d) may be modified or withdrawn at any time by a notice given to that person in such manner as he may require.

(7) An indication, requirement or determination given, imposed or made by a relevant authority for the purposes of this section is to be given, imposed or made by being published in such manner as it considers appropriate for bringing it to the attention of the persons who, in its opinion, are likely to be affected by it.

(8) Where both the recipient and the person making the transmission are relevant authorities –

    (a) subsections (3) and (4) do not apply, and

    (b) the recipient must have indicated to the person making the transmission the recipient's willingness to receive notifications or documents transmitted in the form and manner used.

(9) Subsection (8) of section 303 applies for the purposes of this section as it applies for the purposes of that section.

(10) In this section, 'relevant authority' means the Regulator, the Board or the Secretary of State and in the application of this section to Northern Ireland by virtue of section 323(2)(g)(ii) also includes the Department for Social Development in Northern Ireland.

(11) In this section and section 305, 'electronic communications network' has the same meaning as in the Communications Act 2003 (c. 21).

305 Timing and location of things done electronically

(1) The Secretary of State may by order make provision specifying, for the purposes of any enactment contained in, or made under, this Act, the manner of determining –

    (a)   the times at which things done under that enactment by means of electronic communications networks are done, and

    (b)   the places at which such things are so done, and at which things transmitted by means of such networks are received.

(2) The provision made under subsection (1) may include provision as to the country or territory in which an electronic address is to be treated as located.

(3) An order made by the Secretary of State may also make provision about the manner of proving in any legal proceedings –

    (a)   that something done by means of an electronic communications network satisfies the requirements of an enactment contained in, or made under, this Act for the doing of that thing, and

    (b)   the matters mentioned in subsection (1)(a) and (b).

(4) An order under this section may provide for such presumptions to apply (whether conclusive or not) as the Secretary of State considers appropriate.

General

306 Overriding requirements

(1) Where any provision mentioned in subsection (2) conflicts with the provisions of an occupational or personal pension scheme –

    (a)   the provision mentioned in subsection (2), to the extent that it conflicts, overrides the provisions of the scheme, and

    (b)   the scheme has effect with such modifications as may be required in consequence of paragraph (a).

(2) The provisions referred to in subsection (1) are those of –

    (a)   any order made by the Regulator under Part 1;

    (b)   any regulations made under section 19(7);

    (c)   any regulations made under section 21(4);

    (d)   any regulations made under section 24(7);

    (e)   any direction issued by the Regulator under section 41(4);

    (f)   any direction issued by the Regulator under section 50(4);

    (g)   Part 2 (other than Chapter 1), any subordinate legislation made under that Part and any direction given under section 134 or 154;

    (h)   Part 3 and any subordinate legislation made under that Part;

    (i)   any regulations under section 237;

    (j)   sections 241 and 242, any regulations made under sections 241 to 243 and any arrangements under sections 241 and 242;

    (k)   sections 247 and 248 and any regulations under sections 247 to 249;

    (l)   sections 256 and 258;

    (m)   any ring-fencing notice issued by the Regulator under section 292;

    (n)   any regulations under section 286, 307, 308, 315(6) or 318(4) or (5) and any order under section 322(5).

(3) Subsection (1) is without prejudice to section 32(1) (overriding effect of freezing orders made by the Regulator) and section 154(12) (overriding effect of requirement to wind up pension scheme under Part 2).

(4) In the case of a company to which section 242 (requirement for member-nominated directors of corporate trustees) applies, where any provision mentioned in subsection (5) conflicts with the provisions of the company's memorandum or articles of association –

(a) the provision mentioned in subsection (5), to the extent that it conflicts, overrides the provisions of the memorandum or articles, and

(b) the memorandum or articles have effect with such modifications as may be required in consequence of paragraph (a).

(5) The provisions referred to in subsection (4) are those of –

(a) section 242;

(b) any regulations made under section 242 or 243;

(c) any arrangements under section 242.

307 Modification of this Act in relation to certain categories of schemes

(1) Regulations may modify any of the provisions mentioned in subsection (2) as it applies in relation to –

(a) hybrid schemes;

(b) multi-employer schemes;

(c) any case where a partnership is the employer, or one of the employers, in relation to an occupational pension scheme.

(2) The provisions referred to in subsection (1) are those of –

(a) Part 1 (the Pensions Regulator),

(b) Part 2 (the Board of the Pension Protection Fund), other than Chapter 1,

(c) sections 257 and 258 (pension protection),

(d) sections 259 and 261 (consultation by employers),

(e) section 286 (financial assistance scheme for members of certain pension schemes), and

(f) Part 7 (cross-border activities within European Union).

(3) Regulations may also modify any of the provisions of Part 2 as it applies in relation to an eligible scheme in respect of which a relevant public authority has –

(a) given a guarantee in relation to any part of the scheme, any benefits payable under the scheme rules or any member of the scheme, or

(b) made any other arrangements for the purposes of securing that the assets of the scheme are sufficient to meet any part of its liabilities.

(4) In this section –

'eligible scheme' has the meaning given by section 126;

'hybrid scheme' means an occupational pension scheme –

(a) which is not a money purchase scheme, but

(b) where some of the benefits that may be provided are –

(i) money purchase benefits attributable to voluntary contributions of the members, or

(ii) other money purchase benefits;

'multi-employer scheme' means an occupational pension scheme in relation to which there is more than one employer;

'relevant public authority' means –

(a) a Minister of the Crown (within the meaning of the Ministers of the Crown Act 1975 (c. 26)),

(b) a government department (including any body or authority exercising statutory functions on behalf of the Crown), or

(c) the Scottish Ministers.

308 Modification of pensions legislation that refers to employers

(1) Regulations may modify any provision of pensions legislation for the purpose of ensuring that it, or another provision of pensions legislation, does not purport to refer to the employer of a self-employed person.

(2) Where a provision of pensions legislation contains a reference to an employer in connection with an occupational pension scheme, regulations may modify the provision, or another provision of pensions legislation, for the purpose of excluding from the reference an employer who is a person –

   (a) who does not participate in the scheme as regards people employed by him, or
   (b) who, as regards people employed by him, participates in the scheme only to a limited extent.

(3) For the purposes of this section –

   (a) 'pensions legislation' means any enactment contained in or made by virtue of –
      (i) the Pension Schemes Act 1993 (c. 48),
      (ii) Part 1 of the Pensions Act 1995 (c. 26), other than sections 62 to 66A of that Act (equal treatment),
      (iii) Part 1 of the Welfare Reform and Pensions Act 1999 (c. 30), or
      (iv) this Act;

   (b) a person is 'self-employed' if he is in an employment but is not employed in it by someone else;
   (c) a person who holds an office (including an elective office), and is entitled to remuneration for holding it, shall be taken to be employed by the person responsible for paying the remuneration.

(4) In subsection (3)(b) 'employment' includes any trade, business, profession, office or vocation.

309 Offences by bodies corporate and partnerships

(1) Where an offence under this Act committed by a body corporate is proved to have been committed with the consent or connivance of, or to be attributable to any neglect on the part of, a director, manager, secretary or other similar officer of the body, or a person purporting to act in any such capacity, he as well as the body corporate is guilty of the offence and liable to be proceeded against and punished accordingly.

(2) Where the affairs of a body corporate are managed by its members, subsection (1) applies in relation to the acts and defaults of a member in connection with his functions of management as to a director of a body corporate.

(3) Where an offence under this Act committed by a Scottish partnership is proved to have been committed with the consent or connivance of, or to be attributable to any neglect on the part of, a partner, he as well as the partnership is guilty of the offence and liable to be proceeded against and punished accordingly.

(4) In this section 'Scottish partnership' means a partnership constituted under the law of Scotland.

310 Admissibility of statements

(1) A statement made by a person in compliance with an information requirement is admissible in evidence in any proceedings, so long as it also complies with any requirements governing the admissibility of evidence in the circumstances in question.

(2) But in proceedings to which this subsection applies –

   (a) no evidence relating to the statement may be adduced, and
   (b) no question relating to it may be asked,

   by or on behalf of the prosecution or (as the case may be) the Regulator, unless evidence relating to it is adduced, or a question relating to it is asked, in the proceedings by or on behalf of that person.

(3) Subsection (2) applies to –

(a) criminal proceedings in which that person is charged with a relevant offence, or

(b) proceedings as a result of which that person may be required to pay a financial penalty under or by virtue of –

    (i) section 168 of the Pension Schemes Act 1993 (c. 48) (breach of regulations) or section 10 of the Pensions Act 1995 (c. 26) (civil penalties), or

    (ii) any provision in force in Northern Ireland corresponding to a provision mentioned in sub-paragraph (i).

(4) In this section –

'information requirement' means any statement made in compliance with any duty imposed by or by virtue of –

(a) section 64 (duties of trustees or managers to provide scheme return);

(b) section 70 (duty to report breaches of the law);

(c) section 72 (requirement to provide information to the Regulator);

(d) section 75 (inspection of premises: powers of inspectors to examine etc);

(e) section 78(2)(d) (power of inspector entering under warrant to require a person to provide an explanation of a document);

(f) section 190 (information to be provided to the Board);

(g) section 191 (notices requiring provision of information to the Board etc);

(h) section 192 (entry of premises: powers of appointed persons to examine etc);

(i) section 194(2)(d) (power of inspector entering under warrant to require a person to provide an explanation of a document);

(j) section 209 (power to make order enabling PPF Ombudsman to obtain information, documents etc);

(k) section 213 or 214 (disclosure of information on references made to PPF Ombudsman);

(l) section 228 (failure to make payments in accordance with schedule of contributions);

(m) paragraph 19 of Schedule 1 (power to make regulations enabling Regulator to summon persons to give evidence before it);

(n) paragraph 11 of Schedule 4 (the Pensions Regulator Tribunal: evidence);
'relevant offence' means any offence other than one under –

(a) section 77 (neglect or refusal to provide information etc to the Regulator);

(b) section 80 (providing false or misleading information to the Regulator);

(c) section 193 (neglect or refusal to provide information etc to the Board);

(d) section 195 (providing false or misleading information to the Board);

(e) any provision in force in Northern Ireland corresponding to a provision mentioned in paragraphs (a) to (d);

(f) section 5 of the Perjury Act 1911 (c. 6) (false statements made otherwise than on oath);

(g) section 44(2) of the Criminal Law (Consolidation) (Scotland) Act 1995 (c. 39) (false statements made otherwise than on oath);

(h) Article 10 of the Perjury (Northern Ireland) Order 1979 (S.I. 1979/1714 (N.I. 19)).

311 Protected items

(1) A person may not be required under or by virtue of this Act to produce, disclose or permit the inspection of protected items.

(2) For this purpose 'protected items' means –

(a)   communications between a professional legal adviser and his client or any person representing his client which fall within subsection (3);

(b)   communications between a professional legal adviser, his client or any person representing his client and any other person which fall within subsection (3) (as a result of paragraph (b) of that subsection);

(c)   items which –

(i)   are enclosed with, or referred to in, such communications,

(ii)   fall within subsection (3), and

(iii)   are in the possession of a person entitled to possession of them.

(3)   A communication or item falls within this subsection if it is made –

(a)   in connection with the giving of legal advice to the client, or

(b)   in connection with, or in contemplation of, legal proceedings and for the purpose of those proceedings.

(4)   A communication or item is not a protected item if it is held with the intention of furthering a criminal purpose.

312 Liens

If a person claims a lien on a document, its production under any provision made by or by virtue of this Act does not affect the lien.

313 Crown application

(1)   In this section 'the relevant provisions' means –

(a)   Parts 1 to 5,

(b)   sections 306, 307, 310, 311, 312, 314, 315, 318(4) and (5) and 322(5).

(2)   The relevant provisions apply to a pension scheme managed by or on behalf of the Crown as they apply to other pension schemes; and, accordingly, references in those provisions to a person in his capacity as a trustee or manager of, or person prescribed in relation to, a pension scheme include the Crown, or a person acting on behalf of the Crown, in that capacity.

(3)   The relevant provisions apply to persons employed by or under the Crown in like manner as if such persons were employed by a private person; and references in those provisions to a person in his capacity as an employer include the Crown, or a person acting on behalf of the Crown in that capacity.

(4)   This section does not apply to any of the relevant provisions under or by virtue of which a person may be prosecuted for an offence; but such a provision applies to persons in the public service of the Crown as it applies to other persons.

(5)   Nothing in the relevant provisions applies to Her Majesty in Her private capacity (within the meaning of the Crown Proceedings Act 1947 (c. 44)).

Regulations and orders

314 Breach of regulations

The following provisions of the Pensions Act 1995 (c. 26) apply to regulations under this Act as if they were regulations made by virtue of Part 1 of that Act –

(a)   section 10(3) to (9) (power to impose civil penalties for contravention of regulations under Part 1 of that Act);

(b)   section 116 (power to provide for contravention of regulations under that Part to be criminal offence).

315 Subordinate legislation (general provisions)

(1) Any power conferred by this Act to make subordinate legislation is exercisable by statutory instrument, except any order-making power conferred on the Regulator.

(2) Any power conferred by this Act to make subordinate legislation may be exercised –

    (a) either in relation to all cases to which the power extends, or in relation to those cases subject to specified exceptions, or in relation to any specified cases or descriptions of case;

    (b) so as to make, as respects the cases in relation to which it is exercised –

        (i) the full provision to which the power extends or any lesser provision (whether by way of exceptions or otherwise),

        (ii) the same provision for all cases in relation to which the power is exercised, or different provision for different cases or different descriptions of case or different provision as respects the same case or description of case for different purposes of this Act, or

        (iii) any such provision either unconditionally or subject to any specified condition.

(3) Any power conferred by this Act to make subordinate legislation –

    (a) if it is expressed to be exercisable for alternative purposes, may be exercised in relation to the same case for any or all of those purposes, and

    (b) if it is conferred for the purposes of any one provision of this Act, is without prejudice to any power to make subordinate legislation for the purposes of any other provision.

(4) A power conferred by this Act to make subordinate legislation includes power to provide for a person to exercise a discretion in dealing with any matter.

(5) Any power conferred by this Act to make subordinate legislation also includes power to make such incidental, supplementary, consequential or transitional provision as appears to the authority making the subordinate legislation to be expedient.

(6) Regulations may, for the purposes of or in connection with the coming into force of any provisions of this Act, make any such provision as could be made by virtue of section 322(5) by an order bringing those provisions into force.

316 Parliamentary control of subordinate legislation

(1) Subject to subsections (2) and (3), a statutory instrument containing regulations or an order or rules under this Act is subject to annulment in pursuance of a resolution of either House of Parliament.

(2) A statutory instrument which contains –

    (a) regulations under section 117(1) or (3) (administration levy in respect of expenditure relating to the Board of the Pension Protection Fund);

    (b) regulations under section 167 (modification of Chapter 3 of Part 2 where liabilities discharged during the assessment period);

    (c) regulations under section 174 (the initial levy);

    (d) regulations under section 175 (pension protection levies);

    (e) an order under section 177(6) (orders relating to amounts to be raised by pension protection levies);

    (f) an order under section 178(1) (the levy ceiling);

    (g) an order or regulations under section 209 (the PPF Ombudsman);

    (h) regulations under section 213 (reference of reviewable matter to the PPF Ombudsman);

    (i) regulations under section 214 (investigation by PPF Ombudsman of complaints of maladministration);

    (j) regulations under section 237 (combined pension forecasts);

    (k) regulations under section 238 (information and advice to employees);

(l) an order under section 243(1) (power to provide for minimum fraction of member-nominated trustees or directors to be one-half);

(m) regulations which make provision by virtue of section 261(2)(f) (power to make amendments etc to certain Acts);

(n) regulations under section 286 (financial assistance scheme for members of certain pension schemes);

(o) regulations which make provision by virtue of section 314(b) (power to provide for contravention of regulations to be criminal offence);

(p) regulations under section 318(4)(b) (power to extend meaning of employer);

(q) an order under section 319(2)(a) (power to make consequential amendments to Acts);

(r) an order under paragraph 24(8) of Schedule 7 (power to vary percentage of periodic compensation that can be commuted);

(s) an order under paragraph 26(7) of that Schedule (orders specifying the compensation cap in respect of payments from the Pension Protection Fund); or

(t) an order under paragraph 30(1) of that Schedule (power to vary percentage paid as compensation from the Pension Protection Fund);

must not be made unless a draft of the instrument has been laid before and approved by a resolution of each House of Parliament.

(3) Subsection (1) does not apply to –

(a) an order under section 91(9) (commencement of code of practice);

(b) an order under section 126(2) (schemes winding up before day appointed by order not eligible schemes for purposes of Part 2);

(c) an order under section 182(10) (order appointing day after which losses of non-trust schemes are relevant for fraud compensation purposes);

(d) an order under section 322 (commencement).

317 Consultations about regulations

(1) Before the Secretary of State makes any regulations by virtue of this Act (other than Part 8), he must consult such persons as he considers appropriate.

(2) Subsection (1) does not apply –

(a) to regulations contained in a statutory instrument made for the purpose only of consolidating other instruments revoked by it,

(b) in a case where it appears to the Secretary of State that by reason of urgency consultation is inexpedient,

(c) to regulations contained in a statutory instrument made before the end of the period of six months beginning with the coming into force of the provision of this Act by virtue of which the regulations are made, or

(d) to regulations contained in a statutory instrument which –

   (i) states that it contains only regulations which are consequential upon a specified enactment, and

   (ii) is made before the end of the period of six months beginning with the coming into force of that enactment.

Interpretation

318 General interpretation

(1) In this Act, unless the context otherwise requires –

'active member' has the meaning given by section 124(1) of the Pensions Act 1995 (c. 26);

'the Board' has the meaning given by section 107;

'contravention' includes failure to comply;

'direct payment arrangements', in relation to a personal pension scheme, has the same meaning as in section 111A of the Pension Schemes Act 1993 (c. 48);

'earnings' has the meaning given by section 181(1) of the Pension Schemes Act 1993;

'employee' has the meaning given by section 181(1) of the Pension Schemes Act 1993;

'employer' –

    (a)   in relation to an occupational pension scheme, means the employer of persons in the description of employment to which the scheme in question relates (but see subsection (4)), and

    (b)   in relation to a personal pension scheme, where direct payment arrangements exist in respect of one or more members of the scheme who are employees, means an employer with whom those arrangements exist;

'enactment' includes an enactment comprised in subordinate legislation (within the meaning of the Interpretation Act 1978 (c. 30));

'managers', in relation to an occupational or personal pension scheme (other than a scheme established under a trust), means the persons responsible for the management of the scheme;

'member', in relation to an occupational pension scheme, means any active, deferred, pensioner or pension credit member within the meaning of section 124(1) of the Pensions Act 1995 (c. 26) (but see subsection (5));

'modifications' includes additions, omissions and amendments, and related expressions are to be construed accordingly;

'money purchase benefit' has the meaning given by section 181(1) of the Pension Schemes Act 1993 (c. 48);

'money purchase scheme' has the meaning given by section 181(1) of the Pension Schemes Act 1993;

'occupational pension scheme' has the meaning given by section 1 of the Pension Schemes Act 1993;

'pension credit' has the meaning given by section 124(1) of the Pensions Act 1995;

'personal pension scheme' has the meaning given by section 1 of the Pension Schemes Act 1993;

'the PPF Ombudsman' has the meaning given by section 209(1);

'prescribed' means prescribed by regulations;

'professional adviser', in relation to an occupational pension scheme, has the meaning given by section 47 of the Pensions Act 1995;

'the register' has the meaning given by section 59(1);

'regulations' means regulations made by the Secretary of State;

'the Regulator' has the meaning given by section 1;

'the Tribunal' has the meaning given by section 102(1).

(2)   In this Act, unless the context otherwise requires, references to the scheme rules, in relation to an occupational pension scheme, are references to –

    (a)   the rules of the scheme, except so far as overridden by a relevant legislative provision,

    (b)   the relevant legislative provisions, to the extent that they have effect in relation to the scheme and are not reflected in the rules of the scheme, and

    (c)   any provision which the rules of the scheme do not contain but which the scheme must contain if it is to conform with the requirements of Chapter 1 of Part 4 of the Pension Schemes Act 1993 (preservation of benefit under occupational pension schemes).

(3)   For the purposes of subsection (2) –

    (a)   'relevant legislative provision' means any provision contained in any of the following provisions –

      (i)   Schedule 5 to the Social Security Act 1989 (c. 24) (equal treatment for men and women);

     (ii)   Chapters 2 to 5 of Part 4 of the Pension Schemes Act 1993 (c. 48) (certain protection for early leavers) or regulations made under any of those Chapters;

    (iii)   Part 4A of that Act (requirements relating to pension credit benefit) or regulations made under that Part;

    (iv)   section 110(1) of that Act (requirement as to resources for annual increase of guaranteed minimum pensions);

     (v)   Part 1 of the Pensions Act 1995 (c. 26) (occupational pensions) or subordinate legislation made or having effect as if made under that Part;

    (vi)   section 31 of the Welfare Reform and Pensions Act 1999 (c. 30) (pension debits: reduction of benefit);

   (vii)   any provision mentioned in section 306(2) of this Act;

  (b) a relevant legislative provision is to be taken to override any of the provisions of the scheme if, and only if, it does so by virtue of any of the following provisions –

      (i)   paragraph 3 of Schedule 5 to the Social Security Act 1989 (c. 24);

     (ii)   section 129(1) of the Pension Schemes Act 1993;

    (iii)   section 117(1) of the Pensions Act 1995;

    (iv)   section 31(4) of the Welfare Reform and Pensions Act 1999;

     (v)   section 306(1) of this Act.

(4) Regulations may, in relation to occupational pension schemes, extend for the purposes of Parts 1, 2 and 4 to 7 and this Part the meaning of 'employer' to include –

  (a) persons who have been the employer in relation to the scheme;

  (b) such other persons as may be prescribed.

(5) Regulations may for any purpose of any provision of this Act –

  (a) prescribe the persons who are to be regarded as members or prospective members of an occupational or personal pension scheme, and

  (b) make provision as to the times at which and circumstances in which a person is to be treated as becoming, or as ceasing to be, such a member or prospective member.

Miscellaneous and supplementary

319 Minor and consequential amendments

(1) Schedule 12 (which makes minor and consequential amendments) has effect.

(2) The Secretary of State may by order make provision consequential on this Act amending, repealing or revoking (with or without savings) any provision of –

  (a) an Act passed before or in the same session as this Act, or

  (b) an instrument made under an Act before the passing of this Act.

320 Repeals and revocations

The enactments mentioned in Schedule 13 are repealed or revoked to the extent specified.

321 Pre-consolidation amendments

(1) The Secretary of State may by order make such modifications of –

  (a) this Act,

  (b) the Pension Schemes Act 1993 (c. 48),

  (c) the Pensions Act 1995 (c. 26),

  (d) Parts 1 to 4 of the Welfare Reform and Pensions Act 1999 (c. 30), and

(e)   Chapter 2 of Part 2 of the Child Support, Pensions and Social Security Act 2000 (c. 19),

as in his opinion facilitate, or are otherwise desirable in connection with, the consolidation of those enactments or any of them.

(2)   No order is to be made under this section unless a Bill for repealing and re-enacting –

(a)   the enactments modified by the order, or

(b)   enactments relating to matters connected with the matters to which enactments modified by the order relate,

has been presented to either House of Parliament.

(3)   An order under this section is not to come into force until immediately before the commencement of the Act resulting from that Bill.

322   Commencement

(1)   Subject to subsections (2) to (4), the provisions of this Act come into force in accordance with provision made by the Secretary of State by order.

(2)   The following provisions come into force on the day this Act is passed –

(a)   in Part 4, sections 234, 235 and 236 and Schedule 10 (provisions relating to retirement planning);

(b)   in Part 5, section 281 (exemption from statutory revaluation requirement);

(c)   in Part 8 –

   (i)   section 296 (entitlement to more than one state pension),

   (ii)   section 297(3) (commencement of amendments of state pension deferment provisions made by Pensions Act 1995),

   (iii)   section 298 (disclosure of state pension information), except subsections (4) and (5)(b), and

   (iv)   section 299 (claims for certain benefits following termination of reciprocal agreement with Australia);

(d)   in this Part (miscellaneous and general) –

   (i)   sections 303 to 305 (service of notifications etc and electronic working), and

   (ii)   this section and sections 313, 315 (other than subsection (6)), 316, 317, 318 (other than subsections (4) and (5)) and 323 to 325;

(e)   the repeal by this Act of section 50(2) of the Welfare Reform and Pensions Act 1999.

(3)   Section 297 (and Schedule 11) (deferral of retirement pensions and shared additional pensions), other than the provisions coming into force in accordance with subsection (2) –

(a)   come into force on the day this Act is passed so far as is necessary for enabling the making of any regulations for which they provide, and

(b)   otherwise, come into force on 6th April 2005.

(4)   The repeals by this Act of section 134(3) of, and paragraph 21(14) of Schedule 4 to, the Pensions Act 1995 (c. 26) come into force on 6th April 2005.

(5)   Without prejudice to section 315(5), the power to make an order under this section includes power –

(a)   to make transitional adaptations or modifications –

   (i)   of the provisions brought into force by the order, or

   (ii)   in connection with those provisions, of any provisions of Parts 1 to 7 of this Act or of the Pension Schemes Act 1993 (c. 48), the Pensions Act 1995, Parts 1, 2 or 4 of the Welfare Reform and Pensions Act 1999 (c. 30) or Chapter 2 of Part 2 of the Child Support, Pensions and Social Security Act 2000 (c. 19), or

(b) to save the effect of any of the repealed provisions of those Acts, or those provisions as adapted or modified by the order,

as it appears to the Secretary of State expedient, including different adaptations or modifications for different periods.

323 Extent

(1) Subject to the following provisions, this Act extends to England, Wales and Scotland.
(2) The following provisions of this Act also extend to Northern Ireland –

(a) in Part 1 (the Regulator) –

(i) sections 1, 2, 4 (other than subsection (2)(b)), 8, 9, 11, 59, 102 and 106,
(ii) in Schedule 1, paragraphs 1 to 19, 20(1) to (3) and (7), 21 (other than paragraph (b)), 22 to 25 and 27 to 35, and section 3 so far as it relates to those provisions, and
(iii) Schedule 4,

(b) in Part 2 (the Board) –

(i) sections 107, 108, 109, 110(1) and (3), 112, 113, 114, 115, 118, 119, 161(2)(a), (3) and (5) to (8), 173, 188, 209 (other than paragraphs (b) to (d), (f) and (g) of subsection (4), subsection (6) so far as relating to any of those paragraphs and subsections (7) and (8)), 210, 211(3) and (4), 212 and 220,
(ii) section 111 so far as that provision has effect in relation to functions of the Board conferred by any provision of, or made under, this Act which extends to Northern Ireland,
(iii) Schedule 5 (other than paragraph 18), and
(iv) Schedule 6 (other than paragraph 7),

(c) in Part 4 (retirement planning), sections 234 and 235 and paragraph 2 of Schedule 10 (and section 236 so far as it relates to that paragraph),
(d) in Part 5 (personal and occupational pension schemes: miscellaneous provisions), sections 274 and 277(2)(b),
(e) Part 6 (financial assistance scheme for members of certain pension schemes),
(f) in Part 8 (state pensions), section 299, and
(g) in this Part –

(i) sections 300(1) and (2), 301, 302(1) and (2), 307, 308 and 310,
(ii) sections 303 to 306, 309, 313, 315, 316 and 318 so far as those provisions have effect for the purposes of provisions which themselves extend to Northern Ireland, and
(iii) this section and sections 319(2), 321, 322, 324 and 325.

(3) Section 106 (legal assistance scheme) does not extend to Scotland.
(4) An amendment or repeal contained in this Act has the same extent as the enactment to which it relates and sections 236 (except so far as it relates to paragraph 2 of Schedule 10), 319(1) and 320 have effect accordingly.

324 Northern Ireland

(1) An Order in Council under paragraph 1(1) of the Schedule to the Northern Ireland Act 2000 (c. 1) (legislation for Northern Ireland during suspension of devolved government) which contains a statement that it is made only for purposes corresponding to those of this Act –

(a) is not subject to paragraph 2 of that Schedule (affirmative resolution of both Houses of Parliament), but
(b) is subject to annulment in pursuance of a resolution of either House of Parliament.

(2) Where an Order in Council to which subsection (1) applies makes provision ('the NI provisions') which corresponds to the GB transfer provisions, regulations may make provision to secure that any transfer of property, rights and liabilities, or modification of a term of a contract of insurance, by virtue of the NI provisions is recognised for the purposes of the law of England and Wales and the law of Scotland.

(3) In subsection (2) 'the GB transfer provisions' means section 161(1), (2)(a), (3) and (5) to (8) and Schedule 6 (other than paragraph 7).

325 Short title

This Act may be cited as the Pensions Act 2004.

SCHEDULES

SCHEDULE 1   THE PENSIONS REGULATOR

Section 3

PART 1

MEMBERS OF THE REGULATOR

Terms of appointment and tenure of members

1   (1)   The members of the Regulator appointed by the Secretary of State under section 2(1)(a) or (c) are to be appointed on such terms and conditions as are determined by the Secretary of State.

(2)   Subject to sub-paragraph (3), such a member –

(a)   is to hold and vacate office in accordance with the terms and conditions of his appointment, and

(b)   may resign or be removed from office in accordance with those terms and conditions.

(3)   A person must cease to be a member of the Regulator where –

(a)   in the case of the chairman, he ceases to hold that office or becomes a member of the staff of the Regulator;

(b)   in the case of any other non-executive member, he becomes a member of the staff of the Regulator;

(c)   in the case of an executive member appointed under section 2(1)(c), he ceases to be a member of the staff of the Regulator.

2   Where a person ceases to be employed as Chief Executive, he ceases to be a member of the Regulator.

3   No person is to be prevented from being a member of the Regulator (whether as chairman or otherwise) merely because he has previously been such a member.

Remuneration etc of members

4   The Regulator may pay, or make provision for paying, its non-executive members such remuneration as the Secretary of State may determine.

5   The Regulator may –

(a)   pay to or in respect of any person who is or has been a non-executive member such pension, allowances or gratuities as the Secretary of State may determine, or

(b)   make such payments as the Secretary of State may determine towards provision for the payment of a pension, allowance or gratuity to or in respect of such a person.

6   Where –

(a)   a non-executive member ceases to be a member otherwise than on the expiry of his term of office, and

(b)   it appears to the Secretary of State that there are circumstances which make it right for that person to receive compensation,

the Regulator may make a payment to that person of such amount as the Secretary of State may determine.

PART 2

STAFF OF THE REGULATOR

The staff

7 (1) The staff of the Regulator consists of –

    (a) the Chief Executive of the Regulator appointed under paragraph 8,

    (b) the other employees of the Regulator appointed under paragraph 9, and

    (c) any additional staff made available by the Secretary of State under paragraph 10.

  (2) No member of the Board of the Pension Protection Fund is eligible for appointment as a member of the staff of the Regulator.

The Chief Executive

8 (1) The Regulator is to employ a person as its Chief Executive.

  (2) The Chief Executive's main function is to be responsible for securing that the functions of the Regulator are exercised efficiently and effectively.

  (3) The first appointment of a Chief Executive –

    (a) is to be made by the Secretary of State, and

    (b) is to be on such terms and conditions as to remuneration and other matters as are determined by the Secretary of State.

  (4) Subsequent appointments of a Chief Executive –

    (a) are to be made by the Regulator with the approval of the Secretary of State, and

    (b) are to be on such terms and conditions as to remuneration and other matters as are determined by the Regulator with the approval of the Secretary of State.

  (5) By virtue of subsection (2) of section 8 (non-executive functions), the function conferred on the Regulator by sub-paragraph (4)(b), so far as it relates to the terms and conditions as to remuneration, is exercisable on its behalf by the committee established under that section.

Other employees

9 (1) Other employees of the Regulator may be appointed by the Regulator with the approval of the Secretary of State as to numbers.

  (2) Any such appointments are to be on such terms and conditions as to remuneration and other matters as are determined by the Regulator with the approval of the Secretary of State.

Additional staff etc

10 (1) The Secretary of State may make available to the Regulator such additional staff and such other facilities as he considers appropriate.

  (2) The availability of such staff and facilities may be on such terms as to payment by the Regulator as the Secretary of State may determine.

PART 3

MEMBERS OF THE DETERMINATIONS PANEL

Nomination of the chairman of the Panel

11 (1) On each occasion when the Regulator is required to appoint a person as chairman of the Determinations Panel, the chairman of the Regulator must establish a committee (in this Schedule referred to as 'the appointments committee').

(2) The appointments committee must consist of –

(a) a chairman appointed by the chairman of the Regulator from the non-executive members of the Regulator, and

(b) one or more persons appointed by the chairman of the Regulator.

(3) At least one of the persons appointed under sub-paragraph (2)(b) must be a person who is not a member of the Regulator.

(4) But a person appointed under sub-paragraph (2)(b) must not be a person who is a member of the staff of the Regulator.

(5) The committee must nominate a person suitable for appointment as chairman of the Panel.

Terms of appointment and tenure of members of the Panel

12 (1) The members of the Determinations Panel are to be appointed on such terms and conditions as are determined by the Regulator with the approval of the Secretary of State.

(2) Subject to sub-paragraph (3) such a member –

(a) is to hold and vacate office in accordance with the terms and conditions of his appointment, and

(b) may resign or be removed from office in accordance with those terms and conditions.

(3) A person must cease to be a member of the Panel where –

(a) in the case of the chairman, he ceases to hold that office, or

(b) in the case of any member, he becomes a member of the Regulator or a member of the staff of the Regulator.

13 No person is to be prevented from being a member of the Panel (whether as chairman or otherwise) merely because he has previously been a member of the Panel.

Remuneration etc of members of the Panel

14 The Regulator may pay, or make provision for paying, the members of the Determinations Panel such remuneration as the Secretary of State may determine.

15 The Regulator may –

(a) pay to or in respect of any person who is or has been a member of the Panel such pension, allowances or gratuities as the Secretary of State may determine, or

(b) make such payments as the Secretary of State may determine towards provision for the payment of a pension, allowance or gratuity to or in respect of such a person.

16 Where –

    (a)   a member of the Panel ceases to be a member otherwise than on the expiry of his term of office, and

    (b)   it appears to the Secretary of State that there are circumstances which make it right for that person to receive compensation,

the Regulator may make a payment to that person of such amount as the Secretary of State may determine.

PART 4

PROCEEDINGS AND DELEGATION ETC

Committees

17 (1) The Regulator may establish committees for any purpose.

    (2) Any committee so established may establish sub-committees.

    (3) The members of such committees or sub-committees may include persons who are not members of the Regulator.

    (4) The members of such sub-committees may include persons who are not members of the committee.

    (5) But the majority of the members of a committee or a sub-committee must consist of persons who are members of the Regulator or members of the staff of the Regulator.

    (6) Sub-paragraphs (2) to (5) do not apply to –

        (a)   the committee established under section 8 or any of its sub-committees, or

        (b)   the Determinations Panel or any of its sub-committees (see section 9).

    (7) Subject to that, references in this Schedule to the committees of the Regulator are to –

        (a)   the committee established under section 8 and any of its sub-committees,

        (b)   the Determinations Panel and any of its sub-committees,

        (c)   the appointments committee, and

        (d)   any committees or sub-committees established under this paragraph.

Procedure

18 (1) The Regulator may determine –

    (a)   its own procedure (including quorum), and

    (b)   the procedure (including quorum) of any of its committees (other than the Determinations Panel and any of that Panel's sub-committees).

    (2) The Determinations Panel may determine –

    (a)   its own procedure (including quorum), and

    (b)   the procedure (including quorum) of any of its sub-committees.

    (3) This paragraph is subject to –

    (a)   sections 93 to 104 (procedure in relation to the regulatory functions) and any corresponding provisions in force in Northern Ireland, and

    (b)   any regulations made by the Secretary of State under paragraph 19.

19 (1) The Secretary of State may make regulations –

    (a)   as to the procedure (including quorum) to be followed by the Regulator or any of its committees;

(b)   as to the manner in which the functions of the Regulator are to be exercised.

(2)   Such regulations may in particular –

(a)   make provision as to the hearing of parties, the taking of evidence and the circumstances (if any) in which a document of any prescribed description is to be treated for the purposes of any proceedings before the Regulator, as evidence, or conclusive evidence, of any prescribed matter;

(b)   make provision as to the manner in which parties to any proceedings before the Regulator may or are to be represented for the purposes of the proceedings;

(c)   provide for enabling the Regulator to summon persons –

(i)   to attend proceedings before the Regulator and give evidence (including evidence on oath) for any purposes of proceedings in connection with a determination whether to exercise, or the exercise of, a regulatory function (or any corresponding function under any provisions in force in Northern Ireland corresponding to this Act), or

(ii)   to produce any documents required by the Regulator for those purposes.

(3)   In this paragraph references to proceedings before the Regulator include references to proceedings before the Determinations Panel and any of the Panel's sub-committees.

Delegation

20   (1)   The Regulator may authorise –

(a)   any executive member of the Regulator,

(b)   any other member of the staff of the Regulator, or

(c)   any of its committees (other than the appointments committee, the Determinations Panel and any of that Panel's sub-committees),

to exercise, on behalf of the Regulator, such of its functions, in such circumstances, as the Regulator may determine.

(2)   But sub-paragraph (1) does not apply to –

(a)   the non-executive functions of the Regulator listed in subsection (4) of section 8 (which, by virtue of subsection (2) of that section, must be discharged by the committee established under that section),

(b)   the duty of the Regulator to appoint the chairman and other members of the Determinations Panel under section 9,

(c)   the duty of the Regulator to determine the terms and conditions of their appointments under paragraph 12(1), and

(d)   the functions of the Regulator which are exercisable only by the Panel by virtue of –

(i)   section 10(1) (the power in certain circumstances to determine whether to exercise the functions listed in Schedule 2 and to exercise them) or any corresponding provision in force in Northern Ireland, or

(ii)   section 99(10) (the functions concerning the compulsory review of certain determinations) or any corresponding provision in force in Northern Ireland.

(3)   The Regulator may authorise the appointments committee to exercise the power under paragraph 18 to determine the committee's own procedure (including quorum).

(4)   The Regulator may authorise the Determinations Panel, in such circumstances as the Regulator may determine, to exercise on behalf of the Regulator –

(a) the power to determine whether to exercise one or more of the regulatory functions listed in sub-paragraph (5), and

(b) where the Panel so determines to exercise the regulatory function in question, the power to exercise it.

(5) The regulatory functions mentioned in sub-paragraph (4) are –

(a) the power to issue an improvement notice under section 13;

(b) the power to issue a third party notice under section 14;

(c) the power to issue a clearance statement under section 42;

(d) the power to issue a notice under section 45(1) approving the details of arrangements;

(e) the power to issue a clearance statement under section 46;

(f) the power to make an order under section 154(8);

(g) the power to make an order under section 219(4);

(h) the power to grant or revoke authorisation under section 288;

(i) the power to grant or revoke approval under section 289;

(j) the power to issue a notice under section 293(5);

(k) the power by direction under section 2(3)(a) of the Welfare Reform and Pensions Act 1999 (c. 30) to refuse to register a scheme under section 2 of that Act;

(l) the power to appoint a trustee under any of the following provisions of section 7 of the Pensions Act 1995 (c. 26) –

(i) subsection (1) where a trustee is removed by reason of his disqualification;

(ii) subsection (3)(b);

(m) the power to appoint an independent trustee under section 23 of that Act;

(n) the power to give directions under section 72B of that Act facilitating a winding up.

(6) The Regulator may also authorise the Determinations Panel, in such circumstances as the Regulator may determine, to exercise on behalf of the Regulator such functions (other than those mentioned in sub-paragraph (2)(a) to (c)) as the Regulator considers necessary for the effective exercise by the Panel of –

(a) a function of the Regulator which it is authorised to exercise by virtue of sub-paragraph (4),

(b) a function of the Regulator mentioned in sub-paragraph (2)(d) (functions exercisable only by the Panel), or

(c) a function of the Panel under section 93(3), section 99(11) or paragraph 18(2) of this Schedule (procedure).

(7) This paragraph is subject to any regulations made by the Secretary of State under paragraph 21.

21 The Secretary of State may make regulations –

(a) limiting the extent to which any of the functions mentioned in subsection (8) of section 8 may be delegated by the committee established under that section to any of its members or any of its sub-committees under that subsection;

(b) limiting the extent to which any of the functions mentioned in subsection (9) of section 10 may be delegated by the Determinations Panel to any of its members or any of its sub-committees under that subsection;

(c) limiting the extent to which functions of the Regulator may be delegated under paragraph 20;

(d) limiting the delegation under paragraph 20 of any power to delegate contained in that paragraph;

(e)   permitting the Regulator in prescribed circumstances to delegate to prescribed persons prescribed functions of the Regulator.

Application of seal and proof of instruments

22   (1)   The fixing of the common seal of the Regulator must be authenticated by the signature of a person authorised for that purpose by the Regulator (whether generally or specifically).

(2)   Sub-paragraph (1) does not apply in relation to any document which is or is to be signed in accordance with the law of Scotland.

23   A document purporting to be duly executed under the seal of the Regulator or purporting to be signed on its behalf –

(a)   is to be received in evidence, and

(b)   is to be taken to be so executed or signed unless the contrary is proved.

PART 5

FUNDING AND ACCOUNTS

Funding

24   The Secretary of State may pay the Regulator out of money provided by Parliament such sums as he may determine towards its expenses.

25   (1)   The Secretary of State may make regulations authorising the Regulator to charge fees to meet the costs incurred by the Regulator in connection with applications made for –

(a)   the modification of an occupational pension scheme under section 69 of the Pensions Act 1995 (c. 26) or under any corresponding provision in force in Northern Ireland, or

(b)   the issuing of a clearance statement under section 42 or 46 or under any corresponding provision in force in Northern Ireland.

(2)   Regulations under sub-paragraph (1) may prescribe, or authorise the Regulator to determine, the time at which any fee is due.

(3)   Any fee which is owed to the Regulator by virtue of regulations under this paragraph may be recovered as a debt due to the Regulator.

26   (1)   Section 175 of the Pension Schemes Act 1993 (c. 48) (levies towards certain expenditure) is amended as follows.

(2)   In subsection (1) omit 'or' at the end of paragraph (b) and for paragraph (c) substitute –

'(c)   of the Regulatory Authority (including the establishment of the Authority under the Pensions Act 2004), or

(d)   of the Lord Chancellor in meeting the costs of the legal assistance scheme established by virtue of section 106 of the Pensions Act 2004 (legal assistance in connection with proceedings before the Pensions Regulator Tribunal),'.

(3)   In subsection (3), in paragraph (a), for the words from 'any amounts paid' to the end of the paragraph substitute ' –

      (i)   any amounts paid to the Secretary of State under section 168(4) of this Act or section 10 of the Pensions Act 1995 (civil penalties), and

      (ii)   any fees paid to the Authority under paragraph 25 of Schedule 1 to the Pensions Act 2004 (fees for certain applications), and'.

Accounts

27   (1)   The Regulator must –

      (a)   keep proper accounts and proper records in relation to the accounts, and

      (b)   prepare in respect of each financial year a statement of accounts.

    (2)   Each statement of accounts must comply with any directions given by the Secretary of State with the approval of the Treasury as to –

      (a)   the information to be contained in it and the manner in which it is to be presented;

      (b)   the methods and principles according to which the statement is to be prepared;

      (c)   the additional information (if any) which is to be provided for the information of Parliament.

    (3)   The Regulator must send a copy of each statement of accounts –

      (a)   to the Secretary of State, and

      (b)   to the Comptroller and Auditor General,

before the end of the month of August next following the financial year to which the statement relates.

    (4)   The Comptroller and Auditor General must –

      (a)   examine, certify and report on each statement of accounts which he receives under sub-paragraph (3), and

      (b)   lay a copy of each statement and of his report before each House of Parliament.

    (5)   In this paragraph 'financial year' means –

      (a)   the period beginning with the date on which the Regulator is established and ending with the next following 31st March, and

      (b)   each successive period of 12 months.

Other expenses

28   (1)   The Regulator may –

      (a)   pay, or make provision for paying, persons attending proceedings before the Regulator at its request such travelling and other allowances (including compensation for loss of remunerative time) as the Secretary of State may determine, and

      (b)   pay, or make provision for paying, persons from whom the Regulator may decide to seek advice, as being persons considered by the Regulator to be specially qualified to advise it on particular matters, such fees as the Regulator may determine.

    (2)   In this paragraph references to proceedings before the Regulator include references to proceedings before any committee of the Regulator.

PART 6

STATUS AND LIABILITY ETC

Status

29   (1)   The Regulator is not to be regarded –

    (a)   as the servant or agent of the Crown, or

    (b)   as enjoying any status, privilege or immunity of the Crown.

  (2)   Accordingly, the Regulator's property is not to be regarded as property of, or held on behalf of, the Crown.

Validity

30   The validity of any proceedings of the Regulator (including any proceedings of any of its committees) is not to be affected by –

    (a)   any vacancy among the members of the Regulator or of any of its committees,

    (b)   any defect in the appointment of any member of the Regulator or of any of its committees, or

    (c)   any defect in the appointment of the Chief Executive.

Disqualification

31   Schedule 1 to the House of Commons Disqualification Act 1975 (c. 24) is amended as follows –

    (a)   in Part 2 (bodies whose members are disqualified) at the appropriate place insert –

      'The Pensions Regulator.', and

    (b)   in Part 3 (other disqualifying offices) at the appropriate place insert –

      'Member of the Determinations Panel established by the Pensions Regulator under section 9 of the Pensions Act 2004.'

32   Schedule 1 to the Northern Ireland Assembly Disqualification Act 1975 (c. 25) is amended as follows –

    (a)   in Part 2 (bodies whose members are disqualified) at the appropriate place insert –

      'The Pensions Regulator.', and

    (b)   in Part 3 (other disqualifying offices) at the appropriate place insert –

      'Member of the Determinations Panel established by the Pensions Regulator under section 9 of the Pensions Act 2004.'

The Parliamentary Commissioner for Administration

33   In Schedule 2 to the Parliamentary Commissioner Act 1967 (c. 13) (departments and authorities subject to investigation), at the appropriate place insert –

    'The Pensions Regulator.'

The Superannuation Act 1972

34 (1) The persons to whom section 1 of the Superannuation Act 1972 (c. 11) (persons to or in respect of whom benefits may be provided by schemes under that section) applies are to include –

the chairman of the Regulator
the employees of the Regulator.

(2) The Regulator must pay to the Minister for the Civil Service, at such times as he may direct, such sums as he may determine in respect of the increase attributable to sub-paragraph (1) in the sums payable out of money provided by Parliament under that Act.

Exemption from liability in damages

35 (1) Neither the Regulator nor any person who is a member of the Regulator, a member of any of its committees, or a member of its staff is to be liable in damages for anything done or omitted in the exercise or purported exercise of the functions of the Regulator conferred by, or by virtue of, this or any other enactment.

(2) Any person who is –

(a) the chairman of the Regulator,
(b) the Chief Executive of the Regulator, or
(c) the chairman of the Determinations Panel,

is not to be liable in damages for anything done or omitted in the exercise or purported exercise of any function conferred on the office in question by, or by virtue of, this Act or any provisions in force in Northern Ireland corresponding to this Act.

(3) Any person who is a member of the committee established under section 8 or of any of its sub-committees is not to be liable in damages for anything done or omitted in the discharge or purported discharge of the duty to prepare a report under subsection (5) of that section on the discharge of the non-executive functions.

(4) Any person who is a member of the Determinations Panel is not to be liable in damages for anything done or omitted in the exercise or purported exercise of the functions of the Panel under –

(a) section 93(3) (procedure in relation to regulatory functions) or any corresponding provision in force in Northern Ireland,
(b) section 99(11) (procedure in relation to exercise of functions on a compulsory review) or any corresponding provision in force in Northern Ireland, or
(c) paragraph 18(2) of this Schedule (general procedure).

(5) But sub-paragraphs (1) to (4) do not apply –

(a) if it is shown that the act or omission was in bad faith, or
(b) so as to prevent an award of damages made in respect of an act or omission on the ground that the act or omission was unlawful as a result of section 6(1) of the Human Rights Act 1998 (c. 42).

SCHEDULE 2　THE RESERVED REGULATORY FUNCTIONS　Section 10

PART 1

FUNCTIONS UNDER THE PENSION SCHEMES ACT 1993 (c. 48)

1　The power by direction under section 99(4) to grant an extension of the period within which the trustees or managers of a scheme are to carry out certain duties.

2　The power by direction under section 101J(2) to extend the period for compliance with a transfer notice.

3　The power under regulations made by virtue of section 168(4) to require a person to pay a penalty.

PART 2

FUNCTIONS UNDER THE PENSIONS ACT 1995 (c. 26)

4　The power to make an order under section 3(1) prohibiting a person from being a trustee.

5　The power to make an order under section 3(3) revoking such an order.

6　The power to make an order under section 4(1) suspending a trustee.

7　The power to make an order under section 4(2) extending the period for which an order under section 4(1) of that Act has effect.

8　The power to make an order under section 4(5) revoking an order under section 4(1) of that Act suspending a trustee.

9　The power to make an order appointing a trustee under any of the following provisions of section 7 –

(a)　subsection (1) where a trustee is removed by an order under section 3 (prohibition orders);

(b)　subsection (3)(a) or (c).

10　The power under section 9 to exercise by order the same jurisdiction and powers as the High Court or the Court of Session for vesting property in, or transferring property to, trustees in consequence of the appointment or removal of a trustee.

11　The power to require a person to pay a penalty under section 10 (including under regulations made by virtue of subsection (3) of that section).

12　The power to make an order under section 11 directing or authorising an occupational pension scheme to be wound up.

13　The power to give directions to trustees under section 15.

14　The power under section 29(5) to give a notice waiving a disqualification under section 29 of that Act.

15　The power under section 30(2) to exercise by order the same jurisdiction and powers as the High Court or the Court of Session for vesting property in, or transferring property to, the trustees where a trustee becomes disqualified under section 29 of that Act.

16　The power to make an order under section 67G(2) by virtue of which any modification of, or grant of rights under, an occupational pension scheme is void to any extent.

17　The power to make an order under section 67H(2) prohibiting, or specifying steps to be taken in relation to, the exercise of a power to modify an occupational pension scheme.

18　The power to make an order under section 69 authorising the modification of an occupational pension scheme or modifying the scheme.

19   The power to make an order under section 71A modifying an occupational pension scheme with a view to ensuring that it is properly wound up.

PART 3

FUNCTIONS UNDER THE WELFARE REFORM AND PENSIONS ACT 1999 (c. 30)

20   The power by direction under section 2(3)(b) to remove a scheme from

PART 4

FUNCTIONS UNDER THIS ACT

21   The power to make or extend a restraining order under section 20.
22   The power to make an order under section 20(10) permitting payments out of an account that is subject to a restraining order.
23   The power to make a repatriation order under section 21.
24   The power to make a freezing order under section 23.
25   The power to make an order under section 25(3) extending the period for which a freezing order has effect.
26   The power to make an order under section 26 validating action taken in contravention of a freezing order.
27   The power to make an order under section 28 directing that specified steps are taken.
28   The power to make an order under section 30 giving a direction where a freezing order ceases to have effect.
29   The power to make an order under section 31(3) directing the notification of members.
30   The power to issue a contribution notice under section 38.
31   The power to issue a direction under section 41(4) to the trustees or managers of an occupational pension scheme.
32   The power to issue a revised contribution notice under section 41(9).
33   The power to issue a financial support direction under section 43.
34   The power to issue a contribution notice under section 47.
35   The power to issue a direction under section 50(4) to the trustees or managers of an occupational pension scheme.
36   The power to issue a revised contribution notice under section 50(9).
37   The power to make a restoration order under section 52.
38   The power to issue a contribution notice under section 55.
39   The power to issue a notice under section 71 requiring a report to be provided to the Regulator.
40   The power to make a direction under section 76(8) extending the retention period for documents taken into possession under section 75.
41   The power to make a direction under section 78(10) extending the retention period for documents taken into possession under that section.
42   The power to make an order under section 231 modifying a scheme, giving directions or imposing a schedule of contributions.
43   The power to issue a ring-fencing notice under section 292.
44   The power to vary or revoke under section 101 –

(a)   a determination made by the Determinations Panel whether to exercise one of the other functions listed in this Schedule, or

(b)   an order, notice or direction made, issued or given in the exercise of one of those functions –

    (i)   by the Panel, or

    (ii)   by the Regulator in compliance with a direction of the Tribunal under section 103.

SCHEDULE 3   RESTRICTED INFORMATION HELD BY THE REGULATOR: CERTAIN PERMITTED DISCLOSURES TO FACILITATE EXERCISE OF FUNCTIONS

Section 86

Persons	Functions
The Secretary of State.	Functions under – (a) Part 14 of the Companies Act 1985 (c. 6), (b) the Insolvency Act 1986 (c. 45), (c) Part 3 of the Companies Act 1989 (c. 40), (d) Part 1 of the Export and Investment Guarantees Act 1991 (c. 67) (apart from sections 5 and 6), (e) Part 3 of the Pension Schemes Act 1993 (c. 48), (f) Part 5 of the Police Act 1997 (c. 50), (g) the Financial Services and Markets Act 2000 (c. 8), or (h) this Act, and functions of co-operating with overseas government authorities and bodies in relation to criminal matters.
The Bank of England.	Any of its functions.
The Financial Services Authority.	Functions under – (a) the legislation relating to friendly societies, (b) the Building Societies Act 1986 (c. 53), or (c) the Financial Services and Markets Act 2000 (c. 8).
The Charity Commissioners.	Functions under the Charities Act 1993 (c. 10).
The Pensions Regulator Tribunal.	Any of its functions.
The Pensions Ombudsman.	Functions under – (a) the Pension Schemes Act 1993 (c. 48), or (b) the Pension Schemes (Northern Ireland) Act 1993 (c. 49).
The Ombudsman for the Board of the Pension Protection Fund.	Any of his functions.

Persons	Functions
The Comptroller and Auditor General.	Any of his functions.
The Auditor General for Wales.	Any of his functions.
The Auditor General for Scotland.	Any of his functions.
The Comptroller and Auditor General for Northern Ireland.	Any of his functions.
The Commissioners of Inland Revenue or their officers.	Functions under – (a) the Income and Corporation Taxes Act 1988 (c. 1), (b) the Taxation of Chargeable Gains Act 1992 (c. 12), (c) Part 3 of the Pension Schemes Act 1993, (d) Part 3 of the Pension Schemes (Northern Ireland) Act 1993, or (e) the Income Tax (Earnings and Pensions) Act 2003 (c. 1).
The Commissioners of Customs and Excise.	Functions under any enactment.
The Official Receiver or, in Northern Ireland, the Official Receiver for Northern Ireland.	Functions under the enactments relating to insolvency.
An inspector appointed by the Secretary of State.	Functions under Part 14 of the Companies Act 1985 (c. 6).
A person authorised to exercise powers under – (a) section 447 of the Companies Act 1985, (b) Article 440 of the Companies (Northern Ireland) Order 1986 (S.I. 1986/1032 (N.I. 6)), or (c) section 84 of the Companies Act 1989 (c. 40).	Functions under those sections or that Article.
A person appointed under – (a) section 167 of the Financial Services and Markets Act 2000 (c. 8), (b) subsection (3) or (5) of section 168 of that Act, or (c) section 284 of that Act, to conduct an investigation.	Functions in relation to that investigation.
A body designated under section 326(1) of that Act.	Functions in its capacity as a body designated under that section.
A recognised investment exchange or a recognised clearing house (as defined by section 285 of that Act).	Functions in its capacity as an exchange or clearing house recognised under that Act.

Persons	Functions
A body corporate established in accordance with section 212(1) of that Act.	Functions under the Financial Services Compensation Scheme, established in accordance with section 213 of that Act.
The Panel on Takeovers and Mergers.	Functions under the City Code on Takeovers and Mergers and the Rules Governing Substantial Acquisitions of Shares for the time being issued by the Panel.
The General Insurance Standards Council.	Functions of regulating sales and advisory and service standards in relation to insurance.
A recognised professional body (within the meaning of section 391 of the Insolvency Act 1986 (c. 45)).	Functions in its capacity as such a body under that Act.
A person on whom functions are conferred by or under Part 2, 3 or 4 of the Proceeds of Crime Act 2002 (c. 29).	The functions so conferred.
The Counter Fraud and Security Management Service established under the Counter Fraud and Security Management Service (Establishment and Constitution) Order 2002 (S.I. 2002/3039).	Any of its functions.
The Department of Enterprise, Trade and Investment in Northern Ireland.	Functions under – (a) Part 15 of the Companies (Northern Ireland) Order 1986 (S.I. 1986/1032 (N.I. 6)), (b) the Insolvency (Northern Ireland) Order 1989 (S.I. 1989/2405 (N.I. 19)), or (c) Part 2 of the Companies (No. 2) (Northern Ireland) Order 1990 (S.I. 1990/1504 (N.I. 10)).
The Department for Social Development in Northern Ireland.	Functions under Part 3 of the Pension Schemes (Northern Ireland) Act 1993 (c. 49).
An Inspector appointed by the Department of Enterprise, Trade and Investment in Northern Ireland.	Functions under Part 15 of the Companies (Northern Ireland) Order 1986.
A recognised professional body within the meaning of Article 350 of the Insolvency (Northern Ireland) Order 1989.	Functions in its capacity as such a body under that Order.
The Gaming Board for Great Britain.	Functions under – (a) the Gaming Act 1968 (c. 65), or (b) the Lotteries and Amusements Act 1976 (c. 32).

SCHEDULE 4   THE PENSIONS REGULATOR TRIBUNAL   Section 102

PART 1

THE TRIBUNAL

The Panels

1   (1)   The Lord Chancellor must appoint a panel of persons for the purpose of serving as chairmen of the Tribunal ('the panel of chairmen').

(2)   A person is qualified for membership of the panel of chairmen if –

(a)   he has a 7 year general qualification within the meaning of section 71 of the Courts and Legal Services Act 1990 (c. 41),

(b)   he is an advocate or solicitor in Scotland of at least 7 years' standing,

(c)   he is a member of the Bar of Northern Ireland of at least 7 years' standing, or

(d)   he is a solicitor of the Supreme Court of Northern Ireland of at least 7 years' standing.

(3)   The panel of chairmen must include at least one member who is a person of the kind mentioned in sub-paragraph (2)(b).

(4)   The Lord Chancellor must also appoint a panel of persons who appear to him to be qualified by experience or otherwise to deal with matters of the kind that may be referred to the Tribunal ('the lay panel').

The President

2   (1)   The Lord Chancellor must appoint one of the members of the panel of chairmen to preside over the exercise of the Tribunal's functions.

(2)   The member so appointed is to be known as the President of the Pensions Regulator Tribunal (in this Schedule referred to as 'the President').

(3)   The Lord Chancellor may appoint one of the members of the panel of chairmen to be the Deputy President.

(4)   The Deputy President is to have such functions in relation to the Tribunal as the President may assign to him.

(5)   The Lord Chancellor may not appoint a person to be the President or Deputy President unless that person –

(a)   has a 10 year general qualification within the meaning of section 71 of the Courts and Legal Services Act 1990,

(b)   is an advocate or solicitor in Scotland of at least 10 years' standing,

(c)   is a member of the Bar of Northern Ireland of at least 10 years' standing, or

(d)   is a solicitor of the Supreme Court of Northern Ireland of at least 10 years' standing.

(6)   If the President ceases to be a member of the panel of chairmen, he also ceases to be the President.

(7)   If the Deputy President ceases to be a member of the panel of chairmen, he also ceases to be the Deputy President.

(8)   If the President is absent or otherwise unable to act, his functions may be exercised –

(a)   by the Deputy President, or

(b)   if there is no Deputy President or he too is absent or otherwise unable to act, by a person appointed for that purpose from the panel of chairmen by the Lord Chancellor.

Terms of office etc

3 (1) Subject to the provisions of this Schedule, each member of the panel of chairmen and the lay panel –

(a) is to hold and vacate office in accordance with the terms and conditions of his appointment, and

(b) may resign or be removed from office in accordance with those terms and conditions.

(2) A member of either panel is eligible for re-appointment if he ceases to hold office.

Remuneration and allowances

4 The Lord Chancellor may pay, or make provision for paying, out of money provided by Parliament, any person in respect of his service –

(a) as a member of the Tribunal (including service as the President or Deputy President), or

(b) as a person appointed under paragraph 7(4) (appointment of experts),

such remuneration and allowances as the Lord Chancellor may determine.

Staff

5 (1) The Lord Chancellor may appoint such staff for the Tribunal as he may determine.

(2) The remuneration of the Tribunal's staff is to be paid by the Lord Chancellor out of money provided by Parliament.

Expenses

6 The Lord Chancellor may pay, out of money provided by Parliament, such expenses of the Tribunal as the Lord Chancellor may determine.

PART 2

CONSTITUTION OF THE TRIBUNAL

7 (1) On a reference to the Tribunal, the persons to act as members of the Tribunal for the purposes of the reference are to be selected from the panel of chairmen or the lay panel in accordance with arrangements made by the President for the purposes of this paragraph ('the standing arrangements').

(2) The standing arrangements must provide for at least one member to be selected from the panel of chairmen.

(3) If, while a reference is being dealt with, a person serving as a member of the Tribunal in respect of the reference becomes unable to act, the reference may be dealt with –

(a) by the other members selected in respect of the reference, or

(b) if it is being dealt with by a single member, by such other member of the panel of chairmen as may be selected in accordance with the standing arrangements for the purposes of the reference.

(4) If it appears to the Tribunal that a matter before it involves a question of fact of special difficulty, it may appoint one or more experts to provide assistance.

(5) For the purposes of this Schedule, a 'reference to the Tribunal' means a reference to the Tribunal under this Act or any provisions in force in Northern Ireland corresponding to this Act.

PART 3

TRIBUNAL PROCEDURE

General

8   For the purpose of dealing with references, or any matter preliminary or incidental to a reference, the Tribunal must sit at such times and in such place or places as the Lord Chancellor may direct.

9   Rules made by the Lord Chancellor under section 102 may, in particular, include provision –

   (a)   as to the manner in which references are to be instituted;
   (b)   for the holding of hearings in private in such circumstances as may be specified in the rules;
   (c)   as to the persons who may appear on behalf of the parties;
   (d)   for a member of the panel of chairmen to hear and determine interim matters arising on a reference;
   (e)   for the Tribunal to deal with urgent cases expeditiously;
   (f)   as to the withdrawal of references;
   (g)   as to the registration, publication and proof of decisions and orders.

Practice directions

10   The President may give directions as to the practice and procedure to be followed by the Tribunal in relation to references to it.

Evidence

11   (1)   The Tribunal may by summons require any person to attend, at such time and place as is specified in the summons, to give evidence or to produce any document in his custody or under his control which the Tribunal considers it necessary to examine.

   (2)   The Tribunal may –

      (a)   take evidence on oath and for that purpose administer oaths, or
      (b)   instead of administering an oath, require the person examined to make and subscribe a declaration of the truth of the matters in respect of which he is examined.

   (3)   A person who without reasonable excuse refuses or fails –

      (a)   to attend following the issue of a summons by the Tribunal, or
      (b)   to give evidence,

   is guilty of an offence.

   (4)   A person guilty of an offence under sub-paragraph (3) is liable on summary conviction to a fine not exceeding level 5 on the standard scale.

   (5)   A person who without reasonable excuse –

(a) alters, suppresses, conceals or destroys a document which he is or is liable to be required to produce for the purposes of proceedings before the Tribunal, or

(b) refuses to produce a document when so required,

is guilty of an offence.

(6) A person guilty of an offence under sub-paragraph (5) is liable –

(a) on summary conviction, to a fine not exceeding the statutory maximum;

(b) on conviction on indictment, to imprisonment for a term not exceeding two years or a fine or both.

(7) In this paragraph 'document' includes information recorded in any form and, in relation to information recorded otherwise than in a legible form, references to its production include references to producing a copy of the information –

(a) in a legible form, or

(b) in a form from which it can readily be produced in a legible form.

Decisions of the Tribunal

12 (1) A decision of the Tribunal may be taken by a majority.

(2) The decision must state whether it was unanimous or taken by a majority.

(3) The decision must be recorded in a document which –

(a) contains a statement of the reasons for the decision, and

(b) is signed and dated by the member of the panel of chairmen dealing with the reference.

(4) The Tribunal must inform each party to the reference of its decision.

(5) The Tribunal must as soon as reasonably practicable send a copy of the document mentioned in sub-paragraph (3) –

(a) to each of the parties to the reference, and

(b) to such other persons as appear to the Tribunal to be directly affected by the decision.

(6) The Tribunal must send the Secretary of State and the Department for Social Development in Northern Ireland a copy of its decision.

(7) In this paragraph 'document' includes information recorded in any form.

Costs

13 (1) If the Tribunal considers that a party to any proceedings on a reference has acted vexatiously, frivolously or unreasonably it may order that party to pay to another party to the proceedings the whole or part of the costs or expenses incurred by the other party in connection with the proceedings.

(2) If, in any proceedings on a reference, the Tribunal considers that a determination of the Regulator which is the subject of the reference was unreasonable it may order the Regulator to pay to another party to the proceedings the whole or part of the costs or expenses incurred by the other party in connection with the proceedings.

PART 4

STATUS ETC

Disqualification

14   In Part 3 of Schedule 1 to the House of Commons Disqualification Act 1975 (c. 24) (other disqualifying offices), at the appropriate place insert –

'Any member, in receipt of remuneration, of a panel of persons who may be selected to act as members of the Pensions Regulator Tribunal.'

15   In Part 3 of Schedule 1 to the Northern Ireland Assembly Disqualification Act 1975 (c. 25) (other disqualifying offices), at the appropriate place insert –

'Any member, in receipt of remuneration, of a panel of persons who may be selected to act as members of the Pensions Regulator Tribunal.'

The Parliamentary Commissioner for Administration

16   In Schedule 4 to the Parliamentary Commissioner Act 1967 (c. 13) (relevant tribunals for the purposes of section 5(7) of that Act), at the appropriate place insert –

'The Pensions Regulator Tribunal constituted under section 102 of the Pensions Act 2004.'

Judicial Pensions and Retirement Act 1993

17   (1)   The Judicial Pensions and Retirement Act 1993 (c. 8) is amended as follows.
       (2)   In Schedule 1 (offices which may be qualifying offices), in Part 2, at the appropriate place insert –

'President or Deputy President of the Pensions Regulator Tribunal.'

       (3)   In Schedule 5 (relevant offices in relation to retirement provisions), at the appropriate place insert –

'Member of the Pensions Regulator Tribunal.'

Disclosure of information

18   In section 449(1) of the Companies Act 1985 (c. 6) (exceptions from restrictions on publication and disclosure), after paragraph (m) insert –

'(n)   for the purposes of proceedings before the Pensions Regulator Tribunal.'

19   In Schedule 15D to that Act (permitted disclosures of information) (as inserted by Schedule 2 to the Companies (Audit, Investigations and Community Enterprise) Act 2004), after paragraph 44 insert –

'44A A disclosure for the purposes of proceedings before the Pensions Regulator Tribunal.'

20   In section 87(2) of the Companies Act 1989 (c. 40) (exceptions from restrictions on disclosure), after paragraph (c) insert –

'(d)   proceedings before the Pensions Regulator Tribunal.'

21   In section 50(2) of the Courts and Legal Services Act 1990 (c. 41) (exceptions from restrictions on disclosure), after paragraph (s) insert –

'(t)   the Pensions Regulator Tribunal to discharge any of its functions.'

SCHEDULE 5   THE BOARD OF THE PENSION PROTECTION FUND

Section 109

PART 1

MEMBERS OF THE BOARD

Appointment of chairman

1   The chairman of the Board is to be appointed by the Secretary of State.

Appointment of ordinary members

2   (1)   The appointments of the first five ordinary members are to be made by the Secretary of State.

(2)   Subsequent appointments of ordinary members are to be made by the Board, subject to sub-paragraph (4).

(3)   In making any appointment by virtue of sub-paragraph (2) the Board must act in accordance with any procedure for making such appointments that may be prescribed.

(4)   If, at any time, there are less than five ordinary members, the Secretary of State must appoint such number of ordinary members as is required to bring the number of ordinary members to five.

Terms of appointment

3   (1)   The chairman and the ordinary members appointed by the Secretary of State are to be appointed on such terms and conditions as are determined by the Secretary of State.

(2)   The ordinary members appointed by the Board are to be appointed on such terms and conditions as are determined –

(a)   in the case of a non-executive member, by the chairman with the approval of the Secretary of State, and

(b)   in the case of an executive member, by the Chief Executive.

(3)   This paragraph is subject to paragraph 7 (remuneration of members).

Tenure of members

4   (1)   Subject to the following provisions, the chairman and any ordinary member –

(a)   is to hold and vacate office in accordance with the terms and conditions of his appointment, and

(b)   may resign or be removed from office in accordance with those terms and conditions.

(2)   A person must cease to be a member of the Board where –

(a)   in the case of the chairman, he ceases to hold that office or becomes a member of the staff of the Board;

(b)   in the case of any other non-executive member, he becomes a member of the staff of the Board;

(c)   in the case of an ordinary member who is an executive member, he ceases to be a member of the staff of the Board.

5   Where a person ceases to be employed as Chief Executive, he ceases to be a member of the Board.

6   No person is to be prevented from being a member of the Board (whether as chairman or otherwise) merely because he has previously been such a member.

Remuneration etc of members

7   The Board may pay, or make provision for paying, its non-executive members such remuneration as the Secretary of State may determine.

8   The Board may –

    (a)   pay to or in respect of any person who is or has been a non-executive member such pension, allowances or gratuities as the Secretary of State may determine, or

    (b)   make such payments as the Secretary of State may determine towards provision for the payment of a pension, allowance or gratuity to or in respect of such a person.

9   Where –

    (a)   a non-executive member ceases to be a member otherwise than on the expiry of his term of office, and

    (b)   it appears to the Secretary of State that there are circumstances which make it right for that person to receive compensation,

the Board may make a payment to that person of such amount as the Secretary of State may determine.

Interpretation of Part 1

10   In this Part 'ordinary member' has the same meaning as in section 108.

PART 2

STAFF OF THE BOARD

The staff

11   (1)   The staff of the Board consists of –

    (a)   the Chief Executive of the Board appointed under paragraph 12,

    (b)   the other employees of the Board appointed under paragraph 13, and

    (c)   any additional staff made available by the Secretary of State under paragraph 14.

    (2)   No member of the Regulator, or of the Determinations Panel established by the Regulator under section 9, is eligible for appointment as a member of the staff of the Board.

The Chief Executive

12   (1)   The Board is to employ a person as its Chief Executive.

    (2)   The Chief Executive's main function is to be responsible for securing that the functions of the Board are exercised efficiently and effectively.

    (3)   The first appointment of a Chief Executive –

(a)   is to be made by the Secretary of State, and

(b)   is to be on such terms and conditions as to remuneration and other matters as are determined by the Secretary of State.

(4)   Subsequent appointments of a Chief Executive are to be made by the Board with the approval of the Secretary of State.

(5)   Appointments under sub-paragraph (4) are to be –

(a)   on such terms and conditions as to remuneration as may be determined by the Board with the approval of the Secretary of State, and

(b)   on such other terms and conditions as may be determined by the Secretary of State.

(6)   By virtue of subsection (2) of section 112 (non-executive functions), the function conferred on the Board by sub-paragraph (5)(a) is exercisable on its behalf by the committee established under that section.

Other employees

13   (1)   Other employees of the Board may be appointed by the Board with the approval of the Secretary of State as to numbers.

(2)   Subject to sub-paragraph (3), an appointment under sub-paragraph (1) is to be on such terms and conditions as may be determined by the Chief Executive.

(3)   The terms and conditions relating to remuneration are –

(a)   in the case of an appointment of an employee who is also to be an executive member of the Board, to be determined by the Board with the approval of the Secretary of State,

(b)   in the case of an appointment of an employee of a prescribed description, to be determined by the Board.

(4)   By virtue of subsection (2) of section 112 (non-executive functions), the functions conferred on the Board by sub-paragraph (3)(a) and (b) are exercisable on its behalf by the committee established under that section.

Additional staff etc

14   (1)   The Secretary of State may make available to the Board such additional staff and such other facilities as he considers appropriate.

(2)   The availability of such staff and facilities may be on such terms as to payment by the Board as the Secretary of State may determine.

PART 3

PROCEEDINGS AND DELEGATION ETC

Committees

15   (1)   The Board may establish committees for any purpose.

(2)   Any committee established by the Board may establish sub-committees.

(3)   The members of such committees or sub-committees may include persons who are not members of the Board.

(4)   The members of a sub-committee may include persons who are not members of the committee.

(5)   Sub-paragraphs (3) and (4) do not apply to the committee established under section 112 or any of its sub-committees.

Procedure

16 The Board may determine –

    (a)   its own procedure (including quorum), and

    (b)   the procedure (including quorum) of any of its committees or sub-committees.

Delegation

17 (1) The Board may authorise –

    (a)   any executive member of the Board,

    (b)   any other member of its staff, or

    (c)   any of its committees or sub-committees (other than the committee established under section 112 or any of its sub-committees),

to exercise on behalf of the Board, such of its functions, in such circumstances, as the Board may determine.

    (2) But sub-paragraph (1) does not apply to the non-executive functions of the Board (which must, by virtue of subsection (2) of section 112, be discharged by the committee established under that section).

18 (1) The Board may make arrangements for any of its functions mentioned in sub-paragraph (2) to be exercised, in accordance with those arrangements, by a person on behalf of the Board.

    (2) The functions are those conferred by or by virtue of –

    (a)   the pension compensation provisions (see section 162);

    (b)   section 163 (adjustments to be made where Board assumes responsibility for a scheme);

    (c)   section 165 (duty to notify Inland Revenue in relation to guaranteed minimum pensions);

    (d)   section 166 (duty to pay scheme benefits unpaid at assessment date);

    (e)   sections 169 and 170 (discharge of liabilities in respect of compensation or money purchase benefits);

    (f)   section 191 (notices requiring provision of information);

    (g)   section 203(1)(a) (provision of information to members of schemes etc);

    (h)   section 111 (supplementary powers), so far as that section relates to any function conferred by or by virtue of any provision mentioned in paragraphs (a) to (g).

    (3) Where arrangements are made under this paragraph for any functions of the Board to be exercised by another person on its behalf –

    (a)   section 195(1)(b) (offence of providing false or misleading information to the Board) and section 196 (use of information) apply in relation to that person and any functions of the Board exercised by him as they apply in relation to the Board and its functions;

    (b)   subject to paragraph (c), sections 197 to 202 and 203(2) to (6) (disclosure of information) apply in relation to that person and any information obtained by him in the exercise of the Board's function as they apply in relation to the Board and information obtained by it in the exercise of its functions;

    (c)   nothing in paragraph (b) authorises any person to determine on behalf of the Board under section 201(1) whether the disclosure of any restricted information is desirable or expedient in the interests of members of occupational pension schemes or in the public interest.

19 (1) Where the Board makes arrangements under paragraph 18(1) for any of its functions to be exercised by a person on its behalf, those arrangements may also provide for that person to exercise on behalf of the Board any delegable review
function.

   (2) Where the Regulator is required to or may exercise any function on behalf of the
Board by virtue of –

   (a) section 181(4) or 189(8) (administrative functions relating to levies),
   (b) section 181(7)(b) or 189(10)(b) (recovery of levies), or
   (c) regulations under section 181(8) or 189(11) (collection, recovery and
waiver of levies),

the Board may also require the Regulator to exercise on behalf of the Board any
delegable review function.

   (3) In this paragraph, 'delegable review function', in relation to a delegated function,
means –

   (a) any function, by virtue of section 207(1)(a) or (3)(a), to give a review
decision in respect of any reviewable matter arising from the exercise of the
delegated function;

   (b) in relation to any function exercisable by virtue of paragraph (a) above, any
other function under regulations under section 207(1) in connection with
the giving of a review decision;

   (c) any function conferred by section 111 (supplementary powers), so far as
that section relates to any function mentioned in paragraph (a) or (b).

   (4) In sub-paragraph (3) –

'delegated function' means a function which is exercisable on behalf of the Board
as mentioned in sub-paragraph (1) or (2);
'review decision' has the meaning given by section 207(1).

Application of seal and proof of instruments

20 (1) The fixing of the common seal of the Board must be authenticated by the signature of a person authorised for that purpose by the Board (whether generally or
specifically).

   (2) Sub-paragraph (1) does not apply in relation to any document which is or is to
be signed in accordance with the law of Scotland.

21 A document purporting to be duly executed under the seal of the Board or purporting
to be signed on its behalf –

   (a) is to be received in evidence, and
   (b) is to be taken to be so executed or signed unless the contrary is proved.

PART 4

ACCOUNTS

Accounts

22 (1) The Board must –

   (a) keep proper accounts and proper records in relation to the accounts, and
   (b) prepare in respect of each financial year a statement of accounts.

(2) Each statement of accounts must –

    (a)   contain an acturial valuation of the Pension Protection Fund, and

    (b)   comply with any accounting directions given by the Secretary of State with the approval of the Treasury.

(3) For the purposes of sub-paragraph (2) –

    "acturial valuation", with respect to the Fund, means a valuation, prepared and signed by the appointed actuary, of the assets and liabilities of the Fund;

    "accounting direction" means a direction regarding –

        (a)   the information to be contained in a statement of accounts and the manner in which it is to be presented;

        (b)   the methods and principles according to which the statement is to be prepared;

        (c)   the additional information (if any) which is to be provided for the information of Parliament.

(4) In sub-paragraph (3) –

    (a)   "the appointed actuary" means a person with prescribed qualifications or experience, or a person approved by the Secretary of State, who is appointed by the Board for the purposes of this paragraph, and

    (b)   the liabilities and assets to be taken into account in preparing the acturial valuation, and their amount or value, are to be determined, calculated and verified by the appointed actuary in the prescribed manner.

(5) The Board must send a copy of each statement of accounts –

    (a)   to the Secretary of State, and

    (b)   to the Comptroller and Auditor General,

before the end of the month of August next following the financial year to which the statement relates.

(6) The Comptroller and Auditor General must –

    (a)   examine, certify and report on each statement of accounts which he receives under sub-paragraph (5), and

    (b)   lay a copy of each statement and of his report before each House of Parliament.

(7) In this paragraph "financial year" means –

    (a)   the period beginning with the date on which the Board is established and ending with the following 31st March, and

    (b)   each successive period of 12 months.

Other expenses

23 The Board may –

    (a)   pay, or make provision for paying, persons attending proceedings of the Board at its request such travelling and other allowances (including compensation for loss of remunerative time) as the Board may determine, and

    (b)   pay, or make provision for paying, persons from whom the Board may decide to seek advice, as being persons considered by the Board to be specially qualified to advise it on particular matters, such fees as the Board may determine.

PART 5

STATUS AND LIABILITY ETC

Status

24   (1)   The Board is not to be regarded –

(a)   as the servant or agent of the Crown, or

(b)   as enjoying any status, privilege or immunity of the Crown.

(2)   Accordingly, the Board's property is not to be regarded as property of, or held on behalf of, the Crown.

Validity

25   The validity of any proceedings of the Board (including any proceedings of any of its committees or sub-committees) is not to be affected by –

(a)   any vacancy among the members of the Board or of any of its committees or sub-committees,

(b)   any defect in the appointment of any member of the Board or of any of its committees or sub-committees, or

(c)   any defect in the appointment of the Chief Executive.

Disqualification

26   In Schedule 1 to the House of Commons Disqualification Act 1975 (c. 24), in Part 2 (bodies whose members are disqualified), at the appropriate place insert –

'The Board of the Pension Protection Fund.'

27   In Schedule 1 to the Northern Ireland Assembly Disqualification Act 1975 (c. 25), in Part 2 (bodies whose members are disqualified), at the appropriate place insert –

'The Board of the Pension Protection Fund.'

The Superannuation Act 1972

28   (1)   The persons to whom section 1 of the Superannuation Act 1972 (c. 11) (persons to or in respect of whom benefits may be provided by schemes under that section) applies are to include –

the chairman of the Board
the employees of the Board.

(2)   The Board must pay to the Minister for the Civil Service, at such times as he may direct, such sums as he may determine in respect of the increase attributable to sub-paragraph (1) in the sums payable out of money provided by Parliament under that Act.

Exemption from liability in damages

29   (1)   Neither the Board nor any person who is a member of the Board, a member of any of its committees or sub-committees, or a member of its staff is to be liable in damages for anything done or omitted in the exercise or purported exercise of the functions of the Board conferred by, or by virtue of, this or any other enactment.

(2) Any person who is the Chief Executive of the Board is not to be liable in damages for anything done or omitted in the exercise or purported exercise of any function conferred on the Chief Executive by, or by virtue of, this Act or any provisions in force in Northern Ireland corresponding to this Act.

(3) Any person who is a member of the committee established under section 112 or of any of its sub-committees is not to be liable in damages for anything done or omitted in the discharge or purported discharge of the duty to prepare a report under subsection (5) of that section on the discharge of the non-executive functions.

(4) Sub-paragraphs (1) to (3) do not apply –

   (a)   if it is shown that the action or omission was in bad faith, or
   (b)   so as to prevent an award of damages made in respect of an act or omission on the ground that the act or omission was unlawful as a result of section 6(1) of the Human Rights Act 1998 (c. 42).

(5) This paragraph does not prevent the Board being required to pay compensation on a direction of the PPF Ombudsman by virtue of regulations under section 213(1) or 214 or any provision in force in Northern Ireland corresponding to either of those provisions.

SCHEDULE 6   TRANSFER OF PROPERTY, RIGHTS AND LIABILITIES TO THE BOARD   Section 161

1   This Schedule applies where the property, rights and liabilities of an occupational pension scheme are transferred to the Board in accordance with section 161.

2   (1) Subject to sub-paragraph (2), the property, rights and liabilities so transferred include –

   (a)   property, rights and liabilities that would not otherwise be capable of being transferred or assigned,
   (b)   property situated anywhere in the United Kingdom or elsewhere, and
   (c)   rights and liabilities under the law of any part of the United Kingdom or of any country or territory outside the United Kingdom.

   (2) Where, but for this sub-paragraph, any rights or liabilities under a contract of employment between the trustees or managers of the scheme and an individual would be transferred to the Board under section 161, this sub-paragraph operates to terminate the contract of employment on the day preceding the day on which the transfer notice is received by the trustees or managers of the scheme.

3   (1) Without prejudice to the generality of section 161 and subject to sub-paragraph (2), any legal proceedings or applications to any authority pending immediately before the transfer by or against any of the trustees or managers of the scheme in their capacity as trustees or managers shall be continued by or against the Board.

   (2) The liabilities transferred by section 161 do not include any liabilities in respect of an existing or future cause of action against the trustees or managers of the scheme if, disregarding the transfer, the trustees or managers would have been personally liable to meet the claim and would not have been indemnified from the assets of the scheme.

4   The transfer is binding on all persons, even if, apart from this paragraph, it would have required the consent or concurrence of any person.

5   No person shall have any power, in consequence of the transfer, to terminate or modify any interest or right which was vested in the trustees or managers of the scheme.

6   Any reference in any agreement, document or instrument of any description to the trustees or managers of the scheme shall have effect so far as necessary for the purposes of giving effect to the transfer as a reference to the Board.

7   (1) The Board must take all such steps as may be required to secure that the vesting in the Board, by virtue of section 161, of any foreign property, right or liability is effective under the relevant foreign law.

   (2) Until the vesting of any foreign property, right or liability in the Board is effective under the relevant foreign law, the persons who were the trustees or managers of the scheme immediately before the transfer effected by section 161 must hold that property or right for the benefit of, or discharge that liability on behalf of, the Board.

   (3) Nothing in this paragraph prejudices the effect under the law of England and Wales or of Scotland of the vesting in the Board, in accordance with section 161, of any foreign property, right or liability.

   (4) In this paragraph references to any foreign property, right or liability are references to any property, right or liability as respects which any issue arising in any proceedings would have to be determined (in accordance with the rules of private international law) by reference to the law of a country or territory outside the United Kingdom.

SCHEDULE 7   PENSION COMPENSATION PROVISIONS   Section 162

Introductory

1   This Schedule applies for the purposes of determining the compensation payable where the Board assumes responsibility for an eligible scheme ('the scheme') in accordance with this Chapter.

2   In this Schedule references to 'the assessment date' are to the date on which the assessment period in relation to the scheme, or (where there has been more than one such assessment period) the last one, began.

Pensions in payment at assessment date

3   (1) Compensation is payable in accordance with this paragraph where, immediately before the assessment date, a person is entitled to present payment of a pension under the admissible rules of the scheme.

   (2) That person ('the pensioner') is entitled to periodic compensation in respect of that pension ('the pension') commencing at the assessment date and continuing for life or, in a case to which sub-paragraph (8) applies, until such time as entitlement to the pension would have ceased under the admissible rules.

   (3) The annual rate of the periodic compensation is the appropriate percentage of the aggregate of –

      (a) the protected pension rate, and

      (b) any increases under paragraph 28 (annual increases in periodic compensation).

   (4) In sub-paragraph (3) 'the appropriate percentage' means –

      (a) in a case to which sub-paragraph (7) applies, 90%, and

      (b) in any other case, 100%.

   (5) In sub-paragraph (3) 'the protected pension rate' means the annual rate of the pension, under the admissible rules, immediately before the assessment date.

   (6) In determining for the purposes of sub-paragraph (5) the annual rate of the pension immediately before the assessment date, any recent discretionary increase is to be disregarded if paragraph 35(3) applies.

   (7) This sub-paragraph applies where the pensioner has not attained normal pension age in respect of the pension before the assessment date and his entitlement to the pension –

(a)   is attributable to his pensionable service, and

(b)   did not arise by virtue of any provision of the admissible rules of the scheme making special provision as to early payment of pension on grounds of ill health.

(8) This sub-paragraph applies where the pension was not attributable –

(a)   to the pensioner's pensionable service, or

(b)   (directly or indirectly) to a pension credit to which the pensioner became entitled under section 29(1)(b) of the Welfare Reform and Pensions Act 1999 (c. 30).

(9) This paragraph does not apply if compensation is payable in respect of the pension in accordance with paragraph 5 (pension benefits postponed at assessment date).

(10) This paragraph is subject to –

paragraph 26 (compensation cap), and

paragraph 30 (power of Secretary of State to change percentage rates by order).

4   (1) This paragraph applies where –

(a)   the pensioner dies on or after the assessment date, and

(b)   the pension was attributable –

(i)   to the pensioner's pensionable service, or

(ii)   (directly or indirectly) to a pension credit to which the pensioner became entitled under section 29(1)(b) of the Welfare Reform and Pensions Act 1999.

(2) Subject to sub-paragraph (4), the pensioner's widow or widower is entitled to periodic compensation commencing on the day following the pensioner's death and continuing for life.

(3) The annual rate of the periodic compensation at any time is half of the annual rate of the periodic compensation (including any increases under paragraph 28) to which the pensioner would at that time have been entitled under paragraph 3 in respect of the pension had the pensioner not died.

(4) The pensioner's widow or widower is not entitled to periodic compensation under this paragraph in such circumstances as may be prescribed.

(5) In this paragraph 'the pension' and 'the pensioner' are to be construed in accordance with paragraph 3.

Pension benefits postponed at assessment date

5   (1) Compensation is payable in accordance with this paragraph where immediately before the assessment date –

(a)   a person is entitled to present payment of a pension under the admissible rules of the scheme,

(b)   payment of that pension is postponed, and

(c)   he has attained normal pension age in relation to the pension.

(2) That person ('the postponed pensioner') is entitled to periodic compensation in respect of that pension ('the pension') commencing at the assessment date and continuing for life or, in a case to which sub-paragraph (7) applies, until such time as entitlement to the pension would have ceased under the admissible rules.

(3) The annual rate of the periodic compensation is 100% of the aggregate of –

(a)   the protected pension rate, and

(b)   any increases under paragraph 28 (annual increases in periodic compensation).

(4) In sub-paragraph (3) 'the protected pension rate' means what would have been the annual rate of the pension, under the admissible rules, if the postponement of payment had ceased immediately before the assessment date.

(5) In determining for the purposes of sub-paragraph (4) the annual rate of the pension immediately before the assessment date, any recent discretionary increase is to be disregarded if paragraph 35(3) applies.

(6) Where the pension is attributable (directly or indirectly) to a pension credit, the reference in sub-paragraph (1)(c) to 'normal pension age' is to be read as a reference to 'normal benefit age'.

(7) This sub-paragraph applies where the pension was not attributable –

   (a) to the postponed pensioner's pensionable service, or
   (b) (directly or indirectly) to a pension credit to which the postponed pensioner became entitled under section 29(1)(b) of the Welfare Reform and Pensions Act 1999 (c. 30).

(8) This paragraph is subject to –

   paragraph 24 (commutation), and
   paragraph 30 (power of Secretary of State to change percentage rates by order).

6 (1) This paragraph applies where the postponed pensioner –

   (a) dies on or after the assessment date, and
   (b) the pension was attributable –

      (i) to the postponed pensioner's pensionable service, or
      (ii) (directly or indirectly) to a pension credit to which the postponed pensioner became entitled under section 29(1)(b) of the Welfare Reform and Pensions Act 1999.

(2) Subject to sub-paragraph (4), the postponed pensioner's widow or widower is entitled to periodic compensation commencing on the day following the postponed pensioner's death and continuing for life.

(3) The annual rate of the periodic compensation at any time is half of the annual rate of the periodic compensation (including any increases under paragraph 28) to which the postponed pensioner would at that time have been entitled under paragraph 5 in respect of the pension had the postponed pensioner not died.

(4) The postponed pensioner's widow or widower is not entitled to periodic compensation under this paragraph in such circumstances as may be prescribed.

(5) In this paragraph 'the postponed pensioner' and 'the pension' are to be construed in accordance with paragraph 5.

7 (1) Compensation is payable in accordance with this paragraph where immediately before the assessment date –

   (a) a person is entitled to present payment of a lump sum under the admissible rules of the scheme ('the scheme lump sum'),
   (b) payment of that lump sum is postponed, and
   (c) he has attained normal pension age in relation to the lump sum.

(2) That person is entitled to compensation in the form of a lump sum of an amount equal to 100% of the amount of the scheme lump sum which would have been payable had the postponement ceased immediately before the assessment date.

(3) The compensation is payable at the assessment date.

(4) Where the scheme lump sum is attributable (directly or indirectly) to a pension credit, the reference in sub-paragraph (1)(c) to 'normal pension age' is to be read as a reference to 'normal benefit age'.

(5) This paragraph does not apply in relation to a lump sum to which a person is entitled by reason of commuting any part of a pension under the scheme.

(6) This paragraph is subject to paragraph 30 (power of Secretary of State to change percentage rates by order).

Active members over normal pension age at assessment date

8   (1)   Compensation is payable in accordance with this paragraph where a person who, under the admissible rules, is (immediately before the assessment date) an active member of the scheme has, before that date, attained normal pension age in respect of his rights under the admissible rules of the scheme to a pension.

(2)   The active member is entitled to periodic compensation in respect of that pension ('the pension') commencing at the assessment date and continuing for life.

(3)   The annual rate of the periodic compensation is 100% of the aggregate of –

(a)   the protected notional pension, and

(b)   any increases under paragraph 28 (annual increases in periodic compensation).

(4)   In sub-paragraph (3) 'the protected notional pension' means the aggregate of –

(a)   the accrued amount, and

(b)   any increases in the pension to which the active member would have been entitled under the admissible rules (by virtue of the fact that the pension did not come into payment at normal pension age) if he had ceased to be an active member of the scheme immediately before the assessment date.

(5)   Subject to sub-paragraphs (6) and (7), the accrued amount is –

$$AR \times PE \times PS$$

where –

AR is the active member's annual accrual rate in respect of the pension under the admissible rules,

PE is the active member's annual pensionable earnings in respect of the pension under the admissible rules, and

PS is the active member's pensionable service in respect of the pension under the admissible rules in years (including any fraction of a year).

(6)   If the accrual rates or pensionable earnings differ in respect of different parts of the active member's pensionable service relating to the pension, an amount is calculated in accordance with the formula in sub-paragraph (5) in respect of each of those parts and the accrued amount is the aggregate of those amounts.

For this purpose the references in that sub-paragraph to the active member's pensionable service, accrual rate and pensionable earnings are to be read as references to the part of his pensionable service in question and to his accrual rate and pensionable earnings in respect of that part.

(7)   In any case where the Board is satisfied that it is not possible to identify one or more of the elements of the formula in sub-paragraph (5), the Board may, having regard to the admissible rules, determine how the accrued amount is to be calculated.

(8)   This paragraph is subject to –

paragraph 20 (compensation in respect of scheme right to transfer payment or contribution refund),

paragraph 24 (commutation), and

paragraph 30 (power of Secretary of State to change percentage rates by order).

9   (1)   This paragraph applies where the active member dies on or after the assessment date.

(2)   Subject to sub-paragraph (4), the active member's widow or widower is entitled to periodic compensation commencing on the day following the member's death and continuing for life.

(3) The annual rate of the periodic compensation at any time is half of the annual rate of the periodic compensation (including any increases under paragraph 28) to which the active member would at that time have been entitled under paragraph 8 in respect of the pension had the member not died.

(4) The active member's widow or widower is not entitled to periodic compensation under this paragraph in such circumstances as may be prescribed.

(5) In this paragraph 'the pension' and 'the active member' are to be construed in accordance with paragraph 8.

10 (1) Compensation is payable in accordance with this paragraph where an active member of the scheme has, before the assessment date, attained normal pension age in respect of his rights under the admissible rules of the scheme to a lump sum ('the scheme lump sum').

(2) The active member is entitled to compensation of an amount equal to 100% of the aggregate of –

(a) the accrued amount, and

(b) any increases to which the active member would have been entitled under the admissible rules (by virtue of the fact that the lump sum was not paid at normal pension age) had the active member ceased to be an active member immediately before the assessment date.

(3) The compensation is payable at the assessment date.

(4) Subject to sub-paragraphs (5) and (6), the accrued amount is –

$$AR \times PE \times PS$$

where –

AR is the active member's annual accrual rate in respect of the scheme lump sum under the admissible rules,

PE is the active member's annual pensionable earnings in respect of the scheme lump sum under the admissible rules, and

PS is the active member's pensionable service in respect of the scheme lump sum, under the admissible rules, in years (including any fraction of a year).

(5) If the accrual rates or pensionable earnings differ in respect of different parts of the active member's pensionable service relating to the scheme lump sum, an amount is calculated in accordance with the formula in sub-paragraph (4) in respect of each of those parts and the accrued amount is the aggregate of those amounts.

For this purpose the references in that sub-paragraph to the active member's pensionable service, accrual rate and pensionable earnings are to be read as references to the part of his pensionable service in question and to his accrual rate and pensionable earnings in respect of that part.

(6) In any case where the Board is satisfied that it is not possible to identify one or more of the elements of the formula in sub-paragraph (4), the Board may, having regard to the admissible rules, determine how the accrued amount is to be calculated.

(7) This paragraph does not apply in relation to a lump sum to which a person is entitled by reason of commuting any part of a pension under the scheme.

(8) This paragraph is subject to –

paragraph 20 (compensation in respect of scheme right to transfer payment or contribution refund), and

paragraph 30 (power of Secretary of State to change percentage rates by order).

Active members who have not attained normal pension age at assessment date

11 (1) Compensation is payable in accordance with this paragraph where a person who, under the admissible rules, is (immediately before the assessment date) an active member of the scheme has not, before that date, attained normal pension age in respect of his rights under the admissible rules of the scheme to a pension.

   (2) If the active member survives to attain normal pension age in respect of that pension ('the pension'), he is entitled to periodic compensation in respect of the pension commencing at that age and continuing for life.

   (3) The annual rate of the periodic compensation is 90% of the aggregate of –

   (a) the protected notional pension, and

   (b) any increases under paragraph 28 (annual increases in periodic compensation).

   (4) In sub-paragraph (3) 'the protected notional pension' means the aggregate of –

   (a) the accrued amount, and

   (b) the revaluation amount for the revaluation period (see paragraph 12).

   (5) Subject to sub-paragraphs (6) and (7), the accrued amount is –

$$AR \times PE \times PS$$

where –

   AR is the active member's annual accrual rate in respect of the pension under the admissible rules,
   PE is the active member's annual pensionable earnings in respect of the pension under the admissible rules, and
   PS is the active member's pensionable service in respect of the pension under the admissible rules in years (including any fraction of a year).

   (6) If the accrual rates or pensionable earnings differ in respect of different parts of the active member's pensionable service relating to the pension, an amount is calculated in accordance with the formula in sub-paragraph (5) in respect of each of those parts and the accrued amount is the aggregate of those amounts.

   For this purpose the references in sub-paragraph (5) to the active member's pensionable service, accrual rate and pensionable earnings are to be read as references to the part of his pensionable service in question and to his accrual rate and pensionable earnings in respect of that part.

   (7) In any case where the Board is satisfied that it is not possible to identify one or more of the elements of the formula in sub-paragraph (5), the Board may, having regard to the admissible rules, determine how the accrued amount is to be calculated.

   (8) This paragraph is subject to –

   paragraph 20 (compensation in respect of scheme right to transfer payment or contribution refund),
   paragraph 24 (commutation),
   paragraph 26 (compensation cap), and
   paragraph 30 (power of Secretary of State to change percentage rates by order).

12 (1) This paragraph applies for the purposes of paragraph 11(4)(b).

   (2) The revaluation period is the period which –

   (a) begins with the assessment date, and

   (b) ends with the day before the day on which the active member attains normal pension age in respect of the pension.

(3)   The revaluation amount for the revaluation period is –

(a)   in a case where the revaluation period is less than one month, nil, and
(b)   in any other case, the revaluation percentage of the accrued amount.

(4)   In sub-paragraph (3) 'the revaluation percentage' means the lesser of –

(a)   the percentage increase in the general level of prices in Great Britain during the revaluation period determined in the prescribed manner, and
(b)   the maximum revaluation rate.

(5)   For the purposes of sub-paragraph (4)(b) 'the maximum revaluation rate' in relation to the revaluation period is –

(a)   if that period is a period of 12 months, 5%, and
(b)   in any other case, the percentage that would be the percentage mentioned in sub-paragraph (4)(a) had the general level of prices in Great Britain increased at the rate of 5% compound per annum during that period.

This is subject to paragraph 29 (power of Board to determine maximum revaluation rate etc).

(6)   In this paragraph 'the active member', 'the accrued amount' and 'the pension' are to be construed in accordance with paragraph 11.

13   (1)   This paragraph applies where the active member dies on or after the assessment date.

(2)   Subject to sub-paragraph (4), the widow or widower of the active member is entitled to periodic compensation commencing on the day following the active member's death and continuing for life.

(3)   The annual rate of the periodic compensation at any time is –

(a)   where the active member died after attaining normal pension age, half of the annual rate of the periodic compensation (including any increases under paragraph 28) to which the member would at that time have been entitled under paragraph 11 in respect of the pension had the member not died, and

(b)   where the active member died before attaining normal pension age, half of the annual rate of the periodic compensation (including any increases under paragraph 28) to which the member would have been entitled at normal pension age under paragraph 11 if –

(i)   normal pension age had been the member's actual age immediately before the date of the member's death, and
(ii)   the member had not died.

(4)   The active member's widow or widower is not entitled to periodic compensation under this paragraph in such circumstances as may be prescribed.

(5)   In this paragraph 'the pension' and 'the active member' are to be construed in accordance with paragraph 11.

14   (1)   Compensation is payable in accordance with this paragraph where immediately before the assessment date, under the admissible rules of the scheme, an active member of the scheme has not attained normal pension age in respect of his rights to a lump sum ('the scheme lump sum').

(2)   If the active member survives to attain normal pension age in respect of the scheme lump sum, he is entitled to compensation in respect of the scheme lump sum when he attains that age.

(3)   The compensation is a lump sum equal to 90% of the protected amount.

(4)   In sub-paragraph (3) 'the protected amount' means the aggregate of –

(a)   the accrued amount, and
(b)   the revaluation amount for the revaluation period.

(5) Subject to sub-paragraphs (6) and (7), the accrued amount is –

$$AR \times PE \times PS$$

where –

AR is the active member's annual accrual rate in respect of the scheme lump sum under the admissible rules,

PE is the active member's annual pensionable earnings in respect of the scheme lump sum under the admissible rules, and

PS is the active member's pensionable service in respect of the scheme lump sum, under the admissible rules, in years (including any fraction of a year).

(6) If the accrual rates or pensionable earnings differ in respect of different parts of the active member's pensionable service relating to the scheme lump sum, an amount is calculated in accordance with the formula in sub-paragraph (5) in respect of each of those parts and the accrued amount is the aggregate of those amounts.

For this purpose the references in that sub-paragraph to the active member's pensionable service, accrual rate and pensionable earnings are to be read as references to the part of his pensionable service in question and to his accrual rate and pensionable earnings in respect of that part.

(7) In any case where the Board is satisfied that it is not possible to identify one or more of the elements of the formula in sub-paragraph (5), the Board may, having regard to the admissible rules, determine how the accrued amount is to be calculated.

(8) Paragraph 12 applies for the purpose of determining the revaluation amount except that –

(a) in that paragraph the references to the pension are to be read as references to the scheme lump sum, and

(b) in sub-paragraph (6) of that paragraph the reference to paragraph 11 is to be read as a reference to this paragraph.

(9) This paragraph is subject to –

paragraph 20 (compensation in respect of scheme right to transfer payment or contribution refund),

paragraph 26 (compensation cap), and

paragraph 30 (power of Secretary of State to change percentage rates by order).

Deferred members who have not attained normal pension age at assessment date

15 (1) Compensation is payable in accordance with this paragraph where, under the admissible rules of the scheme, a person who is a deferred member immediately before the assessment date has not attained normal pension age, in respect of his rights to a pension under the scheme, before that date.

(2) If that person ('the deferred member') survives to attain normal pension age in respect of that pension ('the pension'), he is entitled to periodic compensation in respect of the pension commencing at that age and continuing for life.

(3) The annual rate of the periodic compensation is 90% of the aggregate of –

(a) the protected pension rate, and

(b) any increases under paragraph 28 (annual increases in periodic compensation).

(4) In sub-paragraph (3) 'the protected pension rate' means the aggregate of –

   (a) the accrued amount,
   (b) the revaluation amount for the first revaluation period (see paragraph 16), and
   (c) the revaluation amount for the second revaluation period (see paragraph 17).

(5) In sub-paragraph (4) 'the accrued amount' means an amount equal to the initial annual rate of the pension to which the deferred member would have been entitled in accordance with the admissible rules had he attained normal pension age when the pensionable service relating to the pension ended.

(6) This paragraph is subject to –

   paragraph 24 (commutation),
   paragraph 26 (compensation cap), and
   paragraph 30 (power of Secretary of State to change percentage rates by order).

16 (1) This paragraph applies for the purposes of paragraph 15(4)(b).

   (2) The first revaluation period is the period which –

   (a) begins with the day after the day on which the deferred member's pensionable service in respect of the pension ended, and
   (b) ends with the day before the assessment date.

   (3) The revaluation amount for the first revaluation period is –

   (a) where that period is less than one month, nil, and
   (b) in any other case, the amount determined in the prescribed manner.

   (4) In this paragraph 'the deferred member' and 'the pension' are to be construed in accordance with paragraph 15.

17 (1) This paragraph applies for the purposes of paragraph 15(4)(c).

   (2) The second revaluation period is the period which –

   (a) begins with the assessment date, and
   (b) ends with the day before the day on which the deferred member attains normal pension age in respect of the pension.

   (3) The revaluation amount for the second revaluation period is –

   (a) where that period is less than one month, nil, and
   (b) in any other case the revaluation percentage of the aggregate of –

      (i) the accrued amount, and
      (ii) the revaluation amount for the first revaluation period (see paragraph 16).

   (4) In sub-paragraph (3) 'the revaluation percentage' means the lesser of –

   (a) the percentage increase in the general level of prices in Great Britain during the second revaluation period determined in the prescribed manner, and
   (b) the maximum revaluation rate.

   (5) For the purposes of sub-paragraph (4)(b) 'the maximum revaluation rate', in relation to the second revaluation period, is –

   (a) if that period is a period of 12 months, 5%, and
   (b) in any other case, the percentage that would be the percentage mentioned in sub-paragraph (4)(a) had the general level of prices in Great Britain increased at the rate of 5% compound per annum during that period.

   This is subject to paragraph 29 (power of Board to determine maximum revaluation rate).

(6)   In this paragraph 'the deferred member', 'the accrued amount' and 'the pension' are to be construed in accordance with paragraph 15.

18   (1)   This paragraph applies where –

(a)   the deferred member dies on or after the assessment date, and

(b)   the pension was attributable to the deferred member's pensionable service.

(2)   Subject to sub-paragraph (4), the widow or widower of the deferred member is entitled to periodic compensation commencing on the day following the deferred member's death and continuing for life.

(3)   The annual rate of the periodic compensation at any time is –

(a)   where the deferred member died after attaining normal pension age, half of the annual rate of the periodic compensation (including any increases under paragraph 28) to which the deferred member would at that time have been entitled under paragraph 15 in respect of the pension had the member not died,

(b)   where the deferred member died before attaining normal pension age, half of the annual rate of the periodic compensation (including any increases under paragraph 28) to which the deferred member would have been entitled at that time under paragraph 15 if –

(i)   normal pension age had been the deferred member's actual age immediately before the date of the deferred member's death, and

(ii)   the deferred member had not died.

(4)   The deferred member's widow or widower is not entitled to periodic compensation under this paragraph in such circumstances as may be prescribed.

(5)   In this paragraph 'the deferred member' and 'the pension' are to be construed in accordance with paragraph 15.

19   (1)   Compensation is payable in accordance with this paragraph where, under the admissible rules of the scheme, a deferred member has not attained normal pension age in respect of his rights to a lump sum under the scheme ('the scheme lump sum') before the assessment date.

(2)   If the deferred member survives to attain normal pension age in respect of the scheme lump sum, he is entitled to compensation under this paragraph on attaining that age.

(3)   The compensation is a lump sum equal to 90% of the protected amount.

(4)   In sub-paragraph (3) 'the protected amount' means the aggregate of –

(a)   the accrued amount,

(b)   the revaluation amount for the first revaluation period, and

(c)   the revaluation amount for the second revaluation period.

(5)   In sub-paragraph (4) 'the accrued amount' means an amount equal to the amount of the scheme lump sum to which the deferred member would have been entitled in accordance with the admissible rules had normal pension age been the actual age attained by the deferred member when the pensionable service relating to the lump sum ended.

(6)   Paragraphs 16 and 17 apply in relation to this paragraph as if in those paragraphs –

(a)   references to the pension were to the scheme lump sum, and

(b)   'the deferred member' and 'the accrued amount' had the same meaning as in this paragraph.

(7)   This paragraph does not apply in relation to a lump sum to which a person is entitled by reason of commuting any part of a pension under the scheme.

(8)   This paragraph is subject to –

paragraph 26 (compensation cap), and

paragraph 30 (power of Secretary of State to change percentage rates by order).

Compensation in respect of scheme right to transfer payment or contribution refund

20 (1) Compensation is payable in accordance with this paragraph where –

    (a) a person's pensionable service terminates on the commencement of the assessment period,

    (b) as a result, he has rights, under the admissible rules, to –

        (i) a transfer payment calculated by reference to the value of benefits which have accrued to him under the scheme ('the protected transfer payment'), or

        (ii) a cash payment calculated by reference to the amount of contributions made by him or on his behalf to the scheme ('the protected contribution repayment'),

    (c) Chapter 5 of Part 4 of the Pension Schemes Act 1993 (c. 48) (early leavers: cash transfer sums and contribution refunds) does not apply to him, and

    (d) he does not have relevant accrued rights to benefit (within the meaning of section 101AA(4) of that Act).

(2) That person is entitled to compensation in the form of a lump sum in respect of the protected transfer payment or protected contribution repayment.

(3) The amount of the compensation is 90% of the amount of the protected transfer payment or protected contribution repayment (whichever is the greater).

(4) For the purposes of sub-paragraph (3), the amount of the protected transfer payment or protected contribution repayment is to be calculated in accordance with the admissible rules, which are to be applied for this purpose subject to any prescribed modifications.

(5) The compensation is payable immediately after the transfer notice given under section 160 is received by the trustees or managers of the scheme.

(6) This paragraph is subject to paragraph 30 (power of Secretary of State to change percentage rates by order).

(7) Regulations may modify any provision of paragraph 8, 10, 11 or 14 (compensation for persons who were active members immediately before assessment date) as it applies in the case of a person who is entitled to compensation under this paragraph.

(8) Regulations may modify any provision of sub-paragraphs (1) to (6) as it applies in the case of a person who is entitled to compensation under paragraph 8, 10, 11 or 14.

Pension credit members who have not attained normal benefit age at assessment date

21 (1) Paragraphs 15, 18 and 19 apply in relation to a pension credit member of the scheme who has not attained normal benefit age at the assessment date as they apply to a deferred member who has not attained normal pension age at that date, subject to the modifications in sub-paragraph (2).

(2) The modifications are as follows –

    (a) in paragraph 15(1) and (2) the references to normal pension age are to be read as references to normal benefit age,

(b)   in paragraph 15(4) for the words from 'the aggregate of' to the end substitute 'the accrued amount',

(c)   for paragraph 15(5) substitute –

'(5)   In sub-paragraph (4) "the accrued amount" means an amount equal to the initial annual rate of the pension which, under the admissible rules, the deferred member is entitled to receive at normal benefit age by virtue of his pension credit rights.',

(d)   for paragraph 18(1)(b) substitute –

'(b)   the pension was attributable (directly or indirectly) to a pension credit to which the deferred pensioner became entitled under section 29(1)(b) of the Welfare Reform and Pensions Act 1999 (c. 30).',

(e)   in paragraph 19(1) and (2) the references to normal pension age are to be read as references to normal benefit age,

(f)   in paragraph 19(4) for the words from 'the aggregate of' to the end substitute 'the accrued amount',

(g)   for paragraph 19(5) substitute –

'(5)   In sub-paragraph (4) "the accrued amount" means an amount equal to the amount of the scheme lump sum which, under the admissible rules, the deferred member is entitled to receive at normal benefit age by virtue of his pension credit rights.',

and

(h)   paragraph 19(6) does not apply.

Survivors who do not meet conditions for scheme benefits at assessment date

22   (1)   Compensation is payable in accordance with this paragraph where –

(a)   a member of the scheme has died before the assessment date,

(b)   as a result of that death, a pension, which is attributable to the member's pensionable service, is payable to that person's widow or widower or any other person ('the survivor') if conditions specified in the scheme rules are met, and

(c)   the survivor first satisfies those conditions on or after that date.

(2)   The survivor is entitled to periodic compensation in respect of that pension ('the pension') –

(a)   commencing if, and when, the pension would have become payable under the admissible rules, and

(b)   continuing until such time as entitlement to the pension would have ceased under the admissible rules.

(3)   The annual rate of the periodic compensation is 100% of the aggregate of –

(a)   the initial rate of the pension which would have been payable in accordance with the admissible rules had the conditions mentioned in sub-paragraph (1)(c) been satisfied, immediately before the assessment date, and

(b)   any increases under paragraph 28 (annual increases in periodic compensation).

(4)   This paragraph is subject to paragraph 30 (power of Secretary of State to change percentage rates by order).

Compensation in form of dependants' benefits

23   (1)   Regulations may provide for compensation to be payable, in such circumstances as may be prescribed, to or in respect of –

    (a)   partners of prescribed descriptions of persons of prescribed descriptions who were members of the scheme immediately before the assessment date;

    (b)   dependants of prescribed descriptions of persons of prescribed descriptions who –

        (i)   were members of the scheme, or had rights to benefits payable under the scheme rules in respect of a member, immediately before the assessment date,

        (ii)   became entitled to benefits under the scheme rules in respect of a member on or after the assessment date but before the time the trustees or managers of the scheme received a transfer notice under section 160, or

        (iii)   have become entitled to compensation under paragraph 22 (survivors who do not meet conditions for scheme benefits at assessment date), in relation to the scheme.

    (2)   Regulations may in particular –

    (a)   provide for compensation in the form of periodic or lump sum payments;

    (b)   provide for periodic compensation to be payable for a prescribed period;

    (c)   apply paragraphs 28 and 29(2) (annual increases in respect of periodic compensation) in respect of compensation in the form of periodic payments (with or without modifications).

Commutation of periodic compensation

24   (1)   In prescribed circumstances, a person entitled to periodic compensation under paragraph 5, 8, 11 or 15 may opt to commute for a lump sum a portion of the periodic compensation with effect from the time it becomes payable.

    (2)   Except in such circumstances as may be prescribed, the portion commuted under sub-paragraph (1) must not exceed 25%.

    (3)   Any reduction required to be made under paragraph 26 (compensation cap) must be made before determining the amount of a person's periodic compensation which may be commuted under this paragraph.

    (4)   Where a person opts to commute any part of his periodic compensation under this paragraph, the lump sum payable under sub-paragraph (1) is the actuarial equivalent of the commuted portion of the periodic compensation calculated from tables designated for this purpose by the Board.

    (5)   The Board must publish in such manner as it considers appropriate the tables designated by it for the purposes of sub-paragraph (4).

    (6)   Regulations may prescribe the manner in which an option to commute periodic compensation under this paragraph may be exercised.

    (7)   This paragraph does not apply where –

    (a)   before the assessment date, the person concerned has received benefits under the scheme rules which were in the form of a lump sum (otherwise than as a result of the commutation of any part of a pension) and were attributable to his own service under the scheme, or

    (b)   immediately before the assessment date, the person concerned has rights to a lump sum under the admissible rules (otherwise than by commutation of any part of a pension) and those rights are attributable to such service.

(8)   The Secretary of State may, by order, amend sub-paragraph (2) to substitute a different percentage for the percentage for the time being specified in that sub-paragraph.

Early payment of compensation

25   (1)   Regulations may prescribe circumstances in which, and conditions subject to which, a person may become entitled to –

   (a)   periodic compensation under paragraph 11 or 15, or
   (b)   lump sum compensation under paragraph 14 or 19,

   before he attains normal pension age (or, in a case to which paragraph 21 applies, normal benefit age).

   (2)   The Board must determine the amount of the actuarial reduction to be applied to compensation where a person becomes so entitled by virtue of regulations under this paragraph.

   (3)   Where, by virtue of this paragraph, periodic compensation is payable to a person under paragraph 11 or 15 before that person attains normal pension age –

   (a)   paragraph 12(2) applies as if the reference to the date on which the active member attains normal pension age were a reference to the date on which the compensation is payable by virtue of this paragraph, and

   (b)   paragraph 17(2)(b) applies as if the reference to the date on which the deferred member attains normal pension age were a reference to the date on which the compensation is payable by virtue of this paragraph.

Compensation cap

26   (1)   Where –

   (a)   a person becomes entitled to relevant compensation in respect of a benefit ('benefit A') under the scheme, and

   (b)   sub-paragraph (2)(a) or (b) applies,

   the amount of the compensation must be restricted in accordance with sub-paragraph (3).

   (2)   For the purposes of sub-paragraph (1) –

   (a)   this paragraph applies if –

      (i)   the annual value of benefit A exceeds the compensation cap, and
      (ii)   paragraph (b)(i) does not apply, and

   (b)   this paragraph applies if –

      (i)   at the same time as the person becomes entitled to relevant compensation in respect of benefit A he also becomes entitled to relevant compensation in respect of one or more other benefits under the scheme or a connected occupational pension scheme ('benefit or benefits B'), and

      (ii)   the aggregate of the annual values of benefit A and benefit or benefits B exceeds the compensation cap.

   (3)   Where the relevant compensation in respect of benefit A is required to be restricted in accordance with this sub-paragraph –

   (a)   if that compensation is within sub-paragraph (4)(a), the protected pension rate for the purposes of paragraph 3(3)(a) is the cap fraction of the rate determined in accordance with paragraph 3(5);

(b)   if that compensation is within sub-paragraph (4)(b), the protected notional pension for the purposes of paragraph 11(3)(a) is the cap fraction of the rate determined in accordance with paragraph 11(4);

(c)   if that compensation is within sub-paragraph (4)(c), the protected amount for the purposes of paragraph 14(3) is the cap fraction of the amount determined in accordance with paragraph 14(4);

(d)   if that compensation is within sub-paragraph (4)(d), the protected pension rate for the purposes of paragraph 15(3)(a) is the cap fraction of the rate determined in accordance with paragraph 15(4);

(e)   if that compensation is within sub-paragraph (4)(e), the protected amount for the purposes of paragraph 19(3) is the cap fraction of the amount determined in accordance with paragraph 19(4).

(4)   For the purposes of this paragraph 'relevant compensation' means –

(a)   periodic compensation under paragraph 3 (in a case to which sub-paragraph (7) of that paragraph applies),

(b)   periodic compensation under paragraph 11,

(c)   compensation under paragraph 14,

(d)   periodic compensation under paragraph 15, or

(e)   compensation under paragraph 19.

(5)   For the purposes of this paragraph, 'the cap fraction' means –

$$\frac{C}{V}$$

Where –

C is the compensation cap, and

V is the annual value of benefit A or, in a case to which sub-paragraph (2)(b) applies, the aggregate of the annual values of benefit A and benefit or benefits B.

(6)   For the purposes of this paragraph the 'annual value' of a benefit in respect of which a person has become entitled to relevant compensation means –

(a)   if the relevant compensation is within sub-paragraph (4)(a) and neither paragraph (b) nor (c) below applies, the amount of the protected pension rate for the purposes of paragraph 3(3)(a);

(b)   if the relevant compensation is within sub-paragraph (4)(a) and is in respect of a pension of which a portion has been commuted for a lump sum, the amount which would have been the protected pension rate for those purposes had that portion not been commuted;

(c)   if the relevant compensation is within sub-paragraph (4)(a) and the person became entitled to a relevant lump sum under the scheme at the same time as he became entitled to the pension to which that compensation relates, an amount equal to the aggregate of –

   (i)   the protected pension rate for the purposes of paragraph 3(3)(a), and

   (ii)   the annualised value of the relevant lump sum;

(d)   if the relevant compensation is within sub-paragraph (4)(b), the amount of the protected notional pension for the purposes of paragraph 11(3)(a);

(e)   if the relevant compensation is within sub-paragraph (4)(c), the annualised value of the protected amount for the purposes of paragraph 14(3);

(f)   if the relevant compensation is within sub-paragraph (4)(d), the amount of the protected pension rate for the purposes of paragraph 15(3)(a);

(g)   if the relevant compensation is within sub-paragraph (4)(e), the annualised value of the protected amount for the purposes of paragraph 19(3);

and for the purposes of determining the annual value of a benefit any reduction required to be made by this paragraph is to be disregarded.

(7) In this paragraph –

'annualised value' of a lump sum or amount means the annualised actuarially equivalent amount of that sum or amount determined in accordance with actuarial factors published by the Board;

'the compensation cap', in relation to the person who becomes entitled to relevant compensation in respect of benefit A, means –

    (a)   the amount specified by the Secretary of State by order, or

    (b)   where the person –

        (i)   has not attained the age of 65, or

        (ii)   has attained the age of 66,

at the time he first becomes entitled to that compensation, that amount as adjusted by the Board in accordance with actuarial adjustment factors published by it;

and for the purposes of this paragraph, except in prescribed circumstances, the scheme is connected with another occupational pension scheme if the same person is or was an employer in relation to both schemes.

(8) For the purposes of sub-paragraph (6)(c) a lump sum under the scheme is a relevant lump sum if the person's entitlement to the lump sum –

    (a)   is attributable to his pensionable service, and

    (b)   did not arise by virtue of any provision of the admissible rules of the scheme making special provision as to early payment of pension on grounds of ill health.

(9) Regulations may provide for this paragraph to apply with prescribed modifications where a person becomes entitled to relevant compensation in respect of a benefit and he has previously –

    (a)   become entitled to relevant compensation in respect of a benefit or benefits under the scheme or a connected occupational pension scheme, or

    (b)   become entitled to one or more lump sums under the scheme or a connected occupational pension scheme.

(10) Regulations may prescribe sums which are to disregarded for the purposes of this paragraph.

Increasing the compensation cap in line with earnings

27   (1) This paragraph applies where, on a review under subsection (2) of section 148 of the Social Security Administration Act 1992 (c. 5) (review of general level of earnings obtaining in Great Britain) in a tax year, the Secretary of State concludes that the general level of earnings obtaining in Great Britain ('the new level') exceeds the general level at the end of the period mentioned in paragraph (a) or, as the case may be, the date determined under paragraph (b) of that subsection ('the old level').

    (2) The Secretary of State must make an order under sub-paragraph (7) of paragraph 26 which has the effect of increasing the amount specified for the purposes of that sub-paragraph by the percentage by which the new level is greater than the old level.

    (3) The order must provide for the increase to have effect on and after the 1st April next following the end of the tax year to which the review relates.

Annual increase in periodic compensation

28 (1) This paragraph provides for the increases mentioned in sub-paragraph (3)(b) of paragraphs 3, 5, 8, 11, 15 and 22.

(2) Where a person is entitled to periodic compensation under any of those paragraphs, he is entitled, on the indexation date, to an increase under this paragraph of –

   (a) the appropriate percentage of the amount of the underlying rate immediately before that date, or

   (b) where the person first became entitled to the periodic compensation during the period of 12 months ending immediately before that date, 1/12th of that amount for each full month for which he was so entitled.

(3) In sub-paragraph (2) –

'appropriate percentage' means the lesser of –

   (a) the percentage increase in the retail prices index for the period of 12 months ending with the 31st May last falling before the indexation date, and

   (b) 2.5%;

'indexation date' means –

   (a) the 1st January next falling after a person first becomes entitled to the periodic compensation, and

   (b) each subsequent 1st January during his lifetime;

'underlying rate' means, in the case of periodic compensation under any of the paragraphs mentioned in sub-paragraph (1), the aggregate of –

   (a) so much of the amount mentioned in sub-paragraph (3)(a) of the paragraph in question as is attributable to post-1997 service, and

   (b) the amount within sub-paragraph (3)(b) of that paragraph immediately before the indexation date.

(4) Where paragraph 26(3) (compensation cap) applies to restrict the amount of periodic compensation under one of the paragraphs mentioned in sub-paragraph (1), the amount mentioned in sub-paragraph (3)(a) of the paragraph in question is attributable to post-1997 service and pre-1997 service in the same proportions as the amount so mentioned would have been so attributable had paragraph 26(3) not applied.

(5) Where a portion of periodic compensation under one of the paragraphs mentioned in sub-paragraph (1) has been commuted under paragraph 24 –

   (a) for the purposes of sub-paragraph (2), the definition of 'underlying rate' in sub-paragraph (3) applies as if the reference in paragraph (a) of the definition to the amount mentioned in sub-paragraph (3)(a) of the paragraph in question was a reference to that amount reduced by the commutation percentage, and

   (b) that amount (as so reduced) is attributable to post-1997 service and pre-1997 service in the same proportions as that amount would have been so attributable had no part of the periodic compensation been commuted.

(6) In this paragraph –

'post-1997 service' means –

   (a) pensionable service which is within paragraph 36(4)(a) and occurs on or after 6th April 1997, or

   (b) pensionable service which is within paragraph 36(4)(b) and meets such requirements as may be prescribed;

'pre-1997 service' means –

    (a)   pensionable service which is within paragraph 36(4)(a) and occurred before 6th April 1997, or

    (b)   pensionable service which is within paragraph 36(4)(b) and meets such requirements as may be prescribed;

'the commutation percentage', in relation to periodic compensation, means the percentage of that compensation commuted under paragraph 24.

(7)   But in this paragraph, in relation to any relevant pension credit amount, 'post-1997 service' and 'pre-1997 service' have such meanings as may be prescribed.

(8)   In sub-paragraph (7), 'relevant pension credit amount' means an amount mentioned in sub-paragraph (3)(a) of –

    (a)   paragraph 3,

    (b)   paragraph 5, or

    (c)   paragraph 15 as it applies by virtue of paragraph 21,

which is attributable (directly or indirectly) to a pension credit.

(9)   This paragraph is subject to paragraph 29 (Board's power to alter rates of revaluation and indexation).

Board's powers to alter rates of revaluation and indexation

29   (1)   The Board may determine the percentage that is to be the maximum revaluation rate for the purposes of paragraphs 12(4) and 17(4), and where it does so paragraphs 12(5) and 17(5) do not apply.

    (2)   The Board may also determine the percentage that is to be the appropriate percentage for the purposes of paragraph 28 (and where it does so the definition of 'appropriate percentage' in paragraph 28(3) does not apply).

    (3)   Before making a determination under this paragraph the Board must –

       (a)   consult such persons as it considers appropriate, and

       (b)   publish details of the proposed determination in such manner as it considers appropriate and consider any representations made in respect of it.

    (4)   The rate determined under this paragraph may be nil.

    (5)   A determination under this paragraph may be expressed so as to have effect for a limited period.

    (6)   A determination under sub-paragraph (2) –

       (a)   has effect in relation to future increases under paragraph 28 only, and

       (b)   may be expressed to have effect –

          (i)   in all cases (whether the entitlement to the periodic compensation first arose before or after the date the determination is made), or

         (ii)   only in cases where entitlement to the periodic compensation first arose on or after a date determined by the Board.

    (7)   Notice of any determination under this paragraph must be published in such manner as the Board considers appropriate.

Secretary of State's powers to vary percentage paid as compensation

30   (1)   The Secretary of State may, on the recommendation of the Board, by order provide that any of the provisions mentioned in sub-paragraph (2) is to have effect as if a different percentage were substituted for the percentage specified in the provision on the passing of this Act ('the original percentage').

494 Pensions Act 2004

(2) The provisions are paragraphs 3(4)(a) and (b), 5(3), 7(2), 8(3), 10(2), 11(3), 14(3), 15(3), 19(3), 20(3) and 22(3) of this Schedule (percentage used to calculate periodic or lump sum compensation entitlement).

(3) Subject to sub-paragraph (4), an order under sub-paragraph (1) has effect only in respect of any period for which the Board has, under paragraph 29 –

    (a) reduced the maximum revaluation rate for the purposes of paragraphs 12(4) and 17(4) to nil, and

    (b) reduced the appropriate percentage for the purposes of paragraph 28 to nil in all cases.

(4) Sub-paragraph (3) does not prevent an order under sub-paragraph (1) having effect to the extent that it provides for paragraph 3(4)(a), 11(3), 14(3), 15(3), 19(3) or 20(3) (provisions where the original percentage is 90%) to have effect as if for the original percentage there were substituted a higher percentage.

(5) Before making a recommendation for the purposes of sub-paragraph (1) the Board must –

    (a) consult such persons as it considers appropriate, and

    (b) publish details of the proposed recommendation in such manner as it considers appropriate and consider any representations made in respect of it.

(6) Subject to sub-paragraph (3), an order under this paragraph may have effect –

    (a) for a limited period specified in the order;

    (b) in relation –

        (i) to all payments of compensation which fall to be made after such date as may be specified in the order (whether the entitlement to the periodic compensation first arose before or after that date), or

        (ii) only to payments of compensation to which a person first becomes entitled after such a date.

(7) The date specified under sub-paragraph (6)(b)(i) or (ii) must not be earlier than the date of the order.

Special provision in relation to certain pensions in payment before the assessment date

31 (1) The powers conferred by this paragraph are exercisable in relation to cases where –

    (a) immediately before the assessment date, a person ('the pensioner') is entitled to present payment of a pension under the scheme rules ('the pre-assessment date pension'), but

    (b) the effect of disregarding rules within paragraphs (a) and (b) of paragraph 35(2) is that the pensioner is not entitled to compensation under paragraph 3(2) by reason of the pension or a part of the pension.

(2) Regulations may provide –

    (a) for the pensioner to be treated, for the purposes of the pension compensation provisions, as entitled, immediately before the assessment date, to present payment of a pension under the admissible rules, and

    (b) for the compensation payable under paragraph 3 in respect of that pension to be determined in the prescribed manner and, for this purpose, for any provision of this Schedule to be applied with such modifications as may be prescribed.

(3) Regulations may also provide, in cases where –

    (a)   the pensioner is not treated as entitled to present payment of a pension by virtue of regulations under sub-paragraph (2), but

    (b)   he is or may become entitled to compensation in respect of the pre-assessment date pension otherwise than under paragraph 3,

for any provision of this Schedule to apply with such modifications as may be prescribed.

Short periods of service which terminate on commencement of assessment period

32   (1) This paragraph applies to a member of the scheme if –

    (a)   his pensionable service terminates on the commencement of the assessment period, and

    (b)   as a result, he has rights, in relation to the scheme, under Chapter 5 of Part 4 of the Pension Schemes Act 1993 (c. 48) (early leavers: cash transfer sums and contribution refunds).

   (2) Where this paragraph applies, for the purposes of this Schedule the member is to be treated as if, immediately before the assessment date, he –

    (a)   had relevant accrued rights to benefits under the scheme (within the meaning of section 101AA(4) of that Act), and

    (b)   did not have any other rights to benefits (other than benefits attributable (directly or indirectly) to a pension credit) under the scheme.

Power to modify Schedule in its application to certain schemes

33   Where the scheme is a prescribed scheme or a scheme of a prescribed description, this Schedule applies with such modifications as may be prescribed.

Normal pension age

34   (1) In this Schedule 'normal pension age', in relation to the scheme and any pension or lump sum under it, means the age specified in the admissible rules as the earliest age at which the pension or lump sum becomes payable without actuarial adjustment (disregarding any admissible rule making special provision as to early payment on the grounds of ill health).

   (2) Where different ages are specified in relation to different parts of a pension or lump sum –

    (a)   this Schedule has effect as if those parts were separate pensions or, as the case may be, lump sums, and

    (b)   references in relation to a part of the pension or lump sum to the normal pension age are to be read as references to the age specified in the admissible rules as the earliest age at which that part becomes payable under the scheme without actuarial adjustment (disregarding any special provision as to early payment on grounds of ill health or otherwise).

   (3) In any case where the Board is satisfied that it is not possible to identify the normal pension age from the admissible rules of the scheme, it may, having regard to those rules, determine how the normal pension age is to be determined.

Scheme rules, admissible rules etc

35 (1) In this Schedule, in relation to the scheme, the following expressions have the meaning given by this paragraph –

'admissible rules';
'recent rule changes';
'recent discretionary increase'.

(2) The 'admissible rules' means the scheme rules disregarding –

(a) in a case where sub-paragraph (3) applies, the recent rule changes, and

(b) in any case, any scheme rule which comes into operation on, or operates by reference, to the winding up of the scheme or any associated event.

(3) This sub-paragraph applies if the combined effect of the recent rule changes and recent discretionary increases is such that, if account were taken of those changes and increases in calculating the protected liabilities in relation to the scheme at the relevant time, those protected liabilities would be greater than they would be if all those changes and increases were disregarded.

(4) In sub-paragraph (3) 'the relevant time' means the time immediately before the assessment period which begins on the assessment date.

(5) Subject to sub-paragraph (6), 'recent rule changes' means –

(a) changes to the scheme rules which took effect in the period of three years ending with the assessment date, or were made in that period and took effect by reference to an earlier time, and

(b) any scheme rules which come into operation on, or operate by reference to –

(i) an insolvency event in relation to the employer or any associated event, or

(ii) any prescribed event relating to the future of the employer as a going concern.

(6) 'Recent rule changes' does not include –

(a) any scheme rules or changes attributable to paragraph 3 of Schedule 5 to the Social Security Act 1989 (c. 24), section 129 of the Pension Schemes Act 1993 (c. 48), section 117 of the Pensions Act 1995 (c. 26), section 31(4) of the Welfare Reform and Pensions Act 1999 (c. 30) or section 306 of this Act (overriding requirements),

(b) any enactment, or any scheme rules or changes which are required or reasonably necessary to comply with an enactment,

(c) any scheme rules or changes that come into operation on, or operate by reference to, the winding up of the scheme or any associated event, and

(d) any scheme rules or changes of a prescribed description.

(7) 'Recent discretionary increase' means an increase in the rate of any pension in payment or postponed pension under the scheme rules which took effect in the period mentioned in sub-paragraph (5)(a).

(8) For the purposes of sub-paragraph (7) an increase ('the relevant increase') in the rate of a pension in payment or postponed pension is to be disregarded to the extent that it does not exceed –

(a) the amount by which the pension in question is required to be increased by virtue of –

(i) the admissible rules, or

(ii) sections 13(1) and 109 of the Pension Schemes Act 1993 (requirement to index and pay guaranteed minimum pensions), or

(b) if greater, the appropriate percentage of the rate of that pension.

(9) For the purposes of sub-paragraph (8)(a), no increase in the rate of a pension which is made at the discretion of the trustees or managers of the scheme, the employer or any other person is to be regarded as an increase required by virtue of the admissible rules.

(10) For the purposes of sub-paragraph (8)(b), 'the appropriate percentage' is the percentage increase in the general level of prices in Great Britain during the period –

(a) beginning when the rate of the pension was last increased or, if there has been no previous increase, the date the pension first became payable (or would have been payable but for its being postponed), and

(b) ending with the time the relevant increase was made.

Accrual rate, pensionable service and pensionable earnings

36 (1) In this Schedule, in relation to a member's entitlement to benefits under the scheme, each of the following expressions has the meaning given by this paragraph –

'accrual rate';
'pensionable earnings';
'pensionable service'.

(2) 'Accrual rate' means the rate at which under the admissible rules rights to the benefits accrue over time by reference to periods of pensionable service.

(3) 'Pensionable earnings' means the earnings by reference to which the benefits are calculated under the admissible rules.

(4) Subject to sub-paragraph (5), 'pensionable service' means –

(a) actual service in any description of employment to which the scheme applies which qualifies the member for benefits under the scheme, and

(b) any notional service allowed in respect of the member under the admissible rules which qualifies the member for such benefits.

(5) The service within sub-paragraph (4)(b) does not include –

(a) service attributable (directly or indirectly) to a pension credit, or

(b) service of a prescribed description.

Other definitions

37 (1) In this Schedule –

'deferred member', in relation to the scheme, means a person who, under the admissible rules, has accrued rights other than –

(a) an active member, or

(b) a person who in respect of his pensionable service is entitled to the present payment of pension or other benefits;

'normal benefit age', in relation to the scheme and a person with rights to a pension or lump sum under it attributable (directly or indirectly) to a pension credit, means the age specified in the admissible rules as the earliest age at which that pension or lump sum becomes payable without actuarial adjustment (disregarding any scheme rule making special provision as to early payment on grounds of ill health or otherwise);

'pension credit member', in relation to the scheme, means a person who has rights under the scheme which are attributable (directly or indirectly) to a pension credit;

'pension credit rights', in relation to the scheme, means rights to future benefits under the scheme which are attributable (directly or indirectly) to a pension credit;

'retail prices index' means –

(a) the general index of retail prices (for all items) published by the Office for National Statistics, or

(b) where that index is not published for a month, any substituted index or figures published by that Office;

'the scheme' is to be construed in accordance with paragraph 1.

(2) For the purposes of this Schedule the accrued rights of a member of the scheme at any time are the rights (other than rights attributable (directly or indirectly) to a pension credit) which, in accordance with the admissible rules, have accrued to or in respect of him at that time to future benefits.

(3) In this Schedule references to a pension or lump sum under the admissible rules of the scheme, or a right to such a pension or lump sum, do not include a pension or lump sum, or right to a pension or lump sum, which is a money purchase benefit.

(4) In this Schedule references to 'ill health' are to be construed in accordance with regulations under this sub-paragraph.

SCHEDULE 8   RESTRICTED INFORMATION HELD BY THE BOARD: CERTAIN PERMITTED DISCLOSURES TO FACILITATE EXERCISE OF FUNCTIONS

Section 200

Persons	Functions
The Secretary of State.	Functions under – (a) Part 14 of the Companies Act 1985 (c. 6), (b) the Insolvency Act 1986 (c. 45), (c) Part 3 of the Companies Act 1989 (c. 40), (d) Part 1 of the Export and Investment Guarantees Act 1991 (c. 67) (apart from sections 5 and 6), (e) Part 3 of the Pension Schemes Act 1993 (c. 48), (f) Part 5 of the Police Act 1997 (c. 50), (g) the Financial Services and Markets Act 2000 (c. 8), or (h) this Act, and functions of co-operating with overseas government authorities and bodies in relation to criminal matters.
The Bank of England.	Any of its functions.

Persons	Functions
The Financial Services Authority.	Functions under – (a) the legislation relating to friendly societies, (b) the Building Societies Act 1986 (c. 53), or (c) the Financial Services and Markets Act 2000.
The Charity Commissioners.	Functions under the Charities Act 1993 (c. 10).
The Pensions Regulator Tribunal.	Any of its functions.
The Pensions Ombudsman.	Functions under – (a) the Pension Schemes Act 1993, or (b) the Pension Schemes (Northern Ireland) Act 1993 (c. 49).
The Ombudsman for the Board of the Pension Protection Fund.	Any of his functions.
The Comptroller and Auditor General.	Any of his functions.
The Auditor General for Wales.	Any of his functions.
The Auditor General for Scotland.	Any of his functions.
The Comptroller and Auditor General for Northern Ireland.	Any of his functions.
The Commissioners of Inland Revenue or their officers.	Functions under – (a) the Income and Corporation Taxes Act 1988 (c. 1), (b) the Taxation of Chargeable Gains Act 1992 (c. 12), (c) Part 3 of the Pension Schemes Act 1993 (c. 48), (d) Part 3 of the Pension Schemes (Northern Ireland) Act 1993 (c. 49), or (e) the Income Tax (Earnings and Pensions) Act 2003 (c. 1).
The Commissioners of Customs and Excise.	Functions under any enactment.
The Official Receiver or, in Northern Ireland, the Official Receiver for Northern Ireland.	Functions under the enactments relating to insolvency.
An inspector appointed by the Secretary of State.	Functions under Part 14 of the Companies Act 1985 (c. 6).

Persons	*Functions*
A person authorised to exercise powers under – (a) section 447 of the Companies Act 1985, (b) Article 440 of the Companies (Northern Ireland) Order 1986 (S.I. 1986/1032 (N.I. 6)), or (c) section 84 of the Companies Act 1989 (c. 40).	Functions under those sections or that Article.
A person appointed under – (a) section 167 of the Financial Services and Markets Act 2000 (c. 8), (b) subsection (3) or (5) of section 168 of that Act, or (c) section 284 of that Act, to conduct an investigation.	Functions in relation to that investigation.
A body designated under section 326(1) of that Act.	Functions in its capacity as a body designated under that section.
A recognised investment exchange or a recognised clearing house (as defined by section 285 of that Act).	Functions in its capacity as an exchange or clearing house recognised under that Act.
A body corporate established in accordance with section 212(1) of that Act.	Functions under the Financial Services Compensation Scheme, established in accordance with section 213 of that Act.
The Panel on Takeovers and Mergers.	Functions under the City Code on Takeovers and Mergers and the Rules Governing Substantial Acquisitions of Shares for the time being issued by the Panel.
The General Insurance Standards Council.	Functions of regulating sales and advisory and service standards in relation to insurance.
A recognised professional body (within the meaning of section 391 of the Insolvency Act 1986 (c. 45)).	Functions in its capacity as such a body under that Act.
A person on whom functions are conferred by or under Part 2, 3 or 4 of the Proceeds of Crime Act 2002 (c. 29).	The functions so conferred.
The Counter Fraud and Security Management Service established under the Counter Fraud and Security Management Service (Establishment and Constitution) Order 2002 (S.I. 2002/3039).	Any of its functions.

Persons	Functions
The Department of Enterprise, Trade and Investment in Northern Ireland.	Functions under – (a) Part 15 of the Companies (Northern Ireland) Order 1986 (S.I. 1986/1032 (N.I. 6)), (b) the Insolvency (Northern Ireland) Order 1989 (S.I. 1989/2405 (N.I. 19)), or (c) Part 2 of the Companies (No. 2) (Northern Ireland) Order 1990 (S.I. 1990/1504 (N.I. 10)).
The Department for Social Development in Northern Ireland.	Functions under Part 3 of the Pension Schemes (Northern Ireland) Act 1993 (c. 49).
An Inspector appointed by the Department of Enterprise, Trade and Investment in Northern Ireland.	Functions under Part 15 of the Companies (Northern Ireland) Order 1986.
A recognised professional body within the meaning of Article 350 of the Insolvency (Northern Ireland) Order 1989.	Functions in its capacity as such a body under that Order.
The Gaming Board for Great Britain.	Functions under – (a) the Gaming Act 1968 (c. 65), or (b) the Lotteries and Amusements Act 1976 (c. 32).

SCHEDULE 9   REVIEWABLE MATTERS

Section 206

1   The issue of a determination notice under section 123 approving a notice issued under section 122.
2   The failure to issue a determination notice under section 123.
3   The issue of, or failure to issue, a notice under section 122 by the Board by virtue of section 124 (Board's duty where failure to comply with section 122).
4   The issue of, or failure to issue –
   (a)   a scheme failure notice under subsection (2) of section 130 (scheme rescue not possible), or
   (b)   a withdrawal notice under subsection (3) of that section (scheme rescue has occurred).
5   Any direction given under subsection (2) of section 134 (directions during an assessment period) or any variation or revocation of such a direction under subsection (4) of that section.
6   The issue of a notice under section 136(2) (power to validate contraventions of section 135).
7   The making of a loan under section 139(2) (loans to pay scheme benefits), the amount of any such loan or the failure to make such a loan.
8   The failure by the Board to obtain an actuarial valuation of a scheme under section 143(2).
9   The approval of, or failure to approve, a valuation in respect of an eligible scheme under section 144(2).

10   The issue of, or failure to issue, a withdrawal notice under or by virtue of –

   (a)   section 146 (schemes which become eligible schemes), or
   (b)   section 147 (new schemes created to replace existing schemes).

11   The issue of, or failure to issue, a withdrawal notice under section 148 (no insolvency event has occurred or is likely to occur).

12   The issue of, or failure to issue, a determination notice under section 152(3) (whether value of scheme assets less than aggregate of liabilities etc).

13   The issue of, or failure to issue, a determination notice under section 153(6) (authorisation to continue as closed scheme).

14   Any direction given under section 154(7) (directions about winding up of scheme with sufficient assets to meet protected liabilities) and any variation or revocation of such a direction.

15   The failure by the Board to give a transfer notice under section 160.

16   Any determination by the Board of a person's entitlement to compensation under the pension compensation provisions or the failure in any case to make such a determination.

17   Any failure by the Board to make a payment required by section 163(4)(b) (adjustments to be made where Board assumes responsibility for a scheme).

18   Any determination by the Board under section 181(3)(a) (the eligible schemes in respect of which the initial levy or the pension protection levy is imposed) or the failure to make such a determination.

19   The amount of the initial levy or any pension protection levy payable in respect of an eligible scheme determined by the Board under section 181(3)(b).

20   The making of a fraud compensation payment under section 182(1), the amount of any such payment or the failure to make such a payment.

21   The issue of, or failure to issue, a notice under section 183(2) (scheme rescue not possible or having occurred in case of scheme which is not eligible etc).

22   Any settlement date determined by the Board under section 184(2) (recovery of value) or the failure to determine a settlement date under that provision.

23   Any determination by the Board under section 184(4) (recovery of value: whether amount received in respect of particular act or omission) or the failure to make such a determination.

24   The making of a payment under section 186(1) (interim payments), the amount of any such payment or the failure to make such a payment.

25   Any term or condition imposed by the Board –

   (a)   under section 185(2) on the making of a fraud compensation payment, or
   (b)   under subsection (4) of section 186 (interim payments) on the making of a payment under subsection (1) of that section.

26   Any determination by the Board under section 186(3)(b) (interim payments) that the amount of a payment was excessive.

27   Any date determined by the Board under section 187(4) (earliest date for making a fraud compensation transfer payment).

28   Any determination by the Board under section 187(6) (fraud compensation transfer payments: whether payment is received in respect of particular act or omission).

29   Any determination by the Board under section 189(7)(a) (occupational pension schemes in respect of which any fraud compensation levy is imposed) or the failure to make such a determination.

30   The amount of any fraud compensation levy payable in respect of an occupational pension scheme determined by the Board under section 189(7)(b).

SCHEDULE 10   USE AND SUPPLY OF INFORMATION: PRIVATE PENSIONS POLICY AND RETIREMENT PLANNING

Section 236

Use of information held by Secretary of State etc

1   (1)   Section 3 of the Social Security Act 1998 (c. 14) (use of information) is amended as follows.

    (2)   In subsection (1), for the words from 'social security' to 'training' substitute 'any of the matters specified in subsection (1A) below'.

    (3)   After subsection (1) insert –

       '(1A) The matters are –

          (a)   social security, child support or war pensions;
          (b)   employment or training;
          (c)   private pensions policy;
          (d)   retirement planning.'

    (4)   In subsection (2)(a), for the words from 'social security' to 'training' substitute 'any of the matters specified in subsection (1A) above'.

    (5)   After subsection (4) insert –

       '(5)   In this section –

          "private pensions policy" means policy relating to occupational pension schemes or personal pension schemes (within the meaning given by section 1 of the Pension Schemes Act 1993);

          "retirement planning" means promoting financial planning for retirement.'

Supply of information held by tax authorities

2   (1)   This paragraph applies to information which is held –

        (a)   by the Commissioners of Inland Revenue;
        (b)   by a person providing services to the Commissioners of Inland Revenue, in connection with the provision of those services;
        (c)   by the Commissioners of Customs and Excise;
        (d)   by a person providing services to the Commissioners of Customs and Excise, in connection with the provision of those services.

    (2)   Information to which this paragraph applies may be supplied –

        (a)   to the Secretary of State or the Northern Ireland Department, or
        (b)   to a person providing services to the Secretary of State or the Northern Ireland Department,

    for use for the purposes of functions relating to private pensions policy or retirement planning.

    (3)   In this paragraph –

       'private pensions policy' means policy relating to occupational pension schemes or personal pension schemes;

       'retirement planning' means promoting financial planning for retirement;

       'the Northern Ireland Department' means the Department for Social Development in Northern Ireland.

Supply of housing benefit and council tax benefit information

3   (1)   Section 122D of the Social Security Administration Act 1992 (c. 5) (supply of information by authorities administering housing benefit or council tax benefit) is amended as follows.

(2)   In subsection (1) for 'or employment or training' substitute 'employment or training, private pensions policy or retirement planning'.

(3)   After subsection (2) insert –

'(2A)   Information supplied under subsection (2) may be used for any purpose relating to private pensions policy or retirement planning.'

(4)   After subsection (5) insert –

'(6)   In this section –

"private pensions policy" means policy relating to occupational pension schemes or personal pension schemes (within the meaning given by section 1 of the Pension Schemes Act 1993);

"retirement planning" means promoting financial planning for retirement.'

SCHEDULE 11   DEFERRAL OF RETIREMENT PENSIONS AND SHARED ADDITIONAL PENSIONS   Section 297

PART 1

PRINCIPAL AMENDMENTS OF SOCIAL SECURITY CONTRIBUTIONS AND BENEFITS ACT 1992 (c. 4)

1   In this Part of this Schedule 'the principal Act' means the Social Security Contributions and Benefits Act 1992.

2   Schedule 5 to the principal Act (increase of pension where entitlement is deferred) is amended as follows.

3   For the heading, substitute 'PENSION INCREASE OR LUMP SUM WHERE ENTITLEMENT TO RETIREMENT PENSION IS DEFERRED'.

4   Before paragraph 1 insert –

'Choice between increase of pension and lump sum where pensioner's entitlement is deferred

A1   (1)   Where a person's entitlement to a Category A or Category B retirement pension is deferred and the period of deferment is at least 12 months, the person shall, on claiming his pension or within a prescribed period after claiming it, elect in the prescribed manner either –

(a)   that paragraph 1 (entitlement to increase of pension) is to apply in relation to the period of deferment, or

(b)   that paragraph 3A (entitlement to lump sum) is to apply in relation to the period of deferment.

(2)   If no election under sub-paragraph (1) is made within the period prescribed under that sub-paragraph, the person is to be treated as having made an election under sub-paragraph (1)(b).

(3)   Regulations –

   (a)   may enable a person who has made an election under sub-paragraph (1) (including one that the person is treated by sub-paragraph (2) as having made) to change the election within a prescribed period and in a prescribed manner, if prescribed conditions are satisfied, and

   (b)   if they enable a person to make an election under sub-paragraph (1)(b) in respect of a period of deferment after receiving any increase of pension under paragraph 1 by reference to that period, may for the purpose of avoiding duplication of payment –

      (i)   enable an amount determined in accordance with the regulations to be recovered from the person in a prescribed manner and within a prescribed period, or

      (ii)   provide for an amount determined in accordance with the regulations to be treated as having been paid on account of the amount to which the person is entitled under paragraph 3A.

(4)   Where the Category A or Category B retirement pension includes any increase under paragraphs 5 to 6, no election under sub-paragraph (1) applies to so much of the pension as consists of that increase (an entitlement to an increase of pension in respect of such an increase after a period of deferment being conferred either by paragraphs 1 and 2 or by paragraph 2A).'

5   For paragraph 1 (increase of pension where pensioner's entitlement is deferred) substitute –

'1   (1)   This paragraph applies where a person's entitlement to a Category A or Category B retirement pension is deferred and one of the following conditions is met –

   (a)   the period of deferment is less than 12 months, or

   (b)   the person has made an election under paragraph A1(1)(a) in relation to the period of deferment.

(2)   The rate of the person's Category A or Category B retirement pension shall be increased by an amount equal to the aggregate of the increments to which he is entitled under paragraph 2, but only if that amount is enough to increase the rate of the pension by at least 1 per cent.'

6   (1)   In paragraph 2 (calculation of increment), in sub-paragraph (5)(b), for '83 or' substitute '83A or'.

(2)   In relation to any incremental period (within the meaning of Schedule 5 to the principal Act) beginning before 6th April 2010, the reference in paragraph 2(5)(b) of that Schedule to section 83A of that Act is to be read as a reference to section 83 or 84 of that Act.

7   After paragraph 2 insert –

'2A   (1)   This paragraph applies where –

   (a)   a person's entitlement to a Category A or Category B retirement pension is deferred,

   (b)   the pension includes an increase under paragraphs 5 to 6, and

   (c)   the person has made (or is treated as having made) an election under paragraph A1(1)(b) in relation to the period of deferment.

(2)   The rate of the person's Category A or Category B retirement pension shall be increased by an amount equal to the aggregate of the increments to which he is entitled under sub-paragraph (3).

(3)   For each complete incremental period in the person's period of deferment, the amount of the increment shall be 1/5th per cent. of the weekly rate of the increase to which the person would have been entitled under paragraphs 5 to 6 for the period if his entitlement to the Category A or Category B retirement pension had not been deferred.'

8   (1)   After paragraph 3 insert –

'Lump sum where pensioner's entitlement is deferred

3A   (1)   This paragraph applies where –

(a)   a person's entitlement to a Category A or Category B retirement pension is deferred, and

(b)   the person has made (or is treated as having made) an election under paragraph A1(1)(b) in relation to the period of deferment.

(2)   The person is entitled to an amount calculated in accordance with paragraph 3B (a "lump sum").

Calculation of lump sum

3B   (1)   The lump sum is the accrued amount for the last accrual period beginning during the period of deferment.

(2)   In this paragraph –

"accrued amount" means the amount calculated in accordance with sub-paragraph (3);

"accrual period" means any period of seven days beginning with a prescribed day of the week, where that day falls within the period of deferment.

(3)   The accrued amount for an accrual period for a person is –

$$(A + P) \times 52\sqrt{\left(1 + \frac{R}{100}\right)}$$

where –

A is the accrued amount for the previous accrual period (or, in the case of the first accrual period beginning during the period of deferment, zero);

P is the amount of the Category A or Category B retirement pension to which the person would have been entitled for the accrual period if his entitlement had not been deferred;

R is –

(a)   a percentage rate two per cent. higher than the Bank of England base rate, or

(b)   if regulations so provide, such higher rate as may be prescribed.

(4)   For the purposes of sub-paragraph (3), any change in the Bank of England base rate is to be treated as taking effect –

(a)   at the beginning of the accrual period immediately following the accrual period during which the change took effect, or

(b)   if regulations so provide, at such other time as may be prescribed.

(5)   For the purposes of the calculation of the lump sum, the amount of Category A or Category B retirement pension to which the person would have been entitled for an accrual period –

(a)   includes any increase under section 47(1) and any increase under paragraph 4 of this Schedule, but

(b)   does not include –

    (i)   any increase under section 83A or 85 or paragraphs 5 to 6 of this Schedule,

    (ii)   any graduated retirement benefit, or

    (iii) in prescribed circumstances, such other amount of Category A or Category B retirement pension as may be prescribed.

(6)   The reference in sub-paragraph (5)(a) to any increase under subsection (1) of section 47 shall be taken as a reference to any increase that would take place under that subsection if subsection (2) of that section and section 46(5) of the Pensions Act were disregarded.'

(2)   In relation to any accrual period (within the meaning of Schedule 5 to the principal Act as amended by this paragraph) ending before 6th April 2010 the reference in paragraph 3B(5)(b) of that Schedule to section 83A of that Act is to be read as a reference to section 83 or 84 of that Act.

9   After paragraph 3B (inserted by paragraph 8 of this Schedule) insert –

'Choice between increase of pension and lump sum where pensioner's deceased spouse has deferred entitlement

3C   (1)   Subject to paragraph 8, this paragraph applies where –

(a)   a widow or widower ("W") is entitled to a Category A or Category B retirement pension,

(b)   W was married to the other party to the marriage ("S") when S died,

(c)   S's entitlement to a Category A or Category B retirement pension was deferred when S died, and

(d)   S's entitlement had been deferred throughout the period of 12 months ending with the day before S's death.

(2)   W shall within the prescribed period elect in the prescribed manner either –

(a)   that paragraph 4 (entitlement to increase of pension) is to apply in relation to S's period of deferment, or

(b)   that paragraph 7A (entitlement to lump sum) is to apply in relation to S's period of deferment.

(3)   If no election under sub-paragraph (2) is made within the period pre-scribed under that sub-paragraph, W is to be treated as having made an election under sub-paragraph (2)(b).

(4)   Regulations –

(a)   may enable a person who has made an election under sub-paragraph (2) (including one that the person is treated by sub-paragraph (3) as having made) to change the election within a prescribed period and in a prescribed manner, if prescribed conditions are satisfied, and

(b)   if they enable a person to make an election under sub-paragraph (2)(b) in respect of a period of deferment after receiving any increase of pension under paragraph 4 by reference to that period, may for the purpose of avoiding duplication of payment –

    (i)   enable an amount determined in accordance with the regula-tions to be recovered from the person in a prescribed manner and within a prescribed period, or

(ii)   provide for an amount determined in accordance with the regulations to be treated as having been paid on account of the amount to which the person is entitled under paragraph 7A.

(5)   The making of an election under sub-paragraph (2)(b) does not affect the application of paragraphs 5 to 6 (which relate to an increase in pension where the pensioner's deceased spouse had deferred an entitlement to a guaranteed minimum pension).'

10   (1)   Paragraph 4 (increase of pension where pensioner's deceased spouse has deferred entitlement) is amended as follows.

(2)   For sub-paragraph (1) substitute –

'(1)   Subject to paragraph 8, this paragraph applies where a widow or widower ("W") is entitled to a Category A or Category B retirement pension and was married to the other party to the marriage ("S") when S died and one of the following conditions is met –

(a)   S was entitled to a Category A or Category B retirement pension with an increase under this Schedule,

(b)   W is a widow or widower to whom paragraph 3C applies and has made an election under paragraph 3C(2)(a), or

(c)   paragraph 3C would apply to W but for the fact that the condition in sub-paragraph (1)(d) of that paragraph is not met.

(1A)   Subject to sub-paragraph (3), the rate of W's pension shall be increased –

(a)   in a case falling within sub-paragraph (1)(a), by an amount equal to the increase to which S was entitled under this Schedule, apart from paragraphs 5 to 6,

(b)   in a case falling within sub-paragraph (1)(b), by an amount equal to the increase to which S would have been entitled under this Schedule, apart from paragraphs 5 to 6, if the period of deferment had ended immediately before S's death and S had then made an election under paragraph A1(1)(a), or

(c)   in a case falling within sub-paragraph (1)(c), by an amount equal to the increase to which S would have been entitled under this Schedule, apart from paragraphs 5 to 6, if the period of deferment had ended immediately before S's death.'

11   (1)   After paragraph 7 insert –

'Entitlement to lump sum where pensioner's deceased spouse has deferred entitlement

7A   (1)   This paragraph applies where a person to whom paragraph 3C applies ("W") has made (or is treated as having made) an election under paragraph 3C(2)(b).

(2)   W is entitled to an amount calculated in accordance with paragraph 7B (a "widowed person's lump sum").

Calculation of widowed person's lump sum

7B   (1)   The widowed person's lump sum is the accrued amount for the last accrual period beginning during the period which –

(a)   began at the beginning of S's period of deferment, and

(b)   ended on the day before S's death.

(2) In this paragraph –

"S" means the other party to the marriage;

"accrued amount" means the amount calculated in accordance with sub-paragraph (3);

"accrual period" means any period of seven days beginning with a prescribed day of the week, where that day falls within S's period of deferment.

(3) The accrued amount for an accrual period for W is –

$$(A + P) \times 52\sqrt{\left(1 + \frac{R}{100}\right)}$$

where –

A is the accrued amount for the previous accrual period (or, in the case of the first accrual period beginning during the period mentioned in sub-paragraph (1), zero);

P is –

    (a)   the basic pension, and

    (b)   half of the additional pension

to which S would have been entitled for the accrual period if his entitlement had not been deferred during the period mentioned in sub-paragraph (1);

R is –

    (a)   a percentage rate two per cent. higher than the Bank of England base rate, or

    (b)   if regulations so provide, such higher rate as may be prescribed.

(4) For the purposes of sub-paragraph (3), any change in the Bank of England base rate is to be treated as taking effect –

(a) at the beginning of the accrual period immediately following the accrual period during which the change took effect, or

(b) if regulations so provide, at such other time as may be prescribed.

(5) For the purposes of the calculation of the widowed person's lump sum, the amount of Category A or Category B retirement pension to which S would have been entitled for an accrual period –

(a) includes any increase under section 47(1) and any increase under paragraph 4 of this Schedule, but

(b) does not include –

    (i)   any increase under section 83A or 85 or paragraphs 5 to 6 of this Schedule,

    (ii) any graduated retirement benefit, or

    (iii) in prescribed circumstances, such other amount of Category A or Category B retirement pension as may be prescribed.

(6) The reference in sub-paragraph (5)(a) to any increase under subsection (1) of section 47 shall be taken as a reference to any increase that would take place under that subsection if subsection (2) of that section and section 46(5) of the Pensions Act were disregarded.

(7) In any case where –

(a) there is a period between the death of S and the date on which W becomes entitled to a Category A or Category B retirement pension, and

(b) one or more orders have come into force under section 150 of the Administration Act during that period, the amount of the lump sum shall be increased in accordance with that order or those orders.'

(2) In relation to any accrual period (within the meaning of Schedule 5 to the principal Act) ending before 6th April 2010 the reference in paragraph 7B(5)(b) of that Schedule to section 83A of that Act is to be read as a reference to section 83 or 84 of that Act.

12 After paragraph 7B (inserted by paragraph 11 of this Schedule) insert –

'Supplementary

7C (1) Any lump sum calculated under paragraph 3B or 7B must be rounded to the nearest penny, taking any 1/2p as nearest to the next whole penny above.

(2) In prescribing a percentage rate for the purposes of paragraphs 3B and 7B, the Secretary of State must have regard to –

(a) the national economic situation, and

(b) any other matters which he considers relevant.'

13 For the heading immediately preceding paragraph 8 substitute 'Married couples'.

14 In paragraph 8 (married couples) –

(a) in sub-paragraph (3) for 'the reference in paragraph 2(3) above' substitute 'the references in paragraphs 2(3) and 3B(3) and (5)', and

(b) for sub-paragraph (4) substitute –

'(4) The conditions in paragraph 3C(1)(c) and 4(1)(a) are not satisfied by a Category B retirement pension to which S was or would have been entitled by virtue of W's contributions.

(5) Where the Category A retirement pension to which S was or would have been entitled includes an increase under section 51A(2) attributable to W's contributions, the increase or lump sum to which W is entitled under paragraph 4(1A) or 7A(2) is to be calculated as if there had been no increase under that section.

(6) In sub-paragraphs (4) and (5), "W" and "S" have the same meaning as in paragraph 3C, 4 or 7A, as the case requires.'

15 After Schedule 5 to the principal Act insert –

'SCHEDULE 5A   PENSION INCREASE OR LUMP SUM WHERE ENTITLEMENT TO SHARED ADDITIONAL PENSION IS DEFERRED

Choice between pension increase and lump sum where entitlement to shared additional pension is deferred

1 (1) Where a person's entitlement to a shared additional pension is deferred and the period of deferment is at least 12 months, the person shall, on claiming his pension or within a prescribed period after claiming it, elect in the prescribed manner either –

(a) that paragraph 2 (entitlement to increase of pension) is to apply in relation to the period of deferment, or

(b) that paragraph 4 (entitlement to lump sum) is to apply in relation to the period of deferment.

(2) If no election under sub-paragraph (1) is made within the period prescribed under that sub-paragraph, the person is to be treated as having made an election under sub-paragraph (1)(b).

(3) Regulations –

(a) may enable a person who has made an election under sub-paragraph (1) (including one that the person is treated by sub-paragraph (2) as having made) to change the election within a prescribed period and in a prescribed manner, if prescribed conditions are satisfied, and

(b) if they enable a person to make an election under sub-paragraph (1)(b) in respect of a period of deferment after receiving any increase of pension under paragraph 2 by reference to that period, may for the purpose of avoiding duplication of payment –

(i) enable an amount determined in accordance with the regulations to be recovered from the person in a prescribed manner and within a prescribed period, or

(ii) provide for an amount determined in accordance with the regulations to be treated as having been paid on account of the amount to which the person is entitled under paragraph 4.

Increase of pension where entitlement deferred

2 (1) This paragraph applies where a person's entitlement to a shared additional pension is deferred and either –

(a) the period of deferment is less than 12 months, or

(b) the person has made an election under paragraph 1(1)(a) in relation to the period of deferment.

(2) The rate of the person's shared additional pension shall be increased by an amount equal to the aggregate of the increments to which he is entitled under paragraph 3, but only if that amount is enough to increase the rate of the pension by at least 1 per cent.

Calculation of increment

3 (1) A person is entitled to an increment under this paragraph for each complete incremental period in his period of deferment.

(2) The amount of the increment for an incremental period shall be 1/5th per cent. of the weekly rate of the shared additional pension to which the person would have been entitled for the period if his entitlement had not been deferred.

(3) Amounts under sub-paragraph (2) shall be rounded to the nearest penny, taking any 1/2p as nearest to the next whole penny.

(4) Where an amount under sub-paragraph (2) would, apart from this sub-paragraph, be a sum less than 1/2p, the amount shall be taken to be zero, notwithstanding any other provision of this Act, the Pensions Act or the Administration Act.

(5) In this paragraph "incremental period" means any period of six days which are treated by regulations as days of increment for the purposes of this paragraph in relation to the person and pension in question.

(6)   Where one or more orders have come into force under section 150 of the Administration Act during the period of deferment, the rate for any incremental period shall be determined as if the order or orders had come into force before the beginning of the period of deferment.

(7)   The sums which are the increases in the rates of shared additional pension under this paragraph are subject to alteration by order made by the Secretary of State under section 150 of the Administration Act.

Lump sum where entitlement to shared additional pension is deferred

4   (1)   This paragraph applies where –

(a)   a person's entitlement to a shared additional pension is deferred, and

(b)   the person has made (or is treated as having made) an election under paragraph 1(1)(b) in relation to the period of deferment.

(2)   The person is entitled to an amount calculated in accordance with paragraph 5 (a "lump sum").

Calculation of lump sum

5   (1)   The lump sum is the accrued amount for the last accrual period beginning during the period of deferment.

(2)   In this paragraph –

"accrued amount" means the amount calculated in accordance with sub-paragraph (3);

"accrual period" means any period of seven days beginning with a prescribed day of the week, where that day falls within the period of deferment.

(3)   The accrued amount for an accrual period for a person is –

$$(A + P) \times 52 \sqrt{\left(1 + \frac{R}{100}\right)}$$

where –

A is the accrued amount for the previous accrual period (or, in the case of the first accrual period beginning during the period of deferment, zero);

P is the amount of the shared additional pension to which the person would have been entitled for the accrual period if his entitlement had not been deferred;

R is –

(a)   a percentage rate two per cent. higher than the Bank of England base rate, or

(b)   if a higher rate is prescribed for the purposes of paragraphs 3B and 7B of Schedule 5, that higher rate.

(4)   For the purposes of sub-paragraph (3), any change in the Bank of England base rate is to be treated as taking effect –

(a)   at the beginning of the accrual period immediately following the accrual period during which the change took effect, or

(b)   if regulations so provide, at such other time as may be prescribed.

(5)   For the purpose of the calculation of the lump sum, the amount of the shared additional pension to which the person would have been entitled for

an accrual period does not include, in prescribed circumstances, such amount as may be prescribed.

(6) The lump sum must be rounded to the nearest penny, taking any 1/2p as nearest to the next whole penny.'

PART 2

CONSEQUENTIAL AMENDMENTS

Social Security Contributions and Benefits Act 1992 (c. 4)

16   The Social Security Contributions and Benefits Act 1992 is amended as follows.

17   In section 62(1) (graduated retirement benefit) –

(a)   in paragraph (a), for 'paragraphs 1 to 3' substitute 'paragraphs A1 to 3B and 7C', and

(b)   after paragraph (b) insert –

'(c)   for amending that section in order to make provisions corresponding to those of paragraphs 3C, 4(1) and (1A) and 7A to 7C of Schedule 5 to this Act enabling a widowed person to elect to receive a lump sum, rather than an increase in the weekly rate of retirement pension, in respect of the graduated retirement benefit of his or her deceased spouse.'

18   In section 122(1) (interpretation of Parts 1 to 6) –

(a)   before the definition of 'beneficiary' insert –

'"Bank of England base rate" means –

(a)   the rate announced from time to time by the Monetary Policy Committee of the Bank of England as the official dealing rate, being the rate at which the Bank is willing to enter into transactions for providing short term liquidity in the money markets, or

(b)   where an order under section 19 of the Bank of England Act 1998 is in force, any equivalent rate determined by the Treasury under that section;', and

(b)   for the definitions of 'deferred' and 'period of deferment' substitute –

'"deferred" and "period of deferment" –

(a)   in relation to a Category A or Category B retirement pension, have the meanings given by section 55(3), and

(b)   in relation to a shared additional pension, have the meanings given by section 55C(3);'.

19   In section 176 (parliamentary control of subordinate legislation) in subsection (1) (affirmative procedure), after paragraph (b) insert –

'(bb) regulations prescribing a percentage rate for the purposes of –

(i)   paragraph 3B(3) or 7B(3) of Schedule 5, or

(ii)   paragraph 5(3) of Schedule 5A;'.

Social Security Administration Act 1992 (c. 5)

20   The Social Security Administration Act 1992 is amended as follows.

21   In section 150 (annual up-rating of benefits) –

    (a)   in subsection (1), after paragraph (d) insert –

       '(dza)   which are lump sums to which surviving spouses will become entitled under paragraph 7A of that Schedule on becoming entitled to a Category A or Category B retirement pension;',

    (b)   in subsection (1)(da), for 'section 55C of' substitute 'paragraph 2 of Schedule 5A to', and

    (c)   in subsection (3)(b), after '(d),' insert '(dza),'.

22   In section 151 (up-rating – supplementary) in subsection (2) –

    (a)   for 'subsection (1)(d) or (e)' substitute 'subsection (1)(d), (dza) or (e)', and

    (b)   after 'apart from the order and' insert ', in the case of the sums mentioned in subsection (1)(d) or (e) of that section,'.

Welfare Reform and Pensions Act 1999 (c. 30)

23   The Welfare Reform and Pensions Act 1999 is amended as follows.

24   In section 50, omit subsection (2) (which amends provisions relating to the deferment of shared additional pensions and is superseded by Part 1 of this Schedule).

25   In section 52(2) (power to make regulations preserving rights in respect of additional pensions), in paragraph (b) –

    (a)   after 'increase of pension' insert 'or payment of lump sum', and

    (b)   after 'constituent element of an increase' insert 'or of a lump sum'.

PART 3

TRANSITIONAL PROVISIONS

Widowers' entitlement to increase of pension or widowed person's lump sum

26   In the case of a widower who attains pensionable age before 6th April 2010, paragraphs 3C, 4 and 7A of Schedule 5 to the Social Security Contributions and Benefits Act 1992 (c. 4) (entitlement to increase of pension or widowed person's lump sum) shall not apply unless he was over pensionable age when his wife died.

Transitional provision

27   (1)   The Secretary of State may by regulations make such transitional provision as he thinks fit in connection with the coming into force of this Schedule.

    (2)   Regulations under this paragraph may, in particular, modify the preceding provisions of this Schedule in relation to cases where the retirement pension or shared additional pension of a person is deferred and the period of deferment begins before 6th April 2005 and continues on or after that day.

    (3)   In this paragraph 'deferred' and 'period of deferment' are to be read in accordance with section 55 or 55C of the Social Security Contributions and Benefits Act 1992, as the case requires.

SCHEDULE 12   MINOR AND CONSEQUENTIAL AMENDMENTS

Section 319

Public Records Act 1958 (c. 51)

1   In Schedule 1 to the Public Records Act 1958 (definition of public records), in Part 2 of the Table in paragraph 3 insert at the appropriate place –

'The Pensions Regulator.'
'The Board of the Pension Protection Fund.'
'The Ombudsman for the Board of the Pension Protection Fund.'

Superannuation Act 1972 (c. 11)

2   (1)   Schedule 1 to the Superannuation Act 1972 (kinds of employment in relation to which pension schemes may be made) is amended as follows.

(2)   At the appropriate place in the list of 'Other Bodies' insert –

'The Board of the Pension Protection Fund.',
'Employment by the Ombudsman for the Board of the Pension Protection Fund.', and
'The Pensions Regulator.'

(3)   At the appropriate place in the list of 'Offices' insert –

'Chairman of the Board of the Pension Protection Fund.',
'Chairman of the Pensions Regulator.',
'A deputy to the Ombudsman for the Board of the Pension Protection Fund.',
'A deputy to the Pensions Ombudsman.', and
'The Ombudsman for the Board of the Pension Protection Fund.'

Matrimonial Causes Act 1973 (c. 18)

3   After section 25D of the Matrimonial Causes Act 1973 (pensions: supplementary) insert –

'25E   The Pension Protection Fund

(1)   The matters to which the court is to have regard under section 25(2) include –

(a)   in the case of paragraph (a), any PPF compensation to which a party to the marriage is or is likely to be entitled, and

(b)   in the case of paragraph (h), any PPF compensation which, by reason of the dissolution or annulment of the marriage, a party to the marriage will lose the chance of acquiring entitlement to,

and, accordingly, in relation to PPF compensation, section 25(2)(a) shall have effect as if "in the foreseeable future" were omitted.

(2)   Subsection (3) applies in relation to an order under section 23 so far as it includes provision made by virtue of section 25B(4) which –

(a)   imposed requirements on the trustees or managers of an occupational pension scheme for which the Board has assumed responsibility in accordance with Chapter 3 of Part 2 of the Pensions Act 2004 (pension protection) or any provision in force in Northern Ireland corresponding to that Chapter, and

(b)   was made before the trustees or managers of the scheme received the transfer notice in relation to the scheme.

(3) The order is to have effect from the time when the trustees or managers of the scheme receive the transfer notice –

    (a)   as if, except in prescribed descriptions of case –

       (i)   references in the order to the trustees or managers of the scheme were references to the Board, and

       (ii) references in the order to any pension or lump sum to which the party with pension rights is or may become entitled under the scheme were references to any PPF compensation to which that person is or may become entitled in respect of the pension or lump sum, and

    (b)   subject to such other modifications as may be prescribed.

(4) Subsection (5) applies to an order under section 23 if –

    (a)   it includes provision made by virtue of section 25B(7) which requires the party with pension rights to exercise his right of commutation under an occupational pension scheme to any extent, and

    (b)   before the requirement is complied with the Board has assumed responsibility for the scheme as mentioned in subsection (2)(a).

(5) From the time the trustees or managers of the scheme receive the transfer notice, the order is to have effect with such modifications as may be prescribed.

(6) Regulations may modify section 25C as it applies in relation to an occupational pension scheme at any time when there is an assessment period in relation to the scheme.

(7) Where the court makes a pension sharing order in respect of a person's shareable rights under an occupational pension scheme, or an order which includes provision made by virtue of section 25B(4) or (7) in relation to such a scheme, the Board subsequently assuming responsibility for the scheme as mentioned in subsection (2)(a) does not affect –

    (a)   the powers of the court under section 31 to vary or discharge the order or to suspend or revive any provision of it, or

    (b)   on an appeal, the powers of the appeal court to affirm, reinstate, set aside or vary the order.

(8) Regulations may make such consequential modifications of any provision of, or made by virtue of, this Part as appear to the Lord Chancellor necessary or expedient to give effect to the provisions of this section.

(9) In this section –

"assessment period" means an assessment period within the meaning of Part 2 of the Pensions Act 2004 (pension protection) (see sections 132 and 159 of that Act) or an equivalent period under any provision in force in Northern Ireland corresponding to that Part;

"the Board" means the Board of the Pension Protection Fund;

"occupational pension scheme" has the same meaning as in the Pension Schemes Act 1993;

"prescribed" means prescribed by regulations;

"PPF compensation" means compensation payable under Chapter 3 of Part 2 of the Pensions Act 2004 (pension protection) or any provision in force in Northern Ireland corresponding to that Chapter;

"regulations" means regulations made by the Lord Chancellor;

"shareable rights" are rights in relation to which pension sharing is available under Chapter 1 of Part 4 of the Welfare Reform and Pensions Act 1999 or any provision in force in Northern Ireland corresponding to that Chapter;

"transfer notice" has the same meaning as in section 160 of the Pensions Act 2004 or any corresponding provision in force in Northern Ireland.

(10) Any power to make regulations under this section is exercisable by statutory instrument, which shall be subject to annulment in pursuance of a resolution of either House of Parliament.'

Matrimonial and Family Proceedings Act 1984 (c. 42)

4 (1) The Matrimonial and Family Proceedings Act 1984 is amended as follows.

   (2) In section 18 (matters to which the court is to have regard in exercising its powers under section 17) –

   (a) in subsection (3A) –

      (i) in paragraph (a) after 'have' insert 'and any PPF compensation to which a party to the marriage is or is likely to be entitled,',

      (ii) in paragraph (b) after 'include' insert ' –

         (i) ', and

      (iii) at the end of that paragraph insert ', and

         (ii) any PPF compensation which, by reason of the dissolution or annulment of the marriage, a party to the marriage will lose the chance of acquiring entitlement to', and

   (b) in subsection (7), after paragraph (b) insert ', and

   (c) "PPF compensation" means compensation payable under Chapter 3 of Part 2 of the Pensions Act 2004 (pension protection) or any provision in force in Northern Ireland corresponding to that Chapter.'

   (3) In section 21 (application to orders under sections 14 and 17 of certain provisions of Part 2 of the Matrimonial Causes Act 1973), after subsection (1)(be) insert –

   '(bf) section 25E(2) to (10) (the Pension Protection Fund);'.

Companies Act 1985 (c. 6)

5 (1) The Companies Act 1985 is amended as follows.

   (2) In section 449 (provision for security of information obtained by the Secretary of State under section 447), for subsection (1)(dg) substitute –

   '(dg) for the purpose of enabling or assisting the Pensions Regulator to exercise the functions conferred on it by or by virtue of the Pension Schemes Act 1993, the Pensions Act 1995, the Welfare Reform and Pensions Act 1999 or the Pensions Act 2004 or any enactment in force in Northern Ireland corresponding to any of those enactments;

   (dh) for the purpose of enabling or assisting the Board of the Pension Protection Fund to exercise the functions conferred on it by or by virtue of Part 2 of the Pensions Act 2004 or any enactment in force in Northern Ireland corresponding to that Part;'.

   (3) In Schedule 15D (permitted disclosures of information) (as inserted by Schedule 2 to the Companies (Audit, Investigations and Community Enterprise) Act 2004) –

   (a) for paragraph 13 substitute –

   '13 A disclosure for the purpose of enabling or assisting the Pensions Regulator to exercise the functions conferred on it by or by virtue of any of the following –

   (a) the Pension Schemes Act 1993;

   (b) the Pensions Act 1995;

(c) the Welfare Reform and Pensions Act 1999;

(d) the Pensions Act 2004;

(e) any enactment in force in Northern Ireland corresponding to any of those enactments.', and

(b) after that paragraph insert –

'13A A disclosure for the purpose of enabling or assisting the Board of the Pension Protection Fund to exercise the functions conferred on it by or by virtue of Part 2 of the Pensions Act 2004 or any enactment in force in Northern Ireland corresponding to that Part.'

Companies Act 1989 (c. 40)

6   In section 87 of the Companies Act 1989 (exception from restriction on disclosure of information obtained from overseas regulatory authorities etc), in the table in sub-section (4) for the entry relating to the Occupational Pensions Regulatory Authority substitute –

'The Pensions Regulator	Functions conferred by or by virtue of –
	(a) the Pension Schemes Act 1993,
	(b) the Pensions Act 1995,
	(c) the Welfare Reform and Pensions Act 1999,
	(d) the Pensions Act 2004,
	or any enactment in force in Northern Ireland corresponding to an enactment mentioned in paragraphs (a) to (d) above.
The Board of the Pension Protection Fund	Functions conferred by or by virtue of Part 2 of the Pensions Act 2004 or any enactment in force in Northern Ireland corresponding to that Part.'

Social Security Administration Act 1992 (c. 5)

7   In section 122AA of the Social Security Administration Act 1992 (disclosure of contributions etc information by Inland Revenue), in subsection (2)(d), for 'Occupational Pensions Regulatory Authority' substitute 'Pensions Regulator'.

Tribunals and Inquiries Act 1992 (c. 53)

8   (1) The Tribunals and Inquiries Act 1992 is amended as follows.

(2) In section 7 (concurrence required for removal of members of certain tribunals), in subsection (2) for '(g) or (h)' substitute '(i), (j), (k) or (l)'.

(3) In section 14 (restricted application of Act in relation to certain tribunals), for subsection (1A) substitute –

'(1A) In this Act –

(a) references to the working of the Pensions Regulator referred to in paragraph 35(i) of Schedule 1 are references to its working so far as relating to the exercise of its regulatory functions (within the meaning of section 93(2) of the Pensions Act 2004) or any corresponding function conferred by a provision in force in Northern Ireland, and

(b) references to procedural rules for the Pensions Regulator are references to regulations under paragraph 19 of Schedule 1 to that Act (Secretary of State's powers to make regulations in respect of Regulator's procedure) so far as they relate to the procedure to be followed when exercising those functions.'

(4) In Schedule 1, in Part 1, in paragraph 35, after paragraph (h) insert –

'(i) the Pensions Regulator established by section 1 of the Pensions Act 2004;

(j) the Pensions Regulator Tribunal established by section 102 of that Act;

(k) the Board of the Pension Protection Fund established by section 107 of the Pensions Act 2004 in respect of its functions under or by virtue of section 207 of that Act or any enactment in force in Northern Ireland corresponding to that section;

(l) the Ombudsman for the Board of the Pension Protection Fund in respect of his functions under or by virtue of section 213 of that Act or any enactment in force in Northern Ireland corresponding to that section.'

Pension Schemes Act 1993 (c. 48)

9 The Pension Schemes Act 1993 is amended as follows.

10 In section 53 (supervision: former contracted-out schemes), after subsection (1B) insert –

'(1C) But where a direction under subsection (1) conflicts with a freezing order made by the Regulatory Authority under section 23 of the Pensions Act 2004 in relation to the scheme then, during the period for which the freezing order has effect, the direction to the extent that it conflicts with the freezing order –

(a) is not binding as described in subsection (1), and

(b) is not enforceable as described in subsection (1B).'

11 (1) Section 56 (provision supplementary to provision relating to payment of state scheme premiums) is amended as follows.

(2) In subsection (4) for the words from the beginning to 'another scheme' substitute –

'(4) Where under the rules of the scheme, transfer credits have been allowed –

(a) in respect of the earner's rights under another scheme, or

(b) in respect of the earner by reference to the payment of a cash transfer sum (within the meaning of Chapter 5 of Part 4) to the trustees or managers of the scheme by the trustees or managers of another occupational pension scheme,'.

(3) After subsection (6) insert –

'(7) Where a premium under section 55 is payable by the Board of the Pension Protection Fund by virtue of a transfer under section 161 of the Pensions Act 2004 (effect of the Board assuming responsibility for an occupational pension scheme), then, subject to subsection (8), sections 55 to 68 apply with such modifications as may be prescribed in relation to that premium.

(8) A premium under section 55 in respect of an earner ceases to be payable if –

(a) the liability to pay the premium is transferred to the Board of the Pension Protection Fund by virtue of section 161 of the Pensions Act 2004, and

(b) prescribed requirements are met.'

12 In section 61 (deduction of contributions equivalent premium from refund of scheme contributions), after subsection (9) insert –

'(9A) Where under section 101AH the trustees or managers of an occupational pension scheme may pay a contribution refund to a member of the scheme, the member is to be treated for the purposes of this section as being entitled to the contribution refund.'

13 (1) Section 94 (right to cash equivalent) is amended as follows.

(2) In subsection (2), for the definition of 'the applicable rules' substitute –

'"the applicable rules" means –

(a) the rules of the scheme, except so far as overridden by a relevant legislative provision;

(b) the relevant legislative provisions, to the extent that they have effect in relation to the scheme and are not reflected in the rules of the scheme; and

(c) any provision which the rules of the scheme do not contain but which the scheme must contain if it is to conform with Chapter 1 of Part 4 of this Act;'.

(3) After that subsection insert –

'(2A) For the purposes of subsection (2) –

(a) "relevant legislative provision" means any provision contained in any of the following provisions –

(i) Schedule 5 to the Social Security Act 1989 (equal treatment for men and women);

(ii) this Chapter or Chapters 2, 3 or 5 of this Part of this Act or regulations made under this Chapter or any of those Chapters;

(iii) Part 4A of this Act or regulations made under that Part;

(iv) section 110(1) of this Act;

(v) Part 1 of the Pensions Act 1995 (occupational pensions) or subordinate legislation made or having effect as if made under that Part;

(vi) section 31 of the Welfare Reform and Pensions Act 1999 (pension debits: reduction of benefit);

(vii) any provision mentioned in section 306(2) of the Pensions Act 2004;

(b) a relevant legislative provision is to be taken to override any of the provisions of the scheme if, and only if, it does so by virtue of any of the following provisions –

(i) paragraph 3 of Schedule 5 to the Social Security Act 1989;

(ii) section 129(1) of this Act;

(iii) section 117(1) of the Pensions Act 1995;

(iv) section 31(4) of the Welfare Reform and Pensions Act 1999;

(v) section 306(1) of the Pensions Act 2004.'

14 In section 99 (trustees' duties after exercise of option) –

(a) in subsection (4) after 'circumstances,' insert 'by direction', and

(b) in subsection (4A) for 'in relation to applications for extensions under subsection (4)' substitute 'requiring applications for extensions under subsection (4) to meet prescribed requirements'.

15 In section 101J (time for compliance with transfer notice) –

(a) in subsection (2) after 'circumstances,' insert 'by direction', and

(b) in subsection (6)(a) for 'in relation to applications under subsection (2)' substitute 'requiring applications for extensions under subsection (2) to meet prescribed requirements'.

16 In section 111A (monitoring of employers' payments to personal pension schemes) omit subsection (10).

17 In section 113 (disclosure of information about schemes to members etc), after subsection (2)(d) insert –

'(e) persons of prescribed descriptions.'

18 After that section insert –

'113A Disclosure of information about transfers etc

Regulations may provide that, where –

(a) a payment is made out of an occupational pension scheme to the trustees or managers of another occupational pension scheme, and

(b) transfer credits are allowed to a member of that other scheme in respect of the payment,

the trustees or managers of the first scheme must, in prescribed circumstances and in the prescribed manner, provide to the trustees or managers of the other scheme prescribed information relating to the payment.'

19 In section 123 (interpretation of Chapter 2 of Part 7) omit –

(a) the definition of 'occupational pension scheme' in subsection (3), and

(b) subsection (4).

20 In section 124 (duty of Secretary of State to pay unpaid contributions), after subsection (5) insert –

'(6) In this section "on his own account", in relation to an employer, means on his own account but to fund benefits for, or in respect of, one or more employees.'

21 In section 129(1) (overriding requirements), –

(a) for 'and IV' substitute ', IV and V', and

(b) after 'under' insert 'any of those Chapters or'.

22 In section 130(b) (extra-statutory benefits), for 'or IV' substitute ', IV or V'.

23 In section 145 (the Pensions Ombudsman), after subsection (1) insert –

'(1A) Provisions conferring power on the Pensions Ombudsman to conduct investigations as mentioned in subsection (1) are to be read as conferring power that –

(a) in a case of a prescribed description, or

(b) in a case involving a scheme that is prescribed or is of a prescribed description,

may be exercised whatever the extent of any connections with places outside the United Kingdom.

(1B) In subsection (1A) 'scheme' means occupational pension scheme or personal pension scheme.

(1C) Subsection (1A) shall not be taken to prejudice any power of the Pensions Ombudsman apart from that subsection to conduct investigations in a case having connections with places outside the United Kingdom.'

24 In section 146 (functions of the Pensions Ombudsman) –

(a) for subsection (1)(f) substitute –

'(f) any dispute, in relation to a time while section 22 of the Pensions Act 1995 (circumstances in which Regulatory Authority may appoint an independent trustee) applies in relation to an occupational pension scheme, between an independent trustee of the scheme appointed under section 23(1) of that Act and either –

        (i)   other trustees of the scheme, or

        (ii)   former trustees of the scheme who were not independent trustees appointed under section 23(1) of that Act, and',

  (b)   after subsection (6) insert –

     '(6A) For the purposes of subsection (6)(c) –

       (a)   a description of complaint may be framed (in particular) by reference to the person making the complaint or to the scheme concerned (or to both), and

       (b)   a description of dispute may be framed (in particular) by reference to the person referring the dispute or to the scheme concerned (or to both).', and

  (c)   in subsection (8), in paragraph (a) of the definition of 'independent trustee' for the words from 'section 23(1)(b)' to the end substitute 'section 23(1) of the Pensions Act 1995 (appointment of independent trustee by the Regulatory Authority)'.

25   In section 149 (procedure on investigation by Pensions Ombudsman), in subsection (6) –

  (a)   for paragraph (b) substitute –

     '(b) the Board of the Pension Protection Fund,

     (ba) the Ombudsman for the Board of the Pension Protection Fund,', and

  (b)   at the end insert –

     '(n) a person who, in a member State other than the United Kingdom, has functions corresponding to functions of the Pensions Ombudsman.'

26 (1) Section 158A (other disclosures by the Secretary of State) is amended as follows.

    (2) In subsection (1), for the words from 'any information' to 'Pensions Act 1995' substitute 'any regulated information'.

    (3) In the Table in that subsection –

      (a)   in the entry for the Regulatory Authority in the second column of the Table for the words from 'or the' to the end substitute ', the Pensions Act 1995, the Welfare Reform and Pensions Act 1999 or the Pensions Act 2004 or any enactment in force in Northern Ireland corresponding to any of those enactments.', and

      (b)   for the entry for the Pensions Compensation Board substitute –

'The Pensions Ombudsman.	Functions conferred by or by virtue of this Act or any enactment in force in Northern Ireland corresponding to it.
The Board of the Pension Protection Fund.	Functions conferred by or by virtue of Part 2 of of the Pensions Act 2004 or any enactment in force in Northern Ireland corresponding to that Part.
The Ombudsman for the Board of the Pension Protection Fund.	Functions conferred by or by virtue of Part 2 of the Pensions Act 2004 or any enactment in force in Northern Ireland corresponding to that Part.'

    (4) After that subsection insert –

     '(1AA) In subsection (1), "regulated information" means information received by the Secretary of State in connection with his functions under –

       (a)   this Act,

       (b)   the Pensions Act 1995, or

       (c)   the Pensions Act 2004,

other than information supplied to him under section 235(2) of, or paragraph 2 of Schedule 10 to, the Pensions Act 2004 (supply of information for retirement planning purposes etc).'

27 In section 168(4) (penalties for contravention of regulations) after 'the provision' insert 'to be required by notice in writing'.

28 In section 175 (levies) –

    (a)   for subsection (8) substitute –

    '(8)   An amount payable by a person on account of a levy imposed under this section shall be a debt due from him to the Secretary of State, and an amount so payable shall be recoverable by the Secretary of State accordingly or, if the Secretary of State so determines, by the Regulatory Authority on his behalf.', and

    (b)   in subsection (9) for 'subsections (1) and (4)' substitute 'subsection (1)'.

29 In section 178 (power to make regulations as to the persons to be regarded as trustees or managers of schemes for certain purposes), in paragraph (b) for 'to 26C' substitute 'to 26'.

30 (1) Section 179 (linked qualifying service) is amended as follows.

    (2) In subsection (1)(a) –

    (a)   for 'the rules of a scheme' substitute 'Chapter 4 or 5 of Part 4 or under the rules of a scheme',

    (b)   for sub-paragraph (i) substitute –

    '(i)   there was made a transfer of his rights (including any transfer credits allowed) under that scheme, or a transfer payment in respect of those rights, to, or to the trustees or managers of, another scheme applying to him in the later period of service;',

    (c)   for 'and' at the end of sub-paragraph (ii), substitute 'or', and

    (d)   after that sub-paragraph insert –

    '(iii)   a cash equivalent (within the meaning of Chapter 4 of Part 4) or cash transfer sum (within the meaning of Chapter 5 of that Part) was paid in respect of him to the trustees or managers of another scheme applying to him in the later period of service; and'.

    (3) In subsection (1)(b), after 'second scheme,' insert 'or the payment to the trustees or managers of that scheme,'.

31 In section 181(1) (general interpretation), in the definition of 'transfer credits', for the words following 'by reference to' substitute ' –

    (a)   a transfer to the scheme of, or transfer payment to the trustees or managers of the scheme in respect of, any of his rights (including transfer credits allowed) under another occupational pension scheme or a personal pension scheme, other than rights attributable (directly or indirectly) to a pension credit, or

    (b)   a cash transfer sum paid under Chapter 5 of Part 4 in respect of him, to the trustees or managers of the scheme;'.

32 In section 183(3) (sub-delegation), after '97(1)' insert ', 101AF(1)'.

33 In section 192(2) (provisions extending to Northern Ireland) –

    (a)   for 'section 145 (except subsections (4)' substitute 'section 145 (except subsections (4A) to (4C)', and

    (b)   at the appropriate place insert –

    'section 145A (except subsection (6)(b)),'.

Pensions Act 1995 (c. 26)

34 The Pensions Act 1995 is amended as follows.

35 In section 4 (suspension orders), in subsections (3) and (5) for 'class' substitute 'description'.

36 In section 7 (appointment of trustees) –

    (a) in subsection (1) omit 'a trustee of such a scheme ceases to be a trustee', and

    (b) in subsection (2) for 'section 23(1)(b)' in both places substitute 'section 23(1)'.

37 In section 9 (removal and appointment of trustees: property), after 'exercise' insert 'by order'.

38 In section 10 (civil penalties), in subsection (5)(a) omit 'as a trustee of a trust scheme'.

39 In section 15(4) (failure to comply with Authority's direction) for 'sections 3 and 10 apply' substitute 'section 10 applies'.

40 In section 22 (circumstances in which independent trustee provisions apply), in subsections (1) and (3) for 'to 26A', in each place, substitute 'to 26'.

41 In section 25 (appointment and powers of independent trustees: further provisions) –

    (a) in subsection (1) for 'section 23(1)(b)' substitute 'section 23(1)',

    (b) in subsection (2) –

        (i) after 'a scheme' insert 'and there is an independent trustee of the scheme appointed under section 23(1)', and

        (ii) omit from 'but if' to the end,

    (c) in subsection (3) for ', no independent trustee of the scheme may' substitute 'and there is an independent trustee of the scheme appointed under section 23(1), the independent trustee may not', and

    (d) in subsection (4) –

        (i) for 'section 23(1)(b)' substitute 'section 23(1)', and

        (ii) after 'person' insert '(within the meaning of section 23(3))'.

42 In section 26 (insolvency practitioner or official receiver to give information to trustees), in subsection (1) after 'a scheme' insert 'by virtue of subsection (1) of that section'.

43 Sections 26A to 26C are hereby repealed.

44 In section 28 (consequences of prohibition on trustee being auditor of scheme etc) omit subsection (4).

45 In section 29 (persons disqualified for being trustees), in subsection (5) for 'class' substitute 'description'.

46 In section 30 (persons disqualified: consequences) –

    (a) in subsection (2), after 'exercise' insert 'by order', and

    (b) omit subsections (7) and (8).

47 Omit section 30A (accessibility of register of disqualified trustees).

48 In section 32 (decisions of trustees by a majority) –

    (a) in subsection (4) for ', 16(3)(b) and 25(2)' substitute 'and 25(2) of this Act and section 241(6) of the Pensions Act 2004', and

    (b) in subsection (5) for 'sections 3 and 10 apply' substitute 'section 10 applies'.

49 In section 34 (powers of investment and delegation) in subsection (1) after 'subject to' insert 'section 36(1) and to'.

50 (1) Section 38 (power to defer winding up) is amended as follows.

(2) In subsection (2) –

(a) in paragraph (a) after 'scheme' insert '(other than those due to be paid before the determination is made)', and

(b) in paragraph (b) omit 'new'.

(3) After subsection (3) insert –

'(4) This section also does not apply in relation to a trust scheme where the trustees are required to wind up, or continue the winding up, of the scheme under section 154(1) of the Pensions Act 2004 (requirement to wind up certain schemes with sufficient assets to meet protected liabilities).'

51 In section 40 (restriction on employer-related investments), in subsection (4) for 'sections 3 and 10 apply' substitute 'section 10 applies'.

52 In section 41 (provision of documents for members) –

(a) for subsection (3) substitute –

'(3) The documents referred to in subsection (1)(b) are –

(a) any statement of funding principles prepared or revised under section 223 of the Pensions Act 2004,

(b) any valuation or report prepared by the actuary under section 224 of that Act,

(c) any certificate given by the actuary under section 225 or 227 of that Act.', and

(b) in subsection (5B) for 'sections 3 and 10 apply to any trustee, and section 10 applies' substitute 'section 10 applies to any trustee, and'.

53 In section 47 (professional advisers), in subsections (3), (8) and (11) for 'sections 3 and 10 apply to any trustee, and section 10 applies' substitute 'section 10 applies to any trustee, and'.

54 In section 49 (other responsibilities of trustees, employers, etc) –

(a) in subsection (6) for 'sections 3 and 10 apply' substitute 'section 10 applies', and

(b) in subsection (10) –

(i) omit paragraph (a) and the word 'and' immediately after it, and

(ii) in paragraph (b) for 'such steps' substitute 'reasonable steps to secure compliance'.

55 In section 49A (record of winding up decisions) omit subsection (4).

56 In section 68 (power of trustees to modify schemes by resolution), in subsection (2) –

(a) in paragraph (b), for 'section 16(1) or 17(2)' substitute 'section 241 of the Pensions Act 2004', and

(b) for paragraph (c) substitute –

'(c) to enable the scheme to comply with such terms and conditions as may be imposed by the Board of the Pension Protection Fund in relation to any payment made by it under section 185 or 186 of the Pensions Act 2004,'.

57 In section 69 (grounds for applying for modifications) –

(a) in subsection (2) for 'about the manner of dealing with applications under this section' substitute 'requiring applications under this section to meet prescribed requirements',

(b) in subsection (3) omit paragraph (a),

(c) in subsection (4)(a) omit '(a) or', and

(d) in subsection (5)(a) omit 'either of' and for 'subsection (3)(a) or (b)' substitute 'subsection (3)(b)'.

58   In section 71A(4)(d) (power to make provision in relation to applications for the purposes of that section) –

    (a)   for 'before such time as may be prescribed' substitute 'before an application is made for the purposes of this section', and

    (b)   for 'an application for the purposes of this section' substitute 'the application'.

59   In section 72A (reports to Authority about winding up) omit subsection (9)(a) and 'and' immediately after it.

60   In section 72C (duty to comply with directions for facilitating winding up) omit subsection (2).

61   In section 73 (preferential liabilities on winding up) in subsection (6), omit paragraph (a) and 'and' immediately after it.

62   In section 76 (excess assets on winding up) –

    (a)   in subsection (3), omit paragraph (c) (but not the word 'and' immediately following it),

    (b)   omit subsection (5), and

    (c)   in subsection (6) for 'sections 3 and 10 apply' substitute 'section 10 applies'.

63   In section 77 (excess assets remaining after winding up: power to distribute) –

    (a)   omit subsections (2) and (3),

    (b)   in subsection (4) –

        (i)   for the opening words substitute 'Where this section applies –', and

        (ii)   in paragraph (a) for 'those assets' substitute 'the undistributed assets', and

    (c)   in subsection (5) for 'sections 3 and 10 apply' substitute 'section 10 applies'.

64   In section 87 (schedules of payment to money purchase schemes) omit subsection (5)(a) and 'and' immediately after it.

65   In section 88 (provision supplementary to section 87) omit subsection (4)(a) and 'and' immediately after it.

66   In section 89 (application of further provisions to money purchase schemes) –

    (a)   in subsection (1)(a) –

        (i)   for 'sections 56 to 60' substitute 'Part 3 of the Pensions Act 2004', and

        (ii)   for 'those sections' substitute 'that Part', and

    (b)   in subsection (2) omit 'insolvency'.

67   In section 118 (powers to modify Part 1 of the Pensions Act 1995) –

    (a)   in subsection (2) for 'to 26C' substitute 'to 26', and

    (b)   omit subsection (3).

68   In section 119 (calculations etc under regulations: sub-delegation), for '73(3)' substitute '73B(4)(a)'.

69   (1)   Section 124 (interpretation of Part 1) is amended as follows.

    (2)   In subsection (1), in the definition of 'transfer credits', for the words following 'by reference to' substitute ' –

    (a)   a transfer to the scheme of, or transfer payment to the trustees or managers of the scheme in respect of, any of his rights (including transfer credits allowed) under another occupational pension scheme or a personal pension scheme, other than pension credit rights, or

    (b)   a cash transfer sum paid under Chapter 5 of Part 4 of the Pension Schemes Act 1993 (early leavers) in respect of him, to the trustees or managers of the scheme,'.

(3) In subsection (3A), after '(3E)' insert 'and to sections 28, 154 and 219 of the Pensions Act 2004'.

(4) In subsection (3B), after '(3E)' insert 'and to sections 154 and 219 of the Pensions Act 2004'.

Bank of England Act 1998 (c. 11)

70 In Schedule 7 to the Bank of England Act 1998 (restriction on disclosure of information), in the table in paragraph 3(1), for the entry relating to the Occupational Pensions Regulatory Authority substitute –

'The Pensions Regulator	Functions conferred by or by virtue of –
	(a) the Pension Schemes Act 1993,
	(b) the Pensions Act 1995,
	(c) the Welfare Reform and Pensions Act 1999,
	(d) the Pensions Act 2004, or
	(e) any enactment in force in Northern Ireland corresponding to an enactment mentioned in paragraphs (a) to (d) above.'

Welfare Reform and Pensions Act 1999 (c. 30)

71 The Welfare Reform and Pensions Act 1999 is amended as follows.

72 In section 1 (stakeholder pension schemes), in subsection (6), after 'members etc)' insert 'and of regulations under section 237 of the Pensions Act 2004 (combined pension forecasts)'.

73 In section 2 (registration of stakeholder pension schemes) –

(a) in subsection (1) for 'Occupational Pensions Regulatory Authority ("the Authority")' substitute 'Authority',

(b) in subsection (3) after 'may' insert 'by direction', and

(c) in subsection (4) for the words from 'Section 3' to 'Act applies' substitute 'Section 10 of the Pensions Act 1995 ("the 1995 Act") (civil penalties) applies to any trustee of a pension scheme which is or has been registered under this section, and'.

74 In section 8(2)(a) (providing for stakeholder pension schemes to be treated as personal pension schemes), after 'is' insert 'prescribed or is'.

75 In section 38 (treatment in winding up) –

(a) in subsection (2), for 'section 56 of the Pensions Act 1995' substitute 'this section', and

(b) after that subsection insert –

'(2A) This section applies to an occupational pension scheme other than –

(a) a money purchase scheme, or

(b) a prescribed scheme or a scheme of a prescribed description.'

76 (1) Paragraph 1 of Schedule 1 (application of enactments relating to occupational schemes to certain stakeholder schemes) is amended as follows.

(2) In sub-paragraph (2), in paragraph (b) –

(a) in sub-paragraph (i) for the words from 'except' to the end substitute 'except sections 7(5A)(b), 8(1)(a) and (c) and (2), 11(3A) and (3B) and 15(1),

(b) in sub-paragraph (ii) for '31' substitute '30',

        (c)   in sub-paragraph (iii) omit the words from 'except' to the end,

        (d)   for sub-paragraph (v) substitute –

        '(v)   section 47 (professional advisers);', and

        (e)   in sub-paragraph (vii) for 'section 50' substitute 'sections 50 to 50B'.

  (3) After that paragraph insert '; and

        (c)   the following provisions of the Pensions Act 2004 –

           (i)   section 67 (accessibility of register of prohibited trustees);

          (ii)   Chapters 4 and 5 of Part 2 (fraud compensation and information gathering);

         (iii)   sections 247 to 249 (requirements for knowledge and understanding); and

         (iv)   section 318 (interpretation).'

  (4) In sub-paragraph (5), after '1995 Act' insert ', and section 318(1) of the Pensions Act 2004,'.

  (5) After sub-paragraph (5) insert –

    '(6) Chapters 4 and 5 of Part 2 of the Pensions Act 2004 (as applied by sub-paragraph (1)) shall have effect with such modifications as the Secretary of State may prescribe by regulations.'

77 (1) Schedule 5 (pension credits: mode of discharge) is amended as follows.

  (2) In paragraph 8(1)(b), for the words from 'section 56' to 'related schemes)' substitute 'Part 3 of the Pensions Act 2004 (scheme funding)'.

  (3) After paragraph 13 insert –

'13A The provisions of this Schedule are subject to –

        (a)   section 73A(3) and (6) of the Pensions Act 1995 (prohibition on new members during winding up of scheme: exception for discharge of pension credit derived from the scheme), and

        (b)   section 133(2) and (8) of the Pensions Act 2004 (prohibition on new members during an assessment period in relation to a scheme: exception for discharge of pension credit derived from the scheme).'

Terrorism Act 2000 (c. 11)

78 In Schedule 3A to the Terrorism Act 2000 (regulated sector and supervisory authorities), for paragraph 4(1)(f) substitute –

    '(f)   the Pensions Regulator;'.

Freedom of Information Act 2000 (c. 36)

79 In Schedule 1 to the Freedom of Information Act 2000 (public authorities), in Part 6 insert at the appropriate place –

'The Pensions Regulator.'
'The Board of the Pension Protection Fund.'
'The Ombudsman for the Board of the Pension Protection Fund.'

Proceeds of Crime Act 2002 (c. 29)

80 In Schedule 9 to the Proceeds of Crime Act 2002 (regulated sector and supervisory authorities), for paragraph 4(1)(f) substitute –

    '(f)   the Pensions Regulator;'.

SCHEDULE 13   REPEALS AND REVOCATIONS

Section 320

PART 1

REPEALS

Short title and chapter	Extent of repeal
Parliamentary Commissioner Act 1967 (c. 13)	In Schedule 2, the entries relating to – (a) the Occupational Pensions Regulatory Authority, and (b) the Pensions Compensation Board.
House of Commons Disqualification Act 1975 (c.24)	In Schedule 1, in Part 2, the entries relating to – (a) the Occupational Pensions Regulatory Authority, and (b) the Pensions Compensation Board.
Northern Ireland Assembly Disqualification Act 1975 (c.25)	In Schedule 1, in Part 2, the entries relating to – (a) the Occupational Pensions Regulatory Authority, and (b) the Pensions Compensation Board.
Tribunals and Inquiries Act 1992 (c. 53)	Section 10(5)(ba) and the word 'or' immediately preceding it. In Schedule 1, in Part 1, paragraph 35(g) and (h).
Pension Schemes Act 1993 (c. 48)	Section 6. In section 28 – (a) in subsection (4), paragraphs (a) and (b) and the word 'and' in paragraph (c), (b) subsections (4A) and (4B), and (c) in subsection (8), the words ', which must not be earlier than the member's 60th birthday,' in the definition of 'the starting date'. In section 29(1)(aa)(ii), the words from 'and is not' to '75th birthday,'. In section 34(1)(a)(ii), the words 'or category'. Section 99(6). Section 101J(3). Section 111. Section 111A(10). Section 111B. In section 123, the definition of 'occupational pension scheme' in subsection (3), and subsection (4). In section 129 – (a) in subsection (2) the words from 'and Chapter IV' to the end, and (b) subsection (3)(b).

Short title and chapter	*Extent of repeal*
Pension Schemes Act 1993	In section 131(b), the words 'payable at any earlier time or'.
	In section 132, the words from 'or the voluntary' to third 'requirements'.
	Section 148(5)(ba) and (bb).
	Section 149(1), (1A) and (1B).
	In section 149(3) –
	(a) paragraph (ba), and
	(b) paragraph (d) and the word 'and' immediately preceding it.
	In section 149(6) –
	(a) paragraph (c), and
	(b) the word 'and' at the end of paragraph (k).
	Section 149(8).
	In section 151(1), paragraph (c) and the word 'and' immediately preceding it.
	In section 151(3) –
	(a) paragraphs (ba) and (bb), and
	(b) in paragraph (c) the words 'any of paragraphs (a) to (bb)'.
	In section 158 –
	(a) in subsection (6), the words 'Subject to subsection (7)', and
	(b) subsection (7).
	Section 168A.
	In section 175 –
	(a) in subsection (1), paragraph (a) and the word 'or' at the end of paragraph (b), and
	(b) subsections (4) to (7).
	In section 177(5) –
	(a) the word 'and' at the end of paragraph (a), and
	(b) paragraph (b).
	In section 181 –
	(a) in subsection (1), the definitions of 'the register', 'the Registrar', and 'voluntary contributions requirements',
	(b) in subsection (3), the words 'section 6,', and
	(c) in subsection (4), the word '6,'.
	In section 192(2), the words 'section 6(1) and (2) (except paragraph (a)(ii)), (3), (4), and (8),'.
	In Schedule 9, paragraphs 5 and 7(2).

Short title and chapter	Extent of repeal
Pensions Act 1995 (c. 26)	Sections 1 and 2.
	Section 5.
	In section 7(1), the words 'a trustee of such a scheme ceases to be a trustee'.
	Section 7(4).
	In section 10(5)(a), the words 'as a trustee of a trust scheme'.
	Section 11(3).
	Section 13.
	Sections 16 to 21.
	In section 22(1)(b), the word 'or' at the end of sub-paragraph (i).
	In section 25(2), the words from 'but if' to the end.
	Sections 26A to 26C.
	Section 28(4).
	In section 29 –
	(a) subsections (3), (4) and (5)(b), and
	(b) in subsection (6), the words 'or revocation made'.
	In section 30 –
	(a) in subsection (2), paragraph (b) and the word 'or' immediately preceding it, and
	(b) subsections (7) and (8).
	Section 30A.
	Section 31.
	Section 36(2).
	In section 38(2)(b), the word 'new'.
	Section 41(2)(c).
	Section 48.
	In section 49, subsection (10)(a) and the word 'and' immediately after it.
	Section 49A(4).
	In section 51(1), the word 'and' at the end of sub-paragraph (i) of paragraph (a).
	In section 54(3), the definition of 'appropriate percentage'.
	Sections 56 to 61.
	In section 63(4)(c), the words 'or category'.
	In section 69 –
	(a) subsection (3)(a),
	(b) in subsection (4)(a), the words '(a) or', and
	(c) in subsection (5)(a), the words 'either of'.
	In section 71A(4), paragraphs (f) and (g).
	Section 72A(9)(a) and the word 'and' immediately after it.
	Section 72B(7) and (8)(b).
	Section 72C(2).

Short title and chapter	*Extent of repeal*
	Section 73(6)(a) and the word 'and' immediately after it.
	In section 74 –

(a) in subsection (2) the words '(including increases in pensions)',

(b) in subsection (4) the words '(including increases in pensions)', and

(c) subsection (5)(b) and the word 'or' immediately preceding it.

Section 75(9).
In section 76 –

(a) subsection (3)(c) (but not the word 'and' immediately following it), and

(b) subsection (5).

Section 77(2) and (3).
Sections 78 to 86.
Section 87(5)(a) and the word 'and' immediately after it.
Section 88(4)(a) and the word 'and' immediately after it.
In section 89(2), the word 'insolvency'.
Sections 96 to 114.
In section 117(2) –

(a) at the end of paragraph (b), the word 'or', and

(b) paragraph (c).

Section 118(3).
In section 119, the word '56(3),'.
In section 124(1) –

(a) in the definition of 'employer', the words 'or category',

(b) the definitions of 'member-nominated director', 'member-nominated trustee' and 'minimum funding requirement', and

(c) in the definition of 'pensionable service', the words 'or category'.

Section 134(3).
Section 142(5).
In section 162(1), the word 'and' at the end of paragraph (a).
In section 175(2), the word 'or' at the end of paragraph (c).
In section 178(2), the words '1, 2, 21(3)' and '78, 79, 80(4)'.
Schedules 1 and 2.
In Schedule 3, paragraphs 12, 21, 23 and 44(a)(ii).
In Schedule 4, paragraph 21(13) and (14).

Short title and chapter	Extent of repeal
Pensions Act 1995 (c.26) – *cont.*	In Schedule 5 – (a) paragraph 20, and (b) paragraph 77(b) (but not the word 'and' immediately following it). In Schedule 6, paragraph 6(d).
Criminal Procedure (Consequential Provisions) (Scotland) Act 1995 (c. 40)	In Schedule 4, paragraph 98.
Employment Rights Act 1996 (c. 18)	In section 58(3)(b), the words 'or category'.
Bank of England Act 1998 (c. 11)	In Part 4 of Schedule 5, paragraph 71.
Social Security Contributions (Transfer of Functions, Etc.) Act 1999 (c. 2)	In Schedule 1, paragraphs 67 and 68.
Welfare Reform and Pensions Act 1999 (c. 30)	Section 2(5) and (6). Sections 4 and 5. Section 17. Section 38(1). In section 46(1), in the definition of 'pensionable service', the words 'or category'. Section 50(2). In Schedule 1 – (a) paragraph 1(2)(a), (b) in paragraph 1(2)(b)(i) the word ', 13', (c) in paragraph 1(2)(b)(iii), the words from 'except' to the end, (d) paragraph 1(2)(b)(ix) and (xi) to (xiii), and (e) paragraphs 2 and 3. In Schedule 2, paragraphs 3(1)(a), 9 and 13 to 16. In Schedule 12, paragraphs 39(3), 44, 45 to 49, 53, 55 and 60.
Child Support, Pensions and Social Security Act 2000 (c. 19)	In section 42(7), the word 'and' at the end of paragraph (c). Sections 43 to 46. Section 47(1), (2) and (4). Section 54. In Schedule 5 – (a) paragraph 3(3) and (4), (b) paragraph 10, (c) paragraph 11, and (d) paragraph 12(2), (3) and (4). In Schedule 9, Part 3(10).

Short title and chapter	Extent of repeal
Freedom of Information Act 2000 (c. 36)	In Schedule 1, in Part 6 the entries for – (a) the Occupational Pensions Regulatory Authority, (b) the Pensions Compensation Board, and (c) the Registrar of Occupational and Personal Pension Schemes.
Anti-terrorism, Crime and Security Act 2001 (c. 24)	In Part 1 of Schedule 4, paragraph 37.
Employment Act 2002 (c. 22)	In Schedule 6, paragraph 1(a) and (b).

The repeals in sections 148, 149 and 151 of the Pension Schemes Act 1993 (c. 48) relate to those provisions as amended by section 54 of the Child Support, Pensions and Social Security Act 2000 (c. 19) to the extent that those amendments have been brought into force for the purpose of making regulations and rules.

PART 2

REVOCATIONS

Title and number	Extent of revocation
Pensions (Northern Ireland) Order 1995 (S.I. 1995/3213 (N.I. 22))	Article 78(4).

INDEX

Execution of Documents

A Practical Guide

Mark Anderson and Victor Warner

This practical and user-friendly book provides all of the tools required to execute the more commonly encountered legal documents, including:

- deeds
- contracts
- powers of attorney
- documents used in litigation.

A step-by-step guide to the correct procedure is provided for each type of document, together with a commentary on the underlying legal principles.

Fully up-to-date, the book considers the introduction of electronic signatures and the Law Commission's proposals for changes to the execution of documents by corporations. It also features a helpful range of execution clauses and signature blocks. The book will be invaluable to any practitioner conducting commercial or property transactions or private client work.

Available from Marston Book Services:
Tel. 01235 465 656.

1 85328 980 9
416 pages
£39.95
January 2005

The Law Society

Pensions and Marriage Breakdown

David Davidson

This book provides a practical guide to the powers the Courts have in relation to pension funds and the way they can exercise those powers when granting financial relief following a decree of judicial separation, divorce or nullity of marriage.

Practical and up-to-date, the third edition includes:

- summary of the main private and public pension schemes and benefits for members
- an introduction to the new tax regime for pension schemes brought in by the Finance Act 2004
- practical problems that arise on implementing Pension Sharing Orders
- helpful analysis of the latest cases
- provisions for pension sharing including registered same sex couples as contemplated in the Civil Partnerships Bill

Available from Marston Book Services:
Tel. 01235 465 656.

1 85328 951 5
216 pages
£29.95
February 2005

The Law Society